WOMEN'S REALITIES, WOMEN'S CHOICES

WOMEN'S REALITIES, WOMEN'S CHOICES

An Introduction to Women's and Gender Studies

FOURTH EDITION

Hunter College Women's and Gender Studies Collective

Linda Martín Alcoff

Jacqueline Nassy Brown

Sarah Chinn

Florence L. Denmark

Dorothy O. Helly

Shirley Hune

Rupal Oza

Sarah B. Pomeroy

Carolyn M. Somerville

New York   Oxford

OXFORD UNIVERSITY PRESS

Oxford University Press is a department of the University of Oxford.
It furthers the University's objective of excellence in research,
scholarship, and education by publishing worldwide.

Oxford   New York
Auckland   Cape Town   Dar es Salaam   Hong Kong   Karachi
Kuala Lumpur   Madrid   Melbourne   Mexico City   Nairobi
New Delhi   Shanghai   Taipei   Toronto

With offices in
Argentina   Austria   Brazil   Chile   Czech Republic   France   Greece
Guatemala   Hungary   Italy   Japan   Poland   Portugal   Singapore
South Korea   Switzerland   Thailand   Turkey   Ukraine   Vietnam

For titles covered by Section 112 of the US Higher Education
Opportunity Act, please visit www.oup.com/us/he for the latest
information about pricing and alternate formats.

Published by Oxford University Press
198 Madison Avenue, New York, NY 10016
http://www.oup.com

Library of Congress Cataloging-in-Publication Data
Women's realities, women's choices : an introduction to women's and gender studies / Hunter College Women's
and Gender Studies Collective (Linda Martin Alcoff [and eight others]).—Fourth edition.
   pages cm
ISBN 978-0-19-984360-2
1. Women's studies—United States.   I. Hunter College. Women's and Gender Studies Collective.
HQ1181.U5W653 2015
305.40973—dc23
2013033932

Printing number: 9 8 7 6 5 4 3 2 1

Printed in the United States of America
on acid-free paper

To our teachers, colleagues, and students
Our parents and children
Our spouses, partners, and friends
And our sisters and brothers both literal and metaphorical
We dedicate this book in the spirit of collaboration, intellectual engagement, political commitment, lively debate, and love in which it was written.

CONTENTS

BOXES AND TABLES

Tables

PREFACE

In the three decades since the first publication of this introductory textbook in women's studies, there has been an extraordinary transformation in scholarship. Consideration of gender as it interacts with race, ethnicity, class, and sexuality has become an essential factor of analysis in every field, while the issues raised by the modern women's movement have reshaped much of public discourse around the world.

Unlike single-authored books by a scholar trained in one discipline and anthologies by many authors each tackling one subject, *Women's Realities, Women's Choices* has been written by nine authors from as many disciplines, calling upon a further author for a specific chapter. The authors have shared with each other and share with the reader the multiple perspectives they bring to this examination of women's lives and experiences, treating women as subjects rather than objects, looking at the world through women's eyes. In addition, in this fourth edition of the book, we expanded our examination of the workings of gender to many more aspects of women's everyday lives as well as across the globe.

As in earlier editions, we also have a Foreword written by a leading feminist, this time the transnational scholar Chandra Talpade Mohanty. Strikingly, her Foreword both inspired us and led to some serious debate within the collective. Her commentary on the Israeli–Palestinian conflict caused significant disagreement, with some collective members citing the violence on both sides of the conflict as worthy of inclusion in Mohanty's text and others arguing that her Foreword represents an anti-colonial struggle that should be taken on its own terms. It is proof of the power of the collaborative process that despite these differences we could come together as a group and respect each other's deeply felt disagreements.

Rethinking the world through women's eyes has affected the very basis of knowledge in our universities. Until this revolution in scholarship, only men's experiences, and especially those of privileged men, were seriously studied, with the assumption that to understand them was to understand all that was worth knowing. Over 40 years of research focused on women has not only added new information about their lives historically and cross-culturally but also changed our understanding of what happened in the past and how our world works today across cultures.

As the Introduction makes clear, the writing of this book has continued to be a collaborative effort, with each author contributing to all chapters. The organization of the book, as set out in the introductions to each of its three parts, deals with women as individuals, as family members, and as members of society. In every chapter we point out the contradictions between social or cultural "givens" that generally have been structured by men in their own interest and what we perceive to be women's realities. At each point we consider what changes would be required to ensure better choices for women. The title of the book acknowledges our awareness of the gap between women's realities and women's choices, and the book sets out to analyze that gap and to find ways of bridging it.

The history of this book goes back to 1978–79, when a year-long interdisciplinary seminar for faculty members at Hunter College met weekly and taped their discussions. The purpose was to design an introductory course for the women's studies program instituted in 1976. As the outline for such a course emerged, so did a core group of faculty willing to carry the project forward into published form. With a grant to Sarah B. Pomeroy from the National Endowment for the Humanities, eight authors proceeded to turn these materials into a text and were able to test it out in various campus situations before completion of the manuscript. Oxford University Press published it in 1983.

The founding co-authors were Ülkü Ü. Bates, Florence L. Denmark, Virginia Held, Dorothy O. Helly, Susan H. Lees, Sarah B. Pomeroy, E. Dorsey Smith, and Sue Rosenberg Zalk. The second edition was published in 1995 without Dorsey Smith and with the addition of Shirley Hune and Carolyn M. Somerville as authors. For the third edition in 2005, dedicated to our late co-author Sue Rosenberg Zalk, we added as author Frances E. Mascia-Lees. Changes in this fourth edition, which has nine co-authors, include as new authors Hunter College faculty Linda Martín Alcoff, Jacqueline Nassy Brown, Sarah Chinn, and Rupal Oza, while those choosing to retire from the project included founding authors Ülkü Ü. Bates, Virginia Held, and Susan H. Lees and third-edition author Mascia-Lees. In this book we can at times still recognize the voices of past authors, making it also collaboration between past and present.

After the first edition, it became necessary to consult a Hunter College colleague to update the chapter on women's health and the health system. In this fourth edition, we are again grateful to Kathryn Rolland for Chapter 9 on Health.

From the beginning, a great many people have been generous to us with their support, time, and expertise. At Hunter College, Provost Jerome Schneewind, in 1978–79, funded the seminar that launched this project from overhead monies from a Mellon grant obtained by the Humanities Dean, Gerald Freund. Donna Shalala, president of Hunter in the 1980s, encouraged its completion and wrote the Foreword to its first three editions. We are still grateful to our earliest reviewers who helped shaped the book when it was a project funded by NEH—Nancy Hartsock, Joyce Ladner, and Catherine Stimpson.

Our labors on the fourth edition have also been aided by Dr. Emily Fairey, who helped us prepare the manuscript for the press, including merging all references into a single bibliography. At Oxford University Press, we are grateful to our fourth edition editor Sherith Pankratz and to her assistants at various times, Richard Beck, Cari Heicklen, Caitlin Greene, and Katy Albis. We are also delighted to note that Niko Pfund, whom we first met years ago as an editorial assistant, is now president of Oxford University Press (USA).

We would also like to thank the following reviewers:

Christina S. Brophy, Triton College
Teresa Collard, University of Tennessee at Martin
Patricia Hill Collins, University of Maryland, College Park
Mary Duarte, Cardinal Stritch University
Wendy K. Kolmar, Drew University
Robin Powers, Gannon University
Anita Storck, Chapman University

CHANGES TO THE FOURTH EDITION

In this edition, we have placed the study of women in a far more inclusive perspective by presenting issues and drawing from examples worldwide and by attending to transnational feminism (defined in the Introduction) and globalization. Another broad change is in the text's conceptualization. The previous edition was divided into three parts: "Defining Women," "Families," and "Women in Society." While the construct of Part III remains, Part I has become "Defining Women and Gender." Here the revised chapters (see below) examine gender as a social construct and consider how it shapes the experiences of both women and men. Section II, formerly "Families," is now "Women's Relationships, Women's Selves." We sought to move beyond traditional understandings and categories of families and familial roles and to reflect more on the fluidity of the roles that women inhabit and on differences worldwide. This section now includes "Women's Health" as Chapter 9 (formerly Chapter 11) so that we might better expose the ways in which women's well-being, or lack thereof, shapes their ability to navigate through their life course and within and on behalf of their families.

Several chapters are completely new or substantially reworked.

Chapter 1, "Imagery and Symbolism in the Definition of Women," is now "Cultural Representations of Women." Feminist scholars increasingly focus on gender as a representation: that is, as a complex of images, mandates, vocabularies, and systems of power that construct our sense of selves in the world as women and men. We reworked this chapter to show a fuller sense of how women and men see themselves reflected in appropriately gendered identities and also participate in reproducing them.

"Diversity Among Women" (formerly Chapter 5) has become "Intersectionality" and is now Chapter 3. While every chapter considers the diversity among women, the old chapter on gender, race, and class has been replaced with an entirely new one. In addition to tracing the history of intersectionality, we emphasize the difference that this approach makes to feminist inquiry, feminist theory and methodology, and feminist practice and to our understanding of women's identities, oppression, and activism.

Chapter 4, formerly "Women's Personalities," is now "Learning, Making, and Doing Gender." In this edition, we recognized that women's identities are organized around more than personalities. We explore here how gender as a cultural phenomenon is learned, created, and enacted by women and men every day across cultures.

"Daughters and Sisters" (formerly Chapter 6) is now incorporated into a new Chapter 8, "Growing Up and Growing Older." Accordingly, we have integrated recent findings on girlhood across the globe and included a new section on women and aging and their changing identities and roles.

Every chapter has been updated to reflect changes in the field and in the world. Here is a sampling of changes in chapters not discussed above. Chapter 2, "Ideas and Theories about Women and Gender," draws on non-Western sources as well as nineteenth- to twenty-first-century black, Chicana, and Euro-American feminist thought to present a variety of trends in the study of women and gender. Chapter 5, "Gender and the Politics of the Body," applies recent work in anthropology and philosophy to show bodies as cultural and not strictly biological entities and contains new material on female genital cutting and sexual violence during wartime. There is also new material on changes in family configurations worldwide in Chapter 6, "Families and Their Configurations," and on the culture and politics of being a mother in Chapter 7, "Mothers." Chapter 10, "Women and Education," reassesses women's gains in schooling and provides a new section on their struggles to become scientists. Chapter 11, "Women and Religion," now contains a discussion of secularism and various forms of fundamentalism. In Chapter 12, "Women and Work," there is a new discussion on work–life balance and women in the military and in sex work. Finally, Chapter 13, "Feminism and Politics," includes an extended analysis of transformations in U.S. electoral politics with attention to women's participation.

Every chapter has a revised set of recommended readings and new discussion questions. We have updated the data presented in tables and added some 39 new boxes (short excerpts from books, speeches, and the like) and new photographs. In summary, the 4th edition of *Women's Realities, Women's Choices* is an extensively reimagined text from the 3rd edition and includes new theoretical approaches, research findings, data, and issues that place women at the center locally and globally in a gendered context.

FOREWORD TO THE FOURTH EDITION

Chandra Talpade Mohanty

January 2, 2013

Written by a diverse, brilliant collective of feminist scholars at Hunter College, this new, revised edition of *Women's Realities, Women's Choices* engages the history of feminist thought and practice, and includes brand new chapters on the epistemological shifts and complexities of gender, race, nation, class, and sexuality that are a hallmark of the current knowledge base of women's and gender studies. As I write, at the dawn of a new year, the mainstream media and alternative/progressive news outlets review the "highlights" of the past year, and I am convinced, once again, that books like this one are necessary to our health and survival!

News stories about the everyday (and the extraordinary) violence in all our lives, from the school massacre in Newtown, Connecticut, and the gang rape/murder of a young woman in Delhi to the minute and unnoticed everyday abuses of power in families, communities, and streets, continue to haunt us. And then there are the so-called "high points." Recent political milestones have included Barack Obama, the first African American president of the United States, upon being elected to his second term, announcing his support for gay marriage, and Nobel Laureate Aung San Suu Kyi being sworn into parliament in Burma after almost 20 years of house arrest! And of course there were the 2011–12 Occupy movements that changed the U.S. political landscape and engendered conversations about Wall Street, capitalism, and the 99%. Remember also the corresponding occupy and un-occupy movements around the globe: Occupy Nigeria with its focus on corruption, Occupy Hiroshima with its focus on anti-nuclear proliferation, Occupy your food supply, Un-occupy Palestine and Native lands, and so on.

We have witnessed the rise of social movements against autocratic governments, the prison-and-terror industrial complex, colonial occupations, and neoliberal economic policies in many parts of the globe. The last two years have profoundly changed the landscape of democratic and social justice struggles in the Arab world, and while women are perhaps less visible than we would like, gender politics remain at the center of these human rights struggles. I believe we need better lenses, better feminist analytics to "see" women's participation and leadership in these revolutions and to bring women's critical agency to the forefront of our social justice struggles. The mobilization of transnational organizing and knowledge networks is readily acknowledged in the current anti-authoritarian social movements, and women's significant participation in creating sustainable infrastructures is evident to some of us. But, many of us still ask: Where are the women, what are they doing, and how have they transformed their everyday realities? And this precisely is why books like *Women's Realities, Women's Choices* remain necessary to our survival!

Big changes continue to occur because ordinary people struggle in their homes and communities, march in the streets, and dream of justice. The historical resistance to the

Israeli occupation and state-sponsored settler colonial violence against Palestinians, and the ongoing mobilization of indigenous peoples and allies by the Idle No More movement inspired by Attawaspiskat Chief Theresa Spence's hunger strike protesting the Canadian government's abuse of indigenous treaty rights are just two instances of anti-colonial social movements that necessitate a feminist analysis. In all of these instances, the anti-racist, intersectional feminist analysis of this text is key to making sense of the fact that gendered bodies, capitalist/racist/masculinist ideologies, and heteronormative state and civil society practices are central to understanding these ongoing struggles, as well as the "highlights" of the past year.

The largest generation of young people in human history is about to come of age. Nearly half the world's population is under the age of 25. This generation inherits a world of global crises in climate, health, poverty, violence, wars, and environmental destruction. But it is also poised at a moment of great hope and possibility. We do, however, need productive analytic tools and gender-just visions that allow us to acknowledge both the inheritances of colonial legacies, and of movements for emancipation—to hold on to the contradictions in our lives and act with accountability to improve the lives of people in our own neighborhood as well as across the world in communities thousands of miles away. The sustained histories of feminism, the analyses of women's bodies, families, communities, and institutions found in this text gift us with the sharp analytic literacy necessary to understand the contradictions and inheritances of gendered violence and inequity at multiple scales, and to envision gender justice in all its complexity. Addressing epistemological questions about the invisibility and misrepresentation of diverse communities of women, providing anti-racist, intersectional, and postcolonial analyses of gender and sexuality in the context of intimate lives, families, communities, and public spaces, engaging questions of education, health, work, religion, and the state in historicized and nuanced ways is a hallmark of this text.

Almost two years ago, a woman carried a sign in the Occupy Wall Street movement that said: "Women are ½ the world's population, working 2/3rds of the world's working hours, receiving 10% of the world's income, owning less than 1% of the world's property. We are part of the 99%!" Another woman carried one that said: "Warning: Don't mistake the complexity of this moment for chaos!" It is the urgency and complexity of this historical moment that *Women's Realities, Women's Choices* helps us understand. This book is an invaluable companion for anyone interested in making feminist sense of our world.

THE AUTHORS

Linda Martín Alcoff is Professor of Philosophy at Hunter College and the Graduate Center, CUNY. She is a past President of the American Philosophical Association, Eastern Division. Her writings have focused on social identity, race, gender, knowledge, sexual violence, and Latino issues. She has written two books: *Visible Identities: Race, Gender and the Self* (Oxford, 2006), which won the Frantz Fanon Award in 2009, and *Real Knowing: New Versions of the Coherence Theory* (Cornell, 1996). And she has edited 10 books including several important collections on feminist topics. She is currently at work on two projects, one on the future of white identity and one on effective resistance to rape. She was named the Distinguished Woman in Philosophy for 2005 by the Society for Women in Philosophy, in 2006 she was named one of the 100 Most Influential Hispanics in the United States by *Hispanic Business* magazine, and in 2011 she was awarded an honorary doctorate from the University of Oslo. She is a high school dropout and a college dropout who had children early but managed to go back and get her degrees. She is originally from Panama, but lives today happily in Brooklyn.

Jacqueline Nassy Brown is Associate Professor of Anthropology at Hunter College and the Graduate Center, CUNY. Her academic passions concern the intersection of race, place, and nation; diasporic formations of black culture and identity; and feminist geography. She is the author of *Dropping Anchor, Setting Sail: Geographies of Race in Black Liverpool* (Princeton University Press, 2005). She has published in *American Anthropologist, American Ethnologist, Cultural Anthropology,* and *Social Text.* She earned an Excellence in Teaching Award from the University of California, Santa Cruz. With her contribution to the present book, Jackie pays tribute to her beautiful late mother, who was her first feminist role model. She also taught Jackie most of what she knows about writing—and about life.

Sarah E. Chinn teaches in the English Department at Hunter College, CUNY. She is the author of two books, *Technology and the Logic of American Racism: A Cultural History of the Body as Evidence* (2000) and *Inventing Modern Adolescence: The Children of Immigrants in Turn-of-the-Century America* (2008). She's currently working on a book on the representation of masculinity in early American drama. She has published widely in American literature and culture, LGBTQ studies, and disability studies. From 2007 to 2011 she was the Executive Director of the Center for Lesbian and Gay Studies (CLAGS) at the CUNY Graduate Center. She lives in Brooklyn with her partner and two children and is finally learning to play the guitar.

Florence L. Denmark is the Robert Scott Pace Distinguished Research Professor at Pace University in New York, where she has served as chair of the Psychology Department for 13 years. She previously taught at Hunter College for 26 years. A social psychologist who received her doctorate from the University of Pennsylvania, she has published extensively on the psychology of women and gender. She is a fellow of the American Psychological Association (APA) and served as its eighty-eighth president in 1980. In addition, she was president of the International Council of Psychologists, the Eastern Psychological Association, the New York State Psychological Association, and Psi Chi. She was vice president of the New York Academy of Sciences. She has six honorary doctorates and is the recipient of many awards including APA's Distinguished Contributions to Education and Training, Public Interest, and the Advancement of International Psychology. Professor Denmark is currently an APA nongovernmental organization representative to the United Nations and continues to teach graduate courses at Pace University. She has one surviving child, three stepchildren, four grandchildren, and one great-grandchild. She is also a frustrated sports writer.

Dorothy O. Helly is Professor Emerita of History and Women's Studies at Hunter College and the Graduate School at the City University of New York. She is associated with St. Antony's College and the Institute for Gender Studies (Lady Margaret Hall) at Oxford University, has been a scholar in residence at the Rockefeller Foundation Study Center at Bellagio, Italy, and on the boards of the Feminist Press, the *Journal of Women's History*, and *Women's Studies Quarterly*. She co-chaired the program committee of the Seventh Berkshire Conference on the History of Women (1987) and the Fourth International Interdisciplinary Congress on Women (1990). The author of *Livingstone's Legacy: Horace Waller and Victorian Mythmaking* (1987) and coeditor of *Gendered Domains: Rethinking the Public and Private in Women's History* (1992), she has published in the fields of history, women's studies, and higher education, including curriculum transformation. She is finishing a biography of Flora Shaw, Lady Lugard (1852–1929), the first woman on the staff of *The Times* of London in the 1890s, serving as its colonial editor. Her articles on Shaw appear in four anthologies and in the *Oxford Dictionary of National Biography* (2004). She enjoys Pilates, playing Scrabble™, and reading mysteries.

Shirley Hune is Professor Emerita of Urban Planning at UCLA where she also served as Associate Dean of the Graduate Division and PI of several NSF grants to increase graduate diversity in science, technology, engineering, and mathematics (STEM) and social sciences doctoral programs. Previously, she was an Associate Provost at Hunter College and Professor of Social Foundations of Education. She has authored many publications on nonaligned countries (Global South), the human rights of international migrant workers, and on Asian Americans, notably their historiography and race and gender issues in higher education. She has been involved in the development of ethnic studies for more than three decades and is a past president of the Association for Asian American Studies. Her writings on Asian American women include *Teaching Asian American Women's History* (1997), *Asian Pacific American Women in Higher Education: Claiming Visibility & Voice* (1998), and *Asian/Pacific Islander American Women: A Historical Anthology* (2003). Her recent publications focus on the experiences of women students, faculty, and administrators of color. She lives with her husband in Seattle, where she teaches at the University of Washington and enjoys gardening, traveling, walking her dog, and visits with her large extended and blended family.

Rupal Oza is the Director of the Women's and Gender Studies program at Hunter College, CUNY. Her work focuses on political economic transformations in the Global South, the geography of the right-wing politics, and the conjuncture between development and security. Her first book, *The Making of Neoliberal India: Nationalism, Gender, and the Paradoxes of Globalization*, was published in 2006 by Routledge, New York, and by Women

Unlimited, India. She has several articles in peer-reviewed journals. She is currently working on three projects: the first examines the mobilizing of particular human rights and feminist discourses against "Muslim extremism" in an age of terror and empire; the second explores security beyond its conventional mooring in law and order to examine its deployment at different scales in south Asia; and the third examines the link between special economic zones, the discourse of security, and Hindutva politics in Gujarat, India. She is on the Board of the Brecht Forum and has been involved in South Asian political organizing in New York for 10 years.

Sarah B. Pomeroy is Distinguished Professor of Classics and History, Emerita, at Hunter College and the Graduate School, CUNY. She was the first coordinator of the Women's Studies Program at Hunter, the first coordinator of the certificate program in women's studies at the City University of New York Graduate Center and the first Chair of the Women's Classical Caucus. She is the author of many publications on Greek and Roman women and on ancient history including *Goddesses, Whores, Wives, and Slaves: Women in Classical Antiquity* (1975, 1995); *Women in Hellenistic Egypt from Alexander to Cleopatra* (1984, 1990); *Spartan Women* (2002); *The Murder of Regilla. A Case of Domestic Violence in Antiquity* (2007); and *Pythagorean Women. Their Lives and Their Writings* (2013). Her books have been translated into Italian, Spanish, German, and Chinese. Professor Pomeroy has received fellowships from the Ford Foundation, the Guggenheim Foundation, the Mellon Foundation, and the National Endowment for the Humanities and is an Honorary Fellow of St. Hilda's College, the University of Oxford. She likes to play the harpsichord. She has seven grandchildren and is writing a book for them about the seventeenth-century artist and entomologist Maria Sibylla Merian.

Carolyn M. Somerville is Associate Professor of Political Science at Hunter College. Her research, writing, and teaching interests include African politics, international relations, and international human rights. She has published in the *International Journal of Middle East Studies*; *Sex Roles: A Journal of Research*; *PS: Political Science and Politics*; *The Oxford Companion to Politics of the World*; and *Globalization and Survival in the Black Diaspora*. She has also served as acting director of the Women's Studies Program at Hunter College. Somerville practices Nichiren Buddhism. She has a daughter and a son.

Kathryn Rolland, who contributed Chapter 9 on women's health, is now an Associate Professor Emerita of Public Health/Community Health Education whose fields of concentration are women's health, sexuality, and curriculum development and is proud to have created one of the first multidisciplinary courses for undergraduates on HIV/AIDS in the United States. She also enjoys reading poetry and mysteries and thinks that in an alternative life she would have been a swimming instructor who "never left the water."

Introduction

The "woman question" is not just one among many raised by injustice, subordination, and differentiation. It is basic. The denigration and segregation of women is a major mechanism in reinforcing male bonds, protecting institutions that favor them, and providing the basic work required for societies to function. To ignore this great social divide is to ignore a missing link in social analysis.

CYNTHIA EPSTEIN, 2007

We are the daughters of feminist privilege. The gains of the Feminist Movement (the efforts of black, white, Latin, Asian, and Native American women) had a tremendous impact on our lives—so much we often take it for granted. We walk through the world with a sense of entitlement that women of our mothers' generation could not begin to fathom. Most of us can't imagine our lives without access to birth control, legalized abortions, the right to vote, or many of the same educational and job opportunities available to men. Sexism may be a very real part of my life but so is the unwavering belief that there is no dream I can't pursue *and achieve* simply because "I'm a woman."

JOAN MORGAN, 2012

The academy has always been the site of feminist struggle. It is that contradictory place where knowledges are colonized but also contested—a place that engenders student mobilizations and progressive movements of various kinds. It is one of the few remaining spaces in a rapidly privatized world that offers some semblance of a public arena for dialogue, engagement, and visioning of democracy and justice.

CHANDRA TALPADE MOHANTY, 2003

Why Women's Studies?

In the single year 2012, a host of books was published proclaiming that women are "the richer sex" and that they dominate in the new knowledge economy—and even that "the end of men" has arrived (Hymowitz, 2012; Mundy, 2012; Rosin, 2012). One might imagine that these books provide advocates for women's equality with a cause for celebration. And one certainly couldn't be blamed for concluding that since a bright new day seems finally to be dawning for women, there is no longer a need for women's studies—or even for feminism, a movement defined, at the very least, by its attention to gender inequality. And yet, the publication of these books (and there are many more like them) provides one of the most critical rationales for women's studies now.

Let's take an ever-so-brief look at a specific claim found in such books: that women in their 20s in certain large cities are now out-earning their male counterparts of the same age. That conclusion is based on a very particular set of demographic and economic realities. For the particular cities in question are those with a relatively high number of well-educated, single white women and an also high number of poorly educated, low-wage-earning Latino men (Coontz, 2012). Entailed in this singular corrective are at least two reasons why women's studies is more important than ever. First, such books as *The Richer Sex* (Mundy, 2012), because they seem to contain such great news for women, contribute to the growing tendency to dismiss or underestimate continuing gender discrimination and inequality. And in so doing, they also bolster claims that feminism, as a social movement and an approach to critiquing society, is no longer necessary. Second, this corrective dramatizes the central role that factors of race and class play in the understanding not only of women but of gender, a power relation that implicates and affects men in myriad ways. A final corrective is also in order: these texts, with their sensationalist titles, encourage a damaging misconception of feminism, which is that its goal is to bring about, for example, economic domination of women over men or even "the end of men."

Women's studies is not only the study of women. Rather, it is a way of studying society writ large through the lens of gender. Women's studies examines the gendered power relations that shape the experiences of women *and* men. And because not all women's and men's lived experiences are the same, women's studies also sheds light on the ways that social differences—in race, ethnicity, nationality, sexual identity, generation, class, religion, and physical ability—shape and are shaped by the politics of gender. Women's studies brings together scholarship on the place of women in all realms of society, while also drawing on men's experiences in order to provide a truly comprehensive set of perspectives on our world. Insofar as it highlights and critiques the power relations called gender, women's studies is an explicitly feminist enterprise. As we shall see in Chapter 2, there have been many brands of feminism. Broadly speaking, though, the women's studies approach to feminism reflects its status as a scholarly field, for it has focused on developing concepts and theories that can identify, explain, and contest the ways that men and women come to occupy disparate social positions vis-à-vis each other.

Knowledge about ourselves and our world has usually been divided into disciplines such as history, sociology, and philosophy. Each involves a relatively distinctive approach to knowledge, characterized both by explicit observations concerning what is "true" and implicit assumptions and ethical views. These observations and assumptions provide us with guidelines for human action, as if they were universally applicable. Yet on close inspection, such premises often reveal a predominantly masculine perspective on reality. Women's studies offers both a complement and correction to established disciplines. It requires other fields to reexamine and revise the basic assumptions and methods on which they rest.

By crossing the boundaries between established fields, women's studies provides fresh views of their subject matter and creates coherent new ways of seeing the world. Like other disciplines, it has its own history of theories, its intellectual arc, and its core concepts. And like other fields of scholarly inquiry, women's studies has undergone a series of major shifts since its inception. Many of the programs and departments that emerged across the United States and in universities across the world as "women's studies" have over the past decade begun to change their name to "women's and gender studies," or even "feminist studies." Such changes are the outcome of debates over whether to continue focusing on women exclusively, or whether to also reflect the ways that men are affected by patriarchy. Other programs have chosen to retain the name "women's studies" highlighting their continuing investment in the focus on women, lest women manage to become marginalized anew in the process of expanding the scope of the field to include men. This textbook maintains a critical balance between both perspectives. Our emphasis on women is communicated in our title, *Women's Realities, Women's Choices.* Yet our attention to men reflects our view that gender is a fundamentally relational social category and axis of power and identity. It affects and implicates us all, even if in different ways.

Adding to Our Knowledge about Humans

A major goal of women's studies is to add to what we know about humans by filling in "missing information" about women. For example, for many years archaeologists of prehistory refined theories about human origins based on increasing knowledge about tools and behavior associated with what is generally considered a man's activity: hunting. They concluded that hunted animals provided the entire food supply for these ancient populations; but when feminist anthropologist Sally Slocum (1975) asked what women were doing, it was realized that little or nothing was known of women's activities in foraging communities. This led to the discovery that among some "hunting" societies up to 80% of the diet consisted of vegetable foods gathered by women (Tanner, 1981; Haraway, 1989). Our ancestors are now referred to as "hunter–gatherers." And in contrast to the common view that women only gathered, feminist research in archaeology now suggests that women in the Paleolithic period also excelled in the art and craft of producing all-important stone tools (Arthur, 2010).

The invisibility of women's labor continues to this day. In industrialized societies, women's domestic labor contributes substantially to the economic functioning of members of her household. Yet economists certainly do not factor such work as childrearing, cleaning, cooking, and doing the laundry into the gross domestic product. In the world of literary criticism, male scholars have long rendered women invisible by universalizing the experience of men. Historians, for their part, may have imagined that they knew a great deal about the Renaissance until feminist historian Joan Kelly asked whether *women* had a Renaissance. What were women doing during that period in Europe? It was discovered that developments that were gains for men of the upper classes were losses for women and that if women were taken as the basis for conceptualizing periods of history, the periods would have to be divided very differently (Ferguson et al., 1986; Kelly, 1987).

One reason women have been "invisible" has to do with the way their silence has been sustained. Women have generally been excluded from recorded public discourse. White middle-class women in particular were confined to the domestic sphere of home and family and to less valued "woman's work." Because women of previous centuries were only rarely taught to write, there is relatively little direct documentary material about their lives. Unlike male artists, women were actively discouraged from creating the painting, sculpture, and architecture that historians traditionally study, and work of lasting value done by women was often forgotten through neglect. Many creative women tended to use such forms as music, dance, weaving, tapestry making, quilting, and gardening—forms that were fragile, ephemeral, and anonymous. Women are still poorly represented in the arts establishment among those who decide which paintings will be hung in museums and which books published.

Not only have women had fewer opportunities to express themselves to others, but scholars and critics, usually men, in the past have not selected as interesting the things that women recorded or did. They have felt that the restricted set of activities open to women was simply not very important: what was important was what men did—governing, fighting, and producing "great" works of art. The work of women was often ignored because it was done by women. Indeed, women were often subjected to ridicule for even venturing into the public sphere. Knowing that they would be derogated, some women chose to write under male pen names, such as nineteenth-century novelists George Eliot (Marian Evans) and George Sand (Amandine Aurore Lucie Dupin Dudevant). Even Harriet Beecher Stowe gave God credit for *Uncle Tom's Cabin.*

It is a distortion of history to think that the course of social events has been directed by men's activities alone. Men's wars could not have been fought and male-controlled industrialization could not have taken place without the integral support of women's work and activities. Economic and social changes in men's lives could not have taken place in the same way without the concurrent—if different—changes in women's lives, but these have been largely overlooked. Correcting that invisibility is double-edged, however. Women participate in social processes and world-historical events in ways that warrant a critical perspective. Just as many of the people who argue that feminism is no longer necessary are women—such as the authors of the three books that opened this introduction—so too have women often ranked among the world's most conservative politicians and also among the chief supporters of war.

Today, economic planners are beginning to ask what the impact of technological development is on women around the world. Educators are looking at the effects of particular pedagogical methods on girls' learning of mathematical concepts. In this way they are gaining a new view of phenomena they once thought they understood—from explanations of the origins of culture to the events of a historical period to the processes of social development to the impact of primary school teaching to the development and use of ideologies like that of public and private spheres (Helly and Reverby, 1992). Such critical knowledge is opening our eyes to the realities that have shaped the lives of women and men and constrained their interactions.

Changing Views of Women and Men

The discovery that a great deal of information is missing about humans has contributed to another discovery: some very serious misconceptions about humans, particularly about women, are widely believed. Feminist research has uncovered a large number of mistaken views about women's bodies, mental capacities, activities, and achievements. This book addresses many of these misconceptions and their implications for a better and broader understanding of what it means to be human.

The discipline of women's studies aims to understand how these misconceptions in other disciplines came about, how they affect these disciplines today, and how we might improve the processes of inquiry to develop more reliable knowledge. The historian who wishes to understand why we know so little about women's activities during a particular period might observe that only a limited set of written documents was used to study that time and place, primarily those relating to "public" events or leaders. This historian might then look for other kinds of sources, such as those dealing with local and family records. These records add new kinds of information and yield new insights into the previously used materials. The researcher who asks how women contributed to development in postcolonial African nations might observe that calculations of gross national product were based on men's wage labor and ignored unpaid agricultural production largely done by women. To find out what that production was, the researcher might have to develop new means of collecting data and new types of analysis. It might be necessary to reexamine such basic concepts as "work" and "production" and to rethink the whole notion of how an economy functions.

Women's studies may begin with questions about women, but it leads to many other questions about men and societies and about the methods used to study them. When questions such as these are pursued, they can radically alter the way whole areas of knowledge can be conceptualized (Zalk and Gordon-Kelter, 1992). For instance, most moral theory can be seen to be gender-biased; it has given priority to the norms of "public" life where men have predominated and has discounted as of little moral significance the "personal" interactions largely conducted by women; it has given priority to the rules and rationality traditionally associated with men and denigrated the sensitivity and caring traditionally associated with women (Held, 1993). Not only have feminists disputed this priority, but they have also shown how an ethics of care can be applied to major social institutions for the benefit of society as a whole (Tronto, 2010).

Once we recognize the degree to which gender informs our assumptions and expectations about basic human activities and social relations, we become better equipped both to critique the knowledges that produced and supported such limited views as well as to understand societies past and present, here and around the world, in a more complex way. Our assumptions about how sexual desire operates can obscure the sexual arrangements that have been taken for granted in other cultures or at other historical moments but that feel foreign or even unnatural to us. We can also recognize how masculinity and femininity are expressed and understood that might differ significantly from our own norms. Basic human relations between and among women and men, young and old, majorities and minorities look very different when we bring a feminist perspective.

Women's studies raises questions about all that we have been taught and all that we have learned. It has become increasingly clear that if women are not well understood, neither are men. Just as social systems based on beliefs about "natural" gender roles perpetuate stereotypic female roles, pressuring women to conform to a "feminine" ideal, so do they perpetuate stereotypic male roles, pressuring men to conform to a "masculine" ideal. Women's studies teaches us that gender liberation is for both women and men.

Gender Now

There is a great deal of evidence of growing gender equality worldwide. Consider the following points:

- More women than ever serve as members of their country's legislative bodies at the local, regional, and state levels. As of

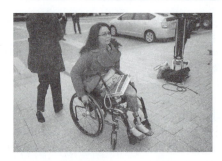

In 2012, Tammy Duckworth (D-Illinois), a veteran of the Iraq War, became the first Asian American from Illinois elected to the House of Representatives. Here she is arriving to pose for a group photo of new members of the 113th Congress.

Judge Nitza I. Quinones of Puerto Rico (left), whom President Barack Obama nominated to the federal judiciary. If confi rmed, she will be the fi rst openly gay Latina appointed to a federal court.

Newly elected U.S. senators Elizabeth Warren (D-Massachusetts) and Tammy Baldwin (D-Wisconsin). In 2012 Baldwin became the first openly gay person elected to the Senate.

2012, women in Rwanda account for 56% of local government officials—the first time in history they have outnumbered men. In Cuba, women make up more than 45% of the legislators at the national level (Inter-Parliamentary Union, 2012). As of 2013, 98 women are serving in the United States Congress, a number representing one third of the total number of women who have ever served. Hence, whereas women have long had a sparse presence in the halls of Congress, they are becoming, for the first time ever, a critical mass.

- In contrast to 1950, when only 34% of working-age women worked in the U.S. labor force, today almost 60% of all women do (Bureau of Labor Statistics, 2011A: 1). And career opportunities have expanded considerably for women.
- In the past, wartime rape was just considered an unfortunate byproduct of armed conflict. In 2002, 60 countries ratified a treaty that created the International Criminal Court at The Hague, which will treat wartime rape as a crime against humanity.

Women are active politically, economically, and socially in ways that were previously unimaginable. Political and economic rights acquired by women now allow them to live their lives quite differently from earlier generations of women. Yet the progress and changes in women's lives that are almost taken for granted today have a long and uneven history, one in which social change was not always to women's benefit.

While women in the United States gained the right to vote in 1920 and entered the worlds of politics and work in unprecedented numbers in the 1920s and 1930s, a few decades later their possibilities shrank and women were actively discouraged from pursuing a life beyond marriage and children. A similar process occurred in the sphere of education. By 1930, 1 in 7 Ph.D.s was earned by a woman, but by 1960, the figure had dropped to about 1 in 10 (Howe, 2000). In Britain and the United States, women entered the workforce en masse during World War II, alleviating a great labor shortage and contributing to the war effort. Yet in the 1950s and 1960s they were sent back to the kitchen. Sexual double standards were rampant, particularly in white middle-class families; because such families could afford it, mothers were expected to care for their children full-time until they were grown. This history shows us that rights and achievements gained can be lost, and hence part of the work of gender studies is to expose, explain, and critique such processes.

While the consciousness that feminism generated in the 1970s and later is still relevant to contemporary society, gender politics themselves are becoming ever more complex and contradictory, requiring us to develop an even sharper gender analysis. Let's consider the following caveats to the statistics that opened this section.

Yes, women are increasingly being elected to political office around the world. But many female elected officials are conservative; we cannot assume that female politicians will always make public policy that is beneficial to women. Yes, women are entering the labor force in ever greater numbers. Yet full-time female workers in the United States, as a group, make only 81.2% of what their male counterparts make (Bureau of Labor Statistics, 2011B). While that figure reflects progress (in 1979 the figure was 62%), that progress has leveled off since the 1990s. Furthermore, consider the fact that much of the labor that women do fails to be remunerated at all; globally, this unpaid labor is estimated to be worth $11 trillion (United Nations Development Fund for Women, 2007). And yes, the use of rape as a weapon of war is now prosecuted as a crime against humanity. That is a recognition, on an international scale, that women's rights are human rights. Yet on a national scale, the picture is bleak. One hundred and twenty-seven countries, including Norway and Britain, have yet to criminalize marital rape (UN Women, 2011–2012). In 2003 dozens of women cadets at the U.S. Air Force Academy reported that they had been raped at the academy and that when they reported the incidents they were subjected to retribution. According to an official Pentagon study conducted in 2011, a violent sex crime occurs in the military every six hours, and 3,192 sexual assaults were reported by U.S. military service personnel (Department of Defense, 2012).

Women's studies attends to new complexities of gender, such as the fact that so many actors of various and often opposing political positions all claim to be working on behalf of women's equality. Events in Afghanistan in 2001–2 brought the plight of women to the attention of the whole world. The Taliban prevented women from going to school and from working outside the home. Women around the world organized in support of Afghan women. Capitalizing on feminist sentiment, the U.S. military and government sought to justify their occupation of Afghanistan and later Iraq by claiming to want to liberate women. These "feminist" justifications are reminiscent of colonial narratives in which, to paraphrase theorist Gayatri Spivak, white men seek to save brown women from brown men. Another example of how the quest for gender equality gets drawn into larger political crises—often in problematic ways—lies in the case of Ayaan Hirsi Ali, a Somali woman who resisted her parents' attempt to marry her to a man she did not know. After successfully gaining political asylum in the Netherlands, she wrote a bestselling memoir, *Infidel* (2007). Ali describes why and how she defied her parents and her religious community on an issue that indeed affects many women. Yet she couches her resistance in a wholesale denunciation not just of Islamic fundamentalism, but of Islam in its totality. In so doing, Ali has become the

darling of the political right and the secular left—and the bane of millions of moderate Muslims around the globe. Perhaps now more than ever, the study of gender—and the seemingly straightforward goal of gender equality—requires careful and critical attention to a broader set of political dynamics and historical relations than those focused solely on the categories "male" and "female."

The continuing study of gender is also warranted by the fact that the categories "male" and "female" are becoming increasingly unstable. In terms of gender roles, feminists have long argued that it is our culture, not our biology, that assigns different attributes to males and females. Feminists reject evaluations that esteem presumably "masculine" qualities, such as being aggressive and autonomous, when found in men while deploring these qualities in women, and they affirm the moral importance, for men as well as for women, of various presumably "feminine" qualities, such as being caring and compassionate. Any quality may appear in any human being and should be evaluated on its own merits, not in terms of the gender of the person in whom it appears.

The wisdom that biology is not destiny is also being examined anew in the realm of gender identity. People who are born with female bodies can become men and vice versa—and not simply through medical procedures, but through a thorough-going practice and performance of masculinity or femininity (respectively). Importantly, the term "transgender" refers not only to the adoption of the "opposite" gender identity, but also to the crafting of an identity that seeks to defy binary notions of gender altogether. In 2012, Argentina became the first country in the world to allow people to alter their gender designation on official documents without having to first undergo surgery or psychotherapy. The law defines gender identity as "the inner and individual gender experience as each person feels it" (Schmall, 2012: 8).

Women's studies today is dedicated to apprehending new ways that gender identities are being expressed and embodied, as well as to analyzing the new social and political questions that arise in the process.

The terrain of feminist activism—where it literally takes place—has also undergone a shift. The growth of social networking websites has arguably made feminist activism more powerful than ever. Facebook, Twitter, and the blogosphere have been critical to this process. As feminist author and blogger Kate Harding notes, "When your brand's Facebook wall is overtaken by feminist outrage, you can't just write it off as a few man-hating cranks and continue on as usual" (quoted in Watson, 2012). In 2012, when the Komen Foundation—a conservative organization that developed the famous pink ribbon campaigns in the fight against breast cancer—decided to withdraw funding from Planned Parenthood because of its position on abortion, the issue became a huge controversy within hours. On Facebook, not only did people spread the news, creating a public relations nightmare for the Komen Foundation, but they also encouraged their "friends" to donate to Planned Parenthood. The organization received $400,000 from 6,000 online donors the day after the news broke (Kliff and Sun, 2012). The challenge of women's studies is to examine both the complexities of gender in the twenty-first century and the myriad tactics that are emerging in relation to them.

History of Women's Studies

The development of an academic manifestation of feminism has been a relatively recent addition to the history of feminism. Although there were scattered courses in areas such as women's history or women in literature, women's studies was not taught under that name on U.S. college campuses until 1970. In the late 1960s, concurrent with the civil rights, students' rights, and antiwar movements and the creation of black studies, courses sprang up around the country exploring the status of women, discrimination experienced in public roles and private lives, and gender bias in general in society, literature, and learning (Buhle, 2000). Dozens of courses, some official and some unofficial, were launched in a variety of contexts by instructors with many different academic backgrounds but most often in the liberal arts: humanities, sociology, psychology, and history. During the next six years, such courses proliferated on American campuses. Instructors exchanged syllabi and ideas about how to teach with a critical feminist pedagogy. Scholar-activists brought their organizing skills and experiences in the movements of the 1960s to the struggle to have women's studies institutionalized on college campuses.

From 1970 to 1976, women's studies began to be articulated as a distinctive, increasingly integrated field. Journals in women's studies were established, including, in the United States alone, *Feminist Studies, Quest, Sex Roles, Signs, Women's Studies,* and *Women's Studies Quarterly.* Anthologies and books in women's studies were published, heralding the birth of the discipline. The National Women's Studies Association was founded in 1977 to facilitate the sharing of information among individuals involved in women's studies and other feminist pursuits. In 1984 with the publication of *This Bridge Called My Back: Writings by Radical Women of Color* by Cherríe Moraga and Gloria Anzaldua, the centrality of women of color's experiences and voices fundamentally changed feminism. Writings by Adrienne Rich, Barbara Smith, Gloria Anzaldúa, and others critiqued heterosexual privilege and focused on the multiple experiences of lesbian and bisexual women.

The publication of Edward Said's *Orientalism* (1978) spawned an entire field of inquiry on postcolonialism, which had a major impact on feminist scholarship. Said's work exposes and critiques the way colonizing societies constructed an east/west binary that continues to operate, even after the official end of colonialism. Postcolonial theory examines the continuing manifestations of a false dichotomy between the "the west and the rest" and other related binaries such as "traditional/modern." Non-Western (African, Asian, Latin American, and indigenous) societies are always "traditional," a euphemism for "backward," while Western societies (the United States and Europe) are represented as advanced or "modern." Contemporary postcolonial feminism, exemplified in the work of Gayatri Spivak (1988) and Trinh T. Min-ha (1989), has developed these critiques, applying them to Western feminism.

Other feminist scholar-activists focus instead on the ways in which historical and contemporary forms of imperialism impact women in the Global South. Transnational or global feminism is premised on a broad critique of the assumption that there is a universal form of feminism, one that Western women should or will teach to women of the Global South (Grewal and Kaplan 1994; Abu-Lughod, 1998; Mohanty, 2003). Transnational feminism is especially attuned to the influence of racism, nationalism, and global capitalism on the production of inequalities and other forms of structural violence within and across societies, as well as to their heterogeneous expressions and effects. Central to its vision is the need to recognize and meet the challenges that such differences pose to feminist practice—that is, to the project of building "a noncolonizing feminist solidarity across borders" (Mohanty, 2003: 224) One concrete example of these kinds of dynamics lies in the discussion above about Ayaan Hirsi Ali. A transnational feminist perspective would insist that we not simply see her as a woman resisting patriarchy, but as someone whose words and actions are seized upon in ways that collude with (and

even spring from) bigoted views of Muslims, lending justification to the violation of their civil and human rights.

Queer theory, which emerged in the 1990s, was another major influence on feminist analysis. Indeed, it posed a serious challenge to it by arguing that a primary focus on gender constrains the study of sexuality—or better, sexualities. Queer theorists were interested in all marginalized sexualities, which is to say all forms of sexual practice that fell outside of the norm, not just homosexuality (Rubin, 1993). And unlike women's studies, which originally emerged as the study of women, queer theory scholars refused to name a single population—again, such as gay men, lesbians, and bisexuals—as the subject of study. The contingency of the term "queer," Judith Butler wrote, "allows it to take on meanings that cannot now be anticipated by a younger generation whose political vocabulary may well carry a very different set of investments" (1993: 21). But women's studies also had a critical impact on queer theory. As described above, women's studies scholars began fully incorporating race and class analyses back in the 1980s. Feminist scholars brought those critical perspectives to bear upon queer theorists, who had often focused on sexualities to the exclusion of other axes of social difference (Jagose, 2009).

The roots of women's studies are in feminist critiques not only of existing scholarship, but of higher education. A distinctive characteristic of women's studies, inherited from its earliest days, has been the development of collective modes of production. The first women's studies courses were often collaborative efforts involving both faculty and graduate students. These courses also introduced critical new pedagogies to decenter power in the classroom. For example, instructors encouraged students to draw upon their life experiences in order to aid the learning process and to promote participatory democracy (Buhle,

2000). Although women who are scholars, professionals, artists, and the like often work alone, they also often pool their resources of skills and energy for collective work that does not emphasize individual achievement but rather the shared product made possible only by cooperative group effort. This book is one example.

Since the inception of women's studies in the 1970s, there has been a virtual explosion of scholarly books and articles on women, and feminist perspectives have transformed much of the work in fields as varied as literature and poetry, health and medicine, history, psychology, philosophy, law, political science, economic development, communications, and management. Many university and trade presses have adopted book series on women and gender, finding an increasing demand for them. Women's and gender studies have produced a proliferation of scholarly works on feminist theory across all fields.

By 2007, there were over 900 women's/gender/feminist studies programs worldwide: more than 600 undergraduate programs exist in the United States at public and private institutions, large and small, single-sex and coeducational (NWSA, 2007). These programs enroll the largest number of students in any interdisciplinary field. Undergraduates can take majors and minors in the field, and there are well over 100 programs at the master's-degree level and a small but growing number of doctoral programs. Part of the price that feminists have had to pay for their success in academe has been intellectual harassment of their teaching and scholarly

Co-authors of *Women's Realities, Women's Choices*

Box I.1   WOMEN'S EDUCATION AT HUNTER COLLEGE

Established in 1870 as New York City's first public normal (teacher training) college for women, by 1914 Hunter had developed into a full liberal arts college named after its first president, Thomas Hunter. In 1964 it became coeducational. Hunter College ranked first in a study of the number of female graduates of undergraduate institutions who obtained doctorates in the period 1920–73 (Tidball and Kistiakowsky, 1976). Now a part of the City University of New York, the student body at Hunter has always been at least 70% female, with a large proportion of adult women. Its diverse student body reflects the many cultural, ethnic, and religious groups that make up New York City. The women's studies program, initiated in 1971, became official by 1976, offering now both a major and a minor. In 2006 after a series of meetings with students and faculty and in response to the changes in the discipline, the name was formally changed to The Women and Gender Studies Program (WGS). The program has also grown tremendously and currently has over 85 majors. Since 2009, students and faculty have campaigned to make WGS into a department. In 2013, the program was granted departmental status.

publications (Clark et al., 1996; Vargas, 2002; Hune, 2011) and continued marginalization in the profession as a whole (Eisenhart and Finkel, 1998). Just as women students were often in the forefront of initiatives to establish women's studies, so too must they take the responsibility, along with committed faculty, for ensuring that women's/gender/feminist studies programs do not become obsolete— a real danger considering the ever-present reality of cutbacks in university funding, the declining support for academic programs related to subordinated groups, and the growing viewpoint, described earlier, that feminist goals have been achieved.

The U.S. Women's Movement: A Brief History

Although the history of the U.S. women's movement will be presented in Chapter 13, here we outline the ways that it tends to be periodized, which is in terms of three broad eras known as "waves."

The first wave of the women's movement occurs between the late nineteenth and the early twentieth centuries and is most associated with the struggle for women's suffrage. Elizabeth Cady Stanton (1815–1902) and Susan B. Anthony (1820–1906) were early pioneers in what became known as "the woman movement" (Cott, 1987). Having begun their activist careers as abolitionists, they developed a critical perspective on the subordinate place of women in American society, eventually giving speeches and otherwise campaigning on a wide range of issues from family law to birth control to voting rights. The latter issue became the rallying cry of a mass movement in the 1910s, drawing strength from the political climate of the times when, for example, the rights of industrial workers were also actively being asserted. The term "feminist" emerged in this period, both as a reaction against the forms of Christian respectability and moral uplift that animated "the woman movement" and as an explicit strategy to forge a common political identity for women as a group in the hopes of maintaining focus and momentum in the period after the suffragists won the franchise (Cott, 1987). Indeed, that signature achievement in 1920 is generally marked as the end of the first wave, for the radical and mainstream branches of the suffrage movement then split and pursued separate goals (Cott, 1987). Although not commonly recognized, women's activism continued well after 1920. To provide just one example, in the 1940s a small, elite group of feminists struggled for the passage of an Equal Rights Amendment to the Constitution (Taylor, 1989).

The mid-1960s marks the beginning of second-wave feminism, which, unlike common understandings of the first wave, does not have a clear-cut end. The 1963 publication of *The Feminist Mystique* by Betty Friedan is often credited with effectively sparking feminism's second wave (Davis, 1991). In "one of the most influential nonfiction books of the 20th century" (Fox, 2006), Friedan proffered a political analysis for a pervasive sentiment among middle-class, white American housewives living in the suburbs: they were deeply dissatisfied with their lives. Contemporary scholarship argues that *The Feminist Mystique* did not quite start the movement as much as it capitalized upon growing attention to women's rights that was already emerging in society writ large—even within the halls of government (Coontz, 2011). Betty Friedan founded the National Organization for Women in 1966, serving as its president until 1970.

The 1960s was an era of profound cultural transformation in American society, owing to widespread political agitation occurring across the entirety of the social landscape. The civil rights and antiwar movements inspired myriad other political struggles—and not only in the name of reform but increasingly in the revolutionary name of "freedom." The women's movement found a revolutionary voice in the work of Australian feminist Germaine Greer, whose 1970 book *The Female Eunuch* became a bestseller. Unlike Friedan, Greer did not couch her feminism in terms of equality but rather liberation. As indicated above, women's studies courses emerged during this period. Gloria Steinem and others founded *Ms.* magazine, and figures like tennis champion Billie Jean King became pop icons.

Whether in the name of equality or liberation, second-wave activism employed a wide-ranging set of methods. It did not focus solely on laws and policies—although it did do that, for example by reviving the campaign for an Equal Rights Amendment to the Constitution. The movement also took aim at the culture as a whole. Women's liberationists tossed out their bras, calling dramatic attention to the ways their bodies had been sexualized and constrained. Feminists believed that in order to effect fundamental social change, ordinary women needed to learn to recognize gender oppression; the formation of women-only "consciousness-raising" groups became one strategy for achieving that goal. The slogan "the personal is political" encouraged women to make the connection between their own life experiences and the larger forces that produced them. Women's solidarity was framed in the idiom of sisterhood, and explicit historical links were forged with first-wave feminists, who were claimed as foremothers. One powerful example of this reclaiming is in the writings of Shulamith Firestone, author of a seminal text, *The Dialectic of Sex* (2003 [1970]). Firestone resuscitated interest in the nineteenth-century women's movement by detailing the true radicalism of their work.

Second-wave feminism has long been critiqued for being a white middle-class movement blind to the ways that gender is lived by poor women, lesbians, and women of color, again as suggested above. Yet the fact that women of marginalized groups may have been outsiders within mainstream feminist circles does not mean that they did not participate in the movement. In the 1970s, black and Chicana women's feminist activism more often took place in organizational arenas revolving around race. While not hostile to white women's liberation efforts, feminists of color prioritized their work in organizations where they could forge a politic consistent with their view that race, class, and gender were inseparable bases of oppression (Roth, 2004). White-run women's organizations that did attract black women were those that operated from that point of view (Valk, 2008). Among the most enduring achievements of women of color's second-wave activism is the scholarship they produced. In addition to some of the anthologies cited above (e.g, Moraga and Anzaldua, 1983), there is also the groundbreaking theoretical-cum-political treatise by the Combahee River Collective (1979) called "A Black Feminist Statement" (see Chapter 3).

Feminists of the second wave generally belong to the "baby boomer" generation, a term for people born between 1946 and 1964. Feminism's third wave—again speaking very generally—belongs to "Generation X," which refers to people born between 1963 and 1974. Some third wavers passionately distinguish themselves from their predecessors (Walker, 1995; Astrid, 2004). In general, these third wavers seek to redress what they see as the shortcomings of the second wave—such as its singular focus on women, as opposed to a larger, more complex set of politics and social positions. They couch their critique of the movement in terms of a generational split, which is both poignant and fitting considering that many of them are the actual daughters of second-wave activists. Rebecca Walker, daughter of the author Alice Walker, famously proclaimed the very dawn of the third wave when, in 1992, she wrote the following in

Ms.: "I am not a post-feminist feminist. I am the Third Wave" (Walker, 1992: 41). In so declaring, Walker heralded the arrival of an entirely new incarnation of feminists, one that was clearly not a continuation of the second wave (this, despite the fact that her important proclamation appeared in the second wave's pathbreaking magazine). Nor did Walker mean for the third wave to be confused with "postfeminist feminists." The term "postfeminist" is a slippery term, sometimes referring to conservative feminists and other times referring to the view that, having achieved its goals, feminism is over.

As was the case with the previous waves, the third is not monolithic. Some third wavers do recognize and celebrate their continuities with the second wave. They locate the bridge between eras in the scholarship of U.S. women of color, such as that which has already been cited in this chapter. Scholars such as Gloria Anzaldua, Angela Davis, Cherrie Moraga, Chela Sandoval, and, very importantly, bell hooks all wrote critically important works in the 1980s and the early 1990s. These women's works argued for the inextricability of race, class, sexuality, and gender, both as axes of power and as bases of identity, community, and solidarity. And their works, each in its own way, emphasized both the difficulty and the importance of respecting difference and negotiating across it for the purposes of forming political coalitions. Yet, whereas the second wave would simply acknowledge difference by proclaiming that "sisterhood is powerful" (Morgan, 1970), this new generation dispensed altogether with the language of "sisterhood" and of "foremothers" (Hewyood and Drake, 1997; Astrid, 2004) since those terms assume a common identity among women. The third wave, after all, came of intellectual-cum-political age in women's studies classes in the 1990s. The brand of feminist theory they would have been reading was dominated by postmodernism

and poststructuralism. In short, these two perspectives posed a serious challenge to essentialism—or the view that any identity category, such as "woman," has a set of irreducible, stable, and universally-agreed-upon meanings.

The two expressions of third-wave feminism sketched above share the view that gender cannot be a stand-alone basis of identity, community, or political activism. Third-wave feminists on the whole seek to transcend a narrow focus on gender. Walker, herself a black woman, founded the Third Wave Foundation, whose mission statement indicates that it supports "groups and individuals working towards gender, racial, economic and social justice" (http://www.thirdwavefoundation.org/about-us/mission/). The third wave also opposes the kind of identity policing that would restrict young women's desires in the realm of fashion and lifestyle. They seek instead to broaden ideas of what an independent woman with control over her life might look like. They are sex-positive—a position that eschews censorship or other ways of restricting the free expression of sexuality—and they embrace nonnormative gender identities including transgender.

One of the cornerstones of third-wave feminism is its technology: its message is often spread through websites, blogs, and social networking sites. And it is not the traditional organizations and publications, such as the National Organization for Women (NOW) or *Ms.* magazine, that are galvanizing young women on feminist issues through digital media, but rather sites such as Reel Girl, The Crunk Feminist Collective (rooted in southern black hip-hop culture), and Jezebel, a site proudly proclaiming to be about "Celebrity. Sex. Fashion for Women. Without Airbrushing." Jezebel consistently delivers irreverent but wholly feminist messages. It can also boast more "likes" on Facebook than NOW and *Ms.* combined. The instantaneous nature of Internet communication also facilitates the efficacy of protests and boycotts, allowing them to sprout up immediately from an individual woman's blog or Facebook post, rather than depending on the slow-moving mechanisms of traditional organizations.

The image of waves has become fundamental to the way the U.S. women's movement is understood. However, it has some very serious drawbacks. Chief among them is the fact that, like most attempts at historical periodization, it creates a false sense of coherence within one era and downplays continuities across eras. And as a metaphor, the image "of waves crashing onto land and then receding" does a disservice, if not outright damage, to the movement as a whole (Fernandes, 2010: 114). For example, it creates the impression that nothing of significance happened in the gaps between eras, which could not be more untrue (Harrison, 1988; Taylor, 1989). Moreover, the wave idiom overvalorizes mass mobilization and concrete victories such as the passage (or repeal) of laws, and hence renders the movement's less visible triumphs—for example, in the sphere of social transformation or shifts in attitudes—less important. The apparent lack of spectacular achievements invites detractors to glibly announce the death of feminism (Nicholson, 2010). Finally, the wave narrative normalizes the American experience, promoting a nationalist view of the world.

In closing, our own (the authors) personal experiences suggest that wholesale distinctions between the waves is overdrawn, the result of cultural misrepresentations. Some of us who came of age in the 1980s and 1990s were taught by the surrounding culture that the pioneers of the second wave of the feminist movement were angry, man-hating, and anti-sex (see Box I.2). When we explored this history for ourselves we discovered how courageous, creative, and forward-thinking these women were about every aspect of life. Likewise, the older women among us

remember that when we were young, the suffragettes who demonstrated and won the vote for women were no models of who we wanted to be. And here the work of Shulamith Firestone, mentioned above, was pivotal, for she railed against the common stereotyping of feminists that served to inhibit women from defining themselves as such (see Box I.3). Our own image of the suffragists was of women who were dowdy, frumpy, and definitely not sexy. We wanted to be attractive, contemporary, and focused on our own lives. We thought we were interested in the same things as men. Only later did we appreciate the achievements of the suffragists and begin to see how far we still needed to go to achieve the equality for which gaining the vote was only a beginning.

How This Book Presents Women's Studies

We begin with a focus on the ways that the category "woman" and gender more broadly have been culturally constructed in different times and places and within different kinds of representations and socio-political contexts—all with an eye toward showing the ways these constructions have affected lived experience. We then move on to study women in the context of their various social relationships, with special reference to their positions within ever-changing family forms; and lastly, we examine the gendering of key social arenas and institutions—specifically, the domains of education, work, religion, and politics. Inevitably, we found that certain topics could just as easily have appeared in the work chapter as in the one on politics. At times we opted in favor of slight repetition in order to highlight the way a single phenomenon or event (such as the U.S. Supreme Court decision of 2011 favoring Wal-Mart in a class action suit filed by women employees) could focus important attention on different

Box I.2   ARE FEMINISTS ANTI-SEX?

One of the most persistent stereotypes of feminists is that they are anti-sex. Over the centuries, however, the pursuit of sexual fulfillment unbound by social conventions has proven to be a cornerstone of feminism. Sappho, Mary Wollstonecraft, George Sand, and many other early feminists lived and loved outside the bonds of marriage and heteronormativity. And in the contemporary era, we need only examine the life and legacy of Helen Gurley Brown to further dispel the myth.

In the early 1960s, an era defined by conservative gender ideals dictating that marriage should be a young woman's highest goal in life, Brown authored *Sex and the Single Girl* (1962). That book boldly proclaimed that single women should claim and control their sexuality, rather than keeping it under wraps only to be revealed and expressed in the marital boudoir. She turned the dominant view of (hetero)sexual power relations on its head, writing, for example, that: "Theoretically a 'nice' single woman has no sex life. What nonsense! She has a better sex life than most of her married friends. She need never be bored with one man per lifetime. Her choice of partners is endless and they seek *her*. They never come to her bed duty-bound. Her married friends refer to her pursuers as wolves, but actually many of them turn out to be lambs—to be shorn and worn by her" (1962:7). The book sold 2 million copies in three weeks.

Brown's influence on American culture is evident in the rise of television programs depicting this young, urban, unmarried, career woman who had her own apartment in the big city: there was *That Girl* (starring Marlo Thomas) in the late 1960s and early 1970s, followed by the eponymous *The Mary Tyler Moore Show*. Brown's version of feminism is also evident in the more recent and indeed era-defining HBO series *Sex and the City*. The creators of the AMC television series *Mad Men*, set in an advertising agency in the 1960s, specifically cite Brown's life as a model for the character Peggy Olson. Brown began her career in an advertising agency, rising to become one of the highest paid copywriters in the country. After hitting the glass ceiling there, she was hired as editor-in-chief for the then fledgling magazine, *Cosmopolitan*.

Some might consider Brown an unlikely feminist heroine. Indeed, her name scarcely emerges on lists of feminist icons of our time. Even her contemporaries in the quest for women's liberation did not embrace her particular vision of it. After all, "Cosmo," as it is affectionately called, addressed its readership in terms of glamour and sexuality, seemingly at the expense of other dimensions of women's lives. Yet those were only the most conspicuous aspects of its content, for the magazine also included career and financial advice in every issue. Brown, who very much saw herself as a feminist, emphasized that "the single girl," in order to be fabulous, must be financially independent.

The status of Brown as a feminist worth looking up to, as well as the sexy vision of feminism that she espoused, are matters of debate—as is every other vision of feminism. Brown emphasized financial independence but came short of identifying and denouncing the economic and political structures that stand in the way of it for many women. While celebrating glamour, she failed to critique the social pressures involved in meeting impossible bodily ideals. Brown herself took the desire for eternal youth to extremes, with numerous surgeries and an apparent eating disorder. Women of color have been exceedingly rare both on the cover and in the magazine's pages. Finally, the *Sex and the City* version of how to be a modern woman is often cited as a prime example of postfeminism for emphasizing, for example, "a woman's right to shoes"—a phrase actually uttered in one episode. Just as one might question how the flaunting of sexuality could possibly serve as the grounding of a feminist way of life, so too have fashion and consumerism been recurring themes in contestations over legitimate expressions of feminist identity (Tasker and Negra, 2007).

Source: Based on Jennifer Scanlon, *Bad Girls Go Everywhere: the Life of Helen Gurley Brown.* New York: Oxford University Press, 2009.

Box I.3   STEREOTYPING THE FEMINIST: A VIEW FROM 1968

What does the word "feminism" bring to mind? A granite-faced spinster obsessed with a vote? Or a George Sand in cigar and bloomers, a woman against nature? Chances are that whatever image you have, it is a negative one. To be called a feminist has become an insult, so much so that a young woman intellectual, often radical in every other area, will deny vehemently that she is a feminist, will be ashamed to identify in any way with the early women's movement, calling it cop-out or reformist or demeaning it politically without knowing even the little that is circulated about it.…I would like to suggest a reason for this.…[W]omen's rights (liberation, if you prefer) has dynamite revolutionary potential.

[A] real women's movement is dangerous. From the beginning it exposed the white male power structure in all its hypocrisy. Its very existence and long duration were proof of massive large-scale inequality in a system that pretended to democracy. Both the Abolitionist Movement and the Women's Rights Movement, working at times together, at times separately, threatened to tear the country apart, and very nearly did during the Civil War.

Source: "The Women's Rights Movement in the U.S.A.: New View," in Shulamith Firestone, *Notes from the First Year.* New York: The New York Radical Women, 1968.

---

aspects of women's experience and the politics of gender.

Women are not one group of people with common backgrounds, experiences, and perspectives. When we wrote the first edition of this book in the early 1980s, there was much more information on white, middle-class women and women in the majority classes of more industrialized countries than on other women, including women from industrially developing parts of the world and in earlier periods of history. As women's studies has grown and as more women with diverse backgrounds are contributing to it, literature and scholarly work continue to be developed by and about women who had previously not received enough attention. This fourth edition of the book incorporates many rich insights, new points of view, and added information provided by such material. Clearly, understanding women and women's experiences historically, across cultures, races, classes, generations, and sexual orientations—indeed, across all the barriers that potentially divide women—requires a heightened awareness of both their differences and their similarities.

The co-authors of this textbook are all current or past professors at Hunter College. Since this is the fourth edition, we can still read some of the words of the women who worked on previous editions but who either have died, have been unable to continue, or are now engaged in other scholarly pursuits. All of the current authors—some more, some less—worked on all the chapters, using a unique "round robin" method of cooperative composition. Two members of the collaborative were in charge of each chapter. The entire group commented on the first draft, both online and in plenary meetings. Next, groups of three other authors were assigned to review and revise the chapters in each of the three subsections. In addition, Oxford University Press solicited comments from teachers of women's studies in educational institutions of various types. They remain anonymous, but we are grateful for their contribution.

In keeping with the new insights and points of view on women, the fourth edition has removed references to women as an undifferentiated whole. In the previous editions, the term "we" was often used to describe all women, minimizing differences across categories of women. In this latest edition, we avoid claiming a universal woman. Another term we struggled over was that for countries once referred to as the "Third World." Historically, the "First World" referred to the industrialized Western countries; the "Second World" included the Soviet Union

and its allies in eastern Europe and Central Asia; and the "Third World" included Africa, Asia, and Latin America. With the collapse of the "Second World" as a distinctive grouping, and with the recognition that the term "Third World" represents a problematic lumping together of the majority of the world's people, the latter term has fallen out of favor. After much discussion and in recognition of the new political realities and current thinking on Africa, Asia, and Latin America, we have substituted "developing" for "Third World." However, since much of the "developing" world is heavily industrialized (think of how much of our technology is manufactured in "developing" countries), we also refer to those regions as the "Global South" and the "developed" world as the "Global North." While these geographic labels are imperfect, they do fairly accurately describe the way in which resources and power have been concentrated and exercised. This edition also uses the terms "African American" and "black" interchangeably. Despite the popularity of the former term, "black" remains important for naming a political identity. "Black" refers to the manifold politics of race, racism, and racialization over and above those of ethnicity, with which the term "African American" is associated.

Women's studies is devoted to the study of all women. For this, one needs to understand the consequences of being assigned membership in a human group socially labeled "women" and the enormous differences among women. Women's studies seeks to understand the possibilities of what one can make of one's life as a human being.

Part *I*

Defining Women and Gender

Women's and Gender Studies today are committed to understanding the social, political, economic, historical, and cultural factors that give rise to different conceptualizations and differential practices concerning women, men, and gender both across cultures and within the same society. Our first task is to understand how women and gender have been understood and how the dominant ideas and practices concerning women and gender are reproduced from one generation to the next. This will help us to determine whether these ideas and practices need to be changed as well as how they can be changed.

The long history of ideas about women and gender provides a case study for how power can infect philosophy and scholarship in general. Until very recently, women's own ideas and experiences have been overlooked and omitted within academic disciplines. Privileged men, with the power and authority to control ideas and their dissemination, have been the main producers of knowledge about the world and about how gender identities should operate. One important consequence of this control of knowledge has been that in nearly every society the male has been viewed as the "ideal" and, thus, characteristics associated with men have been more highly valued than characteristics associated with women.

Women have long been defined as "not men" or as the "other" to men. Because women were viewed as defective or incomplete males, inherently inferior and even less than human, their characteristics, their work, and their contributions to society have been devalued. In Western thinking, for example, women have been seen as less rational, more frivolous, closer to nature, more emotional, and less aggressive than men. The conceptualization of women as "other" has led to an emphasis in much thinking and research on the differences between women and men rather than the similarities shared by all humans. In many cases there are more differences within genders than between genders, and yet gender differences continue to be emphasized. Since the most obvious differences between women and men are anatomical, it has not been unusual for women to be defined in terms of their reproductive systems and for their biological differences to be taken as the explanation and rationalization for their social subordination.

Thus, women have been understood and studied as the "other" for centuries; only recently, with the advent of the modern women's movement and women's and gender studies, has there been a sustained effort to understand women from the perspective of women themselves, to put the elements of women's daily lives at the center of analysis, to value women's contributions to ideas, to acknowledge their creativity, and to document the central role women play in the maintenance, reproduction, and development of their society, wherever they may live. There is also a growing scholarship on the actual variety that has existed historically and across cultures in regard to the social ideas and practices of gender and the many different formations gender has taken. Gender arrangements and gender-based divisions of labor have been varied, and not all societies have assumed that there are only two genders.

Today there are lively debates among feminist scholars, especially in the humanities and social sciences, over how we should understand how gender identities and roles have historically worked and what sort of future we would like to work toward. They have shown that just as gender has differentially privileged men over women and heterosexuals over nonheterosexuals, so too have such social structures involving race and ethnicity, class, ability, age, religion, national origin, and culture differentially privileged some women over others and even some women over some men. In many cases lesbians have not only been subordinate but rendered invisible, defined as both "not men" and "not women."

These insights have led to the development of intersectional approaches to scholarship, in which multiple categories of analysis are understood to be necessary for any explanation. The experience of sexism, for example, differs not just in degree—or how much of it one might have to bear—but also in kind or in the form that it takes. There is no lowest common denominator of sexism or any other form of discrimination. Thus, feminist scholars today study and analyze how ideas about "woman" and gender maintain and reproduce power relations and how ideas about race, ethnicity, and other forms of difference intersect with ideas about gender to produce social stratification.

Women, from whatever social group, need not read the scholarly literature on women to know how they have been seen and understood. Definitions of women, ideas about women's bodies and the biological basis of gender categories, and assumptions about race, ethnicity, sexuality, and differential ability are communicated in multiple ways in all nations. They are communicated through images, language, and nonlinguistic symbols in myths, rituals, folklore, and the media. In the course of socialization and education, whether in a household, a classroom, or a movie theater, we are all told how we should act, what we should desire, who we should strive to be, and how we should value our-selves. The implications and consequences of such definitions affect our daily lives, mold-ing our identities and sense of self from child-hood to old age. Such definitions impose on women and men the expectations of society and provide a framework within which to cen-sor those who do not, or will not, conform to those expectations.

The chapters in Part I investigate how the questions about women and gender have tra-ditionally been answered. They focus on how these beliefs have been constructed through images and ideas about women's "nature," their bodies, personalities, and "proper" social roles. They assess how these images and ideas vary cross-culturally and how they differen-tially affect the lives and choices of all of us.

chapter **1**

Cultural Representations of Women

Identity is not as unproblematic as we might think. Perhaps instead of thinking of identity as an already accomplished fact...we should think, instead, of identity as a "production" which is never complete, always in process, and always constituted within, not outside representation.

STUART HALL, 1992

Culture, Representation, and Gender

Experience, Perception, and the Construction of Reality

Think about what you know about gender. What is it that makes a woman a woman or a man a man? What physical, psychological, emotional, professional, and other characteristics combine to create what we understand as "woman" or "man"? Now think about *how* you know what you know. Was there a moment in which an adult in your life told you that a behavior, toy, or article of clothing was not for boys or for girls? Or a classmate made fun of your clothes, appearance, or taste in books or music as not appropriate for your gender? What books did you read as a child that laid out what girls should do? What television programs did you watch that had girls as central, active participants in the action, or were they mostly hanging around in the background? When you play video games, how many of the protagonists are girls or women? How about in music videos: How are women represented either at the forefront or in the background? What kind of clothes are they wearing?

Much of this book will discuss where our ideas of gender come from, how they play out in the United States and elsewhere, and how they have changed over time and vary across cultures. In this chapter we'll be talking about how these ideas are communicated and absorbed through *cultural representation*: through myths, books, music, television, movies, magazines, the Internet, fashion,

and other cultural phenomena. While representation can seem trivial compared to nuts-and-bolts politics and policies affecting women's lives, in fact it pervades our lives in a way unparalleled in our history. Almost from birth we are surrounded by images from a variety of media, and none of those images is free from assumptions about appropriate gender behaviors and self-presentation.

"Culture" is a concept that comes in large part from the field of anthropology. It embraces the behaviors and attitudes that we learn from our communities, systems of symbols like language and religious practices, and complex social organizations such as families, friendship groups, and voluntary associations (Tomasello, 1999). Our earliest learning comes through imitation: babies watch and imitate parents and other children, and that pattern continues throughout childhood. In order to make sense of the world around us, we absorb our culture's literal and figurative languages: not just the words "woman" and "girl," but the *concepts* of womanhood, girlhood, and femininity.

The Construction of Gender in Culture and in Ourselves

Many of the images that we see today have deep roots in U.S. culture; some are of more recent vintage. Cultural representation is tricky to negotiate, particularly when it comes to gender. There are ongoing debates about cause and effect: Do the images of women that we encounter simply reflect women's experiences in the world, or do they also actively construct what we believe we know about women and men? While it is clear that representation provides a mirror, however distorted, of how we understand gender, it is also true that the images we see around us shape our expectations of how the world *should* be, how women *should* look, behave, and interact with each other and with men and children. Representation is also culturally specific even as we might absorb it as universally true and natural—for example, in the United States skirts and dresses are represented and worn as female clothing, something that might come as a surprise to an Egyptian man wearing a *djellaba*, an Indonesian boy wearing a sarong, or a Scotsman wearing a kilt.

While representations of gender may feel self-evident and natural, they are on the whole constructed and sometimes even arbitrary. For example, it seems obvious to us that children wear specific colors depending on gender, with blue being assigned to boys and pink to girls. This seemingly inevitable color-coding is an invention of the twentieth century. In fact, before World War I, pink was associated more with boys: one newspaper in 1914 suggested: "If you like the color note on the little one's garments, use pink for the boy and blue for the girl, if you are a follower of convention," and even as late as 1918 the *Ladies Home Journal* declared: "There has been a great diversity of opinion on the subject, but the generally accepted rule is pink for the boy and blue for the girl. The reason is that pink being a more decided and stronger color is more suitable for the boy, while blue, which is more delicate and dainty, is pertier for the girl" (http://histclo.com/gender/col/col-pink.html).

There is no logical reason that men should be more adept at repairing cars or solving mathematical equations than women or that women should be responsible for keeping homes clean or worrying about their children's academic achievement. Yet it is hard to find media representations of men mopping a floor or women fixing cars. And it is a short step from not seeing these images to believing that a woman shouldn't want to fix cars or a man should see mopping a floor as not his responsibility.

As important as external images of women and men, representation shapes our inner lives as well. The images that we see of women's lives, women's work, love, sexuality, relationships with others, mothering, and overall place in society shape the ways we understand our own lives. From the earliest stories we hear of Cinderella and Sleeping Beauty, who are rescued by a prince and live "happily ever after," to romantic comedies in which the happy ending is the pairing up of male and female protagonists, we learn that women's satisfaction in life depends upon marriage. As we'll see in Chapter 5, even (or especially) the ways in which women experience our bodies are powerfully shaped by the images we see of female beauty and attractiveness in that idealized bodies—slim, curvaceous, hairless, able bodies—are represented not just as the ideal but as the norm. For decades, almost all images of idealized women and men were of white people: film producers, television writers, and advertisers could not even imagine that people of color lived complex, interesting, attractive lives with which white viewers could identify. It was only in the wake of civil rights organizing that the popular media represented people of color in any meaningful way, and this lack of representation is still a major problem in the United States. When we don't have access to a variety of images of masculinity and femininity across class and race, it is difficult—although not impossible—to generate those concepts for ourselves.

The problem with these images is not that they exist. After all, there's nothing objectively wrong with a man fixing a car or a woman mopping a floor. The problem is that these images act as *norms*: sets of social and cultural rules that everyone is expected to follow. Norms are so powerful that we enforce them not just in others but in ourselves, even when no one else is there to correct us. A norm defines an activity and erases the possibility of other definitions, so that mopping a floor becomes an activity identified only with women and femininity. Cultural representations then reinforce that norm: advertising for floor cleaners features women who are thrilled with their sparkling floors; women's blogs complain about men who don't understand how important clean floors are; male comedians make fun of women's seeming obsession with keeping their kitchen floor clean, and so on and so on. In addition, since housekeeping is seen as a private matter, rather than one of political and national importance, the norm that women are concerned about clean floors reinforces the norm that women are not serious enough to participate on the same level as men in public life. The norm becomes the only possible reality.

Language as a Cultural System

The Relationship between Language and Culture

Language is one of our most basic systems of representation. In fact, language is pretty much *only* representation: a set of sounds and written shapes that take the place of actual things and ideas in the world around us. As with most cultural forms, there's no necessary relationship between most words and the thing or idea they represent, no reason that C-A-T means a furry four-legged creature (any more than C-H-A-T or G-A-T-O or Q-I-T-T-A does, or that we use these shapes to represent sounds rather than other shapes). And like other systems of representation, language is both descriptive and normative. Since

we live in a male-dominated society, *man* has come to mean all people, rather than just male people, whereas *woman* means only female people. One *masters* material; one does not *mistress* it. *Patrons* support the arts; *matrons* serve as custodians in prisons. *Patrimony* describes an inheritance from one's ancestors, including women, while *matrimony* refers to marriage. We speak of "a farmer and his wife," although it is probably safe to assume that a woman living on a farm with a husband who is a farmer is most likely a farmer herself. Until recently, there was no gender-neutral way to describe people who fought fires, chaired meetings, policed communities, or spoke for others: they were firemen, chairmen, policemen, and spokesmen. The word "maid," which originally meant a young woman, has come to mean someone who cleans other people's houses. Even nongendered words have gendered connotations: since nurses, babysitters, fashion models, and housekeepers are assumed to be female, we modify them with the word "male" when describing men in those roles.

When language operates in this way, the messages about gender and its norms are clear: men are doers and producers, women are watchers, caretakers, and consumers. When there are only postmen and firemen and spokesmen, the cultural assumption is that only men "man" these posts. This assumption stretches from adults down to children, reproduced in children's games. Girls play house, looking after children and cooking and cleaning, and boys pretend to be policemen and firemen. Boys who want to play house or dress-up are quickly told by adults or by other children that this kind of play isn't appropriate for boys, and representation of a norm becomes a reality.

Inequalities in language extend to concepts of masculinity and femininity, and we see the asymmetry between cultural representations of the masculine versus the feminine. Concepts attached to women are more often negative, particularly for men, but concepts attached to men can be positive not just for men but also for women. *Effeminate* is always a "bad" word, meaning weak, flaccid, irresolute. Women can *emasculate* men by undermining their power, but there's no equivalent term for a process by which women are rendered more powerful. *Feminine* is a "nice" word as applied to women, but applied to anything else it is likely to be uncomplimentary. Masculinity in little girls is tolerated when they are "tomboys" (as long as they grow out of it), but femininity in boys is always represented negatively—"sissy" is always pejorative. And doing anything "like a girl"—throwing, screaming, running—is problematic for boys and girls.

Changes in Language

In recent years we have seen changes in the gendering of language, as terms like *firefighter, police officer*, and *congressperson* enter the public discourse. Often these changes in language accompany actual social change, as more women join police forces or become our political representatives. The term *Ms.*, which, like *Mr.*, refers to an adult regardless of marital status, is gradually replacing *Miss* and *Mrs.* in public life to the extent that the exceptions stand out. The increasing numbers of women in the armed forces has led to the adoption of "service men and women" as a common phrase. However, most of these changes involve women joining traditionally male fields of action, rather than vice versa. The phrase "stay-at-home father" has entered the cultural vocabulary (somewhat ahead of the reality), but integrating men into traditionally female roles has moved as slowly as associated changes in language.

As some parts of our language become more egalitarian, other parts have become more gendered. Specifically gendered insults have become more common: calling someone a "pussy" to indicate that he is weak or cowardly turns what has long been slang for a vagina into a slur that attributes negative femininity to men. Similarly, the term "douchebag," a device for washing out the vagina, has become increasingly popular to mean a despicable person, usually male.

Enduring Symbols of Women

Stereotypical images of women have existed since the beginnings of human communication, particularly since women have rarely had the same levels of literacy and literary and artistic opportunity as men. If only men, not women, are the artists, writers, historians, and performers, then the images of women depicted in visual arts, literature, and performance will be men's. More importantly, if male experience is believed to be universal for all people and women's experience specific only to women, then even when women do create art, it will have a narrower audience and even be trivialized as "women's art" or "women's writing." If women have access to the products of this creativity only as "consumers"— if, for example, they listen and read but do not speak or write—then the perceptions of women who listen and read will be shaped by a one-sided view of reality. While there have been some cultures in which women have been valued as the creators of stories, songs, art, and performance, cultures that have left significant legacies of artistic production have been dominated by and have privileged men and male perspectives.

Images of Women in Mythical and Religious Texts

Normative images of women did not come into being only in the age of mass media. Every culture has a series of myths and legend representing ideal or "typical" female behavior, from which women and men are supposed to learn how womanhood works and what it means. In one version of the story of Adam and Eve, an origin myth for Christians and Jews, man is created by God "in his own image." Here, we learn that man came first and that God is like man (because man is like God). Eve was made as a companion to Adam and constructed from his rib, deriving from him, rather than directly from divine origins, and designed as his "helpmeet," or assistant. The next event in this creation myth is that Eve, defying God, eats the fruit from the forbidden tree of knowledge and convinces Adam to do the same, bringing evil into the world. From this, women learn that they are morally weak, that they cannot resist temptation, and that their weakness leads men into trouble. In this case, the trouble is great: Adam and Eve are expelled from paradise and cursed. The curse itself is interesting: Adam's curse is that he shall have to work for a living, and Eve's is that she shall bear children in pain. This suggests that it is men, not women, who engage in productive labor and that women deserve the pain of childbirth (see Chapter 8).

Similarly, in Greek mythology, Pandora cannot resist opening her box of gifts from the gods, which she was explicitly commanded not to open. The box contains all of the evils that afflict humanity, attributing the troubles of the world to a woman who could not control her curiosity. And Greek and Roman myths are full of stories of women (e.g., Leda, Europa, Selene) abducted and impregnated by male gods to fulfill the gods' desires and of women (e.g., Clytemnestra, Deianeira, Medea) motivated by jealousy or infidelity to murder their husbands or children.

Ancient mythology rarely has a single origin, since much of it emerged in cultures that were preliterate. However, such myths reflect the assumptions about male dominance and the role of women of the time when they originated and were written down. The Hebrew Bible makes clear that women are predominantly men's property, useful for cementing connections between tribes by marriage, and that their sexuality is men's possession. Chapter 19 of Leviticus, which lays out forbidden sexual practices, for example, takes for granted that it is *men's* sexuality that is being regulated, since it speaks only to men, forbidding a man from having sex with various relatives or from putting other men in the sexual position to which women are relegated. The messages that these ancient stories and laws convey are complex; there may be contradictions and multiple aspects and many levels of communication. Moreover, these beliefs are played out in more than written texts or explicit doctrines: they find their way into sculpture, painting, literature, dance, drama, ritual, clothing, gesture, words (spoken and written), and other ways in which humans use their imaginations to express ideas.

More recent religions that came into being in literate societies are more easily traced to the person or people who wrote their holy books and the historical moment and geographic location from which the religion emerged. The Q'uran, which Muslims believe the prophet Muhammad transcribed from the words of the angel Gibreel, does not indicate the order in which the first couple was created. However, in Islamic traditionalist literature inscribed in the period following the Muslim conquests, Eve is once again referred to as created from a rib. This is an example, among others, of how Islam conformed to religions that were already established in adjoining regions and in which segregation of the sexes and use of the veil were already common practices (Ahmed, 1992).

Changing Representations of Women's Sexuality

The "Sexual Revolution" and Its Legacies

Representations of women's sexuality have changed significantly since the middle of the twentieth century with the discovery of antibiotics that could easily cure sexually transmitted infections and birth control pills that could more effectively disconnect heterosexual intercourse from pregnancy. Pioneers in sex research like Alfred Kinsey and the team of William Masters and Virginia E. Johnson studied women's sexual response in detail and demonstrated that women were not only not less interested in sex than men but also that women's sexual response was far more varied and intense than the divide between asexual "good girls" and voracious "bad girls" allowed for. Kinsey's 1953 study *Sexual Behavior in the Human Female*, which was based on thousands of interviews with American women, made a huge splash in popular culture with its findings about women's diverse sexual activities inside and outside marriage and with other women. Similarly, Masters and Johnson's 1966 book *Human Sexual Response*, which talked in detail about women's orgasms, turned the conventional wisdom about women's sexuality upside down in its focus on the clitoris as the source of women's sexual pleasure.

These developments contributed to what was called the "sexual revolution" of the late 1960s and 1970s, and the belief that only "bad women" were sexually active before, outside of, or in the absence of marriage faded. Feminists embraced sexual self-determination as an important goal, and women began producing sexually explicit materials that put women's desires at the center, rather than focusing on men's fantasies about women. *Our Bodies, Ourselves*, a self-help and informational book about women's health first published by the Boston Women's Health Collective in 1973, advised women to claim their sexualities for their own pleasure and featured chapters about lesbian sexuality, reproductive health and rights, and sexual independence (including a section teaching women about masturbation).

The change in cultural values was not wholly positive for women's sexuality, however.

Representations of women in mass media became increasingly sexualized. The American Psychological Association defines "sexualization" as occurring when "a person's value comes only from his or her sexual appeal or behavior, to the exclusion of other characteristics; a person is held to a standard that equates physical attractiveness (narrowly defined) with being sexy; a person is sexually objectified— that is, made into a thing for others' sexual use, rather than seen as a person with the capacity for independent action and decision making; and/or sexuality is inappropriately imposed upon a person." These processes were clearly in effect in the 1970s and beyond: images that were usually found only in pornography made their way into the mainstream. On the one hand, women were shown initiating and enjoying sex. On the other hand, the growing explicitness of sexual representations suffused the culture, reducing the complex feelings people can have about sexual desire and sexual practice into a depersonalized social mandate to have sex.

Feminist responses to the sexualization of representations of women and the popularization of pornography varied considerably in these years. A significant group of feminists opposed pornography, arguing that it is degrading to women, encourages violence, and perpetuates sexist images of women in general (Russell, 1993). Some antipornography feminists (notably Andrea Dworkin, 1979, and Catharine MacKinnon, 1993) promoted legislation against images deemed to be degrading to women. Others took a position based on their belief that First Amendment protections on speech and images protected even offensive representations of women (Burstyn, 1985; Ellis et al., 1986; Vance, 1990) and argued for social policies that promote nonsexist education and the protection of women from sexual violence or its effects (by establishing rape crisis centers, battered women's shelters, and abortion services). An enduring legacy of this debate is the emergence of "pro-sex" feminists, who argued that rather than limiting the production of sexually explicit images, women should create their own sexual materials and claim their sexuality for themselves (Califia, 1988; Bright, 1992; Jaker et al., 1992; Duggan and Hunter, 1995).

Enter the category of "feminist porn." The (assumed) privacy of the Internet has shaped how women engage in sex, for now there are myriad websites dedicated to feminist pornography to help them along. Any rigid definition of what counts as either "feminist" or "porn" would defeat the radically open nature of the category itself. Yet according to the website "Feministe," some of the highlights include: an openness to all body types and to queer and trans-friendly sexuality; consensual sex that might include rape fantasies; women engaging in sexual acts that involve active menstruation; and the eroticization of safer sex (creative use of dental dams, for example). Although "second-wave" feminists such as Gayle Rubin (1993) argued brilliantly against narrow ideas about what counts as appropriate, nondegrading sex acts and sex expert Annie Sprinkle (2005) has been doing pro-sex feminist educational performances for decades, the category of feminist porn is emerging as if it were a "third-wave" innovation. Popular texts, such as *Jane Sexes It Up: True Confessions of Feminist Desire* (Johnson, 2002), address the question of how to reconcile one's sexual fantasies with one's feminism. What may indeed be an innovation, however, is the Feminist Porn Awards, also known as the Emmas. The brainchild of a women-run sex toy store in Canada, the award was inaugurated in 2006 to honor women directors of erotic films for particularly revolutionary work. The namesake of the award? Emma Goldman, the late nineteenth-/early twentieth-century anarchist, who championed the cause of free love decades before it became a 1960s rallying cry.

Women's Sexuality in Recent Popular Culture

One of the most powerful mass media instruments of this sexualization has been the cable channel MTV, which in the 1980s and 1990s was one of the few places for music videos, which had barely existed before then. Music videos produced and reproduced sexualized images of women, particularly very young women, and reinforced the idea that women's sexuality existed for men's benefit. As music videos expanded to the Internet in the 1990s and into the twenty-first century, this trend of representing women as sexualized accessories to men has not abated.

At the same time, female musicians laid claim to the power of representation of women's sexuality. The most influential figure in this phenomenon has without a doubt been Madonna, who appeared on the scene in the early 1980s. Madonna pushed the limits of how women's sexuality could be represented on television, mixing erotic imagery with images of religion, race, and class, bringing previously marginalized sexual practices like sadomasochism into the mainstream and claiming ownership of her sexual desires. In response to white rock-and-roll musicians, who traded in images of pliable, receptive sex objects, Madonna insisted on her own independence, sexual and commercial.

In the same period, Janet Jackson asserted herself as a sexual being who was fully in control, as her first breakthrough album emphasized. Echoing the 1970s disco queen Donna Summer, Jackson often moaned and groaned provocatively in her songs, emulating the sound of intense sexual arousal. Yet even as she celebrated the pleasure principle and reimagined the sexual body by putting "abs" (abdominal muscles) on the map, her songs also alluded to issues of sexual responsibility in the age of AIDS. Britney Spears, the pop diva of the early 2000s, pushed the sexual envelope

---

Box 1.1   MAKING FEMINIST SENSE OF LADY GAGA: TWO VIEWS

... Gaga is explicit in her insistence that, since feminine sexuality is a social construct, anyone, even a man who's willing to buck gender norms, can wield it.

Gaga wants us to understand her self-presentation as a kind of deconstruction of femininity, not to mention celebrity....."Me embodying the position that I'm analyzing is the very thing that makes it so powerful." Of course, the more successful the embodiment, the less obvious the analytic part is. And since Gaga herself literally embodies the norms that she claims to be putting pressure on (she's pretty, she's thin, she's well-proportioned), the message, even when it comes through, is not exactly stable. It's easy to construe Gaga as suggesting that frank self-objectification is a form of real power.

Real young women, who, as has been well documented, are pressured to make themselves into boy toys at younger and younger ages, feel torn. They tell themselves a Gaga-esque story about what they're doing.

Source: Nancy Bauer, http://opinionator.blogs.nytimes.com/2010/06/20/lady-power.

Lady Gaga is a symbol for a new kind of feminism....Gaga Feminism, or the feminism (pheminism?) of the phony, the unreal, and the speculative, is...a monstrous outgrowth of the unstable concept of "woman" in feminist theory, a celebration of the joining of femininity to artifice....[G]aga feminism is not totally new, it does not emerge from nowhere, but it certainly strives to wrap itself around performances of excess; crazy, unreadable appearances of wild genders; and social experimentation....[T]his version of feminism looks into the shadows of history for its heroes and finds them loudly refusing the categories that have been assigned to them: these feminists are not "becoming women" in the sense of coming to consciousness, they are unbecoming women in every sense—they undo the category rather than rounding it out, they dress it up and down, take it apart like a car engine and then rebuild it so that it is louder and faster. This pheminist takes it upon herself to "occupy gender" as the new terminology of our politcal moment might phrase it.

Source: J. Jack Halberstam, *Gaga Feminism: Sex, Gender and the End of Normal.* Boston: Beacon Press, 2012: xii–xiv.

---

by trampling over societal taboos about age. She cultivated a teen audience with danceable hits while flaunting a too-early sexuality that was meant as a turn-on to everyone else. With the rise of Lady Gaga in 2009, the issues of sexual self-fashioning entered a new phase. It is Lady Gaga's style of self-presentation, as opposed to her music, that is sexually unconventional. Apropos of her tendency to speak on stage about the virtues of freedom and of having choices in life, Lady Gaga flouts convention with hair and makeup that present an edgy, harsh, and indeed parodic approach to feminine beauty, even as she puts her body on display with barely there peek-a-boo costumes and bare-butted looks. Despite the fact that all of these pop artists have crafted daring sexual personas, they have never done so with complete freedom. First, their messages, no matter how creative, always engage on some level with the predominant view of women as irreducibly sexual beings. And second, they

While there's no feminist consensus on whether Lady Gaga's image challenges or reinforces norms about femininity, she certainly makes her viewers think about the limits of acceptable femininity.

craft their self-images so as to succeed in a highly corporatized arena that is attuned to the market—that is, to the need to sell records.

The achievement of female sexual empowerment in hip-hop is also ambiguous. Black women have worked hard to establish their place within a culture that has sexualized them in problematic ways—not simply as sex objects but as "video hoes" (or "whores"), for example. That term indexes the highly circumscribed space that black women have been allowed to occupy in the male-dominated culture of hip-hop. However, there has always been a critical female presence in that world. In the 1980s, artists such as Salt-N-Pepa, Queen Latifah, and MC Lyte both criticized misogyny in rap music and advanced their own female-centered views of society, including more affirmative expressions of their own sexuality. This struggle has continued into the twenty-first century. Certainly, more and more black women such as L'il Kim (famous for the lyric "I can make a Sprite can disappear

in my mouth"), Missy Elliot, Foxy Brown, and Nicki Minaj have become extremely successful rap artists—for women. Even though they often go toe-to-toe with men in expressing their sexual bravado, and they rap just as well, they often garner less label support and lower record sales than male rappers. As one record producer explained: "males just don't want to hear hard things from women" (quoted in Rivera, 2012: 428). Becoming businesswomen in the rap industry might be a boon to female artists— unfortunately, while there are many excellent "femcees," there is, as of yet, no female equivalent to the rap-star-turned-mogul Jay-Z.

We live in a media-saturated culture, surrounded by television, movies, the Internet, music, magazines, and billboards. For that reason, the trend of sexualization seems to be expanding around the world instead of receding. In addition, in the United States the processes of sexualization are trickling down to younger and younger women and girls: a recent report by the American Psychological Association found a disturbing upswing in sexualized representations of young girls or the use of images associated with childhood in sexualized contexts, and recent research bears them out. Toy manufacturers produce dolls wearing black leather miniskirts, feather boas, and thigh-high boots and market them to 8- to 12-year-old girls (La Ferla, 2003). Clothing stores sell thongs with sexually suggestive slogans printed on them, sized for 7– to 10-year-old girls (Cook and Kaiser, 2004; Brooks, 2006); other thongs sized for women and late adolescent girls are imprinted with characters from Dr. Seuss and the Muppets (Pollett and Hurwitz, 2004; Levy, 2005). A whole subculture of child beauty pageants encourages young girls to wear extensive make-up and imitate their adult counterparts with sexualized costumes and gestures (Cookson, 2001). This excessive sexualization can have negative effects on girls and adolescents, particularly teenagers, who are in the process of working out what sexual desire and sexual behavior mean (Tolman, 2002). And the sexualization of girls encourages adults to see children as appropriate objects of sexual desire well before they themselves understand how sexuality operates.

Can We Change Reality by Changing Images?

If our sense of ourselves and of the ways we feel and act is shaped by predominant social images of gender, then presumably our perceptions, feelings, and behavior can be changed in part by a change in representation. In the 1980s and 1990s, feminists focused on contesting images perceived to represent women negatively, often by creating diverse alternatives in academia, art, literature, and the media (Rakow, 1992). A short-lived but influential movement of the 1990s, Riot Grrrl focused on the similarities between feminist and punk rock values: rebellion and resistance to mainstream standards of beauty, do-it-yourself aesthetics, collective action and collaborative creativity, sexual self-determination, and self-expression of all kinds (Monem, 2007). Through zines and live shows, Riot Grrrl bands like Team Dresch, Bikini Kill, and Bratmobile created confrontational, explicitly feminist and pro-lesbian music and culture. They reclaimed misogynistic terms like "bitch," "dyke," and "slut" as empowering labels and challenged the male-dominated music scene of the era. While their radical message was soon co-opted by less political musicians and by the music industry in general and watered down into "girl power," Riot Grrrl relaunched radical feminism for a new generation.

Another powerful example of how women can and do overturn conventional, media-driven standards of beauty lies in the realm of body politics. Despite the "thin ideal" that is prevalent in American society

writ large and despite the rise of eating disorders among young black and Latina women (National Eating Disorders Association, 2005), they have historically responded to a different set of aesthetic pressures. They, along with an increasing number of other women, cultivate the "thick" and "bootylicious" look of such stars as Jennifer Lopez, Beyoncé, and Nicki Minaj. While that look offers a liberating alternative to thinness, it also establishes yet another difficult ideal, one dictating that women be "phat" (meaning "plenty hips, ass, and tits") without being fat; it is no coincidence that "phat" is slang for "good." Along similar lines, one recent popular film set in a Mexican American community announced that *Real Women Have Curves.* Hence, even ostensible alternatives to convention can usher in difficult new standards. We will return to the politics of the booty in the next chapter.

Hence, as the need to produce alternative images became a goal in the 1980s and 1990s, a new consideration came to the fore. What, in fact, constitutes an alternative? Are alternatives de facto "positive"? And who gets to decide? After all, "the production of meaning is inseparable from the production of power" (Chadwick, 1990).

Although feminists from the 1960s to the present day have focused a great deal of energy on producing images that, whether "positive" or "negative," represent the complexities of women's lives, in the past couple of decades feminism itself has been subject to a new kind of misrepresentation. Under the rubric of "postfeminism," the dominant culture has twisted feminism's central concerns—opening up the range of women's opportunities, reclaiming our sexuality on our own terms, expanding women's economic and political power—into far less threatening solutions. Rather than claiming actual power, postfeminism focuses on the fuzzy goal of "empowerment"; instead of leveling the playing field between girls and boys in popular culture, postfeminism gives us "girl power," which we can exercise by buying more products and wearing sexier clothes.

Reshaping Representation

Despite the significant challenges discussed above, important changes have occurred in the years since second-wave feminism began exerting its influence on public discourse. In part these changes in representation have followed political and economic change, but in some cases remaking representation itself has led to larger cultural shifts in both the mainstream and in subcultures.

Television provides a case in point. It is undoubtedly the most powerful and influential medium of communication in the world, cutting across national and class barriers. The number of women who work as news anchors and correspondents on major channels has been steadily rising and includes some of the best paid, most successful people in the business (Marlane, 1999; Gutgold, 2008). Christiane Amanpour and other women have been reporting from the front lines of wars and upheavals, showing how women are no longer confined to "soft" topics. Women also serve as political pundits and as hosts of mainstream political talk shows. *The View*, a popular daytime program featuring five female co-hosts, has become an important vehicle for national conversations about major social issues and current events. Guests are almost as likely to be national political figures as international celebrities. That program has also become an essential campaign stop for any presidential candidate. Openly lesbian news commentator Rachel Maddow began helming her own news analysis show in 2008.

Such developments have undoubtedly made a difference to millions of viewers, male and female, who can now watch and hear women in positions of authority speaking about business, international politics, and men's sports. Even so, women in the media still have to contend with gendered expectations about what signifies seriousness. Interviewing Katie Couric about her historic selection as the first woman to anchor the CBS Evening News, CNN's Larry King said: "We've got to begin with the most important question that all, everybody wants to know: your hair. What have you done with your hair?" (Gutgold, 2008: 16).

Women's Search for Self through Art

Historical Perspective. In the past, the designation of much of women's work as mere "craft" rather than "high art" has caused their creations to be devalued. Consider needlepoint, quilt making, and painting on porcelain. These have been termed *crafts* or *arts*, as in "arts and crafts," rather than art. Such terms demonstrate that political power dictates the assignment of labels and categories. Some contemporary women are reviving such skills as weaving and quilting and (like the authors of this textbook) finding a special pleasure in the collaborative nature of much of their creative work. Fiber arts like knitting, crocheting, and embroidery are being adapted into the world of "fine art" by organizations like the Fiber Artists Collective.

Since the first edition of this textbook was published, art historians have brought women's work into the mainstream of art history, making it no longer possible for critics to ask, "Why were there no great women artists?" (Harris and Nochlin 1977). Though much frustration remains, some contemporary women artists have seen their works installed in prestigious museums like the Museum of Modern Art in New York. The National Museum of Women in the Arts in Washington, D.C., which was founded in 1981, displays works exclusively by women artists from the Renaissance to the present. Not only painters

Judith and Maidservant with the Head of Holofernes, Artemisia Gentileschi (c. 1625). A very successful artist and confident in her own talent, Gentileschi often portrayed herself in her art. In this Baroque painting, the artist casts herself as the heroine Judith.

Artist Maria Montoya Martinez, one of the most celebrated of all Native American potters.

The Smithsonian Institute commissioned Martinez to produce work such as this, a recreation of pottery discovered in a 1908 excavation in her pueblo.

but also silversmiths, textile makers, potters, and others are given due attention (Heller et al., 1980:158–9). Included in the collection is a jar by one of the most prominent Native American artists of the twentieth century, Maria Martinez (1887–1980). Martinez

was born into a family of artists and taught to make pottery by her grandmother and aunt, who made pots for practical and ritual use. Martinez did not even sign her pots until collectors began to recognize them as works of art. Pottery making is often a collaborative effort. Martinez's fame brought prosperity to her family and pueblo in New Mexico.

Contemporary Feminist Imagery. Feminism has created a new context within which women artists may work, with feminist and mainstream critics commenting on their work. Feminist artists now flourish. The multiplicity of their work demonstrates that there is no single form of expression that must be labeled "feminist."

In the 1980s, feminist artists explored a variety of genres to critique consumerism,

A striking image created by Maya Lin, a Chinese American woman and one of the foremost landscape artists currently working in the United States. Her most famous work, the Vietnam Memorial in Washington, D.C., is also one of the most frequently visited and celebrated national monuments in the country. Lin was in her early twenties and a student in the School of Architecture at Yale University when, in 1981, she won the design competition for that memorial. Having completed several other memorial works since then, Lin, as of 2012, is currently working on what she calls her final memorial, titled "What Is Missing?," a piece that will address "the current crisis surrounding biodiversity and habitat loss." http://www.mayalin.com/. She was awarded the National Medal of Arts in 2009.

media constructions of femininity, and government inaction in response to the AIDS crisis. The rise of performance art in the 1980s and 1990s provided an arena for explicitly political artists like Karen Finley, who used her own body as a canvas, Holly Hughes, who put her experience as a lesbian at the center of her work, and Annie Sprinkle, a former porn actress who transformed sexually explicit material into feminist performance (Carr, 2006). Others, such as Jenny Holtzer, Cindy Sherman, Barbara Kruger, Silvia Kolbowski, Marie Yates, and Mary Kelly, have criticized dominant media constructions of women through their own art (Chadwick, 1990). The exclusion of women artists from mainstream museums and galleries has also come under attack from feminist artists, scholars, and curators. Starting in 1985, a group of women formed the Guerrilla Girls. Taking the names of women artists as their pseudonyms, they protested outside museums to draw attention to the lack of women represented on the walls. They produce posters, stickers, books, printed projects, and actions that expose sexism and racism in politics, the art world, film, and the culture at large. More recently, Mickalene Thomas has created enormous, elaborate portraits of her mother and other black women, and Yolanda Lopez has recast the traditional image of the Virgin of Guadalupe as a contemporary Chicana.

Women's Search for Self through Literature

The earliest woman writer in Western literature whose works are extant is Sappho, who lived on the Greek island of Lesbos in the sixth century B.C.E. She wrote poetry for and

---

Box 1.2 WOMEN, WRITING, AND LANGUAGE

I shall speak about women's writing: about *what it will do*. Woman must write her self: must write about women and bring women to writing, from which they have been driven away as violently as from their bodies—for the same reasons, by the same law, with the same fatal goal. Woman must put herself into the text—as into the world and into history—by her own movement.

Every woman has known the torment of getting up to speak. Her heart racing, at times entirely lost for words, ground and language slipping away—that's how daring a feat, how great transgression it is for a woman to speak—even just open her mouth—in public. A double distress, for even if she transgresses, her words fall almost always upon the deaf male ear, which hears in language only that which speaks in the masculine.

It is by writing, from and toward women, and by taking up the challenge of speech which has been governed by the phallus, that women will confirm women in a place other than that which is reserved in and by the symbolic, that is, in a place other than silence. Women should break out of the snare of silence. They shouldn't be conned into accepting a domain which is the margin or the harem.

Source: Excerpted from Helene Cixous, "The Laugh of the Medusa," *Signs* 1 (1976): 875–93. Chicago: University of Chicago Press. Reprinted in Cixous, 1981: 245, 251. Keith Cohen and Paula Cohen, translators.

about a group of younger women who spent time with her before they departed for marriage. The emotions expressed by Sappho run the gamut from love to jealousy to hate, and they were all inspired by women. Although she lived in a male-dominated culture, Sappho asserted woman-centered values. She would not trade her daughter for limitless treasure, she appreciated the beauty of other women, and she preferred love to war. Despite her preoccupation with women's culture, Sappho was admitted into the mainstream of classical literature because of her technical versatility. Male poets could adopt her erotic imagery for homosexual or heterosexual purposes.

Sappho's poetry is an artistic rearrangement and interpretation of reality, though it appears to be frank and personal. In fact, most women's literature is personal to such a degree that the confessional style of writing has been labeled "feminine" even when men employ it. Because of the circumstances of their lives, women writers have often turned inward to explore the private sphere.

Women as Heroes

In male-dominated societies, heroism is often identified by actions that are specific to men: battles, hunts, quests, and long journeys. For women, who have long been limited in their mobility by social mandates to care for home and children, it has been harder to identify (and identify with) heroes in literature. Is Penelope in *The Odyssey* heroic because she waits for her warrior husband Odysseus and resists demands to remarry? Is Cordelia in *King Lear* heroic because she is honest about her love for her father and suffers death because of her sisters' treachery? While men's heroism is associated with action, women's heroism is often hard to distinguish from suffering. At the same time, historically, few women have been able to participate in the kinds of activities that mark men as heroic.

Many women writers, as a result, have had to create new and woman-centered ways of thinking about heroism.

Alice Walker's groundbreaking novel *The Color Purple* (1982) does exactly this. By focusing on a young black woman, Celie, who has been raped by her stepfather and given away to be married to an abusive older man, Walker rethinks how we define heroism. Celie finds her own voice not through the violence and conquest modeled by the men around her, but by finding love with another woman, Shug, and renouncing aggression. While surrounded by white racism and male violence, Celie transforms herself and the men around her through love and self-determination. Some writers claim traditional heroic models for their female characters. In *The Woman Warrior* (1976), Maxine Hong Kingston conjures up a myth derived from stories told by women in her family. A Chinese American girl raised in a hard-working family that earned a living by operating a laundry envisions herself as a warrior woman in China fighting barbarians, bandits, and even the emperor. She takes vengeance on behalf of the people of her village, whose grievances were inscribed on her back with knives, thus avenging her family for grievances experienced in the United States, such as being called "chink" and "gook." Heroines are women who do not accept their fate passively. They think, choose, and act.

Kingston's creation and/or adaptation of women-oriented legends is a strategy that several writers have embraced. In *Oranges Are Not the Only Fruit* (1985), Jeanette Winterson combines the story of a young girl raised in a fundamentalist Christian home who grows into a lesbian teenager with a mythical quest subplot that runs parallel to the autobiographical plot of the novel. Similarly, Toni Cade Bambara's *The Salt Eaters* (1980) calls upon African American rural traditions of faith healing to grapple with urban racism, and poet Audre Lorde used images of goddesses of the African Dahomey people to reimagine the place of black women in the modern world. In a powerful combination of political manifesto and reclamation of the space of the border, Gloria Anzaldúa reinterpreted Mexican legends in *Borderlands/La Frontera* (1987) to analyze her experiences as a Chicana lesbian growing up on the Texas/Mexico border.

It's not surprising that all these women are marginalized in some way—through race, sexuality, class, and/or national origin. If, as we've already seen, myths are powerful tools to transmit cultural messages, then so too are the marginalized histories that lesbian writers and women writers of color draw upon in their effort to craft new ways of situating themselves in the world. And in an uplifting development, a 16-year-old olive-complexioned girl featured as the protagonist in Suzanne Collins's *The Hunger Games* (2008), a futuristic young adult novel that, despite also having several black characters, is not about race at all.

Telling Other Stories

Many women writers have been more inclined to reject the model of heroism and myth-making altogether. As the novel, a genre that focuses much of its attention on the domestic sphere and ordinary lives, became the dominant literary genre in the Global North in the nineteenth century, women characters moved into greater focus. Unlike epic poems, myths, and legends, which primarily focus on the acts of men, the novel often features women in central roles. This did not mean that women writers were welcomed, however: Jane Austen, one of the great novelists of the early nineteenth century, initially published her books anonymously; the Brontë sisters published under male names; and Mary Anne Evans, one of the most well-regarded novelists in the English language, is still best known by her male pen name, George Eliot. In the United

States, women writers published mostly under their own names but disavowed any ambition for their own sake. Harriet Beecher Stowe claimed that her best-selling antislavery novel *Uncle Tom's Cabin* was written by God, and the popular novelist Fanny Fern argued that women writers were forced into publication by economic need, not artistic drive.

Nonetheless, women did find increasing opportunities as writers beginning in the nineteenth century. Indeed, in the twentieth century, women writers were among the most adventurous and experimental, seeing literary self-expression as the way to represent the many varieties of women's lives (Dickie and Travisano, 1996). Virginia Woolf, writing in the 1920s to 1940s, focused on the everyday experience of women's lives through a stream-of-consciousness technique that put women's thoughts and feelings at the center. Nella Larsen's novels *Quicksand* (1928) and *Passing* (1929) explored urban black women's lives in similar ways. In poetry in particular, women writers were intensely experimental: Gertrude Stein, Hilda Doolittle (also known as H.D.), Laura (Riding) Jackson, and Angelina Weld Grimké embraced complex poetry to represent the particularity of their lives as lesbians (Stein and H.D.), women of color (Grimké), and feminists ([Riding] Jackson).

While women continued writing throughout the twentieth century, the growing antifeminism of the years after World War II dismissed the representation of women's experiences as "trivial" or "boring." It's not surprising, then, that the second wave of feminism brought with it an explosion of writing by women about women. Women of color were especially productive, creating magazines, journals, poetry, novels, essays, and journalism to represent their experiences and create community. It is one of the great achievements of second-wave feminism that women writers around the world are approaching a level of recognition equal to their male counterparts. Women writers have won the Nobel Prize for literature six times in the past two decades—certainly not equal to male writers but considerably better than the previous 90 years during which five women won or between 1955 and 1990, when none did.

Writing as Political Activism

Women writers around the world have used literature as a form of political activism. Under apartheid in South Africa, Nadine Gordimer used her novels to protest the cruel and unequal treatment of nonwhite people. In Egypt, Nawal El Saadawi's novels have dramatized the abuse of women and the ways in which they fight back. Women writers have often explored the genres of science fiction and fantasy to imagine better (or dramatically worse) worlds in which gender difference has either been eradicated or has become even more unequal. Marge Piercy's *Woman on the Edge of Time* (1976) uses the science fiction genre to suggest two opposing possible futures, one sexist and one nonsexist. Her vision is conveyed in part through terms that underscore social inequality and equality. In *The Handmaid's Tale* (1986), Margaret Atwood describes a feminist dystopia called Gilead in which a totalitarian regime imposes roles on women that are extensions of what some people have always believed women should be.

In more recent years, women writers have also engaged political issues through their writing. Arundhati Roy, an Indian writer, explored class and sexual castes in her 1997 novel *The God of Small Things* and has taken a leading role in writing about the degradation of the natural world, neo-imperialism, and nuclear proliferation. For many women writers, issues that were controversial in the early years of feminist and liberation movements in the 1960s and 1970s are now integrated into their writing. Zadie Smith, a leading British novelist of mixed European and Afro-Caribbean descent, represents a multicultural, multilingual England grappling with the changes wrought by the end of the British Empire and immigration of Caribbean and Asian people to Britain (2000). Alison Bechdel's graphic memoir *Fun Home* (2006) uses the insights of lesbian politics to meditate on Bechdel's father's life and death as a closeted gay man. And in a rare move, Bechdel produced a follow-up memoir, *Are You My Mother?* (2012), in which she even incorporates her mother's comments upon the evolving text. "I don't know why everyone has to write about themselves," her mother remarks at one point.

Representation in the Internet Age

Each generation has its defining medium that has both been shaped by and transformed the representation of gender. Visual art, literature, movies, radio, and television have all been deeply implicated in representations of gender and sexuality and made mass distribution of images of dominant models of masculinity and femininity more easy and widespread. At the same time, feminists have been able to take hold of these different technologies to generate alternative and resistant representations of women and gender and then spread these representations to a larger public. For example, the work of feminist filmmakers like Yvonne Rainer, Julie Dash, and Lizzie Borden made space for more mainstream women directors such as Kathryn Bigelow, Nancy Meyers, and Lisa Cholodenko. Groundbreaking comedians Joan Rivers, Phyllis Diller, Danitra Vance, and Kate Clinton created the conditions in which Roseanne, Ellen DeGeneres, Wanda Sykes, Margaret Cho, and Sarah Silverman could flourish. However, as we've seen, cultural representation, particularly that of mass culture, has historically been transmitted from the top down—that is, from dominant cultural groups. The production and distribution of cultural products is usually separated from the people who consume those products; the majority of people listening to music, watching movies or television, reading books, and looking at art are consumers, not musicians, filmmakers or actors, writers, or artists themselves.

The Internet has changed this balance between producers and consumers of culture. While someone would need significant money, influence, and connections to produce a TV show and actually have it appear, pretty much anyone with access to a computer can create a website or blog; anyone with a cellphone can make a YouTube video and post it; anyone with a digital camera and access to a computer can upload photographs and make them public to billions of viewers. Indeed, the Internet has proven a significant challenge to authoritarian political regimes, who struggle hard to control the proliferation of information and images that can spread worldwide in hours. The Internet is not unique in its do-it-yourself format: resistant political movements from anticolonial struggles to U.S. antislavery organizations to second- and third-wave feminists to Riot Grrrl punk rockers have created their own cultural products and distribution networks. However, what distinguishes the Internet is that an image created by one person is accessible to anyone with an Internet connection. Distribution is effortless and immense. And fast.

What effect will this have on cultural representations of women and gender? It's hard to predict. There are some promising signs, however, particularly the emergence of organizations that focus on media literacy and awareness of the messaging of gender in the media and online. The Girls, Women + Media Project is "a 21st century, nonprofit initiative and network working to increase awareness of how pop culture and media represent, affect, employ, and serve girls and women—and to advocate for improvement in those areas"

(www.mediaandwomen.org). Young women, who are most familiar with new media technologies, are creating blogs and e-zines like Feministing, What About Our Daughters, and Velvet Park. But as we have seen, cultural representations are produced by larger social systems, and the Internet has become a place not just for bottom-up culture making but also for sex trafficking, demeaning images of women, and misogynist business as usual. As feminists we have our work cut out for us to make spaces on the Internet that resist male dominance, racism, and heterosexism.

Gender in Film: A Case Study

In considering cultural representations of gender in film, we present here an extended case study of a single genre rather than presenting a survey. This section examines gender in the context of a global phenomenon of cultural representation: Bollywood cinema. In so doing, it emphasizes that "gender is always already constituted by other forms of difference," especially, in the case at hand, the nation (Sinha, 2004: 233).

Bollywood is a term coined in the late 1970s to refer to the Hindi film industry centered in Mumbai (formerly Bombay), India. As the world's largest film industry, Bollywood produces some 900 films per year and reaches millions of people, not only in India but also the South Asian diaspora, a term referring to the millions of people of South Asian descent (the term "South Asia" is inclusive of the entire subcontinent) living in the Middle East, the Caribbean, Africa, England, Canada, Australia, the United States, and other parts of Asia. Since the 1950s—long before the current era of globalization—Indian films have enjoyed an impressive global reach (Gokulsing and Wimal Dissanayake, 2004: 3).

Not all Indian films are a product of Bollywood. Rather, certain conventions define the genre. Chief among these is the use of melodrama and grand spectacle. Sumptuous visuals abound, famous Indian locales often serve as backdrops, and every film features several song-and-dance sequences that contribute to a film's fantastical effect. For its themes and plot lines, Bollywood draws promiscuously from a variety of sources: from ancient Indian epics (*The Ramayana* and *The Mahabharata*) and Parsi theater to recent American films and classics of Western literature. For example, *The Ramayana* provided the religious basis of one of the most popular Bollywood films of all time, *Hum Aapke Hain Koun!* (dir. Sooraj Barjatya, 1994), a film celebrating traditions of marriage and family. *Bride and Prejudice* (dir. Gurinder Chadha, 2004) took up the theme of the patriotic family romance 10 years later, with a cheeky send-up of Jane Austen's classic novel. No matter its inspiration, though, the essence of a Bollywood film lies in its gloriously larger-than-life representation of India itself.

Popular Hindi film has long associated the Indian woman with the Indian nation, drawing on a symbolic relation dating at least as far back as the mid-nineteenth century (Chaterjee, 1993). In the mid-twentieth century, the first generation of Hindi filmmakers reinvigorated that association in critical response to the politics of culture under British colonialism. The British justified their rule over India, in part, by representing certain rare though oppressive practices such as *sati* (the immolation of widows) as if they were the cornerstones of Hindu tradition (Chatterjee, 1993). In an effort to lend support to British rule, an American woman, Katherine Mayo, a member of the Society of Mayflower Descendants, wrote a book called *Mother India* (2000 [1927]), in which she provided sensationalist details of the oppression of Indian women. Child marriage, early sexuality, early maternity, and unsafe midwifery practices were all, in her view, signs that India lacked the fundamentals of civilization (Sinha, 2004).

Mayo's book became a cause célèbre within India and in international circles. In India, the text lent impetus to a nascent women's movement around such issues as child marriage, even as Indian women activists denounced Mayo's diatribe against India. In Britain it was proclaimed "the most powerful defense of the British raj that has ever been written" (Mishra, 2002: 67) and has even found its way into more recent books by American feminists—yet with no reference to its imperialist origins (Sinha, 2004). In sum, books about women in non-Western contexts written for popular Western audiences are powerful forms of cultural representation in their own right. The example of *Mother India* shows that knowledge produced about women in colonial contexts often derive less from ideologies of sexual difference per se than from politically motivated representations of cultural difference.

With independence in 1947, Indian nationalists promoted ideas of Indian culture as if there were a single, pure, authentic form of it—one that was spiritual (and Hindu) to the core and hence distinct from and superior to materially oriented Western culture (Chatterjee, 1993). And given the gendered and highly damning criticism of Indian culture that sought to justify British imperialism, postcolonial nationalism in India became powerfully gendered in kind. There was a premium on exalted images not simply of Indian womanhood, but of motherhood. Mothers were represented as paragons of Indian values, keepers of Indian traditions, and protectors of the nation.

The crowning example of this phenomenon lies in a film titled, ever so strategically, *Mother India* (dir. Mehboob Khan, 1957), which was a remake of the same director's *Aurat* (1940), or "Woman." *Mother India* centers on Radha, a woman raising four sons in extremely adverse circumstances. The film dramatizes her heroism by quickly dispensing with her husband,

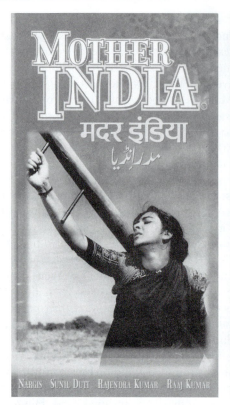 

These movie posters capture the stark contrast between the chaste Indian woman, represented as the very personification of the nation in "Mother India," and the more sultry diasporic Indian woman of "London Dreams," who invites fantasy and desire.

Diaspora provides a crucial context for understanding the production of patriarchal themes and narratives. Whereas the South Asian world beyond India was previously an afterthought for Bollywood filmmakers, this huge, worldwide audience is currently their primary target, providing at least 65% of the industry's revenues (Ninian, 2003). Filmmakers play to their viewers' desires for depictions of India, but they do so in ways that refer to diasporic life as culturally inauthentic. Whether the films are set in India or, say, England, the films portray diasporic families as in need of cultural education. And here again, the burden of maintaining Indian tradition falls exclusively to the female characters (Hirji, 2011). Men's burden, meanwhile, is to support the nation's pocketbook. Both in their global travels and in their messages, films depicting diasporic Indian life participate in a largely successful Hindu nationalist agenda within India aimed at attracting capital investment among "nonresident Indians." In light of the millions of dollars that Indian American corporate elites have invested in Indian enterprises, some Bollywood films have recast the image of immigrant men from disloyal sons to national heroes coming to the rescue of Mother India (Mankekar, 1999).

To the degree that Bollywood satisfies a desire for cultural connection, one might expect its conservative representations of women and gender relations to be readily embraced and perhaps emulated by its viewers. However, the opposite is often true. In one study of South Asians in Canada, young women expressed "annoyance with sexist plot lines and portrayals," reporting that they used such depictions "as a starting point for discussion and debate with parents, relatives and peers" and that the films inspired them to identify as feminists (Hirji, 2011: 160). And as an antidote to the presentation of ostensibly authentic Indian culture in ways that normalize heterosexuality, Bollywood's queer diasporic viewers subject the films to transgressive interpretations, reading female homosexual desire into scenes and songs that might otherwise pass as straightforwardly heterosexual (Gopinath, 2005A). Diasporic filmmakers, working well outside of the Bollywood machine, who leaves the family in shame after an accident renders him dependent on his wife. (As the loyal wife, though, she pines for him throughout the film.) Radha is left to work the land, a task made all the more difficult by the floods that ravage her home and her harvest, killing two of her sons. An evil moneylender offers to erase her considerable debts if she marries him. In the name of her chastity, she declines. When one of her son grows up, he avenges the earlier insult against his mother's honor by killing the moneylender and threatening to abduct his daughter. Instead, Radha kills her son in order, again, to preserve her honor, which collapses with that of the village, its women, and the nation. Indeed, the actress who played Radha, Nargis, was effectively rendered one and the same with her film character. As Salman Rushdie wrote of Nargis, "she became, until Indira-Mata supplanted her, the living mother-goddess of us all" (Rushdie, 1995: 138–9). More than 50 years after its release, *Mother India* remains "the quintessential Indian film" (Gokulsing and Dissanayake, 2004: 79), influencing Bollywood cinema for decades. It is shown somewhere in India every day of the year (Mishra, 2002: 66).

Bollywood has long portrayed the ideal Indian woman as a loyal wife and self-sacrificing mother. Her moral stature was also enabled by constrained representations of her sexuality. Until the early 1990s, filmmakers were bound by censorship codes prohibiting the depiction of "excessively passionate love scenes" or "scenes suggestive of immorality" (Prasad, 1998: 88). Onscreen kissing, sex, and nudity were associated with low Western morals and were hence constituted as a threat to the nation (Prasad, 1998: 91). Filmmakers commonly circumvented these codes by, for example, featuring titillating "wet sari scenes." In large measure, the films trafficked in dichotomous depictions of women as sexual beings: the appearance of an occasional vamp (a Westernized woman) functioned to throw into stark relief the real (that is, culturally pure) Indian woman's virtue (Gangoli, 2005).

The liberalization of the Indian economy in the 1990s and the advent of satellite television—a harbinger of globalization—ushered in a new era for Bollywood films. As heavily sexualized images from abroad began circulating within India, filmmakers of the "new Bollywood" (Durham, 2007) were licensed and inspired to revise their images of women. Now they are far less demure than in the past—even to the point of having a profession and a premarital

---

more freely resist its most powerful norms. Deepa Mehta's *Fire* (1996) famously represented the "traditionally" female space of the middle-class Indian home as a site of homosexual desire—a move that was met with complete outrage from the nationalist rightwing and from the political left within India. Together, then, the practices of diasporic queer viewers and diasporic filmmakers transform the significance of "India" from its would-be status as an object of nostalgic longing and source of authentic originary culture to a touchstone of alternative sexuality for South Asian women (Gopinath, 2005A).

Bollywood has recently been "discovered" by the American mainstream. Andrew Lloyd Weber's Bollywood-themed musical *Bombay Dreams* appeared on Broadway in 2004. It appropriated and readjusted Bollywood conventions to fit the narrative expectations of white American audiences. Yet this happy attempt to mainstream South Asian people, rendering theirs one among many "ethnic" American stories, belies the unique reality they face. In post-9/11 American society, South Asian men have been subjected to intense surveillance and detention in another poignant example of the ways that gender and nation intersect—in this case, through race (Gopinath, 2005B).

Despite the pronounced degree of historical, political, economic, cultural, and social contextualization necessary to apprehend the dynamics of such globally popular genres as Bollywood films—and here we could add Latin American telenovelas and hip-hop—they bear studying precisely because they shape and reflect the ever-shifting experience of gender in so many parts of our interconnected world.

sex life. But the old association of women and tradition persists. Where she is made into a doctor, an Indian woman must still manifest exceptional beauty while cooking classic Indian dishes and being a consummate caregiver (Hirji, 2011). Where she is made to share men's lust for money and power, shamelessly using her body as a means to achieve those, she becomes an antiheroine and meets with a violent end (Durham, 2007). The continuing conflation of women with tradition affects the actresses who now choose between what they themselves call "admirable" or "trashy" roles; those who choose the latter often disavow the personas they create on film, publicly claiming to be quite different in real life (Govindan and Dutta, 2008). Critics of Bollywood's turn to sex and nudity decry these as "Western assaults on Indian culture," while directors (all male) defend these moves as feminist and modern (Durham, 2007: 47). Meanwhile, it is largely in the work of India's "parallel cinema" where women directors do their work, raising difficult social issues such as surrogacy or otherwise critiquing the gendered status quo as well as the Indian political system writ large (Chakravarty, 1993; Pudasaini, 2009).

Summary

The ideas that women and men have had about who they are, how they relate to one another, and their potential are the products of their cultures. An important part of any culture is its representation of reality. We (or our cultures) shape our perception of what is "out there" on the basis of the ways in which we have learned to interpret reality. These perceptions, or images, are social creations whose shape and origin need to be explained rather than accepted at face value.

Notions of what women are have been shaped by representation. Society conveys imagery through ordinary language, social behavior, and creative works. The images themselves have served to set women aside from humanity by reducing them to one or a few aspects of their personalities, physiologies, or behavior. The sexualization of women and girls transforms women into vessels for sexuality rather than people with complex human desires. The image of woman in singular, stereotypical terms reduces all women to something less than whole, individual human beings. Conversely, the use of woman to represent an entire group—whether it be a nation, an ethnic, racial or religious group—places an inordinate burden on the women of that group. Popular media both produce and reflect these dynamics.

Most cultural representations have been created by dominant groups and disseminated through established networks. This means that women, particularly marginalized women (women of color, working-class women, colonized women, and lesbians and bisexual women, to name a few) have rarely been fairly or accurately represented. However, women have always been writers, artists, and cultural participants, and as they have claimed opportunities to share their work, ideas about women and gender have expanded. In such realms as popular music and feminist pornography, women lay claim to express their sexuality on their own terms. Yet women's agency and their claims to freedom of expression are not necessarily devoid of political implications or repercussions. While feminists have been analyzing and critiquing all forms of cultural representation for generations, the Internet presents new challenges: it is highly democratic, meaning that it can be used effectively toward progressive ends as well as to advance the many harmful agendas that we seek to thwart.

Discussion Questions

1. Describe a woman and a man as portrayed in a popular song, television show, or film. Note the difference in language and

imagery both the writer and you have used to describe each.

2. Can you provide an example of the ways in which a particular group is represented through the image of its female members? Or through gendered imagery more broadly? In what form(s) (music, art, television?) do such representations come? How do you imagine that the group's male and female members might be differently affected by those images?

3. Images of women's sexualization are everywhere. Where, if at all, do we see the sexualization of men's bodies? Are these images the subject of social critique? Should they be?

4. What opportunities exist for the Internet to expand different kinds of representations of women and gender? What are its limitations?

Recommended Readings

Gross, Larry P. *Up From Invisibility: Lesbians, Gay Men and the Media in America.* New York: Columbia University Press, 2001. Traces the history of popular representations of gay men and lesbians since the mid-twentieth century. Gross identifies shifts in the ways homosexual characters have been depicted in mainstream popular culture, from the era of the Stonewall demonstrations in 1969 and the AIDS crisis that began in the late 1980s through to the 1990s, when middle-class gays and lesbians were suddenly recognized to constitute "a market," one with great purchasing power. The author questions whether the newfound visibility of gays and lesbians in the media is a completely positive development.

Mendible, Myra, editor. *From Bananas to Buttocks: The Latina Body in Popular Film and Culture.* Austin: University of Texas Press, 2007. With articles from sociologists and media studies and women's studies scholars, this interdisciplinary text shows how Latino cultures have been stereotyped and essentialized through rigid ideas about Latina women's bodies. The book examines a host of case studies, focusing on such popular figures as Salma Hayek, Shakira, and Jennifer Lopez while also examining gendered and racialized images of Latinas who appear in the news and in Spanish language television programs airing in the United States. The authors further discuss the ways in which audiences receive and challenge representational norms.

Radner, Hilary, and Rebecca Stringer, editors. *Feminism at the Movies: Understanding Gender in Contemporary Popular Cinema.* New York: Routledge, 2011. Essays cover such wide-ranging themes as masculinity, consumer culture, violence, and transgenderism. The authors identify and analyze the gender implications of such recent cinematic trends as the wedding film, the "lad flick," women lawyer films, and films adapted from young adult novels.

Tasker, Yvonne, and Diane Negra, editors. *Interrogating Postfeminism: Gender and the Politics of Popular Culture.* Durham, NC: Duke University Press, 2007. Proffers a feminist critique of postfeminist trends in the media. This volume argues that many film and television plotlines, as well as reality show premises, tend to promote a singularly consumer-oriented lifestyle, one seemingly reserved for a young, middle-class, white audience.

chapter **2**

Ideas and Theories about Women and Gender

What does it mean to be, as in the famous Aretha Franklin song, a "natural woman"? Do women and men have naturally different characteristics, styles of parenting, ways of relating to others, or values? Or are men and women essentially the same? Is sexism the idea that women *are not the same as men*, or is it sexist to demand that women *have to act and think the same as men* if they want to be treated equally? Many philosophers and other thinkers have addressed these questions over the centuries, and the ideas they developed about women and gender differences continue to be debated today. Although many thinkers in the past supported male dominance, some opposed it even over 2000 years ago. The eighteenth- and nineteenth-century revolutionary movements of liberalism and socialism began a more systematic challenge to the subordination of women. In this chapter we consider both historical ideas and theories about women and gender and newer analyses from the perspectives of feminist philosophers and thinkers. We focus on the critical analysis of sexism while emphasizing the many varied positions feminists writers have held.

Why Ideas and Theories Are Important

Why read about old ideas and theories concerning the nature of women and gender differences in the face of the rapid changes in women's social roles globally? It is important to study these because (1) they represent not just the beliefs of the thinkers who developed them but also the widely held beliefs in their societies at those times, and (2) they still influence current debates. Although most people today agree that women should be able to have control over their lives, many continue to believe, as in the past, that men and women have different roles to play in the family, in society, and in the workplace and that these roles are justified by the essential nature of gender differences. Old ideas and theories about women and gender have been around for a very long time and may still influence us even when we think we are beyond them.

The question of whether there are natural facts about women and gender is a scientific question, but scientific inquiry has to begin with *concepts and definitions* so that we know what we are studying. These change over time as usage changes and social ideas change. *Fathering* used to mean begetting a child by impregnating a woman; today it means something comparable to *mothering*, involving the actual care of a child. *Marriage* used to signify more of an economic unit than a romantic partnership. New concepts can also emerge in our language, such as *sexual harassment* or *date rape*, to indicate new ways of interpreting events and experiences that used to be called *seduction*. A shared way of speaking reflects a society's values and how it understands the world. Using more inclusive gender terms, such as *firefighter* rather than *fireman*, indicates that society has begun to believe that this occupation can be performed by any qualified person. Fighting over language is not trivial, since our language indicates what we believe and can sometimes reveal that old ideas about gender are still influential. Children who are learning the language of their communities are also learning about social roles, expectations, and beliefs. Many of the commonly accepted ways to talk about women and gender have contained hidden, implicit sexism (Daly, 1978; Vetterling-Braggin, 1981).

49

We also need to distinguish between *descriptive* and *prescriptive* aspects of the way we use concepts and definitions. In developing theories, we aim not merely to understand the way human beings have generally done things but also to consider how things *should* be done. Human beings are always striving to improve our selves and our lives: from decreasing

---

Box 2.1   MEN'S IDEAS ABOUT WOMEN

The glory of a man is knowledge, but the glory of a woman is to renounce knowledge.

—CHINESE PROVERB

Whenever a woman dies there is one less quarrel on earth.

—GERMAN PROVERB

Women are sisters nowhere.

—WEST AFRICAN PROVERB

I thank thee, O Lord, that thou hast not created me a woman.

—DAILY ORTHODOX JEWISH PRAYER

There is a good principle which created order, light, and man, and an evil principle which created chaos, darkness, and woman.

—PYTHAGORAS

When a woman thinks, she thinks evil.

—SENECA

Wives, submit yourselves unto your husbands…for the husband is the head of the wife, even as Christ is the head of the church.

—ESPHESIANS 5:23–24

In childhood a woman must be subject to her father; in youth, to her husband; when her husband is dead, to her sons. A woman must never be free of subjugation.

—THE HINDU CODE OF MANU, V

A man in general is better pleased when he has a good dinner than when his wife talks Greek.

—SAMUEL JOHNSON

The difference between men and women is like that between animals and plants.

—G.W. F. HEGEL

Nature intended women to be our slaves.

—NAPOLEON BONAPARTE

Women have great talent, but no genius, for they always remain subjective.

—ARTHUR SCHOPENHAUER

Regard the society of women as a necessary unpleasantness of social life, and avoid it as much as possible.

—LEO TOLSTOY

Women, in general, want to be loved for what they are and men for what they accomplish. The first for their looks and charm, the latter for their actions.

—THEODOR REIK

violent tendencies to overcoming disease. Just because something is natural does not prove that it is good, or even inevitable. Humans are intensely imaginative and creative animals with innovative capacities to change, adapt, and learn.

Thus, it is important to consider how we use language since this may actually inhibit change or conceal aspects of something we are trying to understand. Much of written "women's history" has actually been white women's history. By acknowledging this we can more clearly see the work that still needs to be done. Anthropologists once assumed that it was perfectly justifiable to study a culture by talking only to the men. They believed that women's lives are determined by nature rather than culture and that women do essentially the same sorts of things in every society. Feminist anthropologists questioned this assumption and argued that interviewing only men could produce a skewed theory about the community, about how harmonious it really is, or how power relations operate. And anthropologists could only discover whether their assumptions about "natural women" were true by actually talking to the women.

Definitions of *woman* and *gender* have often reflected faulty theories. Yet these ideas were always contested.

Ancient and Early Modern Ideas about Women and Gender

Like many ancient thinkers, Confucius (551–479 B.C.E.) held that women's proper place was in the home and that their proper attitude should be one of obedience. Women must be obedient first to their fathers, then to their husbands, and then to their grown sons. Confucius believed in maintaining a clear division between the private, or domestic, and public spheres that continues to shape much thought about women: "the woman's correct place is within; the man's correct place is

outside." On the other hand, the public sphere was modeled on the private sphere: the family was seen as a microcosm of the state, and just as the state was ruled by a male emperor with the divine mandate, so too the father's authority was seen as part of the natural order.

By contrast, the founder of Buddhism, Gautama Buddha (c. 563–c. 483 BCE), supported women joining monastic sects as teachers alongside men and even believed women could achieve enlightenment. Buddhism taught that the highest state of *nirvana* was achieved through gender neutrality, or transcending one's gender identity. However, it was thought to be harder for women to achieve nirvana than men, indicating what most scholars believe today was a rather ambivalent attitude toward women in early Buddhism.

Although the Greek philosopher Plato (427–347 B.C.E.) was a well-known critic of democracy, he held remarkably egalitarian views about women. He believed that the natural capacities of individuals were not determined by their gender and that women could become rulers or physicians or philosophers. In *The Republic* he says, "…if it appears that [the male and the female sex] differ only in just this respect, that the female bears and the male begets,…no proof has yet been produced that the woman differs from the man for our purposes, but we shall continue to think that our guardians and their wives ought to follow the same pursuits" (Plato 2005: 454). Equality of education followed from this: if women are to be assigned similar duties as men, Plato said, "We must also teach them the same things" (453).

Aristotle (384–322 B.C.) was Plato's pupil, yet he developed some of the most notoriously sexist views about women in the history of philosophy. He believed that "[t]he female is as it were a deformed male," meaning that females have male features but in impure and undeveloped form. Aristotle believed women to be intellectually and morally inferior to men, but much of his account was based in mistaken biological claims, the most important of which was that the pregnant female is simply a vessel or incubator for the human form that has been implanted by the man's seed. A woman, he thought, makes no formative contribution to the child but only provides its sustenance (Aristotle, 1943; Bell, 1983: 63).

Susan Bordo's (1993) analysis of recent laws regarding pregnant women reveals some surprising resonances with Aristotle's views. Pregnant women are treated in U.S. law as mere vessels; their role as incubators overrides

Hypatia: 370–415 C.E. philosopher, astronomer, and mathematician of northern Africa, in Alexandria, Egypt. In the early sixteenth century, the famous Italian painter Raphael (1483–1520) wanted to honor Hypatia by including her image among the famous philosophers of the past in his *The School of Athens.* When the Bishop of Rome disapproved of including her, since she had been killed by Christian monks of Alexandria for heretical teachings, Raphael was unwilling to give her up, "disguising" her by lightening her skin color and painting her face to resemble a favored nephew of the Pope.

Sources: http://pages.prodigy.net/fljustice/hypatia.html and http://www.newbanner.com/AboutPic/athena/raphael/nbi_hypa.html.

consideration of their own health, needs, or life choices. Although forcible bodily intrusion must generally meet high standards for the general population (for example, we cannot force people to give blood even to save a life), the standards are noticeably lower for pregnant women (cesarian sections can be forced even at risk to the mother's health).

Many of the most important Christian theologians viewed sexuality as sinful and women as unclean. According to the African bishop Saint Augustine (354–430), given the depraved nature of women and human sexuality, the best form of life would be absolute chastity, with marital sex only for the purposes of reproduction a second best alternative. Maimonides (1135–1204), philosopher and Jewish theologian, provides an interesting alternative view. He held that the conjugal rights of wives are so important that "a wife may restrict her husband in his business journeys to nearby places only, so that he would not otherwise deprive her of her conjugal rights." Neither can a husband change his occupation to one involving a less "frequent conjugal schedule…as for example, if an ass-driver seeks to become a camel-driver, or if a camel driver seeks to become a sailor" (Maimonides, 1972; Bell, 1983: 95). No mention is made of reproduction, indicating that it is sexual fulfillment that is the wife's right. Despite this acknowledgment of female sexual needs, Maimonides supported a husband's right to all of his wife's earnings and to restrict her public movements, and he held that in cases of rape compensation should be paid to the woman's father at an amount based on her beauty.

In the eighteenth century, a lively debate ensued concerning women and rationality. Most intellectuals, such as David Hume (1711–1776) and Immanuel Kant (1724–1804), held views that women reason very differently than men. They thought that women's rationality is "related to the finer feeling" of sentiment and delicate discernments, such as the capacity to distinguish jealousy from envy. Others, such as Diderot (1713–1784) and Rousseau (1712–1778), held that women have little rationality of any sort and are driven more by visions and hysteria. Others in the eighteenth century disagreed with both of these types of view and argued that women's different capacities were the result of being treated and educated differently, rather than the result of innate differences.

This anti-naturalist view about gender differences began to influence the wider revolutionary movements that were developing in Europe and throughout the Americas against the landed aristocracy, colonialism, and monarchy. Feminism, as the new ideas about women came to be called, became an integral part of the two main theoretical developments that emerged during this period of ferment: liberalism and socialism.

Classical Liberalism and Feminism

Enlightenment philosophers of the eighteenth century first began to criticize the idea that the hierarchy of men that had dominated Western thought since the ancient slave societies of the Greeks was a natural phenomenon. They also rejected much of the religious teachings that used the doctrine of original sin to reject the idea that human beings can improve themselves. They emphasized instead the essential equality of men, the importance of liberty, the right of self-governance, and the possibility of social change. If men are essentially equal and each deserves liberty, then it followed that the only form of government that is justifiable is democracy. Liberals thus began to argue for free elections, an independent judiciary, laws that respect the right of citizens to be treated fairly, and a government that is accountable to the will of its citizens as expressed through the political process. This is the basis of classical, liberal political thought.

Classical liberalism, as it developed further in the nineteenth century, viewed liberty in the private sphere as the cornerstone of a just society. This implied a *laissez-faire* approach to the economy, or the idea that government should not interfere with the economic activity of private businesses. The very term *private enterprise* indicates that economic activity is considered to be part of the private rather than the public sphere and outside of democratic political control. This form of liberalism predominates in the United States and Europe among both what we today call "liberals" and "conservatives." The question still under debate within classical liberalism is how exactly these principles are to be applied to women and to the sphere of sexuality and reproductive activity.

Feminists often take for granted the principles that liberalism first espoused, such as that people have the right to be free and to be treated as equals and that social arrangements ought to be based on the consent of all. Yet these ideas were not applied to women until recently. For example, women were only given the vote, the absolute minimum of political equality, starting at the end of the nineteenth century: first in New Zealand in 1893, and then in most countries across the world slowly through the twentieth century. Not until 2006 was women's suffrage granted in the United Arab Emirates (see Chapter 13).

Despite this slow progress, liberal ideas are still considered by many to be the foundation upon which feminism is built, since they stress freedom and equality. But many liberal theorists acknowledge the need to reconsider how we understand these concepts in order to make them more effective forces for women's liberation. Women cannot live freely if they are sexually or physically or economically dominated in the "private" sphere of either the home or the workplace. How we treat the private sphere, as well as how we define its boundaries, is a political issue.

Liberal ideas were generally developed with male citizens in mind. Most of the theorists believed that women's interests would be taken care of automatically once we took care of men's interests. As James Mill (1773–1836) expressed in 1820 with respect to who should be permitted to vote: "all those individuals whose interests are indisputably included in those of other individuals, may be struck off without inconvenience....In this light also, women may be regarded, the interest of almost all of whom is involved in either that of their fathers or in that of their husbands" (James Mill, [1820] 1992).

Most liberal thinkers also assumed that the family was *necessarily* hierarchical. They did not consider the possibility of women acting in the political realm as free and equal citizens, nor did they consider that relations within the family needed to change to become more egalitarian and consensual, even though they argued for such changes in society. As Susan Moller Okin (1979: 202) wrote, "Whereas the liberal tradition appears to be talking about individuals as components of political systems, it is in fact talking about male-headed families....Women disappear from the subject of politics."

Some of the architects of liberalism and social equality for men vigorously opposed gender equality. Jean-Jacques Rousseau (1712–1778), one of the most important figures of the Enlightenment, argued that women are simply unfit for self-governance

---

Box 2.2   WHAT IS FEMINISM?

In the most basic sense, feminism is exactly what the dictionary says it is: the movement for social, political, and economic equality of men and women. Public-opinion polls confirm that when women are given this definition, 71 percent say they agree with feminism, along with 61 percent of men. We prefer to add to that seemingly uncontroversial statement the following: Feminism means that women have the right to enough information to make informed choices about their lives. And because *women* is an all-encompassing term that includes middle-class white women, rich black lesbians, and working-class straight Asian women, an organic intertwining with movements for racial and economic equality, as well as gay rights, is inherent to the feminist mandate. Some sort of allegiance between women and men is also an important component of equality. After all, equality is a balance between the male and female with the intention of liberating the individual.

Breaking down that one very basic definition, feminism has three components. It is a *movement*, meaning a group working to accomplish specific goals. Those goals are *social* and *political change*—implying that one must be engaged with the government and law, as well as social practices and beliefs. And implicit to these goals is *access* to sufficient information to enable women to make responsible choices.

The goals of feminism are carried out by everyday women themselves, a point that is often lost on the media.

Source: Jennifer Baumgardner and Amy Richards, Excerpt from "What Is Feminism" from "A Concise History of the F Word" from *ManifestA: Young Women, Feminism, and the Future.* New York: Farrar, Straus, and Giroux, 2000: 56; italics in original. Copyright © 2000, 2010 by Jennifer Baumgardner and Amy Richards. Reprinted by permission of Farrar, Straus and Giroux, LLC.

or political participation. In *Émile* (1762), he maintained that women should be educated in such a way that they will learn that their happiness requires submitting to men's will.

Along with many others, Rousseau invoked nature to justify democracy, arguing that social hierarchies are man-made, not ordained by God. Yet he also used nature to justify women's subordination: "Nature herself has decreed that woman, both for herself and her children, should be at the mercy of man's judgment....When the Greek woman married, they disappeared from public life;...[and] devoted themselves to the care of their households and family. This is the mode of life prescribed for women alike by nature and reason" (Rousseau, [1762] 1966: 328–30).

Since the essence of being human for Rousseau is to be free, it follows that he believed women to be less than fully human. He argued, like Confucius, that the father must be the dominant authority within the family, and without this "proper order" both the family and society would fall apart.[1] But if Rousseau was right that not even two persons who have common concerns and ties of affection can reach decisions on the basis of mutuality rather than domination and submission, there is little hope for the democratic, consensual decision making in the larger society that he so passionately advocated. On the other hand, if governments should be based not on tradition or force but on consent between free and equal individuals, then this liberal and democratic approach must be extended to women inside families as well (Okin, 1989).

Wollstonecraft

Mary Wollstonecraft (1759–1797), an Enlightenment philosopher writing in England in the late eighteenth century, disputed Rousseau's views on women and gender relations. Wollstonecraft was a journalist and author who struggled to live on her own earnings, and she was critical of the social conventions that created barriers to women's ability to achieve economic independence. She developed philosophical counterarguments against the widespread beliefs about women's "natural" idleness, weakness, and irrationality (Eisenstein, 1981). Wollstonecraft pointed out that women had been *taught* to be creatures of emotion rather than reason. Even if one accepts Rousseau's belief that women are responsible for the raising of children, women need an education to raise children well. Wollstonecraft further reasoned that if women's childlike status was truly innate and women are truly incapable of being educated, why does professional education for women have to be prohibited by law? Why do we need laws to ensure what conservatives believe to be natural? "Men, indeed, appear to me to act in a very unphilosophical manner when they try to secure the good conduct of women by attempting to keep them always in a state of childhood....It is a farce to call any being virtuous whose virtues do not result from the exercise of its own reason. This was Rousseau's opinion respecting men: I extend it to women" (Wollstonecraft, [1792] 1967: 50, 52)

Wollstonecraft was not discouraged by the magnitude of the changes needed in her society; along with other Enlightenment thinkers, she was optimistic about social change. Unfortunately, conservative ideas about gender such as Rousseau's appealed more to the male elites in power. Although the French Revolution of 1789 opened up a debate about gender equality, Olympe de Gouges, author of *Declaration of the Rights of Woman*, went to the guillotine in 1793, and whatever gains women had made in the political turmoil of the eighteenth century were soon lost in the subsequent conservative reaction to the revolution. Mary Wollstonecraft died at the young age of 38 giving birth to her daughter Mary Shelley (the author of *Frankenstein*).

Her death was part of an epidemic of deaths in childbirth across Europe caused when obstetrics was wrested away from midwives in favor of doctors who unknowingly carried the germs of their ill hospital patients to the bedsides of women in labor. Midwives were seen as ignorant and dirty despite their high level of skill, and their replacement by trained male physicians led to the loss of generations of women due to septicemia (Ehrenreich and English, 2010; see also Chapter 9).

Various European rationalist philosophers continued to maintain that women have a defective rationality. In Germany, Kant developed a theory that an act is moral if it is done on the basis of rationally determined duty, but not if it is done on the basis of feelings, such as feelings of sympathy or love. Since he believed women are emotional rather than rational beings, they are not capable of fully moral action. Kant's identification of reason with traits most people associated with masculinity were powerful precursors of later psychological and developmental theories that also identified human nature in masculine terms, for example, as emotionally independent of others (Lloyd, 1984). Kant's moral principles became a cornerstone of the liberal tradition, with his emphasis on respect for individual rights and the duty not to instrumentalize or objectify other persons. Yet most believed these did not apply to women.

Mill and Taylor

Almost all the main figures of the liberal tradition excluded women from the political realm, but there were a few exceptions. In his treatise *On the Subjection of Women* (Mill, [1869] 1970), John Stuart Mill (1806–1873), the son of James Mill (quoted above), took the radical position that equal rights and opportunities should be extended to women. He argued that women ought to be able to own property, vote, attend schools and colleges, and enter into any profession for which they were qualified. Such ideas went against the beliefs of his day and, as a result, were until recently often omitted from philosophy textbooks covering Mill's views. His lifelong companion, collaborator, and eventual wife, Harriet Taylor Mill (1807–1858), helped him develop his feminist arguments.

Mill's arguments ran counter to those of the French philosopher Auguste Comte (1798–1857), who is often considered the "father of sociology." Comte believed that biology was already "able to establish the hierarchy of the sexes, by demonstrating both anatomically and physiologically that, in almost the entire animal kingdom, and especially in our species, the female is formed for a state of essential childhood" (Okin, 1979: 220). Mill took Comte on, arguing, like Wollstonecraft, that observable deficiencies found among women cannot be attributed to innate inferiority when their life circumstance is so different from men's. Until women are given a chance to have the same education as men, Mill reasoned that we cannot claim to know what their real capacities are.

Although Mill believed that society would benefit if women were given equal educational opportunities and that women should be free to choose a career, he also believed that marriage itself was a career for women and if they married they should not work. Not surprisingly, he and Harriet Taylor disagreed on this issue. It was not until a century later that feminist movements declared this double standard to be unfair and unnecessary.

Harriet Taylor demanded equality for women even more forcefully than Mill. She derided the faulty arguments through which men tried to justify their dominance:

> The world were once persuaded that the supreme virtue of subjects was loyalty to kings, and are still persuaded that the paramount virtue of womanhood is loyalty to

men....Self-will and self-assertion form the type of what are designated as manly virtues, while abnegation of self, patience, resignation, and submission to power...have been stamped by general consent as preeminently the duties and graces required of women...power makes itself the center of moral obligation...a man likes to have his own will, but does not like that his domestic companion should have a will different from his. (Mill, [1851] 1970: 97)

Contemporary Liberal Feminism

Liberal feminists, past and present, view biological differences as irrelevant to the question of women's rights (Jaggar, 1983; Littleton, 1987). They proposed a constitutional amendment in the 1970s—the Equal Rights Amendment (ERA)—as a way of ending all sex-biased laws once and for all in the United States (see Chapter 13). Although the ERA did not pass, today liberal feminists continue to fight for women's equality by opposing gender discrimination in workplaces, protecting the equal rights of lesbians, and working toward more effective laws concerning rape, domestic violence, and sexual harassment (Rhode, 1989; Smith, 1993; Nussbaum, 1999).

Liberal feminists continue the task begun by Wollstonecraft, Taylor, and J. S. Mill to extend liberal principles of self-governance and equality to women and family relations. Equality can never be realized for most women if the primary responsibility for household tasks, child care, and elder care falls on them while the opportunities for economic independence are much greater for men (Okin, 1989). Liberal feminists hold that women have a right to choose whether or not to have children, but if they choose to become parents they should have adequate social supports for their mental health and self-development. Modern-day liberals realize that making our legal rights effective requires us to regulate the private sphere, whether this involves private enterprise or family relations, in order to ensure that it is both fair and equal for all.

For example, to make equality of opportunity a reality, liberals supported policies of "affirmative action" as a proactive way to force employers to give access to qualified women as well as qualified men from racial and ethnic groups who have experienced patterns of discrimination. Advocates of affirmative action argue that (1) white males have been receiving an unacknowledged preference in hiring for a long time, and affirmative action is a way of leveling the playing field, and (2) we can most effectively change people's attitudes about who can perform what type of job when they see the jobs performed well. Yet affirmative action has been strongly opposed by some of those who previously enjoyed employment preferences based on racism and sexism. Despite some advances made in opening up opportunities previously closed, most types of work remain highly segregated by gender and race (on affirmative action in education, see Chapter 10).

Those who do housework and who care for children and the elderly perform for long hours hard work that is vital to the functioning of the economy. Yet often neither the value nor the difficulty of this work is recognized (Folbre, 2001). Starting in the nineteenth century, some feminists began to argue that the oppression of women, especially the devaluing of women's work, could not be sufficiently explained or solved in the terms of classical liberal theory. They argued for a more systematic analysis that links the political sphere to the economic sphere. Thus began the development of socialist feminism.

Socialism and Feminism

Socialist feminists aim for a society with a more rational, just, and democratic system of economic production. If socialism were to develop in countries with strong democratic traditions, they argue, it would be different than what was developed in the USSR or Eastern Europe. Yet we must not forget that, although those societies had their problems, current capitalist societies are causing environmental destruction, encouraging wars for profit, derailing democracy by the influx of money in electoral campaigns, and continuing to wantonly exploit vulnerable populations in the labor market, which includes large numbers of women. Surely, they argue, we can do better than this.

Socialist feminists fear that the feminism that develops in liberal capitalist societies simply encourages women to scramble for self-advancement up the corporate hierarchy, leaving most women out. Because liberal feminists focus on individualism and individual *legal rights*, their reforms leave most women *economically* disadvantaged. Liberal feminism does not even aim to address the oppressive structure of a global economy dominated by corporate power.

The situation of women worldwide is centrally connected to their labor. Women's labor in the home is unpaid and often undervalued (for example, it is never included in a country's gross domestic product [GDP]), while women's labor outside the home is routinely underpaid. The large majority of women work in a gender-segregated workforce, as office workers, retail employees, seamstresses, teachers, nurses aids, hotel maids, waitresses, etc., with low wages and benefits and fewer unions. The focus on individual liberties for women provides neither an adequate analysis nor an effective solution to this problem.

Marx and Engels

Karl Marx (1818–1883) and Friedrich Engels (1820–1895) argued that relations between men and women under capitalism are similar to relations between the bourgeoisie and the proletariat: one side is always negotiating from a position of weakness (*Communist Manifesto*, 1848). They held that women's economic dependence on men is neither natural nor inevitable. In *The Origin of the Family, Private Property and the State* ([1884] 1972), Engels argued that the particular institutions, laws, and ideas of a given historical period—including forms of the family and gender relations—arise as a by-product to the form of the economy. Moreover, men became dominant not through any natural superiority but through historical happenstance. Although some of the anthropological data Engels drew from is outdated, he was right that women were not always unequal but lost power as social change advantaged men who controlled the tools of production. Men's subsequent material dominance then led to their cultural dominance, or their ability to create belief systems in their interests. Engels described the bourgeois wives of the nineteenth century as little more than legally sanctioned prostitutes, bought and sold in marriages that legally ceded all power and property to their husbands. With no right to seek a job or education, travel freely, have their own bank account, or go to the authorities when they were raped or beaten, wives were essentially a form of property themselves, and their husbands, as the owners of that property, could do with them what they wished.

Women of the lower classes were economically exploited at a rate even greater than male workers during the industrial revolution. Marxists argued that the capitalist class had no interest in overturning sexist views about women's worth given that they could reap greater profits off their labor as well as commodify their sexuality and profit from their unpaid reproductive labor (defined not just as bearing and raising children but all the domestic work necessary to sustain workers in an ongoing way). Capitalism's profit motive ensured that women would remain underpaid and oppressed. Socialism would liberate women by reorganizing the system of production to make it more rational and more just, basing wages, for example, on the difficulty of a job and its value to society.

Clara Zetkin (1857–1933), leader of the German socialist movement, wrote in 1896 that the struggle of proletarian women was very different from the struggle of bourgeois women: the former, unlike the latter, are not struggling *against* the men of their class. Because the vast majority of women are workers, Zetkin thought the struggle for women's liberation should aim to bring about a political rule of the proletariat in which men's and women's interests would be aligned. She agreed with the reforms demanded by the bourgeois women's moment, but for her these demands were mainly to help working-class women in their battle alongside working-class men for shared goals of social justice (Zetkin, 1984).

Gilman

Although Marxism or "scientific socialism" was the dominant strain of socialist thought in the nineteenth century, there were also other versions, including "utopian socialism," Christian communism, market socialism, and others. Charlotte Perkins Gilman (1860–1935), born in the United States, became an influential writer and feminist lecturer who developed original ideas about how society could be creatively reorganized along utopian socialist lines.

In her widely read story, "The Yellow Wall-Paper," Gilman ([1899] 1973) describes how the constricting lives of women could lead to madness. In the story, a young woman whose interest in writing is taken as "abnormal" is restricted by her physician and her husband to bed rest for three months. The woman begins to focus obsessively on the room's ugly wall-paper, eventually losing her sanity. Such treatments were commonly diagnosed for women who had independent and creative aspirations.

Gilman analyzed the oppression of women in a series of nonfiction books, such as *Women*

and Economics ([1898] 1966), and in *Herland* (1979), one of the first works of feminist utopian fiction. She believed the key was to change women's work in the home: "We see the human mother…laboring her life long in the service, not of her children only, but of men; husbands, brothers, fathers, whatever male relative she has.…The human female, the world over, works at extra-maternal duties for hours enough to provide her with an independent living, and then is denied independence on the ground that motherhood prevents her working!" (Gilman, [1898] 1966: 10, 19–20).

Gilman urged women to overcome their dependent state and cease being martyrs to their children's needs by socializing housework and child care so that it was done by professionals. Keeping the care of children under the exclusive domain of mothers (or mothers and fathers) makes them vulnerable to the happenstance of their parents' abilities, and it so restricts women's lives that it stunts their capacities. Domestic chores, she argued, should be made communal by creating cooperative kitchens and laundry rooms. These ideas are not so outlandish: food and daycare cooperatives today operate by shared work assignments, and middle-class working women often hire professionals to do their child care and housework and buy take-out meals. Gilman simply wanted these options to be more universally available. She thought feminists should develop concrete proposals for transforming both the workplace and the home, but she also knew that such changes required changing how women understood their identity both as women and as mothers.

Other Marxist feminists such as Alexandra Kollontai (1872–1952), a leader of the Russian revolution, focused on women's sexual liberation. Kollantai argued that we should rethink the "moral codes" that govern our sexual relationships, including monogamy. She chastised socialist leaders who neglected the issue of sex as a "private matter" unworthy of "the effort and the attention of the collective" (Kollontai, [1911] 1972). In reality, she pointed out, the state of our personal, sexual relationships always has a significant effect on social struggle, sometimes disabling social movements. Socialists are sometimes guilty of assuming values of individualism and possessiveness in sexual relationships, she believed, and need to think more expansively about how to maximize freedom, equality, and genuine friendship between the sexes.

Goldman

Emma Goldman (1869–1940), a Russian Jew who immigrated to New York when she was 16, began work in a clothing factory and quickly became involved in union organizing. She became one of the most influential anarchist writers and leaders of all time. Like Kollantai, Goldman believed that sexual freedom was central to women's liberation. Like Marx and Engels, she believed that most women were forced to provide sexual favors in exchange for their livelihood. "To the moralist, prostitution does not consist so much in the fact that the woman sells her body, but rather that she sells it out of wedlock" ([1911] 1996: 181).

Yet, Goldman pointed out, despite women's need to sell their sex, they were kept systematically ignorant about sex. As a result, their own desires were usually thwarted. Anticipating theories of sexual liberation that came much later, Goldman wrote in 1911 that people's capacity to freely pursue their sexual desires was linked to their capacity to resist oppression and imagine a more just world: "…If the world is ever to give birth to true companionship and oneness, not marriage, but love will be the parent" ([1911] 1996: 213).

The idea of a woman condemning marriage and espousing free love and anarchism struck terror in the hearts of conventional society.

When Goldman traveled to small towns to give a lecture, sometimes riots would erupt and she was often arrested, but thousands of people continued to flock to hear her speak. In her early 20s, Goldman was imprisoned for a year for advocating that the starving poor should steal food, and during World War I she was imprisoned again for organizing against the draft. After the war the U.S. government deported her to Russia, where she soon became a critic of the Soviet's suppression of open debate. By 1921 she and her long-time lover Alexander Berkman left Russia. Goldman lived her life in a way that was consistent with her ideals, continuing to write no matter what it cost her. She predicted that the greatest obstacles to women's freedom would prove to be not man-made laws, but "internal tyrants": women's internalization of the social conventions that oppress them.

Contemporary Socialist Feminism

In the 1970s dissatisfaction with corporate capitalism as well as the gender conservatism of much orthodox Marxism led to an explosion of new socialist feminist organizations and theoretical writings (Eisenstein, 1981; Jaggar, 1983; Hartsock, 1998; Holmstrom, 2002). Socialist feminists wanted a theory that could integrate race and class oppression alongside the gender concerns of liberal feminists. Feminists began to debate whether patriarchy, white supremacy, and capitalism constituted *independent* systems of oppression, or whether racism and sexism were caused by economic forces and the profit motive. Socialist feminism came to represent the idea that both Marxism and feminism were insufficient on their own: Marxism provided a class analysis, but, as Heidi Hartmann (1981) argued, it was "blind" to gender- and race-based forms of discrimination. And classical Marxism underplayed cultural forces that were independent of the profit motive.

But liberal feminism was also stunted in its focus on individual preferences and rational choices and could not explain why we sometimes oppress ourselves. Socialist philosophy espoused the idea that human beings are historical creatures, the product of the praxis— or collective economic labor—of their time. On this view, our current preferences (for example, our excessive consumerism) may not express our "real" natures or our highest potential. We need to change our collective praxis in order to create the social conditions for new desires and new capacities for equality.

Simone de Beauvoir

The philosopher Simone de Beauvoir (1908–1986) developed an innovative feminist theory in the 1940s that incorporated insights from both liberalism and socialism. Her book *The Second Sex* ([1949] 2011) began with the socialist idea that human nature *changes* through history, at least in part. If human nature can change, she reasoned that we should be wary of ideas about natural femininity or natural masculinity.

Woman as "Object"

Being human means that we are subjects: *we* choose what has value and what is meaningful, whether in the realm of art, ideas, or ways of living. But women are viewed as more object-like than subject: women's lives are determined by their biology, that is, by their bodies more than their minds. Men alone have been thought to escape being objects by creating culture and deciding how to live their lives.

This sharp distinction between men and women serves men well. It is easy for men to feel secure in their rationality when contrasted with an inferior female, just as a man self-conscious about his height might prefer to be with a much shorter woman. Thus de Beauvoir suggested that ideas about "woman"

are really motivated by the desire to construct man as comfortably superior and justifiably dominant. Men resist feminism because changing ideas about women necessarily changes ideas about men.

Women, de Beauvoir argued, are encouraged to embrace their object-like status and to follow their male partners' life plans rather than making their own. They are discouraged from thwarting gender conventions by the threat of family disapproval and the possibility of a life lived alone. Women are not biologically determined to be obsessed with their appearance, de Beauvoir argued, but it makes sense to be so when that is the primary source of one's desirability and worth.

Woman as "Other"

De Beauvoir argued that male-dominant cultures have also conceptualized women as the "other," or the second sex. Women are never taken to be central to a society's history and formation, and their lives are never taken to be paradigmatic of the human condition, rather, women are seen as a supporting cast to men who are the real protagonists. The norm of human psychology, biology, etc., is the male experience; women are an afterthought.

When women grow up in cultures that take the male as the norm, they learn to take the man's point of view. Thus women come to accept the idea that history is the unfolding of male activity, to value men's opinions above women's, and to have a generally negative assessment of women. "The representation of the world as the world itself is the work of men; they describe it from a point of view that is their own and that they confound with the absolute truth." (de Beauvoir, [1949] 2011: 162)

On the other hand, de Beauvoir believed women have long seen through the contradictions of conventional gender practices, such as the hypocrisy of men who publicly espouse a

---

Box 2.3   DE BEAUVOIR LOOKS BACK

This book was first conceived…almost by chance. Wanting to talk about myself, I became aware that to do so I should first have to describe the condition of woman in general; first I considered the myths that men have forged about her.…[I]n every case, man put himself forward as the Subject and considered the woman as an object, as the Other.

…I began to look at women with new eyes and found surprise after surprise lying in wait for me. It is both strange and stimulating to discover suddenly, after forty, an aspect of the world that has been staring you in the face all the time which somehow you have never noticed. One of the misunderstandings created by my book is that people thought I was denying there was any difference between men and women. On the contrary, writing this book made me even more aware of those things that separate them; what I contended was that these dissimilarities are of a cultural and not of a natural order.

Source: Simone de Beauvoir, *The Force of Circumstance.* 1964: 185–7. ©Editions Gallimard, Paris, 1960.

---

high-minded morality while privately pursuing sexual adventure and infidelity. So she believed that the more women interpret their experiences themselves, the less likely they will be to accept the misconceptions that have prevailed throughout history about "woman" and "women's nature." Women can then begin to truly make their own lives.

For de Beauvoir this process requires women to seek meaningful work outside the home in order both to develop their capacities and to gain social recognition free from their social relations to others. She viewed the life of the housewife as too cloistered and monotonous to be truly rewarding. She also believed we need a social transformation to make jobs outside the home truly meaningful, jobs in which we can be subjects and not mere objects.

Contemporary Feminist Debates

Socialist feminism and liberal feminism continue as trends today, but since the 1960s there have been numerous other theoretical and political trends within feminism.

Radical Feminism and Cultural Feminism

Radical feminists sought an analysis focused on *misogyny* or the systematic derogation of everything associated with women and the feminine. In their view, the problem is not simply discrimination against women, but an all-out war on women including their very right to have bodily autonomy, to live free from violence, and in some cases just to live.

Radical feminists began to use the concept of patriarchy to define societies, broadening this term from its traditional anthropological usage of "father-right" to mean male dominance in general. Kate Millett's important book *Sexual Politics*, published in 1970, introduced this idea: "…our society, like all other historical civilizations, is a patriarchy…the military, industry, technology, universities, science, political office, and finance—in short, every avenue of power within the society, including the coercive force of the police, is entirely in male hands" (1970: 25). Patriarchy may vary greatly across time and cultures, but Millett insisted male dominance is global, and males as a group, no matter their class, benefit from the oppression of women.

Millett advocated androgyny as central to the liberation of women. If sexism exaggerates gender differences, and in some cases creates differences where there are none, feminism should aim to overcome gender differences. Though many feminists agreed with Millett, some radical feminists began to develop a critique of androgyny in the 1970s. Mary Daly (1978) and Adrienne Rich (1976, 1980) argued that patriarchy mischaracterized and unfairly devalued feminine traits and that feminism should be wary of rejecting traditions associated with women such as the domestic arts and crafts, empathetic relationships, and a value on peace over violence.

Although it may seem that societies have one unified culture, radical feminists find two cultures: the visible and documented world of male culture, which is divided by national boundaries, and the invisible world of women's culture, which exists universally "within every culture" (Jaggar, 1983: 249). Dominant male culture portrays a picture of social reality in which men are, and should be, aggressive, dominant, objective, strong, and intellectual, while women are, and are valued as, passive, emotional, intuitive, dependent, and submissive. Many liberal and socialist feminists view such differences as socially constructed rather than natural and believe that in an egalitarian future we will discover that men and women are basically the same and that women have as much potential for autonomy and rationality as men.

Some radical feminists, by contrast, began to develop a form of "cultural feminism," arguing that while male culture honors competition and aggression even to the point of killing, "woman culture" celebrates birth, connection, and peace. They pointed out that feminists who espoused androgyny rarely aimed for a true mix of traits but generally aimed to make women more like men. In *The Second Sex*, for

Barbara Smith, leading Black Feminist and member of the Combahee River Collective established in 1975. As a lesbian and a socialist, she has stressed the intersectionality of racial, gender, heterosexist, and class oppression in the lives of all women of color. In 1980, she was a cofounder of the Kitchen Table Press created to publish works by Black women. Her own writings throughout the rest of the century opened up the field of Black women's literature. Since 2005, Smith has carried her ideas and principles into politics in New York State.

example, de Beauvoir takes meaningful work outside the home as the only route to becoming truly human. By contrast, cultural feminists promoted a woman-centered approach for women that would value relationships with the women in one's life and create new forms of culture that affirm women.

Radical feminists also initially coined the slogan "the personal is political" (Jaggar, 1983: 255). This was meant to criticize leftist and anti-racist men with whom women were engaged in shared political struggle but whose personal lives continued to be sexist. The slogan encouraged activists to analyze the politics of housework, childrearing, and sexual relationships alongside war, racism, and capitalism, rather than viewing the former as trivial or irrelevant to the important work of revolutionary change.

Radical feminists viewed patriarchy as a system of pervasive domination most clearly expressed in the efforts to control women's bodies. Conservative attitudes about contraception or abortion aim at maintaining a system of compulsory motherhood. Pervasive sexual harassment, rape, prostitution, and pornography are other ways by which men dominate women and channel their sexuality for their own needs or profit (MacKinnon, 1987).

For some radical feminists, heterosexual relationships are always in danger of becoming oppressive to women. Separatism may be an answer and can take the form of sexual celibacy or lesbianism. In this way lesbianism came to be associated with a political stand, as when Charlotte Bunch argued that "[b]eing a Lesbian means ending identification with, allegiance to, dependence on, and support of heterosexuality. It means ending your personal stake in the male world so that you join women, individually and collectively, in the struggle to end your oppression. Lesbianism is the key to liberation and only women who cut their ties to male privilege can be trusted to remain serious in the struggle against male dominance" (Bunch, 1975: 36).

Some feminists also argued that the hatred and fear of lesbians is politically motivated in a way that distinguishes it from a general homophobia, as indicated by the fact that "uppity" women were often called "dykes." As Adrienne Rich (1980: 648) expresses it: "Lesbianism is a threat to the ideological, political, personal, and economic basis of male supremacy. The Lesbian threatens the ideology of male supremacy by destroying the lie about female inferiority, weakness, passivity, and by denying women's 'innate need for men.'"

Box 2.4   CHICANA VIEWPOINTS

Chicana feminist Sonia Saldívar-Hull (2000) points out that it is essential not to lose sight of specific ethnic distinctions in feminist theory.

I use *Third World feminism* to indicate how our histories as Chicana/Latina feminists force us to examine geopolitics as well as gender politics. As our alignment with women of the Third World indicates, our subject position exists in the interstices of national borders. More to the point, we are aligned as women whose specific needs have largely been ignored by most of our own male theorists as well as by many Euro-American feminists….We Chicanas, along with other previously unlistened-to subaltern women, now insist on our agency to speak for ourselves. The question remains—who will listen and how well equipped with relevant information is that audience?

Source: Sonia Saldívar-Hull, *Feminism on the Border: From Gender Politics to Geopolitics,* p. 55. Berkeley: University of California Press, 2000. Copyright © 2000 The Regents of the University of California.

Some radical feminists also came to believe that racial and class oppression is derived from gender domination. As the oldest form of social domination, gender oppression became the model and organizational structure on which all others were developed.

Black Feminism

Many women of color were actively writing theory and influencing the development of liberal feminism, socialist feminism, radical feminism, and other trends. By the 1970s, some began to name specific forms of feminism that were based on the experiences and conditions of women of color. "Black feminism" became one of the most influential and well developed of these theories, though in the United States there has also been a development of Latina feminism, Asian American feminism, Arab feminism, Indigenous Feminism, and "women of color feminism." Given the different conditions of women's lives, these feminists argued we need specific theories to understand specific groups, as well as to develop realistic strategies for change.

"Black feminism" was not accepted by all African American feminists. Some rejected the need for a separate form of feminism while others, following Alice Walker, advocated for the term "womanism" rather than "feminism." But many agreed that (1) the legacy of slavery continues to have an impact on black communities and gender relations, and (2) some of the common cultural representations of black women pose unique obstacles, such as the idea that they are "too strong" and "too dominant" (hooks, 1984; Davis, 1998).

Conventional gender practices were very different in black communities. As most slaves were not allowed to marry or to form or maintain familial relationships, many black women have cherished the right to have families and children and have experienced this sphere as, at least potentially, a domain of freedom rather than the domain of oppression and monotony that de Beauvoir described. Moreover, black feminists pointed out that the form of femininity conventional to white women was largely denied black women, who were rarely put on a pedestal or "protected" from long hours of grueling labor. Cheryl Clarke (1983), Audre Lorde (1984), and others also argued that homophobia and lesbophobia took on specific forms based on the false claim by some nationalists that homosexuality was a European invention. But because of the oppression of African American heterosexual families, those who wanted to defend gay rights needed to address the specific history of African Americans.

This difference in feminist priorities and orientation became very clear early on in regard to the issue of rape and reproductive rights. An early feminist work, "Rape: An All-American Crime," by Susan Griffin (1971), uncritically repeated racist myths about the desire of African American men to rape white women. Moreover, the book omitted any discussion of the legacy of lynching black men, which in most instances used the charge of rape as the pretext for their sexual torture and public murder. Thus, Angela Davis (1998) argued that overcoming the problem of rape in African American communities requires attending to both race and gender issues. There has been an institutionalized acceptance of the rape of black women by men of all races since slavery, when rape was legal and common as a means of enforcing submission, and still today this is among the least punished crimes in the country.

The "myth of matriarchy" has also beset African American gender relations. In 1965, while assistant secretary for labor, Daniel Patrick Moynihan (1927–2003) issued a report to Congress that blamed black women for the "dysfunction" of black families based on analyses that, at the time, were well respected by sociologists. The Moynihan Report (1965)

Vandana Shiva, scientist, ecofeminist, global activist. Born in India in the middle of the twentieth century, Shiva has written over 20 books to become a leading figure in the movement to bring issues of global ecology to the scientific and political communities of the world. Trained as a physicist, with a Ph.D. in philosophy, she has argued for the need to pay attention to the advantages of traditional practices. In 1993 she was awarded the Right Livelihood Award, which recognizes personal courage and the work of social transformation. It ensures the winner an international audience.

charged that the legacy of slavery and ongoing discrimination kept black men from becoming the rightful heads of their families and created a matriarchal tradition. Black feminists pointed out that this report assumed male dominance as the natural order, necessary for social success, and, furthermore, that there is no matriarchy: African American women have neither economic nor political power and suffer some of the highest rates of poverty and violence.

Black feminists differed over whether they should pursue organizational autonomy from other feminist groups. Some, such as Barbara Smith (1983), argued that the specific conditions of black women's oppression required a period of organizational independence so that they could develop and deepen their theoretical and political analysis. For others, like bell hooks (1984) and Angela Davis (1998), having separate groups would prolong the struggle and might wrongly imply that the oppression of black women has different causes from other forms of social oppression.

Black feminists generally agreed, however, on the importance of having an intersectional analysis that could make visible the interconnections of multiple oppressions of social identities including race, gender, class, sexuality, and so on. This has become an important trend in feminist theory and will be discussed in Chapter 3.

Postmodern Feminism

Postmodern and psychoanalytic trends in feminist theory were motivated by a sense that existing theoretical analyses were not going deep enough. Many of the legal reforms that liberal feminists had fought for were beginning to be won by the late 1970s. Women were legally guaranteed equal employment free from sexual harassment, abortion in the first trimester was made legal, and many women benefited from affirmative action in male-dominated areas of work. Yet sexual violence and a general cultural sexism persisted. As some feminists argued, a poststructuralist analysis of how the culture is organized by gender relations would reveal that the roots of misogyny are not in explicit beliefs that can be legislatively addressed but in deep structural formations that exist in language and belief systems.

Postmodern feminists looked to the work of European poststructuralist philosophers like Derrida (1978) and Foucault (1978) as a way to analyze the persistence of gender divisions. Poststructuralists shared the structuralist view that some social dynamics cannot be explained by the aggregated conscious choices of individuals; rather, as Marx and other structuralists argued, individuals are caught up in structures over which they have little control. Structuralism was thus able to provide better explanations of many social phenomena like war, environmental destruction, and gender hierarchies without relying on evil intentions or conspiracies. Sometimes dominant groups pursue actions that are against their own best interests, and sometimes outcomes are unintended consequences; structuralism explained how this is possible.

The great structuralists like Marx (see above), Freud (see Chapter 5), and Lévi-Strauss (1908–2009) believed that structures represent deep mechanisms that operate like laws of history: they cannot be changed, although we can become aware of them and in this way might be able to subvert their damaging effects. Poststructuralists disagreed on just this point: they saw structures as changeable rather than absolute. Structures do not represent stable patterns of human behavior but variable systems of meaning and ways of producing meaning and what we take to be truth (Lévi-Strauss, 1963).

Conventional ideas and ways of life are not the natural developments of human nature or of human experience, but the effect of what Foucault called "discourses": systems of meaning that connect language and practice such that we come to experience things differently through them. He rejected the idea of false consciousness, since this assumes there is a true consciousness beneath the veil of social convention. Rather, discourses are fully determinative of experience and not simply a means of concealing reality. To understand experience as socially constructed—constituted by specific discourses—is to understand that experience is neither natural nor inevitable. Discourses are the variable manifestations of power structures and relations and thus can be critically evaluated, not on the grounds of whether or not they express the "truth" about human experience, but on the grounds of *how* they produce experience, and with what effects. Poststructuralism took the feminist critique of naturalist approaches to gender to the next level.

Other feminists in this trend argued that deconstructing existing discourses is not a guarantee of decreasing oppression and that the poststructuralist view generally, like Marxism, is gender-blind and race-blind. These feminists turned to psychoanalysis for a deeper explanation of sexism and a more fully developed plan for subversion.

Psychoanalytic Feminism

Psychoanalysis, feminists argued, is a sexist theory. Freud believed women naturally have penis envy, are naturally sexually submissive, "evolve" (if they are normal) from clitoral to vaginal orgasms, and are naturally less rational than men. But feminists like Juliet Mitchell (1973) argued that, as a theory, psychoanalysis helpfully describes the effects of patriarchy, even if Freud himself did not understand his theory in this way. Freud beautifully captured what male dominance does to the psyche of both men and women.

Nancy Chodorow (see Chapter 1) took up this approach and used Freud to develop an account of why males can be irrationally afraid of commitment and monogamy and why they fear being swallowed by female power even when in most cases males have greater ability than females do to leave their relationships. Growing up with mothers who are socialized to take their parenting as the central focus of their life, males often struggle to achieve independence. When a tight connection with obsessive mothers leaves little room for separate development, and when masculinity is defined as the *opposite* of femininity, males are indeed psychically threatened. This effect is not an inevitable feature of mother–son relationships but caused by societies that have oppositional concepts of gender and parenting practices that make mothers the exclusive caregivers of young children. Chodorow thus concluded that these dynamics are changeable.

Feminists working with psychoanalysis in Europe, notably Luce Irigaray ([1974] 1985), Hélène Cixous (1976), and Julia Kristeva (1980), developed further ways to analyze the implicit sexism in our language and culture. They traced the erasure of mothers throughout societies that worship male deities and inscribe males as the givers of life: the (male) God giving life to Adam, Zeus giving birth to Athena (from his head), and Aristotle's influential view that mothers are merely the vessels of male seed. Defining sex as intercourse includes male orgasm as part of sex but not women's: whether or not a woman has an orgasm is irrelevant to how we define sex. The experiences of women and mothers are not only objectified, they are erased.

Psychoanalysis provided a way to understand this widespread removal of women as well as irrational fears about what the female represents. Cixous argued that the antidote to such social patterns is for women to begin to write themselves back into language, not through following the style of male writers, but by freeing themselves to develop their own *écriture feminine*.

Ecofeminism

Also in the 1970s feminists began to make connections between the oppression of women and the disregard for the environment based on the historical associations between women and nature, both of which were viewed as unruly, unpredictable, and irrational forces that need to be tamed and controlled. Carolyn Merchant (1980) traced this attitude to the rise of industrialization in Europe between the fourteenth to seventeenth centuries. Whereas in medieval times Europeans believed nature was given to man by God as a kind of sacred trust, the emerging capitalist societies viewed nature as either a dangerous nuisance or exploitable resource. Merchant also links the witch craze that swept Europe, putting tens of thousands of women to death, to ideas of both women and nature as dangerous and diabolical forces needing to be controlled. Many so-called witches were in fact healers who relied on natural herbs and midwives who assisted women in a full range of reproductive needs. During this period women suffered a significant loss of social status and economic power in European societies, losing their ability to join guilds or own land. Overturning the view of nature as divine and mysterious and worthy of reverence was correlated to a similar demotion of women.

Ecofeminists sought to understand the connections between feminism and ecology and to develop a unified vision of social change. Some argued, like cultural feminists, that women have a stronger connection to life-affirming values because of their reproductive experiences, such as childbirth. Organizations like Mothers against Nuclear Disarmament made explicit reference to motherhood as a motivation for disarmament.

Other ecofeminists avoided reinforcing the association between women and nature. Ynestra King argued that the goal of ecofeminism should be to create a more integrative culture that combines "intuitive, spiritual and rational forms of knowledge" accessible to all (King, 1995: 19). The obstacle to this is not men per se, but a particular way of defining gender identity. Dorothy Dinnerstein (1923–1992) argued similarly that the current system of gender is a threat to the planet. By defining masculinity in terms of violent aggression and restricting nurturance and emotional caregiving to femininity, expressions of nurturance for the earth are viewed as feminine, rather than human or even rational (1977).

Ecofeminists agreed, however, that our treatment of wombs and female bodies as generally subject to state control and exchange for profit is connected to our view of nature. We need to learn to respect both women and nature, to recognize the sacred rhythms and harmonies of life, and to respect and *work with* these natural processes rather than always trying to control or alter them.

Postcolonial theorists like Vandana Shiva emphasized the connections between the oppression of women, global imperialism, and the ideology of development. Development along a capitalist model that emphasizes excessive materialism and consumerism is neither possible nor desirable on a global scale.

Shiva argues that there is a mistaken identification of the growth of commodity production as better satisfaction of basic needs. In actual fact, there is less water, less fertile soil, less genetic wealth as a result of the development process. Since these natural resources [e.g. water, soil] are the basis of nature's economy and women's survival economy, their scarcity is impoverishing women and marginalized peoples in an unprecedented manner." (Shiva, 1988: 89)

Women hold the key to a sustainable agricultural model, Shiva argues. Women across the world practice a form of subsistence economics in which they provide basic needs through self-provisioning, including making their own houses, clothing, and seed supplies, without having to participate in the market for everything they need. Sometimes women are perceived as poor only because they participate less in the market economy. Ecofeminism must combine its critique of gender ideology with a critique of capitalism and imperialism and learn from the struggles of rural women who have fought to protect natural resources like water, seeds, and herbal remedies as communally shared rather than as private property or subject to patents so that corporations can make profits.

Transnational Feminism

Along these lines, transnational feminist theory seeks to develop a feminism "without borders," as Chandra Talpade Mohanty puts it (2003). This requires addressing the challenges of creating global feminist solidarity so that we can unite around international issues such as sex trafficking or women's sweatshop labor. It can be a challenge to identify sexism across differences of religion and values. Is the veil, or hijab, worn by some Muslim women a sign of oppression or a testament to their religious piety that others should respect? Is there one universalizable model for achieving women's equality or many different ones?

Before we can develop transnational feminist solidarity, Mohanty and others argue we must understand the ways in which feminism can be used by colonialism and imperialism. Some leading Western feminists have viewed women from the Global South as powerless victims who need "our" help, implicitly assuming that women from the Global North are the vanguard of the movement for women's equality. Thus, they have judged women's lives from the perspective of their own cultural values, associating feminism with individualism, for example, and in opposition to family or community-centered identities.

Uma Narayan (1997) has identified a tendency to downplay the way in which sexism in the West is *culturally* mediated. While women in India are portrayed as victimized by their culture, the epidemic of male violence against women in the United States is not seen as connected to its pro-gun culture or the commodification of women's bodies in market societies. Thus, the first task for transnational feminism is to analyze the assumptions of Western feminism that may inhibit solidarity.

Yet transnational feminists remain optimistic that solidarity is possible. Mohanty argues that it is vital to develop a global analysis of the conditions of women's lives that can explain the connections between the diverse structures and institutions that oppress women. We need to understand, for example, how the global assembly line—or division of labor in commodity production—takes advantage of women's social vulnerability in many societies to increase profits and how birth control devices intended for U.S. markets have been tested on poor women in the Global South before they were deemed safe (see Chapter 9).

Transnational feminism is especially urgent in a period where military interventions are justified on the basis of protecting women or improving their lives. Many women from war-torn countries point out that war destroys communities and infrastructure and increases sexual violence. Most importantly, the effort to advance the cause of women in any part of the world must rely on *their* leadership and *their* knowledge of local conditions. Transnational alliances can only be built through communicative networks with equal and meaningful participation. True feminism cannot be imposed unilaterally, and a strategy of women's liberation must work for all and not just some women.

Contemporary Feminist Philosophy

Feminist philosophers argue that feminist analyses are relevant to every sphere of inquiry. Historically, moral theories started from the idea that we have to find a way to justify the claim that independent individuals have moral obligations to others. They ignored the obligations that exist within families and communities, in which there are relations of interdependence. Theories of knowledge had similar blind spots, defining "reason" in such a way that it mirrored conventional ideas about masculinity and femininity. Reason came to be defined in such a way that it excluded the realm of the emotional and the intuitive. Philosophers today are trying to formulate broader notions of rationality that are less distorted by social ideologies of gender and more realistic about what it means to reason well.

One common idea about reasoning is that it should ideally be value-free, interested only in the facts. But many "facts" advanced about women and gender purport to show that gender hierarchies are natural and therefore normal and right. Defining reason as neutral assessments of facts can obscure the ways in which values and goals structure our projects of inquiry, influence our assessment of what evidence is relevant, and provide support for our conclusions.

As we've seen in this chapter, there is a long tradition of thinking that women's subordination is natural and inevitable. Today there are new versions of this argument. For example, some claim that because women are biologically disposed to be less aggressive than men, it is therefore natural that men should be the dominant leaders in societies. Even if it were true that men are innately more aggressive, however, society might be organized so as to restrain and discourage the aggressiveness of men rather than to reinforce and reward it.

Because women are the ones who give birth, it has often been supposed that this is their primary function and thus fitting that they be confined to the role of mother, nurturer, or homemaker. Yet, again, no such conclusion follows from the biological facts. There is no reason to believe that the person who gives birth must be the person who spends the following 20 years doing the primary parenting, or that giving birth provides automatic knowledge about how to parent effectively. Nor does being a dedicated parent exclude a person from pursuing other interests and activities.

Sexual organs are obviously functional for reproduction, but is reproduction their singular or primary purpose? Sexual organs have at least three possible functions: to reproduce, to give pleasure, and to express love. Most human beings use their sexual organs most of the time for the latter two functions, not the former, which means that homosexual sexual activity is coherent with the proper functions of our sexual organs. Reasoning about matters such as sexuality and gender roles thus requires us to reason about what we value, and why. Without attending to values, our reasoned arguments may well go off course.

Rethinking "Knowledge" and Values of Inquiry

Feminist theorists have shown that we need to rethink how we attain knowledge if we are to overcome the gender biases built into what has been taken to be "knowledge." Moreover, traditional fields of study will have to be rethought if they are to reflect the perspectives of women as fully as they reflect those of men (Harding, 1987; Zalk and Gordon-Kelter, 1990; Alcoff and Potter, 1993; Fausto-Sterling, 2000). Not only have many topics been neglected that are of interest to women, but the very concepts and assumptions with which inquiry has proceeded have often reflected a male rather than a universal point of view. Bringing in perspectives on race, gender, and global issues requires radical rethinking of what has been thought of as impartial and objective knowledge (Williams, 1991; Narayan, 1997; Collins, 2000).

As it turns out, all values are not equal when it comes to the search for truth. Remember the earlier example in this chapter about the anthropologist who only interviewed men in his effort to study a foreign cultural system. Feminist philosophers of science like Elizabeth Anderson (2004) have argued that anti-sexist or feminist values would have improved his research. Anti-sexist values would have led the anthropologist to talk to the women, even if the men had told him that the women were unimportant and uninformed. And anti-sexist values would have led him to develop a more complete database of information that included women's perspectives and experiences.

Helen Longino (1990) argues that values enter at multiple stages in the pursuit of scientific knowledge. Each stage of inquiry—formulating questions, developing plausible hypotheses, developing methods of testing, and deciding when the evidence is conclusive—involves a judgment call. Sexist values may hinder research at any of these stages, whereas anti-sexist values may enhance the likelihood of reaching more reliable conclusions. We need to rethink the assumption that knowledge is best attained through impartial or politically neutral methods.

Feminists are increasingly concerned with the ways in which mainstream practices around knowledge and science are exclusionary. Everyday people have knowledge and often a thoughtful analysis, but both are underappreciated and underutilized. Feminists began asking how to proceed in ways that will include as part of the process those groups often excluded not only by gender but also by race, class, and sexual identity (Spelman, 1988; Anzaldúa, 1990; Card, 1995).

From the beginning, feminist theorists and social scientists used women's experiences to question received wisdom and develop new hypotheses. Sandra Harding developed this approach into a "feminist standpoint epistemology," based on the idea of starting inquiry from women's actual lives and work (Harding, 1987; 1991). Harding reasoned that understanding and overcoming social oppression of all sorts would be much higher on the agenda of inquiry given women's material labor in most societies and women's presence in every oppressed group, from the disabled to the working class. She also argued that women's "outsider status" in many social positions of power and dominance would give them an epistemic privilege: outsiders can often detect the unfounded assumptions that insiders may be too immersed in to see.

Poststructuralist feminist theorists voiced concern at this approach, however. They argued that women's experiences are socially constructed, influenced by culture, and repositories of ideology and cannot be taken as reliable knowledge (Scott, 1992). Other feminist epistemologists defended the importance of taking women's experience into account, no matter its constructed nature. Experience need not be a timeless universal or completely pure of social influences to have value for inquiry. And some experiences, especially bodily ones such as rape and pregnancy, can only be socially constructed so far. It remains important to take women's experiences

---

Box 2.5   GLORIA STEINEM ON FEMINIST LABELS

In the label department…I would prefer to be called simply "a feminist." After all, the belief in the full humanity of women leads to the necessity of totally changing all male-supremacist structures, thus removing the model and continuing support for other systems of birth-determined privilege. That should be radical enough. However, because there are feminists who believe that women can integrate or imitate existing structures (or conversely; that class or race structures must be transformed first, as a precondition to eliminating sexual caste), I feel I should identify myself as a "radical feminist." "Radical" means "going to the root," and I think that sexism is the root, whether or not it developed as the chronologically first dominance model in prehistory….The tolerance of a habit as pervasive as male-dominance not only creates an intimate model for oppression as "natural," but builds a callousness to other dominations—whether based on race, age, class, sexuality, or anything else.

Source: Steinem, 1978: 92–3.

seriously, even if approached with a critical analysis (Alcoff, 1997; Wylie, 2004).

The Ethics of Care

An approach that has influenced some contemporary feminists, especially radical ones, concerns morality: the ethics of care. It involves reevaluating activities and practices long associated with women and appreciating both their enormous importance in society and the neglected moral values they incorporate. Theorists have been exploring how the importance and value of caring relations should be applied to other areas in society beyond those associated with women: for instance, to medical practice, public and political life, even international relations (Sherwin, 1992; Tronto, 1993; Held, 1995; Kittay, 1999; Robinson, 1999; Tong, 2001).

In the 1970s feminists began to reconsider traditional ideals of morality. Carol Gilligan (1982) showed that the most widely accepted theory of moral development, developed by Lawrence Kohlberg, is as male-biased as Freud's theories. Proposed as a universal theory but based on a study of the cognitive development of 84 boys, Kohlberg's scale of moral development was supposed to describe the way in which moral reasoning moves from an immature stage of concern for others to a more mature stage where moral reasoning was based on formal, abstract principles or rules of justice.

Gilligan set out to study women to determine why they seemed to become stalled at the middle stage of Kohlberg's scale, which implied that women are deficient in the development of moral judgment. She found that many women reason very differently about moral issues. She called this a "different voice" from the one that Kohlberg identified as definitive of mature judgment (Kittay and Meyers, 1987). Studying a group of women making real-life decisions regarding abortion, Gilligan discovered that instead of applying abstract rules of justice, her subjects were concerned with preserving human relationships and expressing care for those for whom they felt responsible. This "ethic of care" was a different way of interpreting moral problems from the "ethic of justice" Kohlberg described. As Gilligan (1982: 19) put it: "This conception of morality as concerned with the activity of care centers moral development around the understanding of responsibility and relationships, just as the conception of morality as fairness ties moral development to the understanding of rights and rules."

Although Gilligan's analysis suggests how women and men act and think differently, it does not explain whether an "ethic of care" is equivalent, inferior, or superior to an "ethic of justice." One danger, according to some of Gilligan's critics, is that the idea of a morally "different voice" lends itself to biological typecasting that has been used for centuries to keep women in their "place" by praising their capacities for selfless devotion to others. Some feminists also suggested that women's different moral expression may result from their historically subordinate social position.

Joan Tronto draws on studies showing that African Americans tend to construct morality in terms that resemble an ethic of care. She notes that people of color do a disproportionate amount of the work of caring for the ill and elderly—for instance, as in nursing homes and hospitals. Thus, tendencies to use an ethic of care may depend less on gender than on restricted job options (Tronto, 1993). Yet Tronto and others continue to argue that the ethic of care developed in these conditions is something society in general can learn from. Moreover, a lack of caregiving experiences by privileged males can leave them morally deprived, misleading them into thinking that moral beliefs can be expressed in abstract, universal terms as if they were purely cognitive questions, like mathematical ones.

Some feminist moral philosophers have argued that caring may not be enough to address issues of fairness and justice: parents may care for their daughter but still impose greater restrictions on her than on her brother. Perhaps an "ethic of care" should be combined with an "ethic of justice," or perhaps we need to expand our understanding of what care involves in actual social conditions of inequality (Noddings, 1984; Ruddick, 1989; Held, 1995; Clement, 1996). Other feminists have been examining those aspects of the practice of care that should be changed because they are too often performed with little power or remuneration.

Many feminists argue today that a moral approach based in care is suitable not just for the household but for the wider society. Feminists have also come to a different view of persons. Whereas the ethic of justice can sometimes view persons as abstract individuals who are all equal, the ethic of care necessarily understands persons as relational, embedded in human relationships and in an actual historical context, as well as embodied (Clement, 1996; Meyers, 1997; Mackenzie and Stoljar, 2000).

The Nature of Gender

Feminist thinkers have also vigorously debated gender concepts and whether feminism should aim to deconstruct the very category of women. But all feminists generally agree that the history of ideas about women and gender show a pattern of falsely naturalizing gender roles and essentializing gender differences. Essentialism is the view that there is an essential, innate set of traits that all women share based on their biology. Essentialism thus forces all women into a single grouping, underemphasizing the differences among women as well as differences among men and overemphasizing men's and women's differences from each other, as well as ignoring the great variety of gendered and transgendered experiences. Critics of

essentialism have emphasized that "women's nature" has been socially and culturally constructed and is subject to significant change over time and place. Increasingly, it has been recognized that the question of defining "women" must now be broached in terms of a multitude of racial, ethnic, religious, class, and sexual identities and histories.

Still, without falling into essentialism, women can affirm their distinct contributions. Feminist philosopher Linda Martín Alcoff suggests they take a "positional perspective":

> The concept of positionality allows for a determinate though fluid identity of woman…woman is a position from which a feminist politics can emerge rather than a set of attributes that are "objectively identifiable." Seen in this way, being a "woman" is to take up a position within a moving historical context. (Alcoff, 1988: 435)

Those who are classified as women have a distinct experience of society the world over, and there is much shared sexism in the history of multiple cultures. Beyond the legacy of ideas there is also a real material difference in embodied experience concerning the division of labor in reproduction, menstruation, and menopause. Thus, gender categories continue to help us make sense of our historical, experiential, and material differences. The future of gender may yet change radically as new social practices unfold that accept more various ways to be in the world and new technologies transform the practices of human reproduction. Feminist theoretical analyses will be needed at every step of the way to question assumptions and to develop concepts and values that make sense for the people of the future.

Summary

Definitions of *woman* have often reflected faulty theories about the "nature" of women. Distorted definitions result from men seeing women as more biologically determined than and inferior to men, especially in their capacity to reason. Women are deemed less like active subjects making their own lives and more like passive objects.

Philosophers of the Enlightenment rejected hierarchical traditions of Western political thought—but not for women. The liberal principles of equality and freedom that helped to shape democracy applied to men and to male heads of households. Many liberal thinkers were silent on the subject of women or, like Jean-Jacques Rousseau, operated with a double standard of condemning social hierarchies everywhere but in relations between women and men.

The Enlightenment philosopher Mary Wollstonecraft argued that women's rational capacities would be increased if they had an education comparable to men's. Contemporary liberal feminists favor equality in the home as well as in the public realm, advocating that wives and husbands share equally in child care and household tasks. Affirmative action programs may be needed to provide women and minorities with equal job opportunities.

Socialist feminists argue that while liberal feminists underemphasize the role of the economy in sexism, traditional Marxists underestimate the role of sexism in the economy. They argue that we need to focus on the oppression of women as both women and workers, paying special attention to the economic structures around the world that oppress the disadvantaged.

Radical feminism emphasizes patriarchy as a fundamental structure organizing every aspect of society. Cultural feminism advocates for valuing the strengths of women's traditional practices and interrelationships. Black feminism contends that the specific conditions of African American women's lives require a specific analysis and set of solutions. Poststructuralist and psychoanalytic feminisms stress the implicit deep structures of gender that operate to produce misogyny without people's intentions. Ecofeminism looks at the relationship between the domination of women and the domination of nature. Transnational feminism seeks the basis for a global solidarity of women and a global analysis of women's oppression.

What has been thought to be impartial and objective "knowledge" has often represented the views and values of men only. Feminist theorists call for radical reconceptualizations of both knowledge and the values of inquiry to address gender biases.

Feminist standpoint theory advocates starting theory from women's lives to value women's experience and marginalized status as epistemically useful. The ethics of care has developed as an influential feminist approach to moral issues and to questions about how society should be organized. It especially values caring relations between persons and emphasizes these in both personal and social contexts.

Although feminists frequently disagree, all share one goal: to overcome the oppression of women. They are interested in work that meets human needs, with the work fairly divided and cooperatively organized, and believe society should be governed with a minimum of domination and subordination.

Women no longer have to accept the conceptions that others have had about them and about society. They can choose for themselves what ideas to accept and what their goals should be.

Discussion Questions

1. Do women have a "choice"? Discuss the ways in which women can or cannot choose to (*1*) "accept" subordinate roles, (*2*) believe in the "natural" inferiority of women, (*3*) act as free and responsible persons, and (*4*) do what they would like rather than what others would like them to do.

2. In what ways can you see a male rather than a universal point of view as predominant in

(1) traditional moral or political theory and (2) a social science with which you are familiar?
3. What would be needed for women to have (1) legal equality, (2) equal opportunities, (3) equality within the family, and (4) full equality?
4. What sorts of governmental policy might be recommended by an ethic of care?
5. Discuss the importance of feminist theory in your own experience. Has it helped you to understand, to choose, to act? If so, how? What are the major areas in which you think feminist theory needs to be improved?

Recommended Readings

De Beauvoir, Simone. *The Second Sex*, translated by Constance Borde and Sheila Malovany-Chevallier. New York: Vintage, [1949] 2011. A classic book about how the ideas and social conditions of women have affected women and how they can begin to think for themselves about themselves.

Hypatia. A Journal of Feminist Philosophy. Bloomington: Indiana University Press. This is the premier women's philosophy journal with continuing new theorizing about women's issues.

McCann, Carol R., and Seung-Kyung Kim, editors. *Feminist Theory Reader: Local and*

Global Perspectives. New York: Routledge, 2003. A sample of classic and current theoretical analyses of gender in relation to class, sexuality, nation, and race, including sections on standpoint theories and poststructuralism.

Lloyd, Genevieve. *The Man of Reason: "Male" and "Female" in Western Philosophy.* Minneapolis: University of Minnesota Press, 1984. Lloyd demonstrates that Western philosophers have celebrated the ideal of "reason" in ways that required the rejection of whatever was associated with the female at various stages of history.

Tong, Rosemarie. *Feminist Thought*, 3rd ed. Boulder, CO: Westview Press, 2009. A comprehensive introduction to varieties of feminist thinking, such as liberal feminism, socialist feminism, radical feminism, psychoanalytic feminism, ecofeminism, global feminism, and postmodern feminism.

Note

1. Rousseau's views on protecting the family have always been taken with a grain of salt by readers of his autobiography, who learn that he ordered his mistress to deliver all five of the children she bore with him to the steps of the local orphanage.

Intersectionality

> I find I am constantly being encouraged to pluck out some one aspect of myself and present this as the meaningful whole, eclipsing or denying the other parts of self. But this is a destructive and fragmenting way to live. My fullest concentration of energy is available to me only when I integrate all the parts of who I am, openly....
>
> AUDRE LORDE, 1984

In April 1989, a white woman jogging in Central Park was brutally beaten and raped. For months the story was in the headlines not just in New York City, but around the nation, as the woman lay in a coma, fighting for her life. The five African American and Puerto Rican teenagers accused of the crime were referred to throughout the media as savages, barbarians, and wild animals. Real estate tycoon Donald Trump paid for $85,000 worth of advertisements calling for a reinstatement of the death penalty in New York State so they could be executed (Smith, 1998). During the same week that this rape occurred, 28 other first degree or attempted rapes were reported in New York City, nearly all involving black and Latina victims.

As this series of events makes clear, there is wide disparity in the public responses to crimes of sexual violence (Dowd Hall 1983; Morrison 1992; Lubiano 1997). We continue to observe today that both victims *and* perpetrators are treated differently depending on the specifics of their identities and not just the specifics of the crime. In order to understand the problem of sexual violence, then, and the challenges we face in addressing it, we need to consider more than the ideas and norms that govern our practices around gender and sexual violence. At a minimum we need to bring in race and class along with gender in order to unpack the varied public responses to rape, why some victims who report are considered credible and others

are not, and why some victims elicit wide public sympathy while others are blamed or ignored. If we cannot adequately understand the problem, we cannot expect to find effective solutions.

In the Central Park case, the victim was an upper-class white investment banker, and the accused rapists were five young men of color from poor and working-class parts of the city. All five were convicted in a highly politicized climate and sent to prison, but all were exonerated years later based on DNA evidence and a confession from the real rapist. (This case was documented in the 2012 film *The Central Park Five*.) Importantly, this rape did not take the usual form that most rapes take: it did not occur between people of the same race and class, and the victim did not know her assailant. By contrast, the vast majority of sexual violence occurs between victims and assailants who know each other and thus typically share the same class and race background. These more typical rapes are rarely considered newsworthy. When women are victimized by men they know or with whom they have had relationships, their charges are often viewed skeptically by police, by courts, and even by their own family and friends. Poor women are often assumed to have economic motivations to make false rape charges against rich men. The patterns by which women are accorded credibility and justice requires an intersectional analysis (see Box 3.1).

Box 3.1   THE FRENCH POLITICIAN AND THE HOTEL HOUSEKEEPER

Dominique Strauss-Kahn, French economist, lawyer, politician, and Managing Director of the International Monetary Fund (IMF) from 2007, was accused of sexual assault by Nafissatou Diallo, an African immigrant working as a hotel housekeeper, in New York City in 2011. Strauss-Kahn had enormous power as well as wealth from his third wife, the heiress Anne Sinclair. Diallo, a Muslim single mother living in the Bronx who came to the U.S. in 1998 from Guinea, had been working at Sofitel for three years when she accused Strauss-Kahn of forcing her to have oral sex when she went to clean his hotel room. After Diallo came forward, other women began to report stories that indicated a history of sexual coercion on the part of Strauss-Kahn, and one young journalist in France brought a second suit against him. Defense attorneys in New York, meanwhile, began to unravel her credibility, charging her with lying to get asylum in the U.S. and with conniving a plot to get money out of Strauss-Kahn. Some of the media in the U.S. characterized Diallo as a prostitute, while some of the French media defended Strauss-Kahn's sexual appetites and suggested a conspiracy. The New York prosecutor's office subsequently decided to drop the case before it came to trial. Strauss-Kahn resigned from the IMF and retreated from his political aspirations, and Diallo had to leave her job as well. The intersections of power, race, gender, and money made this case a complex story in which Diallo's and Strauss-Kahn's different identities produced contrasting credibility, access to legal experts, influence on the media, and appeals to public sympathy and feminist outrage.

Diallo pursued justice through the civil courts and was awarded a confidential financial settlement from Strauss-Kahn in December 2012.

Source: "Hotel Worker Settles Claim Strauss-Kahn Forced Sex." *New York Times,* December 10, 2012.

Sexism and Racism

Feminists like Princeton professor Valerie Smith, who analyzed the Central Park case and its surrounding media responses, argue from these and similar cases that feminist theory and women's studies scholarship must begin to adopt an *intersectional approach*. Such an approach holds that "ideologies of race, gender…class, and sexuality are *reciprocally constitutive categories* of experience and analysis" (Smith, 1998: xiii; emphasis added). The particular language of racism, in other words, will differ depending on whether it is targeting a male or female, a working-class or a middle-class group. Males may be called savages, while females may be called hot tamales, depending on their race and gender. Both gender discrimination and racial oppression take different forms when these occur in different configurations. An intersectional approach takes into account these multiple dimensions of identity and experience operating in a given context and the ways in which these dimensions *interact*.

Without an intersectional approach, the experiences of women of color cannot be adequately understood, as writers such as Audre Lorde (1984), bell hooks (1984), and the philosopher Elizabeth Spelman (1988) argued, and as the legal theorist Kimberlé Crenshaw (1989, 1991) showed in her work on domestic violence: "[T]he experiences of women of color are frequently the product of intersecting patterns of racism and sexism, and…these experiences tend not to be represented within the discourses either of feminism or antiracism." As a result, "women of color are marginalized within both" (Crenshaw, 1991: 1243–4). African American women in particular are rarely viewed as victims: the stereotype of the "strong black woman" creates unique obstacles to their ability to receive justice from juries who cannot see them as vulnerable. Without an intersectional approach, Crenshaw argued, neither feminism nor

Kimberlé Crenshaw, professor of law, divides her time teaching at UCLA and the Columbia School of Law. A distinguished scholar of race and gender issues, she is one of the earliest contemporary analysts of intersectionality as a valuable tool for making visible and addressing the needs and concerns of women of color, such as in the situation of domestic violence.

anti-racism will be able to address adequately the specific obstacles that women of color in the United States face.

Intersectional approaches are just as important in understanding the situation of white women, or any group of women from the dominant social groups in a society, since their particular experiences of sexism are also affected by the multiple aspects of their identity. While working-class black women were long treated as "the mule of the world," as the Harlem Renaissance writer Zora Neale Hurston put it, upper-class white women were put on a pedestal and viewed as delicate flowers in need of paternal protection (Wallace, 1978). But both are forms of sexism: being "protected" from the dirty world of work and politics was hardly liberation since it denied autonomy to this group of women or their right of self-determination. Yet whether one is treated as a mule or a delicate flower produces quite a different set of practices and ideologies, a difference in kind and not merely in degree. The ideology of the pedestal elicits patriarchal protection and interference into the decisions a woman makes about her own life, while being treated as a mule means one is mercilessly exploited. In the one case there is excessive and paternalistic oversight, and in the other case, a brutal neglect of well-being. Again, this is not a difference in degree, but in kind. There is no generic sexism meted out to women in varying degrees depending on their specific status and identity. Rather, there are different *forms* of sexism depending on one's race, class, sexuality, religion, able-bodiedness, nationality, ethnicity, age, and legal or citizenship status. This is what Smith means when she claims that these categories are co-constitutive. One's racial identity can constitute how one's gender identity is understood, whether as a form of fragility or as an excuse for mistreatment.

Taking an intersectional approach does not dilute or disable the possibility of making sexism a political priority. Smith herself advocated for what she called a "woman-centered rape law policy that seeks to police violent, coercive sexual behavior as a crime in and of itself, one that recognizes that rape is part of a system of aggression against all women…" (1998: 20).

Nonetheless, Smith argued that developing a woman-centered policy requires an intersectional approach. Otherwise, the full dimensions of the problem cannot be understood or addressed. In the weeks and months after the Central Park case, various African American and Puerto Rican media effectively criticized the racist portrayals of the alleged rapists but also attacked the credibility of the victim. In contrast, the white-dominated media continued to play on the racist stereotypes that have been used throughout U.S. history to justify lynching, such as stereotypes of dark men desiring and preying on innocent white womanhood. In the meantime, as Smith points out, the "systemic violence and misogyny that makes women unsafe in this society" went unanalyzed in the media brouhaha. The Central Park victim appeared only as an objectified image, without her own voice, simply used by diverse groups for their own competing purposes that had nothing to do with reducing the crime of rape. The other 28 women who were victimized that month remained completely invisible.

Sexism and Heterosexism

Considerations of race and class were not the only motivators behind the development of an intersectional approach in feminist theory and activism. Lesbian feminists began to argue throughout the 1970s and 1980s that the oppression of lesbians takes a different form than the oppression of straight women. Heterosexual women who express a desire for children or who demonstrate a loving devotion to their partners are praised; the same behavior in lesbians is reinterpreted as perverse and even monstrous and makes them subject to homophobic attack. Such double standards indicate that a society is *heterosexist*: that is, it considers only heterosexual relationships and heterosexual love or desire acceptable.

For these sorts of reasons some theorists argued that lesbian oppression needs an entirely separate analysis as well as a different set of solutions than the oppression of straight women. French feminist writer Monique Wittig (1935–2003) argued that lesbians are not really women at all by the commonly understood concepts in the dominant cultural imaginary. Neither the term "woman" nor "womanliness" invoke the mental image of a lesbian, and may even invoke a contrast (Wittig, 1992). Moreover, Wittig held that lesbians exist outside the patriarchal system of work in which heterosexual women's biological and socially reproductive labor is managed and organized. The traditional feminine roles in gender-segregated societies are caregiver, helpmate, and nurturer, but these are implicitly understood to be providing service to men and boys. Even the nurturing of children is assumed to be part of a system in which heterosexual mothers are taking care of families headed by heterosexual fathers, and in which daughters are socialized into the tasks of housekeeping, child raising, and caregiving.

The exclusion of lesbians from the domain of the family is the basis of their exclusion from the domain of "woman." The Belgian philosopher Luce Irigaray has argued that this exclusion from the conventional domain of women's separate sphere explains why lesbians have had very little representation in Western history (1985). While there are records and discussions concerning male homosexual and homoerotic relationships that date back thousands of years, there is much less mention of lesbianism. Women were visible in historical records only as the mothers and wives of important men; thus lesbian lives were invisible.

Wittig held that these considerations should make us realize that, in reality, lesbians represent a different sort of gender category in Western culture that does not fit into either the categories of male or female, man or woman, masculine or feminine.

Lesbian is the only concept I know of which is beyond the categories of sex (woman and man), because the designated subject (lesbian) is *not* a woman, either economically, or politically, or ideologically. For what makes a woman is a specific social relationship to a man, a relation that we have previously called servitude, a relation which implies personal and physical obligation as well as economic obligation ("forced residence," domestic corvée, conjugal duties, unlimited production of children, etc.), a relation which lesbians escape by refusing to become or to stay heterosexual. (Wittig, 1992: 20)

In the conceptual framework of Western culture, Wittig wrote, lesbians constitute the category of *not-women* (1992). Many of the usual sorts of attacks on lesbians confirm this: they are criticized for not being feminine and for having masculine characteristics, but their masculinity is considered an abomination rather than an accepted form of individual expression. Any woman who resists servitude and submission to male dominance is suspected of lesbian tendencies. Yet lesbians are not accepted into the category of males either. If the meaning of "woman" is servitude, the meaning of "man" involves a right of access to women's labor, sexuality, and care. Lesbians are not accorded such rights. "Thus a lesbian *has* to be something else, a not-woman, a not-man, a product of society, not a product of nature, for there is no nature in society" (Wittig, 1992: 13).

Lesbians thus constitute a kind of third category that is defined against both the conventional, naturalistic understanding of "woman" and of "man," yet a category that has not been given a substantive or positive definition with its own distinct content. Lesbians are always defined as almost-men or not-quite-women, as overly masculine and not feminine enough—thus, only in terms that compare and relate them to heterosexuals. Wittig therefore defines lesbians as "not-women." This lack of a positive definition, Wittig suggests, could provide an opportunity to escape the constraints imposed by naturalist approaches to gender distinctions that constrain the possibilities for change and transformation and the proliferation of differences.

More recent work on heterosexism has further developed the idea that heterosexism takes a fundamentally different form than sexism. Where heterosexual women are pushed into organizing their lives around marriage, family, and motherhood and may feel "unnatural" if they opt out of such life choices, most societies deny lesbians and gay men the very ability to form families and marriages. Some theorists argue that this stems from the view that lesbians and gays are not "normal" and that until societies accept the right of gays and lesbians to form marriages and families, homophobic attitudes will continue. Attaining civil rights in the public domain of employment and political participation will be insufficient to change attitudes if the familial and affective spheres remain construed as "naturally" heterosexual (Calhoun, 2003).

Some theorists of heterosexism have disagreed with Wittig's account that lesbians are outside of the category of women. Suzanne Pharr, for example, has argued that the oppression of lesbians is directly tied to the oppression of heterosexual women because both are disciplined by an ideology of natural self-sacrificing femininity (1997). This ideology punishes both heterosexual women and lesbians who refuse to accept the role as the primary nurturer for families and men. Sexism and heterosexism, Pharr argues, are thus connected by an ideology about natural gender differences and a natural gender-based division of social and reproductive labor. The vilification and punishment of lesbians is in fact necessary to the system of sexism as a means of threatening heterosexual women, providing an example of what befalls all women who fall out of line. Heterosexual women who evidence feminist leanings are disciplined by being called lesbian and threatened with subsequent social exclusion and disapproval. Although Pharr argues that *the cause* of sexism and homophobia are connected, her analysis does not collapse the different forms that these take. Heterosexual women may be chastised and even shunned if they refuse their proper role in male-dominant societies, while lesbians must hide their relationships, risk

losing their jobs as well as their children, and live with the constant danger of violence.

More recently, theorists have been exploring the intersections of heterosexism and immigration policy as well as nationalist discourses. Many of the policies around immigration that affect the ability to obtain working permits and residency status, attend public school, and so on favor family relationships so that the heterosexual families can stay together. Gay and lesbian family relationships are generally excluded by most national policies. Moreover, persons requesting refugee status because of homophobic violence in their home countries are often denied the ability to make their claims or to obtain safe havens and are forced to return to places where they may be killed. On the other hand, an ostensible commitment to anti-homophobia has been used by some countries to justify anti-Muslim immigration policies as the means to screen whole ethnic or religious groups from entering a country. This "ties the recognition of homosexual subjects…to the national and transnational political agendas of U.S. imperialism" (Puar, 2007: 9). Feminist theorists have argued that the struggle to reduce homophobic violence and heterosexist government policies needs to operate in an intersectional way so that considerations include noncitizens, refugees, the undocumented, as well as communities that may be targeted with Islamophobic or other forms of prejudice. Just as heterosexism must be understood in an intersectional way, so too must the fight against heterosexism so that the movement is not used to support policies that inflict other kinds of discrimination.

What unites these diverse accounts about heterosexism is the idea that we need an intersectional approach that takes into account both gender and sexuality, that is, whether one is gay, straight, bisexual, transsexual, or transgender. The oppression of straight women, gay women, and transgender people cannot be collapsed into a single account. Straight women do not have to hide their sexuality for fear of violence, family rejection, or discrimination on the job market. Their relationships can be public and supported by a variety of social, legal, and economic mechanisms. Their right to form families is taken for granted and factored into immigration policy. None of this can be taken for granted by lesbians, bisexual, or transgender persons. Here, then, is another example where the forms of oppression differ in kind and not merely in degree.

Historical Foundations of Intersectionality

The intersections of race, class, and gender were widely recognized among the more radical and socialist trends of the women's liberation movement that emerged in the 1960s and 1970s. This period of feminist upsurge was largely inspired by women active in the civil rights movement, which had focused on racial and economic oppression, and in the movement against the U.S. war in Vietnam, which had a vision of sweeping social and cultural transformation (Evans, 1980). Feminism in this period had multiple sites of development as women were beginning to articulate their own demands within labor organizations such as the Coalition of Labor Union Women (CLUW), the Chicano and black power movements, radical Asian American organizations such as I Wor Kuen, various anti-imperialist groups, gay and lesbian rights organizations, and student organizations such as Students for a Democratic Society (SDS) (Roth, 2003). Many of the women active in these organizations took the links between gender oppression and other forms of oppression as an obvious starting point and began trying to formulate a way to understand the connections between identities and oppressions. Organizations of women of color took the lead here out of the necessity to address multiple and interlocking systems of discrimination. Debates emerged over whether multiple systems of oppression were interdependent or distinct, or whether they could all be traced to capitalism or to patriarchy.

However, within the United States the history of taking an intersectional approach to the oppression of women actually began with the influential writings and speeches of African American women in the late nineteenth century, including Sojourner Truth (1797–1883), Ida Wells-Barnett (1862–1931), and Anna Julia Cooper (1858–1964) (Guy-Sheftall, 1995; May, 2007). Their writings addressed the multiple issues of structural oppression as a matter of course. For example, as early as 1900 Ida Wells-Barnett advanced a shrewd analysis about the crisis of lynching (Giddings, 2009). She showed how conventions of belief around both race *and* gender produced the atrocities of lynching by rendering every liaison between black men and white women rape by definition. This required a specific construal of the heterosexual desires of black men as well as white women that was not applied to all men, all women, or all whites. It was the intersections of certain identities that made the difference.

Elise Johnson McDougald (1884–1971), contributing to the special issue on the Harlem Renaissance in the anthropological journal *Survey Graphic*, edited by Alain Locke, was the first to name the experience of black women who faced both sexism and racism a "double burden." McDougald's sociological description further divided black women into four distinct categories by class, analyzing the specific social and economic challenges and cultural attitudes as these varied for each group. She recognized that the intersectional identities of black women vary significantly by their class and social status (1995).

Yet the principal source of the concept of intersectionality is generally agreed to be Anna Julia Cooper.

Anna Julia Cooper

Born to a slave mother, Cooper (1858–1964) lived a remarkable life as a leader in education and politics. In 1892 she published a collection of her essays entitled *A Voice from the South*, which addressed racism, sexism, and colonialism. Instead of addressing racism and sexism as general problems throughout society, Cooper made very specific criticisms of sexism within the African American communities she inhabited as well as very specific analyses of racism as she observed it in the white women she worked with. She noted how the various social reform campaigns that different groups advanced to undermine racial and sexual oppression systematically ignored some of the most egregiously injured parties. She showed, for example, how the campaign to improve the working conditions of women was really only concerned with white women:

> One often hears in the North an earnest plea from some lecturer for "our working girls" (of course this means white working girls)…how many have ever given a thought to the pinched and down-trodden colored women bending over wash-tubs and ironing boards.…Will you call it narrowness and selfishness, then, that I find it impossible to catch the fire of sympathy and enthusiasm for most of these labor movements at the North?([1892] 1988: 254–55)

From this, Cooper began to give voice to the idea that a particular subgroup of women should not be characterizing their cause as "the" cause of women, especially when their demands were put forward as more important than the demands of other groups who have also experienced enslavement or colonialism (because their lands were annexed, for example).

> Is not woman's cause broader, and deeper, and grander, than a blue stocking debate or an aristocratic pink tea? Why should woman become plaintiff in a suit versus the Indian, or the Negro or any other race or class who have been crushed under the heel of Anglo-Saxon power and selfishness?([1892] 1998: 123).

Some white feminists had indeed argued for making the cause of "women's" suffrage a greater priority than suffrage for African Americans or other nonwhites. But, Cooper asked, how could the cause of black women even be visible in such a debate, much less defended?

Cooper began to develop the idea that the specific experience of black women at the nexus of race, class and gender oppression afforded them a unique social position from which to analyze the obstacles to progress as well as to judge the effectiveness of a movement's victories. The male leadership of the anti-racist movement of her time generally ignored the topic of sexism. African American male leaders were ignorant about the conditions of women's lives, Cooper forthrightly stated, just as the white suffragists and white labor leaders were limited by their racism and their ignorance about the lives of African Americans. Black women did not have the luxury of such limited perspectives or single-issue politics. In the following famous passage, Cooper concluded from this that the social position of black women is unique in this respect: "Only the BLACK WOMAN can say 'when and where I enter, in the quiet, undisputed dignity of my womanhood, without violence and without suing or special patronage, then and there the whole *Negro race enters with me*'" ([1892] 1998: 31).

Cooper's arguments in *A Voice from the South* ultimately supported a version of the feminist standpoint theory, as described in Chapter 2, through her argument that black women's social position has important political and epistemic implications. Just as Sandra Harding (2004) argued a century later, Cooper held that addressing the oppression of African

Anna Julia Cooper

Anna Julia Cooper earned her own living as a teacher and eventual principal of the famous Dunbar School in Washington, D.C., the first high school in the United States for African Americans. She also raised five orphaned children, was one of the first black women to receive a doctorate, and wrote numerous essays.

American women would require understanding racism, sexism, class exploitation, and the history of colonialism. Developing a political project from the starting point of black women's lives would necessarily produce an intersectional analysis. For black women to enter society as equals and full participants, many forms of oppression would have to be overcome.

Cooper was not the only African American woman theorist advancing an intersectional approach during this period. Besides Wells-Barnett and McDougald, similar arguments were made by Sojourner Truth, Frances Harper, Mary Church Terrell, and later, Alice Dunbar-Nelson, among others, from the second half of the nineteenth century through the first half of the twentieth century, though none with the sustained elaboration of Cooper's.

Still, these concerted efforts to make the conditions of black women's lives visible, and to complicate the oversimplified pictures of racial and sexual oppression that were written even by the best theorists of the day, had surprisingly little influence. Outspoken women writers of the Harlem Renaissance were often unsupported and isolated, and the organizations advancing women's rights remained focused on white women. It would take another several decades and the sustained efforts of the civil rights and new feminist movements of the 1960s to push an intersectional approach further.

Angela Davis

The influential work of Angela Davis, Audre Lorde, and bell hooks developed intersectional approaches in important respects. Angela Davis is a philosopher and political activist who wrote her first essays in 1970–71 while in prison on a charge of conspiracy involving her support for the Soledad brothers, three African American men accused of murder. She was acquitted and went on to become an influential theorist on the specificity of the oppression of black women. Davis (1971) provided critical historical and sociological analyses of black women's lives under slavery, arguing that we will not understand their treatment unless we know it as the result of both sexism and racism. Within the growing nationalist discourses of the 1960s, histories of slavery often viewed slave women as suspect for consorting with the enemy by having babies by their white masters. Davis showed how this analysis was misguided precisely because it did not take into account the role of rape and sexual violence under slavery. Rather than "reproducing with the enemy," women under slavery were treated as conduits for reproducing the slave population, as "breeders" rather than human beings. Through these kinds of examples and many others, Davis inaugurated the methodology of taking race, class, and gender into account in the study of any group of women.

Davis (1983) also made important early criticisms of liberal views about poverty in the black community. Liberals such as Daniel Patrick Moynihan blamed black poverty rates on a matriarchal family structure that was said to have arisen during slavery, when men had been emasculated and kept from becoming providers or heads of families. In this analysis, African American women were blamed for being too strong and too dominant in their families, and the solution to ending poverty was argued to be in empowering African American men over "their" women and children. Davis argued that this "myth of matriarchy" was based on nonsense, given that African American women were among the most impoverished and disempowered in the United States. African American women didn't have too much power, but too little. The solution was not to establish male dominant families, as if this is the natural order, but to address the unfairly depressed wages of all African Americans as well as other people of color and working class people and to address the serious problem of unemployment that she believes is an inevitable, and necessary, feature of capitalist economies.

Davis also began to provide important critiques of the ways in which some of the mainstream feminist theories of the time ignored issues of race and class, undermining the legitimacy of their analyses of issues such as domesticity, rape, and reproductive technologies. For many African American women, Davis argued, the ability to nurture and provide domestic labor for their own families was experienced as liberatory rather than oppressive, given the generations who had had to serve and care for white children and white families instead of their own. The demand to increase criminal penalties for sexual violence also needed to be analyzed in relationship to racist court systems that were biased against black defendants. Davis's work (1983) showed that every feminist topic and policy proposal needed to be analyzed in a context sensitive to the historical and sociological dimensions of race, class, and gender.

Audre Lorde

Audre Lorde (1934–1992) was a Caribbean-American poet, writer, and activist and one of the earliest out lesbian black activists. Both her poetry and her theoretical writing consistently drew from elements of her experience in the gay community as well as in anti-racist and feminist communities (De Veaux, 2006). During a period in the 1960s and 1970s when many feminist groups wanted to put the differences among women aside in order to articulate a unified women's politics and culture, Lorde insisted on the critical importance of acknowledging the differences among women: "it is not those differences [of race, age and sex] between us that are separating us. It is rather our refusal to recognize those differences, and to examine the distortions that result from our misnaming them…" (1984: 115).

Lorde argued that movements for social justice and transformation will be derailed not by acknowledging and exploring the different experiences and interests of the persons engaged in struggle, but in trying to pretend that these differences have no significance. This leads to misunderstanding others and misinterpreting their actions and motives. It also leads to a poor theoretical and political analysis. Those on the margins of power, she said, "often identify one way in which we are different, and we assume that to be the primary cause of all oppression, forgetting other distortions around difference, some of which we ourselves may be practicing" (1983: 116). The project of an organization or group to render some differences as less important than others may be motivated by the desire of some of its members to deemphasize the way they are privileged. Whether this comes from white women who deemphasize race, or African American women who deemphasize homophobia, or African American men who refuse to engage with gender oppression, Lorde declared that the result is the same: trust and understanding are reduced, and solidarity is broken.

As Anna Julia Cooper had done decades before, Lorde explained the personal impossibility of separating out the multiple aspects of her identity by explaining that, for women of color, no such separation is even conceivable:

> I find I am constantly being encouraged to pluck out some one aspect of myself and present this as the meaningful whole, eclipsing or denying the other parts of self. But this is a destructive and fragmenting way to live. My fullest concentration of energy is available to me only when I integrate all the parts of who I am, openly, allowing power from particular sources of my living to flow back and forth freely through all my different selves, without the restrictions of externally imposed definition. (1984: 120–1)

The Combahee River Collective

In the 1970s a group of black lesbian activists, including Barbara Smith, came together to form the Combahee River Collective, taking this name from an anti-slavery action led by Harriet Tubman on the Combahee River in South Carolina. This group was one of many small feminist collectives around the country that were engaging in activism alongside theoretical work. They issued "A Black Feminist Statement" in 1977 outlining their theoretical and political position, which has become one of the most influential documents of feminism in the twentieth century.

The statement of the Combahee River Collective outlines a defense of the concept of intersectionality and also the concept of identity politics. They held that identity is relevant to one's political understanding as well as to

one's political interests and that black women needed to assert their own needs within the anti-racist and feminist struggles: "We realize that the only people who care enough about us to work consistently for our liberation is us....This focusing upon our own oppression is embodied in the concept of identity politics" (Combahee River Collective, 1979: 365).

The Combahee Collective was well aware that identities are complicated and multiple, with no simple causal line from one's identity to one's political stance. The very formation of the Combahee River Collective was based on their experience of racism in the white-dominated wing of the women's movement, the sexism in the male-led black liberation movement, and the heterosexism that was virulent everywhere. Yet they continued to assert that identity could make a difference in motivation, experience, and understanding.

The Collective supported the development of solidarity across divisions of race, class, gender, and sexuality, and opposed the "fractionalization" that many separatists were at that time advocating. Barbara Smith had in fact criticized lesbian separatists for having an ineffective strategy that would make no "real political change" (Moraga and Anzaldúa, 121). But despite this critique of separatism as a strategic position, the Combahee Collective branched out to form their own organization for black lesbians, justifying this by the argument that the specific dimensions of black women's oppression required organizational autonomy at least for a certain period of time so that they could develop a more meaningful analysis: "...although we are in essential agreement with Marx's theory as it applied to the very specific economic relationships he analyzed, we know that this analysis must be extended further in order for us to understand our specific economic situation as black women"(1979: 366).

Other black feminists took issue with this position, among them bell hooks, who argued that organizational autonomy would create a political separatism that would divide groups who should be aligned. Barbara Smith continued to hold nonetheless that one could be critical of the philosophy of separatism but recognize the need for groups with shared experiences to come together at certain points in order to develop the analysis of specific forms of oppression as well as an effective agenda for activism.

Gloria Anzaldúa

Chicana lesbian feminist author Gloria Anzaldúa (1942–2004) broke new ground in the development of intersectionality (1987, 2000). In her celebrated and influential book *Borderlands/La Frontera* (1987), she gave a very personal account of the oppression of Chicana lesbians, weaving together considerations of male dominance, colonialism, and heteronormativity. In her account, the interrelations of these three systems of domination take a very specific form.

The expectations of females in her Mexican-Indian community near the United States–Mexico border were clear-cut: "The ability to serve, claim the males, is our highest virtue" (1987: 21). Anzaldúa echoed Zora Neale Hurston in her criticism that her culture "cripples its women, *como burras*, our strengths used against us, lowly *burras* bearing humility with dignity" (1987: 21). Yet she was equally

Gloria Anzaldúa was a poet and activist whose works spanned Chicano, feminist, cultural, and queer theory. Her writings and vision of "mestizas" as a new and positive way of being and future model for oppressed people of mixed backgrounds were based, in part, on growing up as the child of sharecropper/field workers in Texas on the U.S.–Mexico border and her feelings of social and cultural marginalization.

critical of "how my culture makes *macho* caricatures of its men" (1987: 21), inhibiting their emotional growth as human beings. Anzaldúa argues that this gendered organization of values and expected behaviors was overdetermined by the conquest of Mexico by Cortes in the sixteenth century as well as by the conquest of northern Mexico by the United States in the U.S.–Mexican War of 1848. The latter war impoverished Anzaldúa's family, appropriating their land and redistributing it to Anglos.

In Mexican national histories, the Conquest by Cortes in 1531 is often blamed on a mythically embellished story of the consort between Cortes, the Spanish conquistador known as the bloodiest and most ruthless tyrant over the indigenous peoples, and *la Malinche*, or *Malintzin*, the indigenous woman given by the Aztec rulers to Cortes for his use as a concubine when she was a young girl. *La Malinche* developed the capacity to communicate in Spanish and provided crucial translations for the Spaniards and the Aztecs. Her union with Cortes is represented figuratively as the Adam and Eve of the mestizo race that emerged from the Conquest to dominate Mexico and Latin America (Townsend, 2006). But in the mythic portrayal of that union, *la Malinche's* role, like that of Eve in the Genesis story of the Bible, is portrayed as one of betrayal. And like the descendants of Eve, mestiza women today must carry the burden of *la Malinche's* guilt by proving their sexual purity and maintaining their subservience. Men, on the other hand, seek to reestablish their dominance in displays of control over women: "The loss of a sense of dignity and respect in the macho breeds a false machismo which leads him to put down women and even to brutalize them" (Anzaldúa, 1987: 83). Thus, the roots of sexism in Chicano communities, Anzaldúa argued, must be understood in relation to the colonization of Indian and Mexican communities.

Chicanos as a group are today among the poorest in the United States. Connected to their economic exploitation as underpaid laborers is a sense of cultural inferiority. Often unable to speak Spanish as well as Mexicans, and derided by Anglos for not speaking better English, the very term "Chicano" was invented as a form of resistance. To call oneself Chicano was to depart from the usual "Mexican-American" term as a way of declaring the specificity of their intersectional identity as "a politically aware people born and/or raised in the U.S." (Anzaldúa, 1987: 63). Defending all aspects of Chicano communities and culture became the principal tactic of Chicano liberation. This meant that defending conventional practices of sexism and homophobia was required of all radical activists who wanted to be a part of the movement, including women.

Borderlands/La Frontera marked out a new vision of Chicano/Chicana liberation, one that could resist the internal sexism and homophobia of the community as well as Mexican disdain and Anglo exploitation. It is understandable that Chicano liberation activists, Anzaldúa claims, developed a form of cultural nationalism to defend the community and its multilingual dialects and unique cultural practices and to highlight its unique socio-political history. "[A]s a people, we, Chicanos, blame ourselves, hate ourselves, terrorize ourselves. Most of this goes on unconsciously; we only know that we are hurting, we suspect that there is something 'wrong' with us, something fundamentally 'wrong'"(Anzaldúa, 1987: 45). To overturn this sense of innate inferiority, Chicano nationalism elaborated a positive representation of their shared culture. But undermining the strength of women and dividing women from men and gays from heterosexuals only weakens the Chicano communities further, rendering them more, not less, vulnerable to continued abuse.

The lesson of intersectionality from Anzaldúa's work is that the struggle against sexism and homophobia within Chicano communities must understand the specific justifications made for these beliefs in light of the specific history of Chicano peoples. And the alternative vision must be one that addresses the problems of cultural inferiority and economic oppression that besets Chicano communities. Toward this end, Anzaldúa developed an account of the "new mestiza" as a new "consciousness" that will be able to live harmoniously by breaking down borders and dualistic ways of thinking. She wrote that:

> *En unas pocas centurias*, the future will belong to the mestiza. Because the future depends on the breaking down of paradigms, it depends on the straddling of two or more cultures....The answer to the problem between the white race and the colored, between males and females, lies in healing the split that originates in the very foundation of our lives, our culture, our languages, our thoughts. A massive uprooting of dualistic thinking in the individual and collective consciousness is the beginning of a long struggle, but one that could, in our best hopes, bring us to the end of rape, of violence, of war. (Anzaldúa, 1987: 80)

The intersectional approach to understanding and addressing gender and sexual hierarchies is itself an attempt to uproot dualistic thinking. As Anzaldúa and other Chicana feminists such as Cherrie Moraga (1981) emphasized, Chicano men are themselves the object of social, cultural, and economic oppression. Even in situations of violence against women, there are often strong ties of love and solidarity with male abusers because of these shared, complex histories. Dualistic thinking would either put the "community's" interest above women, as if the community has a unified set of needs and interests without internal conflict, or there could be a feminist dualism that puts all women on one side, including women of all ethnic groups, and all men on the other, no matter their social condition. Lumping men together in this way, Anzaldúa

says, "is a gross injustice" (1987: 84). But she also declares that "the struggle of the mestiza is above all a feminist one" (1987: 84). It is a demand for an acknowledgment of the harm and abuse women have suffered, for acts of support and solidarity, and for equal power in the struggle to change society.

Anzaldúa analyzes the dualisms in which homophobia and heterosexism are embedded as equally important to unpack. These forms of oppression no less than sexism have a specific form and purported justification in Chicano communities. "Tenderness, a sign of vulnerability, is so feared that it is showered on women with verbal abuse and blows. Men, even more than women, are fettered to gender roles....We need a new masculinity and the new man needs a movement" (1987: 84). Thus, Anzaldúa links the oppressive conventions of behavior forced on men with the oppression of gay men as a whole and suggests that gay people of color are positioned in an analogous way to the new mestizas: with knowledge of more than one culture, way of being, and gender, they must struggle against dualism on a daily basis. As a result:

> Colored homosexuals...have always been at the forefront (although sometimes in the closet) of all liberation struggles in this country; have suffered more injustices and survived them despite all odds. Chicanos need to acknowledge the political and artistic contributions of their queer. People, listen to what your *jotería* is saying. (Anzaldúa, 1987: 85)

Intersectional Approaches to Feminist Activism

Much feminist activism in the 1960s and 1970s focused on the following sorts of demands: equal pay for equal work, making abortion legal, opening up elite schools and high-paying professions to women, and creating more daycare centers. By the late 1970s these demands had largely been met: the Equal

Employment Opportunity Act was passed in 1972; *Roe* v. *Wade* made abortions legal by 1973; the last male-only Ivy League schools, medical schools, and law schools became coed by the late 1970s; and most communities had daycare centers. Yet many women's lives did not appreciably change. Today there is still a 20% wage gap between men and women doing comparable work, most women do not have effective access to abortion because of geographical or financial obstacles, and although there are many more women in the professions, the ranks of the poor are disproportionately filled by women. Why?

Early feminist demands did not operate in an intersectional way. They were looking at gender issues and women's rights as if these are universals, unaffected by whether one works as an executive or a maid, lives in a rural or urban area, has the money to attend a professional school, or is an immigrant.

Shifting Policy Demands

Consider the demands just listed. Demanding "equal pay for equal work" was construed by the courts and government bodies entrusted with its enforcement as only applying to employees who are engaged in the same exact kind of work, so that female accountants could demand the same pay as male accountants if they worked under identical conditions. Yet most women who work outside the home work in a largely gender-segregated work force, as clerical workers, nurses and nurse-aides, teachers, seamstresses, school cafeteria workers, and domestic workers. The right to demand "equal pay for equal work" has no application to this area of the workforce, and so these workers had no way to make a legal case that their pay scales were discriminatory. Thus feminists began to develop "comparable worth" demands based on the idea of equal pay for comparable work, or work that is comparable in terms of difficulty,

skill level, and the physical challenges of the work (Blum, 1991). By taking an intersectional approach to the problem of gender equity in the labor force, connecting class and gender, comparable worth could reach many more women from the working class who work in the service sector, health care, the needle trades, and other gender-segregated areas of the labor force. Rather than pushing women to change professions if they wanted higher pay, this movement argued that the work most working class women do is highly valuable to society and much more difficult than traditionally acknowledged. Although the movement for comparable worth won only a few victories, it helped to enlarge the public's understanding about what gender equity requires (see Chapter 11). Professional organizations advocating for women's traditional sectors of the labor market began to lobby for industry-wide pay increases that would address gender discrimination.

Although it was important to open the higher-status and higher-paid professions, such as medicine and law, to women, this also proved insignificant for most working women and most women of color, few of whom could effectively take advantage of the newly opened opportunities to attend Ivy League colleges or professional schools. A more important effort with the potential to change more women's lives was unionization. Teachers, healthcare workers, and office workers became unionized throughout the 1980s and 1990s, often with women union organizers leading the way, vastly improving their wages, benefits, and working conditions as well as their ability to participate in democratic governance structures at their work sites. The efforts to unionize these types of jobs were often opposed by those who held gender-related stereotypes about the low skill level these required or the motivations women had to pursue this work. Organizers had to develop new analyses of work to show that being a nursery school teacher was more demanding than being a parking lot attendant, as the government-issued *Dictionary of Occupational Titles* held in the 1960s (Howe, 1978). Today teachers and nurses earn much more in real wages than a generation ago, with the top strata earning annual salaries of more than $100,000.

Perhaps the clearest example of intersectionality changes in feminist activism has been in the sphere of reproductive rights. The legal right to an abortion, won in the United States in 1973 after mass protests throughout the country, did not result in accessible abortion services for all women. Abortion is unavailable in most rural communities and several states, which adds the price of travel to the price of the procedure, and it is not covered by most health insurance plans. Moreover, many poor women and women of color argued that their communities were in desperate need of a full range of reproductive services, including contraception, assistance in childbirth, prenatal care, and health services for infants and children, as well as abortion. Poor women, disabled women, and women of color were also subject to sterilization abuse when medical personnel sterilized them without their informed consent (see Chapter 9). Lesbian advocacy groups advocated for the right to adoption as well as reproductive technologies. Thus, an intersectional approach indicated that much more than legal abortion was required to ensure women's autonomy in their reproductive lives and that the overall demand should be for reproductive rights as a whole—the right to *have* children as well as to *not have* children. Moreover, women needed not merely *legal* rights but *effective* rights, or rights that they could actually enact, to a full range of reproductive healthcare in order to have agency in their reproductive and sexual lives.

Rosalind P. Petchesky, one of the leading analysts of reproductive issues, has argued that separating out the struggles around violence, sexuality, development, work, education, and reproductive needs in the lives of girls and women eliminates the possibility of effective solutions. "The most important operational principle of a human rights framework" is, Petchesky claims, "the principle of *indivisibility*." This requires integrating "civil and political, economic, social and cultural and so-called solidarity rights (such as sustainable human development and environmental safety)." She explains:

> . . . a woman cannot avail herself of her right "to decide freely and responsibly the number, spacing, and timing of her children" if she lacks the financial resources to pay for reproductive health services or the transport to reach them; if she cannot read package inserts or clinic wall posters; if her workplace is contaminated with pesticides or pollutants that have an adverse effect on pregnancy; or if she is harassed by a husband or in-laws who will scorn her or beat her up if she uses birth control. (Petchesky, 2002: 75)

Effective activism that actually changes the conditions of women's lives must be integrative and intersectional. This is not just the case for poor women: women from oppressed religious and ethnic communities report pressure against shaming their communities or airing dirty laundry. Women from communities that experience discrimination in the justice system may be inhibited from reporting abuse to the police. Actual effective policies must take into account the different contexts in which women live.

Global Intersections

Another set of implications for activism concerns the intersectional ways in which structures of discrimination operate. Governments may respond positively to the activism of one part of the community, but in a way that exacerbates the problems in another part. Jasbir Puar, Zillah Eisenstein, and others have shown that if they do not take intersectional issues into account, anti-homophobic and anti-sexist activism can exacerbate Islamophobia and the oppression of Muslim women and become an alibi for imperial military aggressions (Eisenstein, 2004; Puar, 2007). The treatment of gays and lesbians has become a key issue in U.S. and European nationalist discourses, used to bolster claims that the West is modern, enlightened, and protective of human rights while Muslim majority nations are culturally backward with no right to be part of international dialogues and treaties. This hierarchy can be used to justify unilateral military invasions and the abrogation of basic human rights for millions.

Puar argues that the fight against homophobia cannot operate through a single issue lens or ignore the movement's intersections with nationalist rhetoric. In some cases, gay rights provides a cover for other agendas or an alibi that paints a moral face on what is actually an immoral motivation for war—such as profit or power. Eisenstein argues that if feminism is truly concerned with all women, it must work against racism and against military or economic empires.

Intersectional analyses need to be applied within every movement and every constituency. Just as there are important differences among women, differences with implications for their interests, so too are there important differences among gay, lesbian, and transgender people, among Muslims, among people of color, and within every group. Some within a given group may even benefit from the oppression and discrimination of others, such as when rich white women benefit from the typically low wages of domestic workers, or gays and lesbians in the West benefit from distributions of global resources that advantage the West. This does not doom the possibility of coalition, since partial, short-term alliances may continue to be possible across broad differences. But it does call for a clear-eyed, intersectional approach to the complex challenges social movements must face.

Kimberlé Crenshaw conducted a policy analysis of feminist-led organizations. She describes a Latina woman in desperate need of help denied entry to a battered women's shelter because she spoke only Spanish, since the rules of this shelter required that every resident have the capacity to participate in support group meetings deemed vital to their psychological empowerment and mental health. Yet the meetings were only held in English, which resulted in denying services to some of the most vulnerable sectors of the population. Crenshaw (1991) argues that this shelter was operating with a single yardstick model for assisting women fleeing abuse.

As this example showed, intersectional analyses are vital not merely in how we formulate movement goals and demands, but also in how feminist-led organizations are run. Battered women's shelters, rape crisis centers, feminist health centers, women's bookstores, women's studies programs, and women's political organizations all need an intersectional approach in setting their policies and priorities and ensuring that the process of decision making is truly representative. An organization designed to meet the needs of women will not succeed if it does not fully understand the varied conditions of women's lives, much less if it requires women, as did the shelter Crenshaw describes, to conform to a white Anglo norm before they can take advantage of its services. bell hooks (1984) argued that this does not mean that every organization must have a representative diversity in its leadership, because this may not be possible, but it can still take an intersectional approach to its work.

Many organizations today have adopted such an intersectional approach. The National Abortion Rights Action League became the National Abortion and Reproductive Rights

Action League, expanding its scope accordingly. After an initially narrow focus on homophobia, ACT UP, the organization that emerged in the 1980s to engage in militant activism for AIDS research and treatment, began to address the problems of intravenous drug users and the need for free medication for all. And the Service Employees International Union, the largest union of healthcare workers in the United States, has adopted multilingual communications and gender and race quotas for conventions and conducts training workshops on discrimination against transgender people in the workplace.

The widespread influence of intersectionality has yielded new questions about how to understand the complexity of our social identities as well as new questions about research methods. Is it possible to formulate a "women's political agenda" of any sort, given the multiple and conflicting formations of gender identities? Is it possible to study "women" or "men" as a whole, and if not, how fine-tuned do we need to be?

Intersectional Approaches to Feminist Scholarship

Intersectionality has posed new challenges to feminist scholarship and, in particular, to the formulation of projects of inquiry and research. Some question whether it is possible to take one category of analysis—such as disability or heterosexism—as an object of inquiry for a given study or to prioritize one element of a complex social reality in order to study it in a sustained manner (Carby, 1987; Saldivar-Hull, 1998). Others have argued that we can trace the causality of multiple strands of identity-based oppression to a single source such as capitalism or to ideas about what is normal (Davis, 1983; Pharr, 1997; McWhorter, 2009). But the first question that intersectionality raises for feminist scholarship is a simple one: What does it mean to say that one has a gender identity in the first place?

Intersectional Identities

As we have discussed throughout this chapter, the concept of intersectionality is meant to be applied both to the varied forms that sexism can take as well as to our identities.

Intersectional approaches to social categories of identity are often posed as an alternative to additive approaches that assume one can simply add race and gender and other categories together to develop an adequate analysis. Additive approaches do not work because they assume that one can take a singular or nonintersectional approach to understanding any one category and then simply add these up. This assumes that racial identity or sexual identity can be described and explained prior to its intersection with other categories. If we take the additive approach, Elizabeth Spelman explained,

> . . . we may get the impression that a woman's identity consists of a sum of parts neatly divisible from one another. . . . This is a version of personal identity we might call tootsie roll metaphysics: each part of my identity is separable from every other part, and the significance of each part is unaffected by other parts. (Spelman, 1988: 136)

Such an additive approach conflicts with the way Audre Lorde described her life as a black lesbian. Recall that Lorde responded to those who asked her to "simply speak as a woman" by explaining that her life makes up a whole that cannot be subdivided into a racial, sexual, and gendered parts. It also contradicts Valerie Smith's definition of intersectionality, in which one's race and gender are co-constituting, with every aspect of one's identity affected by the others.

The idea that various factors are co-constituting of any given identity leads to new ways of thinking about identity as both historical and relational. Our identities change in relation to specific contexts and are in fact in a constant process of fluid movement. The actual mediation of factors influencing a given social identity varies constantly depending on context. We may be viewed as a budding intellectual among our friends, as a potential thief in stores, as still a child when we are at home, or as a primarily sexual being when we walk down the street. These diverse treatments affect how we actually act and perform in given situations—with easy assurance or pained self-consciousness, or with an expectation to fail.

Minnie Bruce Pratt's autobiographical account of her white lesbian southern identity explains the relational aspect of our social identities very well. Pratt describes how her Washington, D.C. neighborhood in the 1980s provided a complex terrain of shifting power and cultural systems that affected her identity in various ways. Mr. Boone, the African American janitor in her apartment building, said "yes ma'am" to her in a way that signified her privileged race and class standing in relation to him. She found this experience uncomfortable, but discovered to her chagrin that when "he 'yes ma'am's' me in a sing-song: I hear my voice replying in the horrid cheerful accents of a white lady" (1984: 12). In her response Pratt *becomes* the white middle-class woman he sees because this is a part of who she is given how she learned to act and speak while growing up in Alabama. The brief hallway encounter between her and Mr. Boone brings forth or makes manifest this aspect of Pratt's identity. In other, very different interactions, Pratt is viewed as an unfit mother and loses custody of her children simply because of her sexual identity. As a lesbian in the court system of the south, Pratt was far from a privileged white southern lady.

Thus Pratt's identity, including the social privilege and range of life options associated with that identity, as well as the way she sometimes finds herself acting and speaking, is fundamentally relational. Her identity at any

given moment, as well as the degree and type of privilege she enjoys, is shaped by her relations to others in varying contexts. Different elements of her identity are foregrounded, while others may become inactive and even invisible. It therefore makes no sense to ask who is the "real" Minnie Bruce Pratt or what her "real" identity is apart from these social encounters, since her very sense of herself, her confidence and capacity of making herself understood, and her range of choices are dependent on her momentary relational context. She cannot force Mr. Boone to stop acting toward her with deference simply by controlling how she behaves toward him, given the larger historical realities that produced the power systems with which both she and Mr. Boone must contend. In her relations with him, she has real power that cannot be dissolved by sheer force of will or by putting

Minnie Bruce Pratt, born in Selma, Alabama, is an award-winning poet and essayist. She is currently a professor of Women's and Gender Studies, Writing, and Rhetoric at Syracuse University.

on a different performance, just as the courts had the power to deny her custodial rights no matter how she acted or spoke to the judge.

The identities we have are dependent on relational contexts, and as these relational contexts change, our identities can undergo important transformations. One might think that Pratt has a stable identity in the sense that she remains a white, middle-class, southern lesbian. Surely these add up to a set of experiences and options for her that are different from others. Yet what it means to be marked by any one of these categories is both contextually variable and historically evolving. As Wittig (1992) argued, to be designated a "man" in patriarchal societies was to be designated as someone who had the right of access to women's services, and thus even the identity "man" is a relational one. As feminist movements expand women's rights and freedoms and alter their behavior and sense of themselves so that they no longer accept subordinate status, this changes the relations between men and women in workplaces as well as domestic spaces with a subsequent impact on what it means to be a man today. There will undoubtedly continue to be historical shifts in the meanings and practices associated with every element of our identities. It makes no sense to ask who we "truly" are in some final, stable sense, but to ask, rather, who do we want to become? How might we change the meanings of social identity categories, and are there some we might want to eliminate entirely?

Research Methods

Since the 1990s the intersectional approach to gender analysis has become the cornerstone of new research methods in the social sciences as well as the development of postcolonial and transnational feminism. Intersectional approaches have transformed research in women's and gender studies, bringing about

a new epistemological framework for understanding the object of inquiry. Whether a researcher is studying gender, race, class, or sexuality, or whether their project is focused on work, citizenship, families, disability, or the military, a multidimensional approach is increasingly understood to be required.

One way to think about gender, race, and class is that they are social structures that organize individual practices and construct systems of meaning. Consider a soccer game. Individuals are trained to develop the particular skill set that is necessary for the game, rather than just encouraged to develop generic physical abilities. And individual physical achievements are rewarded—with praise or blame—in the context of the rules of the game. A player's beautiful run down the field with perfect control of the ball, but one that is mistakenly going in the wrong direction, will get derision rather than cheers from the crowd. We need to understand the structure before we can understand or assess individual actions and reactions.

Racial and gender systems operate as structures in this sense. There are "gender frames" that predispose us to perform different roles, develop different skills, interact in specific ways, and interpret the actions of others differently (Valian, 1999). For example, in some

New York City, December 17, 2011

communities women may be encouraged to engage in a lot of emotional caregiving of others, such as listening to friends' stories, providing encouragement, advice, and gestures of support. Because this activity has a "gender frame," women who neglect these social expectations may come in for negative judgment. Men who engage in emotional caregiving, in contrast, may be negatively judged as less than masculine. Before we conclude that women are naturally better at caregiving, we need to consider the gender structures that cultivate or discourage these skills.

But are women expected to provide emotional caregiving to everyone? Not really. It is expected within the community of one's peers, a grouping that may be defined by religion, age, race, class, etc. A young woman who provides a lot of emotional caregiving for an older rich man may be subject to suspicion for having less than altruistic motives. A wealthy woman who offers a lot of encouragement and advice to her servants may be viewed as patronizing and interfering. Conventions of gender expectations are modulated by intersecting structures. Thus, the analysis of structures in the social sciences needs to take an intersectional approach.

The relational and contextual nature of social identities has also brought home the idea that dominant identities are just as much in need of analysis as nondominant or marginal ones. Dominant identities in the United States, such as whiteness or maleness or heterosexuality, are relational, context-dependent, and subject to historical shifts and operate to mediate other elements of identity in complex ways. In the past, these dominant identities were generally considered norms of neutrality that required no historicization or political genealogy to understand. One could name a book "women's history" if it covered only white women, but would have to name a book "Chinese women's history" if it covered Chinese women, while a book covering mainly men's history could be called simply "history." Unlike nondominant identities, dominant identities were thought to be the normative, rational way all human beings should be understood and treated. However, once we begin to understand dominant identities as relational and contextual—as taking the specific form that they do because of their relation to other identities—we see that they cannot provide a goal for all to reach, or a standard that can be universally applied. The entitlements of dominant identities to be the center of attention, to control the discussion, to secure the most resources, to have their language enforced on all, to represent what is "normal," etc., are not universalizable.

Analyses of gender, therefore, will require foregrounding the ways in which masculinity is expressed as much as femininity. Analyses of sexuality require making the structure of heterosexual expressions of gender and familial formations more visible. An inquiry into race and ethnicity must include whiteness as well as other identity categories.

One way in which researchers have responded to the fact that identities are relational, contextual, and fluid is to reframe their study to focus not on "men," for example, as if this is a natural category, but on *masculinity* (Blount and Cunningham, 1989; Murphy, 2004). How is masculinity operating in this specific domain, in this specific work site? What characteristics are assumed, and what behavior is enabled for whom? (See Box 3.2.) By reframing it in this way, researchers can recognize that some women may be able to participate in masculinity by performing as managers, bosses, or leaders, radically changing their relations to others and their position within structures of gender. Research in geography has been at the forefront of developing new research methods and altering its approach in light of the complicating factors of intersectionality (see Massey, 1994). Workplaces are conceptualized as highly specific constellations of space-time, affecting the way people interact and understand the relation of the work site to other parts of their lives. High-status healthcare workers, such as surgeons, may bring their sense of self-importance at work to bear on their familial relationships at home, while police work may transform gender identities in non-work settings. Identities and structures are not simply brought to the workplace, but emanate from the specific possibilities that workplaces produce.

Finally, even as scholars and researchers have been exploring difference using the concept of intersectionality, they have found it important to note commonalities. As Margo Wilson and Martin Daly (1998) argue in their study of family violence, men beat their wives in many societies while the reverse happens only rarely, and men are by far the main perpetrators of sexual violence across the globe. Legal theorists Lynn Welchman and Sara Hossain (2005) similarly argue in their analysis of the concept of "honor crimes" that "It is important to identify commonalities as well as differences in the structure of violence."

These efforts to develop intersectional research methods can be summarized in the

---

Box 3.2   GENDER IDENTITY: CHANGING PRACTICES OF MASCULINITY

In this portrait of French monarch Louis XV in 1714, he is wearing the customary clothes of small boys, but would be considered cross-dressed in the 21st century. Conventions of gender expression for all genders need to be understood as intersectional with differences based on class, race, ethnicity, culture, and historical time period.

Source: http://en.wikipedia.org/wiki/Louis_XV

following points: (1) specify the object of inquiry as fine-tuned as the project requires, rather than assuming broad and undifferentiated categories like "women"; (2) do not assume that any one subcategory of a group can serve as the paradigm of the whole or be positioned at the center of the analysis; (3) consider the relational nature of both privilege and oppression; (4) recognize the historically changeable nature of oppression and human agency; (5) account for the fluid nature of identities across contexts and time periods and the possibility that socially recognized categories of identity can come into existence and pass out of existence; (6) avoid the practice of simply averaging the data from representative samples of informants as if this can form a picture of the whole: the median is sometimes meaningless; and (7) while acknowledging the importance of difference, avoid assuming that commonalities across difference never occur.

Debates over Intersectionality

Recently, some feminist theorists have debated the concept of intersectionality. No one disputes the fact that multiple structures of oppression and identity formation are operating in every context, requiring a multistrand analysis, but some are concerned about the term "intersectionality" itself to cover this complexity. The term, after all, implies that single lines of identity meet at a certain point, like roads meet at an intersection under a stoplight as Crenshaw suggested in her original metaphor (1989). This might wrongly imply that race, gender, class, sexuality, etc., can operate independently before they intersect. So some are concerned that the term "intersectionality" is misleading and have suggested alternative terms, such as *interstitiality* or *assemblages*, that have less problems.

The philosopher Maria Lugones, for example, argues that intersectionality implies a logic of purity that values unity, homogeneity, and control over multiplicity, fragmentation, and impurity (2003, 2007). The idea of clearly demarcated lines that only intersect at certain points reveals this problem, she asserts. Moreover, we need a theoretical approach that will show that it is impossible to disconnect gender oppression, capitalism, heterosexism, racism, and colonialism, rather than assume these simply "intersect." In a different line of argument, philosopher Naomi Zack is concerned that the adherence to intersectionality causes too much fragmentation and disables feminist solidarity (2005). Intersectionality implies, Zack argues, that women of different ethnicities will have different genders, obscuring the common ground women share. Still other theorists have been concerned that intersectionality puts too much of an emphasis on identities that have themselves been socially constructed under conditions of oppression. While the second-wave feminist project was to make *identities* visible and then make *intersectional identities* visible, these critics charge that what we really need to do is to deconstruct identities, reveal their fluidity and vulnerable contingency, and find forms of political solidarity and motivation that are not predicated on identity ascriptions (Phelan, 1994).

Feminists have also debated whether intersectionality has mistakenly implied that it is mainly black women who are intersectional subjects (Nash, 2008). For philosopher Kathryn Gines, "[w]hile Black women loom large in the literature on intersectionality, this has more to do with the concept coming out of Black feminist scholarship than an effort to make Black women prototypical intersectional subjects" (2011: 280). It is probably not an accident that the most far-reaching work on the concept of intersectionality has come from women who have experienced their own specific forms of oppression as relatively invisible, such as lesbians of color.

Other feminists argue that the concept of intersectionality itself is only a metaphor and should not be taken too far. Ann Garry argues that intersectionality is "the best strategy we have at the moment for developing truly pluralistic and inclusive" feminist theory and politics (2011: 844). We can develop unity, she argues, via a concept of "family resemblances" taken from Ludwig Wittgenstein to signal the idea of the ways in which members of a biological family may be recognizably related even though there is no single trait that each one shares. Moreover, Garry argues, intersectionality is a more modest idea, in reality, than the critics charge: it is not a fully developed theory of identity formation or a theory of oppression, but a framework or "'method checker' that provides standards that a method or methodology should meet" (2011: 830). Identity categories are not abolished, that is true, but with an intersectional approach their inherent complexity, ambiguity, and fluidity will be revealed (Gines, 2011).

Other theorists such as Jasbir Puar who emphasize the multiplicity and fragmentation of identity categories continue to argue that "intersectionality as a heuristic may well be indispensable" (2007: 125). An approach that takes a single-axis lens toward the oppression of sexuality, Puar holds, creates binaries between oppressor and oppressed that are overly simplistic as well as politically dangerous. The desire for a single-axis approach may well come from those who experience discrimination in only one part of their lives, who have uninterrupted access to public space, who see themselves reflected in the media, and who are not faced with racial profiling or the demand to prove their citizenship. For these reasons Puar holds that intersectionalty remains a critically important guiding framework for every arena of social inquiry.

Chandra Talpade Mohanty has argued that intersectional analyses, rather than inhibiting solidarity, are vital to the very possibility of transnational feminist solidarity, but that we need to go even further to analyze our interwoven histories. Rather than studying women in terms of "discrete and disconnected cultures and nations," we should "frame agency and resistance across the borders of nation and culture" and look for "points of connection and distance among and between communities of women marginalized and privileged along numerous local and global dimensions" (Mohanty, 2003: 243). This means that we need to take a macro analysis that considers the interdependent relationships between groups and structures in different parts of the globe, rather than assuming that we can study one small, discrete unit and ignore the way that it is affected—positively and/or negatively—by its relations with others. Mohanty stresses that solidarity can happen when lines of commonality and shared interest emerge between specific communities or constituencies, whether or not they are geographically contiguous. Solidarity can occur in local contexts or across vast distances over issues of intellectual property rights, the policies of global financial institutions, sexual violence, or occupational health hazards. But to develop strong lines of solidarity, we need to remain attentive to power, to differences, to our mutual interdependencies, and to the intersectionality of identities and structures in every location.

Summary

Intersectionality is a way of approaching both identities and structures of oppression. Its basic premise is that to understand anyone's identity or social position, one needs to take into account more than a single axis, more than their gender—for example, race, class, and sexuality.

Feminist theorist Valerie Smith has shown that the mainstream media rarely provide an adequate analysis of current events because they do not take an intersectional approach. Legal theorist Kimberlé Crenshaw argues that without an intersectional approach neither feminism nor anti-racism will effectively address the specific obstacles experienced by women of color. Sexism must also be interrogated for its heterosexist bias that has excluded lesbians and gay men and defined their personal and family relations as not normal.

The history of intersectionality emerges primarily from African American women. In the nineteenth century, Anna Julia Cooper critiqued sexism within the African American community and argued that campaigns to improve the working conditions of women only addressed the situation of white women. Many women of color and lesbians have built on this approach in recent decades. In the 1970s Angela Davis adopted a methodology of incorporating race, class, and gender to assess the lives of any group of women. Without recognizing differences of race, age, and sex, Audre Lorde argued, we cannot build trust and solidarity across groups. Black lesbian activists Barbara Smith and the Combahee River Collective developed "A Black Feminist Statement" in 1997 to analyze black women's identity, needs, and politics in pursuit of their liberation against racism, sexism, and heterosexism.

It was Gloria Anzaldúa who brought the experiences and struggles of Chicanos and Chicanas into intersectionality studies. Her concepts of borderlands and the "mestiza" have been adopted by other scholarships to counter the ways in which racism, sexism, nationalism, colonialism, homophobia, and other oppressions operate elsewhere to render groups invisible and to marginalize their demands for justice.

Feminist activists have adopted intersectional approaches. For example, the comparable worth movement, by connecting race and gender, could enhance the well-being of many more working-class women in gender-segregated workplaces. In reproductive rights struggles, intersectionality has uncovered the limited type and lack of services made available to low-income women, women of color, disabled women, and lesbians given their particular circumstances. Rosalind Petchesky argues that reproductive rights must operate within a principle of indivisibility whereby effective solutions for girls and women in their reproductive needs must also address violence, sexuality, work, education, and so forth.

Activists working at the global level must also consider intersectional methods but recognize biases that promote the West as modern and superior in its ways. For example, anti-homophobic and anti-sexist activism can exacerbate Islamophobia and the oppression of Muslim women while justifying imperialistic military interventions.

Intersectionality also creates new challenges when applied to the notion of identities. Scholars have begun to consider our multiple identities as not additive but historical, relational, fluid, and contextual.

Research methods in women's and gender studies have been transformed as intersectional approaches are commonly applied to their wide range of projects. Nonetheless, women's commonalities as well as differences must be taken into consideration.

Today intersectionality is a widespread approach throughout feminist theory, gender scholarship, and feminist organizing but remains an emerging framework of analysis. While some scholars argue that the term does not explain the full complexity of the multiple structures of oppression and identity formation in every context, others suggest it is an indispensable tool of analysis. Chandra Talpade Mohanty, for example, finds this approach vital if we are to begin to develop solidarity among feminists transnationally.

Discussion Questions

1. Analyze yourself in terms of intersectionality. What are the multiple parts of your identity? Identify two situations in which a different aspect of yourself plays the predominant role.
2. How should researchers use the concept of intersectionality to design empirical studies? In a survey, for example, is it sufficient to draw from a diverse sample of participants, or is more needed?
3. Is it ever useful or appropriate to focus on a singular category of analysis, such as sexuality or race or gender, without an intersectional approach?
4. Interview someone in your community who you think is very different from you in various ways. Is the theory of intersectionality useful to you in understanding these differences?
5. Imagine how this exercise might work in a different culture elsewhere in the world.

Recommended Readings

Anzaldúa, Gloria. *Borderlands: La Frontera: The New Mestiza*. San Francisco: Spinsters/Aunt Lute, 1987. Anzaldúa's groundbreaking semi-autobiographical work of essays and poems explores her identity as a Chicana, lesbian, and activist through the concept of physical, psychological, sexual, and spiritual borderlands and the celebration of the "mestiza."

Collins, Patricia Hill. "It's All in the Family: Intersections of Gender, Race, and Nation." *Hypatia* 13, no. 3 (1998): 62–82. Collins identifies the family as an example of intersectionality with attention to its gendered system of social organization, racial ideas and practices, and construction of U.S. national identity.

Crenshaw, Kimberlé. "Mapping the Margins: Intersectionality, Identity Politics, and Violence against Women of Color." *Stanford Law Review* 43, no. 6 (1991): 1241–99. The author explores race and gender dimensions of violence against women of color and the failure of scholars to examine the intersections of racism and patriarchy.

Davis, Angela. *Women, Race, and Class*. New York: Random House, 1983. Davis exposes the racist and classist biases of some activists within the second-wave women's movement that contributed to divisions within the membership.

De Veaux, Alexis. *Warrior Poet: A Biography of Audre Lorde*. New York: W. W. Norton and Company, 2006. De Veaux's biography of Lorde, the distinguished African American artist and poet, demystifies her life and highlights her struggles as a first-generation immigrant, feminist, and lesbian and her battle against cancer.

chapter **4**

Learning, Making, and Doing Gender

One is not born a woman, one becomes one.
SIMONE DE BEAUVOIR, *THE SECOND SEX*, 1949

If the rigid social constructions of the masculine have resulted in political and cultural forces of oppression, repression, and denial, can masculinity be rehearsed in a way that alters its ideological boundaries? In other words, can masculinity be performed so as to render it less repressive, less tyrannical?
MAURICE BERGER, BRIAN WALLIS, AND SIMON WATSON, *CONSTRUCTING MASCULINITY*, 2012

One of the most powerful effects of marginalization is that it represents dominant groups as neutral and unremarkable. For example, before the emergence in the mid-twentieth century of political movements fighting for the rights of people of color, women, lesbian, gay, bisexual, and transgender (LGBT) people, disabled people, and others, social inequality was defined as the problem of the minority group. What we would now call racism and sexism were identified as "the Negro Problem," or "the Indian Question," or "the Woman Question." In other words, discrimination against women was not the result of male dominance, but a "problem" with "women." A major contribution of the liberation movements of the twentieth century was to redefine these social issues as the responsibility of the dominating majority: racial segregation was not caused by "the Negro Problem," but was the result of white racism.

This conceptual change has had far-reaching influence. One consequence has been the rethinking of how we imagine race, gender, sexuality, and other categories of social existence. From its beginnings, women's studies has recognized that not only women but also men are shaped by cultural mandates about gendered behavior. Men and women are equally defined, contained, and controlled by social expectations of how they should look, act, speak, move, interact with others, affect their surroundings, and think about themselves. Indeed, many women's studies programs in colleges and universities have made this explicit by including the word "gender" in their names to acknowledge that not only women have gender and that gender as a category of identity constructs all of us, albeit within socially unequal contexts.

In this chapter we'll think about what gender is, how it operates in different cultural and national contexts, how it is enforced, and how it is subverted. We'll examine the ways in which the differences between women and men have been naturalized and normalized. And we'll look at the different ways gender is expressed and inhabited in different historical moments and geographical places.

What Is Gender?

The term "gender" comes from the Latin root *genus*, which originally meant "birth, family, or nation"—that is, where something or someone is born from (a meaning that evolved into words like "generate" and "generation"). Over time "genus" came to be more generally defined as "a kind or type of thing," and the words that derive from it share that sense, such as "genre," meaning a kind or type of music or literature. "Gender" came to mean "a kind of thing defined by sex difference," both biologically, like people and animals, and grammatically (so Spanish nouns can have either masculine or feminine gender, like "el gato" or "la playa").

Gender is embodied by more than just physical characteristics. In contemporary U.S. society, gender also represents a broad network of behaviors, attitudes, activities, prohibitions, mandates, relationships, identities, and beliefs. For example, the English language has only two options in describing someone's gender: male or female. We define gendered activities as either masculine or feminine. Our restricted classification of gender into feminine or masculine qualities or behaviors is prone to damaging stereotypes. Not only is our vocabulary of gender impoverished, but our cultural imagination around gender is constrained. At the same time that it is limited, it is also immensely powerful. Not everyone may agree on every single quality that comprises masculinity or femininity, but it is clear when people break the rules of gender exactly what those qualities are. Though the extent to which gender stereotypes reflect actual gender comparisons between men and women is debatable, gender-associated processes are often so deeply engrained and subtle that most of us do not even realize how strongly they affect our behavior, thoughts, feelings, language, interactions with others, and the structure of social interactions (Denmark, Rabinowitz, and Sechzer, 2005). While gender nonconformity is tolerated in girls more and for longer than it is for boys—girls can be tomboys until puberty, whereas boys beyond toddlerhood who express stereotypically feminine characteristics are often harshly reined in—there is no doubt which qualities "belong" to boys or girls, and which are inappropriate for gender conformity.

As long as there have been rules about gender, however, people have been breaking those rules. As we'll see, some cultures make room for gender nonconformity by creating specific social roles for people who step outside the binary, or want to occupy a role that is not prescribed for their gender. Other cultures try to relegate gender bending to the sphere of performance: drag queens and androgynous pop stars, for example. But in every society we find people pushing against the strictures of gender assignment.

Sex versus Gender

Until the late twentieth century, differences between women and men were defined through the word "sex." Women were called "the fairer sex"; in English-speaking countries in the nineteenth century, women were referred to simply as "the sex" (again reinforcing the idea that women are a sex, and men are just people). However, as feminists have pointed out for centuries, the differences between women and men are created at least as much by social and cultural norms as they are by biology.

Gender entered the cultural vocabulary in several ways. Sociologist John Money adopted the word to describe masculinity and femininity in people whose bodies were not wholly male or female—intersex people, who had incomplete or combined sexual organs. Money and his colleagues (1972) argued that gender was imprinted on the brain at a very young age, and so intersex children, especially those who had undergone surgery to "correct" their ambiguous genitalia, had to be intensely schooled in their assigned gender. These scholars did not challenge how gender was arranged or why certain behaviors and feelings were appropriate to men or women; their principal concern was that children be provided with the "right" gender messages.

In the 1960s, psychoanalyst Robert Stoller coined the phrase "gender identity" to mean the sense that a person is aware of being male or female. Unlike John Money, Stoller did not see a necessary relationship between an internal gender identity and conformity to social expectations of that role (Germon,

2009: 66). At the same time, Stoller had a clear and uncomplicated sense of what constituted appropriate behaviors and activities for girls and boys and women and men.

With the emergence of second-wave feminism, the concept of gender came under intense scrutiny. In 1975, Gayle Rubin offered a new way of thinking about these differences: a mechanism she called the "sex/gender system," which she defined as "the set of arrangements by which a society transforms biological sexuality into products of human activity, and in which these transformed sexual needs are satisfied" (Rubin, 1975: 159). Through the sex/gender system, biological women are turned into commodities that can be traded by men through kinship transactions (we see vestiges of this today in the Global North, in which fathers hand over their daughters to husbands-to-be in many wedding ceremonies, and women exchange their fathers' last names for their husbands') (see Chapter 6).

As second-wave feminism adopted the belief that the social construction of gender was separate from the biological material of sex, many feminists took on the project of reducing gendered difference as much as possible and embraced androgyny. The gay liberation movement was at the forefront of these efforts: politically engaged gay men grew their hair and rejected the confines of masculinity in their actions, dress, and relationships, while lesbians cut their hair short and strove against femininity (Jay and Young, 1992). The influence of transgender activists during the early years of Gay Liberation also challenged assumptions within the movement about the inevitable connections between biology and gender.

Gender Expression

Over the past two decades, feminists have developed a nuanced and sophisticated vocabulary about gender, especially in reference to questions of gender expression. "Gender expression" is a term that refers to how a person enacts gender, regardless of their biological sex: rather than talking about men and women, or male and female, gender expression deals with ideas of masculinity and femininity.

This focus on the expression of gender comes in part from the work of transgender theorists, although it also has roots in early gay liberation and feminist and lesbian writers like Joan Nestle. Just as Gayle Rubin differentiated sex (biology) from gender (culture), theories of gender expression separate gender (behavior, appearance, identification) from sexuality (desire and partner-choice). Heternormativity, the assumption that heterosexual desire is the most natural and inevitable kind of sexuality, assumes not just that men desire women and vice versa, but that masculine people desire feminine people or, at the very least, that masculine women must be lesbians and feminine men must be gay. Theories of gender expression challenge these assumptions.

Gendered identities and expressions take different shapes around the world. Sometimes they fulfill formal social roles like the *hijras* of South Asia. Hijras are born with male bodies but take on feminine identities in dress and social status; while they are often marginalized and impoverished, hijras are also a crucial part of life cycle ceremonies like weddings and baby blessings (Nanda, 1986). In Thailand, *Toms* are masculine women who, while they identify and are seen as women, have strongly masculine gender expression and partner with feminine women (Sinott, 2004). In the Global North the identities *butch* and *femme* have long had currency in lesbian (and some gay male) communities for masculine and feminine gender expression.

It's rare to see authentic representations of gender nonconformity in U.S. popular

South Asian Hijras. Hijras are born as men but identify as female in their dress, behavior, and roles. While often marginalized in their societies and discriminated against, they play important roles in life cycle ceremonies such as weddings and the birth of a male child.

culture. While there are a number of movies in which men take on female identities, they are usually comedies that work to reinforce assumptions of gender difference by showing the impossibility of actually giving up one's own gendered identity. A spate of these films in the 1980s and early 1990s—*Tootsie* (1982), *Mr. Mom* (1983), *Mrs. Doubtfire* (1993)—played with gender reversal mostly to show that men could take on and excel in realms previously assigned to women and that women ultimately could never compete with men's superiority. Alternatively, gender nonconformity is represented as ending in tragedy, as in the 1999 film *Boys Don't Cry*, a movie about the life and murder of female-to-male transgender person Brandon Teena.

Traditional Explanations for Gender Differences

Anatomical and Evolutionary Differences

The oldest explanations for the differences between women and men look to women's and men's different anatomies as the source. In the second chapter of the book of Genesis, God creates the first woman from a rib of the first man. Other creation myths, ranging from as those of the Yoruba in what is now Nigeria to the Menominee in northern Wisconsin to the inhabitants of ancient Egypt, represented their gods as male and female, taking gender differences for granted in both divine and human life (see, for example, Hoffman, 1890; Anderson, 1991; and Ions, 1991).

In the Western tradition, anatomical explanations for gender difference were popularized by the ancient Greek philosopher Aristotle (384–322 B.C.E). Aristotle held two interrelated beliefs about gender: first that women were defective versions of men, and second that women's and men's innate characteristics complemented each other. He argued that in both animals and humans, females were not just generally smaller and less muscular, but that they were more easily trained and controlled, more emotional, more nurturing, and less brave. Men, on the other hand, were naturally stronger and more impulsive, protective, and controlling.

According to Aristotle, men's bodies were hot, and their blood was thin and clear, which made them more noble and valiant. Women's bodies were cool and their blood was viscous, which made them less intelligent and less courageous. However, since men's heat could lead them into excessive acts of impulse and violence, and women's cool blood could render them passive and overprotective of children, the two sexes could complement and regulate each other. This complementarity could never raise women to equality with men, though; for Aristotle, women were mutilated, impotent men, whose biology relegated them to inferior status (Matthews, 1986).

Aristotle's theories were powerfully influential on European thought for centuries. The second-century Greco-Roman physician Galen (c.130–200 C.E.) reinterpreted the complementary theory of gender to mean that women's reproductive organs were men's organs turned inside out (so the testicles became the ovaries, the penis became the vagina, etc). According to Galen, women did not have sufficient heat in their bodies to push these organs outside, and instead provided a cool, protected space first for semen and then for fetuses. These essential, biological differences between women and men's reproductive systems created a whole analysis of sexual difference more generally that lasted in Europe and European colonies until the late eighteenth century, so that whenever women challenged male dominance, their anatomical inversion and cooler system were used as irrefutable arguments for women's subordination (Gallagher and Laqueur, 1987).

Ideas about women's and men's bodies changed in the nineteenth century, shifting from the belief that women were inside-out men to the assumption that women and men were essentially different both biologically and psychologically. Women's bodies were reimagined not as deficient male bodies, but as wholly different and physically fragile. Routine parts of women's biological life cycles such as menstruation, pregnancy, childbirth, and menopause were redefined by doctors as dangerous and draining for women. This fragility also generated moral and psychological purity: women's delicacy meant that they could devote themselves to the nurturing of their children and husbands. Out of this rose what historian Barbara Welter has called the "Cult of True Womanhood," in which women were expected to embody the qualities of "piety, purity, submissiveness, and domesticity" (Welter, 1966: 152). Women who strayed from these values were deemed unnatural and depraved, doomed to a bad end or to a life of poverty and shame. These standards, which were challenging for middle-class women, were impossible for working-class and enslaved women to achieve. Since their survival depended on their ability to perform physical labor, they could not embody the delicate, leisured "True Woman." As a result, working women in the United States were constructed as the opposite of the middle-class white woman: sexually uncontrolled, coarse, and undeserving of respect from men of all classes.

While the Cult of True Womanhood was most powerful during the middle of the nineteenth century, the belief that women were ruled by their bodies retained its explanatory power. Opponents to women's education argued that women were too feeble for the rigors of higher education; in 1873 the U.S. physician Edward Clarke (1820–1877) published *Sex and Education; or a Fair Chance for the Girls*, which claimed that women who engaged in sustained vigorous mental activity, studying in a "boy's way," risked atrophy of the uterus and ovaries, masculinization, sterility, insanity, even death (Palmieri, 1987). Charlotte Perkins Gilman's semi-autobiographical novel *The Yellow Wallpaper* (1899) tells the story of a woman experiencing what we would now call postpartum depression, whose doctor forbids her from reading, writing, or any strenuous physical activity—the "rest cure"—so that her fragile system can recover from childbirth. Women of color, working-class women, and immigrant women were defined not just by sex but also by race, class, and national origin and the scientific racism of the era that insisted that all people outside the dominant class of white, middle-, and upper-class U.S.-born men were biologically and intellectually inferior.

After the horrors of World War II, which were motivated in large part by Nazi beliefs that some populations (such as Jews, Roma, Slavs, the aged, and people with disabilities) were biologically inferior, anatomical and biological arguments for social subordination lost their appeal. However, more recently, evolutionary psychology, a new form of sociobiology, has gained popularity as an approach to explaining gender differences. Sociobiology was first formulated by E. O. Wilson (1975), who argued that psychological traits are selected in a population because they are adaptive and help maintain that population.

As sociobiologist Richard Dawkins explains, male and female gender behavior is motivated by "selfish genes." That is, males and females can be thought of as trying to exploit the other, trying to force the individual of the other sex to invest more in their offspring in order to optimize the chances that

their own genes will be passed down to future generations (Dawkins, 1976: 150). To increase this "genetic fitness," males need to impregnate as many females as possible. Males are thus genetically programmed for behaviors and psychological traits that will ensure this, according to evolutionary psychologists, such as hypersexuality and philandering. These traits propel them to have frequent sex with multiple partners.

Females, however, according to this hypothetical scenario, must be chaste to increase the chances of passing on their genes. Once she does become pregnant and give birth, a female increases the chances of her initial investment paying off by investing even more time and energy in the rearing of her child. To relieve some of this burden, a woman encourages a man to help her care for her dependent child. It is in the female's interest to find such a man since he might also be more willing to remain after the birth of a child and help her with child-care responsibilities than a man who wants sex without commitment.

Evolutionary psychologists discount cross-cultural variation in personality traits and behaviors even though evidence for this variation has been available for decades. For example, Margaret Mead (1901–1978), an anthropologist and pioneer in research on the cultural and social context of personality development, studied men and women in a number of non-Western societies in the early part of the twentieth century. She began with the following question: Do universals of personality development exist? She empirically tested propositions about universals by comparing people in different cultural settings. Comparing men and women in several South Pacific societies with those in her own society, the United States, Mead discovered that what many people think of as feminine and masculine are culturally produced traits, not inherent biological differences (Mead, 1949) (see Box 4.1).

Box 4.1   SEX AND TEMPERAMENT

We have now considered in detail the approved personalities of each sex among three primitive peoples. We found the Arapesh—both men and women—displaying a personality that,
out of our historically limited preoccupation, we would call maternal in its parental aspects,
and feminine in its sexual aspects. We found men, as well as women, trained to be cooperative,
unaggressive, responsive to the needs and demands of others. We found no idea that sex was a
powerful driving force either for men or for women. In marked contrast to these attitudes, we
found among the Mundugumor that both men and women developed as ruthless, aggressive,
positively sexed individuals, with the maternal cherishing aspects of personality at a minimum.
Both men and women approximated to a personality type that we in our culture would find
only in an undisciplined and very violent male. Neither the Arapesh nor the Mundugumor
profit by a contrast between the sexes. . . . In the third tribe, the Tchambuli, we found a genuine reversal of the sex-attitudes of our own culture with the woman the dominant, impersonal,
managing partner, the man the less responsible and the emotionally dependent person. These
three situations suggest, then, a very definite conclusion. If those temperamental attitudes
which we have traditionally regarded as feminine—such as passivity, responsiveness, and a
willingness to cherish children—can so easily be set up as the masculine pattern in one tribe,
and in another be outlawed for the majority of women as well as for the majority of men, we no
longer have any bias for regarding such aspects of behavior as sex-linked. And this conclusion
becomes even stronger when we consider the actual reversal in Tchambuli of the position of
dominance of the two sexes. . . .

 . . . Only to the impact of the whole of the integrated culture upon the growing child can we
lay the formation of the contrasting types. There is no other explanation. . . . We are forced
to conclude that human nature is almost unbelievably malleable, responding accurately and
contrastingly to contrasting cultural conditions. The differences between individuals who are
members of different cultures, like the differences between individuals within a culture, are
almost entirely to be laid to differences in conditioning, especially during early childhood, and
the form of this conditioning is culturally determined. Standardized personality differences
between the sexes are of this order, cultural creations to which each generation, male and
female, is trained to conform.

Source: Excerpt from *Sex and Temperament in Three Primitive Societies*, pp. 279–80, by Margaret Mead.
Copyright © 1935, 1950, 1963 by Margaret Mead. Reprinted by permission of HarperCollins
Publishers, Inc. William Morrow.

Psychoanalytic Theory

Traditional psychoanalytic theory was founded
by Viennese neurologist Sigmund Freud
(1856–1939). Freud became intrigued by the
number of patients he saw, especially women,
whose symptoms appeared to be the result of
sexual conflicts and repressions. Based on case
studies of these patients, Freud developed
a theory of personality development called
"psychosexual development," which explained
what he saw as fundamental characteristics of
the female personality: dependence, passivity,
masochism, and an inferior sense of justice.
For Freud, sexual drives underlie all personality development and arise from a fundamental

difference in anatomy that differentiates males from females: the presence or absence of a penis. Thus, for Freud "anatomy is destiny" (Freud, 1925).

Freudian theory stipulates that the significant turning point in the formation of gender identity occurs at about age 3. Before this time, sensual pleasure is centered first on oral, then on anal, gratification. During the subsequent genital stage, the sexual organs become the source of pleasure. It is then that girls notice that boys and men have penises. According to Freud, this recognition leads girls to develop a sense of inferiority and the desire for a penis, a wish he called "penis envy." Women's supposed tendency to be masochistic was thought to arise from their self-loathing due to this lack. At the same time, boys notice that girls and women do not have penises, and this leads boys to suspect that girls' penises were somehow denied or taken away by the main source of power, fathers. Freud concluded that this produces anxiety in boys that their own fathers will take away their penises. Freud called this anxiety castration anxiety. He argued that girls blame their "inferior anatomy" on the mother. Girls then turn affections toward the father, hoping to get the desired object (a penis) or a substitute (a baby) from him. Girls later learn that the father cannot provide either and must replace him with another man to provide gratification. Boys, on the other hand, possess a desire to have sex with their mothers and replace their fathers but fear that their fathers will retaliate for this desire by castrating them (Freud called this the Oedipal conflict, based on the classical Greek story of Oedipus, who unwittingly murdered his father and married his mother). A resolution of this conflict is generally achieved by relinquishing the mother as love object while identifying with the father. This identification with the father removes a boy from the realm of competitor, thus reducing castration fears. As a result of this identification with the

father, the boy develops a male identity and internalizes dominant moral standards. By contrast, girls must identify with their mothers, a mixed result, since the mother clearly cannot supply a girl with her desired object, a penis. Girls' own moral standards are weaker and less developed than those of boys because they do not evolve in response to castration fears but, rather, to counteract the shame of having been castrated. Because internalization of moral standards is essential to maturity, girls are seen as having more difficulty maturing than boys. So according to this theory, gender identity and the foundation for all later personality development is established in the first 6 years of life and indirectly derived from anatomy.

Neurobiological and Hormonal Explanations

Under pressure from feminist critics (discussed below), and an increased focus on chemical and hormonal influences on personality and behavior, psychoanalytic and anatomical rationales for gender differences have lost their explanatory power in the past few decades. That's not to say that theories about the innate differences have disappeared: far from it. But they've been supplanted in large part by arguments grounded in neurobiology and endocrinology. Numerous scientists who study the brain and hormones have offered arguments for essential differences between women and men that look to brain chemistry, during both gestation and everyday life, to support their claims.

The central thread to neurobiological arguments for the brain as the source of gender identity is that humans are "hardwired" for gender differences by exposure to various hormones in the uterus. Sex differences exist not just in our reproductive organs but also in our brains, a result of hormones that make men and women desire each other and want gender-specific things. Neuroscientists claim that prenatal hormones "organize" the human brain, imprinting it with preferences and behaviors that align with anatomical sex (Jordan-Young, 2010). Psychologist Simon Baron-Cohen pointed to prenatal testosterone as the reason that men are "systemizers," good at mathematical and scientific pursuits, which require systematic thinking, whereas prenatal estrogen causes women to be "empathizers," who rely more on intuition and emotion than scientific method (Baron-Cohen, 2003). Some scientists see their research on brain organization as having direct policy implications: Richard Udry has argued that since "males and females have different and biologically influenced behavioral dispositions . . . , if we depart too far from the underlying sex-dimorphism of biological predispositions, they will generate social malaise" (Udry, 2000: 454).

The belief in a "gendered brain" has extended to speculations about hormonal and neurochemical sources for sexual orientation and transgender identification. In the middle of the twentieth century, the idea that gay men and lesbians had an excess of the "wrong" hormone led to experiments in which men were injected with testosterone to lead them toward the "correct" sexual orientation. Although these efforts failed, neuroscientists continued to look to the brain as the cause of gender and sexual nonconformity. The most prominent study was by Simon LeVay in 1991, who analyzed the different sizes of the hypothalamus (a gland that in part controls sexual activity and desire) in gay and straight men. One shortcoming of this work is that just as it assumes a normative gender arrangement of two "opposite" sexes, men and women, neurological research into sexual desire takes for granted that there are just two kinds of sexual orientation, gay and straight. The research is grounded in the belief that male

and female, gay and straight, transgender and cisgender constitute distinct, opposite groups that remain stable across geography and history and over the course of a person's life, something that many people's experiences contradict (Jordan-Young, 2010).

Needless to say, the actual science is much more complicated than this. First of all, both women and men have a variety of "sex hormones" in their bodies, and even the archetypal hormones— testosterone and estrogen—exist in proportionally low quantities compared to amounts found in other mammals. Moreover, testosterone and estrogen are chemically very similar to each other and have a number of different functions beyond controlling secondary sex characteristics like breast development, body hair, menstruation, and testicular development (Jordan-Young, 2010). Theories of prenatal hormonal formation cannot explain how sexual desire changes over time, or even how people may feel differently about their gender at different moments in their lives. And of course, gendered behavior is strongly linked to cultural and historical context: while in the twenty-first century United States we identify men dressing in women's clothes with homosexuality or at the very least femininity, in seventeenth-century England that same behavior was regarded as hypermasculine, since only a man who powerfully desired women would want to dress like them.

Feminist Critiques of Theories of Gender

Feminist Psychoanalysis

Some psychoanalysts have pointed out the lack of empirical evidence for Freud's theories, noting that findings from both direct-observational studies of children and clinical reports lend little support to Freud's formulation of female psychosexual

Box 4.2 DOING GENDER

When we view gender as an accomplishment, an achieved property of situated conduct, our attention shifts from matters internal to the individual and focuses on interactional and, ultimately, institutional arenas. In one sense, of course, it is individuals who "do" gender. But it is a situated doing, carried out in the virtual or real presence of others who are presumed to be oriented to its production. Rather than as a property of individuals, we conceive of gender as an emergent feature of social situations: both as an outcome of and a rationale for various social arrangements and as a means of legitimating one of the most fundamental divisions of society. . . .

To elaborate our proposal, we suggest at the outset that important but often overlooked distinctions be observed among sex, sex category, and gender. Sex is a determination made through the application of socially agreed upon biological criteria for classifying persons as females or males. . . . Placement in a sex category is achieved through application of the sex criteria, but in everyday life, categorization is established and sustained by the socially required identificatory displays that proclaim one's membership in one or the other category. In this sense, one's sex category presumes one's sex and stands as proxy for it in many situations, but sex and sex category can vary independently; that is, it is possible to claim membership in a sex category even when the sex criteria are lacking. Gender, in contrast, is the activity of managing situated in conduct in light of normative conceptions of attitudes and activities appropriate for one's sex category. Gender activities emerge from and bolster claims to membership in a sex category.

. . . Doing gender also renders the social arrangements based on sex category accountable as normal and natural, that is, legitimate ways of organizing social life. Differences between men and women that are created by this process can then be portrayed as fundamental and enduring dispositions. . . . Thus if, in doing gender, men are also doing dominance and women are doing deference, . . . the resultant social order, which supposedly reflects "natural differences," is a powerful reinforcer and legitimator of hierarchical arrangements.

Source: Candace West and Don H. Zimmerman, "Doing Gender," *Gender and Society* 1 (1987): 126–7, 146.

development. Fliegel (1980), for example, rebukes those analysts who rigidly adhere to this dynamic in the face of contradictory information and notes that a belief in penis envy has "almost become a test of doctrinaire loyalty." However, this has not caused feminists to reject Freud entirely.

A number of feminists have drawn on some aspects of Freudian theory while questioning others. Many reject the androcentric Freudian premise that "anatomy is destiny" but share with traditional psychoanalytical models the belief that individuals form a core gender identity based on early childhood experiences. They argue that psychological development must be understood within the cultural context within which girls and boys develop.

The Importance of Culture

Karen Horney (1885–1952) and Clara Thompson (1893–1958) were among the first women psychoanalysts to diverge from the classical Freudian theory of female psychology and to elaborate on the cultural constraints that contribute to the formation of the feminine personality. Horney suggested that psychological traits, such as women's dependence on men and female masochism, were products of male social dominance, not anatomical difference. Horney argued that the fact that women gained status through fathers and husbands explained why they may seem to be more afraid of losing love than men. Similarly, she saw masochism as an attempt on the part of women to achieve personal safety and satisfaction by appearing inconspicuous and dependent, not as a reaction to the recognition of the lack of a penis.

Horney ([1922] 1973) also suggested that anatomical envy could work in both directions, since men lack women's ability to bear children. She argued that men's envy of women's reproductive capacities is at the root of misogyny and male oppression of females; in fact, research suggests that males in many societies experience feelings of breast and womb envy (Mead, 1949; Zalk, 1980, 1987).

Thompson challenged the classic assumption that discovery of the penis invariably causes psychic trauma for a girl, arguing that what appeared to be penis envy was actually women's awareness of their lower status and fewer privileges within the family, which has historically been the case in many Western societies (Thompson, 1942, 1943). Rather than attribute the adolescent female's renunciation of the "active" role in life to the resolution of penis envy, Thompson attributed it to external social pressures. In his collection of short stories *Tales of Nevèrÿon* (1993), Samuel R. Delany parodies theories of penis envy and points out the social construction of the centrality of the penis in male-dominated cultures by inventing a societal hierarchy organized around the "rult," a wooden carving that boys and men wear around their stomachs. Like the penis, the rult is seen as powerful but rarely referred to by its actual name; it is the domain of men only and explicitly excludes women and girls. In the story, a father comes up with a theory of "rult envy" that exactly mimics Freud's idea of penis envy. In this culture, in which people are naked most of the time, genitals have no symbolic power. But as the dominant class, men have created the rult as a sign of their importance.

The Importance of Relatedness

Attempts by feminists to understand gendered psychological development within a psychoanalytical or psychodynamic framework have led many theorists to explore the mother–daughter relationship and the differential impact on girls and boys of being raised by a female caretaker. These writers focus not on genitals but on the impact on early identity formation of having a same-sex or an other-sex caretaker. The fact that the female child is cared for and raised primarily by a parent or a parent-surrogate of the same sex may engender feelings and conflicts that differ from those elicited in the mother–son relationship (Denmark, 1977).

Chodorow (1978) discusses the effect that predominantly female parenting has on the establishment of the boy's gender identity. In order for him to develop his appropriate gender role, the boy must break away from the female-dominated world from which he emerges. The devaluation of femininity and female activities may represent the male's attempt to differentiate himself from that feminine world. According to Chodorow, males have an easier time establishing autonomy than do females but a less stable gender identity and less access to feelings of empathy, nurturance, and dependence, which are a reminder of their early identification with their mothers.

Other psychodynamic theorists have challenged this claim. Jean Baker Miller (1984) and her colleagues, for example, argue that relatedness is the central goal of development and that it is only within the context of relatedness that autonomy can develop. Miller's self-in-relation theory proposes that it is the give-and-take relationship between the caretaker and the child that forms the core "self" and that this reciprocal relationship is the precursor of empathy, nurturance, and connection with others. Miller notes that females are more likely to be encouraged in these experiences than are males; that, as a result, they possess a greater capacity for emotional connectedness, empathy, and intimacy; and that this relational self is a core self structure for them.

In the 1980s and beyond, a number of psychoanalytical feminists looked beyond anatomy to understand those aspects of the female psyche often overlooked in mainstream psychological theory and studies: women's pleasures, desires, and fantasies. These theorists have tended to draw on the work of French psychoanalyst Jacques Lacan (1901–1981), who reinterpreted aspects of Freud's theory, focusing specifically on how a child comes to be either one sex or the other. Lacan's conceptualization of this process centers on how a child becomes a "subject," or an "I," like the subject of a sentence. In other words, Lacan asks how children come to have a conscious understanding of themselves as distinct from the mother, as possessing their own identity, and suggests that it is through entry into the symbolic realm of culture, through the acquisition of language. This entry, based on the recognition of oneself as distinct, however, splits the child from its mother, producing a sense of loss and a constant desire for this unattainable lost object (see Wright, 2000). To disavow this lack and to make up for the lost object, the male projects fantasies onto the female: she becomes the desired *object*. However, this has different consequences for women because of their differing relationship to language.

Unlike Freud, who saw male and female genital anatomy as the basis of sexual identity and sex difference, Lacan sees no predetermined nature to sex difference; instead, sex difference is a "construction in culture." For him, it is not the penis (the biological organ or lack of one) that is associated with one's actual father that is significant in the development of gender identity but the "phallus," the cultural sign or symbol of the father, a metaphor for society's rules and laws and their imposition. The symbolic order, according to Lacan, is organized around the phallus, meaning that in language the male is taken as the norm (e.g., the word *man* subsumes both men and women) and the female is defined as "lack of maleness." Since coming into language produces subjectivity, however, there is no subject position in language for the female; the female subject is constituted as an exclusion. Constituted by lack and defined by men as an object onto which their fantasies are projected, "woman" does not exist.

Rethinking Biology

Evolutionary biologists have found several weaknesses in traditional evolutionary explanations for gender differences. Perhaps the most important is the role of environment in the broadest sense: not just the physical environment of altitude, temperature, and water sources but also psychological environments of comfort, trauma, separation, and so on (Jordan-Young, 2010). For a developing fetus, environment includes prenatal hormone levels, but it also comprises the pregnant woman's nutrition levels, her sleep patterns, and her rate of activity. Organisms react to a whole host of environmental factors. In one study of rhesus monkeys, scientists found that females took on male-linked spatial skills in a new environment, while in another study, female rats who had never encountered rat pups before seemed not to know how to care for their own children, even though maternal behavior is one of the key characteristics that neuroscientists identify as conditioned by hormones (Leboucher, 1989; Herman and Wallen, 2007).

Recent studies in brain chemistry reveal that the brain is actually fairly malleable. Studies of people with serious brain injury, for example, have shown that the brain has the capacity to adjust and adapt, to shift the function of a damaged part over to an intact section. Even basic activities like playing the piano or doing word puzzles can affect the brain's activity (Zuger, 2007). In light of these findings, it's hard to believe that prenatal hormones have the last word about experiences and expressions of gender.

The field of *epigenetics* has arisen in the early twenty-first century to examine how the nature versus nurture debate not only has the wrong answers but is asking the wrong questions. Evelyn Fox-Keller (2010) uses the analogy of two children filling a bucket with water. If Billy puts 40 liters of water in a bucket and Suzy puts in 60 liters, we can clearly say that 60 liters of the water in the bucket was caused by Suzy. But if Billy turns on the tap and Suzy holds the hose over the bucket, that kind of calculation no longer makes sense. We can't even ask how much water was put in by Billy compared to Suzy, only that both children cooperated to fill the bucket. Likewise, although we can identify various genes and locate them inside specific people, there's rarely a direct causal relationship between a single gene and a single outcome. Just as brain chemistry interacts with experience to create new neural pathways, genes function only when they are expressed, and the conditions under which that expression happens vary widely with environment.

How Do We Learn Gender?

Cognitive–Developmental Theory

One approach to thinking about how we learn gender is cognitive-developmental theory; that is, ideas about how our brains develop from childhood onwards. Cognitive psychologists are interested in how people organize and understand their perceptions of physical and social reality and how these perceptions change at different developmental stages. They argue that the human brain needs to make order out of what it perceives and focus on the individual's internal need to fulfill a learned gender identity in order to categorize different kinds of people coherently (Kohlberg, 1966; Kohlberg and Ullian, 1974). Studies in cognitive psychology have suggested that at age 2 girls and boys begin to learn and reproduce gender categories based on experiences with representatives of each gender, although they are not initially aware of anatomical distinctions and do not conceive them to be unchangeable characteristics. These categories, or gender schemas, are structures that allow a person to organize information related to gender by linking gender labels to objects, traits, and behaviors. Children learn to categorize information based on gender at a young age and demonstrate this knowledge in their preferences for play, toys, and playmates (Denmark, Rabinowitz, and Sechzer, 2005). During this period, young children might "try on" different kinds of gender expression or imitate the gendered behavior of their primary caregiver(s). Once children have classified themselves as female or male and recognize that their gender does not change (at about age 5), they are motivated to approximate to the best of their ability the social definitions of this identity. In the case of female children, the motivation to fulfill their gender identity presses them toward the ideal of femininity (as socially defined), independent of externally mediated rewards or punishments for attaining such a goal. This explanation for gender-role acquisition may account for the fact that often girls and boys will conform to stereotypic gender roles and police the gendered behavior of other children even when their parents or other socializing agents do not differentially reinforce feminine and masculine behavior in them (Kohlberg and Zigler, 1967).

Social Learning Theory

All societies teach their young culturally prescribed gender roles. This gender socialization often begins at the moment of birth. Socialization theories focus attention on the social context of this learning of gender roles that gives rise to characteristically female and male personality traits and behaviors. They are particularly interested in the messages a child receives from others in the social environment and how these messages are conveyed. Parents and peers are powerful socializing agents, informing children that certain activities and toys "aren't for girls/ boys," but gender expectations are communicated in many different ways. Television, school, books, clothing, toys, and even fairy tales operate as socializing agents.

Social learning theory argues that conformity to gender is policed by a series of external reinforcements, either rewards or punishments. This theory holds that individuals learn "female" and "male" behavior by observing others and the world around them. However, the behavior actually performed is a function of whether it is rewarded or punished. Social learning theorist and experimental psychologist Albert Bandura (1965) suggests that the introduction of rewards for cross-sex behavior will enable girls and boys to expand their behavioral repertoires with little difficulty.

One of the most powerful socializing messages in our culture is that men are central to any story worth telling. This is especially true of the mainstream movie industry, which churns out one male-focused narrative after another. Recently, feminist commentators have created a metric by which to evaluate how much a movie focuses on its male characters, which they call the "Bechdel test," after lesbian cartoonist Alison Bechdel, who created it. The test makes three requirements of a movie: that it feature (1) two or more female characters who (2) talk to each other (3) about something other than a man. While this test isn't perfect, it does reveal how few Hollywood movies feature meaningful and self-sustaining relationships between women. More importantly, movies then teach girls and boys that relationships between women are necessarily focused on their connection to men, rather than having value in themselves, and that women are rewarded for organizing their emotional lives around men.

Theories of socialization have long been popular among feminist writers, especially those who are interested in imagining alternative ways of being. Feminist science fiction and fantasy writers have created new worlds in which gender is arranged very differently as a way to think about how what we imagine as natural qualities attached to gender are actually created by social conditions. Charlotte Perkins Gilman's *Herland* (1915) creates a woman-only country in which war has been eradicated, women reproduce by will, and the entire society is organized for the good of all. The second wave of the feminist movement inspired similar thought experiments. Joanna Russ's 1975 novel *The Female Man* follows the lives of four women living in parallel worlds that differ in time and place. When they cross over to each other's worlds, their different views on gender roles challenge each other's preexisting notions of womanhood. In the end, their encounters influence them to evaluate their lives and shape their ideas of what it means to be a woman. Octavia Butler took on the intertwined systems of race and gender in her *Lilith's Brood* series of novels, which features a female human protagonist kidnapped by an alien species to sustain them through reproduction. Through these and other books, Butler examines the legacies of slavery, racism, and sexism by transporting them to unfamiliar environments.

Gender Schema Theory

Sandra Bem (1981, 1983, 1985) proposes a *gender schema* theory, which incorporates cognitive, childrearing, and cultural factors to explain the development of gender identity and personality traits. All people have mental categories that are a network of associations. In order to understand or make sense of information, individuals try to place it into these categories, which form a sort of blueprint in the mind. A schema is descriptive and consists of associations and assumptions. For example, schemas for "teacher" and "student" include the descriptors "one who teaches" and "one who learns," respectively, as well as myriad associations about authority, judgment, power, expertise, interdependence, and more.

One of the most culturally salient categories in which people are grouped is gender, with the development of a gender schema beginning early in childhood. Children learn quickly to categorize people by gender and develop a gender schema that incorporates cultural gender roles, norms, attributes, and definitions of *feminine* and *masculine*. Bem proposes that gender schemas become part of an individual's self-concept.

As children learn the contents of the society's gender schema, they learn which attributes are to be linked with their own sex and, hence, with themselves. This does not simply entail learning where each sex is supposed to stand on each dimension or attribute—that boys are to be strong and girls weak, for example—but involves the deeper lesson that the dimensions themselves are differentially applicable to the two sexes (Bem, 1981: 355).

Bem does not consider gender typing as inevitable; she suggests that raising children in gender-aschematic homes and school environments, in which *sex* refers only to anatomy, results in fewer gender-typed behaviors, traits, and expectations.

(a)   (b)

Children learn "appropriate" gender roles through the toys given to them from birth. A Barbie doll socializes young girls to devote themselves to others, to be passive, not aggressive, and to be overly concerned about their physical appearance. G.I. Joe encourages young boys to be active, aggressive, and adventurous.

Social Interactions and Gender Roles

The above theories attempt to explain how individuals develop gender identities and personality traits and the relationship between gender identity and gender roles. Other theories place greater emphasis on social roles; rather than view gender-typed traits and behaviors as primarily a function of internalized gender identities, they understand them as the result of how gender is assigned and maintained and the unequal distribution of power between females and males. These theories hold that gender-typed personality traits or behaviors are, at least in part, behavioral displays that are shaped by, or result from, social demands, interactions, or oppression, rather than necessarily representing internal or stable characteristics.

Alice Eagly (1987), for example, explains gender-typed traits as compliance to gender-role expectations. Her social/role theory suggests that women and men demonstrate different personality characteristics because the family and occupational roles to which they are assigned require them. Thus, women are communal because of their roles in the family as caretakers and nurturers and men are more active in the world because of their roles in the workplace. Although roles may be changing in much of the world, even in the United States women and men continue to assume different family and workplace responsibilities and roles (for example, see Ruble, 1983). Women are more likely to assume the child-care and domestic work in the home, and half of employed women are in service-related jobs (Levine and Neft, 1997).

Candace West and Don Zimmerman (1987) present a thoughtful argument for conceiving of gender as a verb rather than a noun. In other words, they view gender as something people *do*, not as something they *are*. Other researchers have presented a model that explains the display of gender-typed traits and behavior rather than their acquisition. They propose that the enactment of gender takes place within the context of social interactions, is highly flexible, and is context-dependent (Deaux and Major, 1987). In other words, gender-related traits and behaviors are an outcome of the individual's self-perception, expectations of others, and the context of ongoing social interactions.

That such behaviors are related to the characteristics of social interactions rather than to those of particular individuals is borne out by research on low-status individuals, both male and female. Henley (1977), for example, found that when females relate to males and subordinate males relate to more dominant males, they touch less, smile more, make less frequent eye contact, and are more tentative. The effect of male dominance on women may be a direct and powerful influence on gender-related traits and behaviors in other ways as well. MacKinnon (1987), for example, suggests that women behave differently from men because they grow up and live under the constant threat of physical violence and sexual exploitation. It is understandable that women may behave in ways that minimize a challenge to male dominance and the possibility of being victimized (Zalk, 1987).

Performativity Theory

The theories discussed above identify either cognitive processes inside the body or social pressures outside the self as determinants of gendered identity and behavior. Theories of performativity take a different approach. Based in large part in the work of Judith Butler (1990, 1993, 2004), performative theories of gender critique the idea of "identity" as a single or knowable thing. But if gender is not an identity—that is, a set of attributes and behaviors that belong to a certain kind of person, whether by nature or by training—what is it?

In her 1990 book *Gender Trouble*, Butler took on two basic but not quite identical issues. The first was Gayle Rubin's idea of the sex/gender system, the assumption that biological sex is the raw material that social forces shape into "gender." The second was how "gender," which for Butler meant everything produced by discourse under the binary, opposed pairs of signs "man" and "woman," "masculine" and "feminine," and so on, operates at all. At the foundation of her discussion is the claim that "there is no gender identity behind the expressions of gender;" that identity is performatively constituted by the very "'expressions' that are said to be its results" (Butler, 1990: 25).

Butler moved the argument that gender was produced by social relations into a new arena, claiming that gender "ought not to be conceived merely as the cultural inscription of meaning on a pregiven sex . . . gender must also designate the very apparatus of production whereby the sexes themselves are established. As a result, gender is not to culture as sex is to nature; gender is the discursive/

cultural means by which 'sexed nature' or 'a natural sex' is produced and established as 'prediscursive'"(Butler, 1990: 7). Our bodies are not beings in and of themselves. We understand them through the constructs of binary sex: without the ideas "man" and "woman" our bodies wouldn't make sense to us. In some ways like the cognitive psychologists, Butler argued that "sex" is a mechanism that makes otherwise incomprehensible biological material coherent as male and female bodies.

For Butler, biological sex is not only not a fact of nature, its production through discourse is coercive and prescriptive. "Sex" itself is "a regulatory ideal, a forcible and differential materialization of bodies" (Butler, 1993: 22), not a self-evident explanation for why various bodies look certain ways. "Sex" makes sense of bodies through a regime of binarized difference, and any bodies that do not exactly fit into the binary are denied, rejected, surgically altered, or reassigned (Butler, 2004).

In Butler's view, sex and gender are produced by and perpetuate norms of behavior, feeling, action, and psyche. Part of this process is to repudiate everything that does not conform to this compulsory heterosexuality. At this point, then, Butler makes her most radical move, an analysis that distances her from previous U.S. feminist scholars. Rather than seeing gender as extending from sex, Butler argues that *sex* is produced by *gender*. That is, the construction of masculinity and femininity requires the belief in a naturally bifurcated structure of biological sex. In order for gender to seem inevitable, sex (that is, the ways in which are bodies are made intelligible to us by being assigned as male or female, never neither, never both, and never just something else) must appear self-evident. *Of course* everyone is biologically either male or female. *Of course* anatomy, sex, and gender are mapped directly onto each other. And *of course* sexuality is motivated by gendered desires.

For Butler, there is no "of course" about it. We are conscripted—press-ganged—into gender even before we are conscious of it. We are forced into gender from birth—the words "it's a girl," are in fact a command and a threat: "be a girl; if you want to be a real person with a real identity, act out girlness." Most of the ways to "be a girl" are implicit within discourse, and others must be explicitly enforced by parents, educational institutions, magazines, and so on. And of course, the most effective way in which gender is enforced is the fact that it just feels natural to behave in certain ways, "as a girl."

Butler's central point is that gender performativity is neither optional nor natural. Once a child has been "girled," for example, with the words "it's a girl," she is compelled to perform girlness and (or perhaps because) she doesn't even recognize this compulsion. Gender is performed reiteratively through an array of "acts, gestures and desires" (the girl really *wants* to be a girl) that imply an essential gendered self. But for Butler, these "acts and gestures, articulated and enacted desires create the illusion of an interior and organizing gender core" (Butler, 1990: 136, my emphasis). There's no subject underneath the gender, no universal self. Rather, the self is constructed through its strenuous performance of gender.

How Gender Is Enforced

Many people feel that their gender is the most intrinsic part of them, deeply rooted in their beings. According to Butler, though, nothing could be further from the truth. Gender is "a construction that conceals its genesis; the tacit collective agreement to perform, produce, and sustain discrete and polar genders as cultural fictions is obscured by the credibility of those productions—and the punishments that attend to not agreeing to believe in them" (Butler, 1990: 140). Considering that gender is often represented as a natural outgrowth of biological sex, it's surprising how intense the penalties can be for subverting the gendered order of things.

Gender is enforced in many ways, from the subtle to the violent. From the earliest ages, children's clothes are divided into "boys" and "girls"; there are few options that are not explicitly gendered. Divergence from the norms of gender are often met with a range of responses from gentle correction to shaming and humiliation. As children learn gender, they are often eager to police gender conformity in others: nonconforming children are asked "are you a girl or a boy?"

Gender-nonconforming youth are among the most victimized in the United States and represent a disproportionate number of homeless young people, often because they have run away, have been thrown out by family members, or hve been forced out of school by the violence of schoolmates. Some reports indicate that one in five transgender individuals need or are at risk of needing homeless shelter assistance for these reasons (Ray, 2006). However, since shelters are gender segregated, transgender and gender-nonconforming people are often refused housing or are placed in a hostile environment because they are not "really" women or men.

Discrimination against people who transgress gender boundaries is legal almost everywhere in the United States, despite efforts to include gender expression in anti-discrimination statutes.

Alternative Gender Arrangements

Historical Challenges to Gender

Although the binary gender divide exists in some form in every culture, it has hardly been the only way to define how gender operates. As we've seen, many cultures have names and social roles for women and men who occupy gender outside the norm. If we look back

While still using the conventional signs for "male" and "female," many restrooms are now unisex, allowing people of a variety of genders to use them.

through history, we can find numerous examples of individuals and classes of people who have challenged the gender binary.

Before European colonization, many North American indigenous people integrated the idea of a "third gender" into their social arrangements. These "two-spirit" people (so called because they were thought to contain both male and female spirits) often had specific roles, such as healers, matchmakers, craftspeople, and communicators of traditional songs and wisdom (Jacobs, Thomas, and Lang, 1997). Intersex people, that is, people born with ambiguous primary sexual characteristics, have been chronicled in diverse sources: the Greek myth of Hermaphroditus, Jewish legal debates in the Talmud, and early modern English legal reference books (Greenberg, 2006).

In societies that have been strictly defined by the gender binary, there have been women and men who could not conform to these rules. One of the most famous examples in European history was Joan of Arc, a young woman who grew up in fifteenth-century France. Inspired by religious visions, she dressed in soldier's armor to join the French struggle against

English occupation (Warner, 1981). When she was captured by English troops, Joan was condemned for her cross-dressing as much as for her military efforts; church officials were outraged by her short haircut and male attire, and she was burned at the stake at the age of 19. Joan was not the only woman to see military service as a way to escape the strictures of femininity. Angolan "king" Nzinga ruled in the mid-seventeenth century and led her troops against Portuguese colonizers. Many women in the United States joined the Continental Army in the Revolutionary War and the armies of both sides of the Civil War (Feinberg, 1996). Indeed, times of upheaval and social change often provide gender-nonconforming women with the ideal environment to slip out of femininity. As the documentary film *She Even Chewed Tobacco* (1983) chronicles, the westward expansion of the United States allowed many women to take on male personae and live out much freer lives than they could have as women back East.

Given the higher social status of men and masculinity in many societies, men who challenge the gender binary often suffer significant marginalization. In seventeenth-century England, men who took on women's clothing were subject to hanging. Men at the top of the social hierarchy were freer to express their gender nonconformity: for example, the Chevalier Charles D'eon, an eighteenth-century French nobleman, wore women's clothes almost exclusively, and Edward Hyde, the governor of New York and New Jersey in the first decade of the eighteenth century, was famous for dressing in ornate women's clothes at ceremonial occasions, including his wife's funeral (Bonomi, 2000).

Celebrations and performance have made space for the stretching and bending of gender boundaries, however. In all-male theatrical traditions from Greek tragedy to the early modern British stage to Japanese kabuki, men played female roles. Several of Shakespeare's comedies feature female characters who disguise themselves as men, which must have been quite a challenge for the young male actors in those roles, since they were men playing women playing men. The Jewish holiday of Purim is celebrated by parties, drinking, and dressing up, which often includes cross-gendered costumes, and Halloween and Mardi Gras have a strong element of drag performances for women and men.

Expectations of gendered behavior have always been historically and politically specific. During World War II, for example, a large percentage of adult men in the United States were fighting, and women were encouraged to take their places in farms, factories, and shops. The U.S. government launched propaganda campaigns to convince women that heavy industrial work, which was essential to the war effort, was not in conflict with gendered expectations and that patriotism should trump femininity. However, as soon as the men returned home from war, an equally powerful campaign was initiated to persuade women that the very same work was inappropriate for them and that their patriotic impulses should be channeled into housework and childrearing. While many women lost their jobs, the rates of women working outside the home never fell back to prewar numbers (Field, 1980).

In the years after World War II, gender was policed especially strictly. At the same time, lesbian and gay life flourished, and gender-nonconforming people often found a safe place in gay environments. Especially in working-class communities, butch lesbians and feminine men established footholds, working in the building trades, as bartenders, or in the beauty industry (D'Emilio, 1983; Kennedy and Davis, 1993).

Since the rise of the second wave of feminism and the LGBT rights movement, attitudes about gender have oscillated, but it is unlikely we will return to the rigidity of earlier years. Although U.S. culture in the twenty-first century seems in some ways more inflexible about the gender binary, especially for children and young adults, there are many more venues for experimenting with gender expression than there were even a few decades ago.

Gender outside the Binary

Transgender performer and activist Kate Bornstein has written of her own experiences with gender, "I know I'm not a man—about that much I'm very clear—and I've come to the conclusion that I'm probably not a woman either, at least not according to a lot of people's rules on this sort of thing. The trouble is, we're living in a world that insists we be one thing or the other" (Bornstein, 1994: 8). Bornstein uses the metaphor of a cult to think about gender: like cults, gender has to defend its boundaries, requires continual demonstrations of allegiance to its rules, demands attacks on its enemies, and makes clear hierarchical distinctions between leaders and followers, insiders and outsiders. Instead of the coercive tactics of gender conformity, Bornstein asks what it would be like if we thought of gender as a voluntary organization, like a bridge club or a political party, or a charitable organization: a group that we choose to join, whose rules we can choose to follow or decide to challenge and change, a group we can leave in favor of an alternative.

Of course, this is much easier said than done. But people all over the world, in a variety of settings, are working to make gender less like a cult. In Sweden the University of Umeå has initiated a project called "Challenging Gender," in which a group of international scholars "contribute to more complex and reflexive gender theory" (Umeå Center for Gender Studies, 2011). AIDS activists in the southern African country of Namibia are using a gender analysis to reduce new HIV infections: by questioning gender hierarchies and binaries and opening up honest conversations about how expectations of gendered behavior can increase sexual transmission of HIV, women, men, and transgender people can reduce their risk of HIV infection (Clifton and Feldman-Jacobs, 2011).

Challenges to gender conformity happen in informal and individual contexts as well. The growing visibility and politicization of transgender communities is an encouraging sign that gender boundaries are more elastic than they seem.

Summary

Gender represents a broad network of behaviors, attitudes, activities, prohibitions, mandates, relationships, identities, and beliefs about how men and women should behave and relate to each other. However, feminist theorists have argued that gender is a social and cultural construction, different from biological and anatomical sex. We can see this in varieties of gender expression.

For centuries, explanations of gender differences were rooted in the physical differences between women and men, both real and imagined. Freudian psychoanalysis locates the origins of gender in girls' desire for a penis and boys' need to identify with their fathers to avoid castration, the fate of girls and women. Ideas about the importance of biology found new life in the late twentieth century from evolutionary biologists, who saw gender as part of the evolutionary mandate to pass along genes. Similarly, some neurobiologists argue that hormonal differences create gender.

A central concept in feminist thought is that gender cannot be separated from social and cultural conditions. Feminist psychoanalysts argue that women's psychology is formed by gendered power relations and by the nurturing role played by mothers, rather than orbiting around the presence or absence of the penis. Feminist psychologists more generally have shown that culture teaches us how to inhabit gender. In addition, they have argued that female-identified values of relatedness and care must be integrated into our understanding of how gender works. Other critics have challenged the focus on biology, showing the importance of environment and context for human development.

Gender is learned in a variety of ways.

Discussion Questions

1. List three differences between girls/women and boys/men that have been reported in research. These can be differences in personality, skills, or conduct. What kinds of contrasting explanation can you give for them? Which do you find most convincing and why?
2. Imagine what it would be like to live in a world in which gender was voluntary rather than mandatory. How would your life experiences be different?
3. Theories of personality development offer different explanations for gender identity and gender roles. What experiences did you have as a child that shaped your gender-role behaviors and attitudes? Explain these from two or three different theoretical positions. Are they consistent with the research on gender-role socialization, or do they contradict it?
4. Apply the Bechdel test to this year's Academy Award nominees for Best Picture. Do any of them pass the test? What does this suggest about how the movie industry constructs our sense of who is or isn't important in our culture?
5. Compare a novel written in the nineteenth century with a novel written in the twenty-first century; examine the ways in which gender prescriptions are used.

Recommended Readings

de Beauvoir, Simone. *The Second Sex*. New York: Vintage, 1949, 2011. A classic discussion of male and female identities as social constructions rather than products of nature.

Halberstam, Judith. *Female Masculinity*. Durham, NC: Duke University Press, 1998. Halberstam explores the variety of ways in which women inhabit masculinity through discussions of novels, movies, and cultural phenomena.

Laqueur, Thomas. *Making Sex: Body and Gender from the Greeks to Freud*. Cambridge, MA: Harvard University Press, 1992. A historical examination of how ideas about the biological differences between women and men changed over time and were products of their era.

Lorde, Audre. *Sister Outsider*. New York: The Crossing Press, 1984, reissued 2007. A landmark volume of essays about the intersections of race, gender, and sexuality. Lorde inspired a generation of feminists of all races to think deeply about the meanings of identity.

Sycamore, Mattilda Bernstein, editor. *Nobody Passes: Rejecting the Rules of Gender and Conformity*. Berkeley, CA: Seal Press, 2006. A collection of essays about resisting conformity to the binaries of gender, race, class, and other identities.

Gender and the Politics of the Body

There are a great many people in the world—I dare say most of 'em—who would say I'm a pervert and a bad person because I'm a transsexual woman. I was born male and now I've got medical and government documents that say I'm female, but I don't call myself a woman, and I *know* I'm not a man. That's the part that upsets the pope—he's worried that talk like that—*not male, not female*—will shatter the natural order of men and women. I look forward to the day it does.

KATE BORNSTEIN, 2012

The human body is not merely flesh and bones; it is also constructed by our culture. This means that while our bodies feel natural and self-evident, they are not purely biological entities: the body's meaning and significance are shaped by cultural ideas that vary tremendously across time and space.

It's almost impossible, too, to separate how a culture aesthetically values different kinds of bodies and the ways in which those bodies are gendered. For example, everyone ages, but aging as a cultural construct has profound consequences for how women experience their senses of self, especially their sexuality. In a culture that values youth, particularly in women, what makes a body desirable is not a trivial question. The cosmetic, fashion, and fitness industries are not only built on women's desires to meet an often unattainable ideal, but in large part those industries *create* those desires. And even though the cosmetics, fashion, and fitness industries are multibillion dollar businesses, many women gain pleasure and even power from using makeup, shopping, and working out.

These contradictions originate in the fact that women are disproportionately judged on physical appearance and that women's bodies are *objectified*—that is, made into things to be inspected and evaluated. Objectification shapes the ways in which women (and indeed, all gendered beings) inhabit their bodies and their worlds. But, as we'll see, women also actively participate in processes of embodiment. This chapter is focused, then, on some highly specific forms of power that have effectively—if differently across times and places—produced the gendered body as a social, political, and cultural phenomenon, while also attending to the ways that women are differently implicated in and by those very processes.

Feminism and the Body

Since the first organized women's movement in the United States during the late nineteenth and early twentieth centuries (see Chapter 13), feminists have recognized the body as a site of political domination. They have protested cultural constraints placed on women's bodies and argued for women's rightful control of their own bodies. Women at the First Feminist Mass Meeting in the United States in 1914, for example, argued that the right "to ignore fashion" was a political one. U.S. feminists in 1968 echoed their call; they threw their bras into "a freedom trash can" during a demonstration of the Miss America Pageant to symbolically protest how women's bodies are controlled, whether through codes of fashion, ideal notions of femininity and beauty, forced sterilization, abuse, or rape (Bordo, 1993: 15–23). In the United States today, maintaining a woman's reproductive freedom remains a centerpiece of feminist political struggle (see Chapter 13).

The body is a complex construction: it is a physical thing the movements of which can be controlled explicitly by force and implicitly by social pressures; a place onto which gender is written and from which it is expressed; and a symbolic space in which selfhood, identity, and self-worth are worked through. Understanding how the body is variously constructed and the impact of these constructions on women's lives, experiences, and choices has been essential to feminist scholarship since its beginnings. Yet it was in the late 1980s that the most exciting and theoretically challenging research on the body began to emerge in feminist studies (Conboy et al., 1997: 7–8). Much of this research was premised on the view of the body as a site of struggle on which battles for competing ideologies are waged. As we shall see in the subsequent sections, some of this work has been interdisciplinary, although much of it has come out of particular fields such as biology, philosophy, and anthropology.

Bodies are constructed through language, practices, and representations. Each of these can produce different ways of understanding the body and its relationship to the self, often producing intersecting, overlapping, and contradictory images. Feminists have been at the forefront of research on the way bodies become gendered—or written over with meanings and ideologies concerning masculinity and femininity—and become lived, or experienced. The discussion below focuses on both the constraints placed on women by various constructions of the body and how women have creatively resisted such conceptualizations and altered their bodies in protest against them.

Mind/Body Dualism

In Western thought, at least since Plato, the body has been juxtaposed with the mind and seen as inferior to it. This distinction between mind and body is an aspect of what is often referred to as "Cartesian dualism," named for the Western philosopher René Descartes. Descartes's famous dictum "I think, therefore, I am" vividly encapsulates the widespread association in Western culture of the mind and its reasoning processes with the self. The body places limitations on the self, according to this view, and must, therefore, be transcended. Everyday language encodes this understanding of the body as an entity distinct from the self: a person is likely to say, "I have a body," not "I am a body" (Mairs, 1997: 298). Cartesian dualism is so taken for granted that it can be understood as an unwritten, official doctrine of Western societies.

This mind/body dualism is also part of the Christian tradition that has influenced Western thinking: the body is seen in opposition not only to the mind and the self but also to the "soul" and the "spirit." The body, in this view, represents the animal side of human existence, possessing unruly appetites and desires that must be controlled and suppressed for salvation.

What is most significant for women about this conceptualization is that "woman" has been associated with the body, while "man" has been linked with the mind. "Woman" equated with the body is, therefore, not mind and not self. She is not a self or subject but an object, not spirit but flesh. She is aligned against reason (a woman is more emotional, intuitive, and irrational than a man, we still hear today) and against spiritual salvation (woman, it is still widely believed, is naturally a temptress and seductress, as we saw in Chapter 1). She must be controlled.

This logic has had profound significance for how women have been valued, treated, and constrained in their opportunities and choices. As Simone de Beauvoir argued in *The Second Sex*, the entrapment of women in their bodies means that women have been made "the second sex," defined by a lack of masculine qualities and traits that men assume stem from a natural defectiveness (Conboy et al., 1997). As Susan Bordo has argued:

> The cost for such projections to women is obvious. For if, whatever the historical content of the duality, the body is the negative term, and if woman is the body, then women are that negativity, whatever it may be: distraction from knowledge, seduction away from God, capitulation to sexual desire…failure of will, even death. (Bordo, 1993: 5)

The Body as Natural

The association of women with the body also allies femaleness with the negative term in another set of associations: nature/culture. The body has been seen as natural and the mind as the source of human cultural control over nature's destructive forces. Although in the contemporary United States the environmental and New Age movements might suggest otherwise, the predominant view in Western thinking is that nature acts against human interests and needs to be tamed and subdued. The association of women with nature arises from the function of woman's body in giving birth and nurturing children (see Chapter 1), but de Beauvoir's (1949, 2011) insights are again instructive: she argues that if women's bodies have constrained them, it is not because this is natural or inevitable but because women have been interpreted through the lens of culture, thought of as "natural" by men who have created the very category of "nature" to serve their own aims. Evidence from around the world indicates that women have combined motherhood with almost every task imaginable. This suggests the cultural, rather than the natural, character of such limitations in Western culture where "woman" has been defined by her body and seen as trapped in nature because of it. This has not only rendered her as object not as subject, as other not as self, but has also served as a rationalization for her domination and subordination. In contemporary society, science plays a particularly important role in this subordination because scientific theory and practice are concerned with knowledge of, and mastery over, nature (Jardanova, 1993). In nineteenth-century science, nature was often even conceptualized as a woman "to be unveiled, unclothed, and penetrated by masculine science" (Jardanova, 1993: 376).

The construction of the female as natural has had particular consequences for non-Western women and women of color, who have been seen as doubly natural and "other" due to both gender and race. In Western racial discourse, the "naturalness" of black and brown bodies has been equated with animality, in particular with an animal-like sexuality. This belief was perhaps nowhere clearer than in Victorian England, where, under the guise of scientific interest, the African woman Saartje Baartman, known as the "Hottentot Venus," was displayed nude in a public pornographic exhibition disguised as science. Baartman was probed at by anatomists and stared at by a repulsed but fascinated public audience. Her distinctive bodily traits—enlarged vaginal lips and protruding buttocks—were taken as signs of a rampant and animalistic sexuality (Gilman, 1985). This conclusion reinforced the notion at the time that African women were savages, devoid of the sexual modesty necessary for achieving "true" femininity.

The bodies of Asian women have also been represented as particularly erotic and exotic, but unlike the bodies of black women, they have not been associated with savagery and rampant desire but with smallness, timidity, and subservience, traits that have made them desirable to many men in Western societies. This perception has led to the development of a highly profitable mail-order business in which Asian women are sold to Western male consumers as brides. The sensationalist attention that activists and journalists have paid to this industry and the stereotypes on which it is built elide the variety of strategies that Asian women themselves enact in seeking husbands in the West (Constable, 2005). In the absence of such knowledge, the monolithic and objectifying depiction of Asian women as "mail-order brides" encourages a view of them as either exploitative gold diggers or docile kewpie dolls. In Australia, Filipina women have felt the consequences of these stereotypes in a profoundly bodily form: they are disproportionately the victims of domestic abuse and homicide (Saroca, 2007: 33). One site of resistance to essentialist constructions of Asian womanhood is found in the plays of David Hwang. In *M. Butterfly*, he brilliantly critiques the orientalist view contained in Puccini's opera *Madama Butterfly* that an Asian woman's highest goal in life would be to marry a white man. In that play, his exquisitely demure Asian woman turns out to be a man.

In Western thought, then, the body has been understood not only as the physical ground of gender differences, but also as the gendered ground of racial differences. Because the body has conventionally been understood as a natural, relatively unchangeable entity and gender differences are thought to arise from the body, gender is also seen as natural and, thus, inevitable. The differences between the bodies of women and men have been taken as the justification for treating women and men differently. Yet feminist scholarship on the body in the last 30 years reveals that the body is far from being a stable ground of sex differences, as we will see below. Indeed, the very instability of the body as a ground for gender difference allows people to use their bodies to resist constraining definitions of femininity—and masculinity.

The Nature of Sex Differences

As indicated in Chapter 2, Western philosophical definitions of "woman" have been based on faulty theories and biased cultural

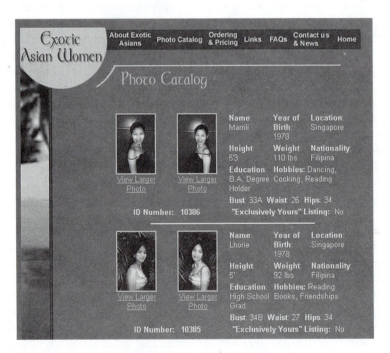

Sample page from online catalog for "exotic Asian women" mail-order brides.

assumptions. This is also true of biological definitions of the sexes focused on the body, but while today it may be easy to see that Aristotle's view of women as "imperfect men" was an ideological construct that served political ends, it is more difficult to conclude the same for definitions of the sexes grounded in scientific research. Is science not, after all, the unbiased, objective pursuit of truth? Are scientific definitions of the sexes not based on biological facts that can be observed and measured with precise and accurate instruments?

Historians of science have documented repeatedly how the gender, race, and class assumptions of scientists influence their supposedly objective, scientific experiments and the conclusions drawn from them (see, for example, Keller, 1985; Longino and Doell, 1987; Martin, 1987, 1994; Haraway, 1989; Fausto-Sterling, 2000; Jordan-Young, 2010). Thus, although science is framed in a language of rationality and objectivity, the apparent neutrality with which it speaks and through which it gains authority conceals its cultural assumptions (Jackson et al., 1993: 363). Because science has until recently been dominated by men and so often been used to "prove" male superiority, revealing its cultural biases has been an important feminist project.

Cultural factors affect the very questions scientists deem important enough to ask and which studies are deemed important enough to fund. That researchers in many Western countries choose to focus on identifying the differences between women and men, rather than the similarities, is itself a product of the history, as well as the social and political agendas, of these nations. This interest in difference is so deeply embedded in U.S. society, for example, that suggesting that the study of gender differences might be misguided and that research on gender similarities might be unproductive tends to strike most people as absurd. Why? Today, most scientists believe it

is wrongheaded to look for biological explanations of many other kinds of difference. Yet, it was not that long ago that learned cultural differences between Jews and non-Jews were attributed to biological causes, an assumption that found its most hideous expression in the notion in Nazi Germany that Jews were so different from non-Jews that they were actually "life unworthy of life" and therefore in need of extermination. Today, most scientists find claims that vast biological differences exist between groups of people to be unwarranted, and the idea that biological factors best explain ethnic and cultural differences between people rightfully strikes many people as ludicrous. Might this not be true for gender as well?

The Gendered Brain

Cultural assumptions affect scientific investigations not only at the level of the questions asked but at every stage of the research process as well. The history of brain research into gender and racial differences clearly indicates this. The claim that women and men have differing brains, and therefore necessarily think differently, has been a longstanding one in Western society. Such supposed natural "brain differences" have been used historically to rationalize and further systems of oppression and to determine social policy. For example, toward the end of the nineteenth century, it was erroneously concluded that white men were naturally superior to women in intelligence because of the larger size of their brains (Fabian, 2010). This assumption was used to justify women's exclusion from higher education. Brain measurements were also taken of African Americans and Native Americans, two other groups assumed to have intelligence levels inferior to those of white men, and a similar "conclusion" was reached: their smaller brain size was taken as evidence of lower intelligence. We know

now, however, that the size differential noted by these scientists was based on measurement techniques affected by pre-existing cultural assumptions about the supposed inferior intelligence of white women and of women and men of color. Craniometrists (the scientists who measured skull sizes) consistently underestimated the cranial capacity of these groups, which biased their results. Even if such measurements had been correct, they would hold no significance today since it has been repeatedly shown that human brain size is not related to intelligence.

In the 1980s and 1990s, differences in brain structure and in the way women and men use their brains became the basis for theories of innate gender differences. In the wake of one study conducted in 1982, which reported a difference in size of the corpus callosum (the band of white matter connecting the left and right hemispheres of the brain) in nine men and five women, a virtual industry of brain lateralization research arose. The popular press was soon awash in feature articles about gender differences in the brain, claiming that they were responsible for everything from women's intuition and difficulties with physics to women's stronger verbal skills and more holistic way of thinking. However, as molecular biologist Anne Fausto-Sterling has detailed in her book *Sexing the Body* (2000), this research is not as straightforward as we might suppose. For example, "[t]he corpus callosum is a structure that is difficult to separate from the rest of the brain, and so complex in its irregular three dimensions as to be unmeasurable" (Fausto-Sterling, 2000: 120–1). Despite the fanfare that accompanies the publication of each new piece of scientific "proof" of binary gender characteristics, the scientific evidence supporting counter arguments generally fail to get the same publicity. The case of the best-selling book *The Female Brain* provides a perfect example (Brizendine, 2006). When it was published, it caused a sensation in the popular media, garnering a lot of very positive

---

Box 5.1 IS THERE A FEMALE BRAIN? TWO SCIENTISTS REVIEW *THE FEMALE BRAIN* BY LOUANN BRIZENDINE

Despite the author's extensive academic credentials, *The Female Brain* disappointingly fails to meet even the most basic standards of scientific accuracy and balance. The book is riddled with scientific errors and is misleading about the processes of brain development, the neuroendocrine system, and the nature of sex differences in general. At the 'big picture' level, three errors stand out. First, human sex differences are elevated almost to the point of creating different species, yet virtually all differences in brain structure, and most differences in behaviour, are characterized by small average differences and a great deal of male–female overlap at the individual level. Second, data on structural and functional differences in the brain are routinely framed as if they must precede all sex differences in behaviour. Finally, the focus on hormone levels to the virtual exclusion of the systems that interpret them (and the mutual regulatory interactions between receptor and secretion systems) is especially lamentable, given the book's clinical emphasis on hormone therapies.

Source: Rebecca M. Young and Evan Balaban, "Psychoneuroindoctrinology," *Nature* 443, 12 (October 2006).

press. Yet it was actually panned in scientific journals like *Nature* (see Box 5.1).

The fact that *The Female Brain* was written by a woman should serve as a crucial reminder that women are often guilty of the scientific phenomenon called "neurosexism" (Fine, 2010). That term refers to the underlying gender bias in the scientific study of so-called "sex differences." The most popular version of neurosexism currently lies in the arena of brain organization research, which hypothesizes that the surge of prenatal hormones delivered to male fetuses in utero explains the ostensibly distinct emotional, intellectual, and sexual characteristics associated with male and female persons. One psychologist argues that men and women are "hard-wired" for systemized thinking and empathic feeling, respectively (Baron-Cohen, 2003). Perhaps because of the cultural value we have come to place on the high-tech and thoroughly computerized dimensions of our lives, the term "hard-wired" has now entered the popular lexicon in the United States to refer to the underlying design features of differently gendered brains. In connoting a blueprint and a function, that term renders supposed male/female brain differences not only natural but also good, and probably permanent. Again, however, there are several serious limitations of this body of work.

Decades of research on brain organization in humans were inspired initially by research on rats, and even there researchers have only found links between differences in hormones and differences in brain size, but never links between differential brain size and behavior (Fine, 2010: 104). Moreover, drawing a clear line from rats to humans is hardly unproblematic. Because studies of hormone delivery cannot be done on pregnant women (for obvious ethical reasons), and because researchers cannot construct controlled experiments on human subjects—administering the hormone and watching its effects, as they do with rats—the only option left is to examine gender-differentiated experiences, personalities, and attitudes that develop in childhood, long after the initial infusion of the hormones that are said to be their cause. Other problems with this research abound. In a close examination of over 300 peer-reviewed scientific articles published between 1967 and 2000 concerning the relationship between brain organization and the development of gender identity and roles among humans, one researcher found a series of patterned flaws in scientific method, reasoning, and use of evidence (Jordan-Young, 2010). Most notably, these studies assume an impossible-to-prove linear path from the initial delivery of hormones to human fetuses, on the one hand, to the development of such complex structures as behaviors, desires, and identities, on the other hand. These studies often cite each other's data, bolstering the number of experiments from which they can draw conclusions. And in the interest of advancing their views about gender difference being rooted in the brain, these studies fail to account for the fact that invariably the majority of research subjects—male and female—occupy the middle ground rather than the two poles on any particular measure of gender (Jordan-Young, 2010).

So are there any foolproof biological signs of the physical differences between women and men? Surely, differences in genital anatomy, hormones, or chromosomes allow us to define women and men as biologically distinct. At first glance, this might seem the case, but a closer look at the range of variation among females and males in basic bodily traits suggests otherwise.

The Sexed Body: Hormones, Chromosomes, and Genitalia

The modern biological definition of a man and a woman is a genetic one: an individual with two X chromosomes is designated a female and an individual with one X and one Y chromosome, a male. But even this seemingly incontrovertible distinction has its exceptions. For example, some "genetic males" with XY chromosomes have a rare mutation of the Y chromosome that results in a lack of male genitalia. These individuals look typically female, including having fully developed breasts at puberty, but don't have female reproductive organs. Other people have a variety of chromosomal combinations—XO, XXY, XXX, and XYY—making their clear assignment as "male" or "female" difficult.

Even in people with standard chromosomal distribution of XX and XY, hormones do not predict identity. The common scientific view that differences in women's and men's behavior are explicable in terms of the presence of differing "sex hormones" in their bodies is a popularly accepted one, often difficult to dislodge. It has, for example, become commonplace to blame complex human behaviors, such as male aggression, on the supposed "male" hormone testosterone or women's unhappiness on fluctuating levels of the supposed "female" hormone estrogen. Some critics of women's participation in politics have even argued that female hormonal fluctuations might cause erratic behavior, which would preclude responsible decision making. During the Cold War it was not unusual to hear that women could never be entrusted with the presidency of the United States since such biologically based erratic thinking might lead to nuclear disaster. How hormones are invoked to explain behavior is also gendered:

> [A]lthough male hormones are used to account for general masculine proclivities (such as aggression) only rarely is any individual man's behaviour explained in these terms. When a man loses his temper we seldom hear anyone say, "It's just an excess of androgen," yet how often women's anger is explained in terms of the "time of the month"…(Jackson et al., 1993: 364)

Such ideas reinforce the image of woman as more trapped in her body than man, even though studies of these hormonal effects have produced contradictory and inconclusive results, and both women and men have both estrogen *and* testosterone in their bodies, although at different levels.

Again, the problem lies with the biases scientists bring to their studies of hormones and gender. Anne Fausto-Sterling (2000), in documenting the history of hormone research, has shown that it has been no less burdened with unproven assumptions and misinterpretations than the history of brain research, which she has also studied. She painstakingly shows how the choices endocrinologists have made about what to name a particular hormone, how to measure it, and how to interpret its effects have been so greatly influenced by cultural ideas about gender as to render the assumption that "sex hormones" exist questionable.

In fact, the primary role of hormones in the bodies of both women and men is not to control behavior but to work at the cellular level to govern cell growth, cell differentiation, cell physiology, and cell death. Hormones may be present in different quantities in males and females and might affect the same tissues differently, but all hormones operate throughout the bodies of both women and men. There is, in other words, no hormone specific to either men or women. Despite this, scientists have labeled some of these chemical secretions "male" hormones (*androgen*, meaning "to create a man") and others "female" hormones (*estrogen*, meaning "to create estrus," which itself means "crazy," "wild," or "insane" and which also refers in animals to the period when females are "in heat"), thus gendering them and infusing them with cultural assumptions about women and men. The results of research on the activities of these substances in the bodies of women and men have been similarly affected by preexisting gendered assumptions, leading Fausto-Sterling and other biologists to call for abandoning the organizing metaphor of the sex hormone in endocrinology studies altogether.

The Politics of "Nature"

The previous discussion shows that defining males and females biologically, that is, determining their "sex," is a complicated business. This is so not just because biology is complex, but also because "our debates about the body's biology are always simultaneously moral, ethical, and political debates about social and political equality and the possibilities for change" (Fausto-Sterling, 2000: 255). The stakes are high in such debates: if women and men can be shown to be different, then it is an easy next step to conclude that such differences, and the benefits and drawbacks associated with them, are natural and we need not do anything to change them. No better example exists than the statement made in 2005 by then Harvard University president Lawrence Summers. At an academic conference about increasing diversity in the fields of science and engineering, Summers suggested that innate differences may explain why women do not succeed in math and science careers at the same rate as men, and why women may be underrepresented in the math and engineering departments of top research universities. That kind of statement turns a social and cultural phenomenon—the fact that women are discouraged from pursuing careers in science and are not offered opportunities equal to their male counterparts—into a biological one: women just aren't as good. Biology is enlisted to make arguments about public policy.

Discourse/Knowledge/Power

In the last few decades, feminist scholarship has focused on how the female body is created through *discourse*: cultural phenomena that include representations, commodification, reproduction, and technology. The role of language in the body's construction has been a particularly fruitful area of feminist inquiry.

Language is a system through which we construct and order reality, interact and live in the world, and transform social existence. It is also a system tied to how power is distributed both socially and materially in any given society. Language is tied to power through *discourse*; that is, systems of knowledge supported by institutions and practices that create a picture for people of what is true and what is not. Historically, various institutions, such as the medical, psychological, and religious establishments, have produced images of women as frail, helpless, dependent, passive, submissive, childlike, and emotional creatures, defining these traits as inevitable, natural, and normal. This "discourse of femininity" not only circumscribes women's lives and choices but also brings them into "the norm," in line with the standard ideas and behaviors desired by adherents with the power to construct and disseminate discourses. In contemporary Western societies, science is a privileged discourse, one that is widely believed to "speak the truth" about sex differences and women's bodies. Individuals who diverge from what science claims is natural, normal, or healthy are labeled "deviant," "abnormal," or "sick" and often feel themselves to be just that.

Gender and the Medicalization of the Body

As we've seen in this chapter, scientific discourse has been central in defining women's bodies. This has occurred primarily through the "medicalization" of the body. In the nineteenth century, as the field of medicine became professionally organized and increasingly the domain of male doctors, the female body became a site of medical knowledge and practice. In earlier years, women had been healers, midwives, and even physicians and surgeons. However, as medicine became an increasingly commercial activity, rather than a part of care-taking centered in the home that had tradi-tionally been part of women's domestic duties, women were excluded, and often forcefully so, from the business of medicine. Medicine became a male-dominated profession charged with gaining "knowledge" of the body. As in many other spheres of Western thought, the male was taken as the norm and the female was found deficient by comparison. Routine bodily functions unique to women such as menstruation, childbirth, and menopause were reinterpreted as diseases, and treated as such.

A number of women authors have worked to dispel such negative notions about meno-pause not only in the United States (Sheehy, 1998), but also in Turkey (Cifcili et al., 2009), Denmark (Hvas, 2001), and Iran (Khademi, 2003). In urban Iran, women consider meno-pause to be a natural and even positive stage of life, particularly for heterosexual women who can now enjoy sex without the fear of pregnancy.

The medicalization of bodies also impacts negatively on intersexed individuals, often subjected to profound and invasive forms of medicalization; yet for them, it largely occurs soon after birth, when they have no ability to protest. Intersexed people have genitalia, chromosomes, and/or gonads in a combi-nation that differs from the most common configuration for either boys or girls. It has been estimated that approximately 1.7% of all births in the United States today are inter-sexed, a rate that would result in a city of 300,000 having 5,100 intersexed individuals in its population (Fausto-Sterling, 2000: 53–4). In other cases, intersex conditions manifest during puberty. Despite the fact, then, that nature presents society with a perfect oppor-tunity to challenge our dichotomized gender categories, physicians and parents usually insist on assigning one of two dichotomized categories to intersexed infants. They may even undergo "clarifying" surgery to bring their external appearance in line with social expectations about masculinity and feminin-ity. Genital surgery is most often conducted on infant girls who are perceived to have an overly large clitoris and on infants who have XY chromosomes and/or male gonads but whose penises are perceived as too small for sexual function. Overwhelmingly, then, the cultural assumptions and expectations that motivate such surgery revolve around hetero-sexual intercourse (vaginal penetration by a penis) and reproduction (Karkazais, 2008).

A further motivation is to enhance what the medical establishment calls "psycho-social functioning," or one's sense of being normal. Over the last 20 years in the United States, an intersex movement has emerged, com-posed of individuals who protest such surgery, claiming that it is a form of genital mutila-tion that ruins future sexual pleasure (Lorber, 2001: 228). Despite that movement, genital surgeries are still a common "solution" to the perceived problem of being intersexed. Often the surgery is performed not at the recom-mendation of doctors, but at the insistence of the parents, who need to "see" the evidence of unambiguous gender in the genitals of their infant child so as to be able to convincingly socialize it accordingly.

Discourses of Sexuality

Since the nineteenth century the discourses of science and medicine have increasingly gained hold over women's sexuality. This process has had significant consequences for how women experience their bodies and their selves. Susan Bordo, following philosopher Michel Foucault (1980), describes how, during this time period, the incessant probing of the body and the mind of the patient for knowledge about sexual practices paradoxically forced sexuality inward. What were understood as sexual *acts* before being subjected to science's scrutinizing eye became transformed into sexual *identities*, which were then represented as immoral and/or diseased:

> (T)he medicalization of sexuality in the nineteenth century…recast sex from a family

matter into a private, dark, bodily secret that was appropriately investigated by such specialists as doctors, psychiatrists, and school educators. The constant probing and interrogation…ferreted out, eroticized and solidified all sorts of sexual types and perversions, which people then experienced (although they had not done so originally) as defining their bodily possibilities and pleasures. The practice

---

Box 5.2   CASTER SEMENYA, ATHLETE

In September of 2009, South African runner Caster Semenya crushed her opponents in the 800-meter race in the World Championships in Athletics, held in Berlin. Immediately thereafter, she was suspended from competition pending the outcome of "gender verification tests" to prove that she is a woman. Under orders of the International Association of Athletics Federation, Semenya was subjected to a series of physically and psychically invasive examinations, which included the photographing of her genitals while her feet were in stirrups. As the controversy unfolded, Semenya chose not speak to broadcast media, fearing that her deep voice would only inspire further discourse over her perceived gender ambiguity. Though she was cleared to compete as a woman 11 long months later, she endured much humiliation in the interim, as details of her tests, suggesting that she had a male genetic make-up, were leaked to the press.

of the medical confessional, in other words, in its constant foraging for sexual secrets and hidden stories, actually created new sexual secrets. (Bordo, 1993: 142–3)

Medical and psychiatric researchers produced "knowledge" of women's bodies and sexual behaviors and declared, based on standard assumptions of ideal femininity, that some of those behaviors were natural and others were deviant. In general, those women with little or no sexual desire but who complied to satisfy their husbands' sexual needs and to have children were deemed "good" women. The sexual woman was viewed as sick, dangerous, and whorelike. Sigmund Freud, perhaps the most significant sex researcher of the day, dissented from this view. He saw women as sexual beings and identified the repression of their sexual desires as a major cause of neurosis. He nonetheless had his own notions of what constituted normal female sexuality: he believed, for example, that women's sexual fulfillment could come about only in the form of vaginal orgasm (as distinct from clitoral orgasm, which Freud considered "masculine" and childish) and the subsequent bearing and nurturing of children. Lesbian sexuality, according to Freud, was a neurosis based on lesbian women's inability to give over their early masculine identification with the clitoris, the "inferior penis," to the vagina, thereby rejecting their true feminine role as passive receptacles in heterosexual vaginal intercourse.

Through such "normalizing discourses," women's sexual appetites and behaviors were tamed and new identities created. Nowhere was this more evident than in the creation of the category of "homosexuality" at the end of the nineteenth century. As people's sexuality became an important focus of study, medical and psychiatric researchers and practitioners sought and gained information about same-sex sexual behaviors, organizing it into a "discourse of homosexuality," deeming desire between

members of the opposite sex normal and same sex desire abnormal. This medicalizing moved beyond mere sexual activity, defining "the homosexual" as a certain kind of person defined not just by sexual desires and behaviors that had always existed, but also by personality traits, physical characteristics, and moral qualities (Foucault, 1980). Medicine and psychiatry created this category of identity through organizing information about same-sex sexual relations under the heading "homosexuality."

What is particularly significant about this and other discourses is that people have great difficulty constructing identities outside of them. Indeed, just the opposite occurs: we find meaning and identity in them. Discourses create categories of identity to sustain power relations and patterns of domination by speaking the supposed truth about an individual's normality. We then internalize and reproduce these norms: their power works from within. If people understand themselves and their desires in terms of these normalizing discourses, they will recognize themselves in talk about normality and abnormality. If their behavior diverges from the norm, they will most likely feel aberrant or deviant and may even secretly believe something is wrong with them, rather than seeing the norms themselves as a form of social control.

Psychoanalytical theories like Freud's dominated Western beliefs about sexuality for many decades and represented a set of assumptions about "normal" sexual behavior and roles for women. In the 1940s and 1950s, Alfred Kinsey conducted an extensive survey of the sexual behavior of women and men (1948, 1953). His findings, based on interviews, astonished his contemporaries. He found that many people engaged in a range of sexual behaviors considered deviant by standards of that time. In fact, the majority of Americans participated in at least one of these supposedly aberrant behaviors, such as masturbation, same-sex sex, and oral–genital sex.

Beginning in the 1960s, sex researchers Masters and Johnson continued to produce unexpected results. Their research was an influential corrective to long-held hetero-sexist and androcentric beliefs about female sexuality. They realized that female orgasms result from clitoral stimulation and that the phases of female sexual response are the same regardless of the source of stimulation, a direct rejection of the notion that a woman's full sexual satisfaction requires sexual intercourse with a man. Their studies indicated that women generally reach orgasm more quickly and with greater intensity from manual stimulation of the clitoris, especially when they stimulate themselves. This finding suggests that delays in achieving or failure to achieve orgasm during intercourse may be a result of techniques that are not compatible with women's physiological responsiveness.

Of course, although laboratory studies of sexuality and physiological sexual responses have discredited many old assumptions and raised new possibilities, sexual desire involves more than just simple physical response. Sexuality is also a complex *social* construction; many feminists have pointed out that focusing solely on biology in our attempts to study and understand sexuality limits our comprehension of the multiple factors that combine to create sexual desire and sexual satisfaction.

Feminist Philosophers and Anthropologists Rethink the Body

Perhaps it is because Western philosophy has constructed so many dualisms that subjugate women that feminist philosophers have set about to wholly rethink the body. They have done so in ways that speak not just to philosophy but also to politics. And since, as philosophers, they tend to operate in a highly abstract and conceptual realm, this section will try to ground their work by putting it in conversation with feminist and queer anthropology.

In the late 1970s and early 1980s, French feminists such as Hélène Cixous and Luce Irigaray theorized that because women's difference from men is located in the body, it is the female body and female sexuality to which women must turn for a source of female creativity that is both authentic and disruptive. Cixous has referred to this as *l'écriture féminine*, "writing in the feminine." In her article "The Laugh of the Medusa," she exhorts women to "write yourself. Your body must be heard. Only then will the immense resources of unconscious spring forth" (Cixous 1981: 250). Many contemporary American women have begun

---

Box 5.3   USES OF THE EROTIC: THE EROTIC AS POWER

The erotic is a measure between our sense of self and the chaos of our strongest feelings. It is an internal sense of satisfaction to which, once we have experienced it, we know we can aspire. For having experienced the fullness of this depth of feeling and recognizing its power, in honor and self-respect we can require no less of ourselves.

Source: Reprinted with permission from *Sister Outsider* by Audre Lorde, 53–4. Copyright © 1984 by Audre Lorde, The Crossing Press, a division of Ten Speed Press, Berkeley, CA. 94707, www.tenspeed.com.

to take this exhortation literally: through tattooing and piercing, they inscribe their own bodies and use them to "write their own stories." Women often explain their body modifications in terms of exerting control over meaning, as a means of replacing the predetermined scripts of what women do with their bodies with their own signifying marks. As Margo DeMello (2000: 173) writes, for women, the tattoo is often "an important step in reclaiming their bodies, and the narrative in which they describe this process is equally important." Frances Mascia-Lees and Patricia Sharpe (1994) have found that women speak of piercing and tattooing as enabling them to control pain, which they could not do in situations where they felt victimized, to dictate some of their own terms in the sexualizing and eroticizing of their bodies, to accept their bodies as desirable, and to resist external control, using the body as a canvas for their own self expression. As one woman writes on a website:

> Tattoos are an important part of who I am. They let me take control of my own body and appearance. They make me feel better about myself, and they improve my self-image. They let me express who I am and what I believe, and they will always be a part of me. (http://www.wiccan-refuge.com/tattoorant.html, September 28, 2004)

Tattooing provides an example of the view that without new ways to imagine the body, there can be no vantage point from which to transform culture (Bordo, 1993: 41). Yet taking control over our bodies may not always be so liberating. Studies of anorexic women show that they, too, see themselves as reclaiming their bodies.

Feminists have critiqued the inherent if unacknowledged maleness that undergirds Western philosophical approaches to "the body" as if it were a single entity, as if *bodies* were not multiple and specific. Philosopher Elizabeth Grosz argues for a theory of corporeal feminism that looks to the politics of experience and a sense of self that emerges from the physical and social construction of sexed bodies. Rather than totally rejecting sex difference as a complete social construction, she analyzes the bodily effects of the way sex is made specific and the ways that our subject positions are rooted in the sexed body. She does not limit her analysis to female bodies, but rather examines the specificity—as opposed to the presumed universality—of male bodies as well. For example, Grosz hypothesizes that heterosexual men experience their sexed bodies in terms that are based on a perceived differentiation from women's bodies, which are defined sexually by passivity and biologically by fluids and flows. She writes that "part of the process of phallicizing the male body, of subordinating the rest of the body to the valorized functioning of the penis, with the culmination of sexual activities occurring, ideally at least, in sexual penetration and male orgasm, involves the constitution of the sealed-up, impermeable body." Unlike women's bodies, which receive penetration and emit fluids and babies, male bodies are constructed as closed circuits, hermetically sealed. Grosz credits gay men for deriving a different kind of sexual subjectivity through their embrace of an open male body: "A body that is permeable, that transmits in a circuit, that opens itself up rather than seals itself off, that is prepared to respond as well as to initiate" is capable of very different kinds of pleasures from the stereotypical heterosexual male body (1994: 200–1). She hopes that straight men will follow suit.

Grosz's analysis of masculinity "phallicized," that is, defined through the penetrating power of the penis, helpfully implies that American men's relationship to their sexed bodies is socially produced—and could thus be altered. There is hope here: men's sexual subjectivity might transgress expected boundaries of bodily experience. And equally importantly, while the cultural construction of men as sexually active, nonpenetrated, closed off is a crucial part of the discourse of male power, it also closes off all kinds of sexual and cultural possibilities that men might explore.

We can see how much the image of the "sealed-off" man is a product of Western culture by looking at the Sambia of New Guinea. They engage in a cultural practice anthropologists call ritualized homosexuality, in which men imbue their semen with a very particular power, attributing to that fluid the ability to grow boys into men. Secret initiation rituals center on young boys' performance of fellatio on adolescents and on the latter's such performance on older men—all so that the younger boys can receive nourishing semen (Herdt, 1999). American men, for their part, imbue not semen but penises with power, claiming that the penis has a mind of its own that often forces its hapless owner to do things he wouldn't do otherwise, such as commit adultery or even rape. This common perception holds that men have a natural, biological, hormonally driven, and utterly insatiable sexual appetite. Hence, some men argue, they themselves are powerless over their bodies, completely lacking control. In the first cultural example, men's power is upheld by maintaining strict secrecy over initiation and inculcating in boys a belief in the superior power of that which differentiates men from women: semen. The second example presents a rare case in which men actually adopt the "body" position in the mind/body dualism and, in so doing, exempt themselves from the rules governing society as a whole. In both cases, men's power in society enables them to sex their bodies in ways that do not transform society but rather reproduce their own privilege.

Judith Butler presents a different view of the body as a site of political transformation. Butler argues that bodies implicitly marked as "normal" have come into being through everyday practices, specifically the acts we go through every day in order to occupy our gendered places. She suggests that bodies are made to seem material and unchangeable through the work we do to inhabit and enforce norms. Yet, she continues, bodies can also be remade by performing those norms in very different contexts. This is particularly relevant to those gendered bodies that exist on the social margins enforced by structures of race, gender, and sexuality. Her model famously rests on the example of black and Latino gay men who appeared in Jennie Livingston's documentary film *Paris Is Burning* (1991). In that film, we see gay men of color competing in drag shows in which they perform various, minutely defined aspects of masculine and feminine dress and bodily comportment. In a prelude to her reading of the film, Butler suggests, first, that these men's "contentious practices of 'queerness' might be understood not only as an example of citational politics, but as a specific reworking of abjection into political agency, thereby explaining why 'citationality' has contemporary political promise" (1993: 21). Second, she proposes that drag is subversive "to the extent that it reflects on the imitative structure by which hegemonic gender is itself produced and disputes heterosexuality's claim on naturalness and originality" (1993: 125). In other words, drag reveals that not only might men perform femininity; indeed, women perform it all the time, just less self-consciously.

By arguing that gender is the result of repeated performances of "male" and "female"—that is, that gender is created through the processes that claim to define it—Butler opened up significant theoretical space to think about gender as both enforced and alterable, as written onto a body but also extricable from it. These insights have been very useful for thinking about categories of gender outside the male/female binary, especially transgender identities.

Like "male" and "female," "transgender" is not a single idea or identity. For some transgender people, such identification opens up the space for more fluid understandings and expressions of gender, ones that intersect with but operate separately from anatomy. At the same time, this argument could get us back to the mind/body split and suggest that the body is something that gender can transcend through rejected binarized sex.

Many anthropologists emphasize the cultural basis of binary sex distinctions—but not without difficulty or contradiction. First, the people whom anthropologists study often (not always!) maintain a strict gender dichotomy based on biology, as they understand it. In Jakarta, Indonesia, "tombois" are born-females who live as males. They define themselves as such based on their sexual desires: they define men as people who are attracted to women. In that way, tombois see themselves as practicing normative gender insofar as they explicitly seek to enact dominant forms of masculinity. But when tombois travel from the urban milieu of Jakarta back to their rural villages, their practice of gender shifts. They find that the pull of family commitments is so intense that they relent to the pressures of being not simply women but daughters, fulfilling the normative obligations associated with that role (Blackwood, 2010). Second, anthropologists themselves, despite their best efforts at deconstructing appeals to biological signifiers in gender studies, sometimes give in to their terms. One anthropologist who conducted an ethnographic study of transgenders in New York City uses the term "male-bodied" to refer to some of his informants (Valentine, 2007). Another anthropologist who did similar work in Brazil refers to his own research subjects as "not-men," a destabilizing term that only works by referring to—and hence reinforcing—a stable biological category (Kulick, 1998). What comes across so clearly in such works is that even the most erstwhile attempts to destabilize appeals to biology sometimes fail, raising the question

of whether we are trapped by our language, our biological reference points, or both.

Ultimately, transgender activists argue, the question of language and of the variety of ways in which transpeople conceive of themselves are less crucial issues than the singular need to develop strategies for attaining social justice. Toward that end "'transgender' refers to a collective political identity. Whether we have psychological features in common or share a particular twist in our genetic codes is less important than the more pressing search for justice and equality" (Currah et al., 2006).

Much of this chapter has emphasized the work of feminist philosophers, anthropologists, and even biologists who have labored to unsettle biology-based understandings of the categories male and female. But we are still left with the question of how to think about the body as a material, physical entity in relation to the politics of gender. Is there a way of thinking about maleness and femaleness materially—that is, in terms of flesh—without making those categories inevitably just the outcome of cultural construction? On the other hand, can we think about bodies as bodies while at the same time not falling into biological determinism? Linda Alcoff has sought a way out of this conundrum by arguing for a "possible objective basis" for sexed identity: "Women and men are differentiated by virtue of their different relationship of possibility to biological reproduction, with biological reproduction referring to conceiving, giving birth, and breast-feeding, involving one's own body" (2006: 172). What's crucial here is the *potential* for reproduction, not actual reproductive acts, abilities or even desires, and the differences in consciousness that potential produces. Alcoff's proposition differs from Grosz's, cited above, in positing the potential to reproduce as the primary marker of sexual difference, as opposed to a larger set of individual markers such as fluids, permeability, and particular body parts. In terms of politics,

Alfcoff is critical of what she sees as the unhelpful abstractions of much theorizing about the body that offers no stable ground from which one can speak and act politically as a woman about women's experiences and concerns. For example, Alcoff argues that approaches that rely so heavily on Foucault—who has been well cited in this chapter—are, in the end, frustrating because they tend to conclude that "it's turtles all the way down." That is, such approaches essentially present a bottomless pit of discourses about "woman" without ever arriving at "women." Much of Alcoff's work is geared toward redeeming identity politics, which have been maligned in mainstream, progressive, and right-wing political spheres alike. Likewise, Alcoff is very attuned to the multiple sets of power relations (such as race, compulsory heterosexuality, able-bodiedness, age) that differentially shape the lived experience of sex difference, as defined.

The Female Body on the World Stage: Two Case Studies

One of the more difficult challenges of developing a progressive transnational feminist politic has been, on the one hand, to speak out against the forms of oppression that specifically target the bodies of women and girls, while on the other hand arguing against the representation of women—especially women in the Global South—as perpetual victims. The present section develops this chapter's concern for the dynamics of power and agency, highlighting gendered inscriptions that originate not in mind/body, nature/culture, or male/female dualisms, but in complex social institutions and political antagonisms.

Bodies as Battlegrounds

The use of sexual violence during wartime is a historical and worldwide phenomenon. It would be difficult to name either an ancient or modern war in which some form of sexual violence did not regularly occur. Women have often been compelled to work as prostitutes in war zones or other conflict-ridden arenas as part of governments' efforts to provide for male soldiers' presumably natural sexual needs. In an infamous example, Japanese officials forced women in the many Asian countries under its imperial control to work as so-called "comfort women," providing sexual services for Japanese soldiers during World War II. Women were commonly abducted from their homes or were fooled into leaving their homes voluntarily after being told that they would be working in Chinese factories. The government rationalized this program of sexual slavery by arguing that it prevented soldiers from raping local women (Tanaka, 2002).

Rape is so common a feature of armed conflict that it has been called a weapon of war (Card, 1996). The Bosnian war is an important case study in the use of rape as an act of political aggression, one that fits Cynthia Enloe's description of "systematic mass rape" (Enloe, 2000). Yet despite the fact that these forms of sexual violence fit into a larger pattern, it remains crucial to highlight the cultural, historical, and social dynamics that underpin each such instance—lest such terms as "systematic mass rape" and "weapon of war" turn into facile, universalist explanations.

In Yugoslavian society before the war, a common masculinist culture prevailed among Serbs, Muslims, and Croats, characterized by the values of honor and shame found in many southeastern European countries. The honor (or shame) that attached to the behavior of girls and women reflected upon the men and the family as a whole. It was men's duty to protect the honor of the women in their patrilineage (an extended family that traces descent through the father), with special reference to virginity, fidelity, and fertility (Olujic, 1998: 32). Folk culture was dominated, meanwhile, by a highly sexualized discourse on the female body and by men's boastful songs and jokes highlighting their prowess at accessing it. Women and girls were thought to be both lustful and untrustworthy and hence a perpetual risk to the reputation of the family. With such values trenchantly in place, rape proved a highly effective tool through which Serbs could humiliate Muslims (and to a lesser extent, Croats) en masse. Held in "rape camps" for months on end, the women were often victimized bodily and emotionally. Men, held in separate camps, were also sexually tortured. In some instances they were made to witness the rapes of women. It is estimated that at least 14,000 women were so brutalized. The profound shame associated with rape has led many victims to remain silent (Olujic, 1998).

One of the important features of wartime rape is that its victims are civilians and should hence, according to the Geneva Conventions, be spared from military aggression. Yet despite how commonplace rape and other forms of sexual violence have been, these were not recognized as war crimes or crimes against humanity until 1993, when International Criminal Tribunals were established to prosecute the perpetrators of genocide in the former Yugoslavia and Rwanda (Engle, 2005). According to Article 7 of the Rome statute of the International Criminal Court, crimes against humanity now include "rape, sexual slavery, enforced prostitution, forced pregnancy, enforced sterilization, or any other form of sexual violence of comparable gravity." So while neither Japanese nor Nazi perpetrators of sexual slavery and rape were ever brought to justice for those specific crimes, there is hope that perpetrators in the former Yugoslavia will continue to be held accountable for acts of profound sexual violence against Muslim and Croat women and men during the early to mid-1990s.

The Democratic Republic of Congo, meanwhile, has been declared the rape capital of the world and, relatedly, the most dangerous place in the world to be a woman. Congo has been engaged in armed conflict since 1998, when Rwandan and Ugandan militias aided Congolose rebels in the overthrow of the government. Afterward, foreign militias, including the main perpetrators in the Rwandan genocide, became mutual antagonists in a broad-based armed conflict in eastern Congo. With close to 6 million dead by 2008, it is the worst armed conflict since World War II (IRC, 2008).

Since the start of the conflict, at least 10,000 women have been raped—sometimes gang-raped—every single year, and not only by foreign militias but also by the Congolese army, rebel groups, and, increasingly, other civilians. The UN peacekeeping forces in Congo, the largest in the world, have been chastised for being ineffectual at either creating peace (much less "keeping" it) or protecting women.

If the sexual atrocities in Bosnia could be contextualized through its cultural beliefs about women's sexuality, what might possibly explain these horrific, systematic acts of violence? Crucially, the conflict in Congo has its roots in the global demand for a now-common item: cell phones. Tin, tantalum, and tungsten are heat-resistant materials used in cell phones and other everyday electronic devices such as laptops, PlayStations, and DVD players. These materials derive from a mineral ore called columbite-tantalite, which is found in abundance in eastern Congo. The competition for control of mines is intense, and the lack of any kind of political order favors these various armed groups, from the government to various and sundry foreign and domestic militias. In this milieu, the most militarily powerful ones profit. Together, these militias are estimated to reap $180 million in profit a year (Prendergast and Cheadle, 2010: 184).

Through the brutality of sexual violence, an armed group or groups can completely intimidate and subjugate a local population, as well as compelling them into forced labor. As the advocacy group Enough explains, "In the infamous Bisie mines of Walikale controlled by the 85th Battalion of the Congolese army, soldiers guarding the sites steal ore from the miners and intimidate rival tradesmen. They force civilians to dig minerals for them, set up roadblocks, collect illegal taxes from the local diggers, rape women and torture their husbands if they resist" (http://drc.vday.org/conflict-minerals). The fact that sexual gratification is not itself the goal of these rapes is evidenced, arguably, by the preponderance of sexually violent crimes that do not involve a sex act, such as when armed soldiers ram a gun into a woman's vagina—a common occurrence.

Sexual violence is not limited to actual rape, and women are not its only victims (in fact, women can also be perpetrators). It can also include sexually loaded acts of humiliation targeted at men, such as occurred in the infamous prison of Abu Ghraib in Iraq. Again, the roots of these crimes are worth briefly laying out. We might begin by noting the deeply entrenched masculinization that American male soldiers undergo as an informal part of their basic training in which recruits "aggressively practice…the unofficial rites handed down from man to man through the generations" (Burke, 2004: xiv). These rites include the singing of banned songs celebrating rape. And of course, if masculinity has such a high value, that must mean that feminization can be wielded as a weapon in its own right (Enloe, 2007). Feminization is the process through which attributes normally ascribed to women are ascribed to men in order to humiliate and disempower them. The photographs taken at Abu Ghraib, and subsequently shown around the world, featured naked Iraqi male prisoners in denigrating poses as American female military officers looked on (Hersh, 2004). The sexualized nature of this act of humiliation is accomplished through the nudity of the men and the presence of the women. Another deeply gendered cultural dynamic of this incident concerns the way it was processed in the United States. "Women…were conventionally expected by most editors and news watchers to appear in wartime as mothers and wives of soldiers, occasionally as military nurses and truck mechanics, and most often as victims of wartime violence. Women were not…supposed to be the wielders of violence and certainly not the perpetrators of torture. When those deeply gendered presumptions were turned upside down, many people felt a sense of shock" (Enloe, 2007: 100). Such shock should inspire "a feminist curiosity" about war (Enloe, 2007). Or, even more critically, it should force the sober realization that "a uterus is not a substitute for a conscience" (Ehrenreich, 2004).

The Congo case presents a different set of possibilities for our understanding of women's agency. An important book, *The Enough Moment: Fighting to End Africa's Worst Human Rights Crimes*, details numerous activist efforts among Congolese women and men aimed at helping women survive economically and psychologically in the aftermath of rape (Prendergast and Cheadle, 2010). Some local activist efforts work through the transformative power of narratives, especially those that link local Congolese women to each other and to the larger world. For example, one Congolese journalist travels from one remote location to another, giving women radios so that they can hear her radio program in which she features interviews with other women affected by rape. The various stories that Congolese women relay to the Enough Project, as presented online and in the above text, are meant to inform international readers about their experiences. If the local crisis in Congo has its roots in global consumerism, then perhaps local-global activism will bring about its demise.

Female Genital Cutting

It is hard to imagine a more contentious issue relating to the broad question of embodiment than that surrounding what is variously called female circumcision, female genital mutilation (or FGM), female genital cutting (FGC), or female genital surgery. One's choice of term announces one's position, with international agencies and activists choosing the critical term "female genital mutilation" over the more value-neutral term "female circumcision" or, even more neutrally, "female genital cutting." The World Health Organization (WHO), in defining the practice, writes, "Female genital mutilation comprises all procedures involving partial or total removal of the external female genitalia or other injury to the female genital organs for non-medical reasons" (www.who.int/topics/ female_genital_ mutilation/en/). Demographic and Health Surveys (DHS) uses the term "female genital cutting" for the sake of neutrality. That usage is also adopted here less for neutrality than as an acknowledgment, in view of foregoing sections of this chapter, that discourses *about* the body can affect the lived experience *of* the body. Indeed, some women who have undergone the surgery are offended by the implication that their bodies have been "mutilated."

Female genital cutting is commonly practiced in 28 African countries and some in Asia and the Middle East (WHO, 2011: 1). Although popular perception in the West is that the practice predominates among Muslims, most Islamic societies do not practice it, while many non-Muslim groups within Ethiopia, Sudan, and Kenya do. An estimated 3 million girls undergo some form of the procedure per year, and between 130 and 140 million living women have done so (WHO, 2011: 1). Data collected between 2005 and 2008 comparing the prevalence of female genital surgeries among older and younger women in various countries show that the practice has been steadily declining.

Twenty-seven percent of all women and girls worldwide who have undergone the surgery live in Egypt, representing the highest proportion in the world (WHO, 2011: 1). (Ethiopia is in second place, at 17%.) By the time the Egyptian government banned the practice in 1996, 97% percent of women and girls had undergone the surgery, with 82% of mothers expressing continued support for it. Despite being illegal, the practice continues. In 2008,

---

Box 5.4   ON THE HUMAN RIGHTS OF GIRLS

Seen from a human rights perspective, [female genital mutilation] reflects deep-rooted inequality between the sexes, and constitutes an extreme form of discrimination against women. Female genital mutilation is nearly always carried out on minors and is therefore a violation of the rights of the child. The practice also violates the rights to health, security and physical integrity of the person, the right to be free from torture and cruel, inhuman or degrading treatment, and the right to life when the procedure results in death.

Source: Eliminating Female Genital Mutilation: An Interagency Statement. OHCHR, UNAIDS, UNDP, UNECA, UNESCO, UNFPA, UNHCR, UNICEF, UNIFEM, WHO 2008: 1. http://www.un.org/womenwatch/daw/csw/csw52/statements_missions/Interagency_Statement_on_Eliminating_FGM.pdf. Accessed Dec. 20, 2011

a major national demographic and health survey asked mothers about their intention to have their daughters circumcised. The data revealed that by 2023, 45% of girls will have likely undergone FGC, a figure that represents a steady decline in yet continuing support for the practice (El-Zanaty and Way, 2009: 197). Even though there is no doctrinal injunction for the practice in either Islam or Christianity, people most commonly cite religion and tradition as the reasons for supporting the practice. In addition, there is widespread belief that young women are more marriageable and can attract men of higher economic and social status if they have been circumcised.

Efforts to abolish the practice largely center on its negative health effects. Those vary according to the exact kind of cutting performed, the quality and cleanliness of the instruments used, the skill of the person performing the procedure, and the health of the girl or woman. The most commonly cited health consequences include: severe pain and bleeding, sometimes resulting in clinical shock and/or anemia; infections, including potentially fatal ones; urinary retention; abscesses, cysts, and keloids; infertility; and various childbirth complications (WHO, 2011).

Although most anthropological studies are critical of female genital cutting, they have been careful to emphasize the specific cultural values and imperatives deemed to make the surgeries necessary. The work of African anthropologist Fuambai Ahmadu is of interest not only because she voluntarily underwent the surgery but because she provides a cultural analysis that highlights the importance of seeing beyond Western philosophical and cultural constructs about nature and the body. Ahmadu grew up in Washington, D.C., but hails originally from Kono society in Sierra Leone. There, she says, bodies are not born complete; nor is sex a "natural" attribute, given at birth. Rather, a girl achieves those qualities by enduring a variety of rituals,

including the painful experience of having one's genitals cut. In particular, part of the clitoris is removed because it is associated with masculinity and excessive sexuality—that is, superfluous to reproduction. Furthermore, "[r]itual officials and other Kono women adamantly maintain that if left untouched, the clitoris will continue to grow and become unsightly, like a penis…and…will categorically lead to incessant masturbation and sexual insatiability" (2000: 297). Ahmadu, for her own part, reports no noticeable decline in sensations from the nerves that lie beneath her own vaginal surface.

A common perception of female genital surgery is that it supports patriarchy by attempting to control women's sexuality. Yet Ahmadu stresses that there is "no cultural obsession with feminine chastity, virginity, or women's sexual fidelity" because the Kono have a matrilineal kinship principle (2000: 285). That is, women are at the center of many of the society's most crucial roles, and these pass through mothers. Biological fathers are marginal, and society is organized around a hierarchy of women: ritual leaders of female secret societies, elders, one's grandmother, and one's mother. What is at stake, she argues, is fertility and successful procreation, which can only be assured if one's genitals do not become masculine. What is more broadly at stake, though, is one's full membership as an adult woman in all the goings-on of the community. Despite having a physical body, one is not truly a person—in the most meaningful sense of the word—unless one has undergone this process. Hence, according to Ahmadu, "[it] is incumbent on mothers to initiate their daughters properly, according to ancestral customs, in order for the latter to become legally recognized as persons with rights and responsibility in society" (2000: 300). Female genital cutting, in this view, assures that one will become a woman, which is an achieved, and indeed, exalted status.

Even within countries in which female genital cutting has been common, there is hardly a single, monolithic point of view about this issue. Female genital cutting is outlawed in 15 of the 28 African countries where it is practiced. In many of these countries the issue has become an object of political machination. In Sierra Leone, from which the Kono case is drawn, women activists who condemn the practice charge that it is bolstered by corrupt campaign practices. Fearing for their political careers, politicians try to win the support of the same powerful, women-run secret societies described above. And to garner the support of Kono communities, they offer to pay for the cost of the surgeries, which can cost up to $200 per girl. Opposition to the practice can come both from the outside and from the grassroots. In 2007, one Sierra Leonean female gynecologist would travel from one Kono village to the next carrying a doll to use as a model in explaining the dangers of female genital cutting (http://womense-news.org/story/070907/fgm-practitioners-s way-elections-in-sierra-leone). The fact that she was faced with death threats yet carried on with her work anyway shows the deep and strong feelings held by people on both sides of the issue.

Dr. Olayinka Koso-Thomas lives in Sierra Leone and campaigns against female genital cutting.

The Body Beautiful: Of Booties and Biceps

In 1792, Mary Wollstonecraft wrote wryly of women's mind/body predicament: "Taught from their infancy that beauty is woman's sceptre, the mind shapes itself to the body and, roaming round its gilt cage, only seeks to adorn its prison" (Wollstonecraft, 2012 [1792]: 37). One hundred years later, with the rise of industrial society and consumer society in Europe and the United States, women were fashioned into the ideal consumer. With the development of the department store, commodities that offered fantasies of a more desirable self titillated elite women. With the increasing "democratization of consumption" throughout the twentieth century, women from the working classes were offered compensation and respite from the bodily drudgery of their daily lives through purchasing products. Although women were enticed to buy newer and better commodities to improve the home, their "proper" domain, a woman's primary act of consumption was aimed at making herself into an object of desire, sometimes with serious medical consequences (Box. 5.5).

Currently, consumption is fundamental to many women's lives, and shopping is a major leisure activity for women of all classes and races; their diverse bodily wants are largely filtered through mass-produced images in commercial ads found in magazines, on TV, and on the Web. Through such images, women are offered more than simply products; they are promised a more beautiful body, a more gratifying life, and a more gratified self (Rosenblatt, 1999: 8). Today in the United States and around the world, the marketplace is central to women's pursuit of beauty as well as to the construction of women's other bodily needs and desires. Globally, the market in fragrances, cosmetics, and toiletries is worth $330 billion dollars per year (Jones, 2010: 1).

Box 5.5   DEFORMED FEET: BUNIONS, CORNS, AND ARCH PAIN

Bunions are a common problem experienced mostly by women. The deformity can develop from an abnormality in foot function, or arthritis, but is more commonly caused by wearing improperly fitting footwear. Tight, narrow dress shoes…can cause the foot to begin to take the

 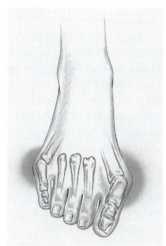

High-heeled shoes and foot deformities.

shape of the shoe, leading to the formation of a bunion. [Bunions] can worsen to the point where surgery is necessary.

Corns…develop from an accumulation of dead skin cells on the foot, forming thick, hardened areas. They contain a cone-shaped core with a point that can press on a nerve below, causing pain. Complications that can arise from corns include bursitis and the development of an ulcer.

Arch pain can be caused from a structural imbalance…most frequently the cause is a common condition called plantar fasciitis…tissue located along the bottom surface of the foot that runs from the heel to forefoot. The inflammation often leads to pain in the heel and arch areas…if left untreated, a bony protrusion (heel spur) may develop.

Source: www.foot.com

Yet a cursory visit to beauty industry websites such as *GCI Magazine*'s www.gcimagazine. com would reveal the growing global importance of men's bodily desires to the beauty industry's growth. For example, Indian men are apparently seeking "male-specific skin care," owing to India's own increasing importance in the global economy. Indian businessmen are in greater contact with their peers in the United States, the United Kingdom, and

Australia, and thus "Indian men are…feeling the pressure." (Bhattacharya, 2008). That same website offers a superlative glimpse into the ways that the globalized beauty industry is constructing new markets through old, orientalist stereotypes, as in the headline of another article, "The Mystique of Mainstream Middle Eastern Beauty" (Grubow, 2010).

Today, women's consumption continues to be critical to the success of a capitalist economy: in the United States, for example, women account for 85% of all purchases (Muley, 2009). Much of this expenditure is directed at the body and, in particular, at the pursuit of beauty. Yet do cosmetics and fashion merely fix women visibly in their oppression? The history of the cosmetics industry in the United States shows that even as women felt increasingly compelled by social pressures to use cosmetics, they also claimed them for their own purposes (Peiss, 1999).

Moreover, the cosmetics industry allowed a few African American women to become entrepreneurs and even, in the case of Madame C. J. Walker, millionaires at a time when black women were among the most economically disadvantaged. To simply see fashion as a "moral feminist problem" is to miss the richness of various forms of self-expression or self-enhancement, some of which might signal one's affiliation with a subcultural group, often with a strong political orientation. The punk fashion of the 1970s, with its torn and slashed clothing, vinyl, bondage gear, and outrageously dyed, spiked, and sculpted hair, for example, presented a mockery of traditional style. Punk style and other "antifashion aesthetics," such as the slacker styles of the 1980s and the cyberpunk styles of the 1990s, were attempts to resist standard encodings of beauty, femininity, female sexuality, and class.

Women's processes of self-creation, resistance, and transgression through the body and fashion exist within capitalist formations and gendered power relations and, thus, will necessarily be influenced, mediated, and constrained by them. However, women are active creators and, as such, can use the resources offered by these formations, if not to escape or transcend them then to negotiate, protest, and resist them. To understand shopping and fashion only as frivolous, empty-headed feminine activities reproduces the denigration of the body with which women have so long been associated. It devalues a historical sphere of women's activities and concerns, and it does not allow for the diverse ways in which women can use these activities to improve their lives. Some women might starve themselves to death in the pursuit of impossible images of beauty and perfection, but others will playfully adorn themselves and seek pleasure in their own bodies (Mascia-Lees et al., 1990). The manipulation of the body and its adornment can also result in the tangible accumulation of both symbolic and economic capital (Brydon and Niessen, 1998). That said, a disturbing trend lies in the growth of anorexia and bulimia among men, in particular gay men. In Britain, an estimated 10% of people with eating disorders were men, and among those, 20% were gay. The degree of bodily dissatisfaction among gay men stems from a norm that puts a higher premium on attractiveness and bodily musculature than obtains among straight men (Petersen, 2007: 68). And it is hard to separate the pleasure we find in adorning our bodies from the multibillion dollar industries producing fashion, make-up, and diet products, whose goal is not to help women—and increasingly men—feel beautiful but to enrich their CEOs and shareholders.

Pop culture icons who happen to be women of color can revise the standards of beauty in ways that are at once liberating but also problematic. Jennifer Lopez's celebrated booty has allowed black and Latina women to be even prouder of the body shapes that many of them have, for the thinness that is exalted in the world of high fashion and mainstream culture has never been highly valued in black and Latino communities. It is only a slight overstatement to suggest that Jennifer Lopez single-handedly rerouted the aesthetic center of gravity of the female body in America. For this reason, the political and historical importance of Lopez's butt merits some comment.

The cultural construction of Jennifer Lopez includes the objectification and inspection at work, an utter—perhaps even grotesque—fascination with her lower body, as if it were grotesque. "A big culo [butt] does not only upset hegemonic (white) notions of beauty and taste, it is a sign for the dark, incomprehensible excess of 'Latino' and other African diaspora cultures....A big Latin rear is an invitation to pleasures construed as illicit by puritan ideologies, heteronormativity, and the medical establishment through the three deadly vectors of miscegenation, sodomy, and a high-fat diet" (Negron-Mutaner, 1997: 189). Lopez, and by extension other Latina women, are racialized by reference to what are seen as their peculiar biological natures—that is, their butts.

On the other hand, there is Lopez's own repeated, brazen invitations to the world to take a good gander at it. When Lopez first burst onto the pop culture scene, interviewers would unfailingly ask her whether her butt was a prosthetic (Beltran, 2002: 74). She would stand up, do a full turn, pat her butt and give a standard answer: "todo es mio," or "it's all mine" (Negron-Mutaner, 1997: 186). In this way she both encourages and profits from her own exoticization—or even racialization. With her proud declaration she provides the absolute resolution that one seeks through inspection.

The butt phenomenon that Lopez inaugurated was helped along by others, most notably Britney Spears, whose genius was in popularizing a fashion statement to perfectly accentuate her own butt: low-rise jeans. Butt crack became the new cleavage. In addition to its racial dimensions, the politics of all this lay in the creation of a new set of impossible desires and, with them, a new industry: butt implants.

While some women seek out cosmetic surgery, others find empowerment in the strong and sculpted body they build at the gym. Such is very much the case with the American First Lady. Michelle Obama's body is, in a word, buff. In magazine interviews, she has described her workout routine (for which she wakes up at 4:30 in the morning) and some of her favorite exercises (squat thrusts). In all of the pomp and circumstance for the 2009 inauguration, and in the months following, she would wear sleeveless dresses that showed off her biceps. Journalists couldn't get enough, writing headlines declaring her "right to bare arms." Yet not everyone was pleased. On the occasion of the president's first state of the union address, the political commentator David Brooks of the *New York Times* remarked on air that she should cover them up. Michelle Obama's official portrait, taken in a sleeveless dress, was critiqued on the same grounds. Once again, we have intense inspection of a black woman's body; surely, such abundant discourse on a woman's arms is unprecedented in American culture. It was improper for a first lady to show her arms, apparently, because they were so beautiful. Rather than allowing those arms to serve as a clarion call for physical fitness, especially in view of the country's obesity crisis, critics sexualized them. Her arms became such a subject of controversy that one would think she were flaunting cleavage.

It bears noting in this context that athleticism is one of the activities that have, historically, served to differentiate men and women. Femininity and visible musculature have been mutually opposed, and women have often been reluctant to lift weights because doing so might make them "bulk up" and take on a masculine appearance. When Venus and

First lady Michelle Obama, showing off her muscles.

Serena Williams emerged on the tennis scene some years ago, proudly describing their game as "power tennis," they too were criticized for being too muscular, a code word for masculine. One of their competitors, Martina Hingis, was heard to liken playing against one of them to playing against a man. Whether intentionally or not, Venus and Serena work against the masculinization of their athletic bodies by portraying feminine sexuality through often scandalous bodily displays on the tennis court.

Summary

The human body is a cultural construct; its meaning and significance are shaped by differing cultural ideas. Historically, women have been associated with the body and nature and men with "self," "soul," and culture, profoundly affecting how women have been valued, treated, and constrained in their opportunities and choices. The body has also been understood as the physical ground of gender differences, which science has been charged with uncovering. Today it is a subject of continual debate whether there are clear-cut biological sex differences. The debate itself is so politicized that it might make more sense to scrutinize the uses to which biological categories are put, rather than try to definitively assess biology's role in the production of gender.

The female body is created through discourse; that is, practices, representations, commodification, reproduction, and technology. Medical discourse, in particular, has constructed negative notions of the female body and sexuality, representing women's bodies and the natural processes they go through as diseased.

As feminism becomes more and more global, debates have emerged and deepened over the relationship of traditional practices around women's bodies and the Western ideal of the self-realized individual. The integrity of the female body—and by extension, the status of women and girls—has also been a frequent concern in world politics, with forms of feminist activism having different and sometimes contradictory effects. Women, especially women in the Global South, can no longer be seen as only victims and objects in these arenas, but also as agents and subjects.

Bodily needs and desires today are constructed in and inextricable from the marketplace. Through mass-media images, women and men of various sexual orientations around the world are differently promised a more beautiful body through buying products and maintaining time-consuming daily beauty regimens. Women have found places in consumer culture to use their bodies and fashion for self-expression and self-enhancement and to signal political commitments.

Discussion Questions

1. The body can be experienced as a site of control, contestation, and empowerment. Compare and contrast times when you felt cultural pressures controlling your body, when you felt yourself challenging and resisting cultural definitions of your body, and when your body acted as a source of power. What does this analysis reveal about the relationship of the body to culture?

2. Analyze a scientific article that claims that women and men are biologically different for any cultural assumption about masculinity and femininity that may affect its "objectivity." How, for example, do such assumptions influence the question asked, research methodology employed, or conclusions reached?

3. Analyze a description of one of women's biological or physiological processes in a popular magazine. How does the language affect the interpretation of that process?

4. Interview women from diverse backgrounds about the clothes they wear. What is the relationship of their clothing to their experiences of their bodies? How do popular images of women in the media affect these experiences?

5. Choose a Hollywood film and pay close attention to how it constructs a viewing position for you as spectator, especially in relationship to the women's bodies on the screen. Interview spectators for their reactions to the film, paying particular attention to how factors such as race, class, sexual orientation, and ethnicity affect them. Compare your analyses of the film based on these two approaches for their strengths and weaknesses regarding the "visibility politics of the female body."

6. Examine the coverage of sports events on television or in the newspaper. Are men and women athletes described in the same way? Does the question of appropriate masculinity arise in regard to male athletes as often as the issue of appropriate femininity arises for female ones?

Recommended Readings

Bordo, Susan. *Unbearable Weight: Feminism, Western Culture, and the Body.* Berkeley: University of California Press, 1993. A cultural analysis of the contemporary female body and the myths, ideologies, and practices that construct, manipulate, and constrain it. It focuses on the commodification of the female body, analyzing how consumption "normalizes" women's bodies and leads some to discipline their bodies so rigorously that it produces dangerous extremes in behavior that might harm or even kill them.

Conboy, Katie, Nadia Median, and Sarah Stanbury, editors. *Writing on the*

Body: Female Embodiment and Feminist Theory. New York: Columbia University Press, 1997. A collection of essays by leading feminist theorists. It uses the metaphor of "writing on the body" to investigate how the body can and has been "read," how bodies are produced, how they speak women's experience, and how they are performed.

Fausto-Sterling, Anne. *Sexing the Body: Gender Politics and the Construction of Sexuality.* New York: Basic Books, 2000. An in-depth analysis of the role of science in constructing "truths" about sexuality, sex differences, and sexual identity. It focuses specifically on past and current research on intersexed individuals, sex-based brain differences, and "sex hormones," showing how the gender politics have been, and continue to be, at work in each of these areas.

Hall, Kim Q., editor. *Feminist Disability Studies.* Bloomington: Indiana University Press, 2011. A series of essays that brings a feminist perspective to disability and chronic illness. The book is particularly interested in how able-bodiedness interacts with sexuality and assumptions about female desire.

Tovar, Virgie, editor. *Hot & Heavy: Fierce Fat Girls on Life, Love & Fashion.* Seattle: Seal Press, 2012. An edited volume of essays that rethink body size and its relationship to gender. The book takes a fat-liberation perspective and celebrates the variety of women's bodies.

Part *II*

Women's Relationships, Women's Selves

In Part II we focus on women's relationships within family configurations, traditional and fictive. Doing so, we also deal with women in roles they inherit and those they create for themselves. The section concludes with a focus on women's ability to lead healthy lives.

Throughout time and across the globe, the socially accepted roles and relationships for young females, those deemed best suited for her, within her household, community, and society, have been to become first a wife and then a mother. Moreover, these roles were to be established through a conventional marriage of a woman and a man and assumed within a traditional nuclear family or an extended family household. Such beliefs still exist and continue to be idealized and pursued. Yet readers may be surprised to learn how much has changed over time for women and men, young and old, in their family roles through their life course. At the same time we will consider how much has not changed in terms of women's domestic and familial responsibilities.

Chapter 6 examines different types of family configurations worldwide, the changing notions of an ideal marriage, and how women's and men's choices and roles and relationships within families have evolved.

The challenging responsibility of being a mother, although some women do not or cannot choose this role, is the focus of Chapter 7, especially how motherhood is defined, constructed, marketed, and contested. Chapter 8 gives attention to two other components of a woman's life. It first explores being a daughter and a sister during girlhood and adolescence and the different treatment given to girls and boys in families. It then examines women's experiences as they grow older and the role transitions that occur in their familial and work lives. Finally, Chapter 9 considers gender disparities in women's physical and mental health in the context of life processes, including the ways in which women have been all too often disempowered by the professional medical community.

Part II therefore explores women's roles and relationships as wives, mothers, grandmothers, daughters, and sisters and the widening options available to them as they negotiate their lives from girlhood to late adulthood. Throughout we consider the persistence of women's inequalities in these roles while highlighting their struggle globally for gender equity and enhanced well-being within family contexts and throughout their lifetime.

chapter 6

Families and Their Configurations

The Family as an Evolving Social Organization

What has constituted the ideal marriage between a wife and husband over the centuries in the United States has changed from institutional, to companionate, to individualized marriage. Marriage has become less of a necessity, more of a choice, and hence less conventional. Many young adults have lived on their own prior to marriage. Changes in family configurations, such as the increase in single-parent households, which we discuss below, has contributed to heated debates and vociferous protests, especially from religious and political leaders, often in the name of "family values." These debates persist in the agendas of national political parties in the United States today (Taylor, 2010a).

The family is the most ancient and universal unit of social organization. Until recently, it has generally been seen as comprised of people related to one another by marriage or "blood." In the past, in small-scale societies, all social life took place within or between families: childrearing, food production, exchange of goods, religion and rituals, and power struggles. A woman's place within the family as wife and mother has defined her role in most societies. Although more women participate outside the home in paid work and in public activities, adult women worldwide still bear the primary responsibility for their family's daily routine and maintenance. Fulfilling these obligations influences what else women might do with their lives.

The *nuclear family* is the most common family type in human history. It is based upon the union or marriage, commonly recognized through societal custom, religion, law, or blood kinship of an opposite-sex couple, a woman and man and their offspring. In some societies the nuclear family is part of a larger entity, sometimes called the *extended family*, consisting of one or more nuclear families and other relatives, often living in the same household as a multigenerational unit. Marriage, as we shall see, is only one way by which people create families.

At best, feminists have been ambivalent about the family but more often have been critical of it. Viewing the family as a political institution, a site of power, sexual inequality, and constricted gender roles where women are subordinated in the home and in the larger society, feminists also call attention to variations in family forms and situations, some of which provide opportunities for more equitable roles for women (Satz, 2011).

Families are fluid, flexible, and socially constructed by individuals, circumstances, state policies, and cultural practices. They vary across the globe and have changed over time. In contemporary industrialized societies, what constitutes a family has expanded beyond marriage, biology, and adoption to include those who are related emotionally, that is, share affection and commitment, as well as those who are legally related.

In the United States, the nuclear family comprised only 22.5% of all household types in 2007, a steep decline from 40.3% in 1970 (see Table 6.1). Many people who are less educated and have low incomes are more likely to form alternative family configurations. Current public opinion reflects the new reality of multiple household types (see Box 6.1).

TABLE 6.1 Household Types in the United States by Percentage, 1970 and 2007

	1970	*2007*
Singles living with nonrelatives	1.7	5.6
Women living alone	11.5	15.2
Men living alone	5.6	11.7
Adults living with children or other relations	10.6	16.8
Married without children	30.3	28.3
Married with children	40.3	22.5

Source: Rose M. Kreider and Dianna B. Elliot. *America's Families and Living Arrangements: 2007*. Washington, DC: U.S. Census Bureau, September 2009, p. 4.

Box 6.1 WHO COUNTS AS FAMILY IN THE UNITED STATES TODAY?

A recent Pew Research Center survey found that the American public is accepting of many family forms. Further, marriage is not the sole path to forming a family; same-sex unions can also be families; and the husband provider/wife homemaker nuclear family model is less relevant. Children, however, do matter: 99% say a married couple with children is a family; 86% consider a single parent and child to be a family; 80% say a cohabiting unmarried couple with a child is a family; and 63% view a lesbian or gay couple with a child to be a family. Marriage still matters, but differently: 88% consider a married but childless couple to be a family. The dual income/shared homemaker family as a satisfying marriage model also gained in value: 62% favored this change in gender roles in 2010 compared to 30% in 1977. Most adults value their own family and find it to be a most satisfying component of their lives. While family in its many configurations is important, marriage is less so.

Source: Paul Taylor, ed. *The Decline of Marriage and Rise of New Families*. Washington, DC: PEW Research Center, 2010a. (c) 2010 Pew Research Center, Social & Demographic Trends Project. The Decline of Marriage and Rise of New Families. http://www.pewsocialtrends.org/2010/11/18/the-decline-of-marriage-and-rise-of-new-families/.

We begin this chapter on family configurations with broad historical trends and a focus on the nuclear and extended family. We then explore alternative communities to the family for women. In the last section we discuss how families in the early twenty-first century have changed from previous eras, especially in terms of their forms and gendered division of labor. We identify other common family types found in the United States and elsewhere today. Throughout, we consider women's choices in forming families, including remaining single or becoming unmarried because of divorce or widowhood, and how gender roles have been affected by changing social, economic, and political conditions.

The Nuclear and Extended Family

As noted above, the nuclear family for the most part is founded upon a marriage between a woman and man who become wife and husband. Marriage, then, has served to legitimate heterosexual relationships

(Hunter, 2011). Such a marriage is so customary that it is seen as conventional. Only recently have same-sex marriages been increasingly accepted in civil law, primarily in a few Western countries and in some states in the United States.

Conventional Marriage: Why Marry?

For most of human history, marriage was economically necessary; women and men needed what the other provided in terms of work to form a stable family. In general, men provided food in the form of large game and protection against marauders, while women gathered nearby plants, tended small animals for food, and cared for children. To a certain extent, this obtains even in today's societies. Some people, however, can purchase household services traditionally performed by one gender or another (a woman can hire a plumber to do what husbands used to be expected to do; a man can hire a cook to do what wives used to be expected to do), and of course they can learn to perform these tasks themselves. Yet it can be a struggle for a woman to manage without a partner. Regulating sexuality is another reason why people marry, although this is much less evident in large, mobile, industrialized societies than in smaller ones. In every known society there is a prohibition against incest, generally defined as sexual relations among close kin: parents and children, siblings, and other family members. In order to have sexual relations and bear children, people must seek a mate outside the family circle. In earlier times and in small-scale societies, this often meant marrying outside the local community, where people were likely to be closely related. As most societies have been patrilineal, typically daughters were sent away and the young bride would begin her married life in the home of her husband's family. Less commonly, in a few matrilineal groups, the groom went to live with his wife's family.

One can imagine how the dynamics of these households would differ.

In such situations, parents decided where to send their daughters or sons based not only on the expected compatibility between their children and those of the other family but also on what was anticipated in an alliance between the two families brought together by their children's marriage. In these cases, the bride and groom had little to say about the match and could only hope that it would be tolerable. In cases where marriages were arranged, the families of the bride and the groom generally exchanged gifts. Sometimes, the much larger gift would be given by the groom's family, especially when the bride was leaving her birth family to join his parents' household. The gift (sometimes known as *brideprice* or *bridewealth*) was in compensation for the loss of her economic contribution to her natal family and would be used to help her brothers to acquire wives. It was also a kind of marriage insurance for the husband's family: the bride's own family, having accepted a substantial gift, would be reluctant to return it, thus discouraging her from leaving her husband if she felt inclined to do so. In some societies, notably in historical Europe among elite families but also in contemporary India, it is the bride's family that is expected to give the groom, or the groom's family, a gift, known as *dowry*. Families without sufficient funds to provide a dowry despair of finding a good marital match for their daughters. Some daughters might spend years weaving a large carpet to sell for a dowry, as in Turkey. In modern times, young women in Sri Lanka are strongly motivated to find work in factories to make money to contribute toward their dowry so that they can marry.

Whether in arranged marriages or not, couples who marry usually anticipate having children. Most people think this is the purpose of marriage. Marriage generally legalizes a man's claim to his children, a woman's claim to support for her children by a man, and the children's claim to some part of their father's income or property. Childlessness is often seen as tragic for both men and women and frequently regarded as justification for divorce or, in polygynous societies (see below), for taking another wife on the assumption that it is she who is unable to conceive children.

Sexual intimacy is also desired, and until recently marriage was commonly seen as the only legitimate realm for this activity. Not all societies confine sex to marriage, and in practice, even in societies where sex for respectable women outside marriage is strictly forbidden, premarital and extramarital sex do occur. Nevertheless, infidelity is generally prohibited, particularly for women (who might bear another man's child), and is often a cause of strife. In some societies, the punishment for women's adultery is severe, ranging from gang rape to death by stoning. Sometimes a woman accused of infidelity will prefer death by suicide to social ostracism and the other sanctions that will result from this accusation. A double standard in sexual conduct usually prevails, however, and most societies are more lenient to male adulterers.

In the past, people were expected to marry for mutual economic support, to have children, to allow families to make alliances, and to engage in socially approved sexual intimacy. These social functions of marriage have been superseded in industrial, urban society by other social, political, and economic institutions, which have undermined many of the earlier reasons for marriage. Arranged marriages for family alliances are no longer common in Western societies (ultra-Orthodox Jewish communities are an exception to this); but in Asia, the Middle East, Africa, and elsewhere, these persist, as they do to a certain extent among immigrant communities from these regions in the Western world. Especially in large urban sectors in the West, sexual relations and having children without

being married are more acceptable, but in most regions, the sanction of marriage is preferred for both sexual unions and parenthood. Just because unmarried sex and parenthood are more common in some societies does not mean that there is no longer pressure to marry.

Whom to Marry?

Girls and young women globally are educated in anticipation of their assuming the roles of wife and mother, regardless of what else they might do. Women who do not (or have not yet) become wives and then mothers are, more often than not, disparaged or pitied (unless they assume other socially esteemed roles, such as being a nun) and more likely than not feel a sense of inadequacy or deprivation. Consequently, most families strive to ensure that their daughters become married, and most women do marry. Though there have always been women who did not marry, only in recent decades have a significant number of women in the world had the option not to be married and not to be mothers as a matter of personal choice.

In some societies, the parents turned to professional matchmakers to pair up their children with an appropriate mate and to smooth the path from betrothal up to the wedding itself. In some cases, children are betrothed in infancy or childhood; in others, the prospective couple is allowed to meet before betrothal. When marriage concerns whole families, the suitability of the individuals to be married as a couple is considered of less importance than the appropriateness of the tie between the families. Families are chosen for their wealth, stability, and social standing. Often, a family has an obligation to marry their daughter to an appropriate kinsman—say, the father's sister's son—if one is available (*cross-cousin marriage*); in other societies, cousin marriages are forbidden. Sometimes, a family has the right or obligation to provide a close kinsman as a husband to a young widow (*levirate marriage*). In societies where such marriage forms are practiced, individual choice is simply not an issue. It is hoped that the bride and groom will develop a fondness for one another over time so that the marriage will be stable and even happy (Potash, 1986).

In industrialized societies, individual preference has become a primary factor in the choice of a spouse. Young adults, especially in Western countries, seek their own partners, though matchmaking may continue through friends and Internet dating services. Even so, people marry largely within certain socially acceptable boundaries and may be encouraged or compelled to choose somebody within a similar social class, race, caste, religion, or ethnic community and other commonalities, such as their own age group, educational background, and even geographic origin.

Where marriage has come to be understood as a romantic commitment rather than a pragmatic arrangement, much is made of falling in love, getting engaged, preparing for a wedding, and having the wedding itself. Expectations about marriage can often leave couples disappointed when the romance has faded. Divorce has become frequent in societies where it is permitted, partly because of this disappointment and partly because more women are able to support themselves and live independently of a spouse. The practical consequences of divorce for women are complex, something that we will discuss below.

The Traditional Marital Household

As noted above, typically the bride moves into the household of her husband's parents, or, less often, the groom moves into the household of his wife's parents, though there are many variants of each of these practices. The household might be comprised of several generations of couples and their children and various unmarried adult siblings of different ages. The experience for a young married woman, and the way this experience evolves as she matures, depends on the configuration of her household. If she is alone with her husband when she starts out, she might have much to learn about managing the household and might have little or no help. If she is in a large household, while she will have teachers and helpers, she might suffer the criticism of older women, particularly her mother-in-law (Hrdy, 2009). Alternatively, her life as a wife alone might be yet more difficult when she has children, unless she can afford hired help. In a larger household she will have help at hand and her status will rise with motherhood.

Some societies allow *polygamy*, the practice in which an individual may have more than one spouse at the same time. For example, Muslim religious law permits a man to have up to four wives at one time. The ideal of *polygyny* (marriage to more than one wife) is more obtainable by the minority of men who have the wealth to support multiple wives: when Osama bin Laden was shot, he left three widows. In other situations, however, a man might seek multiple wives to enhance his economic advantage because women do and share the majority of the work of farming and herding along with child care. The converse, *polyandry*, in which a woman marries more than one man, is truly rare—a well-known example comes from the Himalayas, where in land-scarce areas several brothers might share one wife rather than splitting up their land holdings to provide for several families (Levine and Silk, 1997).

Polygyny, however, is found on every continent, including present-day United States, where, although now outlawed, it continues to be practiced—for example, among some fundamentalist Mormons. Some women have argued that there are advantages in having co-wives in a large household, particularly in the pooling of wealth and labor. In East Africa, for example, it takes teamwork among a number of wives to cultivate land, care for livestock, and raise the children. Polygyny, however, is not necessarily a happy state for women. There is often jealousy and bitterness among the wives, a subject of poetry and literature from the Hebrew Bible to contemporary novels and essays. Mariama Ba's *So Long a Letter* ([1980] 1985), for example, recounts a modern West African woman's unhappiness upon learning that her husband has decided to take a new, younger wife. Another example is the portrayal of the three wives of a Mormon man, their differences, and negotiations with their husband and each other in the American television series *Big Love* (2006–2011). Even when husbands are limited by law to only one wife, in many parts of the world it is common for them to make second and even third families, and such practices are not limited to the wealthy and powerful. While the husband might keep his mistresses and their children secret from his legal wife, not infrequently the wife knows of them and the children know of one another.

This complex situation reflects the traditional subordination of wives to husbands. Although marriage presumably guarantees a wife certain rights and entitlements, generally, in most parts of the world, these have been secondary to those of her husband (see Box 6.2). She becomes his dependent, often owning very little or no property of her own, lacking in inheritance rights or control over finances except those of immediate household management. In such cases, a wife may have virtually no identity of her own. It is her job to provide her husband with sexual satisfaction when he wishes it, physical comfort in his home, and food for their children, his family, and guests. Living away from her family, she is often without support. She is judged by him, his family, and her own family, as well as the neighbors and society at large, according to how well she performs as a homemaker and mother, for these are the primary roles of a wife. A young bride is often deprived of future schooling that could improve her own and her family's future and is often the target of abusive husbands. She is more likely to bear children early, which places her and her offspring at risk (United Nations, 2010).

This asymmetry in traditional marriage is reflected in myriad ways, from the frequent practice of changing a woman's name to that of her husband upon marriage in Western societies to the unequal household tasks

---

Box 6.2   MONOGAMOUS MARRIAGE AS ECONOMIC EXPLOITATION

The first class opposition that appears in history coincides with the development of the antagonism between man and woman in monogamous marriage, and the first class oppression with that of the female sex by the male. Monogamy was a great historical step forward; nevertheless, together with slavery and private wealth, it opens the period that has lasted until today in which every step forward is also relatively a step backward, in which prosperity and development for some is won through the misery and frustration of others. It is the cellular form of civilized society in which the nature of the oppositions and contradictions fully active in that society can already be studied.

Source: Friedrich Engels, [1884] 1972:129.

allocated wives and husbands today. Wives continue to put in more time daily than husbands do in domestic activities, even when both have full-time jobs outside of the home.

The Incorporated Wife

Many careers and occupations involve not one person but two, and sometimes the whole family. Whatever a man does for a living, his wife is to be his supportive junior partner. If a man is a farmer, his wife is a "farmer's wife." In industrial societies, where most people are employees, the incorporation of a wife (more often than a husband) into a spouse's job is less explicit. Wives are expected to support their husbands' activities by taking care of all their domestic needs and also by taking an active interest in company functions as well. They are expected to entertain (depending on the husband's rank in the company) and to appear with their husband at all social functions run by the company (Callan and Ardener, 1984).

Until recently, the wives of professors, doctors, and clergymen had important roles to play in the conduct of their husbands' work—both assisting with the work itself and making a social life for the husband's work community. The work of a politician's wife is very apparent in today's world, especially at the higher levels. This poses something of a dilemma for professional women married to politicians. Debates about attorney Hillary Rodham Clinton concerning her political role, especially around healthcare policy, during her husband's presidency of the United States (1992–2000), for example, highlighted the importance of the role of "first lady" and its limitations (Caroli, 2010). Michelle Obama, also a successful attorney, carved out her first lady role around more traditional gendered concerns. In her focus on childhood obesity, advocacy for fresh produce for low-income households, and the welfare of military families, she remains a family-centered nurturer, albeit while transforming public policies. Much less scrutiny is made of the few men whose wives are world leaders or corporate executives.

In recent years, because many wives also have careers, some companies posting their employees to different locations or recruiting new personnel have assisted in finding a new job for the wife or, if the employee is a wife herself and her rank is high enough, for the husband. Some organizations have adopted this practice for same-sex couples. Still a female "trailing spouse" is often made to feel less important. As the number of dual-career couples grows, many wives are reluctant to give up their careers and, in some cases, are the primary breadwinners. Husbands then must adjust their roles and careers, as did the husband of British Prime Minister Margaret Thatcher or the spouses of women ministers in other countries. Moreover, among highly public political and celebrity marriages, not all wives are choosing to "stand by their man" in the face of revelations of their husband's infidelity.

Increasingly, in a divorce settlement some wives who have given up their careers to support a spouse have obtained a share of their husband's earnings and pensions because of the role they have played in their husband's careers or businesses. Courts have also awarded "palimony" or compensation in the place of alimony to unmarried women who have made similar sacrifices. Such recognition is a further indication of the value of women's economic and social role in families.

Children in the Family

While having children is one of the expected consequences of a marriage, in the United States the rise in the number of children born to single mothers (discussed later in this chapter) is a profound change. This trend in many developed countries has been politicized and

The Arnolfini Wedding (1434) in Flanders, oil painting by Jan Van Eyck. Marriage vows, called "hand-giving," were performed in private homes or church vestibules, not inside churches, in the fifteenth century in Europe. Here, a wealthy merchant has commissioned a painting to commemorate the occasion. The bride gathers up her skirt to her waist, giving the appearance of pregnancy and alluding to the promise of future motherhood.

reduced to a debate on the acceptable form of "family." In the United States, "for the sake of the children," two-parent marriages are thought to be preferable by political conservatives and by many social scientists as well. For example, Linda Waite and Maggie Gallagher (2000) defend even bad marriages, which they believe, with enough determination and work from both spouses, can improve and become quite satisfactory. Marriage, they argue, benefits a woman and her children financially. Consequently, as divorce economically punishes the wife and her children, they counsel women to work out a marital partnership. Others argue that a bad marriage does not benefit either wife or children, and, if the husband is physically abusive, preserving the marriage can endanger all of them. While some researchers (Wallerstein et al., 2000) fear for the long-term damage that is inflicted on children by divorce, others find that the vast majority of children of divorce are resilient and become relatively well-adjusted adults (Hetherington and Kelly, 2002) (see Box 6.3). Children who experience a single parental divorce are much like

---

Box 6.3   PUBLIC SAYS CHILDREN BETTER OFF WHEN UNHAPPY PARENTS DIVORCE, AND SINGLE MOMS SUCK

Posted by Talyaa Liera, as Karen Murphy, September 20, 2007:

My oh my, the public (whoever they are) certainly is opinionated! Blah-de-blah, we like to shoot off our mouths, apparently, about *anything*. Especially when we can spout off about someone else's business. And the Pew Research Center recently asked a whole bunch of people their very opinionated opinions about a whole bunch of things like marriage and parenting, and this is what they said:

1. **Unmarried moms = bad.** Almost half the Judgy McJudgerpants "public" (whoever they are) says you and your spawn are bad, bad, bad if you're not married, and a full two-thirds says it's bad for society! But only if you're a mom. There's no word on the dads, so I guess they're in the clear.
2. **Premarital sex = bad.** Well, the one goes with the other, I suppose. Though fewer people said premarital sex was the beginning of a long and slippery downward slope to the Land of Evil than got all judgmental about unmarried moms, so I guess the real moral of the story is: *don't get caught*. Oh, and cohabitation is also bad, bad, bad.
3. **Children are your path to happiness.** 85% of the people gave "having a relationship with my minor children" a "10" in Importance in Personal Satisfaction and Fulfillment. Take that, non-breeders!
4. **If you're unhappy in marriage, get a fucking divorce already.** Especially when there's kids involved. Kinda ironic, though, isn't it? It's okay to divorce (and thus become a single parent) if you're *already married*, but it's NOT okay if you were never married to begin with. Have I got that right?

Freakin' public. Who *are* these people, anyway?

Source: Talyaa Liera, as Karen Murphy, http://www.babble.com/CS/blogs/strollerderby/archive/2007/09/20/public-says-children-better-off-when-unhappy-parents-divorce.aspx.

the children of continuously married parents in their psychological well-being. The children who suffer the most are those who undergo multiple family transitions (parents divorcing, remarrying, and divorcing again) and the inevitable parental conflict involved (Amato, 2010).

Changes in cultural traditions, more education, being in the paid workforce, better health care, and higher standards of living have had an impact on the total fertility rate (TFR) or the number of children that a woman will have over her childbearing years. Women are choosing to delay marriage and childbirth and to have fewer children. Worldwide, the TFR was 2.5 children in 2010, half of what it was in 1950, though this varies by region. The TFR was highest in a number of African states in 2010 where women had 5 or more children. In most countries, including the United States, the TFR was 1.5–2.1 children. In a small number of developed states like Germany, Japan, and Switzerland and developing states in Eastern Europe and elsewhere, women were having 1.5 or fewer children, well below the population-replacement level. Small family size in the People's Republic of China reflects the government's one-child policy, which penalizes parents for having more than one child. In other countries, uncertain economic and political times, strict gender roles, and the lack of child care for women who work outside the home also leads them to limit their offspring. Maternity leave with pay before and after childbirth and institutions that provide quality child care and the possibility of free or inexpensive health care and medicine for mothers and their children would benefit working mothers (United Nations, 2010; see also Box 7.1 on maternity leave in Chapter 7).

Elders in the Family

Extended families have always included elders, such as older siblings, parents, and grandparents. In nonindustrial societies, a woman has traditionally assumed the role and responsibility of taking care of elders, typically her husband's parents, in conjunction with child care, although an older woman in the household often would assist with child care. Today, with longer life expectancy and the high cost of living and healthcare, many nuclear families in Western societies are becoming multigenerational as aging parents of either or both the wife or husband move in with their adult children. As women tend to live longer, it is likely that women are taking care of more senior women (see Chapter 8). For African American, Asian American, Latina/o, and Middle Eastern families, living intergenerationally is still common. For many other families, caring for elders is an adjustment, whether a women does it in her own home, in the home of elders, or in visits to assisted living facilities, and an addition to her daily workload, although often done with loving care and concern. Because women tend to provide most of the basic physical and emotional care for elders, like child care, those in the paid workforce may reduce their hours or leave it, while men retain their work hours and contribute more financially. Consequently, the average financial loss for women over the age of 50 in the United States in wages and Social Security benefits is $324,044 compared with $283,716 for men. A woman's caregiving responsibilities, therefore, can seriously affect her well-being and earnings (MetLife, 2011).

Marriage and Gender Roles in the United States in Historical Perspective

In precolonial America and later, the status of the wife was determined by the husband's occupation and place in society. In a 1792 critique of this inequity, the British philosopher Mary Wollstonecraft called for *A Vindication of the Rights of Woman*, advocating education for young women so they would not be subject to the "slavery of marriage" (see Wollstonecraft, [1792] 1975; see also Chapters 2 and 9). Property, family, and social status remained important criteria for selecting a mate. Until the twentieth century, poor women were more likely to have unformalized or "common-law" marriages with the men with whom they lived, and they continued to work both at home and outside it, caring for their men and children and marrying only when and if there were enough leisure time and extra money for a ceremony. The ideal for middle- and upper-class white women was to stay in the privacy of their home. In these classes, the husband was expected to be the sole provider, and his world was in the public arena.

By the late nineteenth century, women were making some gains toward equality. In 1848, feminist reformers including Elizabeth Cady Stanton (1815–1902), who would be a wife for almost 50 years (and a mother of seven), and Quaker Lucretia Coffin Mott (1793–1880) met at Seneca Falls, New York, and proclaimed a *Declaration of Sentiments*, which demanded redress for many inequalities in the legal code. In their view, "the only acceptable marriage was based on love, sympathy, and equality between the sexes" (Stanton, [1898], 1971; Hartog, 2000; see Chapters 8, 11, and 13). In 1871, Elizabeth Cady Stanton declared:

> From a woman's stand-point I see that marriage, as an individual tie, is slavery for woman, because law, religion and public sentiment all combine, under this idea, to hold her true to this relation, whatever it may be, and there is no other human slavery that knows such depths of degradation as a wife chained to a man whom she neither loves nor respects no other slavery so disastrous in its consequence on the race, or to individual respect, growth and development. (http://gos.sbc.edu/s/stantoncady3.html)

Reforms concerning equality, however, were slow to come. By the 1890s, wives had acquired some new legal rights: they could

Elizabeth Cady Stanton.

keep their property and earnings in their own names when married, and if separated or divorced, they could claim custody over their children. So long as she was legally a "wife," however, the state expected a woman's husband to provide for her.

Marriage for women in the southern states was a different story. Until after the Civil War (1860–65), only free women, black and white, could legally marry; slaves, as the property of their owners, could not. After the Civil War, interracial marriage was forbidden by state laws in the South. These laws remained in place until very recently (in Alabama until 2000), despite being overturned by the Supreme Court in 1967 (see Box 6.4). Interracial families have always existed despite laws against miscegenation. One of the most notable and controversial was the 38-year relationship between President Thomas Jefferson (1743–1826) and Sally Hemings (1773–1835), his slave, which produced six children (Gordon-Reed, 2008).

White women of the propertied class in the South were supposed to be treated like rare flowers. They were taught not to "unsex" themselves by acquiring too much learning and

Descendants of Thomas Jefferson and Sally Hemings pose for a photograph during their reunion at the Adena Mansion, an Ohio historical site in Chillicothe, Ohio, Saturday July 16, 2005.

developing aspirations that did not suit their place in society. These southern women generally accepted their dependence upon their menfolk, until the Civil War changed their situation drastically. The loss of more than half a million men in the Confederacy compelled a number of southern women, married or not, to consider some form of work outside their homes, as so many of their northern and western sisters did (Yalom, 2001: 204–8).

A turning point for American women came late in the nineteenth century, when the Civil War and its aftermath had effected changes in social conventions and ideas. In 1874, the writer and poet Abba Goold Woolson (1838– 1931) gave voice to a changing self-definition of women in the United States: "I exist…not as a wife, not as a mother, not as a teacher,

but first of all, as woman, with a right to existence for my own sake" (Yalom, 2001: 280). Women went to work outside the home, although in many cases they had to choose between marriage and a career. Rooming houses and dormitories that were set up in cities or mill towns where women worked provided women with an opportunity to separate themselves from their families, at least until they married. About this time lesbian partnerships, as long as they appeared to be devoid of physical intimacy, came to be somewhat tolerated by the larger society; such unions were called "Boston marriages," though Henry James was scathing in his depiction of them in *The Bostonians* in 1886 (Rothblum and Brehony, 1993; Yalom, 2001). The choice that women were forced to make between working and marrying and having children in the late nineteenth century has not completely disappeared in the early twenty-first century.

From the 1920s through World War II, women's increased public participation through their right to vote and in the paid workforce contributed to a change in the traditional form of marriage in which the husband was the undisputed head of the household and women were sexually ignorant. The "companionate marriage" became a new ideal where spouses shared emotional bonds and intimacies, while maintaining their gendered roles in the workplace, home, and as parents. With men in military service during World War I (1916–18) and World War II (1941–45), large numbers of unmarried and married women filled in the ranks at factories, offices, and shops. Especially after World War II, when the returning servicemen demanded their old jobs, women were forced out of them and married women were told to return home, a message justified by a "new" image of the wife. As depicted in the popular media in the 1950s, the young middle-class wife was now idealized as one who cleans her house, shops and cooks, puts her children to bed, and pretties herself, waiting for her (corporately employed) husband to return from work to drink the cocktail she has prepared for him. This gendered division of labor was supported in the policies and practices of other Western societies as well (Cooke and Baxter, 2010). The decade of the 1950s in America was the high point of the male breadwinner and female homemaker family with two, three, even four children (Cherlin, 2005; Simmons, 2009). These offspring grew up to become the "baby boomer" generation. The U.S. television series *Mad Men* depicts the strivings and anguish of corporate men, single working women, and married women with children in their gendered environments in the next decade, the 1960s.

This devoted homemaker image cloaked the reality that many women worked at sex-segregated and lower-paid jobs. Mirra Komarovsky's 1962 study *Blue-Collar Marriage* depicted the struggles of working-class women who had to work both at low-paying jobs and at home with little appreciation by their husbands, describing how children added to the strains of marriage. Betty Friedan's *The Feminine Mystique*, published in 1963, lay bare what she saw as the monotony, drudgery, and isolation of the suburban wife. The book struck a chord in the lives of discontented wives, many of whom had college degrees and wished to use them and pursue careers. Many women began to rethink their situations as a new women's liberation movement gained momentum by the late 1960s. One outcome was a sharp rise in the divorce rate, with one out of two marriages ending in divorce. Another significant outcome came in 1973: the U.S. Supreme Court's decision in *Roe v. Wade*, which invalidated state laws prohibiting abortion and left the decision largely to the woman and her doctor. This legal decision, along with the development of a contraceptive pill, provided a degree of sexual liberation for women (see Chapters 9 and 11). After a period of acceptance, the decision has recently come under attack by conservative religious and political groups and their largely male spokespersons. Because pregnancy and childbearing were no longer the inevitable outcome of sexual intercourse, a woman had more options available, including having sex without necessarily getting married, as dramatically depicted in the highly successful television series *Sex and the City* (1998–2004).

From this growing resistance to their past subordination, women's choices in relationships, marriage, and family life expanded after the 1970s. There were new trends: women as well as men living on their own, women staying single longer and cohabiting without marrying, a significant increase in divorce, women choosing later motherhood, single parenting, and more women completing college and working outside the home, including after marriage and motherhood. There was also a public recognition of same-sex partnerships. Consequently, a more egalitarian form of marriage that was flexible and negotiable, the "individualized marriage," emerged as an ideal, in which wives and husbands began to consider their own self-development and personal satisfaction with each other as more or equally important as raising children. Such a partnership means that both spouses contribute to the economic and physical maintenance of the home, and both have the opportunity and the responsibility to pursue other interests (Held, 1979; Cherlin, 2005).

Many societies have had alternatives to conventional marriage, but often these have been hidden because of social stigma and because researchers have paid more attention to the dominant forms. More equal relationships between husbands and wives have coexisted with the more common patriarchal family, although in most cases "his" marriage continues to be better than "hers," as when marriage ends in divorce and the woman suffers from loss of earnings and insufficient (if any) child support. A historical precedent to an egalitarian marriage was set in 1855 when Lucy Stone (1818–1893) married Henry Blackwell (1825–1909), seven years her junior, after a long and determined resistance to his suit. In pursuit of women's rights, the pair signed a contract which was a manifesto criticizing and abjuring the legal authority of husbands, their conjugal rights to sex on demand, the female duty of constant childbearing, and the obliteration of the wife's personality (Rossi, 1964).

Extramarital Experiences

Whether love develops before marriage or grows between spouses later, many wives and husbands have sought love in extramarital relations. In medieval Europe, for example, among the elite love was thought to be found only outside marriage, or so it was suggested in many of the songs that the thirteenth-century French troubadours sang (Amt, 1993). After the 1450s, the attitude in Europe toward marriage in the upper classes put renewed emphasis on seeing a wife's role as upholding the family honor by being chaste, attentive to decorum, absolutely faithful to her husband, and by producing heirs to bear the family name. If wedlock was primarily expected to produce legitimate offspring, love need not have anything to do with it. In the nineteenth century a wife, especially a mother, was not meant to stray away from the nuptial bed. Gustave Flaubert and Leo Tolstoy wrote their novels *Madame Bovary* ([1857] 2003) and *Anna Karenina* ([1873–77] 2000), respectively, to remind their readers of the terrible end that awaits married women who search for fulfillment and self-definition through adultery.

Definitions of infidelity vary across and within cultures, types of relationships, and over time, but such actions generally involve violating an expected bond of exclusivity with another person in regard to intimacy and sexual relations. In the United States, the dramatic changes in family life and culture since the late 1960s, combined with the availability of the contraceptive pill, have contributed to the rise in extramarital experiences. Age and gender trends have been identified. Rates of extramarital sex for women 60 years and over increased from 5% to 15% from 1991 to 2006 compared to 20% to 28% for their male counterparts. Among women and men 35 years and younger, their rates increased from 12% to 15% and from 15% to 20%, respectively, during this period (Jayson, 2008). Why are more married women engaged in affairs? Reasons include opportunities in the workplace, financial independence, boredom, feeling underappreciated at home, the availability of Internet technology and personal Web sites, the desire to fulfill hopes of romance and sex in another relationship, and fewer societal penalties compared to Emma Bovary's time. The meaning of sexual fidelity has undergone change and is a more complicated personal issue than it was in the past. While some marriages end in divorce because of infidelity, good marriages can heal with time and often with relationship counseling.

Divorce

Not all societies treat divorce the same way. In one anthropologist's sample, women and men had approximately equal rights to initiate divorce in 75% of societies, while men enjoyed superior rights in only 15%. In 10%, women had superior rights. For example, in a matrilocal society, such as that of the Iroquois nation in North America, wives could divorce husbands by dumping their belongings outside the door (Murdock, 1950). The majority of societies disapprove of divorce, and Western society is no exception—as testified to by the many legal obstacles to divorce in both religious and state laws. In ethnically diverse societies, family law (which is generally where divorce is placed) becomes complex. Some nations assign responsibility for legal decisions about marriage and divorce to special courts from each ethnic or religious group, with no civil law on these matters, while others struggle to devise ways to accommodate religious/ethnic diversity, with varying degrees of success.

In the United States through the 1960s, 1970s, and 1980s, one in two marriages ended in divorce, one of the highest rates among developed nations. More recently, the divorce rate has declined to about 40%, due in part to a decline in marriage (Cherlin, 2005, 2010). Divorce is a primary contributor to an increase in the number of impoverished women and children. Most of the families in the United States living in poverty are

female-headed households, although not all are the consequence of divorce. In 2010, the median income of female householders was $32,031 compared to that of male householders ($49,718) and $72,751 for married-couple families (DeNavas-Walt, Proctor, and Smith, 2011: 6). Gender roles in marriage and the gender gap in the workplace help explain these differences. Married women contribute domestic labor to the household. Though many are stay-at-home wives, others also earn an income working full- or part-time. Despite a wife's increased earning power in recent years (women's full-time year-round median earnings in the United States grew from 60.2% of men's earnings in 1980 to 77.4% in 2010), husbands in general contribute the greater amount to the household because of their larger income (DeNavas-Walt, Proctor, and Smith, 2011: 50). When a marriage or similar union ends, a woman generally loses access to the financial resources and other supports that were available through a spouse. As women continue to be discriminated against in the job market (see Chapter 12) and bear a major responsibility for the care of children (see Chapter 7), divorce can severely reduce their standard of living, just at the moment when they and their children may be emotionally vulnerable.

While the law requires former husbands to pay child support in most cases, fewer than half of divorced fathers in the United States pay anything at all and only a small proportion pay what the court has ordered them to pay. In those states that require an equitable split in the marital assets between wife and husband, divorce may involve a bitter struggle over the division of property and money.

It is relatively easy for opposite-sex couples to marry in the United States, but more difficult, although not as difficult as in the past, to get divorced. To marry, a couple of legal age registers with the local government, has a blood test (in most states), exchanges brief vows in the presence of an official and a witness, and pays a very small fee. Waiting time is usually about 3 days, often less. No parental consent is needed, nor any promise of family support. To get divorced, couples usually require lawyers, legal documents, one or more court hearings, and often a considerable amount of time, even when both parties are in agreement. If the couple disagrees about the terms of divorce, and there are children and property rights in dispute, the legal cost of settlement can be high.

Widowhood

Most marriages worldwide end with death, not divorce. As women generally have a greater life expectancy than men, a larger number of women than men are widowed. In most industrialized countries, the elderly are likely to live alone. In many developing states, where women have few rights, widowhood can result in isolation, exploitation, and poverty. It is especially dire for young widows.

Even in the United States the loss of a close partnership can be devastating. In *The Year of Magical Thinking* (2006), American writer Joan Didion explores her first year as a widow after her husband, writer John Gregory Dunne, died of a heart attack in 2003. This occurred while they awaited news of their ill daughter, who subsequently died. In describing the confusion, sense of loss, and astounding pain and grief that she experienced, Didion seeks to make sense of the end of a four-decade long marriage, and the ebb and flow of their years together. Not every widow has Didion's experience, but for most women widowhood is a mix of emotions.

Alternatives to Conventional Marriage in the Past

The alternative configurations to conventional family roles and lives are diverse. Some

have been devised without women's input or consent, and some have evolved as a "last resort" because women lacked the option not to marry and have children. We consider different types of community for women in the past—religious, educative, work-oriented, and supportive. At times, women were able to join ideological communities based on religious or political convictions rather than be in a traditional marriage. The few we describe here are mainly the options that women have shaped for themselves, the ways of living that they have chosen, designed, or imagined.

Religious Communities

Buddhist and Christian orders of nuns have enabled women to live outside the boundaries of the family circle for centuries. Christian convents go back to the fourth and fifth centuries in the Mediterranean area and, like the churches to which they are attached, have had a complex history (McNamara, 1996). Buddhism also has a long history of monasticism for women in Asia and a comparable complexity (Falk, 1980). Both Buddhism and Christianity are formally male-dominated institutions, and this fact is reflected in the regulation of the lives of nuns.

Christianity has valued chastity above marriage. Many women have had genuine longing for the celibate religious life, to take vows to remain a virgin and "to keep herself for God to serve Him freely and for no man besides" (Amt, 1993:140–2). Such fervent convictions, however, were not always heeded. Medieval annals tell of women whose desires to dedicate themselves to God were frustrated because their poverty and that of their families made impossible the payment of the "dowry" for their "marriage to God" and upkeep in the convent. Nevertheless, convents provided an arena in which many women not only realized religious aspirations but had opportunities to exercise their abilities in administration, handiwork, music, art, literature, and scholarly learning. Convents also offered schooling for girls, especially those whose families preferred that they live a sheltered life. Renunciation of sex was not too high a price for the many women of every rank and condition who desired and were able to choose this alternative.

During the religious crises of sixteenth- and-seventeenth-century Europe, nuns were able to overcome the restrictions of cloistering and to expand teaching, charitable, and nursing activities. The nun of early modern times stood out as a public model for generations of European women seeking a respectable alternative to marriage. With the wider availability of other alternatives and a decline in the authority of organized religion, many nuns today leave orders while relatively few women decide to join. The decline in the numbers of women and men who so dedicate themselves may require the Catholic Church to make changes to allow women in religious life to move into positions of power and authority, but this has not yet happened. Today, convent life takes many different forms; nuns vary widely in work, dress, and social relationships. What has not changed are a dedication to spiritual life, a decision not to marry or engage in any sexual relationships, and a commitment to a community of like-minded women organized in convents and orders. Members of these orders may be committed to teaching, nursing, helping the poor, providing shelter for orphans or single mothers, working with drug addicts, or fighting for human rights. Indeed, some Christian nuns have been in the forefront of the struggle for social justice in the world—and in the Church.

Women who choose to walk the path of Buddha and become nuns must give up family and marriage, take vows of celibacy, abstain from most kinds of food, forsake the external world, and undergo a relentlessly demanding instructional period that includes prayer and study of scriptures. Women can be ordained as nuns in the countries dominated by the Mahayana school of Buddhism. (Female ordination is not practiced, however, in several Buddhist countries, including Japan and Cambodia.) Sometimes novices with shaved heads and white robes are little better than servants for the monks, cleaning and cooking in exchange for monastic shelter and food provided by the men. As in Christianity, the number of women attempting to become Buddhist nuns is on the decline.

Laboring Communities

Social pressure in the form of low wages, abuse of unprotected women, and outright coercion has sometimes led working women to organize on a collective basis. In Belgium and the Netherlands, for example, unmarried women, including widows, formed quasi-religious communities called *beguinages* based on the idea of collective housekeeping and economic enterprise. The religious element in their organizations during the late twelfth and thirteenth centuries ensured their social respectability and enabled members to claim the protection of local ecclesiastical authorities. Nevertheless, women met with hostility and even violence from the men in craft guilds, who would neither admit women to their craft "brotherhoods" nor allow them to compete by working for lower wages or longer hours (Neel, 1989; Gilchrist, 1994).

Industrialization in the nineteenth century in western Europe and the United States brought a major social shift away from the organization of production by the individual artisan to factories owned by industrial capitalists. A feature of early factory communities was the supervision and control of unmarried girls and young women who had left home to work in the mills. The most famous experiment of a protected mill community was located in Lowell, Massachusetts, in the 1820s. The rural young women recruited into the textile factories there lived in company boardinghouses, where their morals and physical needs were carefully monitored. They enjoyed the benefits of urban life; lectures and other culturally enriching events were scheduled in the few leisure hours. Several young women produced a magazine, *The Lowell Offering*, and some were inspired to go on to more rewarding careers (Eisler, 1977). The Lowell experiment lasted fewer than two decades and was not repeated. In *North and South* ([1855] 2008), British novelist Elizabeth Gaskell (1810–1865) described the independence of the factory girls in Manchester, England, who used a bit of their earnings to dress themselves better. For most women, the experience of the factory system was not an idyll but a disciplined life of hard labor, tuberculosis, and sexual exploitation. Nevertheless, for some women in Europe and the United States, industrialization made possible a new image and a new kind of role, an alternative to those of "wife" and "mother."

Utopian and Experimental Communities

"Utopia" was first used by philosopher Thomas More (1478–1535) as a name for an imaginary community whose design would eliminate social ills such as injustice and moral degeneracy. The elements of the design reveal the author's critique of society as it exists as well as providing a proposal for correcting society's flaws, however fanciful or unrealistic that construction might be. Many utopias focus on the conventional family and its assigned roles as the root of many social problems and propose radical alternatives. Some attack marriage itself, while others target the nuclear family.

The "solutions" envisioned are diverse and often inventive: elimination of sexual intercourse, keeping sex but eliminating sexual

exclusivity, communal childrearing, and the most fanciful, eliminating men altogether and/or altering the body so that reproduction does not rely on coupling. While the last of these has not occurred so far, the others have been attempted experimentally as well as described in writing. Some of these literary and real utopian (or "intentional") communities can be described as feminist, and some explicitly so. Two examples from the early days of the second-wave U.S. women's movement are Joanna Russ's *Female Man* (1975) and Marge Piercy's *Woman on the Edge of Time* (1976).

The most influential utopian writer of antiquity is the Greek philosopher Plato. His *Republic*, written in the fourth century B.C.E., is perhaps the prototype of antifamily utopias. He imagined a state governed by an elite group, the "guardians," in which women and men would participate on equal terms. Reproduction would be carefully regulated. When children were born, they would be taken from the mother and put under the supervision of special caretakers, a group that included both women and men. New mothers would breastfeed at random and would be prevented from knowing which infant was theirs. Women would participate in the job of governing and develop concern and affection for all the society's children (Plato, 1998). Plato's *Republic* has sometimes been seen as feminist because it challenges male supremacy, educates women equally with men, and frees women from the constraints of child care.

We know of no utopian constructs written by women in antiquity, but a number of modern utopias have been conceived by women. "Ladyland" is such a place described by the Bengali author Rokeya Sakhawat Hossain in her story *Sultana's Dream* (1905; see Hossain, 1988). It is a land where the private and public roles of women and men have been reversed. Women are able to take control over Ladyland after men prove incapable of defending the country through conventional warfare. Men are relegated to seclusion, thus eliminating both crime and sin. Women take over all public and political functions, while men are assigned the job of child care. Women rule in Ladyland not through the traditional male manner of domination and oppression but through more cooperative means and working with nature for example, to extract the sun's energy. As a result of a less exploitative approach to nature, many disasters, such as drought, are eliminated.

Herland, written by Charlotte Perkins Gilman ([1915] 1979) a decade later, solves the problem of women's inequality through the simple device of eliminating men from society altogether. In her utopia, women find a way to conceive children by *parthenogenesis* (nonsexual reproduction) and motherhood is a venerated achievement. All of society is oriented toward nurturance, of human beings as well as of nature. The women see themselves as potential mothers who are not obliged to become wives (see also Chapters 2, 4, and 7).

Utopias and *dystopias* (the disturbing opposite of utopias) have been imagined by many modern feminist writers in the guise of fantasy and science fiction. Many utopian writers rely on radically modifying not only marriage and the family but also the process of reproduction. This suggests that while social inequality is the "problem," the root of inequality is the biology of reproduction (Lees, 1984). Change this and everything changes; without changing this, they suggest, we have little chance of changing anything else.

Celibacy seems to have been the central rule for many communities based on religious conviction. Celibacy, communitarians have argued, reorders the priorities of a community over those of the individual (Muncy, 1973). For the community of Shakers, celibacy was a theological issue; its founder, Ann Lee (1736–1784) preached equality of women with men, deemed possible only by eliminating sexual relations, which would distract women and men from their religious duties, and motherhood, which would create inequality. There were communities which approved sex but not marriage. The most famous and longest-lasting community (c. 1848–1881) were the "Perfectionists" in Oneida, New York, who practiced "complex marriage," in which each member was married to every other person of the opposite sex and exclusive attachments between couples were forbidden. Young women who were chosen to bear children had to give them up to specialists to raise them. In this community, as in many others, the rights of women were still limited, although equality among the members was advocated. Contrary to theory, friction arose between the mothers and the rest of the community over the control of the children.

Since the nineteenth century experimental communities have attempted to create societies with unconventional marriage and childrearing practices. Few of these have been led by feminists, and few have succeeded for very long. The early Israeli kibbutz was viewed as a success in the tradition of communes based on socialist ideals of equality and shared effort. Everyone worked, and all economic conditions, profits and debts, were shared communally. During that period (1920s to the 1970s), children were raised in "children's houses," seeing their parents at the end of the work day but sleeping apart from them with other children of their age group. Housework was done communally, although mostly by women. The ideology of women's equality with men and the subordination of private interests to those of the collective were fundamental to the kibbutz movement. Over the years, the nuclear family, traditional gender roles, and privatization have reemerged and replaced communal living and shared work. Most kibbutz women now tend to the home and their own children, and fewer of them attend college than kibbutz men (Peres, 1998). Other communal social arrangements have been more short-lived for a variety of reasons, but utopian communities are not the only alternative to conventional family life.

Families in the Early Twenty-First Century

Over the past five decades, societal changes have transformed the way we live, love, work, play, and conduct political change (see Chapters 9, 10, 11, 12, and 13). When small and remote communities are linked to major centers worldwide by cell phones and the Internet, traditional ways, including family life, are affected. Also, global economic restructuring has altered how most women and men earn a living. International efforts to improve individual rights, education, and healthcare, for example, along with demands for equality by women and other members of subordinated racial, ethnic, religious, and indigenous groups, have brought new national policies and cultural shifts with implications for families, their structures, and values.

Changes in the Global South

Many multigenerational families in Africa, Asia, and the Americas are becoming nuclear families. Family members may no longer live in the same household and having relatives who work in Europe and elsewhere is common. Some Malian women are pleased with the end of polygyny but miss being part of a large household of wives and children, although they do not want to have many children themselves. Other women in Egypt, El Salvador, and Thailand, for example, express enthusiasm for new jobs that take them away from their families and communities to urban centers and other nations, not fully aware of the challenges that await them (Huston, 2001). Some single women in Sri Lanka who

left their villages to work in the global assembly line in Colombo have had to defend themselves as "good girls" and hence appropriate marriage partners (Lynch, 2007).

Changes in the Global North

Differences in culture and national policies concerning child welfare, parental leave, and employment benefits, for example, have contributed to variances in family life in Western industrialized societies over the past five decades, but there are also commonalities. In regard to household duties, for example, women's increased participation in paid employment and in political representation has brought only a modest gain in the time men commit to housework. Cohabiting couples, however, have tried to have more open and equal housework loads than married couples. Moreover, as women's earnings increased, both partners did less housework. Many couples who can afford to turned to restaurant or store-prepared meals and used time-saving appliances. More affluent dual-career households hired domestic labor, such as immigrants, some of whom were undocumented. German couples, for example, depended upon an Eastern European *Bügelfrau* "ironing board woman" or *Putzfrau* "cleaning woman" (Cooke and Baxter, 2010: 523). Instead of forming new gender roles and a more equal division of labor in household tasks, families with employed women in Western societies are outsourcing much of the unpaid labor in the home to women of a different national origin, race, ethnicity, and class, thereby converting housework to low-pay labor.

New trends in family formation have emerged. These include delaying marriage, a decline in marriage, and fewer children, along with an increase in cohabitation, non-marital childbearing, and the legalization of same-sex marriage or domestic partnerships. Wide variations do exist. In countries where the male-breadwinner family is still dominant, such as Italy, women are more likely to marry than to cohabit. In countries like Sweden where national policies in health benefits and child care support more female equality, the rate of cohabiting is higher. In Sweden and the United States, which have high rates of female employment, as women increased their earning power they had more choices in partnering and are seen as more desirable marriage partners. In Japan, however, where the male-breadwinner family prevails, women's higher earnings decreased the likelihood of marriage for Japanese women (Cherlin, 2005; Cooke and Baxter, 2010).

The United States is distinct in one area. Although fewer people are marrying than in the past, marriage remains a sought after ideal. Couples marry, divorce, and remarry at higher rates than in other developed nations. This same pattern is found in cohabiting couples in their unions, disunions, and new unions. There is also a reversal of earlier marital patterns. Today, it is the college-educated who are more likely to have married by the age of 30, rather than less educated young adults. Previously, when men were the primary income earners, women gained economically through marriage. Men tended to marry women with less education, and educated women were less likely to marry. In the twenty-first century, college-educated women with their increased earning power are changing the marriage market and the marital household. Many are choosing to delay marriage while developing their careers or maintain their careers while married, and some are out-earning their husbands. In 2007 22% of wives earned more than their husbands compared to 4% in 1970. It is men who are now gaining economically through marriage. Moreover, as college-educated women and men marry each other and combine their incomes and wealth, they contribute to a widening socioeconomic

gap in the United States (Chernin, 2005; Fry and Cohn, 2010: 1).

"New" Family Configurations

Blended Families/Stepfamilies

Blended families likely have always existed in human history when women might die in childbirth, men in warfare, and life expectancy generally was shorter. A new union would be sought for mutual support. In some societies it was the duty of family members to make such an arrangement. Today, blended families, traditionally known as stepfamilies in the United States, are formed through remarriage or cohabitation after a divorce or a death but also may involve a partner who was unmarried and include children. In 2010, more than 4 in 10 people in the United States were in a blended family, as a "stepparent," a "step" or half-sibling, or a "stepchild" (Parker, 2011). Some seek to replace the term "step" with "bonus" because being a stepmother/parent or a stepsister/sibling connotes, historically, a lesser or negative status, when in practice extra adults and children in the family can be positive and welcome additions. As a family form that is based on love as much as economics, women speak of the challenges of merging lifestyles, housing, and child custody and visiting arrangements while developing new traditions that reflect their being a blended family (Morello, 2011; Strong, DeVault, and Cohen, 2011).

Single-Parent Families

Single-parent families, in which children are raised by one parent, usually the mother, are more common and are growing worldwide. In 2007, households comprised of a mother only with children under age 18 made up 12% of total family groups in the United States compared with 2.1% of households consisting of a father only with children under age 18 (Kreider and Elliott, 2009; see Table 6.1). Female-headed single-parent families have too often been negatively depicted because they are assumed to be the result of out-of-wedlock or cohabiting relations, or they are pitied if they are an outcome of divorce or widowhood. Globally, single mothers are more likely to be poor than mothers who live with a partner and even poorer in comparison to single fathers. In the United States, which provides fewer social services and less social support for human needs than almost any other advanced industrial country, single mothers and their children have long faced difficult hurdles unless the women are high income earners themselves (United Nations, 2010; Strong, De Vault, and Cohen, 2011).

Consensual Unions: Cohabitation, Domestic Partners

Cohabiting couples form consensual unions based on an intimate relationship, and many of these families include children. Today women and men living as domestic partners are more acceptable and normal in many parts of the world, without the stigma attached to such relationships in the past. In the United States, there were about 6.8 million opposite-sex couples cohabiting in 2007 and almost 800,000 gay and lesbian couples cohabiting in 2005 (Strong, De Vault, and Cohen, 2011). Couples may cohabit because they cannot marry for financial reasons or because one or both partners may not be free to marry or because it is simply made difficult or is not permitted by their society. Couples may simply prefer cohabiting as a lifestyle or choose it because it is common practice in their social group. In some cases, cohabitation is long-term or permanent; in other cases, it may be relatively short-term, such as when couples are testing out their relationship before marrying or may

not desire to make a long-term commitment (Cherlin, 2010). Some suggest a relationship between the increase in consensual unions in various forms in Europe and North America and the weakening of the institution of marriage. The acceptance of children born out of wedlock in most regions of the world is another contributing factor. Some countries provide some legal rights for consensual unions, deemed domestic partners, such as health benefits. In a few countries, cohabitation may be punishable by imprisonment.

Multiracial Families

Historically worldwide, interracial coupling has occurred too often by force, as when warriors and colonizers, for example, "took" conquered women. From World War I to the present, states have overlooked, sometimes facilitated, interracial sexual relations abroad (deemed unacceptable and even illegal at home) by justifying the need for embattled soldiers to have recreational sex with local women, who, in turn, had limited options in supporting their families. Few men had the intent of forming families. Yet multiracial families have been an outcome. In other cases, people of different races have fallen in love and sought to have their union recognized by custom, religion, or law only to face stern opposition from families and officials, even ostracism, death, and imprisonment. Family and societal fears of miscegenation are found in literature, theater, and film and have been critiqued by feminist scholars (for example, Marchetti, 1993). Notable Broadway musicals have explored cross-race and -gender relations that "threaten" the status quo: they include *South Pacific* (1949), about whites and native Pacific Islanders; *West Side Story* (1957), concerning whites and Puerto Ricans in New York City; and *Miss Saigon* (1989/1991), depicting the romance between a U.S. serviceman and a Vietnamese woman in the

Box 6.4   THE LOVING FAMILY STORY

All that Mildred Jeter and Richard Loving wanted as humble working-class people in a small town in Virginia was to marry and raise their children where they grew up, but she was "colored" (half-black and half-American Indian) and he was white. It was 1958 and Virginia had a Racial Integrity Act passed in 1924 that banned interracial marriage not only between whites and blacks, the primary focus of bans in other states, but also between whites and Asians and Native Americans. In June, they were married in Washington, D.C. where it was permitted, and returned to Virginia only to be arrested in their own home weeks later because the Act also forbade interracial couples married elsewhere to live as husband and wife in the state. The Lovings were given one-year jail sentences, which would be suspended if they left Virginia and promised not to return as a couple for twenty-five years. They moved to Washington, D.C., and had 3 children, returning secretly on occasion to visit family members. They were not activists, but simply in love. In 1963, working through the American Civil Liberties Union upon Mildred's initiative, they sought to end what they experienced as exile and appealed to the Supreme Court of Virginia for the right to live in the state as a married couple. It was denied in 1966 and their case went to the U.S. Supreme Court. In a unanimous ruling in 1967, *Loving v. Virginia*, the Supreme Court overturned Virginia's anti-miscegenation law declaring marriage between a man and a woman to be an individual right and that no state could deny the "fundamental freedom" of marriage based on race. This land-mark civil rights case also invalidated racial intermarriage bans in sixteen other states. The Lovings returned to Virginia to raise their children amongst family forever changing U.S. history.

Sources: Newbeck, Phyl. "Loving v. Virginia." In *Encyclopedia Virginia*, edited by Brendan Wolfe. Virginia Foundation for the Humanities, 2012. Retrieved from www.encyclopediavirginia.org/Loving_v_Virginia_1967; Schwender, Martha. "A Life of Marital Bliss (Segregation Laws Aside)." *The New York Times*, January 27, 2002; *The Loving Story*, HBO Documentary, 2011. Director: Nancy Buirski.

1970s. They have been revived with regularity for new generations.

Today multiracial families are more common globally and often are the result of personal choice as people of different races and ethnicities interact at school, work, and in public spaces on more equal terms. In the United States, it took a 1967 Supreme Court decision, *Loving* v. *Virginia*, to overturn Virginia's law against racial intermarriage and to recognize marriage between a man and woman as an individual and not a state matter (see Box 6.4). By 2010, about 15% of new marriages in the United States were interracial or interethnic, a rate twice that of 1980 (Wang, 2012). Today women are more likely to be "central figures" rather than "pawns" in multiracial family formation as they use their increased education, income, and independence to actively negotiate their life choices (Root, 2001: 170).

Families We Choose

LGBTQ people suffer both economically and emotionally from being rejected by biological families and have created alternative family networks (Schulman, 2009). In *Families We Choose* (1991), sociologist Kath Weston examined how lesbian, gay, and transgender people formed families of unrelated adults to provide emotional and financial support when their families of origin had abandoned them because of their sexual and gender identities. These relationships were especially important during the height of the AIDS crisis (c. 1982–1995), when gay men and lesbians cared for their ailing friends and lovers, taking on the responsibilities family members usually fulfill.

Same-Sex Families

Although couples and groups of women and of men have formed families with each other for centuries, only in the past 150 years as coherent lesbian and gay identities emerged have these families become more structured. The law usually defines a family in terms of blood relationships, heterosexual marriage, shared property, and the legitimization of children. This limited and conventional definition often excludes same-sex unions, especially in places in which marriage, legal co-parenting of children, and even homosexual acts are prohibited. Same-sex marriage has been legalized in a number of countries in Europe, Africa, and the Americas, including the Netherlands, South Africa, Argentina, Canada, and Norway. These changes have not taken place without opposition, but political organizing among LGBTQ people and their allies has been a powerful force.

The picture in the United States is very mixed. Although the federal government does not recognize same-sex marriage, in June 2013, the U.S. Supreme Court ruled the national Defense of Marriage Act (DOMA) unconstitutional. DOMA prevents married same-sex couples from claiming marital status in any federal entitlement (filing taxes, inheritance of Social Security benefits, etc.), and allows states that do not have same-sex marriage not to recognize marriages performed in other states. Nonetheless reflecting changing public views of marriage, the number of states legalizing same-sex marriage is growing steadily. As of August 2013, it was legal in thirteen states and the District of Columbia. Some states such as Florida and Virginia forbid same-sex couples from adopting children, even as in other states individuals may legally adopt the biological children of their same-sex partners. Ironically, even as heterosexual marriage is becoming less popular in other industrialized countries—mainly because the benefits that marriage confers in the United States are provided by the government, so marriage loses its financial advantage—same-sex couples are agitating for marriage in the United States.

Rhonda Otten and Debra Curtis (according to Advocate.com, July 26, 2011) met at a Women's Studies conference at Rutgers University in New Jersey. At the time they married, encouraged to do so by their 10-year-old daughter, they had to arrange the ceremony in New York, because New Jersey did not make same-sex marriage possible.

Visiting Unions—Living Apart Together

The movement of large numbers of people globally has never been so great. Workers, refugees, immigrants, or students may enter into informal unions while retaining a marital union in their original residence. Some informal unions are formalized with or without the knowledge and consent of one or more other partners, thus ending up as polygamous marriages. Holding a higher status or income and being unhindered by pregnancy and small children, men are more likely than women to form more than one union and may pay regular or occasional visits to their various "families." Women in "visiting" unions may be disadvantaged relative to women in legal marriages with respect to financial commitments in case of separation; but, of course, the opposite is true when a woman is wealthier than her partner. Nevertheless, since informal unions are usually more common among poor women, the social and financial consequences of their dissolution are even more severe.

A variation of visiting unions is the "Living Apart Together" family in developed countries. The reasons for couples in an intimate relationship maintaining separate residences include employment factors (for example, one having a job in a different location), complications of merging other family members into a single household, and personal lifestyles, such as the desire for private space, and are not limited to young adults prior to deciding to cohabit or to marry (Schwartz, 2011).

Transnational Families

International migration for employment, family reunification, and physical safety from ethnic, religious, and civil conflicts has contributed to the growth in transnational families where family members may live in different countries for an extended period of time. In their new adopted country, higher-income immigrants have the financial capability of maintaining regular contact with family in their country of origin. Professional Bangladeshi American families, for example, promote intergenerational relations and cultural ties with their homeland by taking their children on regular visits to Bangladesh (Kibria, 2009). For the working poor, increasingly it has been women who have emigrated to support their families and left their children and spouses/partners (in some cases, the marital or cohabitation relationship has ended) behind. Today we find Turkish women in Germany, Colombian women in Spain, Filipinas in Canada, Hong Kong, Italy, and the United States, and Mexican women in the United States, for example, supporting their families by sending remittances home and mothering from afar. Low-income transnational families suffer from split-family relations that contribute to anguish on the part of absentee mothers, increased responsibilities for other womenfolk, including daughters, who now manage the household, and children's resentment for the minimal physical contact with their parent. Despite the sacrifices, many women feel they gain from these new gender roles and opportunities (Parreñas, 2005; Dreby, 2009). In such situations, being in a transnational family is not a choice but is imposed out of economic conditions with mixed results for family relations.

Role Reversals

Crossing gender roles, though not widespread, has been accepted in some societies. A typical example is that of "women marriage" among the Igbo of southeast Nigeria, where women could marry other women by paying a bride price. This Igbo institution provided an opportunity for women who had skills and economic resources to operate as men did, within socially sanctioned patterns (Uchendu, 1965). Role reversal may be available to men, too, as in the case of the *berdaches* of the Cheyenne in the United States, a term for men who adopted the clothing and behavior of women and became "wives" (Hoebel, 1960).

The view in developed countries that men in general would not willingly take on "housewifely" roles and take care of children has weakened considerably. Some men choose to be more involved with parenthood; others are led to be so through unemployment. The traditional low regard conferred on domestic jobs to which women have traditionally been relegated is hard to change, but associations between kinds of work or activity and gender are becoming less rigid.

Choosing Not to Mother

In the United States and elsewhere, until recently wives achieved "adult status" primarily by becoming mothers. While the mandate to mother is still strong, it is fading a little. As has always been true, some women cannot bear children, and some choose not to. A growing movement of women "child-free by choice" argues that child-centric culture limits women's lives and puts enormous stress on the environment. Fewer women in the United States are having children: today nearly one in five American women never bears children during her lifetime, and the number of people who believe that children are essential to a good marriage has dropped more than 20% (from 65% in 1990 to 41% in 2007) in the past 20 years (Livingston and Cohn, 2010).

Women on Their Own

The proportion of women who choose to live alone and to not have children has increased in recent years in the United States (see Table 6.1) and elsewhere. Being a singleton is not the same as being alone or feeling lonely; in many cases, it is a lifestyle choice (Klinenberg, 2012). Some researchers have argued that discrimination exists against single people. Not only are single women often deemed less worthy and pressured to marry, they are penalized in the law. The Family and Medical Leave Act in the United States, for example, does not give a single woman time off to care for a relative or close friend. Furthermore, under that law nobody can take time off to care for a single woman without a child. Single women with or without children often devote more time and energy to community work and maintaining ties to neighbors and other family than married couples, who give their focus to each other. One study showed that 84% of never-married women provided routine assistance to their parents, compared to 68% of married women. Never-married women also are more likely to be community volunteers, collecting signatures for petitions and attending political gatherings, for example, than their married female counterparts (Parker-Pope, 2011).

Today, young women are marrying at a later age than their mothers did, if at all. Economic, educational, and job opportunities have relieved many women from the dependent wifely role. Many married (and divorced or widowed) women who were "housewives" are returning to school or the workplace or are establishing businesses, some performed at home. With improved financial standing, the need to marry or stay married or be coupled for economic security has become less compelling to women. The opportunities for lesbians to partner, marry, or be single and to be public about their relationships are greater than ever before. The first requirement for women's emancipation, and for a larger range of choices, is a source of income—for most, a job that pays enough to live independently (see Chapter 12).

Freedom to find love and emotional sustenance outside of conventional marriage and family and the opportunity to be self-supporting are prerequisites to choosing an alternate arrangement to the marital union. This choice is not available to vast numbers of women in the world in societies that do not readily condone the unmarried status of a woman and that continue to censure the independent and autonomous woman. The search for personal autonomy may be difficult and costly even for women with economic means. The reality of the modern world, especially in Western societies, however, is that families in their multiple forms persist but are less dependent upon a marital union.

Summary

The family is an ancient and universal form of social organization, the nuclear family being the most common. In most societies people form families based on marital heterosexual households. Marriage is often explained as an economic necessity. Its gendered division of labor implies that women and men are interdependent. Regulating sexuality and having children are other reasons for marriage. After marriage, couples may reside with the wife's natal family, the husband's, in a new household of their own, or according to some other pattern. Every society has customary rules and expectations about the formation of households.

Parents and families have in the past usually selected mates for their children, often according to traits desired by the family and according to the economic, social, and political interests of the family. In developed countries today most people expect to make their own choices; in these cases, ideas about personal attraction and love play a greater role.

Marital households usually include a husband, wife, and children and often elders, but some societies allow and even encourage more than one spouse (*polygamy*). Having multiple husbands (*polyandry*) is extremely rare, but having multiple wives (*polygyny*) is a common ideal of men, though the cost of providing for such wives prohibits most men from achieving it. Whether single or multiple, wives in traditional marriages in most societies are deemed to be subordinate to husbands. In contemporary industrial societies, this subordination is illustrated by the concept of the "incorporated wife," such as the wives of politicians (the "first lady").

The question of the role of marriage in the welfare of children is controversial. Most societies, like many social scientists, regard a two-parent household as ideal but are not necessarily in agreement about the effects of single-parent homes after divorce on children. Traditionally, women were expected to marry and stay married for the sake of the children. Today, many women have the option of birth control, which reduces the necessity to marry or stay married. Nevertheless, social pressures on women to marry persist.

Women have always assumed primary responsibilities for eldercare. With longevity, more women are caring for elders longer, causing some to jeopardize their own health and their future welfare by leaving the paid workforce.

By the end of the twentieth century, many people were choosing not to marry, many couples were choosing cohabitation without marriage, and many couples were choosing to delay parenthood, to limit the number of children they have, or to not become parents. The new status of women—individual rights, more education, higher income, and maintaining careers—has changed the character of unions (married or not) and of household organization.

Historically women have been punished for extramarital experiences (as well as premarital experiences), while men tend to be excused. This too has changed, especially in the Global North. Divorce, for marriages that do not work out, is an option in many societies; in the United States it tends to result in unfavorable economic consequences for women. Widowhood remains an often tragic circumstance for women.

Alternatives to conventional marriage have existed in earlier times and in the present. Some couples, for example, have rejected inegalitarian marriages, in which women are subordinates, for true parity. Larger nonmarital communities, such as the convent, have been an option for Buddhist and Christian nuns for centuries. These religious communities have provided opportunities for some women to develop their skills and talents and to serve their societies in ways unrealized as wives and mothers. Utopian communities constructed by male and female writers have critiqued the conventional family and imagined alternative roles for women and men, though often by means of celibacy and eliminating reproduction. Actual "utopian" communities have experimented with similar methods to produce ideal societies, though these have proven very difficult to sustain for any length of time.

Multiple new family forms include blended families, single parenthood, same-sex families, domestic partners, role reversals for women and men, families that cross races, ethnicities, and continents, the choice to remain childless, and the choice to live alone. However, choice is highly limited for most women in the world, and in fact, most women continue to wish for the ideal conventional marriage and family.

Discussion Questions

1. Elizabeth Cady Stanton speaks of the position of women in the family as comparable to that of slaves. What are the historical circumstances underlying this comparison? Was it valid then? Is it valid now?

2. Make a review of current popular journal publications, TV shows, or films on married life, brides and weddings, gender roles in housekeeping, home life, and babies/children. What is the image of the woman's role that emerges? In your opinion, do these media representations have an effect on the definition and formation of the *wifely roles* in the United States, in your own family, in your circles?

3. Draw your own family tree including the birthplace and dates of as many people as possible. What does it tell you about the patterns followed in your family?

4. What, in your view, would be an ideal family configuration? What social conditions would be necessary for this kind of family form to be possible?

5. Contrast the Loving family (described in Box 6.4) with the family tree of Michelle and Barack Obama.

Recommended Readings

Ahmed, Leila. *A Border Passage*. New York: Farrar, Straus, and Giroux, 1999. A memoir by an Egyptian feminist and one of the foremost scholars on women and Islam. In the chapter titled "Harem" she reflects on her experience of Islam in the family as complicated but not entirely oppressive. She contrasts the everyday Islam of women that gave them some autonomy and power to interpret their own lives.

Ba, Mariama. *So Long a Letter*, translated by Modope Bode-Thomas. London: Heinemann, 1981. First published in French in 1980, this long "letter" from a recently widowed Senegalese schoolteacher to her girlhood friend is a story of marriage and polygamy in modern urban Africa. It is a short, deeply moving narrative about the practice and meanings of polygyny.

Huston, Perdita. *Families as We Are: Conversations from Around the World*. New York: The Feminist Press, 2001. Using interviews with multigenerational families of all socioeconomic backgrounds in 11 countries, the author describes how the concept of family worldwide is being expanded and how women's and men's roles are being transformed. Women share their strengths, worries, and hopes about the impact of urbanization, economic changes, immigration, and global culture and information on their family structures and relationships in the twenty-first century.

Mukherjee, Bharati. *Desirable Daughters*. New York: Thelia/Hyperion, 2002. A gripping novel about a Brahmin woman, Tara, whose marriage to an equally privileged young man was arranged in Calcutta when she was 19. After the couple moves to the United States, Tara tries to fight the constraints imposed by her traditional marriage and her Indian heritage and becomes a single mother caught between two cultures. This is a story of familial relationships and the attempts of a woman to transform her identity, her history, her present and future.

Root, Maria P. P. *Love's Revolution: Interracial Marriage*. Philadelphia: Temple University Press, 2001. The author, who has written on multiracial children, explores the social and historical forces and the stresses and supports that interracial couples encounter from their families and society in living their lives and building their own families.

chapter 7

Mothers

Among the social roles that a woman fills, motherhood is the most difficult to define: being a mother is multifaceted and multidimensional. It is the hardest role a woman may play, whether she is the biological (natural/birth) mother or an adoptive or foster mother, mother-in-law, grandmother, stepmother, godmother, or unrelated surrogate mother. While mothers' relationships with their children are often complex and ambivalent, fictional mothers loom large: loved and hated, loving and vengeful, nurturing and destructive, all-giving and completely withholding. Nonetheless, in every individual's life she is potentially the most dominant person. What makes a "mother" so significant and all-powerful in our lives? In this chapter we examine why mothers are central to human emotions, their power to continue the existence of the human species, and how that power affects the other roles that women assume. To ensure the continuity of the human species, which is generally considered of paramount importance, control of a woman's body has been strictly maintained, beginning with legal and theological dicta, which in turn affect social and cultural norms and the medical and other scientific tools that foster, enrich, and inhibit mothering. Since for the most part society agrees that the most important function of a woman's body is to bear a child, motherhood is subject to regulations in all its aspects, biological and social. In the twenty-first century, when we live in an over-populated world with dwindling resources, to focus on women's bodies as reproductive machines may seem misguided, yet we cannot deny the reality that the biological aspect of the female body is intimately intertwined with political and economic realities.

The starting point for understanding motherhood is to investigate how it is constructed, that is, how in any society motherhood is defined by belief systems and visual images, because ideas about motherhood are reflected in and shaped by social processes. Attitudes toward the biological aspects of motherhood are also informative, such as ideas about a "maternal instinct" (Hrdy, 1999). These biological events are also shaped by society at large. Motherhood is such a critical role assignment that many people, particularly men, have been determined to design it according to their own convictions and the cultural mores of the day. The state of becoming and being a mother has fostered heated arguments and feelings from legislators in the U.S. Congress to theologians in the Vatican. Girls in every society learn what it means to be a "good" or "bad" mother: at home from their own parents and from community gossip and unspoken rules; from religious traditions and texts; from media like television, movies, and the Internet. While powerful messages are communicated in the private sphere, men in the public sphere have historically controlled the choices made for motherhood: whether, when, and how often to become a mother.

Human babies are born helpless, often needing a well-placed slap on the back to make their lungs breathe on their own, and remain dependent on their mothers or caretakers longer than do other primates. The long dependence of the human child has often required a mother to seek help to care for herself and her baby. In the last section of this chapter, we shall turn to a consideration of support systems, whether offered by her mate, her neighbors (her "village"), or some other system of networks. The mother and her clinging infant must be sustained by individualized or institutionalized help. Support for mothers has become both a private and a public concern—from grandmothers to commercial establishments—and the help to be extended to mothers and infants is highly politicized. We shall see how society is recruited to institute support systems to guide a mother through her early parenting period. Motherhood is here to stay so long as women are willing to become mothers, and mothering will continue to be political.

Images of Mothers

"Mother" is a multilayered term, implying many concepts depending on the context. It may be a metaphor, as in "the mother of all evil," an adjective denoting the superlative. It appears as a prefix, as in "motherland," meaning the country one identifies as one's home. Even when the term is limited to its most

---

Box 7.1 SAPPHO'S DAUGHTER AND MOTHER

The poet Sappho lived in Mytilene, Lesbos, in the seventh century B.C.E. Lesbos is a Greek island off the coast of Turkey where Lydia and its capital Sardis were located. Both her daughter, who is addressed in the first poem, and her mother, who is the subject of the second, were named Kleïs. Most of Sappho's poetry survives only in fragments.

> I have a beautiful child, her form
> Like golden flowers, beloved Kleis
> Whom I would not trade for all of Lydia
> Or lovely . . .
> . . . My mother . . .
> In her youth it was a great
> Adornment if someone had her hair
> Wrapped round with a purple [braid]
> It really was.
> But for the one with hair
> More golden than a pinetorch
> . . . fitted with garlands
> Of blooming flowers.
> Recently a hairband of many hues
> From Sardis . . .
> . . . cities . . .
> But for you, Kleis, I have no colorful
> Hairband—where will it come from—
> But the Mytilenean . . .

Source: Diane Rayor, *Sappho's Lyre. Archaic Lyric and Women Poets of Ancient Greece.* Berkeley: University of California Press, 1991, pp. 72–3.

common and stereotypical usage, the woman who undertakes that role can evoke multiple images, such as a pretty woman embracing a child, a complaining mother-in-law, or an evil stepmother. Images of mothers, as depicted in mythology, religious texts, and the visual arts, as well as in written and oral literature and the performing arts, are usually of central importance. These images, on the one hand, instruct people about the currently acceptable role ascribed to mothers and, on the other hand, inform us about the notions of motherhood that prevail in a particular culture. From its beginnings, feminism has turned an analytical eye on motherhood as both an institution and an experience central to women's lives, whether they choose to be mothers or not.

Representations of Motherhood in the West

Images project and convey the ideas of their creators, who in turn reflect notions of their culture. In the West, where mass media and representational arts are abundant, the imagery of mothers predominantly represents the idealized bond between mother and child. As the larger numbers of artists and writers have been men, these images evolve from their perspective, informed by their experience as sons or partners of women. Mothers in the past—even if they were literate—have generally had little opportunity to reflect on their condition as mothers or to describe motherhood in formal ways. The time-consuming task of mothering has historically left little leisure for women to engage in creative arts. One major exception was the ancient Greek poet, Sappho, who wrote about her mother and her daughter (see Box 7.1). In the modern era, however, many women have made rich contributions to the imagery of mothers. The poet Adrienne Rich, for example, has written, "Once in a while someone used to ask me, 'Don't you ever write poems about your children?' The male poets of my generation did write poems about their children, especially their daughters. For me poetry was where I lived as no one's mother, where I existed as myself" (Rich, 1976).

Daughters' explorations of their relationships with their mothers are also a relatively new phenomenon in Western literature. In Louisa May Alcott's classic novel *Little Women* (published 1868–69) Mrs. March raises her four daughters virtually by herself while their father is away in the army (see Box 7.2). A modern representation of motherhood is the U.S. dollar coin issued in 2000 to honor Sacagawea.

Sons' relations to their mothers, on the other hand, are more commonly found in both myth and literature. For example, two powerful myths that appeared in ancient Greece more than 2500 years ago express the extreme feelings of sons toward their mothers, one who loves his mother too much and another, too little. The "loving son," Oedipus, without knowing who his biological parents were, murdered his father, married that man's widow (his own mother), and had four children by her. Upon discovering that he had committed patricide and incest, tortured by guilt, he blinded himself. In another myth, Orestes murders his mother, who had killed his father. Orestes, like Oedipus, was tormented by a guilty conscience. The gods then invented the first court of law to try Orestes for murder. The gods declared that a father is more truly a parent than a mother, and Orestes was acquitted. These myths illustrate a more general theme: sons must dissociate themselves from their mothers and identify with their fathers or pay an enormous penalty (Baruch, 1991). Male authors of the twentieth century, heavily influenced by Freudian theories, have written in a similar vein of the destructiveness of their mothers' seductive and engulfing love and of conflicts of interest between growing sons and overpowering mothers. This literature depicts mothers as emasculating, possessive,

Box 7.2 *LITTLE WOMEN*

Louisa May Alcott's *Little Women* was set during the U.S. Civil War and published in 1868 after it was over. It described the lives of Meg, Jo, Beth, and Amy, raised by their mother. The novel's influence on women's self-image was immediate and enduring.

Chapter One

"Christmas won't be Christmas without any presents," grumbled Jo, lying on the rug.

"It's so dreadful to be poor!" sighed Meg, looking down at her old dress.

"I don't think it's fair for some girls to have plenty of pretty things, and other girls nothing at all," added little Amy, with an injured sniff.

"We've got Father and Mother, and each other," said Beth contentedly from her corner.

The four young faces on which the firelight shone brightened at the cheerful words, but darkened again as Jo said sadly, "We haven't got Father, and shall not have him for a long time." She didn't say "perhaps never," but each silently added it, thinking of Father far away, where the fighting was.

Nobody spoke for a minute; then Meg said in an altered tone, "You know the reason Mother proposed not having any presents this Christmas was because it is going to be a hard winter for everyone; and she thinks we ought not to spend money for pleasure, when our men are suffering so in the army. We can't do much, but we can make our little sacrifices, and ought to do it gladly. But I am afraid I don't," and Meg shook her head, as she thought regretfully of all the pretty things she wanted.

"But I don't think the little we should spend would do any good. We've each got a dollar, and the army wouldn't be much helped by our giving that. I agree not to expect anything from Mother or you, but I do want to buy *Undine and Sintran* for myself. I've wanted it so long," said Jo, who was a bookworm.

Source: http://www.gutenberg.org/files/514/514-h/514-h.htm#chap01.

dangerous, and antithetical to adult maleness. Only by overpowering the mother can the son free himself of infantilism and go forth into the civilized world of adult men. The theme of men freeing themselves from the control of a once-powerful mother is similar to some of the myths discussed in Chapter 1.

"The Happy Mother": A Western Image as Political Ideology

For centuries, the predominant representation of mothers in the Christian world was of the Virgin Mary (the Madonna) and the baby Jesus. From the early Christian era, the image of the Madonna looking adoringly at her divine offspring defined the ideal relationship of a mother and her (male) child. Nonreligious depictions of a mother and her child(ren) are relatively rare before the sixteenth century in Europe. Most paintings depicting specific mothers were commissioned by the members of various courts as propaganda for a prince to show off his private riches. Representations of ordinary mothers and their children, both inside and outside of their homes, became popular in seventeenth-century Netherlands, where the Calvinist Dutch eschewed

Box 7.3   SACAGAWEA

This Golden Dollar coin, issued in 2000, shows Sacagawea, a Shoshone Native American, carrying Jean Baptiste, her infant son in a cradleboard on her back. Glenna Goodacre, who drew this portrait, took as her model a Shoshone college student, Randy'L He-dow Teton.

Sacagawea was 15 years old and six months pregnant when she joined the Lewis and Clark expedition. Although her husband Charbono had two wives, Sacagawea was the only woman on the expedition, accompanying 33 men as a guide and translator. She gave birth to Jean Baptiste early in the journey. Meriwether Lewis describes Sacagawea's ordeal:

> About five o'clock this evening one of the wives of Charbono was delivered of a fine boy. It is worthy of remark that this was the first child which this woman had boarn [*sic*], and as is common in such cases, her labour was tedious and the pain violent.

Source: Meriwether Lewis and William Clark, *Journals*, February 11, 1805. Reprinted in Landon Y. Jones, *The Essential Lewis and Clark*. New York: HarperCollins, 2000, p. 31.

---

traditional depictions of the virgin and child. The interiors of houses were represented as places where all the human virtues were combined and cleanliness was held as next to godliness. More often than fathers, it was mothers who figured in Dutch paintings and prints as the protectors of the pure household. One of the most affecting family scenes in Dutch genre painting are of children submitting to their mother's inspection of their head for nits and lice.

Images portraying mothers in blissful ecstasy proliferated in western Europe as wealth spread to the expanding middle class in the eighteenth century (Duncan, 1973). There was a new emphasis on domesticity and the elevation of maternity to an exalted state. This type of genre painting in Europe accompanied a shift in attitudes that reflected intellectual, economic, and social changes beginning in seventeenth-century maritime and mercantile Holland and slightly later among the bourgeoisie of France. Heredity had less to do than before with one's success in life, and the environment of the home took on increasing importance in the education and formation of children for society. Though many mothers and children were subsequently forced to work for pitiful wages in horrendous conditions as the Western world industrialized, the image that was held up for aspiration was that of woman as joyful guardian of the peaceful home. The paintings of this idealized home life convey a clear moral message: a woman's place is in her clean home, a symbol of purity where she cares for her children. This early form of media representation continued to change along with social and cultural conditions, but the core remained unaltered. The image was increasingly popularized in the United States and elsewhere with the mass-media development of women's magazines, advertising, motion pictures, and television. This was the encouraging image that accompanied the burgeoning generation of "baby boomers," who were born during and after World War II and whose mothers were urged to eschew the workplace and devote themselves to raising them. But other ambitions had been unleashed when women entered the workforce during World War II, and that genie was hard to put back in the bottle: these contradictory goals led to real ambivalence and conflict related to the balance between work and home life (see Chapter 12).

The Impact of Class, Race, and Ethnicity in the United States

Of course, idealized (or villainous) representations of motherhood hardly tell the whole story. While dominant images of mothers in the United States have primarily represented white, middle-class women, motherhood is an experience that cuts across lines of race, class, and ethnicity, even as the specifics of that experience are profoundly affected by social hierarchies.

Under slavery (roughly 1620–1865), women of African descent had a very different experience of motherhood from their white and free counterparts. Seen primarily as laborers, black women were expected to integrate pregnancy, childbirth, and motherhood into their working lives. Mothers were crucial to the economy of slavery. Since children "followed the condition of the mother," slave mothers had financial value as reproducers of the workforce. Slave parents had no rights to their own children, who could be sold away from them. In fact, much of the rhetoric of the political movement against slavery focused on the destruction of families and the heartbreak of mothers (see Box 7.4).

Box 7.4   *UNCLE TOM'S CABIN* BY HARRIET BEECHER STOWE (1851)

Chapter XLV: Concluding Remarks

And you, mothers of America,—you who have learned, by the cradles of your own children, to love and feel for all mankind,—by the sacred love you bear your child; by your joy in his beautiful, spotless infancy; by the motherly pity and tenderness with which you guide his growing years; by the anxieties of his education; by the prayers you breathe for his soul's eternal good;—I beseech you, pity the mother who has all your affections, and not one legal right to protect, guide, or educate, the child of her bosom! By the sick hour of your child; by those dying eyes, which you can never forget; by those last cries, that wrung your heart when you could neither help nor save; by the desolation of that empty cradle, that silent nursery,—I beseech you, pity those mothers that are constantly made childless by the American slave-trade! And say, mothers of America, is this a thing to be defended, sympathized with, passed over in silence.

. . . If the mothers of the free states had all felt as they should, in times past, the sons of the free states would not have been the holders, and, proverbially, the hardest masters of slaves; the sons of the free states would not have connived at the extension of slavery, in our national body; the sons of the free states would not, as they do, trade the souls and bodies of men as an equivalent to money, in their mercantile dealings. There are multitudes of slaves temporarily owned, and sold again, by merchants in northern cities; and shall the whole guilt or obloquy of slavery fall only on the South?

Black women's social position as mothers under slavery and beyond was shaped by their cultural role in raising the children of their white owners and later employers. Since the primary nonagricultural work available to them was domestic labor, black women often became proxy mothers to white children, even at the expense of their own families. For many years this relationship—which could be both loving and exploitive—was represented only positively in white media, through the image of the smiling, cheerful "mammy" of *Gone With the Wind* and numerous other movies and television programs. In the wake of black migration to cities and the resultant "white flight," black women were often blamed for the effects of poverty and urban disinvestment. In 1965, Assistant Secretary of Labor Daniel Patrick Moynihan released a report arguing that the rise in single-mother families was not due to a lack of jobs but rather to a destructive vein in black urban culture that could be traced back to slavery and Jim Crow discrimination. Moynihan blamed what he called the "black matriarchy," which deprived young black men of meaningful male role models (Office of Policy Planning and Research, 1965). More recently, though, black and white writers and artists such as Toni Morrison, Kara Walker, and Tony Kushner have complicated this story, showing the terrible sacrifices black women had to make in the conflicts between caring for white families and their loyalties to their own children.

Immigrant narratives often represent friction between mothers and children, especially daughters, over sexual freedom, financial independence, and marriage. During periods of increased immigration to the United States (for example, 1885–1924 and after 1965), the immigrant mother has been represented as a vestige of the "old country." Mothers and grandmothers are seen as the repositories of old customs and values. This can be a positive, loving image, but just as often, immigrant mothers come off as out of touch with the new American reality, as controlling and unnecessarily strict, and as smothering. The Jewish mother, who pushes her children to achieve and insists that they value her above all others; the Italian mother, who smothers her children with food and love, while tightly controlling their emotional and sexual lives; the Chinese mother who will take nothing less than perfect academic achievement from her children and has nothing but distrust for the larger world—these stereotypes find their source in the lives of women who, having been uprooted from their communities and familiar customs and values, had to find ways to help their children succeed in an often hostile and discriminatory environment.

Motherhood and the Media

An ideology of motherhood is "sold" to us along with a variety of commercial products in mainstream media. Online and print advertising and television commercials are blatant in the image they convey of motherhood as "it ought to be." The most effectively designed mothers appear on television. In the last 30 years or so, the representation of the mother has undergone considerable change, but stereotypes have persisted. One of the early images was in the series *I Remember Mama* (1950s), a sentimental reconstruction of immigrant Swedish family life in San Francisco based on memoirs written by a daughter. That "mama" was depicted as gentle and comforting, a moral force, and a hardworking housewife. Up until the 1970s the usual depiction of the U.S. mother figure remained a weak woman who had few significant anxieties or nondomestic functions and was always neat, well dressed, calm, eminently middle class, and suburban. She rarely was shown having a job, making major decisions, and being sexually desirous. As the feminist movement became stronger, so did the image of the mother. Ethnic mothers began to appear in the media, including African American, Jewish, and Italian women; some were "liberated," others divorced or otherwise independent. These mothers voiced opinions, held jobs, and expressed anxieties. In the 1990s, the TV mother varied widely, from the affluent, unflappable, professional Clair Huxtable of *The Cosby Show* to the feisty, plainspoken, working-class Roseanne Conner of *Roseanne*. In recent years, representations of mothers on television have become more diverse, although there is a thin line between the image of a mother as a fleshed-out human being and that of the mother as defined by her faults.

In the best programs, television represents the range of emotions and challenges mothers face in everyday life, negotiating between their roles as mothers and their aspirations outside the home. In *Weeds*, Nancy Botwin attempts to save her family in the wake of her husband's death but ends up embodying the neglectful parent who drags her children into drugs and crime. *Mad Men*'s Betty Draper satisfies external perceptions of the perfect woman while stewing inside over her husband's infidelities and her own lack of intellectual fulfillment. And the comedy *Modern Family* explores the different ways mothers and children can interact in an extended, interracial family.

Despite the growing involvement of fathers in raising children, mothers are the primary target for media about parenting and children. Magazines intended explicitly for parents speak almost exclusively to women. Motherhood is marketable; articles on the Web and magazine stories, like the advertisements that support them, create "needs" by spelling out the requisites of good mothering, and strike fear into mothers that not doing the "right" thing could permanently disadvantage their children. There is a proliferation of information that offers a confusing array of choices and demands, and demonstrates that

mothers are being held to a very high standard. Celebrity mothers tout how they have been "fulfilled" or "completed" by their children, as though their own achievements are meaningless in comparison (Douglass and Michaels, 2004). Meanwhile the media promote the so-called "mommy wars" that pit women who stay at home full time or part time with their children against women who work full time outside the home. Rarely are there meaningful discussions of the diversity of women's feelings about combining mothering and paid work, whether those feelings are positive, negative, or ambivalent. Even breastfeeding has become a site of anxiety for women. Feminist advocacy for breastfeeding, which took on child-care "experts" who argued that breastfeeding was unsanitary, has been transformed by the media and the marketplace into judgment against women who cannot or choose not to nurse. Expensive "breastfeeding kits" with all sorts of equipment are marketed as obligatory for women, even as nursing is represented as completely natural and self-evident, rather than a skill both mother and baby learn together.

In most cases the advertisements and advice that saturate the media foster feelings of personal inadequacy and dependence in women. The onslaught of images of "celebrity moms" who have endless patience for their children while maintaining flawless figures implies that any mother who is less than physically and emotionally perfect has failed. The media largely serve the interests of commercial enterprises, whose goal is to sell products and bolster the view of the professionals, such as obstetricians and pediatricians, who advise women on proper mothering and feeding. If the public image of motherhood reflects women's social position in general, we must conclude that, despite considerable changes in women's economic roles during the last 30 years, much less has changed than we would like to believe.

Mothers Speak Out

One of the central goals of the second wave of the women's movement was to demystify and demythologize motherhood. Feminists have long spoken out about the ways in which their experiences as mothers had been misrepresented or erased. Some of this self-expression has taken the form of autobiographical literature. Adrienne Rich's treatise on motherhood, *Of Woman Born* (1976), and Anne Lamott's diary of her first year of motherhood, *Operating Instructions. A Journal of My Son's First* Year (1993), combine autobiography with analysis of being a mother, exposing it to scrutiny to disrupt ideological assumptions. Rachel Cusk's *A Life's Work: On Becoming a Mother* (2002) and Ayelet Waldman's *Bad Mother* (2009) are part of a wave of "backlash" literature that confesses that negative feelings are part of mothering. More recently, blogs have emerged as an accessible space for women to talk about the contradictions of motherhood, especially for women of color, working-class women, and lesbians. Blogs like loveisntenough.com, latinamombloggers.com, and mombian.com are both intimate and public space for women to challenge social stereotypes about mothering.

Though historically some women have supported wars, women have often used their status as mothers to advocate for peace. For example, in the fifth century B.C. in Aristophanes' comedy *Lysistrata*, the women of Greece (who were disenfranchised and could not hold political office or serve on juries) claim a right to engage in politics and make political decisions because they have produced the men who are dying in a long war. In recent times in Liberia, Muslim and Christian women joined together to protest the ongoing violence of a civil war: they wore white and invoked their importance as mothers, many of whom had lost children in the war. This protest was instrumental in bringing the combatants to the negotiating table, ending the conflict, and eventually electing Liberia's first woman president, Ellen Johnson

Antiwar activist Cindy Sheehan, whose son was killed in Iraq in 2004 at the age of 26. Sheehan, who is popularly known as "Peace Mom," has drawn attention for her extensive protests against the foreign policies and military involvements of George W. Bush and Barack Obama. Through time, mothers have railed and rallied to resist the killing of their children in wars, as have these mothers—and grandmothers—in the Plaza de Mayo in Buenos Aires, Argentina.

Sirleaf. In the United States, women have also led the peace movement: for years, beginning in 2004, grandmothers and other peace activists have showed their opposition to the wars in Afghanistan and Iraq in demonstrations every Wednesday (Haberman, 2010).

Parental Behavior: "Instinct" and Culture

As we have seen, media of all kinds provide a window into the society that produces and receives it; by investigating the constructions of motherhood and mothering in the media, we can learn about cultural attitudes toward parenting. It is true, however, that being a mother is a biological process: as mammals we gestate our young, breastfeed them, and care for them. Most people are raised by mothers, and their relationships with their mothers are the first intimate relationship they experience. At the same time, as the discussion above shows, motherhood is more than just biology: it is inextricable from the social, legal, cultural, religious, sexual, and economic roles women play in their societies and the power relations that structure those societies. How, if at all, can we separate the ideology from the reality of motherhood? Perhaps if we work through the biological reality of mothering, we can, at least in part, separate that from the social and cultural components.

All organisms come from other organisms. In this sense, all organisms have "parents." Even when parents never see a child after birth, they are called its "mother" and "father" (biologically if not practically). For other animals, like birds or cats, we assume parenting activities are "instinctive"; that is, their nervous systems are so programmed by genetic inheritance that, as parents, they will automatically behave in certain ways. Feeding and protecting the offspring are two basic parental instincts. Among mammals, a classification named for the breast (in Latin called *mamma*) of its female members because they *lactate* (produce milk), there is considerable variability in parental roles.

When we consider more complex animals, particularly primates like ourselves, we begin to question the applicability of the notion of "instinct" (Hrdy, 1999, 2009). Studies show that for complex animals maternal behavior must be learned and that its expression by females or males depends on their experience and social conditions, which calls the idea of "maternal instinct" into question. Only women can fulfill the biological elements of motherhood: pregnancy, childbirth, breastfeeding. But these processes are not necessarily the same as the set of behaviors we call "mothering": fulfilling the emotional and developmental needs of children. The desire to care for children is not universal, nor do all women feel instinctively protective or loving towards their own or other children.

Scientific studies of female hormonal changes during pregnancy and motherhood are contradictory. On the one hand, breastfeeding triggers the release of the hormone oxytocin (a hormone also released during orgasm), which can produce feelings of intimacy and nurturance. On the other hand, many women experience rapid hormonal shifts after childbirth, which can result in depression and anxiety and a feeling of alienation from the new baby. Our feelings about motherhood are so strongly determined by how we think we *should* feel about it, that it is difficult to separate biological reactions from cultural expectations.

Humans have innate predispositions for complex and varied sorts of behavior; genetic inheritance provides the general pattern, not the details, of such conduct. Of all primate species, humans are the most utterly helpless at birth and remain dependent on their caretakers for the longest time. When advanced apes, such as the chimpanzee, reach the age at which they can have their own babies, human infants are only beginning to venture away from their parents' arms. The dependent period of the human child lengthens in industrialized countries, where there is less urgency for the child to separate from the family in search of other means of support, be it a job or a spouse. This phenomenon of dependence on the part of the child causes a symbiotic relationship between it and its caretakers/parents in which the child demands

Mothers who breastfeed need to integrate it into daily life, inside and outside the home.

and the parent gives. Because of the necessity even today in most societies for a woman to provide her child with breast milk, it is not uncommon for a woman to form emotional bonds with her baby from the moment of birth. Emotions and biological needs intermingle, and traditions in almost every society work to strengthen mother–child togetherness, to ensure the survival of the child, and to maintain the continuity of the human species.

The expectation that mothers be "selfless" is not far removed from the cultural belief that women's lives should be organized around others. In part, it is true that new babies need constant care: feeding, bathing, protecting from the dangers of the world. What nature starts, society soon takes over: biology creates women's capacity for reproduction, but society dictates the task of *mothering*, assigning a multitude of nurturing tasks to women. But the demands and the rewards of caring for another person need not and should not be limited to women. Anyone can nurture and raise a child: anyone can "mother."

Motherhood: Ideology and Reality

The stereotypical view that motherhood comes naturally to women may have no biological basis in fact, but the acceptance of this view by society does have an influence on women's feelings and attitudes. Many cultures regard motherhood as a, or even *the*, source of fulfillment and satisfaction for women and disapprove of negative attitudes toward childbearing and childrearing. Despite these cultural biases and the general denial that a woman may not want to mother ("it is unnatural"), some women have begun to express feelings of ambiguity, dissatisfaction, fear, resentment, inadequacy, and anger about the experience of mothering (Waldman, 2009; see also Box 7.5). In the mid-twentieth century, the suburban middle class in the United States seemed to carry this to an extreme

(Friedan, 1963). Often isolated at home with children and with no help from spouses or public services, middle-class suburban women in particular had virtually no socially acceptable outlet other than mothering, whether in the form of employment outside the home, intellectual activity, or social purpose. Raising children was their "job" in life; mismanaging this job was seen as a shortcoming. Yet, this job offered no pay, no pension plan, and no paid or unpaid vacation. The mother, conscious of unfulfilled yearnings, could feel like a domestic slave.

The contradictions written into the job of mothering are puzzling: if being a mother is a responsible position subject to high standards and demands, why is it not appreciated as "real work"? If we take a mother who is only doing her "natural" assignment for granted, why is she considered so important and yet so fragile that society has been intensely occupied with the definition of and qualifications for the job? Women may be told, for example, depending on the society in which they live, how many children they can have or if they can have any at all without a husband. They may even be denied any choice in having a baby or terminating an unwanted pregnancy. Society may determine if they can raise a child by themselves, whether they should nurse their children, how often they may do so, where they may do so, and so on.

Because mothering as a job is assigned to women, fathers have traditionally been excluded (or may exclude themselves) from an active role in childrearing (though some younger fathers in recent years have been affected by the messages of the women's movement and the positions taken on the subject by their female partners). Why have fathers traditionally not shared or even helped mothers in the care of their young children? Besides what

---

Box 7.5   A "BAD MOTHER"

Battered by a barrage of advice and criticism from relatives, neighbors, peers, childcare experts, and online correspondents, a woman may consider herself or another woman a "bad mother."

It was when I expanded my Web communities. . . that the level of discourse deteriorated, and what support was on offer began slowly to be outweighed by a toxicity that seemed designed to destroy my sense of well-being rather than encourage it. Web sites like UrbanBaby and Berkeley Parents Network, while still providing plenty of useful tips. . . seem to degenerate with surprising frequency into full-pitched battles, the subtext of which is not only that we disagree but that your opinion, in its utter and fundamental wrongness, makes you the worst mother in the world. . . .

The essay I wrote about loving my husband more than my children, the one that made me the butt of such hysterical fury all over the Web, landed me on Oprah, where I faced down a studio of wrathful mothers, with only the eponymous host at my side. But being defended only by Oprah is like relying for nuclear deterrence only on the U.S. arsenal of nuclear warheads. . . . By the end of the show all the angry mommies were reassuring Oprah that they agreed with me.

Source: Ayelet Waldman, *Bad Mother*, pp. 74–5, copyright © 2009 by Ayelet Waldman. Used by permission of Doubleday, a division of Random House, Inc. Third party usage prohibited.

we saw in Chapter 5, that socialization and ideology have traditionally combined to teach boys that "men do not do a woman's job" and a home and children are a "woman's territory," men are more likely to feel detached from babies (after all, no one gave them baby dolls to play with while growing up) and tend not to spend time with them. Moreover, older brothers are rarely expected to help care for younger siblings in the same way that older sisters are, so they are less likely to have the basic skills of child care. The emotional differences between human females and males in their attitudes toward their offspring have also been detected among other species. The nine-month-long investment in carrying her young, the pains of birthing, and the early bonding with the child may prepare a woman to accept the job of mothering. This seems to be true for most women all over the world. The father/partner may also feel neglected while the new mother spends so much of her time caring for the baby; he may feel jealous because he does not have the claim and access to her that he did before the child was born. According to some evolutionary biologists, men, like some other primates, may roam and look for other mates, but most men who presume they are the biological father are willing to provide for their child (Hrdy, 1999: 226–34).

Are oppressive conditions the inevitable consequence of motherhood? Numerous feminist writers have seen the roots of women's oppression in their reproductive function (Firestone, 1970). Because only women can bear children, men, who are excluded from this creativity, try to create everything else and deny women access to their world (de Beauvoir, [1949] 2011). Other feminist writers argue that it is not motherhood itself but the way that society has institutionalized it that oppresses women, children, and men (Rich, 1976). Charlotte Perkins Gilman's fantasy novel *Herland* ([1915] 1979) depicts a world in which motherhood is gratifying, not oppressive, and does not preclude other forms of creativity and achievement. *Herland*, however, has no men, and women create children by willpower. Other feminists see motherhood as the possible source of the most fundamental pride and empowerment in women; they ask that society be reshaped from the point of view of mothers so that it respects first of all the well-being of children and, thus, of those who care for them (Treblicot, 1984).

In the United States today, as in other countries, diverse forms of family configuration have emerged (see Chapter 6). Families in which men engage equally in the activities of mothering are not uncommon. Families formed as alternatives to traditional monogamous marriages have radically challenged conventional ideas of motherhood. Even within the once-standard Western "family," mothers' roles have changed considerably. With the rise in divorce and remarriage, many women are called upon to mother not just their own children but also the children of their new partners. Adjustment, redefinition, and changing descriptions of mothering and motherhood are being made and remade.

The Assignment of Motherhood: Whose Interest Does It Serve?

A woman's biological contributions to reproduction, though costly in time, energy, and risk, are of relatively short duration compared to the social role of motherhood, which lasts a lifetime. Rearing children is very hard work, and usually it is mothers who have borne the primary responsibility for this indispensable contribution to human society.

Why does a woman want to be a mother? Societal norms everywhere in the world expect a woman to bear children; there are not very many strong-willed and rebellious women who could resist such pressure (see Ratner, 2000). Childless women have been burned as witches, persecuted as lesbians, and refused the right to adopt if unmarried. Because women are physically the primary progenitors and, by social convention, the primary caretakers of the human species, the female psyche has been conditioned and shaped to accept having children. Women are generally brought up to expect the role of motherhood. Once a baby is born, this helpless and needy new person can effortlessly dominate her love; she sees it as an extension of her body, of her self; the possibilities of enabling her baby to have a better life than hers seem endless. However, can mothers alone achieve these goals?

The assignment of long-term, daily child-care responsibilities to mothers rather than to fathers has left men free to acquire economic, political, and social power, which can, and too often has, been used against women (Treblicot, 1984). More importantly, because mothering has been constructed as women's most important task, societies in which women care for their own children without any pay create a huge economic savings: imagine what would happen if every mother was paid a wage for her work. The fact that mothers and others see women's primary job as childbearing helps to justify low levels of job training, high levels of unemployment, and lower pay for many women. Thus, women form a pool of cheap labor. Nowadays in most industrialized societies (with the United States as a notable exception), the provision of paid maternity leave, day care, and family allowances has helped to mitigate some of the costs of motherhood to women, in theory to spread the sacrifice more evenly.

The Cultural Shaping of Biological Events

Attitudes about Pregnancy

A woman's emotional state, attitudes, and reactions to her social environment can influence the way she experiences the physiological process involved with motherhood. How women encounter pregnancy, for example, will depend in part on whether the pregnancy was wanted or not. It will also depend on the social support system she has, her perceptions of motherhood, perhaps her relationship with her own parents, and her relationship with the father of the expected child or with her partner. It will also depend on whether this is a first pregnancy, on the nature of a woman's previous experiences, and on her expectations.

Pregnant women must adjust simultaneously to both physiological changes (in hormones and body shape and weight) and changes in self-perception. These adjustments will effect dramatic changes in other people's reactions to their pregnancy. Most societies have sets of rules and beliefs that dictate how a woman ought to feel and act during pregnancy. Depictions of pregnant women in painting and sculpture are found far back in early antiquity, probably even in the Paleolithic era. Current interpretations suggest that the ancient "Venus" figurines of heavily pregnant women represent the notion of fertility and that pregnancy was a desirable, even a venerated state.

The veneration of pregnant women ceased in societies with patriarchal monotheistic religions as the act of sexual intercourse came to be seen as "the fall of man," a reminder of a sinful event even within marriage, or the consequence of private conduct that should be properly covered up in public; hence, the billowing "maternity dress." In the middle and upper classes of European society, pregnant women were once secluded from public life. Even in the twentieth century, pregnant women who were teachers were obliged to relinquish their jobs, a policy that was only changed by the New York State legislature (and therefore at Hunter College) in the later 1960s. Early in the twentieth century in the United States, obstetricians advised pregnant women to avoid a variety of activities, including bathing, physical exercise, and sexual intercourse. Today, however, healthy pregnant women in the United States and elsewhere are encouraged to engage in all activities until they no longer physically can do so.

Will science soon have the capacity to eliminate pregnancy altogether? It is now possible to fertilize the ovum in a dish. Will it be long before a fetus can be brought to term in an artificial womb? Science fiction (like Marge Piercy's *Woman on the Edge of Time*, 1976) has long considered the possible implications of such a development. Would it help to equalize female–male relations by producing a more balanced parenthood? Much may depend on who controls the technology.

Childbirth: A Cultural or a Natural Event?

We are happy to report, for the first time since this textbook appeared in 1983, a worldwide decline in maternal deaths (Grady, 2010). The reasons include more education for women, reduced rates of pregnancy in some countries, higher incomes (resulting in better nutrition and healthcare), and availability of attendants with some medical training (see Chapters 9 and 10). At the same time, maternal death rates have doubled in the United States over the past two decades, from 6.6 per 100,000 in 1987 to 12.7 per 100,000 in 2010. And for African American women, the numbers are even grimmer: they are 3.2 times more likely to die in pregnancy or childbirth than white women (CDC, 2012).

Most women in the United States give birth in hospitals, where the process is monitored and controlled by medical professionals (see Chapter 9). A significant subset of women have increasingly preferred to have their children in midwife-supervised birthing centers or at home, assisted by a midwife, believing that there is something "unnatural" about hospital births. In general, every society has customs that provide the basis for shaping the birthing event. It is the culture that informs women and other participants about what should be done, who should do it, and how.

Typical birth procedures in the United States are unusual in a number of respects. Hospitalized women generally give birth lying on their backs, for the convenience of

George R

Historically, maternity clothing in the Western world was designed to conceal a pregnancy. Nowadays fashionable women choose to reveal it.

the obstetrician (see Chapter 9); but else-where in the world, more common birth postures are kneeling, sitting, and squatting. Ample evidence shows that the latter positions facilitate the delivery of the child. Hospitals in the United States rarely allow friends and relatives to attend births, although the time when the father would wait anxiously outside the delivery room seems to have come to an end. In many areas of the world, however, a large number of women, midwives, female kin, and friends are present in the room, but no strangers.

The U.S. experience has shown signs of changing attitudes toward giving birth; for instance, photographing or filming the pro-cess was introduced several decades ago, inviting more people, even strangers, to participate in the event through this visual medium. Childbirth varies according to cul-ture. In some, as in the United States, it has been treated like a sickness and the woman is rushed to the hospital to be attended by professionals. In others, it may be a cause for celebration or considered a defiling of the premises as fluids spill from the wom-an's body. The act of giving birth is a part of the general attitude toward women in that society; therefore, the event is influenced by gender politics.

Population growth is a public concern in most countries, but it takes many forms. In the United States during the mid-twentieth century, when a decrease in population among the mostly white middle class rang alarm bells, women were exhorted to have more babies to preserve their race and even "civilization" (Gordon, 1976). To encour-age women to have babies, men in the clergy, medical sciences, and politics took it upon themselves to glorify motherhood, to emphasize that it was a woman's duty, and to promise a near-painless childbirth aided with ether and other drugs like scopolamine that caused the woman to forget the pain she

had experienced. There were also scientists who advised women, contrary to those who promoted the use of drugs, that pain dur-ing childbirth was the result of culturally induced fear.

In Europe after the two world wars, which had caused immense losses in population, French and Russian physicians, attempt-ing to reverse the trend of a low birth rate, introduced a new approach to childbirth. "Prepared childbirth" involved mental con-centration so that women could enhance their awareness of the different stages of muscle contraction involved in giving birth, learning to concentrate on controlling them, rather than just passively experienc-ing them as pain. Learning the stages of labor, they could concentrate on different methods of breathing, orchestrated to man-age their responses to each stage. A French doctor, Fernand Lamaze, who was sympa-thetic to such ideas, adopted the approach. His name came to be commonly associ-ated with prepared childbirth in the United States, where it became popular (Karmel, 1965). In the "Lamaze method" of giving birth, the importance of mental preparation replaced anesthesia, but mechanical moni-toring increasingly complicated the hospital situation.

The concept of childbirth during which the mother is not anesthetized was promoted among pregnant U.S. women by holding group sessions in which the experiences of pregnancy and giving birth were shared and discussed and husbands or partners were encouraged to attend and learn to help the woman monitor her breathing. The increased awareness that resulted from the movement has led to greater demands for individual, private control of childbirth and to a gradual drift away from the more ritualized approach used in prepared childbirth classes. The cur-rent resistance by many women to the vigor-ous demands of "natural" childbirth and the more relaxed attitude toward taking painkillers when needed are manifestations of these new trends. Feminists respect the diversity in childbirthing choices for women but still urge women to be well informed about the process of childbirth and to not let themselves be placed in any particular birthing situation without asking questions of the medical establishment.

Breastfeeding: Attitudes and Choices

Social and cultural factors, as well as the physical context of motherhood, affect breastfeeding practices. The biological aspects of lactation, like the treatment and welfare of babies, are shaped by a combination of physiology and society. Women who are supported by their social environment are more successful at breastfeeding; stress and distractions can interfere with a mother's production of milk. Physiology is on the side of the mother and her child when she breastfeeds. Mother's milk builds immunity in the newborn baby, which it needs vitally at this stage. Mother's milk also contains almost all the nutrients that larger amounts of prepared milk "formula" can provide. Breastfeeding can often delay the resumption of women's fertility and can help space out pregnancies. In those societies where cultural factors place taboos on having sexual intercourse with a lactating mother, a mother is aided by not conceiving another child immediately. This natural contraception, though far from perfect, provides her with some respite from continuous pregnancy and ensures enough milk for the child until another one arrives and claims the breast. And as we have seen above, the release of the hormone oxytocin can make breastfeeding enjoyable and even relaxing.

In the United States fewer than 75% of women breastfeed, and by the time their babies are one year old, only around one fifth are nursing (Bakalar, 2010). Most women, however, in most parts of the world over history have had no choice; breastfeeding has always been the only way to nourish infants. Mothers carry their infants with them wherever they go, to gather food (as do the dwellers of the Kalahari Desert in South Africa) or on their jobs (as do the domestic workers in South and Central America). For working middle- or upper-class women, new devices such as "breast pumps" were introduced so that they can store their milk to be fed to the child in their absence. In many countries, including the United States, there are cultural proscriptions against revealing the breast in public, even for feeding babies. In most professional workplaces, babies and children are still rarely welcome.

The development of prepared milk formula for babies has been a mixed bag for women. On the one hand, formula is essential for women who can't breastfeed or produce enough milk for their babies. It allows women to return to work and men to share in baby care by outsourcing nutrition. But baby formula has become a huge business: until recently, all new mothers were given "gift bags" of formula in American hospitals. In the 1950s and 1960s, when the Swiss company Nestlé pushed its "prepared or fortified" powdered milk in areas of south Asia and Africa, where the water to mix formula powder could not be sterilized or women were not told not to water the formula down to make it last longer, children died from water-borne diseases and malnutrition. Only after a widespread outcry have companies like Nestlé agreed that "breast is best" for babies and mothers.

Baby formula was not the first replacement for mother's milk that some societies have found. Substitutes for breastfeeding (or at least for doing the feeding oneself) actually have a long history. In imperial Rome, as in seventeenth-century France and eighteenth-century England, wealthy women and working women had an option other than nursing: the use of "wet nurses" who were paid to breastfeed other women's infants. Likewise, during slavery in the United States, slave women were wet-nurses for their owners' children.

Though some women find nursing their babies sensually and emotionally gratifying, others resent the idea of being tied down to a nursing schedule or feel that breastfeeding is uncomfortable and exhausting (Rosin, 2009). It should be possible for women to make choices concerning breastfeeding, as well as childbirth, not on the basis of stereotypes or cultural strictures in which they have had no say at all but to suit their own personal beliefs, desires, and circumstances (see Box 7.6).

Box 7.6   THE BACKLASH AGAINST BREASTFEEDING

ABOUT SEVEN YEARS ago, I met a woman. . . who was young and healthy and normal in every way, except that she refused to breast-feed her children. She wasn't working at the time. She just felt that breast-feeding would set up an unequal dynamic in her marriage—one in which the mother, who was responsible for the very sustenance of the infant, would naturally become responsible for everything else as well. . . . I recalled her with sisterly love a few months ago, at three in the morning, when I was propped up in bed for the second time that night with my new baby (note the my). My husband acknowledged the ripple in the nighttime peace with a grunt, and that's about it. And why should he do more? There's no use in both of us being a wreck in the morning. Nonetheless, it's hard not to seethe. *The Bitch in the House*, published in 2002, reframed *The Feminine Mystique* for my generation of mothers. We were raised to expect that co-parenting was an attainable goal. But who were we kidding? Even in the best of marriages, the domestic burden shifts, in incremental, mostly unacknowledged ways, onto the woman. Breast-feeding plays a central role in the shift. In my set, no husband tells his wife that it is her womanly duty to stay home and nurse the child. Instead, both parents together weigh the evidence and then make a rational, informed decision that she should do so. Then other, logical decisions follow: she alone fed the child, so she naturally knows better how to comfort the child, so she is the better judge to pick a school for the child and the better nurse when the child is sick, and so on. Recently, my husband and I noticed that we had reached the age at which friends from high school and college now hold positions of serious power. When we went down the list, we had to work hard to find any women. Where had all our female friends strayed? Why had they disappeared during the years they'd had small children?

The debate about breast-feeding takes place without any reference to its actual context in women's lives. Breast-feeding exclusively is not like taking a prenatal vitamin. It is a serious time commitment that pretty much guarantees that you will not work in any meaningful way. Let's say a baby feeds seven times a day and then a couple more times at night. That's nine times for about a half hour each, which adds up to more than half of a working day, every day, for at least six months. This is why, when people say that breast-feeding is "free," I want to hit them with a two-by-four. It's only free if a woman's time is worth nothing.

Source: Hanna Rosin, http://www.theatlantic.com/magazine/archive/2009/04/the-case-against-breast-feeding/7311/. (c) 2009 The Atlantic Media Co., as first published in *The Atlantic* magazine. All rights reserved. Distributed by Tribune Media Services.

Support Systems: Fathers, Women's Networks, and Institutionalized and Societal Support

If motherhood is a social institution, as we have thus far suggested, support for the woman who has given birth or has become a mother by adoption or fostering ought to be provided by the state. Yet, like almost all aspects of motherhood, support for mothers is highly politicized and debated. Fathers, even when willing to assist their mates, are restricted by society: laws and rules regulate a father's role and his closeness to the mother and their children. In some cases, he may have access to her only if they are legally married; in others, he may have to work away from his family. In the absence of a father's support, women with significant resources may hire a nurse or a nanny. More often, help comes from other women who are kin or friends. The women who help a mother are often older, like grandmothers (Hrdy, 1999: 282–6; 2009). If the mother is forced to seek employment to support herself and her child and has no help at home, she depends on government or community-provided day-care centers. In their absence, a mother may look to other women for informal day-care networks. Otherwise, she may be forced to take her child everywhere she goes, as is the practice among the !Kung of the Kalahari Desert in South Africa, where a mother carries her child with her as she forages for food (Hrdy, 2009: 73–4).

Maternity-leave benefits, now largely replaced by parental leave, are also subject to politics and do not hinge on the wealth of a country (see Box 7.7).

Fathers

The model of the "traditional" family in the Global North has been a wage-earning father providing for his dependents, the mother and children. While, as other chapters in this book show, this is actually a fairly recent development that came into being in the wake of industrialization and has been true for only a specific segment of the population, the image of the breadwinning father and nurturing mother has a great deal of power in our culture.

Historically, women's sexual and reproductive lives could be more easily controlled by restricting women to the domestic sphere. Even today in the United States, not providing mothers with paid maternity leave stems from the effort to control motherhood. An economic and social system that ensures that most women are paid less than men (see Chapter 12) is one way to ensure that they are made financially dependent on their husbands. A federal law passed in May 2003 that rewarded married couples with a greater tax cut was part of such a policy, for in its ramifications it encouraged women to get married and be unpaid workers at home. Often-repeated phrases such as "family values" and "keep the family together" are ultimately meant to segregate women in their homes.

Fathers as parents can share the burdens of mothers. And, indeed, recent studies show that there is a remarkable consensus among women and men that both parents should share in the work and pleasures of raising children: between 90% and 98% of women and men surveyed agreed that mothers and fathers should be equally involved in the emotional and social lives of their children, including discipline, play, helping choose friends and playmates, and so on—although fewer than 70% agreed that both parents should share basic care equally (Bianchi and Casper, 2000). The reality is quite different, however. The same study showed that fathers believe that they do much more child care than either their female partners perceive or than they *actually* do. Women are often surprised by how much the division of labor within the home changes when they become mothers. Rachel Cusk, a British author, tells of how, after the birth of a daughter, she remained with her

Box 7.7 HOW THE ZERO WEEKS OF PAID MATERNITY LEAVE IN THE UNITED STATES COMPARE GLOBALLY

Out of 178 nations, the U.S. is one of three that does not offer paid maternity leave benefits, let alone paid leave for fathers, which more than 50 of these nations offer. Here's how the U.S. stacks up to 14 other countries:

Canada and Norway offer generous benefits that can be shared between the father and mother, France offers about four months, and even Mexico and Pakistan are among the nations that offer 12 weeks paid leave for mothers.

American women are offered 12 weeks of unpaid leave under the Family and Medical Leave Act, which exempts companies with fewer than 50 paid employees, but in 2011, only 11 percent of private sector workers and 17 percent of public workers reported that they had access to paid maternity leave through their employer. For first-time mothers, only about half can take paid leave when they give birth.

At the same time that working women in the U.S. lack a benefit widely available across the globe, almost 50 percent of families had two working parents in 2010, and 26 percent of households were headed by single parents. Without guaranteed paid maternity leave, many of these working women face significant financial hardship by having to choose between their paycheck and their families.

Women are forced to put their careers and financial future at risk simply because they want to have children. During their pregnancy, they face being fired unfairly or not being able to properly care for themselves. They should not have to worry about making ends meet without paid maternity leave on top of that.

Source: Amanda Peterson Beadle, with Adam Peck, *Think Progress*, May 24, 2012, © 2005–2012 Center for American Progress Action Fund. For country-by-country statistics, see http://www.nationmaster. com/red/graph/lab_par_lea_pai_mat_lea-labor-parental-leave-paid-maternity. This material [article] was published by the Center for American Progress Action.

baby while her partner continued to work out-side their home. She came to think that their life began to resemble a kind of feudal rela-tionship, in which she was wholly dependent on the lord of the manor for the maintenance of herself and their child (Cusk, 2001: 5–7). Particularly in the United States, where there is little state-supported child care, it can some-times make financial sense for one partner to work full time and the other to care for their children; the long-established assumption is that a woman will be that caretaker. While the numbers of fathers participating in or even tak-ing on all of the care for children is growing, a more humane social and economic system is necessary to make full collaboration in the rais-ing of children a reality.

Women's Networks, Community, and Institutionalized Support

Next to a child's father, a mother's help comes from other women, sometimes her women kin, especially those who have passed the child-bearing age and have no small children of their own to demand their attention. Widowed or unmarried mothers, aunts, and sisters extend their assistance to a mother in need of help to care for her child. Grandmothers are of spe-cial importance. Anthropologist Sarah Blaffer Hrdy has shown that postmenopausal women still serve evolutionary purposes by helping their daughters raise their offspring (Hrdy, 2009: 233–72). Interestingly, the maternal grandmother is more beneficial to the mother and her children than the husband's mother. In the United States at the beginning of the twenty-first century, grandmothers are the primary caregivers of approximately 4 million children (Hrdy, 1999: 282–6). For example, when the Obamas first moved into the White House, Michelle Obama's mother, Marian Robinson, at the age of 71 accompanied them to help care for her granddaughters, accom-panying them to and from school, helping

with homework, showing up at school events, and babysitting.

When help from mates or kin is unavailable or not forthcoming, mothers turn to friends or the Internet, where online chat groups, parenting websites, and listserves have pro-liferated for parents to share information and resources. Mothers may pool their resources and take turns in caring for each other's small children. This practice has been institution-alized in the form of cooperative day-care centers in many towns in the United States. Unlike kin- and friend-based support sys-tems, institutionalized community support in the form of day-care centers is a fairly recent phenomenon. In socialist countries such as Cuba, and in many European countries, government-supported day-care centers are common, as are privately run day-care cen-ters. The United States stands almost alone among the industrialized societies in having a very limited national family policy with regard to such supports as family allowances, manda-tory parental leaves, and child-care facilities (see Box 7.7). Although a law passed in May 2003 offered an increased child tax credit of $1,000 to families in upper income brackets, about 50 million households—36% of all households in the nation—were to receive only $400 per child; these low-income fami-lies include 2.5 million single parents. This highly politicized "tax reform" punishes poor women, especially those with children, who need to work but receive very little relief from the government.

Political ideologies in the United States have simply not kept up with the social reali-ties, have denied the changes in family con-figurations (see Chapter 6), and have turned a deaf ear to the plight of mothers. As more women and children are pushed into pov-erty, the future of motherhood for millions of women in the United States cannot be very bright. In 2008, the mothers of 41% of babies born in the United States were not married

(Douthat, 2010). Whether divorced or never married, single mothers are overburdened with their workload. The Bush administration's welfare plan (2003) required poor single mothers to work 40 hours a week in addition to caring for children. As for the tasks of caring for children, such as preparing their food, washing their clothes, helping them with their homework, and taking them to doctors, these remain unpaid work, and welfare regulations do not count them as real work.

Anne Lamott, in *Operating Instructions. A Journal of My Son's First Year* (1993), describes the tribulations of being a single mother despite the help of close friends and family. She writes about how little sleep she gets, laments the lack of interest shown by her baby's father, and finally when she runs out of money she returns to work as a writer. Less educated single mothers have fewer options. Lamott is one of the ever more numerous middle-class American women over the age of 20 who choose to become mothers, are the sole support of families of one or two children, and are respected members of their communities (Hertz, 2006). They wish to experience the joys of motherhood even though they have not found (and may not be interested in finding) the perfect mate, and they adopt, or more often bear, young children, using sperm contributed by a friend or purchased from a sperm bank.

Childrearing Experts

Modernity has shaken the roots of traditional families. Since the late nineteenth century, families have been on the move, especially from rural areas to urban centers, in search of work and a better life; education for children has consistently been a foremost consideration. In these moves, mothers have generally lost the direct support and advice of their mothers and other kin in rearing their children. Finding themselves alone and bewildered, mothers have historically turned to manuals, which offer advice about caring for children. Ann Hulbert's *Raising America* (2003) is a history of the major handbooks. According to Hulbert, most of the child-care experts have been men. These theorists, pediatricians, and psychologists have advised women about regulating the behavior of their children, from eating habits to cuddling. The advice "experts" have offered changed dramatically from generation to generation, as philosophies of childrearing have adapted to shifting social values. One of the best known child-care experts was Dr. Benjamin Spock, whose book *The Common Sense Book of Baby and Child Care* first appeared in 1946 and has since gone into an eighth edition. Translated into 39 languages with over 50 million copies sold, this advice book has had the widest influence on mothers (Acocella, 2003). Another source of childrearing advice has been from columnists in women's and parenting magazines. By imposing their views on mothers, the authors, overwhelmingly male, have directed the practice of motherhood. Feminist mothers need to offer their counsel to their sisters, daughters, and granddaughters.

Choices and Control: The Politics of Motherhood

We have seen in this chapter that women's reproductive rights are constructed by laws, customs, governments, and religions. The politicizing of motherhood and the control over women's bodies and lives seem to be directed at curbing the power of women as the sole bearers of children. (Although it is scientifically possible to clone humans, the ethical objection renders this prospect moot for the time being.) Whether it is to ensure the continuity of individual families or the human species, men are in the forefront of regulating women's bodies. It seems childbearing bodies are too precious to entrust their ownership only to women. The regulations imposed on women's reproductive rights limit men's accessibility to women's bodies but also curb women's rights to exercise free will in terms of choice of mates, of when and how and how often to have children, and of how to raise them. Men, when in doubt of paternity, often withdraw their support for the care of their partners' children. They thus attempt to force women to restrict their sexual activities to monogamous relationships.

Women's destinies in almost every society, with the exception of northern European countries where women's rights to their bodies are legally accepted, seem to be centered on their reproductive capacity. Women's control of their bodies must start with their free and unrestricted access to reasonable and sound birth control, including, if necessary, abortion.

Whether, When, and How Often to Become a Mother

Struggles over the development of safe and effective contraceptive methods continue to this day. Contraceptives have been made available to women but only after many battles fought and not all universally won (see Chapters 5 and 9). Literacy and education among women are linked to knowledge about birth control, although women have long shared traditional methods to prevent and end pregnancy through herbal medicine, knowledge that is now being revived.

To regulate the frequency of children and to relieve families from the difficulties of maintaining large numbers of children, couples have taken various types of precaution to control reproduction (see also Chapter 9). Birth-control techniques range from the so-called rhythm method practiced traditionally among Catholics, which takes a woman's ovulation period into consideration, to infanticide, euphemistically called "overlaying,"

when infants are "accidentally" smothered by their caretakers. Coroners' reports for London between 1855 and 1860, for example, list 3,900 deaths, mostly of newborns, from "overlaying" (Hrdy, 1999: 290–1). Aborting a fetus is another form of birth control. Despite the imbalance in responsibility assigned to women and men for having or not having babies, there has been a history of legal obstacles to women's reproductive freedom. In Britain, the first laws banning abortion altogether were passed in 1803; the Catholic Church worldwide banned abortion for its communicants in 1869. In the United States, abortion up until quickening (when a fetus is first felt moving), usually the second trimester of pregnancy, was legal in most states until the middle of the nineteenth century. After the Civil War, probably as a result of the high number of deaths caused by the war, many states adopted pro-natalist policies and outlawed abortion entirely. In 1873, as part of a new restrictive attitude toward sexual expression ("social purity"), the federal government passed the Comstock Law, which banned distribution of pornography, methods of abortion, and all means of preventing conception (Yalom, 2001).

Efforts to open birth-control clinics in Europe and the United States in the late nineteenth and early twentieth centuries were met with strong state and church opposition. The depression of the 1930s, when economic conditions discouraged large families, resulted in the loosening of restrictions on birth control in the United States. By 1940, every state except Massachusetts and Connecticut had legalized access to contraceptive information. Family-planning clinics, some publicly funded, were established. In 1965 the Supreme Court held (*Griswold* v. *Connecticut*) that an individual's right to privacy encompasses a woman's right to decide about whether to conceive children and, therefore, to have unrestricted access to contraception. Elsewhere in the world, some countries that are predominantly

Catholic, like Poland, outlaw abortion and severely limit the use of contraceptives. Other countries, concerned about severe poverty in the midst of a rapidly expanding population, have made it official policy to encourage contraception (as in India or the People's Republic of China) and to restrict by means of serious financial and other disincentives the number of children couples may have.

Limiting the number of children is motivated in a family or in a nation by the acknowledged economic burden of raising children. Little or no attention is paid to the wish or health of women when it is state policy, as in the People's Republic of China. Conversely, the desire to increase women's fertility, as in Nicolai Ceausesceau's Romania, or among some ultra-Orthodox Jewish and fundamentalist Christian communities, rarely takes into account the emotional or physical effects of multiple pregnancies, deliveries, and children upon women. Contraceptive devices have been developed for both women and men, although the majority are for women, upon whom lies the burden of their use. On the other hand, to the extent that there is choice about and responsibility for birth control, these devices emphasize the woman's role. Women, in order to make their own choice about pregnancy, need not only legal backing and access to technical devices but full knowledge and awareness of the options. Social conditions have not fostered an atmosphere conducive to real choices. Rather, women have usually been pressured to become mothers from early childhood. Traditionally, men could divorce women for barrenness, or in polygynous societies take another wife. Women who depended on husbands for economic support and protection had no choice but to try to become mothers. For many teenage girls living in poverty, having a child may seem like a chance for happiness and self-esteem, though many become pregnant from lack of sexual information and knowledge of the difficulties of raising a child alone.

Today, many women, especially in the Global North, have the opportunity to ask themselves whether they want a child. They have become aware of the options available to them and are making choices with regard to reproductive technology. Nevertheless, questions about the rights of women around the world remain. Should such rights be granted to a pregnant woman's parents if the woman is a minor and unable to support a child? The U.S. Supreme Court said no to this question in 1964, but such issues continue to be debated, especially at the state level. Because it is women who undergo the burdens of pregnancy and of giving birth, it seems appropriate to place the sole right to determine conduct over childbearing in their hands. Many, however, including some women, are unwilling to accord this power only to the women involved.

Surrogate motherhood, a form of bearing a child that is on the increase, is when a woman is inseminated with an unrelated man's sperm in order to give birth to a child to be raised by others, for example, if a man and his wife are infertile or if a gay man wants to have a baby. It also is used when a fertilized egg (which may have been contributed by the woman or purchased from an egg "donor") is implanted in the womb of a woman who will carry the embryo to birth for the genetic parents. Some issues involved in surrogate mothering that concern feminists, the courts, and the state legislatures are the likelihood of exploitation of poor women who receive payment for bearing a child, the rights of non–birth parents in same-sex relationships, and whether a surrogate mother who contributes her ovum may be permitted to change her mind about giving up her child. These issues remain to be resolved. There is, at present, almost no help from public sources for infertile women who cannot pay the high fees demanded for the new birth technologies. Even these assisted reproductive technologies, like artificial insemination, may not help or may result in multiple births, often at high risk to mother and babies. Infertility may also be the result of restricted options, such as the lack of parental leave and child care, which make women delay having children until it proves too late to conceive. Furthermore, infertility may be caused by workplace and environmental hazards that need to be controlled (see Chapters 9 and 12).

Control over Children

While women in the past were obligated, for the most part, to bear children if they could, the extent to which they had control over their children once they were born varied in different times, places, and classes. Patriarchal societies, such as the traditional Muslim countries, have often viewed children legally as well as by custom as the "possession" of their father and his kin group, and these relatives have determined how children should be raised, taught, married, and employed. Often, this kin group was not formally obligated to consult or even inform the children's mother about decisions that had been made for them. If women lost their husbands through divorce or widowhood, they were often obliged to leave their children as well. Patriarchal patterns have characterized Europe and the United States until the modern era. Not until 1839, for example, did laws in Victorian England make it possible for women to claim physical custody of children under 7 years old. In the United States, the issue has been dealt with on a state-by-state, case-by-case basis. From the early twentieth century until recently, when marriages ended in divorce, women were for the first time given custody of their children on the grounds that the decision was best for the child. Some states, however, have lately made changes in custody decisions that reflect the changing view of the best interests

of the child. A father, instead of declaring his wife unfit as a mother, now has to argue why his custody is better for the child. The women's movement and concurrent rethinking of parental roles have led more fathers to seek physical and legal custody of their children. For some, the solution is joint custody of children shared equally by their parents.

Mothers who dissolve a partnership with a man and enter into a relationship with another woman have not done well in the courts when they seek the custody of their children. Too often they are viewed as "unfit" mothers by judges. The general tendency to be intolerant of homosexuality in many societies, including the United States, leads judges to put their biases before the welfare of the child. Yet there is every indication that children of lesbian mothers fare as well as if not better than children of heterosexual ones (Park, 2010).

Laws designed to protect children ironically have been used as weapons against poor women and women of color. Because of their poverty, lack of education, or lack of familiarity with local practices, these mothers have often been blamed for abuse, neglect, or simply being slovenly in their care of the house and children. Children may be removed from the custody of their mother because of neglect or abuse and placed in foster homes or put up for adoption, permanently cutting all ties with their mother. Poor women are often unable to fight in the courts because they lack funds for adequate legal help.

International adoption has increased dramatically in recent years. In 2009 the vast majority of international adoptions by Americans involved children from China, Ethiopia, and Russia (Levy, 2010). Madonna's and Angelina Jolie's adoptions of children from Malawi, Cambodia, and Ethiopia attracted a great deal of publicity. While most international adoptions are successful, some are failures. Some of the adopted children have untreatable physical and mental

---

Box 7.8 INTERNATIONAL ADOPTION: "ADOPTION'S DIRTY SECRET"

Stop blaming the mom who sent her adopted son back to Russia, says Susan Scarf Merrell, the author of the novel *A Member of the Family*, about an international adoption which ended with the adoptive parents relinquishing the child permanently for foster parenting.

The untold story of adoptions is that they fail a lot more often than we'd like to admit. Now that Russia has suspended all adoptions to the United States after a Tennessee mother made the unfortunate choice to send back her adopted son, everyone's looking for someone to blame.

But if this boy had been released into the foster care or juvenile justice systems in this country—"returned" in the quiet manner in which such situations like this are normally resolved—we would never have heard a peep about this boy, or his mother. It's a dirty little secret that no one likes to talk about: Adoptions fail. More of them than we'd like to admit. And because we don't talk about it, when they do fail, we look for someone to blame instead of looking at the problem.

. . . Exactly how often adoptions fail is poorly tracked data. A 2003 study by the Government Accounting Office found that about 5 percent of all planned adoptions from foster care "disrupt"—that is, fail after the child was placed with its new parents, but before the adoption is legally finalized. But even legally complete adoptions dissolve at a rate of up to 10 percent. And for older children adopted after infancy, like the 7-year-old Russian boy who came not from foster care but from institutionalized care in an orphanage, the failure rate shoots up to a disturbing 15 percent or more.

Yet despite the fact that adoption failure happens with relative frequency, it remains one of our great unspoken taboos. Instead of acknowledging the systemic problem, we blame the individuals involved. . . .

. . . Nobody's life goes back to its original rhythms after a failed adoption. Nobody forgets. Nobody celebrates.

Source: Susan Scarf Merrell. "Adoption's Dirty Secret," *The Daily Beast. Blogs & Stories*, April 17, 2010. http://www.thedailybeast.com/author/susan-scarf-merrell/.

---

illnesses, in some cases the result of abuse in an orphanage, the biological mother's alcoholism, or simply her poverty, poor nutrition, or lack of education (see Box 7.8).

Working for Wages

In many countries, women with small children spend less time on paid work and more time on unpaid work. The responsibility for child care lies mainly with women, who spend more than twice as much time as men do on it. Compared to men, women spend considerably more time doing unpaid work and much less time doing paid work, almost universally (United Nations, 2000). Even so, in the United States, the percentage of women with young children who do full-time paid work more than doubled from 14% in 1978 to 35% in 1998 (Bianchi and Casper, 2000).

Working women of all backgrounds have had to negotiate the demands of motherhood with the reality of wage-earning. In countries in which child care is provided by the state and new parents receive extended paid leaves, the conflict between working and mothering is much less. In countries like the United States, however, where parents are expected to make child-care arrangements themselves, women have faced significant obstacles. This situation is especially difficult for women in the global labor market, who travel from their homes to other countries as domestics, nurses, factory workers, and the like. For many women, providing for their families means giving up the opportunity of raising their own children, who are left at home in the care of grandparents, aunts and uncles, or other family members (Ehrenreich and Hochschild, 2002).

"Unnatural" Mothers: Mothers Who Give Up Their Children

So far, this chapter has focused on "natural," or "birth," mothers. The idealized picture of the mother is a young woman embracing her infant child. The picture that has been handed down from generation to generation would lead us to believe that mothers are instinctively committed to nurture their children. We do not take into consideration that there are women who, for one reason or another, are unable or unwilling to care for their children; there are unwanted children who are born to single, very young, very poor mothers, sometimes already with more children than they can handle. When a woman gives up her child because she feels unable to bear the responsibility of raising it, she is readily blamed for not behaving in the normal way, for lacking in maternal instincts or being "unnatural." A mother who gives up her child may do it to protect herself from a society that reacts harshly to unwed mothers or to procure a better future for her child and for herself, because she finds that to work or earn an education would be impossible with a small child. There are countries, like the People's Republic of China, that regulate against more

than one child per couple, and because boys are preferred, daughters may often be relinquished (see Chapters 8 and 10).

Orphanages and foundling "hospitals" have existed in many countries. The most complete historical records on infant abandonment exist in Italy; for example, in 1640, 22% of all children baptized in Florence were abandoned babies. In the worst years on record, during the 1840s, 43% of all infants baptized in Florence were abandoned. According to these records, the majority, about 90%, of children abandoned to a foundling home died there (Hrdy, 1999: 304). Babies and children in orphanages in poorer countries, as in Romania at the beginning of the twenty-first century, still die as a result of negligence, malnourishment, lack of funds, and lack of concern for abandoned children. Society judges mothers who relinquish their children as unnatural, but provisions for helping them or their children remain minimal.

Women Other Than Birth Mothers Who Mother

Lesbian Co-mothers

One facet of the second wave of the feminist movement was increased attention to women's sexual self-determination. For some women, this led to a realization of or the ability to finally act upon sexual desires for other women and to come out as lesbian. Many of these women had children from marriages to men and brought these children into their new relationships. This was new territory for the nonbiological mother of the children and for society as a whole. As mentioned above, the children's fathers often fought to have their ex-wives declared "unfit mothers" because of their sexuality. This earlier group of women gave way to a generation of lesbians who grew up with the legacy of gay liberation and chose to raise children in the context of a lesbian relationship. While some couples adopt children, others choose to have one partner become pregnant and bear the child(ren). The legal status of non–birth mothers varies from state to state: in some states they can "adopt" their children and become legal co-parents. In other states lesbians and gay men are prevented from adopting children at all, and non–birth mothers have no legal relationship to the children they raise.

Stepmothers

Any woman who substitutes for the "natural" mother does not fare well in our collective imagination. We learn the story of Cinderella and her stepmother in many languages and versions; the stepmother is not only an ugly woman but also evil. The negative image of the stepmother in myth and fiction, the resentment a child may feel toward the woman who replaces the mother, the absence of an early bonding between the child and the stepmother, and the latter's possible preference for her own children over the stepchild are potential reasons to anticipate the difficult role that awaits the stepmother. In almost every country today, however, "blended families" made up of stepparents and stepchildren are becoming common, and the figure of the "wicked stepmother" seems to be fading in relevance.

What of stepfathers? While many men take on childrearing responsibilities for their stepchildren, studies show that they are less likely to care for the children of another man. Child homicide is uncommon and tolerated nowhere. Yet, in the United States when the father of offspring under 2 years of age no longer lives in the home and an unrelated man or stepfather lives there instead, this rare event is 70 times more likely to occur. Among the Ache of South American forests, mothers themselves sometimes kill fatherless infants after a conscious evaluation of what the future holds (Hrdy, 1999).

Foster Mothers and Adoptive Mothers

In the United States, abandoned children are often placed in foster care. Foster mothers provide children with homes in exchange for wages. Although there is abuse in some foster homes, children can be reasonably well cared for, and intimacy and love can grow between foster mother and child, which in some cases may lead to adoption. Adoptive mothers have usually been married women because most adoptions are governed by the state or by the biological mother. Professionally successful single women, however, are sometimes finding it possible to adopt and find they also can turn to international adoption.

Godmothers

Since human children mature over a very long period, they need to be entrusted to the supervision of some adult if the parents are unable to care for them. The designation of a godmother is made in good will by the parents of the child. Sometimes a baby is given the godparent's name to create a recognizable link between them. In the West, the tradition of asking trusted friends and especially influential people to serve as godparents is widespread. The practice of "othermothering," an effort to build up support networks in the African American community, includes godmothers (Chase and Rogers, 2001). The goal is to create substitute parents who, if needed, will look after the offspring. Elsewhere, in some societies, including the Yanomamo of Brazil and Venezuela, sexual liaisons are part of the way a mother sets up networks of well-disposed men to help protect and provision her offspring (Hrdy, 1999: 246; 2009: 270–72).

Summary

Being a mother is the most significant, contradictory, responsible, intimidating, controversial, and politicized role there is for a woman. Images of motherhood permeate most societies in multiple cultural forms, mostly stereotypical. For example, mothers have been depicted in ancient Greek myths as all-powerful and in European paintings as the center of domesticity. U.S. ethnic literature abounds with depictions of the complex relationships of Jewish, African American, and Asian American mothers with their daughters and sons.

The dominant Western media, in particular, have idealized mothers and depicted them as weak and dependent. With the feminist movement, a more positive image of mothers is evident, yet few women can personify such representations of perfection, which contribute to anxiety, frustration, and isolation. The marketing of motherhood also fosters feelings of personal inadequacy in women. Contemporary feminists are beginning to speak out in media ranging from informal blogs to books about the contradictions of motherhood, including its oppressive conditions.

Although women bear children, mothering is cultural behavior. Because human children are dependent for so long, the role of parenting is extended. Biology dictates women's capacity for motherhood, but society enlarges the task of "mothering."

U.S. society has high expectations and standards of mothering, yet mothers and their tasks remain undervalued, and their role is not appreciated as "real work." Assigning parenting to women almost exclusively contributes to women's dependence and men's superior attitude toward women. Until very recently, fathers have been excluded from and often have not demonstrated an active role in childrearing. Feminists disagree about motherhood. For some, it contributes to women's oppression; for others, it can be a source of pride and empowerment.

Some women become mothers willingly, after consideration; others fall into the role without much thought; and on many women motherhood is foisted. The role of motherhood is everywhere manipulated by society, for example, in the choice a woman makes for her mate and the manner she chooses to give birth, to raise her child, and whether or not to breastfeed. Capitalist economies and men, in particular, have benefited from women being assigned the primary responsibility for childrearing. Men are free to acquire more economic, political, and social power.

The attitudes of women and men toward pregnancy, childbirth, and breastfeeding are culturally shaped by their societies and have changed over time and with the women's movement. Prenatal care varies widely across the globe. Class is also a factor in the United States as poor women suffer most from lack of prenatal care.

Support for mothers is highly politicized. The culture of each society prescribes the definition of motherhood, the fathers' role, and women's support networks. State support for women as mothers, including maternity leave and child-care centers, varies widely globally. In the United States, public policy that requires welfare mothers to work outside the home does not adequately reflect or support the social realities of contemporary families, especially for low-income single mothers, and may even penalize mothers and children. In Western societies, manuals written by "experts," largely men, historically came to dominate childrearing information, but nowadays women's online social networking is helping women feel less alone as they face the challenges of motherhood.

Women's reproductive rights, like the definition and role of motherhood, have been and continue to be constructed by laws, customs, governments, and religions. Safe and effective contraceptive methods have become available only as recently as the latter half of the twentieth century. Although surrogate motherhood is on the increase, feminists and the courts raise concerns about the exploitation of poor women. New technologies are increasing the possibility for infertile women to bear children, but there are health risks and financial costs.

Women's control over the children they have borne has varied in different times, places, and classes. Poor women and women of color are more vulnerable to losing custody. Although by necessity, women in many countries must spend time at paid work, their governments, for the most part, have not recognized the unpaid work that women contribute through the care of small children, which benefits each society.

Women have many reasons for giving up their children; sometimes it is for the children's survival and benefit. Women who do so are often viewed harshly by their cultures as "unnatural" mothers, yet their societies provide little support to help women and children in need. Institutions, such as orphanages, have existed to attend to abandoned children but, for the most part, are not ideal.

Women other than birth mothers also mother. Stepmothers have been maligned in mythology and fairytales. In real life, the stepmother–child relationship varies but can include a close bond. Fostering, adoption, and being a godmother are other ways in which women who do not give birth can mother.

Discussion Questions

1. What are some of the sources from which a woman in the United States learns how to be a mother? How do race, ethnicity, and class matter?
2. Examine the role and image of mothers for your generation, your mother's, and your grandmothers'. What have been the major changes over time?
3. From what you now know, what kind of changes in patterns of mothering would you hope for in the next 25 years? Do you expect any of them to happen?

4. How would you define the past and current role of grandmother and mother-in-law (hers and his)?
5. The "good and nurturing mother" and the "terrible mother" are important mythic figures. Find examples from literature and popular fiction, films, and folk tales that represent—sometimes simultaneously—the devaluation and exaltation of mothers.

Recommended Readings

Angelou, Maya. *I Know Why the Caged Bird Sings* (1969), an autobiographical novel about the relationship of a young girl with her glamorous but elusive mother in contrast to her bonds with the grandmother who cares for her through most of her childhood.

Colette. *My Mother's House and Sido* (1930), translated by Una Vincenzo and Enid McLeod. New York: Farrar, Straus, and Giroux, 1953. The distinguished French writer lovingly reminisces about her mother and the beneficent influence that she had. The author depicts the warm, rich atmosphere of the rural home where she grew up—a product, she claims, of her mother's creation. Her warm memories might be compared to earlier ones by Marcel Proust about his grandmother in *Swann's Way* (1913), the first of his series *Remembrances of Things Past* (1913–22).

Folbre, Nancy. *The Invisible Heart. Economics and Family Values.* New York: New Press, 2001. The author, an economist, provides a wide-ranging theoretical discussion of women as caregivers set in the context of social values.

Hertz, Rosanna. *Single by Chance, Mothers by Choice. How Women Are Choosing Parenthood without Marriage and Creating the New American Family.* New York: Oxford University Press, 2006. Based on interviews with 65 self-supporting middle-class women, including physicians and waitresses, who chose to raise one or two children without partners.

Rich, Adrienne. *Of Woman Born: Motherhood as Experience and Institution*. New York: Norton, 1976. In this book, now a feminist classic, Rich examines motherhood as a social institution and the way that it has evolved from antiquity to the present. She shows how relationships between women and men are reflected in the institution of motherhood and how concepts related to this institution change with changes in women's status. Rich, a feminist and poet, draws from her own experience as well as scholarly literature.

chapter **8**

Growing Up and Growing Older

A son's a son until he gets him a wife. A daughter's a daughter all the days of her life.

OLD ENGLISH PROVERB

I attribute my energy to post-menopausal zest!

MARGARET MEAD, ANTHROPOLOGIST, 1971

Women's and gender studies have focused largely on young and middle adulthood. Growing up and growing older are formative experiences but less studied components of women's lives. Girlhood in most parts of the world today has changed greatly over the centuries. Over the past five decades as part of the global community's efforts to advance the human rights of women and children, states and organizations have sought to end the labor and sexual exploitation of girls. More daughters in developing areas today, for example, are attending school and for longer periods of time. In industrialized states, girls now generally experience an extended period of relatively care-free youth before assuming adult responsibilities. Womanhood also has changed with increased longevity. The quality of those later adult years depends in large part on a woman's health, finances, interests, familial and other relationships, as well as government policies and societal customs pertaining to gender roles and the elderly. In this chapter we consider girlhood and adolescence and later adulthood for women within the context of family or family-like households.

Girlhood

Although girls generally hold a subordinate position in their families and societies compared to boys, their experiences, past and present, vary widely across the globe and within communities given differences in backgrounds, cultures, and family dynamics in specific historical eras. In the United

States, for example, girlhood as a daughter of migrant farm workers differs significantly from girlhood as a daughter of professional parents in a predominantly white middle-class suburb (Forman-Brunell, 2001). Moreover, worldwide girls are negotiating changing and often-competing notions of what it means to be a woman from within their own societies and under the external influence of the globalization of Western culture in media, advertisements, and consumer goods (Leach, 2010).

In the early 1990s, feminist studies of Euro-American middle-class girlhood in the United States emphasized girls' vulnerability, including problems of body image and eating disorders (Chapter 5), loss of confidence as their encounters with the dominant male culture increased during adolescence, neglect by schools (see Chapter 10), and the pressures of consumer culture with its sexualized representations of girls (Brown and Gilligan, 1992; Brown, 2008; Driscoll, 2008). Working-class girls, on the other hand, were deemed at risk to teen pregnancy, drugs, and gangs (Kehily, 2008).

Not all girls are sweet, passive, and "good." They can be "mean" to other girls, bullies, and cliquish (Simmons, 2002). In movies like the 2004 *Mean Girls*, these kinds of behavior are played for laughs, although they can be damaging for both perpetrators and victims. Such verbal and physical acting out may also be a form of opposition to having to conform to expectations of how girls should be (Lamb, 2001). Studies on girls' aggression have been balanced by others that give attention to girls who are emotionally and socially confident, do well in school, are active in sports, have close relationships with their parents and girl-friends, and feel no need to strive to be popular (Meadows, 2002).

Currently, the discourse of girls as disadvantaged and "in crisis" is being countered by the discourse of girls as proactive. "Girl power" recognizes girls' agency as they express their goals, navigate their pathways, and work collaboratively for safe spaces for themselves to develop (Brown, 2008; Driscoll, 2008; Kehily, 2008), although "girl power" rhetoric can often be appropriated in ways that are hardly empowering. Moreover, the marketing of pink "princess" girlie-girl clothes and products to preschoolers is a challenge for many modern U.S. parents seeking to raise their daughters with models other than Cinderella waiting for her prince (Orenstein, 2011). Girlhood, then, is a more complex period than formerly understood.

Teenagers rest near a billboard featuring a woman with a sexy pose on a street in Beijing, China, Monday, July 23, 2007. A Chinese newspaper reported that parents and experts are calling for a rating system and selective timeslots for television ads in a bid to reduce the exposure young children have to sexually suggestive advertisements.

In the following sections, we consider ways in which daughters, past and present, have been treated differently from sons. We also discuss why strategies and programs to support and enhance girls' empowerment are necessary and part of the global effort to end discrimination against females.

Daughter in the Family

The conception and birth of a child is usually a welcome event in a family. Sometimes, however, it is inconvenient or even disastrous to a household's economic survival. A new infant may threaten the health of the mother and older children, especially an unweaned child. Other times, when the child has been conceived in rape, incest, or another form of unsanctioned relationship, or when the mother is very young or single, its arrival may complicate family relations and harm the new mother's future prospects for schooling and marriage. Where contraceptive and abortive methods are unknown, unavailable, or undependable, infanticide, abandonment, giving the baby to others to raise, or simply neglecting a newborn have been options in the past for an unwanted child. Reflecting women's inequality worldwide, the death rate of infant girls far exceeds that of infant boys today as in the past. Male preference, which is almost universal, is manifested in parental and societal discrimination, family resource allocations, and government policy (Kristof and WuDunn, 2009; Rosenberg, 2009; see Chapter 10). Why and how have daughters been seen as more expendable than sons?

Female Infanticide and Neglect

Infanticide has existed since ancient times as a method of population control and sex selection of children, but female infanticide is more widespread. In 1 B.C.E., for example, a husband in Alexandria wrote to his wife in the Egyptian countryside: "I beg you and urge you...if by chance you bear a child—if it is a boy, let it be; if it is a girl, cast it out" (Hunt and Edgar, 1932). The Greeks abandoned many more girls to die than boys, and the Romans had a law requiring fathers to raise all healthy sons but only one daughter (Pomeroy, 1975). In medieval Christian society, where church law strictly forbade infanticide, it was still carried out extensively. Girls were the most common victims of "accidents" where women claim to have "overlaid" (smothered) children at night. When foundling homes were established, as in Florence in the fourteenth century, the records revealed that parents discarded many more females than males (Trexler, 1973).

Those readers who believe in a "maternal instinct" that causes mothers to protect their children must wonder what could prompt women to kill them instead. Inability to care for a child, particularly if it is "illegitimate" by a society's norms or if the other parent or other members of the society are not available for assistance, may be a motive. In some situations, a mother may suffer from postpartum depression or a debilitating physical or mental illness. Where infanticide is a socially recognized option, it may be the father alone who makes the decision and it may be the midwife or another party who carries it out.

Today, when new technologies can reveal the sex of the fetus in early pregnancy, they have been used, for example, by many families in patrilineal societies in East and South Asia to abort fetuses identified as female. In such households, one daughter may be considered ideal to help in the home, and additional ones may be seen as a burden. The "missing girls" in such families contribute to a disparate male–female sex ratio in these states (Das Gupta, 2009; Rosenberg, 2009).

Social practices that allot girls less food and medical care and overwork or abuse them physically help explain why more girls than boys die in infancy and early childhood (Rosenberg, 2009). The neglect of daughters is masked almost everywhere by the assertion that girls require less food than boys. When protein has been scarce, women have customarily stinted themselves and their daughters in favor of the husband and sons. This has prejudiced the daughters' well-being and socialized them to do the same later in their own households. This belief might account more for the differences in the size and physical strength of girls and boys than is generally acknowledged. In other cases, daughters are simply abandoned, put up for adoption, or even sold, often into a life of servitude or prostitution (Kristof and WuDunn, 2009).

Worldwide, more couples still prefer to have a son than a daughter, particularly if it is the first child, and many couples may continue having children until they have a son. There is virtually no society that positively prefers girl babies to boys.

The Value of Daughters

The selective destruction and neglect of female babies by individual families throughout history would not have been possible unless society as a whole condoned it. Many of the answers lie in the social patterns that define women's place and value to their society.

One theory explores the high value of males in societies engaged in chronic warfare. If men are the warriors, sons must be raised and "masculine" qualities stressed. Because investment in daughters detracts from investment in sons, daughters are sacrificed. The evidence supporting this argument shows a systematic correlation between female infanticide, chronic warfare, and male supremacist cultural values (Divale and Harris, 1978).

Another theory speculates about the marital strategies of individual families, which are political and economic decisions. In traditional cultures, the most common way in

Box 8.1 "BACHA POSH:" GIRLS MASQUERADING AS BOYS

Afghans of several generations report knowing a female relation, acquaintance, neighbor, or co-worker who spent her childhood and sometimes her early adulthood dressed up in boy's clothing and participating in activities, such as attending school and going to the market, as a male. In the Dari language, these girls are called "bacha posh" or "dressed up as a boy," a phenomenon that generally occurs in families of many daughters. Why do parents create a "fake son" of one daughter, who is then returned to a woman's dress, role, and place usually upon puberty? The many reasons reflect the greater value and privileges of boys. Societal pressures for male children are so great that having a pretend son offsets expressions of pity and enhances a family's standing even if only for a brief time. Also some families may hold to a superstition that by so doing a real son will be conceived. Moreover, because a *bacha posh* can work in a shop, run errands after school to places females are not permitted without a male escort, and accompany sisters on their outings as is the custom in her male attire, this daughter plays a vital role in the family's economic and social well-being as a son. She may be replaced by younger sister when she grows up and out of her son role.

How do "fake sons" feel about their experiences? For some, living as a boy gave them greater freedom to play sports and be educated, making them more determined to change gender inequities in their society. Others had a more difficult time "changing back" and had to learn to socialize as women. Azita Rafaat, who spent some years as a boy and whose third daughter is a *bacha posh* (see photo), found the experience enhanced her ability to communicate with men. Formerly a health worker, she became a politician and women's rights advocate and was one of 68 women in the 249-member Parliament in 2010. She hopes her own daughter will have a positive experience, but like other women wishes the practice did not have to exist in Afghanistan.

Source: Jenny Nordberg, "Where Boys Are Prized, Girls Live the Part," *The New York Times*, September 21, 2010.

which a family gets a daughter-in-law is in exchange for a daughter. Some societies operate on a rigid one-to-one basis: the exchange of cousins, for example. In many societies, a bride must be accompanied by wealth when leaving her father's house, a costly endeavor. In others, a daughter represents potential wealth that will be paid her parents in exchange for her and can be used to secure a bride for a son, pay off debts, or accumulate wealth (see Chapter 6). Where the potential marital pool is known and limited, parents may sacrifice daughters for whom there are no possibilities of a profitable future marriage settlement (Coleman, 1976). Hence, while daughters are valuable directly or indirectly as producers of grandchildren, the possibilities of enhancing family wealth and power or impoverishing the household play an important role in families' decision making about the value of girls.

Still another theory emphasizes gender ideologies. In patrilineal societies, in particular, where daughters are considered temporary members of a family while sons generally and historically have inherited property, carried on the family line, fulfilled cultural rituals, and had responsibilities for parents and female members of the household, son preference is reinforced (Das Gupta, 2009). In Afghanistan, so great is the social pressure to have a son that some families of girls may have one daughter masquerade as a boy to keep up appearances (see Box 8.1). In more egalitarian societies, subtle family choices can still disadvantage daughters. For example, one study found that U.S. parents invested more of their resources in improving their housing when they had a son (Leonhardt, 2003).

Decisions that favor women seem to exist only in the realm of fantasy. Ancient Greek myths about Amazons tell of women warriors who preferred girl babies to boys. Sons were maimed, killed, or immediately sent to their fathers. Feminists have adopted this myth about strong women but have modified its

ugly features. In *The Female Man* (1975), for example, Joanna Russ created a fictional utopia where women live without men and have only girls. Reproduction is accomplished by the merging of ova, and children are raised communally. More recently, fiction for young adults has given us girls who compete with and outdo their male counterparts: in the *Hunger Games* trilogy (2008), Suzanne Collins created in Katniss Everdeen a daughter who provides for her mother and sister, protects her male peers, and ultimately spearheads a revolution against a totalitarian government.

Naming the Daughter

The (low) status of women in different societies is revealed in naming patterns. A name generally designates the sex of a child. The more emphasis a society places on the difference between girls and boys, the more it distinguishes their names. Medieval Europeans usually got through life with a single name, which often repeated the father's name or embroidered on it, such as *Charles, Charlotte,* or *Charlene*. When named for fathers, daughters were given a close feminine form of his name: for example, *John/Joan, Robert/Roberta*. Boys are almost never given names identified with girls, but the reverse can occur, perhaps reflecting the greater worth attached to male associations. Sons are frequently named for their fathers. Daughters are far more rarely named for their mothers. Today, some daughters in the United States are given gender-neutral names (*Alex, Lee, Jessie,* or *Nicky*) or are named for places (*Jordan* or *Dakota*) and other novelties, which may suggest the desire of parents to reduce gender stereotyping in naming.

The importance of children for the continuity of a lineage is reflected in the use of *patronymics* (fathers' names). For example, the ancient Romans did not give their daughters individual names: they were automatically called by the feminine form of the father's name. Thus, all the daughters of a Claudius were called Claudia and referred to informally in numerical order: *Claudia prima, Claudia secunda, Claudia tertulla*. In some areas, patronymics continued into modern times. The Russian heroine of Tolstoy's novel *Anna Karenina* (first published in 1873–77) was named *Anna Arkadyevna* ("daughter of Arkady") Karenina ("wife of Karenin").

Traditionally in Korea, Confucian custom deemed female status too low for married women to be permitted to use the family name of their husbands. In contrast, Myanmar/Burma, with its Buddhist tradition and a matrilineal past, did not have a family name system. Both females and males were registered using their own individual names, and historically women did not change their names after marriage (Matsui, 1989: 109–10). In Spanish-speaking societies, women often retain their father's name by adding it (with *y*) to the husband's name. In other societies, children will perpetuate the name of their mother's family as a middle name or as a first name.

In the modern Western world, a daughter generally changed her surname to that of her husband's upon marriage. Many women have reported feelings of a loss of identity when they became Mrs. _____. A woman's married name designates a position rather than a person, and a first Mrs._____ may be replaced by a second or third with the same surname. Nowadays women in the United States may keep their family name when they marry, as they are legally entitled to do, and some do so for their professional lives. Many U.S. couples experiment with combining or hyphenating both names as a family name. It is still most common for U.S. children to have the surnames of their fathers. Some women reject the surnames of both fathers and husbands and choose their own.

Daughters' Work

Despite their lower status worldwide, girls can occupy an important position within their natal families based on the work they perform. In most households, including those in the contemporary Western world, daughters are expected to care for younger siblings and assist in food preparation and other domestic chores. In developing societies, where child labor is common, girls fetch water and firewood, feed chickens, go to the market, wash clothes, help with the dairying and agricultural work, and undertake income-producing tasks like garment work.

Historically and today in many parts of the world, daughters are thought to be critical for their parents' old-age security and are expected to provide personal care, affection, and other supports. Although sons are liable for the same responsibilities, too often they limit their contributions to cash, have their wives (the daughters-in-law) undertake much of their obligations, or manage to escape altogether. An old saying among the Turks is that only a daughter can be relied upon on a dark day, an adage similar to the old English proverb that opened this chapter.

In the United States, the value of daughters' (unpaid) work to families is evident in eldercare statistics. Overall women assume 68% of caring for those over age 50, although there are differences among racial/ethnic groups. Asian American households have the most equitable sharing; daughters and sons share 50% of caregiving. Lesbians and gays also provide more eldercare than those in heterosexual households (National Alliance for Caregiving, 2009). While some women may not choose the "mother track," they retain for the most part the "daughter track." The strains of eldercare can affect the daughters' health and personal and professional responsibilities. Many women sacrifice aspects of their daily lives and often give up or cut back on paid work, which decreases their income and retirement benefits (Metlife, 2011).

Parental Relationships

It's a girl! From the moment she is born and named, a girl is started on a track that will take her through her whole life as a daughter. Historically, social conventions tend to prescribe parents' behavior. Although gender roles remain rigid in many parts of the world, the changing structure of families worldwide in the twenty-first century (Chapter 6) has created more flexibility in how mothers, fathers, and other relations are raising daughters and sons. Nonetheless, the family remains a political system comprised of parents, siblings, and others. Daughters struggle for identity and material advantage within a pattern imposed by chance and social convention. We begin with daughters in traditional two-parent households.

Daughters and Mothers

Second-wave (white) Western feminists advanced a psychological development theory that identified three phases in a daughter's relationship with her mother (Applebaum, 2001). First, there is the attachment in early infancy and the power of same-sex bonding. Since the mothering person is nearly always a woman, daughters tend to experience stronger feelings of identity with her than do sons and may have more difficulty than their brothers in becoming their own persons (Chodorow, 1978). In cultures where women's and men's roles are distinctly defined, this is probably not a matter for distress. Mothers act easily as role models for young women. In societies that reward individualism, daughters may suffer much confusion in separating psychologically from their mothers.

Second, during adolescence and early adulthood daughters seek to differentiate themselves from their mothers while also maintaining a

---

Box 8.2 MOTHERS AND DAUGHTERS

They perpetuate themselves
one comes out of the other
like a set of Russian dolls.
Each is programmed to pass on
her methods to the daughter
who in turn becomes a mother.
They learn to cry and get
their way and finally to say
"I did it all for you."
When they are old and can't
be mended they're either burnt
or laid in boxes in the dark.
Sometimes their
sons are sad.
Their daughters go away and weep
real tears for themselves.

Russian Dolls (Photo by Richard Zalk)

Source: Vicki Feaver, 1980, reprinted by permission.

close relationship. Mothers may inhibit the development of a separate sense of identity by expecting daughters more than sons to remain closer to home. This may reflect a traditional pattern in which boys are prepared for roles in the larger world, while girls are expected to help with "women's work." Mother–daughter relationships therefore can be both rich and laden with conflict as daughters struggle for independence (Flax, 1997; Glasman 2002).

Third, after daughters grow up and most marry, work, and become mothers themselves, they often draw closer to their mothers, seeking their support and advice. Mother–daughter relationships become increasingly mutually interdependent and their roles may even reverse when mothers become elderly and daughters often mother their mothers (Beck, 1990) (see Box 8.2).

The psychological development model discussed above is not universal and has been challenged for privileging the mother–daughter dyad and overemphasizing conflict between generations (Henry, 2004). U.S. women of color, such as Patricia Hill Collins (2000) and Gloria Joseph (1981, 1991), have identified the importance of other female figures in mothering, such as grandmothers, siblings, aunts, cousins, and women who are not biologically related, as well as men who "mother" African American children. Joseph writes of the respect and affection of daughters for their mothers and mother surrogates in recognition of the obstacles the women (and occasionally men) confront in holding households together under conditions of racism and economic constraints, in addition to gender discrimination, that often require them to work long hours outside the home. Many African American mothers have purposely raised girls to be strong and independent for themselves and their households.

In short, mother–daughter relationships are varied and complex. (For a poet's and one mother's wishes for sons, see Box 8.3.)

BOX 8.3 WISHES FOR SONS

i wish them cramps
i wish them a strange town
and the last tampon.
i wish them no 7–11.

i wish them one week early
and wearing a white skirt
i wish them one week late.

later i wish them hot flashes
and clots like you
wouldn't believe. let the
flashes come when they
meet someone special.
let the clots come
when they want to.

let them think they have accepted
arrogance in the universe,
then bring them to gynecologists
not unlike themselves.

Source: From *Quilting: Poems 1987–1990.* Copyright © 1991 by Lucille Clifton. Reprinted with the permission of BOA Editions, Ltd.

The daughters of Richard and Emmeline Pankhurst followed their parents' commitment to working for radical social and political reform in England. Christabel, (top left) with her mother, established the radical Women's Social and Political Union in 1906 to gain women's suffrage. Sylvia (top right) established a separate women's suffrage movement among the working class in London's East End. Adela (bottom) emigrated to Australia, where she was active in socialist and labor politics.

Mothers may try to mold daughters in their own images; they may also consciously set out to create daughters who will not repeat their experiences. Mothers are often strong allies in helping daughters to realize their dreams. French author Colette ([1930] 1953) wrote of the encouragement she received as a child in her mother's house. The leader of the militant British suffrage movement, Emmeline Pankhurst (1858–1928), raised her daughters Christabel Pankhurst (1880-1958), Sylvia Pankhurst (1882–1960), and Adela Pankhurst (1885–1961) to live independent and creative lives. Each daughter distinguished herself in her own way as a leader of women's rights and social reformer.

Immigrant women in the United States report extensively of their mothers' support and insistence that their daughters would have educational opportunities they did not have. Anthropologist Cecilia Balli (2002) praised her Mexican working-class mother for teaching her a different kind of feminism from that in her courses at Stanford, one that also values sacrifice, small "everyday victories," and mutual support. Chinese American garment workers' daughters who have become professionals and community activists often speak with pride about their hard-working mothers and view them as role models (Bao, 2003). The theme of daughter–mother interdependence (and tensions) underlies much of American ethnic literature. Paule Marshall's classic novel about the child of West Indian immigrants in Brooklyn, *Brown Girl, Brownstones* ([1959] 1996), puts the mother–daughter relationship at its center—the protagonist Selina feels compelled to break away from her mother's expectations of her in order to forge her own identity, even as she feels close ties to the world her mother has created.

U.S. daughters of many racial and ethnic backgrounds who were raised by second-wave feminist mothers have recognized the new opportunities and rewards, both personal and professional, made available to them by their mothers' choices and activism. Hence, these daughters do not view marriage as their only option in life (Glickman, 1993). Some of them, however, have expressed ambivalence about those feminist mothers who seem to devalue motherhood (Baker and Kline, 1996).

Young women frequently find that breaking away from the pattern of their mothers' lives is difficult. As mature adults some daughters may still be haunted by their mothers' "nagging" voices in their heads telling them how to do everything. Other daughters recognize their mother's voice as they themselves speak and smile as they find themselves becoming more like their mothers (see Box 8.2). Still others, such as an adoptee who experienced the loss of her biological mother at a very young age, seek to fill missing parts of their lives (see Box 8.4).

Daughters and Fathers

Historically, fathers have had social, economic, and political power over their daughters as well as certain obligations, such as arranging for a proper marriage. Under conditions such as slavery, feudalism, and colonialism, many fathers were limited as the head of the household and able neither to provide adequately for their daughters nor to protect them. Daughters, on the other hand, have usually deferred to their fathers. As the historical and legal conditions of a father's power over his children have changed, so has a daughter's relationship with her father (Devlin, 2001). Nowadays, in the United States, for example, more fathers are feminists, shoulder a fair share of parenting, and treat daughters and sons in a reasonably equal way.

A daughter's relationship with her father can also be complicated. Daughters often join up with their mothers against the "foreign" male element represented by their fathers. On other occasions, hunger for a father's approval

---

Box 8.4   BECOMING WHOLE: A KOREAN AMERICAN ADOPTEE SEARCHES FOR HER BIRTH MOTHER

Growing up in Utah as an adoptee from Korea, Katy Robinson looked for her homeland in the darkness, imagined her mother and grandmother waiting for her at the Kimpo Airport, and sought to create an unbroken life out what she experienced as two halves. In the opening paragraphs of a memoir "dedicated to my two mothers," Robinson writes of her early memories and of the few photos of her previous life as she returns to Seoul after twenty years with the blessings of her American adoptive family to search for her birth mother and to make herself whole.

When I was seven years old, my mother and grandmother took me to the airport and watched as I boarded a plane for America.

At first I clung to the scent of roasted seaweed and peppery *kimchee*, the feel of my grandmother's body next to mine, and the last look on my mother's face. But with time, I became convinced my life simply began the moment I stepped off the airplane on the other side of the world. One day I was Kim Ji-yun growing up in Seoul, Korea; the next day I was Catherine Jeanne Robinson living in Salt Lake City, Utah.

When I first learned English, I told people my new name and announced, "I'pose to be Korean!" like I didn't believe it myself. In my new home, there was no face that mirrored my own, no one to describe how I got that dime-sized scar imprinted on my left knee. To tell me, perhaps, that I have my mother's eyes, my father's wit.

Left as I was to my own devices, memories of Korea became little more than blurred visions that flash and skip like a broken movie projector. In times of confusion, I return to the photographs—the undeniable evidence. A baby in a traditional Korean birthday costume. A five-year-old skipping down a brick path in a pink ruffled dress. A solemn face that disguises the scabby red remnants of chicken pox. Pasted to the top right-hand corner of the last photograph is a white label with my adoption number—3833—the one that gave me passage to this new life.

Source: From *A Single Square Picture: A Korean Adoptee's Search for Her Roots* by Katy Robinson, pp. 1-2. New York: Berkley Books, 2002.

---

makes daughters vulnerable to pleasing males at whatever cost. More commonly, daughters receive less focused attention from fathers than do sons, conveying to them that females are less worthy of attention than males (Bronstein, 2006).

Fathers who favor traditional gender roles may actively discourage a daughter's efforts to break out of conventional feminine practices and will compliment girls on pretty clothing and beguiling ways. When feminist-crusader Elizabeth Cady Stanton (1815–1902) won a first-place Latin award in school with the hope of compensating her father for the son he had lost, her father only sighed heavily and said, "You should have been a boy" (Stanton, [1898] 1971: 23).

An extreme form of a father's domination of a daughter is incest, a social taboo in almost all societies and a cruel exercise of power. Other male family members— uncles, stepfathers, brothers, cousins, and grandfathers—also perpetrate sexual abuse of females. Yet father–daughter incest is the most commonly reported type of incest in the United States, and its effects on women include low self-esteem, difficulties in maintaining social relationships, and often deep and lasting trauma. Incest may drive girls away from home as runaways, into a premature and unwanted marriage or pregnancy, or to drug addiction and prostitution (Russell, 1986; White and Frabutt, 2006).

Domineering fathers may provoke reactions in their daughters that release their feminist impulses and creative potential. Fathers can also be very supportive. Many prominent women have noted with gratitude their fathers' role in helping them develop skills and establish careers. Historically, however valuable the emotional support of mothers to aspiring daughters, the sheer material support that the father commands can make the difference in determining their fates. For example, astronomer Maria Mitchell (1818–1889), who became the first woman elected to the American Philosophical Society in 1869, spent many hours with her father gazing at stars through his telescope. In 1847, she discovered the comet that is named for her. Indira Gandhi (1917–1984), prime minister of India (1966–77 and 1980–84), credited her father, Jawaharlal Nehru, with preparing her for a world of politics. He purposely educated Gandhi about world history and took her along to meetings as India's first prime minister after the country gained its independence from Britain in 1947 (Bhatia, 1974).

A pioneering study of the lives and careers of a group of women who were among the few to hold top management positions in U.S. business and industry in the early 1970s revealed a distinct pattern. The women were generally the firstborn of girls or only children, and all had a close daughter–father relationship in which the daughter was given strong support to pursue her interests

(Hennig and Jardin, 1976). Wall Street executive Alexandra Lebenthal, architect Maya Lin, and writer Alexandra Styron are among the many feminists, and women entrepreneurs, artists, scientists, and other creative women, who speak with pride of a father's role in their accomplishments (Hass, 2002).

Daughters in Varied Family Configurations

Not all girls grow up in two-parent households. The 2010 U.S. census data show almost one third of all children in the United States are being raised by single parents (Population Research Bureau, 2010). Because different kinds of family structures often open up nontraditional gender roles, daughters may grow up differently. One study found that U.S. daughters in divorced mother-only households exercised more power and were given more responsibilities than girls in nondivorced two-parent families. As we have noted, daughters of color have long experienced nontraditional gender role divisions of labor and household decision making, where their mothers were prominent. Daughters of lesbians also demonstrate higher rates of leadership and a sense of adventure than their counterparts in heterosexual families (Bronstein, 2006).

Globalization, especially in terms of transnational migration, may disrupt parent–daughter relations but may also work to cement gendered roles in the families left behind by migrant worker parents. A study of Filipino transnational families where one parent migrated overseas for work found that traditional assumptions about the appropriate roles for the mothers and fathers who remained prevailed in both mother-away and father-away households. Moreover, the eldest daughter assumed major domestic responsibilities that often enhanced empathy between mothers and daughters, but also could intensify the daughters' feelings of abandonment (Parreñas, 2005).

Sibling Relationships

Girlhood is defined by sibling relationships as well as relationships with parents and other adults. Sex and age ranking are the most common means of discriminating among siblings. Many societies reserve specific privileges for older children. The upper ranks of British society and feudal Japan long held a tradition of passing the family wealth and property to the oldest male offspring. Parents also discouraged younger daughters from marrying until an older sister was settled. The firstborn female child will tend to be given more responsibility for the care of younger children. The older child will generally go to school first and break the path in obtaining privileges from the parents. Fairy tales are replete with stories like Cinderella and Hansel and Gretel that tell of the plight of younger children making their way in a hostile world controlled by elders.

Studies of U.S. households have even identified personality traits based on birth order. The first-born child will often emerge as the more achievement-oriented and responsible sibling. A younger child likely experiences hand-me-down clothes and toys and being treated as an inferior in the games and conversations of older siblings. Nevertheless, younger children may also emerge as more carefree and the darlings of parents and older siblings; while the middle child often feels neglected by parents and lost among other siblings (Sutton-Smith and Rosenberg, 1970; Leman, 1985).

A fictional illustration of the interaction of age-ranked siblings that conforms to the findings of some modern psychological studies can be found in *Little Women* by Louisa May Alcott (1832–1888). In the book, published in 1873, four sisters struggle to help their mother make ends meet while their father is away at war. Meg, the oldest, is the "little mother,"

the somewhat straitlaced, responsible leader of the flock. Her seriousness and occupation of the adult role leaves the next sister, Jo, free to occupy the part of tomboy, mischief-maker, and eventually liberated woman. The third sister, Beth, is the family saint, whose peace-making role continues even after her pathetic death. Amy is the family beauty, whose childish vanity and self-centeredness is a cause for concern for her censorious older sisters. The Bennet girls in the 1813 novel of English sisterhood *Pride and Prejudice* by Jane Austen (1775–1817) reveal a similar assortment of role assignments, as do the Smolinsky sisters in Anzia Yezierska's (c.1880–1970) 1925 novel about Jewish immigrant life in New York, *Bread Givers* (2003).

More flexible parenting practices and the multiplicity of family configurations today are altering sibling dynamics and concomitantly personality formation (Milevsky, 2011). Nevertheless, sibling dynamics established in childhood may last throughout life. The labeling imposed by parents, rivalry between siblings, and reactions against family roles sometimes influence young adults into certain career paths and life goals. Even late into life, jealousy of one another and rivalry for the attention of parents who may long since have died can mark the relationship.

Sisters as Opposites and Companions

Sisters often view themselves and are viewed by others as alike and not alike. In the New Testament of the Bible, for example, Martha was the careful, domestic sister engaged in making Jesus and his companions comfortable in her house; Mary was the intellectual, visionary sister who cast aside her domestic responsibilities in order to listen to Jesus' teaching.

In the contemporary United States, despite their occasional rivalries and jealousies, sisters have affectionate and long-lasting bonds as well. Swapping of clothes, advice, and support often overshadow competition. Jessamyn

West in her memoir *The Woman Said Yes* (1976) recorded her sister's bout with cancer as she assisted her with home care and a peaceful death. During the long ordeal, the sisters relived their youth together, comparing and reconciling the differences in their experiences. The Delany sisters—Sadie (1889–1999) and Bessie (1891–1995)—documented their long lives together in *Having Our Say* (1993). The memoir portrays their loving and bantering closeness and highlights their struggles to overcome racism and sexism as part of the first generation of black professionals in New York City (see Box 8.5).

Box 8.5 THE DELANY SISTERS

In the following excerpts from their memoir, the Delany sisters talk about how they complement one another yet remain distinct.

Anne Elizabeth "Bessie" Delany (1891–1995) lived to 104 and Sarah Louise "Sadie" Delany (1889–1999) until age 110.

SADIE: Bessie is my little sister, only she's not so little. She is 101 years old, and I am 103....Neither of us ever married and we've lived together most of our lives....After so long, we are in some ways like one person. She is my right arm....Bessie and I still keep house by ourselves. We still do our shopping and banking. We were in helping professions—Bessie was a dentist and I was a high school teacher—so we're not rich, but we get by...

Bessie was what we used to call a "feeling" child; she was sensitive and emotional....I always did what I was told. I was calm and agreeable. The way I see it, there's room in the world for both me and Bessie. We kind of balance each other out.

BESSIE: If Sadie is molasses, then I am vinegar! Sadie is sugar, and I'm the spice. You know, Sadie doesn't approve of me sometimes. She frowns at me in her big-sister-sort-of-way and says it's a wonder I wasn't lynched....Most of the things that make me mad happened to me because I am colored. As a woman dentist, I faced sexual harassment—that's what they call it today—but to me, racism was always a bigger problem....

Now, Sadie doesn't get all agitated like this. She just shrugs it off. It's been a little harder for me, partly because I am darker than she...and because I have a different personality than Sadie.

...I'm alive out of sheer determination, honey! Sometimes I think it's my *meanness* that keeps me going.

Source: Excerpted from *Having Our Say: The Delany Sisters' First 100 Years* by Sarah Delany and A. Elizabeth Delany, with Amy Hill Hearth, pp. 5–11. New York: Kodansha International, 1993. Reprinted by permission of Kodansha America, Inc.

Older sisters provide models and assistance to younger ones. In many cultures, past and present, one of the roles of married sisters is to chaperone younger sisters at social gatherings and to use their husbands' contacts to look for husbands for their sisters. They may also provide a home for younger sisters or brothers. Older sisters who emigrate to another country, relocate to a different city, marry, or become established in jobs often provide a base for younger siblings who seek similar opportunities. In old age, the original bonds may reassert themselves. Divorced, widowed, and singleton sisters often come at last to share households.

Sister–Brother Relations

Age ranking is too often nullified by sex ranking. Many daughters received their first jolt of awareness of a "woman's place" when their leadership role was taken over by a new baby brother by right of his gender alone, as an early Egyptian feminist noted in her memoirs (Shaarawi, 1987). Throughout the early years, girls and boys are almost always routed along different tracks. This is often formalized by the practice of special initiation ceremonies for boys alone, such as the *brith*, a Jewish circumcision ceremony.

In many families, the talents of sisters may be subordinated to the ambitions of brothers. In the nineteenth century, for example, the achievements of Charlotte, Anne, and Emily Brontë far overshadowed those of their brother, Branwell, but they were able to gain recognition only by publishing their novels under male pseudonyms. Before the current generation of Kennedys—a preeminent U.S. political family—it was the brothers and their male offspring, rather than the Kennedy women, who garnered the most family support in the pursuit of their aspirations.

Some sisters conditioned to the inequities faced by women may accept their second-class status. In horticultural communities in Kenya, for example, girls aged 5–7 may spend half their time doing chores, while boys of the same age spend only 15% of their time at work and may never do women's work unless there is no sister available to help the mother (Ember, 1973). Other girls may resent the preference that their families (often backed by the laws of the state) have shown to their brothers and the freedom, education, and favored treatment boys receive at home. Resentments of this kind may open deep gulfs between sisters and brothers and may be reflected in their relationships with their spouses and their own children. Today, the attention that NGOs have been giving to girls' education in developing countries without an equal attention to boys' education is also causing different rifts within families and communities.

Age ranking still plays a role in sister–brother relations. Older sisters may be forced to give precedence to their brothers in the family's strategies. They may also be cast in the role of "mothers" to them, a burden that may last throughout life. On the other side, older brothers tend to play the masculine role with their sisters, being protective in some cases and, in more extreme cases, assuming a bullying tone. Often, societies impose this role on young men whether they like it or not. "A man's honor lies between his sister's legs" is a common saying throughout the Mediterranean world. Young men are thus encouraged to police the behavior of their sisters and personally to avenge any infringement of the customary male code of honor by both the sisters and their chosen lovers. Among some Native American tribes, the brothers take an active role in arranging their sisters' marriages, even if the fathers are still alive, with the understanding that it is they who will likely live longest with the proposed brothers-in-law.

Sisters as Sources of Strength

Siblings can be sources of strength as well as conflict. In a period of widespread divorce and other family uncertainties, many individuals find relationships with sisters and brothers to be a core of stability. It is especially true among those with at least one sister. Sisters help family members be more optimistic, even more ambitious, and better balanced because they are more communicative, while brothers tend to discourage talking about issues. Only children tend to develop supports from outside the family (Bennett, 2009; Tannen, 2010). Continuing and successful sibling relationships appear to have positive effects in heightening women's sense of security and in improving their social skills in the wider community.

Inheritance

A daughter's possibilities from birth through girlhood to adulthood are defined by custom, law, and social institutions. The family, however defined, is the recognized unit that bestows status, class, property rights, privilege, or position upon its members. If the sexual relationships of one's parents have followed a prescribed pattern of propriety or if they have fulfilled a socially approved set of rituals governing formal adoption, daughters will usually be given that approved place. Legitimacy is her first social characteristic.

The inheritance of social status may include legacies from both parents. Women may derive their citizenship in a modern state from either mother or father or from both, depending on the laws set by the state. Jews, for example, inherit Jewish affiliation through the mother's line and, therefore, the right to claim Israeli citizenship. In the United States, children of an unmarried female citizen inherit the mother's position. Often, lower status or dependent status (slavery, serfdom, or noncitizenship) comes through the mother. Thus, in the American South in the era of slavery, daughters and sons of slave women were born slaves, even if fathered by a freeman, slaveholder, or a man who became the president of the United States (in the case of Thomas Jefferson).

Sex affects inheritance among sisters and brothers. Patrilineal societies pass authority, property, and descent directly through the male line from father to son. Matrilineal societies sometimes pass authority and property through males, but descent passes through females; property, like tools for producing clothing and food, often passes from mothers to daughters. Although matrilineal societies, such as the Native American Navajo and Iroquois and the African Bemba, tend to confer greater authority upon women than do patrilineal societies; these societies have a less rigid system of authority in general. Where extensive trade or manufacturing exists, matrilineal systems appear to vanish and even patrilineal systems are modified in favor of a bilateral system, allowing a child to inherit from both parents. One exception to this is the Minangkabau of Indonesia, who are highly educated and integrated into Indonesian society. They pass property exclusively through the mother, and women wield significant power (Blackwood, 2006).

Historically, a household head in Japan without children would often adopt a boy to be raised as the successor to manage the family's economic matters, inherit property, and worship the ancestors. If the household head had only daughters, he would adopt a son-in-law as his successor, who would also assume the head's surname (Yanagisako, 1985). Even in the simplest societies, where personal property is restricted to a few effects that are buried with their possessor, the inheritance of parental skills or privileges will generally be apportioned according to a child's sex. In capitalist societies, patterns of inheritance of property and position have favored sons over daughters. In socialist societies, which typically aim at reducing disparities of private property, it remains possible to inherit status or position informally. There, too, discrimination still favors the male.

Commonly, a system that allows the passage of property to and through women is accompanied by the development of class and caste hierarchies with strict rules for controlling individual heirs, particularly females. Generally, women are admitted to the inheritance of their fathers and/or brothers only when strong measures exist to control their marriages and sex lives in general. These societies are careful to enforce adultery laws against women, to link "honor" with virginity before marriage and fidelity after, and to endow fathers and brothers with strong coercive powers over the female members of their families (Goody, 1977).

Many societies have had laws that restricted the leaving of property. These laws may recognize *primogeniture* (passage of the patrimony to the firstborn son), *entail* (a legal device which establishes a strict line of succession to property, which then cannot be sold off, through the oldest related male), and *coverture* (a husband's legal control over his wife's property). The more wealthy and productive a society has been, the more likely that a social hierarchy of class has formed that has caused women to lose status in a variety of ways. Where it has been possible for women to write wills, they have generally left their personal property to daughters and other women in the family.

Inheritance laws and practices are another area in which girls and women are disadvantaged and through which gender discrimination persists. In the twenty-first century, many individual families are seeking a more equitable distribution of inheritance between daughters and sons. Societies, likewise, must do the same.

Women Growing Older: The Double Standard of Aging

The experiences that shape the growing-up years for girls continue to resonate in the years that mark women growing older. Although men are viewed as retaining their redeeming qualities of autonomy and competence during the aging process, and even increasing in power and status, the process of aging for women in any society that emphasizes the value of youth and beauty is generally accompanied by a stigma and a devaluing of their worth. Women are viewed as losing their most desirable qualities as they age; they are seen as less physically attractive and thus less sexually desirable and, where women are viewed primarily for their reproductive function, less fertile and less capable of producing children (one notable exception, which we mention in Chapter 5, is Suriname, where older women are valued and eroticized). This is referred to as the "double standard of aging" (Sontag, 1979). Since women have been taught that their worth rests upon physical appearance and desirability, more older women than men are dissatisfied with their appearance (Halliwell and Dittmar, 2003) (see Box 8.6).

This double standard can have a negative effect on women's attitudes, motivation, and feelings of self-worth. Women in general, and older women in particular, experience inequalities in terms of their access to care, treatment, assessment, and relevant research related to their well-being (Etaugh and Bridges, 2006). Although women are typically in good health as they age, especially in comparison to men, they are more likely to live with chronic illnesses (Crimmins, Kim, and Hagedorn, 2002) and often struggle more than men with both daily living, such as basic self-care skills, and instrumental activities, including money management, shopping, and meal preparation (U.S. Department of Health and Human

---

BOX 8.6   THE MYTHS OF AGING

1. Increasing age brings about greater psychological distress.
2. Older adults are more depressed than younger adults.
3. As individuals reach old age, they come preoccupied with memories of their childhood and youth.
4. Older adults are less satisfied with their lives than younger adults.
5. Older adults are alienated from the members of their families.
6. Because older adults generally do not reside with their children, they rarely see them.
7. Increasing age brings about a decline in sexual desire and interest.
8. Older adults are not physically capable of engaging in sexual intercourse.
9. Older adults are very isolated from their communities.
10. Social contacts decrease with increasing age.
11. Older women focus mainly on keeping their families together.
12. Older women suffer from poor physical health.
13. Married couples may legally engage in any sexual activity they mutually agree on.

All of these statements are false. With reference to number 13, in many states in America legal statuses prohibit couples from certain sexual acts. For example, in Georgia, the only sexual position that is considered legal is when a male occupies a dominant position and a female occupies a subordinate position. These laws are generally not enforced because the violations occur in private homes and therefore go undetected.

Source: F. L. Denmark, "The Myths of Aging," *Eye on Psi Chi* 7, 1 (2002): 14–21. Copyright 2002 by Psi Chi, the International Honor Society in Psychology.

Services, 2004). Despite the potential health problems that may develop during the aging process, even older women living with disabilities do not always experience diminished life satisfaction; many express feelings of happiness and mastery (Unger and Seeman, 2000). Although it is common for older women to experience negative emotions and a lowered sense of well-being, especially in comparison to men, their overall psychological health improves as they age (Etaugh, 2008) (see Box 8.6). Other experiences related to physical and mental health will be discussed in more detail in Chapter 9. Though no single incident marks this transition, a number of life events and their accompanying role transitions signal that growing older has begun.

Life Events and Role Transitions

Midlife to Later Adulthood

In societies like the United States and elsewhere where youth is revered, there is a popular depiction of growing older as fraught with identity crises and turmoil. It can be quite the opposite, particularly for women. This is a time for women to review their lives and begin to form an independent identity that is separate from their spouses and families. For many women, forging this new identity often involves paid employment; being a part of the workforce is associated with positive psychological well-being (Etaugh, 2008). Many other women focus their full efforts on their home life or being students or volunteering. The exact role a woman pursues does not matter as long as it is a role she is happy with. These developments are among the many role transitions that a woman may confront in later adulthood. In the following sections we focus largely on women in the United States.

Divorce

Divorce is a major transition that is occurring increasingly for older women. Divorce rates do vary by race, ethnicity, and class. For example, Native American women have the highest divorce rate; Latina and African American women are more likely to experience marital disruptions such as separation (Kreider and Simmons, 2003). Divorce is also more likely to occur among poorer women, those with disabilities, and those with lower levels of education (Etaugh and Bridges, 2006).

Divorce can be a distressing experience, particularly for women if they have centered their life on their marriage and lack up-to-date skills for the workplace and have limited financial means. Consequently, divorced women are much more likely to be living in poverty than are divorced men (see Chapter 6). On the other hand, divorced women experience few long-term negative psychological effects, and many actually experience it in positive terms, including renewed feelings of liberation, competence, and independence (Hetherington and Kelly, 2002). Many factors may influence the way a woman feels and functions after a divorce in late adulthood, including the kind of support she receives from those around her (Jenkins, 2003).

Widowhood

In most countries, older women are much more likely to experience the death of a spouse than are older men; this is a reflection of women's longer life expectancy and the fact that they often marry individuals older than

themselves (Kinsella and Velkoff, 2001). In the United States, 22% of men over the age of 75 are widowed compared to 59% of women the same age (U.S. Census Bureau, 2010). Widowers are much more likely to remarry than are widows. While 61% of widowers are in a new relationship within two years and 25% are remarried, only 19% of women are in a new relationship within that time, and only 5% have remarried (Wortman, Wolff, and Bonanno, 2004).

Why this discrepancy? There are many more unmarried older women than there are unmarried older men, and men typically marry women who are younger than themselves. This leaves a small group of available older men. Also, widowed older women may be less interested in beginning a new relationship and report a desire to enjoy their independence. A husband's death does not end a woman's life. As Tomioka Taeko, a Japanese poet and fiction writer wrote in one of her stories: "When a man's left a widower the maggots start to crawl, but when a woman's left a widow flowers come out in bloom!" (Tanaka and Hanson, 1982: 176).

Widowhood is undoubtedly a difficult life experience, particularly immediately following a spouse's death; this holds true for heterosexual individuals as well as lesbians and gay men. While most women become adjusted to their new role within two to four years, up to 20% of widows can experience significant and persistent problems, including depression and substance abuse (Etaugh, 2008). A woman's age, her relationship with her deceased spouse or partner, and her personal and financial resources are influential factors in this transition (Bradsher, 2001). Widows may experience a significant decrease in their financial resources, and elderly women who live alone are much more likely than elderly men to be living in poverty (Jenkins, 2003). The loss of a partner may be particularly difficult for lesbian women; not only do they experience bereavement and a significant loss, but they must contend with a society that did not necessarily recognize and honor their relationship and now does not recognize their loss (Shernoff, 1997).

However, older widows have fewer instances of depression and physical illness and lower rates of suicide than older widowers (Canetto, 2003). This major variation is often attributed to men and women's different support systems; women are both more likely to accept their need for social support

during a difficult time and to have a larger social support network (Nagurney, Reich, and Newsom, 2004). Such choices and supports, however, are not necessarily available to widows in the Global South (see Box 8.7).

Singlehood

Many women, both heterosexual and lesbian, consciously choose not to marry or to live with a long-term partner; 3.6% of U.S. women over the age of 75 have never been married

---

Box 8.7 WIDOWHOOD IN DEVELOPING COUNTRIES: INVISIBILITY, SECLUSION, OR EXCLUSION

…Almost worldwide, widows comprise a significant proportion of all women, ranging from 7 percent to 16 percent of all adult women….[I]n some countries and regions the proportion is far higher. In developed countries, widowhood is experienced primarily by elderly women, while in developing countries it also affects younger women, many of whom are still rearing children. In some regions, girls become widows before reaching adulthood.…

…Widowers, even when elderly, are far more likely to remarry, but this is not the case for widows who, if they do remarry, rarely do so of their own free will. In some communities, widows may be forced into new conjugal relations with a male relative or be forbidden to remarry, even if they wish to do so… .

Today millions of the world's widows of all ages endure extreme poverty, ostracism, violence, homelessness, ill health and discrimination in law and custom. A lack of inheritance and land rights, widow abuse and the practice of degrading, and life-threatening mourning and burial rites are prime examples of human rights violations that are justified by "reliance on culture and tradition.".. .

…[M]any widows in developing countries, in areas of conflict or in communities ravaged by HIV/AIDs are young or middle-aged. Widows of all ages are often evicted from their homes, stigmatized and physically abused—some even killed. Widowed mothers, as sole supporters of their offspring, are forced to withdraw these children from school and to rely on their labor.…

…[R]ecent conflicts elsewhere have created a new class of widows—the product of armed conflict and ethnic cleansing. The disintegration of social security systems and the dismantling of the welfare state in Eastern Europe have produced a further sub-class of impoverished older widows.…

…There are, however, signs of hope that the issue of widowhood may finally be beginning to surface in the international debates on human rights and gender justice.…

Source: Women2000. United Nations Division for the Advancement of Women, Department of Economic and Social Affairs, December 2001: 2–3, 16.

(U.S. Census Bureau, 2010). Though this is increasingly the norm, single women are often perceived in a negative light and may be portrayed as such by various media sources. While both older women and men may feel lonely at times during the aging process, older women report high levels of enjoyment, especially in regard to their freedom and individual development (AARP, 2003). Lacking a husband or partner does not mean a lack of companions. Singletons often have rich social lives and many interpersonal relationships with family, friends, and romantic partners. In comparison to married or partnered women of the same age, older women who have never married or been in a sustained relationship are often better educated and in better physical and mental health (Gottlieb, 1989). They also have more time to focus on self-development, their career, and autonomy. Despite the negative stigma traditionally associated with being a single older woman, it can still lead to life fulfillment and happiness (see Chapter 6).

Parenthood

While many women choose not to have children, it is still much more common for women to become mothers. Some women are choosing motherhood after the age of 40 (Etaugh, 2008). Older motherhood is increasingly possible through better health, adoption, in vitro fertilization (IVF) treatments, and use of a surrogate as well as marrying a spouse or partner with children. Later motherhood is enriching the lives of many women; however, in many cases this role is available only to those with financial means. It can also be fraught with emotional and physical costs when a sought-for pregnancy does not occur.

The later years of life for women are often characterized by a change in their relationship with their children. During this time period, children generally move away from their parents and their homes. Though this is commonly depicted as a time of crisis in the lives of parents, in reality it is a positive time for most women. Not only do women report higher levels of marital satisfaction after their children have left, they also view the "empty nest" time as an opportunity for them to focus on developing their own identities and independence (Etaugh and Bridges, 2006) (see Chapter 7).

Grandparenthood

Grandmothers are essential figures in the lives of families. As women are often the family members that maintain relationships across generations within the group, maternal grandmothers are much more involved grandparents than are paternal grandmothers (Bianchi, 2006). The specific role of a grandmother within a family can vary greatly. Although grandmothers themselves may still be working and have many other responsibilities of their own, they are often highly involved in raising their grandchildren, and in some instances grandparents live within the same household as their grandchildren. There are many cases where there is not a parent present and grandparents become the primary caregivers. Raising a child again as a grandmother can be a difficult task. Those who take on this responsibility often experience more physical, psychological, and financial effects than grandparents who don't, including an overall decline in their perceived physical and emotional health (Gibbons and Jones, 2003). Still, the experience affords the grandparent an opportunity to become especially close to their grandchild and to have a major influence on the child's life. Thus, overall, this new role can be satisfying and emotionally fulfilling.

Housing Transitions

When, and if, their children assume the caregiving position, generally it is daughters who support and take care of their elderly parents (Katz, Kabeto, and Lango, 2000). Often this caregiving position is assumed during women's middle or later adulthood, and it can become an added responsibility to their other roles, including as a mother, wife, employee, or student. Many women sacrifice aspects of their daily lives and often give up or cut back on paid work, which decreases their income and retirement benefits (Metlife, 2011).

In some instances, elderly parents who are ill or unable to care for themselves may move in with their children or other family members. Almost 10% of older men and 20% of older women in the United States live with their children or other relations. Although this occurs across all populations, it is most common among ethnic minorities, and it is very common in developing countries (Bongaarts and Zimmer, 2002). In the United States, white elderly individuals are least likely to live with their relatives, while Asian Americans are most likely to (Armstrong, 2001). Multigenerational living can be a mixed blessing of loss of independence balanced by increased supports for older women. Feminists argue that equality for women calls for eldercare to be recognized as a societal responsibility and not one left to individual women (Harrington, 2000).

Workforce Changes

The number of employed older women reached an all-time high at the beginning of the twenty-first century (Rife, 2001). As women have increased their workforce participation in recent years, they also are working until later adulthood. In contrast, older men are beginning to retire at an earlier age (Etaugh, 2008). The reasons older and young women give for working are similar; it is often out of economic necessity. In addition, as previously mentioned, some women pursue

work, including (unpaid) volunteer work, for self-satisfaction.

Across all ages, and particularly during later adulthood, working is related to women's physical and psychological well-being. It provides opportunities for renewal and social contacts and feelings of competency and accomplishment. Older women who are employed have higher levels of morale than do women who have retired. Women who have never pursued a career outside of their home experience the lowest levels of self-esteem (Etaugh, 2008). Older women must deal with the stigma associated with aging across all contexts of their lives, and work is no exception. They experience age discrimination in terms of hiring, promotion, and wages; they also begin confronting this discrimination at a younger age than men (Rife, 2001).

Retirement

Much past research has focused only on the effects of retirement in the lives of men. However, retirement is just as critical a life event for women, although it may function in their lives in different ways. For example, while men often retire for involuntary reasons, women are more likely to retire by choice; this is often due to family issues, including having sick relatives or a recently retired husband (Canetto, 2003). In addition, newly retired men and women may face this experience with very different resources. Since women earn less than their male counterparts in similar positions, often experience discontinuity in their work throughout their careers, and frequently entered the paid workforce later in life, they generally have fewer resources in retirement. They are also much less likely to be covered by a pension plan; similarly, their Social Security benefits are typically lower (Bethel, 2005).

Women may also be more hesitant about retiring; if they began working at a later age, they may not have accomplished all of their career goals yet (Etaugh, 2008) (see Box 8.8). Other women who strongly identify with their career and their work may not want to retire, particularly women who are self-employed or professionals (Etaugh and Bridges, 2006). In contrast, some women, especially widows, those divorced, and singletons, may be unable to retire until much later in their lives, if at all, due to financial stressors (Duenwald and Stamler, 2004). There are also a number of women who choose to retire early; some may be forced to retire due to poor health, while others may choose to do so to provide care to family members, including a spouse, elders, and grandchildren (Etaugh, 2008). Still other older women (and men) have become unemployed and were forced into early retirement when their companies closed or downsized in the new global economy. Many older women struggle in part-time jobs, if they can find them, to make ends meet. Elizabeth Strout's 2008 novel *Olive Kitteridge* explores the complex feelings and experiences of a retired Maine schoolteacher as she ages.

Retirement not only affects older women as individuals, it also affects their marriages and other relationships. The first two years following retirement are reported as a time characterized by marital conflict. However, women and men who retire at the same time as their partners are happier and experience less conflict. Distress is highest when husbands retire before wives (Etaugh, 2008). Although in the long term women adjust positively to retirement, they may experience a longer initial

---

Box 8.8   EARLY RETIREMENT

Imagine Alice, a healthy 62-year-old, faced with the possibility of early retirement from her position in a large communications firm. Her career has been successful and she has received many steady pay increases. However, she has not been promoted to a higher position in the last twelve years. She feels that the company is waiting for her to announce her retirement so they can fill her position with a younger employee. The firm is offering a desirable early retirement package that is starting to look tempting to Alice. Also, the company recently paid for Alice and other employees in their late fifties and early sixties to attend a retirement seminar. She attended several seminars led by psychologists that emphasized the benefits of early retirement. One psychologist noted, "Early retirement will leave you free to pursue your interests while you still have your health." The sessions were compelling and offered some interesting views on early retirement. What should Alice do?

Alice derives immense satisfaction and pleasure from her job. She is competent to handle the demands of her job and makes valuable contributions to the firm (although she feels these efforts are not always appreciated). Alice feels she is just as sharp as the younger employees in her department. In fact, her experience and expertise in communications have proved invaluable on many occasions when critical decisions were made. Aside from slight arthritis, Alice is in perfect physical condition. She has not missed a single day of work in ten years. Why should Alice retire early?

Source: Denmark, Florence L., V. C. Rabinowitz, and J. A. Sechzer. *Engendering Psychology: Women and Gender Revisited,* 2nd ed. Boston: Pearson Education, 2005.

period of transitioning. Often women have higher levels of depression and reduced levels of morale immediately following retirement in comparison to men (Moen, Kim, and Hofmeister, 2001). This may be because women strongly value and identify with their working role and, as a result, struggle more with the transition. Nevertheless, the time of retirement is generally associated with elevated levels of satisfaction, though this is more likely to happen when the retiree is in good health and good financial standing, and is highly active (Fitzpatrick and Vinick, 2005). Married individuals have a more positive experience with retirement than unmarried individuals; it is important for single retirees to develop and maintain social contacts, whether it is with friends, family, or other members of the community (Dorfman and Rubenstein, 1994).

Later adulthood can be an extremely positive time in a woman's life; not only do most older women maintain their intelligence, competence, beauty, and grace as they age, they also continue to develop their relationships and their sense of self. More research needs to be conducted concerning this stage of development. The current research findings have been based on a specific generation; as time progresses and women's beliefs, attitudes, and practices evolve, new research must be undertaken to reflect these changes in the lives of older women. Further, research must expand its horizons beyond white, middle-class, highly educated women; the focus must be shifted to include the experiences of non-Western women, as well as women with varying educational and financial resources and lifestyles, to obtain a more comprehensive and well-rounded understanding of the lives of older women.

The Sisterhood of Women

One of the challenges that women's studies must meet in redefining women from the center of their own experiences is to expose the power relationships that threaten to oppress them and then to reconstruct womanhood as a positive experience. Many feminists believe that the struggles that mark the relationships between daughters and mothers and between sisters are a consequence of inflexible family, sex, and gender roles and of the oppression of women, including the notion of heterosexuality as the norm. A woman's identity based on the rejection of mothers and sisters contributes to self-denigration and dependence. The early slogan of women's liberation, "sisterhood is powerful," sought to strengthen the bonds between women that male-oriented kinship and political structures have obscured. Reaching past the long and often difficult barriers of age and experience to see their mothers, in particular, and their sisters as full members in the sisterhood of women is a task that all women must undertake to fully appreciate their own selves.

Women must also reach out across the differences of culture, race, class, religion, and nationality without ignoring them. Global efforts in recent decades by women and supportive males to improve the lives of females, young, adult, and elderly, are evidence of the value of collaboration. Every woman is the daughter of another woman. Every mother is a daughter. All women are potential sisters.

Summary

Girlhood is not all sweet and passive but complex and varies widely. Girls worldwide experience societal pressures to conform to gender roles and Western consumerism. Societies globally are seeking to promote policies, strategies, and programs to support girls' empowerment.

Virtually no society expresses a preference for girl babies over boy babies. Female infanticide and neglect are ways of controlling the population on the basis of sex. The devaluation of daughters has its roots in the low value placed on women in society at large. Although sons are privileged, daughters have value as the reproducers of the next generation and in the services they provide to the family.

The names given to daughters indicate their place in the social scheme. Most surnames perpetuate the male lineage.

Many Western feminist studies have emphasized conflict in mother–daughter relationships, especially when a daughter seeks an independent life and identity. U.S. women of color identify strong mother–daughter bonds as mothers help prepare their daughters to survive and thrive in unsupportive racial environments.

A close and supportive father–daughter relationship can enhance a daughter's self-worth and educational and occupational achievements. Father–daughter incest is the most commonly reported type of incest and may cause lasting trauma.

Certain personality characteristics go with one's birth order and often are long-lasting. Sex ranking may nullify age ranking, subordinating a daughter's talents to those of her brother.

Sisters are both opposites and companions. Older sisters often provide role models and assistance for younger siblings. Older brothers frequently play the role of protector of younger sisters. Siblings, especially sisters, are a source of family stability and optimism in adulthood. Women inherit legitimacy and social status from their parents. Sex often determines legal inheritance rights. Most societies favor sons over daughters in the inheritance of property and position.

A double standard of aging exists in which older women are devalued. Life events, such as divorce, widowhood, grandparenthood, eldercare, and retirement affect an older woman's psychological and physical health, lifestyle, and financial resources, both positively and negatively. Work, in particular, enhances her well-being and sense of accomplishment.

Later adulthood overall is a positive time in a woman's life. Older women continue to develop dynamic relationships and a rich sense of self.

"Sisterhood is powerful" calls for collaboration among women in male-oriented kinship and political structures. Global sisterhood calls for women to reach out across cultural and national borders. All women are potential sisters.

Discussion Questions

1. Draw a chart illustrating naming patterns of all the members of your extended family. What conclusions can you draw?

2. What changes occurred in your own relationships with your mother, father, and other parenting figures as you were growing up? Does your experience fit the patterns sketched by Chodorow and Flax or that of Collins and Joseph?

3. Describe your changing relationships with your sisters and brothers as you grew older. If you could, how would you change them now?

4. How do women's responsibilities change as they grow older? What options open up for women? What additional tasks are relegated to women? In your opinion, do women gain or lose options in society as they age?

5. It has been shown that, on average, women live longer than men do. What are the positive and negative consequences of longevity?

Recommended Readings

Bateson, Mary Catherine. *Composing a Further Life: The Age of Active Wisdom.* New York: Vintage Books, 2010. Bateson is the author of the landmark book *Composing a Life* (1990), which developed the theme of life as a work in progress and examined the lives of five extraordinary women. In this new work, she explores a new stage of life, "Adulthood II," where women and men do not simply retire but flourish in a period of extended longevity and good health.

Bell-Scott, Patricia, Beverly Guy-Sheftall, Jacqueline Jones Royster, et al., editors. *Double Stitch: Black Women Write about Mothers and Daughters*. Boston: Beacon Press, 1991. With a foreword by Maya Angelou, 47 African American feminists write about black daughters and mothers, drawing attention to the specific dynamics of the black family, lesbian families, and black women's relationships with men. This book includes stories, poems, and essays by such writers as bell hooks, June Jordan, Audre Lorde, Sonia Sanchez, and Alice Walker.

Makhijani, Pooja, editor. *Under Her Skin: How Girls Experience Race in America*. Emeryville, CA: Seal Press, 20004. This volume is a collection of essays by women of color and white women on their girlhood. It sheds light on how race shaped their lives as children and how they negotiated gender, family, and peer group dynamics in developing their identity in racialized America.

Matteson, John. *Eden's Outcasts: The Story of Louise May Alcott and Her Father*. New York: W.W. Norton, 2007. An exploration of the intertwined lives of Louise May Alcott and her father, Bronson Alcott, displaying the many ways this daughter's life was affected by her father's personality, her family dynamics, and her struggle to express her personal and creative independence.

Woolf, Virginia. *The Three Guineas*. New York: Harcourt Brace, [1938] 1966. As an "educated gentleman's" daughter, Woolf presents a critique of the educated fathers and brothers who monopolize the ruling structures of the state, its government, educational establishments, and professions to the exclusion of daughters and sisters. Her footnotes present a feminist history of the English women of her class from the nineteenth century to her own day.

Women's Health

Clayquet Indian healers were predominantly women and they sang songs to compel the spirits to relinquish control of the sick person. We must investigate how the women's healing songs were lost and displaced and learn how women have begun to reclaim their own songs. One such song cautioned:

Do not listen to the other singing.
Do not be ashamed to sing your own song.

JASKOWSKI, 1981

Health systems reflect the societies that create them. Thus they can either perpetuate or ameliorate the inequities that exist in that particular society.

WORLD HEALTH ORGANIZATION, 2009

The Women's Health Movement

This chapter examines why, in the twenty-first century, women's health matters and why different groups of women have widely differing health outcomes, which then affect the lives of all individuals and their families, regardless of gender. Health issues have galvanized political consciousness among women globally and relate to the most fundamental of political questions: Who is to control women's own bodies, their physical selves? Also, how do healthcare policies reinforce and sustain power hierarchies within class, race, age, and gender structures? As a young physician in Puerto Rico in the 1960s, activist and advocate for the underserved Helen Rodriguez-Trias (1929–2001) witnessed the plight of poor Puerto Rican women who wanted a (then still illegal) abortion. "Many were already infected from incompetent or self-attempted abortions, while women (often from the United States) who could pay for them received safe 'appendectomies.' What brought me to the women's movement was the women's health movement. The cultural elements of feminism didn't resonate with me, but abortion resonated with me" (Wilcox, 2002). Such an experience is not unique. The "genitalizing" of women's health, as one

writer has expressed it, has served as both a motivating and an organizing force in the contemporary women's movement (Seaman, 2012). Understanding the issues involved in women's health helps us to identify an important impetus for women to organize to right the wrongs done to women in society.

The publication in 1971 of *Our Bodies, Ourselves* (OBOS) by the Boston Women's Health Book Collective marked the coming of age of second-wave feminism in the United States (see Introduction). This volume analyzed the implications of patriarchal society for the total well-being of women and provided three critical routes to change: (1) empowerment through self-knowledge, (2) establishment of women's rights and obligation to choose what to do with their own bodies, and (3) reliance on mutual support among women. In 2011, OBOS celebrated the fortieth anniversary of the first printing. There are now copies in more than 25 languages worldwide and additional volumes, such as *OBOS: Menopause* (2006), *OBOS: Pregnancy and Childbirth* (2008), *Nuestros Cuerpos, Nuestras Vidas* (2000), and *The New Our Selves Growing Older* (1994), are also available. In addition, there is now both a website and a blog (www.ourbodiesourblog.org/) available in English.

Such publications have provided essential health information for women. Equally important, women have used this knowledge as a steppingstone to their empowerment. For example, Toyoko Nakanishi founded the Shokado Women's Bookstore in 1975 in Japan. There women found a space where free discussion could take place. In the wake of the Fuimi Hospital scandal in 1981, when more than 1,000 unnecessary hysterectomies were performed, the women who had surgery were informed that it was necessary due to a "rotten" uterus or that their ovaries were "a mess." Initially, many women were embarrassed to even voice the term "uterus" in discussions with other women. The bookstore meetings provided opportunities for discussions with less shame and created shifts in language. The term "shame hair" for genital hair became known as "sexual hair" and "menstruation" (linked in many cultures to pollution) was renamed "monthly occurrence" (Davis, 2007).

In the United States many groups like Sister Song, a reproductive justice collective that focuses on women of color, have formed to organize and educate around women's health issues, often focusing on particular groups of women or particular health concerns. Activists have also addressed how discrimination, both inadvertent and intentional, can have an impact on an individual's health. The wording of medical history forms, for example, can be incomplete or misleading if it is assumed that every patient is a heterosexual woman. For the first time, the U.S. Department of Health and Human Services (USDHHS) now includes lesbian, gay, bisexual, transgender, and queer/questioning (LGBTQ) health as part of its long-term planning, including areas that require specific attention to address the neglect that have become evident from recent studies (USDHHS, 2010).

Most importantly, the women's health movement has been largely responsible for new approaches to healthcare. Health is viewed as not just the absence of disease, but an integral part of a woman's total life experience, inextricably linked to her place in society. This ecological or social embeddedness model analyzes the impact of social factors such as race/ethnicity, gender, educational attainment, and socioeconomic status on health. Each of these factors locates an individual or group in the structure of society, giving differential access to power, privilege, and desirable resources (Williams, 2002).

Redefining and Reframing Health

Definitions of health are culturally variable: what is considered normal and what is considered an illness vary widely across societies and across time frames. Health is not a static state: how we define health reflects a dynamic, shifting adaptation to our environment over our life cycle and is influenced by the values inherent in any specific culture. The reader should evaluate how different definitions (see below) fit (or not) into her or his own life and in what ways the definition/s might be modified to be both more inclusive and reactive to the myriad influences on health that exist.

In 1946, the World Health Organization (WHO) defined health as "a state of complete physical, mental, and social well-being and not merely the absence of disease and infirmity." Today, current Western attitudes have expanded the definition to include the physical, emotional, social, intellectual, and spiritual dimensions of a person's life. Health thus has both subjective and objective components that influence the way it is defined, the nature of the data collected in order to study health and disease and the way different groups of people will be treated by the medical establishment.

Women's health has been defined as distinct from the WHO definition in a number of important ways. Employing the

The Broken Column (1944) by Frida Kahlo (1907–1954), oil on canvas. Kahlo was in a trolley accident as a teenager and had to wear a variety of corsets to support her spine for the rest of her life. In this painting, the scattered pins and her naked and corseted upper body display both her pain and her courage.

broader definition used at the Fourth World Conference of Women in Beijing, the Ontario Women's Health Council defined women's health as "a state of emotional, social, cultural, spiritual and physical well-being, determined by social, political and economic context of women's lives, as well as biology. In addition, the definition…recognizes the validity of women's life experiences and women's own beliefs and experiences of health" (Phillips, 1995).

Another definition, formulated for use in training physicians, states: "Women's health recognizes the importance of the study of gender differences…recognizes the diversity of women's health needs over a life cycle and how these needs reflect differences in race, class, ethnicity, culture, sexual preferences [*sic*] and levels of education and access to medical care; includes the empowerment of all women, as for all patients, to be informed participants in their own health care" (Donoghue, 1996).

Moreover, people with higher levels of education and higher income have lower rates of many chronic diseases compared to those with less education and lower income levels. Women without a high school diploma have an 8.6-year shorter life expectancy than those with a bachelor's degree or higher (Tavernise, 2012). Thus the definition of health is broader than the individual and must consider the multiplicity of factors in a woman's life.

Why "Women's" Health?

In the twenty-first century most women can expect to live longer and healthier lives than their grandmothers did. Though advances have been made, these developments are by no means universal or uniform. Health status, in terms of illness and death rates, varies according to gender as well as being influenced by factors such as income level, ethnicity/race, human environment, geography, lifestyle, and access to healthcare. As a result, some groups of women benefit more from scientific and/or social advances, while other women fall behind.

Women's health has historically been focused on maternal health, ignoring the rest of the woman (Wenger, 2004). Not all women will give birth, and even those who do so have a life before and after childbirth. Because the totality of female life over a life span has not yet been adequately addressed (see Chapter 8), the study of women's health is a necessary corrective, both for theory and practice. Such a focus should not be seen to be exclusionary, as health has a profound influence on the ability to participate fully in life—whether one is female, male, transgender, or intersex.

In the United States, the introduction of oral contraception pills (the "birth control pill"), approved by the Federal Drug Administration (FDA) in 1960, was a watershed moment for American women. For the first time, a woman could have control over conception, even without a partner's awareness. In addition, sexual intercourse could be separated from conception, enabling women to explore their sexuality in new ways.

New areas of study such as *epigenetics* (gene modifications induced by local changes in the environment brought on by stress, diet, behavior, toxins, and other factors) and a life-course approach to health (beginning in utero) influence the manner in which we now study health and health outcomes. These theories place increased importance on the ways that experiences both before birth and throughout one's lifetime have an impact on one's health and the health of one's potential offspring. Studies of the offspring of women living in the Netherlands in the post–World War II famine years, for example, found that the children of these women were more likely to be obese than children born to women before and after the famine (Francis, 2011). It is believed that the fetus physiologically adapted to the uterine environment—in this case, one of starvation—even though born into a world of plenty. Thus, physiological adaptations that take place before birth are manifested over an individual's lifetime. Additional studies done on pregnant women after other stressful events, such as Hurricane Katrina, have provided additional evidence of long-lasting changes in the fetus (Paul, 2010).

As women usually have different roles than men, mediated by social and cultural mores, they are exposed to different risks and experiences by virtue of their gender. The HIV/AIDS pandemic is a stark example of how the different paths of exposure, risk factors, disease pathways, and treatment manifest themselves according to gender. The primary routes of transmission of the HIV virus also vary in different parts of the world. Women comprise a growing proportion of people living with HIV/AIDS (50%). In sub-Saharan Africa three young women (age 15–24) are infected for every one young man. A similar pattern emerges in the Caribbean, where two young women are infected for every one young man (KFE, 2005; UNAIDS, 2006; Amfar.org, 2012; CDC, 2012).

Health, therefore, is a central element in women's lives. Being healthy makes it possible for women to care for themselves and their families, to contribute to their community, to be a productive member of the workforce, and to build a base of economic stability (Kaiser Women's Health Survey, 2010).

Health, Gender, and Human Rights

As Eleanor Roosevelt presciently declared, "Where, after all, do human rights begin? In small places, close to home—so close and so small that they cannot be seen on any map of the world" (Roosevelt, 1958). "The ability to attain the highest possible standard of health is not a privilege for the elite but a right that comes with being human" (Levison and Levison, 2001). If only the wealthy and elite

have access to the factors that enhance health and the prospect of engaging in life's challenges to the fullest from birth, it becomes a privilege and not a right. When male infants are provided with more nourishment than female infants, based on their greater perceived worth to a particular society, children have unequal access to health based on gender (see Chapter 8).

In 1948, the United Nations issued a Universal Declaration of Human Rights, meant to "protect the integrity and dignity of human beings," which has had meaningful repercussions for the health of women globally (Agosin, 2001). Together with the 1979 Convention for the Elimination of All Forms of Discrimination Against Women (CEDAW), these UN instruments are potentially pivotal devices to ensure the implementation of human rights. Both professional and activist groups have increasingly called attention to the inextricable link between health, gender, and human rights. The concept of health as a right is still not universally accepted or applied. Yet the link between health as a human right and the lives of the girls and women who do not yet live as equals with the males in their societies provides an important focus or rationale for women's health as a special area of concern.

One egregious human rights abuse that is gendered has been the unwanted, unnecessary female sterilization of the most vulnerable (the poor, women of color, and the disabled) without their consent.

Reforming the Healthcare System

In the context of reframing women's health as a human rights issue, the women's health movement has undertaken steps on multiple fronts to reform the healthcare system and make it more responsive to women's needs. Feminists have encouraged women to ask: What is a healthy woman? How do women become

Box 9.1a   UNETHICAL TREATMENT: RACE, GENDER AND CLASS

Designed to see if African American men had different bodily responses to syphilis than white men, the U.S. Public Health Service (PHS) and the Centers for Disease Control (CDC)—both government agencies—identified 399 black men in rural Alabama with syphilis and followed them from 1932 to 1972. Initially, the infamous Tuskegee Syphilis Study tested both women and men and treated those infected (before penicillin was discovered as a cure), but ultimately only men were selected for the study. The men were offered "free medical care" and burial expenses but were never told that they had syphilis. Treatment was withheld, even after penicillin became available as a cure in the 1940s. The men, uneducated and living in poverty, were a vulnerable population but they did not live their lives in isolation. The forgotten additional victims were their wives and other sexual partners throughout these years, as well as the children born with congenital syphilis. In 1975, the PHS/CDC very belatedly gave lifetime medical and health care to 22 wives, 17 children, and 2 grandchildren.

In the years after World War II, U.S. and Guatemalan doctors (under the aegis of their governments) *deliberately* infected vulnerable populations (prisoners, mentally disabled asylum inmates, and soldiers) and did provide treatment if they became infected. One case involved developmentally disabled women who were infected with syphilis, even as some were terminally ill. Prostitutes (legal in Guatemala at that time) already infected with syphilis were brought into a Guatemalan prison to infect male prisoners with syphilis through sexual activity. Unlike the Tuskegee study, however, penicillin was provided to cure the men if they tested positive although it is not clear if some were never treated or treated incompletely. In both cases, decades after the research, the U.S. government apologized for both events.

Sources: Susan Reverby, *Examining Tuskegee: The Infamous Syphilis Study and Its Legacy*, Chapel Hill: University of North Carolina Press, 2009; "'Normal Exposure' and Inoculation Syphilis: A PHS 'Tuskegee Doctor' in Guatemala, 1946–48," *Journal of Policy History* 23, 1, (2011): 6–28.

and remain healthy? How should women deal with illness or disease? These questions are essential because women's health has been perceived differently from men's and because women's bodies and biological processes are different from men's in some respects (see Chapter 5). The women's health movement has also called for changes in the services a society provides for women, based on its recognition that women have been discriminated against both as recipients and as providers of healthcare services. As we shall examine in more detail in this chapter, women have been both ignored and exploited in research about medical conditions and medical devices.

Medication and treatment for medical conditions not specific to women, such as heart disease, had long been investigated and norms established primarily on the basis of research on men (Sechzer, Rabinowitz, and Denmark, 1994).

Activists have also struggled to improve accessibility to affordable healthcare for women and to reduce discrimination based on gender, race, sexuality, class, or age. The new and contested U.S. healthcare plan—the Affordable Care Act, passed in 2009 and upheld by the Supreme Court in 2012—provides much-needed parity, including expanded health insurance coverage, extended coverage

Box 9.1b HENRIETTA LACKS

Experimentation and exploitation of the most vulnerable in health research has a long history. Questions arise today concerning who has control over our own biological materials (the tissue from a biopsy, the results of blood tests, etc.).

Henrietta Lacks, a poor southern tobacco farmer, was treated at Johns Hopkins University Hospital for terminal cancer and, after her death, was buried in an unmarked grave. Without her knowledge or consent, her cancer cells were taken and became the first "immortal" human cells grown in a culture and hereafter referred to as HeLa cells (using the first two letters of Henrietta Lacks' name). Although Mrs. Lacks has been dead for more than 60 years, her cells are still living. This gave rise to a multi-million dollar industry which has been vital for development of the polio vaccine, gene mapping, and IVF, among other research areas. Mrs. Lacks' descendants (most of whom had no access to healthcare) only learned of this when Rebecca Skloot, investigating HeLa for a book she was writing, informed them of Mrs. Lacks' enormous contribution to science. Her family has not profited financially from the worldwide industry utilizing her cells.

Henrietta Lacks.

Source: Skloot, Rebecca. *The Immortal Life of Henrietta Lacks.* New York: Broadway Paperbacks, 2011.

---

for maternity care (which 62% of individual market enrollees do not have), preventative well-woman visits, domestic violence screening, and contraception without co-payments. In addition, gender discrimination in premiums is not permitted (Cueller et al., 2012).

The efforts of healthcare movements in many poor nations worldwide are somewhat different from those found in wealthier nations. In developing countries, a primary focus is on delivering basic resources such as food, clean water, and shelter to people as well as provisions to alleviate the suffering of the vulnerable and the poor. Greater use of contraception, access to antiretroviral drugs

for pregnant women, and more birth attendants, such as midwives, particularly in rural areas, has reduced maternal mortality worldwide in the past two decades. However, many countries, especially in sub-Saharan Africa, have not met this goal (KFF U.S. Global Health Policy, 2012). New technologies utilized in assisted reproductive techniques (ART) have created new areas of potential abuse and exploitation. For example, transnational surrogacy has become a lucrative market in which lower-income women in India and Central America are inseminated as surrogates for more affluent women in the Global North.

Uncovering the Gender Dynamics of Western Medicine

In most societies women have been the primary caretakers of human bodies from birth to death. It has been women's work to tend to birthing, to care for infants and children, and to teach basic habits of sanitation and nutrition to young people. Women care for the sick and wounded, the ailing and weak, and the elderly. Thus, when the caretaker herself requires assistance, especially in later years, in many industrialized nations there is often no one to help her. Although regular day-to-day caretaking has been, and continues to be, done largely by women, male authorities in many Western societies have taken control of the more prestigious forms of healing. For men, who do not menstruate, menstruation seemed unhealthy, abnormal, and dangerous. Pregnancy and childbirth were also mysterious, frightening, and threatening. If men are the authorities to whom women turn for information about these events, certainly men's subjective interpretations are conveyed to women, who learn to perceive the world through men's "expert" eyes. Men's ideals of women's health reflected not only gender bias but class, race, and heterosexist biases as well and are deeply embedded in Western ideas of the female body as "other" (see Chapter 2).

Woman as Deviant

The notion that a woman is an aberrant man has deep roots. Galen of Pergamon (c. 129–200 c.e.), a Greek physician whose writings influenced Western medicine for centuries, taught that women were "inside-out men." Accordingly, women had insufficient body heat to force genitals outward. Thus, using man as his measure, Galen viewed women (as had Aristotle) as "defective" persons. Since women were "inferior," it followed that their diseases were caused, almost entirely, by their inferior genitalia (Dean-Jones, 1994) (see Chapter 5).

In later centuries, as the new promoters of "science" and "reason" began to overtake the dominant role of the religious leaders in Western societies, many moral and spiritual concerns became the domain of science.

Woman as "the Weaker Sex"

As the Industrial Revolution began to change the structure of modern Western society, women were placed in an illogical, dichotomous position. While their bodies continued to be considered pathological, women were considered the moral guardians of society (Martin, 1987; Ehrenreich and English, 2005). Upper- and middle-class women were perceived as physically weak, of delicate health, and vulnerable to a great variety of ailments arising from the fact that they had wombs. The uterus was believed to be the source of a vast array of illnesses, both of the body and the mind. Excessive physical and mental challenges were thought to be damaging to women's most exalted function, procreation. By the middle of the nineteenth century, physicians claimed that women of the upper classes had little or no sex drive. If they did exhibit some, this was thought to be symptomatic of severe illness, to be treated surgically. Any form of rebelliousness or deviance from gender prescriptions was met with severe medical measures (Barker-Benfield, 2000). Refusal to be satisfied with housework, a tendency to masturbate, an overeagerness to be educated, or a desire for the vote might be deemed cause for surgical practices ranging from clitoridectomy (the removal of the clitoris) to hysterectomy (the removal of the uterus) (Marieskind, 1977). These actions or their threat kept women of the more privileged classes more or less in line. Women of the lower classes and women of color were less vulnerable to such

---

Box. 9.2   THE FIRST "OFFICIAL" FEMALE DISTANCE RUNNER

Are women the "weaker sex?" In 1961, 19-year-old Sylvia Chase defied the ban by the Amateur Athletic Association on women running in road races (because of fears that females would "risk their femininity and reproductive health") by running the 4.75 mile Manchester (Connecticut) Road Race. Chase started a block behind the men and finished in 128th place, ahead of 10 men. By 2012, there were more U.S. women as members of the U.S. Olympic team than men.

Source: From *New York Times*, October 26, 2011.

---

strictures, for they were not thought to share the weakness of those of privilege.

The Gendered Profession of Medicine

By the end of the nineteenth century, the Western healthcare system had begun to crystallize into the professionalized and gendered form it takes today. Men prevailed as leaders of the professional healthcare system and propagated ideals about what was normal in woman's health. In turn, women healthcare specialists, healers, and midwives were prohibited from practicing even among low-income women (Petchesky and Judd, 1998). This prescription had special repercussions for low-income women, who did not have the same access as wealthy women to professional medical practices.

Today the increase in women's goals to earn advanced degrees (see Chapter 10) is reflected in the medical profession. In 1970, less than 8% of all U.S. physicians were female: by 1990, women were 36% of U.S. physicians, and by 2011, 48.3%. How this phenomenon

is changing the profession, such as the medicalization of women's health discussed below, is understudied at present. Women practice predominantly internal medicine, pediatrics, family medicine, and obstetrics and gynecology. Women of color comprised 38.5% of female physicians whose race/ethnicity was known. In 2007 Nancy Edwards was named Dean of Duke Medical School, the first woman to lead any of the top 10 medical schools in the United States. Of all physicians worldwide, 32% are women (Catalyst, 2012). In many developing nations women are the primary healthcare providers and caregivers, in both formal and informal settings. Yet here, too, women have still to gain substantial positions of power.

The Medicalization of Life Processes

In the following subsections we consider how the "normal" functions in women's life processes have been medicalized and come to be dominated by a patriarchal medical system, leaving many women disempowered. Yet women have consistently organized, both formally and informally, and increasingly have challenged and resisted this encroachment on their bodily integrity with success.

As discussed in Chapter 7, medicalization involves organizing a broad (and ever-expanding) range of behaviors and aspects of everyday life into categories of health and illness (Boston Women's Health Collective, 2011). Western society has medicalized menstruation, childbirth, menopause, and sexuality, even though these are normal parts of the life cycle and experience of most women. Nevertheless, some women rarely, if ever, menstruate; some women never give birth; some women do not experience any symptoms, such as hot flashes, with the onset of menopause. Even among those who do experience these processes, there are wide variations in the experience.

Why, then, has women's health been the object of excessive medicalization? Is premenstrual syndrome (PMS) real? Why are there excessive numbers of hysterectomies in the United States? How did "small breasts" become a *disease* known as "micromastia" (Ratcliff, 2002)? Furthermore, the biomedical model, which has been predominant in the West since the seventeenth century, emphasizes identifying a pathology, seeking biological causes within the individual, and finding a "cure." A sociocultural or ecological approach—one that includes the intra-personal, the personal, the community, and the government and its policies—provides more opportunity to examine the multiple causes of ill health, culturally defined. This shifts the emphasis to prevention from diagnosis and treatment, something the women's health movement advocates for both their families and their communities.

Menstruation to Menopause

Menarche (the onset of menstruation) can occur any time between the ages of 10 and 18. Menstruation also varies by individual: it may occur every 28 days or be less regular; it may last a whole week or only a couple of days; it may be accompanied by a blood flow that is heavy or light, with strong abdominal cramps or none at all; it may be preceded by a variety of changes in a woman's body or emotions or it may not.

It was once thought essential for women of the privileged classes—because they were "finer" in makeup—to take to bed while menstruating, during the latter phases of pregnancy (confinement), and for several weeks after childbirth. No such strictures applied to women of the working classes, whose physical makeup was thought to be "coarser." Despite these class disparities, menstruation was persistently conceptualized as a form of illness. By the late nineteenth century, physicians began to define and treat menstruation, thus sharing with mothers the role of socializing adolescent girls about their bodies, a strategy that enlarged their influence (Brumberg, 1997).

Menopause refers to what happens in a woman's body as she reaches the end of her childbearing years. The increased life span for women means that more women now reach menopause and live long years thereafter. Most women cease menstruating between the ages of 45 and 55, experiencing in the process some irregularity in the timing and character of the menstrual cycle. Women may also experience sensations thought to relate in large part to the reduced production of estrogen, which marks the eventual cessation of the menstrual cycle. Symptoms (usually temporary) may include hot flashes, night sweats, sleep difficulties, psychological distress, and weight gain. In response, the medical profession has intervened with hormonal treatment and even surgical removal of the uterus. Although many women do suffer discomforts that might be relieved medically, today feminists question whether such measures are needed, whether they are worth the cost in terms of health risk, and whether alternative measures have been adequately considered. Lack of substantial funding (reflecting traditional [male] research priorities) has resulted in continuing gaps in our understanding of the mechanisms of menopause as they affect individual women.

Birth Control and Sterilization

The ability to control pregnancy has been an important boon to women in many ways. However, it too has become increasingly medicalized, primarily through the exploitation of test subjects and concerns about safety and access.

Women in many societies, past and present, have been able to control pregnancy through the use of herbal remedies. In nineteenth-century New York City newspapers, abortifacient medication makers, abortion providers, and condom manufacturers advertised freely. However, their services gradually became illegal. The 1873 Comstock Law prohibited the sale of birth-control information and materials (such as condoms) through the U.S. mail (Luker, 1996).

In the 1960s, hormone pills and intrauterine devices were distributed freely among millions of U.S. women before adequate testing and other precautions were taken. Some of these devices were later found to be damaging to women's health (Rathus et al., 2011). New methods of contraception have recently become available or are being developed, including transdermal patches, vaginal rings, and injectables that protect against pregnancy

for 12 weeks. At this stage of their development, such contraceptive methods must be supervised by a physician. Funding levels for research into new methods of contraception, however, remain miniscule relative to other health concerns. The testing of birth-control devices and medications, required by Western nations, all too often is done on women from poorer nations, while research into male contraception, aimed at interrupting the production of sperm, is still in its very early stages (Population Council, 2012).

Sterilization has a long history of use in the United States as a form of birth control, generally in the form of *tubal ligation*, a medical procedure that blocks the tubes carrying a woman's egg to her uterus so it cannot be fertilized, and also in the form of male vasectomy. Sterilization without informed consent continued well into the twentieth century. During the 1960s, Puerto Rican women in both the United States and Puerto Rico were sterilized in large numbers without informed consent. Where other birth control alternatives were lacking, sterilization became the only family-planning "choice," known as "La Operacion" (Lopez, 1987).

Abortion

Abortion is often a last resort for women for whom birth control has failed. The nascent American Medical Association wrested control of abortion from midwives and ultimately suppressed it as a legal option, often on the eugenic argument that the "better" classes were producing too few children in contrast to those who were poor and immigrant (Luker, 1984). There is a consensus within the women's health movement that the decision to have or not to have an abortion should be in the hands of the pregnant woman (Solinger, 2005). The legalization of abortion in *Roe* v. *Wade* (1973) recognized the right of women, with their physicians, to make decisions about their pregnancy and vastly improved the conditions of abortion. Since then, the abusive treatment of women seeking abortions (and those women and men who have aided them) has escalated among abortion opponents, making abortion once again a highly politicized issue.

The shift in many parts of the world from medicalization to politicization provides an additional area of concern (WHO, 1998). While U.S. women's health activists have made important gains in health policy, legal abortion remains both divisive and controversial, and one in which a woman's health is rarely mentioned. In the United States there were 162 legal challenges to abortion access in the first half of 2011 alone (Guttmacher Media Center, 2012). Worldwide, nearly half of all abortions are unsafe (56% in the Global South, 6% in the Global North) (Guttmacher Institute, 2012). In the face of these challenges women continue to demand respectful reproductive choice and accurate information about their bodies.

Pharmaceutical or medical abortion, which does not require surgery, is used in many parts of the world, including the United States. Feminists organized a campaign to get this done, as it provides both a choice of methods and a more private means of terminating a pregnancy and has been used by more than 1.4 million U.S. women (Planned Parenthood, 2012).

The realities of the limitations and failures of birth control make the availability of legal abortion vital to the health of women. In Bangladesh, for example, where the abortion law is rigidly restrictive, menstrual regulation services avert unsafe abortions, one of the leading causes of death there. It is legal, however to use "manual or electric vacuum aspiration to induce abortion, provided within 10 weeks of a woman's last period," and this serves as backup to difficult-to-acquire contraception (Johnston, 2010).

When hygienically and correctly induced, abortion is extremely safe. But when women must resort to clandestine and illegal means of terminating unwanted pregnancies, many of which are poorly performed abortions, at least 47,000–70,000 women die annually and hundreds of thousands more suffer serious complications. Women continue to suffer from a shortage of facilities that can provide safe, prompt, and affordable abortions and that can also safeguard their anonymity if they desire it (World Health Organization, 2011; Guttmacher, 2012).

When conservative politicians are in the majority in the U.S. national government and U.S. Supreme Court, the right to safe and legal abortions and women's reproductive rights are at risk. An anti-abortion backlash from 1997 to 2012 in the United States and Canada has resulted in the murders and attempted murders of abortion providers, death threats, clinic bombings and arsons, and increasingly restrictive state mandates. Despite the fact that "13 percent of global maternal mortality" is attributed to complications from unsafe, illegal abortions, the biggest problem facing women wanting or needing an abortion service is accessibility (Guttmacher, 2012). Worldwide, abortion statues range from legal to illegal or severely restricted only to save a woman's life. Twenty-five to 30 million legal abortions and 20 million unsafe abortions are performed worldwide per year (Seager, 2009).

Childbirth

Pregnancy and childbirth are not diseases, but they do carry risks. As childbirth became the domain of medical specialists, it was experienced even more passively by women in hospital settings. New medicines, instruments, and procedures removed childbirth from the home and normal experience, although home births are once again on a slight increase. In addition, women have once again begun to rely on the medical expertise of nurse midwives as well as utilizing doulas, who provide continuous, nonmedical support through labor and delivery and after birth. Doulas have also begun to support women in miscarriage and abortion procedures. In recent decades, delivery has also frequently meant cesarean sections (surgical delivery of the fetus). Although these procedures are convenient and profitable for physicians and hospitals and extremely useful in medical emergencies, they are disabling for a large number of women (Martin, 1987). The rate of cesarean section (C-section) in childbirth in the United States was 32.9% in 2009 after 13 consecutive years of rising rates. This is more than twice the WHO recommended range of 5–15% (Amnesty International, 2011). The dichotomy remains that women with access to such care have fewer deaths (of both mother and child) while also being subjected to unnecessary risks in some cases.

The acceptance of innovations, such as anesthetics during childbirth, hospital-based births, and use of fetal screening through amniocentesis and other testing, reveals that not all medicalization has been forced upon women. The use of new technologies also reflects a confluence of sociocultural attitudes and the availability of medical procedures. Many women today are grateful that such technologies exist. However, the potential for abuse through such innovations is not always sufficiently evaluated before widespread acceptance occurs; past experiences have made increasing numbers of women and health activists more wary.

Until the twentieth century, the risks of childbirth were grave for women everywhere; they remain serious for low-income women in the modern industrial world as well as in developing countries. Of the half-million women who die each year in childbirth, 99% live in poor countries. Many more women worldwide contract serious illnesses, which result in approximately 62 million grave childbirth-related health problems annually (WHO, 2007; Amnesty International, 2011). Mortality rates for Latinas in the United States and their infants, for example, are higher than for other groups. The health risks for pregnant and childbearing adolescents and their infants are also great, since teenage mothers are disproportionately found among groups with low income (WHO, 2011).

Sexuality

Sexuality has also become a medical concern, one that is closely tied to existing gender ideals and expectations. As sexuality is a "learned and deeply socialized phenomenon," utilizing a medical model to study female sexuality requires an examination of norms and may result in another mode of social control (Tiefer, 2004). Moreover, as sexuality education is by no means comprehensive or accurate globally, it is difficult for girls and women to make educated decisions about their sexual health. In the twenty-first century, blogs (like Scarlateen.com) and 'zines provide more accessible (and explicit) informal sexuality education to those with access to the Internet (see Box 9.3).

The double standard of sexual conduct remains firmly in place in many women's lives, even as some young women explore their sexuality with greater ease and freedom. The medicalization of female sexuality, including discussions of *female sexual arousal disorder* as a diagnosis in the revised Diagnostic

Box 9.3a   TIPS ON SEARCHING HEALTH INFORMATION ON THE WEB I

Searching for current, reliable information in health sites on the Internet is a useful skill but one that requires care. Some suggestions for "health information searching" are repeated here:

Not all health information on the web is credible, timely, or safe. Sites such as MedlinePlus (www.medlineplus.gov) by the National Library of Medicine and Healthfinder (www.health-finder.gov) from the U.S. Department of Health and Human Services are a good place to start. The URL gives you some information right away. The last part of the domain name (.com,. org,.edu) is significant: .com for commercial, .org for nonprofit organizations, and .edu for educational institutions. Educational sites are generally a safe bet, with "org" sites generally reliable (if you can identify the organization and who's funding it) and commercial sites the most problematic, though there are exceptions. Information should be factual, not opinion, and capable of being verified.

Health on the Net (HON) Foundation, a Geneva-based NGO, provides accreditation for websites and can be searched by language. HON-accredited sites provide trustworthy information. Does the site tell who's paying for it? Is there an "About Us" section that provides such information, including their mission? How current is the information? Are addresses provided for visitors that seek further information or support?

Source: Adapted from *Medical Library Foundation Resources: A User's Guide to Finding and Evaluating Health Information* (www.mlanet.org/resources/userguide.html) and *HON Code of Conduct for Medical and Health Web Sites. Health on the Net Foundation* (HON is free and depends on the generosity of internet users and private and public donations); accessed 5/28/2011 (www.hon.ch/HONcode/).

and Statistical Manual-V (2013), is cause for concern, as this may result in greater focus on medication and less emphasis on dealing with the cultural and emotional constraints in women's sexual lives.

The development of Viagra and other medications for erectile or sexual dysfunction in males is one example of the "politics of sexuality" (Vance, 1984). No such drug has been produced for women. Women seeking enhanced sexual pleasure began using Viagra (both with and without a physician's prescription) and increasingly purchase untested over-the-counter drugs that claim to enhance arousal, even though no research had been undertaken to assess their effectiveness and safety in women (Ellen, 2012) (see Box 9.4).

Impact of Social and Cultural Disparities on Women's Health

Health Status and Risks

Women's bodies and men's bodies are more alike than they are different from one another. They are largely subject to the same hazards to their health: illnesses, accidents, and disabilities. However, there are some significant differences, which can be identified by comparing men's and women's health status. Health status is typically depicted according to rates of morbidity (illness) and mortality (death). In the past, men on average had greater access to nutritional foods and lived longer than women. However, worldwide for every age group, women on average outlive men (United Nations, 2010). The leading cause of

Box 9.3b   TIPS ON SEARCHING HEALTH INFORMATION ON THE WEB II

The following discussion on Go Ask Alice, a question-and-answer service available through the Internet from Columbia University in New York, covers many of the concerns a young woman may have about health/gynecological health exams:

Should I Tell My Gyn I'm Having Lesbian Sex?

Dear Alice,

Is it necessary to tell my gynecologist that I am bisexual and engaging in lesbian sex when I go for my yearly checkup?

Dear Reader,

Being honest and complete with the information you give to your health care providers is one of the most important things you can do to insure yourself thorough health care. Of course, it's also understandable that you may be reluctant to tell your gynecologist that you're having sex with another woman, or to talk about your bisexuality. Like other women in your situation, perhaps you are worried that:

- talking about this will be awkward
- you will be misunderstood
- your health care provider will ask a lot of embarrassing questions
- your statement will be ignored
- you will be mistreated
- assumptions will be made about you and/or your behavior
- the provider will refuse to treat you

These are all reasonable concerns since, unfortunately, there are still many people out there, including health care providers, who don't understand or accept same-sex relationships. However, there are also lots of providers who are sensitive and open to all of their patients' needs and issues and, in fact, some who even specialize in providing services to lesbian, bisexual, gay, and/or transgendered people.

   If you already have an established relationship with your gynecologist, you have an idea of how s/he has handled your needs in the past. Has s/he been sensitive when listening to your health concerns? Have you had the time to discuss all of the different aspects of your sexual health? Have the services provided been thorough, gentle, well explained, and followed up? These are some questions to ask yourself. Talking about this issue might be hard at first, but if you don't tell your gyn, it is quite possible, unfortunately, that s/he will assume that you're sexually active with only men (if you discuss being sexually active). This can lead to a lot of confusion, complicated, vague wording on your part, and possibly unnecessary or inappropriate discussion and suggestions for your health care.

   If you have felt comfortable with your gyn up until now, you may want to just go ahead and mention the fact that you are having lesbian sex. Perhaps you consider yourself bisexual, but are currently only involved with women. You might have one partner, or multiple partners. You may have physical relationships with both men and women. Whatever your situation, choose the wording that's most comfortable for you, and that best describes you and your sexual activity. You can say something like, "I have a female partner now," or "I'm bisexual, and sometimes I have sex with women, and sometimes with men," or "I know the last time I saw you I wasn't having sex with anyone. Right now I'm involved with a woman." Your

(Continued)

gynecologist will probably ask some questions to get more specific information. Having a productive discussion with her/him can allow you to explore some or all of the following issues:

- how this affects your need, or lack of need, for contraception
- how to effectively protect you and your partner(s) from sexually transmitted infections (STIs), including HIV
- whether you're also having sex with men, and the health care needs associated with this
- your possible interest in having children some day
- whether there's any stress for you associated with your same-sex relationship(s)
- anything in your intimate relationships, whether with women or with men, which is troubling to you: emotional, physical, or sexual abuse, for example

If you do not yet have a gynecologist that you work with, or are unhappy/too nervous about your current one, you can search out a good match for you in a number of ways. Word of mouth is definitely one of the best ways to find out how a particular provider deals with LGBT health care issues. Ask your friends, school-, or work-mates if they can recommend a gynecologist or nurse practitioner they like. While you're at it, ask about primary care providers, dentists, dermatologists, and others...you never know when you'll need a good specialist.

You can also contact your local gay and lesbian services center for some names. If you're in the New York area, contact The Lesbian and Gay Community Services Center. You can also try The Gay and Lesbian Medical Association.

If you're a Columbia student, all of the providers in Primary Care and throughout Health Services are open to discussing the needs of LGBT students.

Take care of yourself,

Alice

Source: Accessed 9/23/03, http://www.goaskalice.columbia.edu/1709.html. Copyright © Columbia University, 2003.

death for both women and men is coronary heart disease, but each year more women die of it than men, especially in Europe (Gupta, 2003; United Nations, 2010). According to indicators such as disability days, hospitalization, and visits to physicians, women display greater rates of illness than men.

Disparities in health worldwide have been persistent over time. Some hazards are unique to women because they concern the female reproductive organs and female reproductive experiences. Other hazards are shared by women and men but experienced differently because of the different roles assigned to women (such as jobs resulting in different workplace hazards) or because society supports different behaviors that are potentially a threat to health. Behavioral differences that affect health risks, such as substance abuse and driving behavior, also are gendered (Travis, 1988). In addition to the biological component of health, the role of risk factors (see below) requires examination in addressing women's health.

Box 9.4   THE CLITORIS

is 9 cm deep
in the pelvis.

Most of it scrunched & hidden.

New studies show
the shy curl
to be longer
than the penis,
but like Africa,
the continent,
it is never drawn to size.

Mapmakers, and others, who draw
important things for a living,
do not want us to know this.

In some females,
    the clitoris stretches,
    unfurls,
    8 in,
    with 2 to 3.5
    in, shaft free
    outside the body.
    The longest clitoris of record
    has been found in the blue whale.

In water
Desire can rise,
Honor sea levels,
Ignore land-locked cartographers.

In water,
desire refuses to retreat.

Source: From Nikki Finney, *Head Off & Split.* Chicago: TriQuarterly /Northwestern Press, 2011.

Poverty

Poverty is probably the single greatest hazard to women's health; it is often lethal when combined with other serious hazards. Women worldwide are more likely than men to be poor. Vulnerable groups, such as women-headed households, the elderly, and those with disabilities (see Chapters 6 and 8) lack assistance as even economically able nations increasingly cut back on their "safety nets" of social services. At higher rates than others, these more vulnerable women experience such ailments as chronic anemia, malnutrition, severe fatigue, and increased susceptibility to infections of the respiratory and reproductive tracts. Premature death is a frequent outcome of poverty.

Poverty explains many of the health inequities found among different groups of humans. It is directly related to disease incidences and to avenues for cure. For example, low-income women are likely to be poorly educated and may lack sufficient knowledge to identify and avoid risks or to respond adequately to them (even if they had the means to do so). In the United States, health insurance coverage is often employment-linked, and increasingly workers may lack health insurance. Low-income women are unlikely to have the financial resources to pay for medical treatment or the means of obtaining it, even when it is offered free, because of transportation costs or time lost from work. Poverty means inadequate housing for shelter and inadequate clothing and shoes for protection. It means inadequate sanitation due to insufficient or unclean water, food storage, and waste removal. It means exposure to risks of violence as a result of living in unprotected neighborhoods, and it means dependence on others for survival. So "choosing" to avoid a potentially dangerous situation, be it environmental, behavioral, or occupational, as many women are warned to do, may not, in fact, be a choice for many poor women.

Racial/Ethnic Discrimination

Race and ethnicity also affect the health risks of women. African Americans have higher rates of morbidity (such illnesses as cardio-vascular disease, diabetes, and cancer) and mortality (including infant mortality due to low birthweight) than white Americans (Orsi et al., 2009). Even when African Americans and whites earn the same income, African Americans still have higher rates of illness in many categories. As researchers have shown that biological or genetic factors and wealth or lifestyle inadequately explain the persistence of racial differences in health, Dressler (1993) proposes a "social structural model" to explain the health risks faced by African

Americans. The stress of "race" as it plays out in daily life does affect physical disease (such as cardiovascular problems) as well as mental health (as in depression). This stress, combined with preconceptions and misconceptions within the healthcare industry about the health needs and risks of various ethnic/racial groups, conspires to maintain health inequalities even when controlling for heredity, income, and social class. Although all women face additional health risks because of gender, poverty, discrimination, and racial status combine to pose even greater health risks for women of color (Harrell et al., 2003).

Occupational Health Risks

Women suffer from different occupational health risks compared to men. Although men are injured at work more often than women, women suffer illnesses related to work conditions that are harder to detect and less often reported (CDC, 2012). Higher rates of illness among people of color are often attributed to factors related to biology or culture, rather than being sought in their work roles. African American women work in riskier and lower-paying jobs compared to white women; consequently they experience more work-related injuries and illnesses. As part-time or temporary workers, they may not report safety concerns for fear of being fired. A large number of African American women work in low-paid health-service jobs that have a high rate of occupational illness. Many Latinas and Asian immigrant women work in the garment industry in cities like Los Angeles, Miami, and New York, often in sweatshops where workers face health risks from overcrowding, lack of adequate ventilation, danger of fire due to inadequate escape routes and fire-prevention features, and other hazards that result in much higher injury rates (CDC, 2012).

Violence

Physical Abuse. A large proportion of women who show up in hospital emergency rooms for treatment of injuries are victims of intimate partner abuse and sexual violence. Nonfatal violence between intimate partners compromises the health of millions of women worldwide. Studies in 48 countries reveal that 10–69% of women report having been physically assaulted by an intimate partner during their lifetime. Nations and cultures vary in the extent of their domestic violence against women, but the phenomenon appears pervasive worldwide, with few minor exceptions in small societies (Seager, 2009; UN, 2010).

Although some physicians do provide supportive care, others do not. There is a continued need to educate less skilled physicians who may be causing more physical and emotional harm to abused women when they examine women roughly, minimize an injury or the abuse, accuse the patient of lying, or blame the patient for the abuse (Hamberger et al., 1998). Nonsexual and sexual assault result in not only chronic disabilities, both physical and mental, but also death. "In the U.S., 43.8% of lesbian women, 61.1% of bisexual women, and 35.0% of heterosexual women had experienced rape, physical violence, and/ or stalking by an intimate partner" (CDC, 2012). Moreover, at least 1 out of 10 women has been sexually abused as a child (Courtois, 2000), and 1 in 3 continues to be subjected to either physical abuse and/or sexual abuse (WHO, 2010).

Rape and PTSD. Rape has obvious health consequences, both physical and mental, including subjection of the victim to exposure to sexually transmitted diseases, such as acquired immunodeficiency syndrome (AIDS). A further consequence in some cultures is the stigma attached to the loss of virginity by unmarried women. Rape victims may become unwanted, "unmarriageable"

members of the household, further victimized. In some instances, women victims may even be murdered by their own male kin for their loss of "honor" (PLOS, 2009). Rape victims also are among the highest-risk groups for posttraumatic stress disorder (PTSD), a debilitating psychological syndrome that involves detailed reliving of the traumatic event, panic attacks, depression, nightmares, and sleep disorders. Female veterans are nine times more likely to experience PTSD if they have been sexually assaulted in the military, higher than those veterans subjected to other forms of sexual assault (Suris et al., 2004). Women in war zones and refugee women are also at risk (PLOS, 2009). Understandably, many women are reluctant to come forward when they are raped because of the way they believe they may be perceived and/or treated by both legal and medical personnel. The concern with a "second rape" during postassault interactions places unnecessary blame on rape survivors and may result in exacerbating the possibility of long-term health problems (Campbell et al., 2003).

Women and Physical Health: Some Specific Concerns

Heart Disease

One in every two U.S. women will develop heart disease (also known as cardiovascular disease), and cardiovascular mortality in women exceeds that in men (Miller and Best, 2011). Women also have more severe first strokes at an older age than men, require longer hospitalization, and remain disabled (World Heart Federation, 2012). Women appear to be diagnosed with heart disease at later stages, to have their illness treated less aggressively by physicians, and to require different medical and surgical treatment from men. Even risk factors such as cholesterol and triglyceride levels appear to pose different risks according to gender. Clinical trials for cardiovascular disease (CVD) focus on symptoms more typical of males than females and provide more information about men than women (Adler, 2010). Moreover, 8 of the 10 drugs most recently taken off the market had more adverse effects in women than men (U.S. General Accounting Office, 2001). Awareness of the dangers of heart disease to women is underestimated by both professionals and women themselves. Women develop chronic diseases such as coronary artery disease well before menopause; hence, prevention of heart disease must begin young, and early detection and awareness is needed to more effectively manage women with cardiovascular disease (Raymond, Greenberg, and Lieder, 2005).

Cancer

The most common type of cancer among women is breast cancer (which very rarely occurs in men), although it varies substantially among different ethnic groups. As with the majority of cancers, the risk of breast cancer increases with age. This may be due to the long-term effect of exposure to environmental and other toxins. Although scientists and activists have urged greater investigation of the role of environmental factors, a major shift in the focus of research has not yet occurred (Gray, 2008). Nonetheless, more attention has been given to breast cancer, largely because of women's efforts to demand more funds for breast cancer awareness and research, especially related to prevention (see Box 9.5).

Box 9.5   WIND CHILL FACTOR

When my grandmother had hers removed,
She complained of the cold.
We wandered down the windy beach in the evening.
You don't think of that beforehand.
She crossed her arms over the flat plains
Of her chest as she spoke.
Our walks were always after the sun had gone down.
Post radiation, the bright light of day was forbidden.
Her cool, dark bedroom was forever fringed
with the hats she would take off and toss.
Within the mahogany dresser drawers
I glimpsed the bulky white contraptions
She strapped on each morning
After shooing us out and closing the door.
Even her daughters were left outside.

My aunt had to forfeit only one.
Do you want to see?
she asked, six months after the surgery.
She pulled open her soft, pink nightgown,
revealing herself.

She and I both looked, curiously.
I shrugged, was nonchalant,
But privately thought
that I could have done the job just as well myself
blindfolded with a dull hatchet.
My aunt buttoned up her flannel.
I'm too small to need a prosthesis.
But there are times I look down at myself
and it seems like someone has
made the bed and left off a pillow.

Now it has come down to you,
drifting though the air,
the water, the years,
who knows.
Before surgery, you write on the good one:
NO! DO NOT REMOVE!
And draw arrows to the bad one.

Source: From *Women's Studies Quarterly* 31, nos. 1 and 2 (Spring/Summer 2003): 185–6. Copyright ©
2001 by Charlotte McCaffrey, by permission of the Feminist Press at the City University of New York,
www.feministpress.org.

A variety of possible factors causing higher risk for cancer have been investigated. It is not clear whether, or to what extent, either dietary fat or obesity increases the risk of breast cancer. Alcohol consumption has been implicated, but questions remain about how the age at onset of drinking or amount of drinking is related to risk (Porzelius, 2000). Guidelines for the use of hormone replacement therapy (HRT) have been modified to reduce their potential harm to women (Boston Women's Health Book Collective, 2011).

The incidence of breast cancer has gone up dramatically in recent years. If detected before it has spread to other areas, it can often be treated effectively. Performing breast self-examinations, though no longer recommended, contributes to awareness of possible changes in a woman's body and can be important for this reason. Access to healthcare practitioners is necessary as physicians or nurse practitioners may detect breast cancers through manual examination, which should be performed at regular gynecological examinations. The most commonly used technology today to detect breast cancer is mammography, which uses radiation to take an image to see if there are any abnormal tissue masses. Cancers of the ovaries, uterus, and cervix cannot be detected by self-examination. Early detection of cervical cancer is possible, however, by use of a Pap smear, which detects abnormalities in sampled cells. HPV vaccines now provide protection against the most common types of virus that cause most cervical cancers.

Sexually Transmitted Disease Infections Including HIV/AIDS

For women of reproductive age (15–44 years) unsafe sex is the single greatest risk factor for disability and death, as it may result in HIV/AIDS or other sexually transmitted diseases (STDs). STDs are quite prevalent in the world today. They are a major cause of infertility and can contribute to blindness and brain damage as well as to difficulties in childbearing. Chlamydia infection is the most common bacterial sexually transmitted disease in the United States, and the rate for women is 2.5 times the rate among men (CDC, 2010). Untreated chlamydia, which is largely asymptomatic in women, can result in pelvic inflammatory disease, which in turn may cause infertility in at least 24,000 women annually in the United States as well as ectopic pregnancy and chronic pelvic pain (CDC, 2010).

The human immunodeficiency virus (HIV), the precursor of AIDS, is transmitted through genital secretions or through blood. At the end of 2010, an estimated 34 million people worldwide—38.6 million adults and 3.2 million children younger than 15 years—were living with HIV/AIDS. Approximately 70% of them (29.4 million) live in sub-Saharan Africa; another 17% (7.2 million) live in Asia. Approximately 50% of adults living with HIV/AIDS worldwide are women (Seager, 2009). Numbers continue to rise among adolescents. One particular consequence for women with these diseases is that they can transfer them to their fetuses unless medication is available during pregnancy.

Approximately 40,000 new HIV infections occur each year in the United States, about 70% among men and 30% among women. Of newly infected women, approximately 64% are black, 18% are white, 18% are Latinas, and approximately less than 1% involves other racial/ethnic groups. Approximately 75% of women were infected through heterosexual sex and 25% through injection drug use (CDC, 2001). AIDS, like other sexually transmitted diseases, is avoidable for adults *who have control over their own bodies*. Protected sex (using a latex or a female condom) is the most common effective alternative (although "safe sex" alternatives, using fantasy and masturbation, have also been recommended). Although condom use has consistently risen among young Americans, some women do engage in sexual relations without using condoms. The reasons they give include inconvenience, shame, and *refusal* by their male partners (Hinkle et al., 1992). Older women are particularly at risk, as they may have recently begun having new sexual partners after many years of marriage, in the case of heterosexual women, and may be uncomfortable addressing safer sex concerns as well as believing it is not relevant to them. Older women living with HIV are an often-overlooked population.

In sub-Saharan Africa, where problems of HIV transmission are acute, women run high risks of abuse by male partners for insisting on condom use. There, poverty forces large numbers of women into sex work and extreme vulnerability to exposure to AIDS and abuse. Women's lower status also may prevent them from having the control to protect themselves from HIV transmission. Many young women in sub-Saharan African countries have stated that their first experience of sexual intercourse was forced (UN AIDS, 1998). Similar data exist in the United States. Issues such as lack of knowledge, inaccessibility, and lack of concern for one's own safety are some of the reasons for the lack of contraception use.

Women who engage in heterosexual intercourse with an HIV carrier are at greater risk of contracting HIV than are men who have sexual intercourse with an HIV-positive woman. Female condoms, sometimes referred to as "vaginal pouches" (because they are inserted in the vagina), can help women exert greater control over HIV transmission. While these are available in some parts of the world, they require practice to use correctly and can be expensive. Microbicides appear to provide a new means of female protection, and research into them continues.

Hysterectomy

Currently in the United States, hysterectomy, or removal of the uterus, is the most common major nonobstetrical procedure performed on women, with over 600,000 performed each year. One third of all women over age 60 in the United States have had a hysterectomy, the highest rate in the industrialized world (OBOS, 2011). Sometimes the healthy ovaries of women over 45 are removed (oophorectomy) during a hysterectomy, which is inadvisable, as the ovaries will continue to produce some hormones after menopause (Parker et al., 2009).

In the nineteenth century, the uterus was thought to be the principal source of women's ailments; its removal was the obvious cure. Although modern medical science rejects this idea, hysterectomies continue to be performed on women with a healthy uterus. Physicians have offered to perform this "service" for women citing two primary reasons: it is an effective form of sterilization for those who no longer wish to bear children, and it is a preventive measure since the uterus may be the site of cancer at some future time. However, hysterectomies may have long-lasting negative physical, emotional, and sexual effects for women. Nevertheless, as many as 70% of hysterectomies performed in the United States may be recommended inappropriately. Alternative procedures, such as localized treatments and surgery to remove only fibroids, are available but may not be made known to women (OBOS, 2011).

Osteoporosis

Osteoporosis, a process linked to estrogen changes, is associated with a decrease in bone density and occurs in all humans after the age of 35. Increased medicalization of osteoporosis may occur in the form of unnecessary or too frequent bone density screenings and subsequent treatment with medications prescribed for women who are not at risk of osteoporosis. Prevention, in the form of adequate calcium intake as a child and young woman and weight-bearing exercise throughout life, is too often ignored. The rate of occurrence is difficult to gauge, but it is greatly accelerated in some women after menopause, resulting in bone ailments and a highly increased vulnerability to bone fractures. Of the estimated more than 25 million Americans affected by osteoporosis, 80% are women (Galsworthy, 1994). The risk of osteoporosis, however, is not uniform among women: African Americans and some African groups rarely show symptoms of this disease (Doress-Worters and Siegal, 1994; Stoppard, 1999). Osteoporosis is a major cause of physical disability in older women (twice as common as for older men) (Galsworthy, 1994).

Alzheimer's Disease

American women are at the epicenter of Alzheimer's disease, the most common form of dementia characterized by loss of mental ability severe enough to interfere with activities of daily living. Its physiological cause is still unclear. Sixty-five percent of all those with Alzheimer's are women (3.3 million), and 60% (6.7 million) of caregivers for persons with Alzheimer's are women. By mid-century, as many as 8 million women in the United States will have Alzheimer's disease (Skelton, 2010).

Women and Mental Health

Gendered Differences

In the realm of mental health, the interconnections between perceptions of health, diagnoses of the causes of illness, and women's place in society seem unavoidable. From the nineteenth-century novel *The Yellow Wallpaper* (Gilman, [1899] 1973) through Phyllis Chesler's classic work *Women and Madness* (1972), feminists have pointed to the way ideas about "madness" in U.S. society were used to oppress and control women. While the interpretation of human behavior as mentally healthy or mentally ill clearly contains a subjective element, it equally reflects social values. For example, until the mid-1970s homosexuality was listed as an illness in the Diagnostic and Statistical Manual of the American Psychiatric Association.

Gender differences in this phenomenon can be traced to two sources: patients and physicians. Women are more likely than men to go to a physician for help. This may be because they experience more problems, they more readily admit they have problems, they feel less able to cope with these problems without help, or they have readier access to physicians due to more flexible working hours. It may be a combination of some or all of these factors. Physicians, on the other hand, are more likely to attribute problems reported by women to psychic causes and to deal with these problems by prescribing psychotropic drugs (Hebald, 2001). The focus on the individual as the source of the problem ignores the social conditions and processes affecting women that exist outside them and are beyond their direct control. Humans are extremely plastic, and most individuals in a society will tend to fit themselves into a pattern of behavior they are taught is "normal." However, behavior that is considered "normal" in one society might be interpreted as "insane" or "neurotic" in another.

Feminist researcher Karen Pugliesi (1992) depicts two basic positions regarding gender differences in mental health. One, which she terms the "social causation approach," looks at aspects of women's experience in society that affect their mental well-being. The social conditions mentioned earlier, such as greater likelihood of experiencing poverty, sexual abuse, violence, and the double discrimination of gender and race, produce stresses that endanger women's mental as well as physical well-being. Mental health advantages can also be attributed to social conditions that differentially affect women and men. For example, the fact that women are encouraged to express emotions while men are encouraged to repress them might have specific mental health repercussions favoring women (Klonoff and Landrine, 1995).

The second position Pugliesi describes, the "social constructionist approach," focuses on different methods of conception and diagnosis of mental health and illness. Phyllis Chesler's (1972) work falls squarely in this category. Certain behaviors by women are labeled as the product of mental disorders by sexist psychiatrists and psychologists (Lopez et al., 1993). While both approaches locate the source of difference in women's and men's mental health in sexism, one takes the discovery of gender differences as "real," the product of different experiences in a gender-biased society, and the other treats this discovery as an artifact of biased diagnosis, a misinterpretation of what actually exists. These approaches complement one another in possibilities for dealing with treatment.

Behavioral differences between women and men related to mental health also reflect social circumstances. Substance abuse is one area. Women are less likely than men to be abusers of alcohol and tobacco, but when their lifestyles more closely resemble those of men, so do their substance abuse patterns. As women entered the workforce, for example, they more frequently used alcohol and tobacco. On the other hand, women make greater use of prescription drugs and, with greater access to the drugs, are more likely to use and abuse them. Yet women, especially pregnant women and women with children, who seek treatment for substance abuse are more likely than men to be turned away from programs or to encounter problems with the legal system over child custody (Larrieu et al., 2008).

Homophobic Bias

Feminist therapists, to be effective, must recognize homophobia experienced by women, along with gender, race, class, and sexual orientation discrimination (Greene, 1993). For example, the problems facing a lesbian or transgender woman seeking assistance through therapy must be understood in terms of the heterosexist bias in the larger social environment and the struggles the woman may experience with negative self-image resulting from taught prejudice. If therapeutic practices are based on an assumption of heterosexuality, their impact can be devastating for nonheterosexuals (Glassgold and Iasenza, [1995] 2000).

Depression

Women are at about twice the risk for depression as men. This finding applies not only to the United States but also globally. Depression is characterized by the persistence over a prolonged time (two weeks according to current diagnostic procedures) of a number of symptoms from a list. Typical symptoms include feeling sad, anxiety, decreased capacity to experience pleasure, diminished ability to think or concentrate, indifferent grooming, change in appetite, sleep disturbance, and many more. Yet the Institute of Medicine has noted that women are still underrepresented in clinical trials, and in early stages of research in this area, "more than 55% of samples testing animal models of depressions and anxiety (disorders twice as common in women than men) failed to include any female animals" (Institute of Medicine, 2010).

Psychiatrists and psychologists recognize a variety of types of depression. The report of the American Psychological Association's National Task Force on Women and Depression (McGrath et al., 1990) urges a "biopsychosocial" perspective on depression with regard to both diagnosis of causes and prescription for treatment. The biological component of this perspective includes a consideration of the biological and psychological consequences of reproduction-related events, including menstruation, pregnancy, childbirth, infertility, abortion, and menopause. The psychological component refers to characteristics of the female personality as constructed by society and the ways that women are oriented by this construction toward certain patterns of perception, social interaction, and coping with stress. The social component refers to the stresses produced by the roles to which women are assigned and to the risks to which women are subject, such as rape, sexual and gender discrimination, and poverty. Because women are subjected to particular gender expectations, the source of their depression may be misidentified. A woman might feel she needs to seek help because she feels "depressed," locating the source of the problem in herself but not recognizing that her social situation might be the major contributor to her feelings. Her consultant, psychiatrist, or psychologist might compound this by "blaming the victim," characterizing a perfectly normal reaction to a terrible situation as a symptom of mental illness.

If the risk for depression or diagnosis of depression is higher among women than among men, the risk for members of racial and ethnic minority groups is also high and higher for women of these groups than men. The conditions affecting rates of depression for African Americans, Latinas, Asian Americans, and Native Americans vary according to the situation of the groups and subgroups in question; while discrimination produces stress and depression at a greater rate than for the population of women in general, the ways in which they are experienced and expressed are specific to each group. Poverty and homelessness, especially among young mothers, exacerbates the risk of depression (Grant, 2009).

Age is another important and variable dimension. Adolescence and old age are considered high-risk categories for depression. These life stages are characterized by both biological changes accompanying changes in reproductive status and social changes resulting in much adjustment (see Chapter 8).

A final dimension of risk for depression is sexual orientation. Alcoholism and drug abuse continue to affect lesbians, gay men, and transgendered persons at two to three times the rate of the general population. Programs are needed to address the special risks of LGBTQ populations (and those "perceived" to be LGBTQ) who are at greater risk of experiences of violence and victimization and have long-lasting effects, such as PTSD. Lesbians also report higher levels of stress than heterosexual women. Adolescents may be particularly vulnerable. Lack of family and social acceptance can place a significant burden on mental health (U.S. Department of Health and Human Services, 2010).

Addressing institutionalized discrimination is an important factor in reducing the risk of negative health outcomes. Positive factors reducing the likelihood of depression for lesbians include group support from the lesbian community (among those who have come out and have a community to consult), LGBTQ health centers, and the sharing of housework and child care in lesbian households. Legislation supporting same-sex marriage, unions, and adoptions also is beneficial, though still controversial.

Women as Special-Risk/Vulnerable Populations

Life situations may expose particular groups of women to greater levels of ill health and injury as well as more limited access to care. We focus on four groups here.

Refugee Women

Some 80% of the world's 30 million refugees are women and children. Although many refugees are homeless, impoverished, separated from other family members, and terrified, women refugees have special vulnerabilities that include sexual violence and a lack of safe shelter and food. When refugee women are finally resettled, many find themselves in a strange new land, frightened and lonely, not knowing the language and customs, and consulting healthcare workers whose understanding of illness and disease might be very different from their own (Smyke, 1991; Cohn, 2013).

Women with Disabilities

Women who are considered or identify as disabled tend to be stigmatized everywhere. Feminist disability studies aims to denaturalize disability. It thus "defines disability broadly from a social rather than a medical perspective, arguing that disability is a cultural interpretation of human variation. This shows that disability—similar to race and gender—is a system of representation that marks bodies as subordinate" (Garland-Thomson, 2005). Traits we think of as a disability range from vision and hearing differences to various levels of mobility to intellectual functioning (Linton, 2007; Hall, 2011). Poverty and isolation from a supportive family unit generally compound disability. Only recently have many high-income countries made accommodations to empower the disabled to participate "in the mainstream" by providing means of access in public places; poorer countries lag far behind (Boylan, 1991).

Disabled women enter a world of "sexism without the pedestal" (Fine and Asch, 1988).

In contrast to disabled men, who are thought of as weak but interested in sex, women who are disabled are thought of as asexual. Nonetheless, disabled women have claimed the right to sexual lives, to marry, and to bear children and have shown that they, their partners, and their children can thrive as families (Linton, 1997).

Older Women

Much of what has been said of disabled women could also be (and has been) said of older women, who are often treated as disabled persons, with the entire stigma that goes with assumptions about disability (see Chapter 8). With improvements in healthcare, more women are living to advanced ages but frequently become disabled with chronic diseases. Isolation exacerbates their difficulties in coping with a disability as women live longer than their male partners and, in urban areas, often live apart from their families (Fried et al., 2001; Gillick, 2001). Membership in an ethnic or racial minority group may exacerbate the problems women experience as aging persons who are female and poor. In other cases they also have coping strategies and support systems within their families and communities that counteract larger societal disadvantages (Padgett, 1989). Often their families need their help, and they offer one another support.

Incarcerated Women

In the United States, in particular, women have been incarcerated in swiftly rising numbers. There are now more mothers behind bars in the United States than at any other point in history. Their health needs include all the concomitant issues of poverty, violence, and racism that have an impact upon male prisoners; however, institutions must also focus on concerns specific to women,

such as reproductive health, including pregnancy, and mental health needs (Braithwaite, Arriola, and Newkirk, 2006). Recently several cities and states in the United States have banned the shackling of imprisoned women while in labor but the practice still persists. Prenatal care is inadequate in 38 out of 50 states in the United States. HIV testing is not offered in 48 states (NWLC, 2012).

Empowering women to be vigilant in addressing the ways that the medicalization of their life processes affects their health can change attitudes, medical practice, and even behaviors. Through the discipline of women's/gender studies, we can examine how the patriarchal lens has warped women's health and create a new vision for the future.

Summary

Around the globe, women's political consciousness has been galvanized around health issues. The women's health movement has sought to empower women about their own bodies. It has also undertaken to reform the healthcare system and public policy by making them more responsive to women's bodies and women's needs and by ensuring that women's issues are addressed as an integral aspect of human rights. Because women's bodies are often at the crux of politico-socio-cultural battles, constant vigilance and creative strategies are required.

Women's health has been perceived differently from men's because women's bodies and biological processes are different in some respects from men's. Feminists have uncovered biases in the gender dynamics of Western medicine. In the past women were considered to be physically defective; more recently women became viewed as the "weaker sex." With the professionalization of the Western healthcare system in the nineteenth century, men displaced midwives and male "experts" came to predominate in providing guidance and information, previously offered by women kinfolk and other women.

Society has medicalized the normal parts of the life cycle and experiences of most women, such as menstruation, childbirth, and menopause. Male experts and policy makers have enormous influence and control over women's access to health information and healthcare. Control over women's bodies is especially politicized around birth control and abortion and jeopardizes women's right to safe and legal abortions and other reproductive rights.

Childbirth has become the domain of medical specialists, with women as passive consumers of their expertise and medical procedures. In developing countries and among the poor everywhere, childbirth remains a risk to the health of the mother and her child. Male biases are also seen in the treatment of menopause and women's sexuality.

Poverty is probably the single greatest hazard to women's health. The stress of racism contributes to physical disease as well as mental health, contributing to unequal treatment from the U.S. healthcare system and its professionals. Women are frequently employed in low-paying and hazardous conditions that contribute to health risks that are harder to detect and less often reported than men's occupational health risks. Physical abuse and rape are forms of violence that women experience and that are very much underreported.

Heart disease, cancer, sexually transmitted diseases, and osteoporosis should be of special concern to women everywhere. These aspects of physical health are too often underdiagnosed, underresearched, and undertreated in women. Hysterectomies, which occur at a very high rate in the United States, may have long-lasting negative physical, emotion, and sexual effects for women. Women also have mental health issues: they experience depression at a much higher rate than men, and drug

therapy is also prescribed for women more frequently and for longer than for men.

Some groups of women, such as refugees, the disabled, the elderly, and the incarcerated, are especially vulnerable. They are at special risk for violent attacks and neglect and have limited access to good healthcare. Lesbian and transgender women are often at a disadvantage when seeking appropriate care.

The women's health movement has made great strides in bringing women's health issues to the public and to women's own agendas. Working to counter gender, racial, ethnic, sexuality, and class biases will address their issues and improve women's health.

Discussion Questions

1. What would be the consequences for women's health if women had greater control of reproduction? What factors affect their control; how might their control be increased? What concerns might arise in the future?

2. Select a group of women at special risk for health problems as a consequence of disability, age, political status, or other factors. Discuss these problems, their causes, how they are addressed in the present healthcare system, and how healthcare delivery might be improved.

3. Interview a woman *at least* 20 years older than you. Compare your health experiences—healthcare, family remedies, information shared about reproductive health matters, beliefs, etc. Who were the healthcare practitioners? How does treatment differ from that with which you are familiar?

4. Review your health history or that of a member of your family. What are the challenges you have faced in trying to adapt or to change to more healthful behaviors? What are the barriers? What has been helpful? In what way does the society

around you (culture, advertising, role models, etc.) influence you—in both positive and negative ways?

5. Identify a definition of health, either from the text or one that you create yourself. Explain how and why it best fits your experience and understanding of women's health.

Recommended Readings

Angier, Natalie. *Woman: An Intimate Geography*. New York: Anchor Books, 2000. A well-researched, passionate, and pithy discussion of female anatomy and physiology.

Asetoyer, Charon, Katharine Cronk, and Samanthi Hewakapuge. *Indigenous Women's Health Book, within the Sacred Circle: Reproductive Rights, Environmental Health, Traditional Herbs and Remedies*. Volcano, CA: 2003. Referred to as "the indigenous women's *Our Bodies, Ourselves*, it combines native traditional healing with Western medicine. Includes resources.

Gordon, Linda. *The Moral Property of Women: A History of Birth Control Policies in America*. Chicago: University of Illinois Press, 2002. An important text in understanding the interstices of health, politics, and the struggle for gender equity.

Seaman, Barbara, with Laura Eldridge, editors. *Voices of the Women's Health Movement*, vols. 1 and 2. New York: Seven Stories Press, 2012. This two-volume anthology includes writings by a broad range of feminists, from Elizabeth Cady Stanton to contemporary activists and authors. Topics range from history of the women's health movement to self-help, body image, and chronic illness.

Skloot, Rebecca. *The Immortal Life of Henrietta Lacks*. New York: Broadway Paperbacks, 2011. A poor woman's cancer cells fuel scientific advances though she herself dies and her family remains poor, despite the multimillion dollar industry the cells generate. The role of race, gender, and poverty, as well as informed consent, the beginnings of bioethics, as each affects the members of the Lacks family, are examined. In August 2013 a landmark agreement was reached between the the U.S. National Institutes of Health and the Lacks family, giving the Lackses some control of future research proposals using Mrs. Lacks's cells.

Part *III*

Women in Society

The earlier sections of this volume explored the various ways in which women have been defined by others—in society and culture, in the family—and the alternatives they have chosen for themselves. This final section deals with women's relationships to what has often been called the "public sphere."

Women have always participated in the world beyond the family circle, but all too often these contributions and efforts have been undervalued, ignored, or treated as invisible. For many people, the threat of feminism has been the growing claims by women to power in the public domain and the redefinition of women's roles in what has been misleadingly called the "private" domain.

In this section we explore the contributions of women to the fields of education, religion, work, and political power. Education stimulates us to ask questions and search for answers. Too often, those who do not have the advantage of an education do not learn how to question the nature of our environment and experience. In many parts of the world, parents without the necessary resources choose not to educate their daughters, only their sons. Women's education can be a controversial issue. Will education provoke them to challenge the status quo? What is appropriate for women to learn? Access to certain fields often requires specific educational preparation. In

the past, women were not permitted to obtain instruction in the male-dominated professions of the ministry, law, and medicine. Women continue to challenge long-held beliefs about their lack of ability for scholarship. In doing gender-conscious research, feminist scholarly questions differ from the traditional approaches of the past, and such research is adding to the knowledge base about both women and men.

Education is not the only way in which women lay claim to central social and cultural beliefs. Religion has been a continuing force in many women's lives. Varieties of religion prescribe human behavior and provide models for human aspiration. Women have often been viewed as saints or sinners. Many women through history have chosen a "religious life" as an alternative to secular life and marriage. They have not only been involved as worshipers and followers but have also taken leadership roles, ranging from curers to clergy.

Feminists involved in religions and religious life have reinterpreted doctrines, rituals, and practices and have questioned the sexist biases of the language and cultural practices in which these dogmas are framed. Today, feminists also seek a religious expression for self-affirming beliefs in womanhood.

The most dramatic shift of the past century in terms of women's place in the world outside the family and religious institutions has been the enormous increase in the numbers of women working for wages outside the home. Much of the work traditionally done by women has been interwoven with the traditional roles of housewife and mother. Within the context of the household, women have rarely, if ever, been paid or given credit for their daily work. With the advent of industrialization and modernization, much of the work formerly done by women in the home was transformed into activities performed outside the home for wages—for example, spinning, sewing, education of the young, and care of the sick. Some of the traditional areas of women's work were taken over by men in factories, schools, and hospitals. When done by men, the status of the work and the pay received for it rose. In the industrialized world, technology continues to change the nature of work, for better and for worse, and women as workers have been at the forefront of the globalization of industrial labor.

Since women's work lives cannot be separated from their personal and familial lives, the growing number of women and mothers in the workforce has led to demand for changes in the workplace and the family to accommodate women's needs. Child-care facilities, flexible working hours, and parental leave have been implemented by employers and governments in response to the influx of women into the workforce.

Even beyond the workplace, politics has been the final frontier for women's involvement in society. Politics and the power to change society are crucial to women's lives. Where there is power, there are means for exerting social control. In societies where power is accorded to certain groups of people by virtue of race, religion, ethnic origin, or gender, it has been difficult for oppressed groups to gain sufficient power to alter the status quo. This is no less true in women's struggles for their political rights.

Women's struggle for political power is international. In a variety of contexts, both formal and grassroots, women from different countries come together to share their common experiences and work together to improve women's lives. Despite the differences that separate women, the women's movement and feminism are global phenomena.

Should women strive to reform the existing social system, or will nothing less than a radical restructuring be necessary? Certainly, different women and different communities have different political objectives. Moreover, recently feminist political theorists have challenged some of the foundational ideas in political thought, such as human rights, the individual, and the meaning of equality, which are all products of a specific time (the Enlightenment) and a particular place (western Europe). However, although women do not make up a homogeneous group, they can and do support one another in realizing a variety of shared goals.

This book has traveled out from the individual to interpersonal relationships to the larger world, but we also understand that these distinctions are in many ways artificial. We are all individuals in relation to each other and our communities, local, regional, national, and international. Our work as feminists is to recognize the varieties and multiplicities of women's experiences, even as we acknowledge the ways in which patriarchal values have affected women *and* men over time and across geographic space. By knowing our pasts, and analyzing the present, we can use old and new tools to construct a more equitable and juster future.

chapter **10**

Women and Education

> One study after another has shown that educating girls is one of the most effective ways to fight poverty. Schooling is also often a precondition for girls and women to stand up against injustice, and for women to be integrated into the economy.
>
> NICHOLAS D. KRISTOF AND SHERYL WUDUNN, 2009

Why Education Matters

Have you ever thought about the fact that you, as a student in a college course, are a member of a highly elite and privileged group? If this comment seems odd to you, perhaps because of the considerable efforts you have had to make to get to college, consider the following facts. Only a small percentage of the world's population and an even smaller percentage of the world's women ever take a course in college. Two thirds of the adults in the world who cannot read or write are women (774 million in 2007), which means that millions of women are unable to read a book like this one (United Nations, 2010: 54). We need to understand why this is so if we want to change it.

When girls do gain access to formal education, as the quote at the beginning of this chapter suggests, they actually achieve benefits for themselves, their families, their communities, and the world. For example, increased education for women of childbearing ages (15–44 years) has been found to have a direct effect on infant mortality. Why? Because the more education that women get, the more they realize the importance of health services for themselves and their children (Gakidou et al., 2010). Where women achieve a higher level of education, they find opportunities to take on new roles and raise their status in society. Education provides a way to understand our world and helps us achieve our goals.

A Matter of Life or Death

Education can also be a matter of life or death. The devaluation of girls by parents and society, which we explored in Chapter 8, has helped create the problem of "missing daughters," the selective destruction by abortion and neglect of girl babies. When parents believe boys are worth more than girls in the family, they make decisions about how to spend their scarce resources, like who should be vaccinated or taken to the hospital or sent to school, that have a serious impact on the health and education of girls.

The Politics of Knowledge

We acquire knowledge from our experiences, our families, our schooling, and increasingly from many forms of media. What we consider knowledge reflects our assumptions about what is valuable to know. The authors of this textbook believe that knowledge includes an understanding of the world as it is experienced by women. Women are not a homogeneous group; they differ from one another depending on such factors as their class, race, ethnicity, sexuality, or religion. How individuals learn from experience is, as we discussed in Chapter 3, affected by the particular mix of the identities we have as women and men, and we react to the world based on this mix and the way we are socialized by our earliest experiences in our families and communities. These include, from the beginning, our experience of power relationships into which we are born. We learn the "pecking order" of who has power over whom and can tell them what to do (Wylie, 2004). This power relationship applies to what we learn as well. This chapter will show how elite males in the past exercised their power to shape what was called "knowledge" and to create barriers to acquiring that knowledge to women and men over whom they had power. It will also show that acquiring that knowledge empowers learners not only to advance their own lives but to reshape knowledge to make it more inclusive of the experiences of all people. In that sense, knowledge itself becomes power, and power can be used in positive as well as negative ways.

Men as the Measure of Knowledge

Formal education in the past was largely in the hands of men of privilege in their societies worldwide. These men simply assumed that their experiences were "universal." Formal education developed on the basis of such assumptions ensured that these assumptions were accepted as the "truth." The politics of knowledge was based on the conviction that those who had privileged knowledge should control those who did not. It also included the belief that women and men of lower status had inferior intellectual abilities and that their proper place in society did not warrant that they share the kind of education that would prepare them for the educated professions, the occupations monopolized by privileged men with formal training.

As specific academic disciplines emerged in the context of universities, few scholars anywhere questioned the prevailing view that to understand any society and how it changed over time, it was necessary to study primarily the lives and actions of men, especially powerful men. Men's experiences were considered universal, while women's experiences, if considered at all, were thought to be of lesser importance. Scholars—and men as a group— might acknowledge that women had always had important reproductive and family roles, but they viewed these roles as functional and "natural."

The Rise of Feminist Scholarship

Understanding gender and understanding knowledge are linked. When feminist historians in the 1970s tried to find out what women had been doing in the past, they found very little recorded about them in the histories written by men—unless the women were powerful queens. This led to a search for missing information—they asked: Did women have a Renaissance? or What were women doing during the French Revolution? Feminist scholars soon learned that much information about women was available—if you looked for it. For example, there were women who became so-called Learned Ladies during the Renaissance, but such women had to choose between marriage and scholarship, for only as unmarried women living in cloistered convents could they pursue their learning. During the French Revolution, we now know, groups of women asserted political equality with men, but despite the advocacy of equality by male revolutionary leaders, these men resisted including women as political equals. They even sent to the guillotine Olympe de Gouges (1748–1793), the most outspoken of the women who made such claims (Kelly-Godal, 1977; Levy and Applewhite, 1979; King, 1980; Scott, 1996).

Feminist scholars began to examine what questions a particular discipline, like history, did not ask as it was shaped earlier by elite men, since such men believed, with rare exceptions, that women had made no significant contributions to history. Asking questions about women's lives reveals that the notion that women and men always led lives in completely separate spheres was never an accurate description of past reality (Helly and Reverby, 1992). Asking questions about women's activities in the past could begin in earnest only when it became visible that such information had been excluded, and therefore not explained. Becoming visible meant they could no longer simply be ignored. Making women's lives visible has been undertaken by increasing numbers of feminist scholars asking woman- and gender-centered questions. The creation of hundreds of women's studies programs reflected this scholarly revolution of intellectual discovery, asking questions about information that had been neglected and should be included and taught so it would not again be lost (Boxer, 1998).

Women's Choices, Women's Constraints

We grow up learning the lessons taught us by our surroundings, but today we are freer than ever before to make choices about who we want to be. Of course this risks being labeled deviant by those who have different expectations for us. Education plays a role in this process, either confirming our acceptance in the world that has nurtured us or opening up new possibilities that attract us. Making changes is not easy, for there are cultural and structural barriers that may limit and prevent, and certainly add to the cost of, making such choices. This chapter deals with some of these impediments.

Education as a Contested Arena: Who Should Be Taught?

Gender, Educational Participation, and Illiteracy Globally

There has been a long historical debate over *who* should be educated. Information about school enrollment shows the attention that nations have begun to give to educating girls and women. More girls worldwide are attending primary school today than ever before, and in the majority of countries they are at or near parity with boys. The educational gender gap for girls, however, widens in developing countries in terms of secondary school participation (UNESCO, 2005: 21–2). In 2007, women

worldwide comprised 51% of higher education enrollment, but there are wide disparities by region. North American and Western European women have, at 56%, the highest university enrollment. Women in South and West Asia and sub-Saharan Africa make up only 41 and 40%, respectively, of attendance at universities (United Nations, 2010).

Being considered "different" contributes to fewer opportunities for schooling. Among those less likely to be formally educated are women (and men) from socially excluded or marginalized groups, including indigenous peoples (like the aboriginals of Australia), those with physical or mental disabilities, immigrants, members of ethnic, language, and religious minorities, and those who reside in rural areas or in urban poverty (Lockheed, 2008). But enrollment data is only a partial portrait of women's educational access. Who is *not* in school? Of primary school–age children worldwide in 2007, about 72 million were not enrolled, and most (41 million) of them were girls. As formal education is a primary road to literacy, many girls are in danger of becoming illiterate, like so many of the adult women in their communities. Nearly two thirds of the people in the world today who cannot "read and write a short simple statement" are female, a proportion that has remained unchanged since 1990 (United Nations, 2010: 54). Moreover, the United Nations now advocates that in this age of new technology and information media everyone be "functionally literate" in oral expression, numeracy, and problem solving as well so that human beings in any culture can improve their lives and participate fully in economic and civic life (UNESCO, 2005: 15–16).

Unequal access to education is gendered in large part because of continuing disagreements over who should be educated. The pattern of social subordination that women experience globally accounts for some of this disparity. In every society, daughters and wives are still expected to be responsible for domestic duties, even when they undertake income-producing labor outside the home (see Chapter 12). The idea that domestic skills should be the primary goal of any girl's education has a long history. Through the centuries daughters who have aspired to the kind of formal education considered appropriate for their brothers have had to struggle to achieve it (Sicherman, 2010).

An extreme example in our contemporary world has been the views promulgated by the Taliban regime of Afghanistan (1996–2001), absolutely prohibiting the schooling of girls outside their homes. Before this regime took power, a number of Afghani women had acquired a university education and held professional positions. The Taliban's objection to girls and women being educated was drawn from a conservative belief that school was not a "woman's place" (see Box 10.1). Throughout history, elite males of all religions have attempted some measure of control over women's access to reading and writing (see Chapter 11).

Nonetheless, it is important that in learning about the prohibition of girl's and women's access to education in other parts of the world we not fall into the trap of considering our (the Global North) context as more advanced or superior to theirs. As transnational feminism (see Introduction) has alerted us, such comparisons elicit a "rescue fantasy" among feminists in developed states that both emanates from and further encourages imperialism.

Women's Struggles for Formal Education in the Past

The West has long praised the ancient world of Greece, beginning in 800 B.C.E, as the

---

Box 10.1   THE TEENAGE GIRL WHO WANTED TO GO TO SCHOOL

Malala Yousafzai, a 14-year-old who campaigned for girls' right to an education, was targeted and shot on her school bus by the Taliban in Pakistan on October 10, 2012. The following excerpt is from a translation of Malala's diary that was published prior to the shooting under a pseudonym:

I was afraid going to school because the Taliban had issued an edict banning all girls from attending schools. Only 11 students attended the class out of 27. The number decreased because of Taliban's edict…Even if they [the Taliban] come to kill me, I will tell them what they are trying to do is wrong, that education is our basic right.

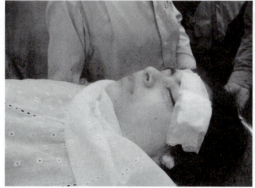

Source: http://www.newyorker.com/online/blogs/newsdesk/2012/10/the-girl-who-wanted-to-go-to-school.html#ixzz29eKlwNeA.

cradle of liberty and political participation among its citizens. When we look closely, however, we find that only Greek males made up its small, privileged citizen class (perhaps 10% of the population) and were educated in athletics, music, and reading. The sisters of elite citizen men were only occasionally taught to read and write. A small number did study and practice poetry, music, philosophy, and even medicine (Pomeroy, 1975, 1977). Formal education was not available to the rest of Greek society, made up of the merchant classes or slave women and men. In ancient Rome, properted citizens similarly educated their sons, but unlike the Greeks they were more inclined to think it desirable that their daughters read Latin and Greek literature, play the lyre, and know how to dance (Pomeroy, 1975; Snyder, 1989).

Late in the ancient world, in Egypt, a truly exceptional woman named Hypatia (c. 370–415 C.E.), taught by her learned father, became a teacher of mathematics, astronomy, and philosophy at the school at Alexandria (see Chapter 2). In the next thousand years (c. 400–1400), formal education in medieval western Europe continued mainly within Christian monasteries and convents and among the Muslims and Jews who settled in Spain. Most European men of titled and properted families were more concerned about swordsmanship and field sports than in learning to read. Formal education was left to male clergy, some of whom used their skills on behalf of their secular rulers, and to cloistered nuns (Lucas, 1983; McNamara, 1996).

There were a few notable learned women in medieval Europe, however. Their intellectual achievements include Latin plays by the German nun Hroswitha of Gandersheim (935–1001), the mystical writings by the abbess Hildegard of Bingen (1098–1179), and song poems by women troubadours in southern France. One woman, Trotula (c. eleventh century), the wife and mother of physicians,

taught at a medical school in Salerno, Italy, where both women and men were allowed to study and teach (Green, 2001). By the thirteenth century, however, when European universities came to dominate formal learning, these institutions were devoted solely to training men in theology, law, and medicine.

Elsewhere in the world during the fifth to fifteenth centuries, some women of aristocratic or royal families could learn to read and write. Several at the Japanese emperor's court in the Heian period (794–1192) kept diaries and wrote letters to each other. One royal woman, Lady Murasaki Shikibu (c. 978–1030), produced the world's earliest epic novel, the *Tale of Genji*, about the love adventures of a prince at court (Jayawardena, 1986). In Islamic Spain, Walladah Bint Mustakfi (c. 1001–1080), the daughter of the caliph (ruler) of Cordoba, composed love poetry in the flourishing intellectual climate established by her father. In the Middle East generally, Islam as a religion required both women and men to study the Qur'an, creating a measure of literacy for girls. A number of Muslim women from scholarly and noble households were educated to a high degree, a few of them contributing to literary and theological writings (Nashat, 1999).

From the 1400s to the 1700s in Europe, the development of government bureaucracies employed men with learning. An urban commercial class, whose trades required a high level of literacy, grew in importance. Knowledge enabled states to govern more efficiently and business enterprises to expand. However, men's assumptions about women's inferior "nature" and impaired mental capacities remained. A few educated women did dare to speak out against this dominant view. Christine de Pizan (c. 1364–1430), a young widow with children at the French court, supported herself by writing lyric poetry, courtly romances, and tracts on moral conduct as well as public matters. In *The Book of the City of*

Ladies (1405), she wrote of the achievements of famous women of the past, chiding male writers who distorted women's abilities (Boxer and Quataert, 2000). With the invention of movable type and the printed book in the late fifteenth century, literacy increasingly flourished among men, who benefited from new schools available to them in their villages and growing cities. These secular schools, reflecting prevailing views about women's inferior intellects, did not admit girls (Lee, 1975).

Two women trained in their fathers' courts in sixteenth-century Europe to be humanist scholars became powerful rulers in their own right: Catherine de Medici (1519–1589) in France and Elizabeth I (1533–1603) in England. Though male Protestant reformers promoted reading the Bible as the proper education for both girls and boys, they soon put restrictions on which women were allowed to be independent readers, based on their higher class position, while placing an increased emphasis on the use of education for women's moral training, not their intellectual development.

European Colonization and Women's Education

After 1500 and until the second half of the twentieth century, Western countries acquired territories overseas through the use of force to control far flung resources, trade, and wealth. In imposing European power, institutions, and practices on many parts of Asia, Africa, the Middle East, and the Americas, the issue of who should be educated became critical. The primary goal of the colonizers was to create an empire with an orderly and disciplined local labor force. For women, the consequences were mixed. Christian missionary schools for girls often provided colonized women with their first opportunity for formal education, but Western education introduced the concepts of European racial and cultural superiority. As the West increasingly began to view the education of women as a symbol of modernity, indigenous elites who identified with their colonial masters sought to redefine their traditional concepts, including that of womanhood (Berger and White, 1999; Edwards and Roces, 2000). In new Latin American nations in the latter part of the nineteenth century, for example, enlightened local leaders expanded secular education for women in order to demonstrate the modern nature of their states (Sànchez Korrol, 1999).

Multiracial British Caribbean colonies followed a pattern that held true elsewhere in imperial systems. Europeans in positions of power sought to replicate hierarchical European codes of conduct. After the abolition of slavery, lower-class black girls and boys attended schools together but studied different subjects. Boys were expected to become skilled and unskilled laborers; girls were prepared to become domestic servants. Upper-class white males were educated for the professions and senior positions in the colonial administration, while middle-class males, many of whom were of mixed race (called "colored" or "mulatto"), received training for the lower ranks of the civil service and commerce. Middle-class and upper-class European girls were groomed to be suitable wives for educated husbands, and while they received more years of schooling, the curriculum, with its emphasis on household subjects such as needlework, differed little from that provided to lower-class black girls (Ellis, 1986).

By the twentieth century, most European colonies had government-supported elementary schools for both girls and boys, increasing general literacy; but boys more than girls were encouraged to take advantage of it. A few private secondary schools and a very small number of universities were established to train indigenous men as professionals and potential political leaders. A handful of women studied at secular and church-related schools in Europe or the United States. Such opportunities enabled a select group of women in India, for example, to return home as teachers, midwives, doctors, and lawyers (Burton, 1998) and a few women in eastern and southern Africa to train for vocations deemed suitable for women, such as teaching and nursing (Berger, 1999).

Some colonial governments, either believing their subjects did not have the intellectual capacity to absorb Western learning or determined to prevent them from doing so, simply neglected to supply any educational services, as in the Portuguese territories of Angola, Guinea-Bissau, and Mozambique (Lindsay, 1980). In the Belgian Congo, discrimination against women in schooling was a matter of colonial law, resulting in one of the lowest literacy rates for women in the world (Yates, 1982). Where it existed, European-sponsored education mirrored traditional European gender values, which meant that secular schools for colonial peoples emphasized formal education for boys only. In conjunction with the elevation of Western learning, traditional languages and knowledge were denigrated in the colonies. In regions where local women in precolonial societies had wielded a measure of political and economic power, colonial regimes diminished their status (see Chapter 13).

Women's Struggles for Education in the Developing World Today

Local reformers and feminist thinkers in the developing world have successfully challenged colonial and traditional views of women's education, in part by gaining access to newer, progressive ideas about women. After 1906, for example, literate Iranian women could obtain a weekly newspaper called *Danish (Knowledge)*, published by one of several women's secret societies aimed at expanding educational opportunities for girls. By 1914, literate Egyptian women could choose from 15 journals in Arabic (Baron, 2005). In 1919 in China, where revolution had removed the ruling dynasty, there were 400 new nationalist and feminist periodicals openly questioning Chinese women's subordination, including foot binding and traditional marriage customs (Jayawardena, 1986).

Like women who took part in the "Arab Spring" uprisings in 2012, women in the three decades after World War II actively supported the independence movements and wars of national liberation that ended Western colonialism, including serving as fighting soldiers (see Chapter 13). Consequently, they expected more inclusion in all sectors of their societies, such as schooling, than their male counterparts were prepared to give them (Disney, 2008).

Poverty and the lack of schools only partially explain gender disparities in developing states. Violence, including rape, directed against girls and women in areas of armed conflict, for example in Rwanda and Sudan, regularly followed by displacement and refugee status, has contributed to a serious decline in their enrollment rates (UNESCO, 2003). Whether because of wars, traditional or renewed religious fundamentalism, or the enormous costs of national reconstruction, social and economic choices are often made at the expense of women's access to formal education.

Even efforts at economic development for poorer countries have sometimes been accompanied by gender inequity. Development planning that upholds male Western and indigenous values has deprived women of access to new resources, ignoring their historic and real but "invisible" contributions to economic growth (Fraser and Tinker, 2004).

In the Global South, most states have focused on providing primary and secondary school access. Given the opportunity, however, women worldwide will pursue higher education. In the post-Taliban era at Kabul University in Afghanistan, for example, women numbered 1,700 of the 7,000 students. Yet, even among these one commented, "I was one of the very few girls in my town allowed to seek higher education. I was lucky that my parents allowed me to study" (Nemtsova, 2010).

As the global community has come to accept access to formal education as a human right for all, feminists throughout the world have expanded the debate about women's education, calling for a curriculum that reflects the values, perspectives, and experiences of women, as well as their full and equal participation at all levels (Martin, 2000; see Introduction).

Broadening U.S. Educational Participation: Racial Desegregation and Title IX

The struggles of white women and women and men of color for educational access and equality are deeply embedded in U.S. history, as are political debates over who should be educated. Their successes are marked by federal legislation adopted to end discriminatory practices of exclusion and marginalization.

Racial segregation in education was a dominant feature in U.S. history for nine decades, especially but not solely in the South. Although Native American, Chinese, Japanese, and Mexican students as well as blacks have been forced to attend schools inferior to and often separate from white students, we focus here on African Americans. Before the Civil War (1861–1865), black slave children in the South were prohibited by state laws from being taught to read and write. For 50 years after the Civil War, the majority of African Americans continued to live in southern states, where economic debt and local laws sustained a system of racial hierarchy and

subjugation. Public facilities were segregated by race, and once the right to vote was fixed by federal law, state barriers were erected to exercising that right. A segregated school system was upheld by the U.S. Supreme Court in *Plessy* v. *Ferguson* in 1896 on the southern claim that their public schools were "separate but equal." It took six decades of struggle to overturn this judicial decision, when the 1954 U.S. Supreme Court decision *Brown* v. *Board of Education* condemned the practice as inherently unequal, based on arguments that demonstrated the adverse psychological effects of segregation.

When many schools and universities in the South resisted the implementation of desegregation, a few courageous African Americans—schoolchildren and university students, both female and male—acted on their new legal rights. Federal troops were sent to protect them in the face of local resistance. A growing civil rights movement in the 1950s and 1960s focused on ending publically sanctioned segregation and winning back African American voting rights. In response, the Civil Rights Act of 1964 condemned all forms of discrimination "based on race, color, religion, sex, or national origin." Title (paragraph) VI called for an end to discrimination by government agencies that receive federal funds, and Title VII prohibited discrimination in hiring and employment, explicitly extending the terms of the act to higher education institutions.

The civil rights movement and the Civil Rights Act of 1964 energized the women's movement. In 1972, Title IX of the Education Amendments was enacted to address sex discrimination. The preamble states: "No person in the United States shall, on the basis of sex, be excluded from participation in, be denied the benefit of, or be subjected to discrimination under any educational program or activity receiving federal financial assistance." The result broadened women's educational participation at all levels and across all programs,

In September 1957, nine black children attempted to integrate Central High School in Little Rock, Arkansas. The young woman in this photo shows the courage necessary to face the jeers and threats of local people encouraged by Governor Orval Faubus. President Eisenhower called on the National Guard to protect these students.

including science and engineering, and as employees, such as faculty and coaches.

Title IX has significantly expanded athletic opportunities for females as well, including scholarships, and increased funding for their sports in high schools and colleges. Such gains, however, have led to considerable resistance to Title IX, because funding for women's sports has been viewed by some administrators and alumni as taking money away from men's sports, rather than as providing equal access and equal treatment (The

National Coalition for Women and Girls in Education, 2008). The large numbers and success of U.S. women athletes at the London Olympics in 2012 made clear the way college women have made use of such access.

Affirmative Action and Diversity in Higher Education Globally

"Affirmative action" is the term commonly applied in the United States to policies adopted by employers and higher education institutions at the behest of Presidential Executive Orders in the early 1960s to conform to anti-discrimination laws. Ending discrimination meant acting affirmatively to compensate for the long-existing patterns of discrimination that barred white women and women and men of color from equal access to studying and teaching in higher education, including professional schools such as law and medicine.

Not everyone has welcomed greater racial, ethnic, and gender diversity in educational institutions. Beneficiaries of the status quo, including its structure, curriculum, and programs, have primarily been white men who have generally sought to preserve their privileged access to education and the opportunities for employment, prestige, and wealth that have accompanied it. Some who have enjoyed this position of privilege, along with others who advocate for individual merit, without recognizing barriers faced by marginalized groups have challenged the premise of affirmative action, preferring to believe that women and racial and ethnic minorities are less qualified and that affirmative action policies give such groups preferential treatment in the new competition for college admissions and academic positions that results from a wider field of applicants. They have therefore claimed that affirmative action serves to lower previous standards.

As the numbers of women and men of color admitted to universities increased, affirmative action has been contested in court cases, with some conservatives arguing it constitutes "reverse discrimination" against whites, particularly white males (Messer-Davidow, 2002). The U.S. Supreme Court in *Regents of the University of California* v. *Bakke* in 1978 sustained affirmative action policies by a single vote. In his deciding opinion, Justice Lewis Powell argued that a diverse student body in terms of gender, race, and ethnicity was a positive value and colleges were within the law to give modest consideration to applicants' race in admissions to contribute to the "robust exchange of ideas" in academe. In *Grutter v. Bollinger*, the U.S. Supreme Court in 2003 upheld Justice Powell's reasoning and affirmed the admissions policy of the University of Michigan Law School, citing Justice Sandra Day O'Connor's ruling that a student body's diversity justified the use of race in university admissions, even as it struck down the point system used by the University of Michigan for undergraduate admissions (see also Chapter 12).

In spite of these challenges, affirmative action continues to have its defenders. Its basic premise has been maintained in the defense of a diverse student body and workforce and the status of diversity in higher education in terms of gender, race, and ethnicity is acknowledged as a positive value in its own right. While the specifics of how to expand educational access are refined, the debate continues about who should be educated in the United States.

The concept of affirmative action that originated in the United States has gained global recognition. In using terms such as "reservation" in India, "positive discrimination" in the United Kingdom, "Charter of Equal Opportunity" in France, or "employment equity" in Canada, strengthened in Brazil's 2012 Law of Social Quotas, many nations have adopted policies to increase the participation of low-income and previously excluded racial, ethnic, caste, language, and religious groups, which include girls and women, in higher education and employment. Broadening access to formal education also means incorporating multiple cultures, social classes, life experiences, values, and individual points of view that are embodied in a diverse nation and world. Diversity up close reveals similarities as well as differences. Experiencing diversity that includes gender and that "robust exchange of ideas" to which Justice Powell referred is a learning experience that we cannot afford to miss.

Education as a Contested Arena: What Should Be Taught?

Women's Traditional Knowledge

The question of *what* should be taught is also basic to the contested arena of educational equity. Through the centuries and across cultures, women have taught themselves and their daughters the knowledge needed to survive. Women's traditional knowledge has played a crucial role in the survival of their families and communities in terms of providing food and clothing as well as healing, birthing, and mourning rituals. Among most nomadic peoples, women designed, built, and transported the tents that housed their families. Among settled villages, women bartered goods and, in some areas, organized long-distance trade. Women's productive role was constant but varied with societies and regions. In some instances, women were acknowledged as crucial to all aspects of village life, but what they contributed to the group's survival could remain relatively invisible to the men around them, subsumed under women's domestic roles.

Formal Knowledge Defined by Men

Women have too often accepted men's devaluation of women's knowledge and men's assertion that their knowledge was the standard of intellectual excellence. As a result, women have sought to gain access to men's formal education on the assumption that it would give them educational equality. One of the achievements of the second wave of feminism in the twentieth century has been to make it clear that what privileged men have defined as formal knowledge in the past is only partial knowledge. It has long excluded large portions of human experiences and achievements, those for which white women and women and men of color are largely responsible. To include this neglected portion necessarily changes the whole.

The Goals of Women's Education Debated

For centuries, men's formal knowledge was the gold standard. Whether it was proper for women to gain access to men's formal knowledge was therefore a matter of hot debate. In Europe, for example, conservatives and progressives vehemently debated the proper goals of women's education. One influential counselor at the court of King Louis XIV of France heartily endorsed the idea that girls should be taught primarily "women's subjects," defined as the duties of a good (obedient) wife (Lougee, 1976). While few contemporaries dared oppose this position, three Englishwomen did and founded schools for girls that provided the more rigorous academic education taught young men, including logic, Greek, Hebrew, math, and poetry. Of these, Mary Astell (1666–1731) boldly asserted that it was solely custom and prejudice that limited women's educational development, while Hannah Woolley made her case in more crude and witty terms (see Box 10.2) (Hill, 1986; Boxer and Quataert, 2000).

In the late eighteenth century the French philosopher Jean-Jacques Rousseau set out his views about the ideal education for a young

---

Box 10.2   THE RIGHT EDUCATION OF THE FEMALE SEX

Hannah Woolley (1622–c. 1675), the daughter of a mother skilled in medical remedies, worked as a servant and then married a schoolmaster when she was 24. Together they ran a grammar school, first in the county of Essex in England and then in London. Widowed in 1661, Woolley wrote The Ladies Directory *and* The Cooks Guide *and used them to advertise her skills. The excerpt is from her book,* The Gentlewoman's Companion, *published in 1675, expressing her mature views about women's right to acquire knowledge.*

The right Education of the Female Sex, as it is in a manner everywhere neglected, so it ought to be generally lamented. Most in this depraved later Age think a Woman learned and wise enough if she can distinguish her Husbands Bed from another. Certainly Man's Soul cannot boast of a more sublime Original than ours, they had equally their efflux from the same eternal Immensity, and [are] therefore capable of the same improvement by good Education. Vain man is apt to think we were merely intended for the Worlds propagation, and to keep its humane inhabitants sweet and clean; but by their leaves, had we the same Literature, he would find our brains as fruitful as our bodies. Hence I am induced to believe, we are debar'd from the knowledge of humane learning lest our pregnant Wits should rival the towering conceits of our insulting Lords and Masters.

Source: From Hannah Wooley in Joan K. Kinnaird, "Mary Astell and the Conservative Contribution to English Feminism," *Journal of British Studies* 19 (1979): 53. Reprinted with the permission of the University of Chicago Press.

---

man in *Émile* ([1762] 1974). For Émile's wife, Sophie, he recommended an education to make her a charming companion, submissive to her husband's will and domestic needs (Keohane, 1980). Rousseau's blatant prescription was challenged by Catharine Macaulay (1731–1791), author of the eight-volume *History of England* (1763–83), who called for women to learn alongside men, sharing the same curriculum and physical exercises (Boos, 1976).

Mary Wollstonecraft (see Chapter 2) opposed Rousseau's views with even more passion. Supporting herself from the age of 19 as a lady's companion, needle worker, governess, schoolmistress, journalist, and translator, the middle-class Wollstonecraft deplored the useless "accomplishments" society thought appropriate for young women.

Her *Vindication of the Rights of Woman* (1792) scornfully pointed out that since Sophie's abilities were left uncultivated, she would make a poor mother for Émile's children. Young women must have the same education as men, she argued, to enable them to be rational, competent, and independent. She claimed not to be radical in her views, for she insisted that women could fulfill their domestic roles best if they learned first to respect themselves as individuals (Sapiro, 1992).

This fierce debate was not limited to European societies. In China, for example, Confucian teachings sustained a deeply patriarchal system, its greatest rewards going to males who mastered the learning required to become scholar-officials. Even here a few independent-minded scholar-officials advocated some modified forms of education for women. One of these was Ch'en Hung-mou (1696–1771), who taught that all people were educable in some fashion and that women should not be neglected. Throughout the world, women of upper and middle ranks were more likely to lead somewhat less restricted lives than conventional prescriptions required, a few managing to become scholars, writers, artists, and poets (for India, see Tharu and Lalita, 1993; for Africa, see Daymond et al., 2003; Sutherland-Addy and Diaw, 2005; Lihamba et al., 2007; Sadigi et al., 2009).

The Debate in the United States

In colonial America, formal education for women beyond their "letters" was considered inappropriate, dangerous, and unsettling to the performance of domestic duties. Male literacy rates may have been as high as 80% at the time of the American Revolution; women's literacy remained as low as 45%. After the Revolution, women were taught that they must be virtuous examples for their brothers, husbands, and sons as well as exemplary mothers for future heroes and statesmen (Kerber, 1980). There have always been women who stood firmly for their beliefs. Emma Willard (1787–1870), for example, helped reshape women's education in the United States. Turned down by the New York State legislature to fund a public female seminary to train teachers, she established a private academy in Troy, New York, in 1821 (Cott, 1977). She told each graduating class that women were capable of studying any academic subject they chose, that they should prepare themselves to be self-supporting in a profession, and—most daring of all—that marriage was not an end in itself. Graduates of her Troy Female Seminary, later renamed the Emma Willard School, formed a widespread network committed to the education of women and to the professionalization of teaching.

By the 1870s, when men found new careers in industry, young women began to replace them in what had been a male-dominated teaching profession. Taught by society to value their own efforts as of less value than men's, the women accepted far lower wages than men had been paid (Kaufman, 1984). One of the early advocates of women's suffrage, Susan B. Anthony, spoke out against this inequity (see Box 10.3). By the twentieth century, women made up over one half of the more than 200,000 teachers in U.S. public elementary and secondary schools. When women sought entry into higher education, they were accepted in a few of the new government-supported "land-grant" state universities being established. By 1870, eight state universities were open to women, but some women were enrolled in separate "female departments" (Newcomer, 1959). Separate private colleges for women were also established and offered a curriculum comparable to that of the colleges for men, which would not admit them. These were Vassar (1861), Smith (1871), Wellesley (1875), Bryn Mawr (1885), and Radcliffe (1894).

Fewer funds were available for the higher education of blacks, but three colleges were opened for African American women: Bennett College (1873), Miner Teachers College (1873), and Spelman College (1881). All were located in the South and established with the assistance of white northern philanthropists and missionary associations (Ihle, 1986: III, IV). Anna Julia Cooper (see Chapter 3), who made the education of girls and women her special concern, wrote eloquently on the need for the higher education of black women (see Box 10.4).

Schools as Socializers of Gender Inequities

Schools have helped socialize girls to be obedient, nice, respectful, and quiet, in contrast

Box 10.3   EQUAL PAY FOR WOMEN TEACHERS, 1853

In 1853, Susan B. Anthony, a teacher and leader in the nineteenth-century women's rights movement, attended an education convention at Rochester, New York. She listened to long discussions of the low prestige in which the teaching profession was held compared to the law, medicine, and the ministry. The discussion was conducted entirely by men, "the thousand women crowding the hall could not vote on the question," nor did they venture to speak. After asking to be heard, and waiting for a further half-hour discussion on whether her request would be granted, she spoke:

It seems to me, gentlemen, that none of you quite comprehend the cause of the disrespect of which you complain. Do you not see that so long as society says a woman is incompetent to be a lawyer, minister, or doctor, but has ample ability to be a teacher, that every man of you who chooses this profession tacitly acknowledges that he has no more brains than a woman? And this, too, is the reason that teaching is a less lucrative profession, as here men must compete with the cheap labor of women. Would you exalt your profession, exalt those who labor with you. Would you make it more lucrative, increase the salaries of the women engaged in the noble work of educating our future Presidents, Senators, and Congressmen.

Source: Gerda Lerner, *The Female Experience: An American Documentary.* New York: Oxford University Press, 1992: 235–6.

---

to attempting to instill in boys a sense of competition and independence of thought. By replicating society's gender prescriptions, schools perpetuate the prevalent structures of sexism in the classroom. Schools do not consciously set out to discriminate in this way, but researchers have found that insofar as teachers and administrators represent the values in which they themselves have been socialized, they propagate these structures in educational settings worldwide.

Elementary Schools

Reading materials prepared to guide children reflect a gendered world. During the 1970s, feminist scholars in the United States found a male world in much-admired children's picture books, including the works of Maurice Sendak, Dr. Seuss, and Richard Scarry (Fisher, 1974). School textbooks in this period reinforced the idea that girls would grow up to be passive and boys to be active. In "new math" texts, which arranged people in sets, groups of men appeared as doctors, firefighters, chefs, astronauts, and letter carriers, ignoring the existence of women in some of these occupations (Federbush, 1974). Not until the 1980s and under pressure from feminist revelations of biases against girls and women did introductory social studies and history texts begin to use more gender-neutral terms, replacing chapter titles such as "political man" and "industrial man" with "political behavior" and "industrial life" (Smithson, 1990).

Efforts to address gender stereotyping in textbooks are ongoing. Worldwide teacher guides and primary school illustrations often reproduce traditional roles, featuring women in the home or as teachers, while men are placed in public spaces and at work in a variety of professional occupations (Lloyd, 2005: 115).

Box 10.4   ANNA JULIA COOPER ON THE HIGHER EDUCATION OF WOMEN

Anna Julia Cooper (1858–1964) was born in slavery in Raleigh, North Carolina, trained as a teacher, earned an undergraduate and a graduate degree from Oberlin College, and wrote A Voice from the South (*1892*) *on the role educated black women should play in their communities. In 1914, she began studying for a doctoral degree at Columbia University; the next year she adopted the five orphans of her half-brother; she completed her degree in 1924 at the University of Paris-Sorbonne. She was by then 65 years old and the fourth black woman in U.S. history to earn a Ph.D. She was president of Frelinghuysen University in Washington, D.C. (1930–1940), an adult education night school. For her, higher education was the path for women to making a mark on the world. The excerpt here is from* A Voice from the South.

In the very first year of our century, the year 1801, there appeared in Paris a book . . . entitled "Shall Woman Learn the Alphabet?" The book proposes a law prohibiting the alphabet to women, and quotes authorities weighty and various, to prove that the woman who knows the alphabet has already lost part of her womanliness. The author declares that women can use the alphabet only as Moliere predicted they would, in spelling out the verb amo; . . . while Sappho, Aspasia, Madame de Maintenon, and Madame de Stael could read altogether too well for their good; finally if women were once permitted to read Sophocles and work with logarithms, or to nibble at any side of the apple of knowledge, there would be an end forever to their sewing on buttons and embroidering slippers.

. . . Now I claim that it is the prevalence of Higher Education among women, the making it a common everyday affair for women to reason and think and express their thought, the training and stimulus which enable and encourage women to administer to the world the bread it needs as well as the sugar it cries for . . . that has given symmetry and completeness to the world's agencies.

Source: Loewenberg and Bogin, 1976, pp. 318–19, 321.

Secondary Schools

Even today girls at the secondary level can be discouraged from intellectual achievement, especially in mathematics and science, where boys are expected to excel. Gender bias subtly influences the use of educational technology, a necessity in the twenty-first century, leaving many girls behind. The digital divide by gender, race, and class is even more pronounced in developing countries where Internet access is more limited (United Nations, 2010).

The 1990s were a turning point in attention to girls' achievement in the United States. Feminist scholars considered how adolescent girls were being hurt psychologically by societal pressures to have them conform to the cultural construction of being female. They described how confident girls experience a loss of their authentic voice and develop low self-esteem and even depression in seeking to be conciliatory and nice (Gilligan, 1993; Orenstein, 1994; Pipher, 1994). Although it has been supposed that adolescents are preoccupied with achieving independence, researchers found that this notion is not sufficient for young women. Finding that girls were conflicted about their desires to find an autonomous self and identity and to establish relationships (Gilligan et al., 1990) or sought both autonomy and connection

(Stern, 1990) galvanized parents and educators to rethink how girls were being taught in and outside the home. One influential report, *How Schools Shortchange Girls* (American Association of University Women, 1992), cited the unequal treatment girls experienced in curricula, testing, and teacher attention, problems identified decades ago. Another study found that girls are sexually harassed in public daily by male classmates and by teachers. It also showed how the high school curriculum continued to teach young women to accept this abuse and how young men continued unchallenged in their intimidating behavior (Stein et al., 1993). This phenomenon is global. In Botswana, for example, where the female dropout rate in secondary school is a national problem, pregnancy is a leading explanation. It is an outcome in part of gender inequity that allows male students, teachers, and other older males to sexually abuse young women (Makwinja-Morara, 2009).

Bullying also reveals gender disparities and is exacerbated through texting and cyberabuse. Although widespread in schools globally, authorities have been slow to address it. Boys tend to be more physically violent and outwardly aggressive; girls use more covert and emotional forms of taunting, such as spreading false stories about individual girls and excluding them from activities. Educators are only just beginning to address how schools are unsafe for LGBTQ students, a situation that has caused some of them to abandon schooling rather than to be harassed (Biegel and Kuehl, 2010).

Media representations present a different portrait of high-school life than research findings. In the widely syndicated American TV show "Glee," high-school youth break out into song and dance with regularity. The show suggests that female and male youth, who might be different from mainstream youth in their race, ethnicity, gender, and sexuality, can find a place for themselves in high school and be supported by peers and teachers. The question is, does this unrealistic representation help the situation by example or does it cover up the problem by failing to address gender and other inequities that still prevail in schools?

One official response to these inadequacies in the United States was the Gender Equity in Education Act of 1964, which recognized girls as an underserved population. In the Global South, advocating for a woman's right to be educated as a human right and the creation of "gender-friendly schools" where girls are physically safe to learn are part of the larger agenda of bringing and keeping them in schools (Mannathoko, 2008).

Higher Education

From the 1970s to the present, the college population in the United States grew enormously and was driven in large part by women of *all* racial/ethnic backgrounds making a concerted effort to be educated, further their career goals, and increase their earning potential. By 2007, women were earning the majority of associate, bachelor's, master's, and doctoral degrees in the United States (see Table 10.1). Women earned 940,345 bachelor's degrees, for example, in 2007 compared with 664,757 in 1997 (Ryu, 2010: 90). Table 10.2 presents an intersectional analysis of *differences* by percentage in women's gains

TABLE 10.1 Percentage of Degrees Awarded to Women in U.S. Higher Education, 1997 and 2007

Degree	1997	2007
Associate	61.5	62.4
Bachelor's	56.0	57.4
Master's	57.1	60.5
Doctoral	43.0	50.5

Source: Mikyung Ryu, *Minorities in Higher Education 2010: Twenty-Fourth Status Report*, pp. 89–92. Washington, DC: American Council on Education, 2010. © 2008, American Council on Education. Reprinted with permission.

TABLE 10.2 Percentage of Bachelor's Degrees Earned in U.S. Higher Education by Race/Ethnicity and Gender, 1997 and 2007

Race/Ethnicity and Gender	1997	2007
White	74.1	67.5
Men	32.8	29.4
Women	41.3	38.1
African American	8.1	8.9
Men	2.8	3.0
Women	5.2	5.9
Hispanic	5.4	7.3
Men	2.3	2.8
Women	3.1	4.5
Asian American*	5.9	6.6
Men	2.7	3.0
Women	3.1	3.6
American Indian**	0.6	0.7
Men	0.3	0.3
Women	0.4	0.4
Foreign Student	3.3	2.9
Men	1.8	1.4
Women	1.5	1.5
Race/Ethnicity Unknown	2.6	6.1
Men	1.2	2.7
Women	1.4	3.4

*Asian American includes Pacific Islanders.

**American Indian includes Alaska Natives.

Source: Mikyung Ryu, *Minorities in Higher Education 2010: Twenty-Fourth Status Report*, p. 90. Washington, DC: American Council on Education, 2010.

by race/ethnicity and in comparison to their male counterparts. Examining advancement in terms of numbers and percentage, however, is not the full measure of women's educational well-being. Gains in access have not eliminated other forms of gender, racial/ethnic, and class inequalities.

In the 1980s and 1990s, a number of studies described the unwelcoming cultural and structural environment that women students, faculty, and administrators experienced in academe as a "chilly climate." They documented how attitudes and actions that marginalized women's intellectual pursuits harmed their academic and career goals (Hall and Sandler, 1982, 1984; Sandler and Hall, 1986; Sandler, Silverberg, and Hall, 1996). Women faculty of color identified policies and practices that made them invisible and dismissed their scholarship, while women students of color emphasized their absence in the curriculum and how intersections of race, gender, class, and anti-immigrant bias compounded their lack of support from faculty, staff, and other students, contributing to everyday inequities in their learning experiences (Moses 1989; Hune, 1998, 2006).

Studies in the 2000s find that college women earn better grades than college men but may experience lower self-esteem about their academic abilities. One cause lies in faculty interactions. If college women feel that faculty, most of whom remain white and male, do not take their scholarly interests and career aspirations seriously, or if they too readily internalize dismissive comments by faculty, they may lower their goals and even make themselves physically ill (Sax, 2008). One consequence worldwide is that women continue to choose traditionally "feminine" fields—education, health, humanities, and social sciences—and remain underrepresented in areas considered "masculine"— science, technology, engineering, mathematics (STEM), and related fields—where they would earn higher wages (United Nations, 2010: 64–5).

New research on and by women of color describes the strategies they have adopted as students, faculty, and administrators to resist their marginalization in academe and being seen as having deficits because of their race, gender, class, sexuality, and culture. Women of color emphasize how their family background and life experiences provide them with cultural strengths to achieve and that their perspectives, community-based knowledge, and leadership qualities need to be viewed as assets (Jean-Marie and Lloyd-Jones, 2011a, 2011b).

Sexual harassment is another form of gender inequity. Female and male students are almost equally likely to experience sexual harassment, but women are more apt to be upset by such encounters. Women find it harder to pay attention in class, have trouble sleeping, and often change their behavior, for example avoiding certain locations. LGBTQ students are deeply affected by sexual harassment, becoming more insecure on campus and anxious about being able to complete their studies (Hill and Silva, 2005).

What would "women-friendly campuses" be like? Lisa Wolf-Wendel (2000) has identified high academic expectations for women, positive role models, a caring, supportive environment, strong student mentorship, leadership opportunities, and connecting students to their communities as among the institutional practices that were "doing right" for women students. Strategies that successfully increase female participation in male-dominated fields include cooperative and hands-on teaching approaches, integration of computer technology into fields like politics and health, supportive mentors, and role models (National Council for Research on Women, 2001).

Educational Institutions as Gendered Workplaces

At every level of formal learning, gender plays a distinctive role, including in the teaching profession. The "feminization" of teaching is a global phenomenon. In countries today where women have a low socioeconomic status, becoming a teacher still offers new and socially accepted opportunities and a role that parents can support (United Nations, 2010: 65). In industrialized nations, like the United States in the nineteenth century, however, a gender hierarchy emerged. As the profession came to be dominated by women and pay was lowered, principals and supervisors remained more highly paid men. In high schools, women have usually taught what men called the "softer" subjects of literature, languages, art, and music, while men became the more highly paid specialists in physics, chemistry, mathematics, and social studies.

More women in developed nations, such as the United States (Table 10.3), now hold faculty positions, but they occupy the lower-paid lower ranks. Women faculty, administrators, and staff, regardless of their race or ethnicity, continue to experience gender bias in being hired, evaluated, and promoted. Today as colleges and universities move away from serving the public to serving the corporate world, a shift described as "academic capitalism," women are being marginalized again despite their greater presence at all levels. Men are seeking out entrepreneurial sectors on campus, rich in rewards of copyrights, patents, and industrial and commercial partnerships, leaving women to do much of the teaching and cope in departments with scarce resources (Metcalfe and Slaughter, 2008). Although more women have achieved the educational credentials traditionally associated with men, they receive disproportionately fewer rewards and less professional acceptance.

Historically, women have argued that equal access to formal education would give them gender equity. Why does gender discrimination in the academy remain subtle, all-encompassing, and persistent into the twenty-first century? Virginia Valian (1998)

TABLE 10.3 Percentage of Full-Time Women Faculty by Rank in U.S. Higher Education, 1997 and 2007

Faculty Rank	1997	2007
Full Professor	19.7	26.5
Associate Professor	33.8	39.7
Assistant Professor	44.6	47.3
Instructors and Lecturers	51.4	53.9

Source: Mikyung Ryu, *Minorities in Higher Education 2010: Twenty-Fourth Status Report*, pp. 114–17. Washington, DC: American Council on Education, 2010.

sought to explain why women do not advance professionally as far and as rapidly as men. In addition to overt discrimination against women, she concludes that in early childhood both women and men acquire the same unconscious hypotheses about sex differences that affect their expectations about women's and men's roles, including how their professional work should be evaluated. These "gender schemas" contribute to small differences in how women and men are treated, but over time they result in pronounced gender disparities in salary, rank, promotion, and prestige.

Women's professional advancement is slowed because women accumulate disadvantages while men accumulate advantages. Letters of recommendation illustrate these schemas. Male applicants are more likely to be described as doers and leaders, while women are characterized in social or emotive terms such as helpful and agreeable, characteristics ranked lower by employers, again to the disadvantage of women in their job search and promotion efforts (Madera, Hebl, and Martin, 2009).

Table 10.4 is a snapshot of associate professors by race/ethnicity and gender. It indicates that more women of all racial/ethnic backgrounds are reaching this rank, which means most are tenured and have some security of employment at their institution. Table 10.3 shows, however, that many will likely not advance to full professor rank, one that would enable them to exercise more decision-making authority on their campuses and positions them for high level administrative and other leadership positions.

Faculty women's advancement is also made more difficult by the challenges of balancing their careers and personal lives, conflicts that male faculty experience to a lesser extent. Ladder-rank women faculty often are forgoing or delaying childbirth to keep to the timeline for tenure, a system that was designed for faculty men with wives at home. Even after

tenure, women report being enormously stressed because they bear the majority of household responsibilities, especially child care and eldercare, duties more daunting if they are the primary or sole breadwinner (see Chapter 6). Consequently, some female doctorates leave the professoriate, choose not to enter it at all, or seek part-time positions (Mason and Goulden, 2004; Wolfinger, Mason, and Goulden, 2009). Other research, however, finds that men have increased their time with chores and children in recent years but are not given credit for this. Moreover, men today too are feeling the pressure to be successful at work and involved as fathers (Konigsberg, 2011).

TABLE 10.4 Percentage of Full-Time Faculty at Associate Professor Rank in U.S. Higher Education by Race/Ethnicity and Gender, 1997 and 2007

Race/Ethnicity and Gender	1997	2007
White	85.8	80.2
Men	56.6	40.8
Women	29.2	32.2
African American	4.7	5.5
Men	2.6	2.9
Women	2.1	2.6
Hispanic	2.3	3.3
Men	1.5	1.9
Women	0.8	1.4
Asian American*	5.5	7.7
Men	4.3	5.3
Women	1.3	2.4
American Indian**	0.3	0.4
Men	0.2	0.2
Women	0.1	0.2
Foreign Faculty	1.1	1.8
Men	0.9	1.3
Women	0.2	0.5

*Asian American includes Pacific Islanders.

**American Indian includes Alaska Natives.

Source: Mikyung Ryu, *Minorities in Higher Education 2010: Twenty-Fourth Status Report*, p. 115. Washington, DC: American Council on Education, 2010.

The need for family-friendly workplaces and policies is universal. Despite the challenges of academia, professional women in other fields, such as law and medicine, point out that women faculty have advantages in balancing work and family because of their flexible work schedules. For women to break through the glass ceiling requires attention to stereotypes and gender biases, hidden and overt, held by both women and men. In the

Rose Tseng, the first Asian American woman to lead a four-year university, served as Chancellor of the University of Hawai'i at Hilo from 1998 to 2010. Her achievements in raising the academic profile of the campus have been widely recognized.

France Cordova became the first Latina president of Purdue University (2007–2012). An astrophysicist, she was born in Paris to a Mexican father and Irish-American mother. She emphasized scholarships for students from around the globe.

Shirley Ann Jackson, the first woman president of the Rensselaer Polytechnic Institute in New York State since 1999, has successfully raised large sums of funds to expand the academic strengths of the campus in both technology and humanities fields. She holds a Ph.D. in theoretical elementary particle physics from MIT.

Drew Gilpin Faust, an historian, became the first woman president of Harvard University in 2007; she followed in the path of other women who became presidents of Ivy League universities: Ruth Simmons at Brown in 2001, Shirley Tilghman at Princeton in 2001, and Susan Hockfield at the Massachusetts Institute of Technology in 2004.

Cassandra Manuelito-Kerkvliet in 2007 became the first Native American Woman to become president of a university outside the tribal college system, Antioch University Seattle. Her doctoral degree is in Educational Policy and Management, and she belongs to the Diné community of the Navajo Nation.

United States, more women are becoming college and university presidents. Of more than 2,000 institutions in one study of American college presidents, women comprised 23% of all presidencies in 2006, more than double the 10% held in 1986 (Ryu, 2010).

Educational Barriers of Girls/Women in Diverse Communities in the Global North

Gender and Cultural Assimilation

To maintain power in multiracial/multicultural societies, dominant groups disempower and marginalize groups they deem different and inferior. One strategy has been to deny or limit indigenous, working-class, and racial/ethnic minority groups from access to formal education. Another is to curtail their resistance by promoting the prevailing language, values, and institutions as superior and treating minority cultures as wanting rather than as an advantage. In the United States, the dominant European American group has long called for the cultural assimilation of those different from them and used the education system to

play a leading role in the "Americanization" process. The schools attended by girls of color up until the last part of the twentieth century have generally been inferior. Moreover, because domestic work, factory work, and entry-level service work were the major positions offered to immigrant women and women of color up until after the civil rights movement, little effort was made to educate them beyond these areas. Women of color and white working-class women have utilized an unequal education system to change their lives and those of their families and communities. We provide examples of their educational struggles in the United States within this context. Readers need to consider the role of intersectionality (see Chapter 3), namely how race, ethnicity, class, language, immigration status, and other identities intersect with gender in advancing and/or limiting one's educational possibilities.

Indigenous/Native Peoples' Experiences

Indigenous peoples, in many cases, have been forcibly incorporated into the dominant culture of many nations and have had their traditional languages and cultures suppressed. In the United States, such groups include American Indians/Native Americans, Native Alaskans, Native Hawaiians, and Pacific Islanders. Native American children were taken from their tribal communities by the U.S. government and placed in boarding schools (1878–1928, 1950–1980) with poor facilities in order to accelerate their assimilation into European American culture. Not only did the academically limited, gendered, and culturally alienating curriculum and pedagogy contribute to high drop-out rates, some girls became disengaged from tribal gender roles and indigenous knowledge that once empowered women (Almeida, 1997).

Other Native American women used their "Western" training to benefit their people, promote Native American rights, and preserve and advance women's participation in tribal matters (Almeida, 1997). Wilma Mankiller (1945–2010), for example, whose family was relocated from Oklahoma to California in 1957, attended the University of Arkansas and returned to her ancestral lands to become a nationally known expert on rural community development (Mankiller and Wallis, 1993). From 1985 to 1995 she served as principal chief of the Cherokee Nation, the second largest tribe in the United States. Today, Native Americans can attend 33 tribally controlled American Indian colleges (the first was founded in 1968) where young women and men can be educated in both indigenous and mainstream subjects (Putman, 2001).

African American Experiences

In a nation that racially segregated them, African American women sought to ensure that black children were schooled. After the Civil War many of them became teachers— low paid by white standards, but high paying and prestigious compared to domestic service. A few opened schools. Lucy Craft Laney (1854–1933), who was born in slavery, graduated from the first class of Atlanta University in 1873 and in 1886 opened Haines Normal and Industrial Institute in Augusta, Georgia, a state that did not provide public high schools for blacks. Her school offered liberal arts courses at a time when southern state educators viewed vocational training as a sufficient education for African Americans (Giddings, 1984). Mary McLeod Bethune (1875–1955) founded Bethune-Cookman College in Florida (Weiler, 1997). Black colleges and universities have played a significant role, past and present, in preparing generations of black women and men for a wide range of professional roles.

Black women have sought education as a tool of liberation: to empower their communities, uplift those in poverty, and become scholars in their own right (Collins, 2001). Only after the civil rights movement and affirmative action have U.S. colleges recruited black students in significant numbers. Today, African American women are attending college at higher rates than their male counterparts and have moved into many professional fields, including as faculty and college presidents.

Immigrant Experiences

Most immigrants leave their homelands reluctantly to escape hunger, war, and religious and cultural persecution and to improve their economic well-being. Recipient states have been ambivalent about immigrants, seeking their "cheap" labor in many cases, while contesting their difference and perceived "cost" to their societies. They also benefit from the skills and expertise of highly educated immigrants, such as scientists and medical personnel. Immigrant communities in the United States throughout its history have relied on the educational system to provide new opportunities for their children, but they are not always welcomed (Suárez-Orozco, Suárez-Orozco, and Todorova, 2008). Current anti-immigrant politics in western Europe and the United States, especially hostility against people of color from Africa, Asia, the Middle East, Latin America, and the Caribbean, whether documented and undocumented, is waged in the education system as well.

Immigrant women often contend with the gender restrictions and conflicting expectations of the dominant society and their own ethnic communities. Work and family responsibilities often hinder their obtaining a formal education. In the United States, it is their daughters who are "Americanized" in the schools. Not all immigrant girls have been joyful about the new worlds opened to them. Memories of adapting, some painful of how they were ridiculed for their accents, dress, and food habits and of being treated as inferior during their school years, abound in the writings of celebrated ethnic authors from Europe, Asia, Africa, and elsewhere (Mendoza and Shankar, 2003).

In the past, higher education for women was viewed globally as a detriment rather than an asset, since marriage was their ultimate goal. Hence a woman's desire for more education could contribute to conflict in immigrant households. Women teachers were among the few role models for immigrant girls until the latter part of the twentieth century. Today, observing the job opportunities and income differences that an education can bring in the United States, immigrant parents are more encouraging of their daughters' educational goals. Their support and their daughters' aspirations contribute to the growth in college participation of women of color (Hune, 1998; Qin-Hilliard, 2003).

Multicultural Education/Ethnic Studies as Resistance

In the United States, communities of color have long resisted European American cultural assimilation and sought to retain their cultures while expressing pride in their contributions to American society. In so doing they have forced educational changes. In the 1970s communities of color initiated new pedagogical approaches and curriculum at the K–12 level, often referred to as "multicultural education." On college campuses, scholars and activists of color and their supporters demanded ethnic studies with women of color, in particular arguing for courses on race and gender issues. Like the scholarly revolution in terms of gender occurring contemporaneously, ethnic studies has aimed at greater inclusion of the knowledge from the various cultures of the nation's diverse population and serves as a more democratic model than that of "Americanization" (Nieto, 2009).

The politics of cultural assimilation, multicultural education, and ethnic studies are part of the historic debates of who is being educated and what should be taught and as such are highly contested. Today, nations everywhere struggle to incorporate their "minority" groups, while communities of difference push back and assert their cultural rights. In France, for example, the aggressive assimilation efforts as exemplified by the implementation of a 2004 law to forbid the wearing of symbols of a religious affiliation that might be considered provocative or proselytizing has come to focus on African-origin Muslim girls. Demanding that they remove their head scarves while in school, an impossible cultural choice for some, or be expelled is one example of how the politics of gender, race, ethnicity, and nationhood creates barriers to women's access to education (Keaton, 2005).

The Contemporary Struggle for Equal Access to Knowledge

The second half of the twentieth century was marked by an extraordinary increase in access to higher education. In the United States, for example, the 1944 GI Bill enabled millions of returning World War II veterans, including a small number of ex–service women, to attend college by paying for their educational expenses. Colleges also expanded in size and type. Women, in particular, took advantage of new opportunities made available in two-year community colleges.

Re-entry/Adult Women

By the 1960s, the number of *re-entry women*—adult women who had previously "dropped out" of college to marry and raise children as was expected of them—was on the rise in higher education. A growing women's movement led more adult women to "drop back in" to prepare themselves for employment or career transitions (Chamberlain, 1988). At this time it was found that attending college even for only one semester helped strengthen a mature woman's concept of her abilities (Denmark and Guttentag, 1967). This principle has been found true at all levels of education for women worldwide.

Adult women today are among the many students who are over 24 years of age, work part or full time, often are single parents, and are attending college for the first time. They are invisible and underserved because they are "nontraditional." Their ability to complete their degrees is complicated by women's limited financial resources and multiple work and family responsibilities (Deutsch and Schmertz, 2011). Consequently, many adult women have turned to and have been targeted for online education and distance learning programs (Kramarae, 2001).

Women: The New College Majority?

Women's strivings to obtain college degrees in the United States is a remarkable achievement (Tables 10.1 and 10.2). A similar phenomenon is occurring in higher education in Canada and several western European states (OECD, 2010). (For how women's education has fared at Hunter College, where this textbook was initiated, see Box I.1 in the Introduction.) Today, the new global economy (see Chapter 12) and changing family structures and gender roles (see Chapter 6) have led more women to secure college degrees to attain economic security as they enter the paid workforce on a permanent basis—often as the main or sole breadwinner. Both adult women and men, finding their jobs eliminated in a time of severe economic recession, are returning to college to be retrained for new jobs, while older women continue to seek education not only for themselves but also as a role model for their families (King, 2010; Deutsch and Schmertz, 2011).

Being a statistical majority overall, however, oversimplifies the notion that gender equity has been achieved. *Full* educational participation requires an examination of different types of gender disparities that persist in higher education. Presently in countries like the United States, despite few, if any, restrictions on the choice of a college major, women remain heavily concentrated in fields identified with "women's work," namely, the "helping professions," such as teaching, healthcare, and social and retail service. These fields of study have long attracted women: they were among the few open to them until recently but generally are lower paying than male-dominated professions (Mason, 2009). Moreover, women are earning the majority of master's degrees—in absolute numbers (Table 10.1)—because they predominate in education and nursing fields, which graduate more students than do the male-dominated fields of engineering and business administration (King, 2010). Why do women choose these fields? Is it to serve their own interests and goals, or are they being directed to these traditionally women-dominated professions? It raises the issue of how much the older debate about women and education and their "proper place" in society continues to affect choices.

Is There a Male Crisis in Educational Access?

That women in several countries in the Global North now comprise the majority of college undergraduates (OECD, 2010) has led to considerable discussion as to why men are not enrolling at the same rates. Research on the academic achievements of girls and boys in the United States concludes that both groups need attention and have different academic and social problems. Boys are more likely to have issues with literacy, low grades, and being inattentive in class. Twice as many boys than girls are diagnosed with attention deficit hyperactivity disorder or as having a learning disability. Elementary school teachers, in particular, who are mostly female, are considered to be less supportive of boys' more active learning styles, perhaps contributing to their disengagement. Nonetheless, middle- and upper-class white males overall continue to perform well and attend college at high rates just as they have done in the past (Kleinfeld, 2009b; The College Board, 2010). What has changed is the increased number of women and men of less privileged status who attend or are expected to attend college today.

Incorporating an analysis of gender, race, class, and other categories provides greater insight into how educational advantage and disadvantage works today in U.S. schools. The educational gender gap lies primarily with low-income young men of color, notably African Americans, Latinos, Native Americans, Pacific Islanders, and Southeast Asian Americans. Many students of color live in low-income households, attend low-performing schools, are less proficient in the English language, basic writing, and reading skills, and lack positive role models. However, many more low-income, immigrant, and minority boys struggle in school and drop out than their female counterparts. More girls of all racial/ethnic and class backgrounds are excelling in their studies, scoring high on standardized tests, and are better prepared for college. Yet girls continue to lag behind boys in the sciences and mathematics, and many experience high rates of depression, eating disorders, and suicide attempts (Corbett, Hill, and St. Rose, 2008; Kleinfeld, 2009b; The College Board, 2010).

If many young men in the United States are not in college, where are they? Historically, low-income and lower-status youth have entered the workforce after high school. Presently, many working-class women are choosing college over work or in conjunction with work to better secure their future, given that jobs offered to women without a postsecondary degree, such as retail and office work, are low paying. Men's options are different. Many men seek high-paying male-dominated jobs that do not require college, such as construction and manufacturing, and until recently could support a family. But these opportunities are shrinking. Some men today, as previously, are choosing the military, as are some women, or just any kind of work. Other men are in prison or have died prematurely because of violence. Hence, educational access is a larger and more complex economic, social, and political issue that affects both women and men and influences their commitment to schooling or lack of it and, concomitantly, future career pathways in distinct ways (Wilson, 2007; Kleinfeld, 2009a; College Board, 2010).

Transforming the Curriculum

Beginning in the late 1960s, second-wave feminist scholars began to question the nature of what was being taught. They discerned that what was labeled as "universal" knowledge had failed to include the activities and achievements of women. Among the efforts to transform this male-centered curriculum were programs undertaken to acquaint faculty in all disciplines with the advances in knowledge being achieved by studies that focused on women, gender, race, ethnicity, class, and sexuality (Fiol-Matta and Chamberlain, 1994). As a debate developed with those who saw their traditional core values being challenged, a backlash against the new curriculum took place—the so-called "culture wars" of the 1990s (Aiken et al., 1988; Boxer, 1998; Messer-Davidow, 2002). Those unsympathetic to the goals of gender inclusiveness and multicultural education accused those who were instituting curriculum changes of watering down the traditional curriculum in terms of the achievements of Western civilization. This catchphrase was used to refer to the long-honored achievements of elite men in the past in the West. It was also meant to denigrate those who favored a more inclusive curriculum, and "political correctness," a phrase used by inclusionists to gently jibe themselves, was taken over by those who opposed them to accuse them of politicizing the curriculum for the first time (Graff, 1994; Levine, 1997). Since the use of power to make policy is always "political," the argument was intense between the two groups, like all politics. The debate was complicated by the concern of feminist scholars that multiculturalism could introduce a cultural relativity that might be used to justify patterns of oppression against women in other cultures (Okin, 1999). The highly public debate aired some of the intellectual ferment stirred up by challenging the traditional European- and male-centered knowledge base and highlighted the importance of the questions of *who* should be taught and *what* should be taught.

Empowering Women Learners

Educational Achievements of Women's Colleges Debated

The increased participation of women in higher education has been accompanied by a shift from single-sex education to coeducation. While the historically selective "Seven Sisters" receive most of the attention, women's colleges vary widely. Today about 60 women's colleges remain in the United States, a decline from a high of 300 institutions in 1960 (Holmgren, 2006). For many, coeducation is seen as a sign of women achieving equality with men, suggesting that women's colleges are inferior and that women who attend them are ill prepared for competing in the larger society. However, these arguments assume that women and men are treated the same in coeducational institutions (Wolf-Wendel, 2003). The research findings on the "chilly climate" for women students, faculty, and administrators, which we have discussed

above, document the persistence of gender disparities in coeducational institutions.

Proponents of women's colleges point to the impressive outcomes for women's academic, professional, and personal development. Women who attended college between 1910 and 1960 and who were listed in *Who's Who of American Women* were more often graduates of women's colleges than of coeducational institutions (Tidball, 1973, 1980). Though they are less than 4% of all college graduate women, women's college graduates comprise 20% of women in Congress and 32% of women board members of Fortune 1000 companies (Holmgren, 2006). They also expressed having a more positive college experience, were more involved in philanthropy, held more advanced degrees, and tended to hold higher positions and earn higher salaries than women at coeducational institutions. Moreover, women's colleges serve women of color and nontraditional-aged women and produce women science graduates in greater proportions than coeducational institutions. Institutional selectivity or admitting the most qualified female students and women's own self-selection are only partial explanations of these positive outcomes. Findings argue that it is women's colleges' consciously adopted mission to serve women, offer them female role models, and provide cooperative learning environments, which are infused in all aspects of classroom and campus life, that produces confident women leaders and intellectuals who excel. Coeducational institutions have much to learn from women's colleges in achieving gender equity (Wolf-Wendel, 2003; Wolf-Wendel and Eason, 2011).

Women's Struggles to Become Scientists

Considering all the educational gains that women have made, why are there still so few women in science? Women's struggles to become scientists and to stay active in the field of science, as well as technology, engineering, and mathematics, remind us that the issue of gender bias remains a many-headed dragon.

The career of Warsaw-born Marie Curie, née Maria Sklodowska (1897–1934), has been held up as a prime example of what a woman in science might achieve. She conducted research with her husband Pierre in France and became the first person to receive two Nobel Prizes for her work in radioactivity: one in Physics in 1903 and the other in Chemistry in 1911. Widowed at a young age, she raised two daughters alone. The eldest, Irene Joliot-Curie, was awarded a Nobel Prize for Chemistry in 1935. Marie Curie's professional achievements, combined with family responsibilities, set a very high standard for women scientists (Kohlstedt, 2004; Des Jardins, 2010).

Whether women possess the intellectual ability to do STEM fields continues to be debated. It is evident both in the way women's achievements remain invisible and the way traditional assertions persist about women's "nature" and intellectual inferiority. To explain women's underrepresentation in STEM fields, feminists have focused on the unsupportive environment of their education, research, and employment. In describing how science became a profession in the United States, Julie Des Jardins (2010) identified its methods and practices identified as "masculine." In the first half of the twentieth century, the few women scientists were relegated to the roles of assistants, technicians, and helpers in men's laboratories and observatories mainly to keep records and clean equipment. A few, like Ellen Swallow Richards, able to work in her husband's laboratory at MIT, struck out on her own to develop the new woman-identified field of home economics (Kohlstedt, 2004).

Until recently women with science degrees found few opportunities to carry out research and hold a full-time university position, except at women's colleges or institutions with few resources and less prestige. Prague-born biochemist Gerty Cori, née Radnitz (1896–1957), worked closely with husband Carl on carbohydrate metabolism. They left Europe because sexism and anti-Semitism denied her research work only to find that anti-nepotism policies and gender bias in U.S. universities kept Gerty in entry-level, low-paying positions. She was not appointed a full professor until 1947, 16 years after Carl, and just months before she received the Nobel Prize in Medicine and Physiology. Although a woman scientist married to another scientist may gain some advantages for opening doors, there are also disadvantages of limited recognition and delayed advancement. Some women scientists chose not to marry, while others partnered with women (Kohlstedt, 2004; Des Jardins, 2010).

Physics and atomic science reigned in the United States between 1941 and 1962. A "cult of masculinity" glorified Albert Einstein, Robert Oppenheimer, and other men for building the first atomic bomb, while largely omitting the contributions of women scientists and engineers (Des Jardins, 2010), many of whom gave up their positions to returning male veterans from World War II (Ambrose et al., 1997). Engineering also became identified with machinery and was promoted as better suited for males (Kohlstedt, 2004). Pressures placed upon women to stay at home and make children their priority (leading to Betty Friedan's analysis of the "Feminine Mystique") in the postwar 1950s also inhibited the ambitions of women in these fields (see Chapter 6). In short, women's scientific work and career decisions were restricted by the highly gendered world of science and society.

Feminist scholars have critiqued the epistemology of science, its masculine and Eurocentric biases, and male-centered views of nature and society as social constructions by men (Harding, 1991; Solomon, 2009;

Alcoff, 2010). In contesting the masculine model of objectivity and the advisability of keeping distance from subjects, feminist scientists often seek to present new ideas about nature and the universe and to develop scientific practices that are nurturing of others and the environment. Marine biologist Rachel Carson (1907–1964) was an early pioneer. Her book *Silent Spring* (1962), now praised as one of the leading science books of all time, brought attention to widespread pesticide use and launched a grassroots environmental movement, but Carson was denounced at the time for challenging established (male) scientific authorities.

Why do many competent women STEM graduates not persevere? Research has pointed to persistent cultural biases of parents, teachers, and school counselors (Hill, Corbett, and St. Rose, 2010) and the continued "chilly climate" that privileges male students and allows only a few women students to advance as possible answers (Fox, 2001; Bystydzienski and Bird, 2006). International students of color, for example, African women in science graduate programs in Canada, Europe, and the United States, have identified racism, gender bias, and their perceived marginality as discouraging factors in their training (Beoku-Betts, 2006). In sum, the overly masculine, authoritarian, and competitive academic and social interactions can alienate many women students (Herzig, 2004; Colyar, 2008; de Pillis and de Pillis, 2008).

The public debate over women's underrepresentation in science escalated in January 2005 after then–Harvard University President Lawrence Summers, attending a diversity conference, commented that a more likely hypothesis than gender discrimination for explaining women's limited presence in mathematics and science lay in women's "innate limitations." His widely reported statement harked back to the centuries-old debate on the subject and eventually contributed to his resignation. The report of MIT senior women scientists also made visible wide institutional disparities that continued to disadvantage them in their careers (see Box 10.5).

Can a woman be a scientist, spouse or partner, and mother at the same time? Marie Curie juggled watching her daughter Irene in the crib placed in the lab and eyeing the test tube of glowing radium, expressing a common tension felt by women who work outside the home. The adult children of Nobel Prize awardees and other women scientists have related how little time they had with their mother given her long hours in the lab away from home and children, dinnertime conversations that centered around work, and often a lack of involvement in their children's lives (Des Jardins, 2010). Does a double standard exist? Do adult children say the same things about their fathers and have the same expectations of them as opposed to their mothers?

Social scientists have asked whether it is or is not a socially learned preference for women to work with people rather than machines or abstractions. One study of mathematically gifted girls and boys found that as adults they chose different career paths. Math-precocious women tended to choose medicine, biological sciences, humanities, and the social sciences. Their male counterparts preferred engineering and the physical sciences (McArdle, 2008). Psychologists also suggest that the pursuit of romantic goals can diminish women's interests in advancing in STEM fields (Park et al., 2011).

Women's participation in STEM fields remains a complex issue, including whether we should give primacy to STEM fields. In an era of DNA, stem cells, biotechnology, and global efforts to solve health and environmental dangers, the biological sciences have gained ground and prestige and have been favored by women in recent decades. Women scientists are transforming the methods of detached, technological "masculine" science

---

Box 10.5   MIT WOMEN EXAMINE THEIR CAREERS IN SCIENCE

In 1999, a small group of senior women science faculty at the Massachusetts Institute of Technology analyzed their situation to reveal the usually invisible gendered hierarchy of their workplace. They found that the percentage of women faculty in the School of Science remained small (8%) despite the existence of a national pool of qualified women scientists. Junior women faculty were certain that gender discrimination had been "solved" by the previous generation, at the same time that senior women faculty reported being marginalized and excluded from important committees and decision-making channels within their departments. The data they compiled, which showed that senior women faculty received less salary, research space, resources, and other supports from MIT than did their male colleagues, had a national impact and their status report has served as a model for other institutions.

MIT responded with new policies to address work and family issues, reduce women faculty's marginalization, and support junior faculty. In 2004, MIT appointed a woman president, Susan Hockfield, a distinguished neuroscientist and former provost of Yale University. A report on women's status in science and engineering in 2011 identified some gains in women faculty recruitment and tenure. Women's record of their achievements also disproved any notion that women lack an aptitude for science, but from the perspectives of many of the women faculty themselves they continue to face challenges. For example, now that every committee must include a woman, with their numbers still small, female professors find they are doing more service and losing valuable research time and consultancy opportunities, a gain for their male colleagues. Stereotypes that women are being hired and advanced because they are simply female still persist.

Sources: MIT Committee on Women Faculty, "A Study on the Status of Women Faculty in Science at MIT," 1999; "Report on the Status of Women Faculty in the Schools of Science and Engineering at MIT," 2011; and Kate Zernike, "Gains and Drawbacks for Female Professors," *The New York Times*, March 21, 2011.

---

through their own methodology and research subjects. Examples include the work of the naturalist Rachel Carson (1907–1964), the geneticist Barbara McClintock (1902–1992), whose research on genes in maize increased crop production and earned her a Nobel Prize in 1983, and Englishwoman Jane Goodall (1934–), who in 1960, beginning without a science degree (later obtaining a Ph.D. in ethology), helped to change primate studies by living among chimpanzees in Tanzania. These women scientists carved new pathways for scientific discovery and the preservation of life and society. They and other women like them are innovators and serve as inspirations

in the twenty-first century in the way Marie Curie did in the previous one.

Women's and Gender Studies

In the Introduction to this textbook, we described the development of women's studies. Its institutionalization on campuses is not monolithic, however, and involves healthy debate among feminists. Women students of all social classes, faculty of color, and LGBTQ members, for example, continue to critique feminist theories and agendas that seem to universalize white middle-class heterosexual women's lives or to exclude the significance, perspectives, and experiences of race, ethnicity, national origin, sexuality, class, and other differences among women. In taking diverse positions, for example, some engage in writing and teaching feminist theory. Others criticize feminist theory and language as being elitist, like many male writers whose work reinforces traditional hierarchies in higher education and ignores the grounding democratic tendency of women's studies (Pesquera and Segura, 1996; Scott, 1997; Messer-Davidow, 2002).

In its focus on women's and gender realities and theories to explain them, the study of women and gender holds the possibility of restructuring knowledge as to make it resonate with women's as well as men's perceptions of the world and consciousness and thereby has the potential of bringing forth a true intellectual revolution.

Summary

Knowledge is not objective but a social construct and part of a political system that has historically marginalized and continues to marginalize women's experiences and taught women to be passive. The rise of feminist scholarship worldwide has challenged a specifically male perspective of knowledge and sought to make women visible and to validate their perspectives.

Societies worldwide always have debated who should be educated. That women's proper place has traditionally been viewed as within the domestic sphere and men's as in the public sphere explains in part why women comprise two thirds of illiterate persons worldwide today. In the ancient world, in Europe, and elsewhere, and through the medieval period, only a few exceptional women became accomplished in literary and scientific endeavors. Religious requirements provided girls and women with opportunities to learn to read; however, the emphasis was on women's moral training, not their intellectual development. Across cultures and over time, women have struggled for access to formal education.

From the 1500s until the 1960s, European colonialism has had varying consequences for colonized women's education. Western ideologies of race, color, class, and gender roles and models for economic development often have contributed to a decline in indigenous women's status from their precolonial period. Today, women in developing countries have gained more schooling, but this varies greatly given the wide range of cultures, political ideologies, and economic resources among these states.

In the United States, *affirmative action* refers to policies enacted to end historic and long-standing discrimination experienced by women and people of color. A diverse student body contributes to the "robust exchange of ideas" that enhances the educational experiences of all students. Title IX has also offered women new access to scholarships, sports activities, and employment.

Societies of all cultures past and present have debated whether girls and women should have the same curriculum as boys and men to achieve equity or be schooled in subjects to prepare them primarily to be traditional wives and mothers. Feminists who sought to provide a rigorous education for women often established their own schools. As more women, including adult "re-entry" women, and students of color are earning degrees at all levels in U.S. higher education and efforts to diversify the curriculum have succeeded since the 1970s, a backlash has occurred to defend Western civilization in the curriculum and to oppose affirmative action.

For the most part, the U.S. educational system at all levels—through textbooks, curricula, and teacher preparation—has socialized women to be quiet and submissive, to accept male authority rather than their own experiences, and to choose traditional women's careers. Schools shortchange girls, and in higher education women experience a "chilly climate," which is even more unwelcoming for women of color. That women and men are evaluated differently, resulting in women accumulating disadvantages and men accumulating advantages, contributes to gendered workplaces. Women faculty are concentrated in the lower ranks and paid less at all ranks than their male counterparts.

Dominant men and groups have maintained their influence in part by limiting the access of women and lesser men to formal education and by using the educational system as a tool of cultural assimilation. In the United States, American Indians, African Americans, and immigrant groups experience pressures to acculturate to the European American values taught in American schools and to suppress their own languages and cultures. Although girls and women of color find new opportunities in schooling, the U.S. educational system continues to treat them as inferior and less capable. Multicultural education and ethnic studies are tools to resist dominant group assimilation and promote inclusivity of communities of difference.

Changes in the global economy and employment, women's aspirations, and greater opportunities account in large part for women earning more college degrees than men in recent decades in the West. Women's colleges, past and present, in their mission, practices, and role models play a significant role in preparing women for careers and leadership. Greater access to higher education has not meant equality in treatment and representation in all disciplines and as faculty and administrators, however. Women remain underrepresented in STEM fields but are making breakthroughs in newer fields, such as the biological sciences. The challenges women experience, past and present, to become scientists and pursue their careers underscore the persistence of gendered notions of who is to be educated and what is to be taught and appropriate career paths for women and men, while also seeking to fulfill family roles.

Feminist scholars have also debated what kinds of educational experience benefit women's academic achievements. Since the 1970s, women's studies as a feminist critique of knowledge has been established as a distinct field of study in higher education and has begun to be taught in traditional disciplines as well. There is also a healthy debate among feminists about the nature and institutionalization of women's and gender studies in the academy. Their future and substance as an intellectual revolution depends on the presence of women students, faculty, and administrators.

Discussion Questions

1. Why did early feminists believe that education was important for women, and why was this idea resisted? How do the world figures for literacy and school enrollment reflect the position of women in various societies?

2. Investigate the statistics for women at your college. Compare the numbers of women and men enrolled, breaking this down by race and ethnicity if possible. How do majors break down? Are there women faculty in all disciplines? If not, why do you think this is so?

3. Do you think there are any special advantages or disadvantages to gender-segregated education? On your campus, what institutional supports and resources, if any, are available to women of color; low-income, lesbian, bisexual, and transsexual women; women who are differently abled; and adult re-entry women?

4. Trace the educational history of the women in your family as far back as you can go. How do their experiences compare with your own, and how do you account for the differences and similarities?

5. What are the opportunities and obstacles you now face in making a career choice? (If you have yet to decide on a career, select an interesting one to think about.) Have your previous educational experiences readily enabled you to pursue this goal? Are there any social expectations by your family and friends that might cause difficulties in carrying out your goal?

Recommended Readings

Des Jardins, Julie. *The Madame Curie Complex: The Hidden History of Women in Science*. New York: Feminist Press at the City University of New York, 2010. The history of women's struggles to be accepted in the fields of science and mathematics, including the life of Marie Curie and how she became an inspiration and standard for other women scientists. The book also explores the cult of masculinity in mid-twentieth-century science and how women scientists have broken new paths and set new goals for achievement.

Howe, Florence. *A Life in Motion*. New York: Feminist Press at the City University of New York, 2011. The autobiography of one of the founders of women's studies. In the 1960s she created a Freedom School in the South, began to teach about women's literature, and founded the Feminist Press in 1970 to recover writings by women to reintroduce them to a new generation eager to read them. Howe then explored the status of women and women's studies throughout the world and became an advocate for critical feminist change everywhere.

Jean-Marie, Gaëtane, and Brenda Lloyd-Jones, editors. *Women of Color in Higher Education: Changing Directions and New Perspectives*. Bingley, U.K.: Emerald Group Publishing, 2011; *Women of Color in Higher Education: Turbulent Past, Promising Future*. Bingley, U.K: Emerald Group Publishing, 2011. These two volumes examine the positionality, status, challenges, and agency of African American, Asian Pacific American, Latina, and Native American women faculty, staff, and administrators in higher education. Written by emerging and established women-of-color scholars, the chapters provide strategies and resources for navigating the academy and being successful.

Lawrence-Lightfoot, Sara. *Balm in Gilead: Journey of a Healer*. Reading, MA: Addison-Wesley, 1988. This biography of an African American woman with educational experiences in the South and North provides a moving personal story behind the analysis offered in this chapter. Born in Mississippi in 1914, she eventually attended Cornell University and went on to become a physician and child psychiatrist.

Woolf, Virginia. *A Room of One's Own* (1929). New York: Harcourt, Brace, 1957. This classic work explores the ways women have been prevented from achieving higher education and what this has meant for their lives, independence, and creativity.

chapter **11**

Women and Religion

As great and educational as this trip was, as inspirational as this trip was, it was also a journey of heartbreak and anguish. And it was a journey of hope....For me, this trip has been totally about touching the pain of the world as real for all these people we've seen, and being hopeful. We have hope that the pain of the world isn't the end of the story. And that frees our imagination to think of our world in a new place. To think of this place between the partisan politics to a center, to think of a church where everyone could be cared for. To think of a lobby like ours, where we could really be voices for the folks who are at the margins. It frees up our imagination. The bus trip was a prophetic imagination, it turns out, and who knew it? It's fabulous....For me, the contemplative life is all about listening deeply to the movement of the spirit among us and to touch the heart of what might frighten me or touch the heart of where Jesus would go in the gospel. And so listening deeply to the needs of the world around us, we've got to be engaged politically in our nation.

SISTER SIMONE CAMPBELL, EXECUTIVE DIRECTOR OF NETWORK, A CATHOLIC
SOCIAL JUSTICE LOBBY AND LEADER OF THE NUNS ON THE BUS, 2012

Religious Beliefs

What Is Religion?

What we call "religion" is something about which people feel passionately. Wars have been fought, people have been maimed and tortured, and some have even sought martyrdom in the name of "religion." The subject has not lost its force in modern times by any means and remains a major element in world politics. Religion is among the most elusive of the concepts we use to describe human societies. Some theorists distinguish religion in terms of its reliance upon a supernatural element, but it is possible to be an adherent to some religions without believing in any god. Furthermore, many religions that have a distinctive label, such as "Hinduism" or "Christianity," incorporate many distinct variants that are so different from one another, occasionally even hostile to one another, that they cannot be described as unitary in any sense. To generalize in any way about women and religion would therefore be futile. In many societies, including U.S. society, religious belief permeates, at least for some women and men, virtually all aspects of life.

Planting a garden, eating a meal, having a baby, and burying the dead have both secular and religious aspects. This is so even in societies that have sought rigorously to establish and enforce a separation between religion and secular society; many societies have not sought to separate in this way but, rather, have combined a mutually reinforcing religious and political establishment.

While many have come to see religion as a relic of the past, representative of older traditions and a bastion of conservatism, it has long been a force for change and continues to be so in the present. Religious believers often seek reform rather than acceptance. They criticize what they see as injustice, oppression, and evil and try to change the behavior both of individuals and of whole societies. At times they attempt to do this through established religious institutions—such as the churches and the clergy—and at times through new religious movements (in which women sometimes play leading roles) within or outside of established religions.

We can speak of varieties of religion just as we can speak of varieties of society. On the one hand, there are the religious beliefs and practices of small-scale societies, which have little social hierarchy or few or no specialized religious institutions. On the other hand, there are the major world religions, diverse in character but each claiming millions of adherents, in state-organized societies that have specialized ordained clergy and that play roles recognized and protected by state-level political institutions. These often contain sects that, though established, are extremely different from one another, some granting prominent roles to women and others being more patriarchal in character. Finally, there are religious movements, often on the fringe or even outside of the established large-scale religions, such as what are called "fundamentalist" religions and "new" religions.

Many religious traditions appeal to a "higher authority," something above human will or desire, for a formulation of right and wrong. For some women and men, this appeal strengthens the dicta about morality. Sometimes this authority involves sanctions, such as blessings for those who, according to that set of beliefs, do right and punishments for those who do wrong. However, the motivations of believers do not lie only in sanctions but also in the wish to do and to see done what they believe is right. Some women and men resort to interpretations of texts for guidance into what is "right" and what is "wrong," while others look to the vision of charismatic leaders or even direct religious experience (though this itself is usually much influenced by leaders and customs). Generally, it is not a live-and-let-live world. Believers are not usually satisfied with following the right path only for themselves or even for themselves and their children. They want others to see and follow the right path and to avoid supporting systems that take the wrong path. The vehemence with which they insist on this in part determines whether outsiders label them as extremely conservative, "fundamentalists," or "fanatics."

Religion and Social Reform

Historically, women have been on the outskirts of religious movements. This is not to say that they have not played a major role, but that the role has not been one equal to that of a man, or one that has come about as easily, since usually religious leaders have been wary of the power that women possess, individually and collectively. Therefore, in much of the history of women and religion, there has been a dichotomy. In some ways, religion has been an impetus for change where women are active, and in other ways the majority of the world's religions have adhered to and prompted sexist standards and mores. There is a paradox, therefore, in how women are viewed in religion. On the one hand, women have been repressed in ways that constrict access to birth control, limit the role they can play in leadership, and denounce women's sexuality. On the other hand, women sometimes are venerated as saints and can be looked upon as pious and worthy of reverence and respect.

Much feminist research and writing has been critical of religious institutions for their treatment and views of women, especially religion's exclusion of women from positions of leadership. Women in male-dominated religions have had to fight to be permitted to be educated in the text or the liturgy and are often banned from participation in central practices of worship. Women's value is connected to their roles as mothers and spouses, roles that support men and help propagate membership in the religion. Many of the world's religions adhere to beliefs and ideas that devalue women and are concerned about women as sexual tempters to men, advocating a mode of dress that covers their sexuality, reserving it only for their husbands. Carried to extremes, this attitude creates a cycle of repression and reinforces a power differential between men and women.

If they are devalued, why should women be attracted to religion? Why do so many remain members of their faiths? In confronting the difficulties of their daily lives, woman may turn to religion for support and spiritual guidance. Religious belief is usually transmitted from older generations to younger ones, and both women and men grow up with the beliefs taught to them as important aspects of their lives. To leave their religions would be to walk away from an important part of themselves, for better or for worse. They are married within religious institutions and raise their own children in them as well. Also, women in particular find a social network of support from other women in their congregations and places of worship. If they are unhappy, they may seek religion for help, seeing in religion a set of beliefs that represent a higher purpose in life, one that offers comfort in times of distress.

In addition to providing comfort and a purpose to life, religion offers individuals a moral code. Through time we have associated doctrines, teachings, and customs concerning right and wrong with religion. Religions not only set standards for good behavior but also tell their adherents how to achieve a state of "goodness," whether this is defined as moral health or conduct that sets things right with the world. Religion is also often associated with healing, a matter that will be explored later in this chapter. Healing, or achieving a better state of being, can be directed toward the individual or society as a whole. When directed toward the individual, it can involve diagnosis (discovery of what is wrong, whether through divination, confession, or some other means) and repair (through penitence, atonement, or restoration—by sacrifice or making amends). The believer in a particular religion is encouraged to improve her life by correcting what is wrong and doing what is right. Women also seek in religion solace for the problems they face or the ill treatment they experience. As individuals they may be deeply unhappy and turn to religion for help. They may also seek change for themselves and others like them, calling upon their communities to establish justice, compassion, harmony, and whatever else their belief system teaches them is right and proper.

Feminists in modern times have critiqued the major world religions for biases against women and have explored the many ways used to control women and keep them in a secondary role, but they have also found the majority of the women around the world have found value in their faith and their religious communities. They have also found that women have devised ways of changing society for the better through their religions. Thus, for example, although their churches may have told Christian women in the United States in the nineteenth century that their place was in the home, it was through their churches that many women fought slavery, organized the abolitionist movement, and spoke out in the name of equality for all under God. Women have used religious platforms to advocate for others and for themselves.

Women have sustained their religious beliefs despite the regulations adopted by all the major religions of the world to repress women's independence by mandating far stronger constraints on women than on men and excluding them from positions of leadership. In fact, even in these religions, some women have asserted their views, sometimes as venerated saints and holy women, sometimes as leaders in the spheres allocated to them. Today, feminist theologians continue to analyze the sexism in major world religious traditions in order to reformulate received doctrines to meet feminist ideals (see Sharma and Young, 1999).

Established Religions

Religions in Small-Scale Societies. Women often play important roles in small-scale societies' religious practices. In these societies, found in Africa, Asia, and Latin America, there may be little specialization in social roles beyond those determined by age and gender. Some women and men are regarded as gifted in their ability to attain communion with spiritual entities and are able to use their gifts and training from more experienced practitioners to perform healing ceremonies for the purpose of enhancing physical as well as spiritual well-being and harmony between humans and nature. In the past, anthropologists and others have sometimes referred to such individuals as "shamans," though many have preferred to use culturally specific terminology that reflects the distinctive understandings of the settings in which such healing practices occur. For example, some Korean women in the United States, coming from a societal hierarchy where women experience marginalization, find that shamanism can be an escape that provides them safety and economic and psychological autonomy (Lee, 2009). Women must learn the rituals associated with their assigned activities and perform them in order to have success. In small-scale societies, the roles of women in the performance of rituals and ceremonies may be regarded as critical to essential elements of social survival, such as fertility, protection from environmental disasters, health, safety, and prosperity.

World Religions. World religions are those that number their adherents in the millions. Some of these are more unitary in their beliefs. Confucianism, Buddhism, and Christianity, for example, trace their origins to their namesakes: Confucius, the Buddha (Siddhartha Gautama), and Christ, and Islam to its Prophet, Muhammad. Judaism traces a common ethnic history as well as a common set of scriptures. Taoism has a coherent set of beliefs. Hinduism, like Judaism, is grounded in an ethnic/national

Muslim women praying.

history, yet it contains immense diversity of belief. Indeed, each of these, with a history of movement through conversion and migration, has been transformed through time into a multitude of different variants, often with different names and different beliefs and practices.

These world religions are frequently associated with political structures, particularly the state itself or an arm of the state. In the past, for example, Christian states recognized an official religion, a particular variant of Christianity, and designated practitioners served important roles in government; conversely, the ruler had to be legitimized by the Church. Today, there are a number of Islamic nations in which Muslim clerics rule (such as Iran) or have great influence (such as Saudi Arabia). While states have varied in their degree of tolerance of other religions, a close linkage between the state and the religious establishment has been the rule, rather than the exception, in the history of complex societies. However, the separation of church and state no doubt has made possible religious tolerance and democratic governance.

As with secular leadership, women have long been excluded from positions of authority in these world religions. Nevertheless, women are adherents of these faiths. If they have access to wealth, they may achieve positions of relative power by becoming patronesses of their religious establishments, endowing religious institutions, supporting the construction of religious edifices, and patronizing sacred arts and artifacts. Regardless of the lower status to which they are assigned, millions of women have found spiritual gratification in the major established religions of the world. Further, they have found the rewards of sisterhood through these religions, gathering together in mutual support and for the purpose of nurturing their own religious communities.

The Nonreligious. While many women acknowledge religion or spirituality as important, there are many women who identify as nonreligious. Why do some women and men choose not to believe in or practice a religion? In the eighteenth century, the intellectual movement known as the Enlightenment offered a critique of the abuse of church and state, namely belief in superstition rather than fact, as well as the intolerance prevalent throughout Europe. Instead, the Age of Enlightenment advocated the application of reason and science to solving society's problems. The Enlightenment movement gained many adherents, who played important roles in the profound changes that shaped how people in Europe and in the North American colonies organized their social and political systems. The growth and advancement of science and technology increased economic development and growth, which provided individuals with higher standards of living and well-being. As economic growth expanded, people's lives improved materially and they became less reliant on religion. In general, people tend to be less religious in societies in which daily survival is not a problem. "Modernized" societies gave rise to secularism, the principles of which have become embedded in democratic societies. Secularism advocates the separation of church and state, the right to be free of a government-imposed religion, the right to be free from religious rules and teachings, and political decision making free of religious influence. The nonreligious incorporates a broad spectrum of beliefs concerning the existence of a supreme being and attitudes toward religious practice. It also includes the antireligious or anticlerical (those who are hostile to religion or religious authorities), agnostics (those who remain skeptical about the existence of God and the importance of religion), and atheists or secular humanists (those who reject religion and the belief in the existence of deities). In the United States, 20% of the population identify themselves as nonreligious, and they account for a growing segment of the population (Pew Forum on Religion & Public Life, 2012). Women make up 47% of those who identify as nonreligious in the United States.

Origin Myths. Most religions provide a creation myth, which tells the story of what are thought to be the first humans and how they came to be. The creation myth to which Jews, Christians, and Muslims subscribe, the story of Adam and Eve, is much more, of course, than a tale of the first humans. Like other people's creation myths, it provides a "charter" and a "plan" for relations between people and the supernatural, between women and men, and between humans and nature. We have already discussed some of the implications for women of the Adam and Eve myth in Chapter 1. One myth that tells of the descent of a group, in this case the Iroquois nation, from females was recorded by Father Louis, a missionary working in New France in the seventeenth century (Québec, 1679–80; see Box 11.1).

Females in the Supernatural World

Most forms of religious belief include some conceptualization of a supernatural world that is inhabited by forces with superhuman qualities.

Box 11.1   THE VARIED CREATION STORIES OF NATIVE AMERICANS

The Cherokee say they came from Corn Mother, or Selu, who cut open her breast so that corn could spring forth, giving life to the people. For the Tewa Pueblo people, the first mothers were known as Blue Corn Woman, the summer mother, and White Corn Maiden, the winter mother. The Iroquois believe that they were born into this world from the mud on the back of the Earth, known as Grandmother Turtle. The essentials of life—corn, beans, and squash—were given to them by the Three Sisters. The Iroquois refer to the Three Sisters when giving thanks for food in everyday prayers. The Apache believe that they are descendants of Child of the Water, who was kept safe by his mother, White-Painted Woman, so that he could slay all the monsters and make the world safe for the Apache people.... For the Sioux, White Buffalo Calf Woman gave the people the gift of the Pipe, and thus a gift of Truth.

[*According to the Western Apache creation myth*] There was a time when White Painted Woman lived all alone....

Longing for children, she slept with the Sun and not long after gave birth to Slayer of Monsters, the foremost culture hero. Four days later, White Painted Woman became pregnant by water and gave birth to Born-of-the-Water (also known as Child-of-the-Water). As Slayer of Monsters and Child-of-the-Water matured, White Painted Woman instructed them on how to live. Then they left home and, following her advice, rid the earth of most of its evil. White Painted Woman never became old. When she reached an advanced age, she walked toward the east. After a while, she saw herself coming toward herself. When she came together, there was only one, the young one. Then she was like a young girl all over again.

Sources: Cherokee story from Rayna Green, *Women in American Indian Society*, p. 21. © 1992 by Chelsea House Publishers, a subsidiary of Haights Cross Communications. Apache story from Thomas E. Mails, *The People Called Apache*, Englewood Cliffs, NJ: Prentice Hall, 1974, p. 76.

These saints, ghosts, and spirits of various sorts are often considered more approachable and more interested in "ordinary" people than the great deities. Although the formal traditions of Judaism, Christianity, and Islam are *monotheistic* (believing in a single divinity), their "folk" or "popular" versions have always included belief in lesser supernatural forces.

Immortal Women: Souls, Saints, and Ghosts.

The question of what happens to the soul after death is a critical one. Many people believe that the soul persists, to occupy a place in the supernatural world or to return to life in another body. The latter, called reincarnation, as represented in Hinduism and Buddhism, involves belief in a scale of perfection that an individual can ascend or descend, through successive lifetimes, depending on how virtuously each life was lived. Individuals are destined to be reborn again and again, to endure the pain of existence, until they reach the pinnacle of perfection, after which they are released. In Hinduism and in some, but not all, Buddhist traditions, the most virtuous life is one devoted to study, meditation, and unconcern about worldly things (like marriage, children, wealth, and comfort, even eating and sleeping). However, women are very unlikely to have the opportunity to pursue a life of study and meditation in Hindu and Buddhist societies. In Hindu mythology, women came to symbolize the eternal struggle that men must wage between materiality and spirit. Kali (the goddess) symbolizes the womb, connected with rebirth and consequent illusion and entanglement in the world (Caldwell, 2000).

In Buddhism the goal is enlightenment, ultimate perfection of the soul, and texts exist for both men and women to study and practice for attaining this goal. *The Lotus Sutra*, a primary text in Buddhist scripture, has influence as a unifying law or truth in Buddhism throughout Asia, including China, Korea, and Japan. The gender imagery in this text provides an inconsistent portrayal of women. Although it states that all people possess a Buddha-nature, and that women, as well as men, are capable of enlightenment, there are also passages suggesting that women are dangerous sources of sexual temptation.

Christianity and Islam teach direct individual immortality, with the soul experiencing punishment or reward in accordance with the virtues and vices of a single lifetime. These religions strongly espouse the idea that souls are essentially without sex and that salvation is open to both women and men. Some souls, because of unusual virtue, become saints. They continue to provide blessings for the living who appeal to them. Fiorenza (1979: 140) argues that "the lives of the saints provide a variety of role models for Christian women. What is more important is that they teach that women, like men, have to follow their vocation from God even if this means that they have to go frontally against the ingrained cultural mores and images of women."

Many religions believe in the existence of ghosts as distinct from immortal souls. A ghost is a spirit that outlasts the physical body for some period. Ghosts are thought to be capable of beneficence, particularly as protectors of their survivors in the family. However, if maltreated or forgotten, they are also believed to be capable of vengeance. Bad luck, sickness, nightmares, and even psychic persecution are often blamed on ghosts. Ghosts differ from saints in that they are interested in their own families and require appeasement and respect, not veneration (Harrell, 1986).

Goddesses.

Many people believe that the supernatural world consists of elevated regions inhabited by deities of wider sway than spirits, saints, and ghosts. This cosmos is generally perceived to be inhabited by a number of divine persons. The goddess, like the unfettered woman of male fantasies, is sometimes envisaged as a threatening and terrible being.

This is the case with the Inuit goddess Sedna. In Hindu mythology, the goddess is dark Kali (see Chapter 1), whose orgiastic dancing brings death and destruction on the world. However, when she submits to her husband, Shiva, the goddess becomes beneficent and her energy is harnessed for good by the rational principle of maleness. In the countryside, peasants in the nineteenth century prayed to Kali alone as the good mother.

Tamed and controlled, a goddess may become a great and well-loved figure, worthy of the worship of men as well as women. Some goddesses, known only in a small geographical space, are respected by local inhabitants because of their protection of the local people and the land (Monaghan, 2011). Goddesses and goddess-like figures are found in all cultures throughout the world.

Buddhism provides a focus for worshipers in figures of *bodhisattvas*, personages whose perfection has freed them from mortal life but who choose to remain in a personalized existence in order to be accessible to the appeals of the struggling faithful. The greatest and most popular of all is Avalokitesvara, the bodhisattva of compassion, who appears as a goddess in one manifestation. Avalokitesvara originated in India but is worshiped in Tibet as Chenresig, in China as Gaunyin, in Japan as Kannon, and by other names throughout Asia. Guanyin is the very quintessence of the compassion of the Buddha. Pregnant women turn to her for help, and she cooperates with mediums seeking communication with ancestors or ghosts.

In the great polytheistic religions of later antiquity, goddesses appear with a variety of powers and attributes. They are patronesses of cities (Athena), marriage (Hera), and sex (Aphrodite). They are in charge of agriculture (Demeter) and human fertility (Artemis). Isis was an amalgam of female deities of the Mediterranean world, gathering their attributes, powers, and myths into her own cult. She began as a local Egyptian goddess associated with the cult of Osiris, who was both her brother and husband. By Hellenistic times, when the Greeks ruled Egypt, her cult was one of the most popular in the ancient world, promising immortality to its adherents. Women were active participants in the cult of Isis as priestesses, members of religious societies, and donors. However, male participants far outnumbered females, and the chief priesthoods were held by men (Pomeroy, 1975).

In the sixth century B.C.E., Jews returning to the Holy Land from their exile in Babylon enforced their belief in one male divinity, outlawing the worship of all other gods and goddesses. When European pagans became Christians, they turned their backs on the gods and goddesses of the Greek and Roman worlds, reducing them to hollow idols. Some second-century Christians favored endowing the Holy Ghost with a feminine persona; this impulse was rejected by the dominant faction, and all three persons of the Christian Trinity became male or without gender. In the seventh century, Muslims in their turn rejected the goddesses of their ancient Arabian tribes in favor of the one (male) god.

For most ordinary worshipers, however, monotheistic religions have not entirely excluded the older idea of a female deity. For example, Christians exalted the memory and attributes of Mary, "mother of God (Jesus)," in direct proportion as God himself became increasingly patriarchal (Fiorenza, 1979, 1983).

Modern-day feminist goddess worship focuses on femaleness, the female body, healing, nature, tolerance, and independence from any central authority. Feminist goddess worship promotes healing and empowerment free from the oppression and pain of male dominance. Rituals serve as a tool to contact the sacred and to align with nature. There is typically no appointed leader during the ritual, and all women are considered priestesses (see Box 12.9) (Stuckey, 2010).

The Gender of God

Some feminists feel that the social position of women can be enhanced by the worship of a goddess and that belief in a female deity would give religion more usefulness and meaning. Such leading theologians and feminists as Mary Daly (1973), Carol Christ (1979, 1987), Naomi Goldenberg (1979), Plaskow (1990), Ruether (2007), and Fiedler (2010) have taken this position. They believe that the image of the deity we worship is important to our understanding and appreciation of ourselves. In patriarchal religions, divinity is male; hence, men see an image of themselves in the divine, while women are denied this identification with divinity. In Islam, for example, although women and men are said to have the same spiritual nature, and superiority is based on religiosity, there have not been any female prophets, and Allah is viewed with a male persona (Badawi, 2003).

Some gods are thought to incite enthusiastic female worship and appear to prefer female devotees. Dionysus, Krishna, and Jesus have all been particularly venerated by women. Dionysus liberated some of the frustrated and confined women of ancient Greece

---

Box 11.2   INVOCATION TO THE GODDESS

Queen of the night
Queen of the moon
Queen of the stars
Queen of the horns
Queen of the earth
Bring to us the child of light.
Night sky rider
Silver shining one
Lady of wild things
Silver wheel
North star
Circle
Crescent
Moon-bright
Singer
Changer!
Teach us!
See with our eyes
Hear with our ears
Breathe with our nostrils
Kiss with our lips,
Touch with our hands,
Be here now!

Source: From *Changing of the Gods: Feminism and the End of Traditional Religions* by Naomi Goldenberg. Copyright © 1979 by Naomi Goldenberg. Reprinted by permission of Beacon Press.

periodically with ecstatic experiences of dancing and frenzied activity. Krishna, who is often represented as a baby, is associated with a sect of female worshipers who call themselves "mothers of God" (Freeman, 1980). As young men, all three gods are represented as attractive and loving of women, posing in their lives as protectors.

The position of goddesses in polytheistic societies varies widely, as did the position of women in ancient Egypt, Athens, and Rome. Similarly, there is such wide variation in the position of women in monotheistic societies that it becomes difficult to generalize about the influence of women's roles on beliefs about the gender of God and vice versa. Not everyone is convinced, then, that a female deity is needed to improve the status and position of women in society or that belief in such a deity would support that goal. While some argue that it is necessary to recognize both "masculine" and "feminine" attributes in the objects of our worship, this compromise is not sufficient to address the social injustice of sexism.

Religion and Social Controls

Religion provides more than the imagery by which we can conceptualize the supernatural world. It provides a basis for a code of ethics to govern human conduct. In highly organized religions, clergy and other specialists interpret and sometimes enforce a code of ethics grounded in religious belief. However, all religious systems have some means for exerting control over human conduct.

Religion and the Family

Laws concerning family matters, particularly marriage, childrearing, and sexual relations, nearly always refer to religious beliefs. In most large-scale societies, such laws have supported patriarchal structures. As an accommodation to multiculturalism, some nations even today bow to the more conservative rights of religious minorities to adhere to "tradition" (usually to the detriment of women's rights), while others override these group rights to protect women (Foblets, 1999; Anantnarayan, 2010; Htun and Weldon, 2011; see Howland, 1999, for many international examples of family law and religion).

Life-Cycle Rituals. As we have already seen, the family provides the framework within which women are confined and socialized. Public performance of rituals during the life cycle—for example, at puberty, marriage, and death—enhances the power of the family, the relationships considered proper for its members, and the control of those individuals in accordance with the decorum of the community. In traditional Greek society from antiquity to the present, death rituals have been almost entirely the responsibility of women (Danforth, 1982). For men, life-cycle rituals are usually occasions that help to define and enhance their potency and social power as they advance toward full adult membership in the community. The major life-cycle rituals for Jewish males, for example, are the brith millah (bris), the circumcision ritual of 8-day-old infant boys, which provides them with a physical identity as Jews, and the bar mitzvah, the ritual of first participation in adult study and prayer, which marks the entry of a 13-year-old boy into the community of adults. For infant girls, there is no equivalent of the bris, but for Conservative and Reform Jews, there is a girls' equivalent to the bar mitzvah, the bat mitzvah. Unlike the bar mitzvah, the bat mitzvah is not essential to girls' membership in the Jewish community, nor does it mark their "coming of age" in the traditional sense.

In patriarchal, patrilineal societies, the most important life-cycle ritual or rite of passage for women is likely to be the wedding ceremony. This marks the major transition from the family of birth to the husband's family. Since divorce and remarriage may be difficult or even impossible for women in such societies, they are likely to undergo this ceremony only once. It may last for days, preceded by months of preparation and preliminary rituals. In Western societies, weddings have traditionally spotlighted the bride. In some matrilineal societies, however, marriage does not substantially alter women's social position since women remain in their own matrilineage for life. If there is a major life-cycle ritual, it is likely to be associated with menarche, when women become of reproductive age, ready to contribute new members to the matrilineage. A good example is the *chisungu* ceremony of the matrilineal Bemba, a large and complex society in Zambia (Richards, 1956). Periodically, all the girls of a district whose first menstruation has occurred since the last *chisungu* participate in the month-long ceremony. The initiates are honored by the whole community; the women sing and dance before these girls, and parents, fiancés, and prospective in-laws contribute to the expenses of the ceremonial feasting.

During the complex ceremony of initiation, Bemba girls pass through several role changes, beginning with separation and seclusion, physical degradation (such as being prohibited from bathing), and testing for strength and courage. The ritual ends with reentry and renewal. After initiation, Bemba girls are prepared for marriage and reproduction, related to other women in a new and more intimate way, and newly knowledgeable about the role requirements of women.

Sexual Controls. At puberty in most cultures, the freedom girls might have enjoyed when they were little is sharply curtailed. Adolescent girls may be told that they are unclean and must learn to control the possible ill effects of their "polluted nature." At the same time, they may be schooled in the hard facts of

their vulnerability to both public censure and physical attack. The leaders of every major literate religion in the world have produced literature against the sexuality of women. Representatives of the major religious hierarchies have continually urged women to contain themselves within the narrow limits of their homes and the narrower limits of female modesty and decorum, threatening them with both earthly and eternal punishments for the sins of their "nature."

The most effective method of controlling the dangers represented by women's sexuality is to ensure that they are kept under the authority of their male kin. At puberty, men are proclaimed mature and ready to undertake public responsibilities. Some societies begin a process of weakening the control of the father over his son at this point, to free the son for service in the greater community. Women, however, are not released from their fathers' power; rather, fathers (or other male kin) are given the right to hand them over to the power of a husband. Even in Christian societies that defended the individual's right of consent to marriage, the economic dependence of daughters usually made them subject to paternal authority.

Religious laws in patriarchal societies often protect men from the "dangers" of pollution inherent in close proximity to women during their menstrual periods. In the Qur'an, the sacred book of Islam, men are ordered to separate themselves from their wives until the women have taken the ritual bath (Box 11.3) at the end of the menstrual period (Delaney et al., 1976). The same religious proscription on sexual relations between husband and wife applies to Orthodox Jews. Some feminists argue that such laws reinforce women's own fears about menstruation and undermine their self-esteem by labeling them as periodically "unclean." However, some adherents to these religions feel quite differently about them. These women feel that the ritual bath enhances their self-regard, the sanctity of their marriages, and even the warmth of their relationships with their husbands.

The codes of most religions urge husbands to use their authority prudently. They warn of the damage that may be caused to a family by the despair of unhappy women. They remind men of the blessings of a home cared for by a contented wife. However, while men are subjected to moral suasion, women are subjected to physical coercion. Nearly every written religious code is based on double-standard morality. Christianity, whose rhetoric consistently states that what is not allowed to women is not allowed to men either, has never made wide practical application of the rule.

Control over women's sexuality and reproduction is a high priority for what are called "conservative religious" groups (Brown, 1994). Conservative religions consist of groups of people who challenge the authority of governments, oppose specific laws or reforms, or impose ideas derived from their interpretations of established religions on others who do not share their beliefs. Such controls on women are often associated with assertions of nationalist or ethnic identity. Women represent holy motherhood, their virtue reflecting

---

Box 11.3   THE RITUAL BATH: POSITIVE AND NEGATIVE

Rachel's experience [with the Jewish observance of mikveh, the ritual bath taken after menstruation] has been one of relative ease. Still even for Rachel, a New York City professional in her 40's, mikveh has always been a "mixed bag...."

Rachel says "I don't resent having to go." She finds something powerful about total immersion in water, a substance connected to the flood of Jewish history and the miracle of the parting sea.

When she emerges from her seventh dunk, she recites personal prayers. Concerning the label, "impure," which defines women during niddah, Rachel says: "I really don't think about it at all. It's not on my radar screen."

When Rachel was younger, in child-bearing mode, she says, "every menstrual cycle became a missed opportunity for life as opposed to seeing myself as impure."

Asked if the observance strengthens her marriage, Rachel closes her eyes to the din of the Upper West Side Starbucks. She thinks.

"Yes, I do," she answers. "There is an element of longing. I liken it to a business trip. When I'm away I miss my husband."

During the days of niddah, before Rachel goes to the mikveh, when physical intimacy with her husband isn't possible, she senses a different dynamic in her marriage. "It makes it easier to talk because you know that's all you are going to do."

[On the negative side], she complains of the long wait at her local mikveh....Often Rachel spends three hours there.

"Even if you have a miraculous experience, even if the spiritual mikveh lady is there, you leave praying your husband hasn't fallen asleep. What kind of date is that?"

Source: ©Elicia Brown. By Permission. Excerpted from Immersed in a Dilemma, *The Jewish Week* Nov. 14, 2003, p. 62.

the purity of the group and their subservence, the source of strength and dignity of men.

Protection of Women. Religious laws generally offer some protection to the "obedient weakling." While they justify authority and preach obedience, they also restrain human authority in the name of a higher power and teach the limits on an insubordinate will.

In this spirit, Jewish, Christian, and Islamic laws are concerned with the economic responsibilities of men toward their wives and daughters. In Islam, for example, a woman is seen first as a mother and wife, so she must seek her husband's permission to work, unless there is absolute necessity (Badawi, 2003). The rights of women to dowries, inheritance, and other economic protections are spelled out carefully. Arbitrary divorce is discouraged, and polygyny is regulated to ensure the rights of co-wives. Catholic canon law sanctifies the consensual basis of marriage and protects wives from repudiation by husbands. It defines rape as a crime of violence against women and denies men the right to kill their wives. In most Christian religions, all the "peoples of the Book" are urged to protect and support widows and orphans and to treat moral and observant women with respect and kindness.

Within that framework, religion acts to establish and enforce the norms of family life. Sexual relationships between wife and husband resulting in the birth of children are universally viewed as divinely ordained. Deviation from that pattern is sometimes considered immoral and sometimes violently punished. While many religious constraints on women were rationalized as being for their protection, this notion has been challenged by feminist critics and sometimes rethought. An Algerian Muslim scholar's analysis has concluded that the function of the veil at the time of Muhammad was to protect women, and thus the veil's most appropriate modern equivalent is education and schooling that

in our times gives the most protection to a woman (Helie-Lucas, 1999: 24).

Beyond the Family

Outside the religious activities of the family, most societies engage in a wider set of ceremonies, celebrations, and rituals devoted to the deities worshiped in the community. These require the services of a professional and trained clergy who enjoy the accoutrements of public art and architecture, conduct time-consuming and often occult rituals (sometimes in a language unknown to the laity), and make use of an extensive tradition of myth and law to enforce their social authority.

Women as Worshipers. Nearly all religions encourage, indeed command, the active participation of women as worshipers. Even as worshipers, though, women are subjected to a variety of restrictions. Lay participation in the performance of rituals is often restricted to men.

Except in Orthodox Judaism, Jewish women are nowadays counted in the *minyan*, the quorum of 10 required for the conduct of certain services. In the past there were no female altar servers in Roman Catholic churches. Yet any traveler in a Catholic country must be struck by the idea of the church as a "woman's space." It may be dominated by an all-male hierarchy, but every day the women spend hours there in devotion and conversation with one another. From earliest times, Christian moralists complained about women's habit of using the church as a social center. Similarly, the shrines of Sufi saints are centers where Islamic women meet daily for rest and relaxation and to confide in the sympathetic saint (Fernea and Fernea, 1972). Underneath the restrictive and apparently prohibitive structure of the great religions— distinguished by monumental places of worship, professional clergy, written literature, and a large following—is the elusive, often undocumented world of women.

Syncretistic and Evangelistic Religions. On the fringes of the "established religions" are hosts of syncretistic religions, each of which combines elements from a variety of others. They flourish today, as they have throughout history. For the sake of simplicity, we shall restrict our discussion to a small sample of groups. However, the findings of historians and anthropologists bear ample witness to the presence of similar "popular" religions throughout the world.

Many syncretistic religions have spun off from Catholicism. Santería, practiced throughout the United States and the Caribbean, and Candomblé, found in Brazil, have both African and Catholic roots. The black leaders of the ancestor religions of the Caribbean see no contradiction between their beliefs and Catholicism. Indeed, they maintain that the one is not possible without the other (Simpson, 1978). Women play important roles of leadership in Santería and Candomblé, outnumber men four to one in these religions, and are the principal dancers in the Shango and Big Drum sects. Similarly, the women of Haiti dominate the popular religions such as Vodun.

In North America, women are also prominent among the Quakers and other nonhierarchical dissenting sects. Women assume much more important places in both leadership and participation in dissenting and popular religions than in established ones, whether or not they see themselves as opponents to established authority. In the United States, women comprise 66% of the participants in the activities of black churches (Parker, 2011). In some denominations of the Sanctified Church, women are equal to men. In the Pentecostal Assemblies of the World, women may offer communion and perform marriages. Even in the denominations that prohibit the ordination of women, they exercise a powerful influence through women's departments. Women's economic contribution and roles in education and community work are essential to the survival of these churches, and women's expression of spirituality is likewise central to their theology.

Women and Religious Movements. Religion often becomes a vehicle for social change. In some cases this involves the formation of a new or the joining of an existing religious movement. Today, unlike in the past, such movements are not necessarily labeled "heretical" and might not risk their members' lives and freedom, but they are often called by pejorative terms, such as "cult," and feared by mainstream religious groups and secular people alike. Religious movements, whether conservative or not, tend to protest and challenge contemporary social conditions, critiquing family and society as well as established religious institutions (Palmer, 1994; Puttick, 1997; Anderson and Young, 2010).

Some such movements, known as "new religious movements," offer women the means to escape traditional family and community constraints and provide alternatives to these structures. In the West, new religious movements are often inspired by Eastern religions, while in the East, (but not always) they are sometimes inspired by Western ones. Others, more conservative or even reactionary in character, called "fundamentalist" or some other label by critics, seek to establish or re-establish traditional structures and roles, placing women in subordinate positions and confining them to the roles of homemaker, wife, and mother. Generally, these latter identify themselves with mainstream religions such as Christianity or Islam yet criticize them for their liberalism and acceptance of "modernism."

The Piety Movement. The women's mosque movement emerged in Egypt in response to the modernization and secularization of society. A group of middle-class, educated women have formed a revivalist movement that involves a return to Islamic traditions of piety. In what is known as the mosque movement, women learn that they cannot separate morality and piety from the ways in which they dress and comport themselves physically; simply believing and practicing Islam is not enough. Although religious instruction is very important, it is through the body and the ritual repetition of particular behaviors that women ultimately achieve piety. For example, weeping during prayer at once expresses the pious virtue of fear of God and at the same time produces that fear. In an echo of Judith Butler's observations about gender, women in the mosque movement believe that continual and exact repetition of physical acts creates emotional and spiritual engagement with faith, so that over time virtuous practice becomes unconscious and inevitable (Mahmood, 2005: 139). This phenomenon challenges Western ideas about what it means to be a woman with agency, especially the assumption that in order to actualize one's identity, women have to resist the physical and cultural restraints imposed by patriarchy.

Modesty is one of the virtues that Muslim women seek to cultivate, and veiling is the practice that not only expresses modesty but produces it. As anthropologist Saba Mahmood writes of participants in the mosque movement:

> While wearing the veil serves at first as a means to tutor oneself in the attribute of shyness, it is also simultaneously integral to the practice of shyness: one cannot simply discard the veil once a modest deportment has been acquired, because the veil itself is part of what defines that deportment. This is a crucial aspect of the disciplinary program pursued by the participants of the mosque movement, the significance of which is elided when the veil is understood solely in terms of its symbolic value as a marker of women's subordination or Islamic identity." (Mahmood, 2005: 158)

By advocating for piety in dress and comportment, Egyptian women seek to retain Islamic values throughout all sectors of their society (Mahmood, 2005).

Besides the women's religious movement in Egypt, Hindu women in India look to traditional Hindu religious values to mobilize political support for Hindu nationalist parties. These Hindu nationalist women have gained prestige for themselves by aligning with right-wing political groups, attracted to their nationalist Hindu ideology that rejects Western values and affirms the traditional roles of women in Hinduism (Basu, 1993; Bacchetta, 2004). As supporters of Hindu nationalism, such women have become very prominent, even though the beliefs of the group may relegate women to secondary status and bar them from public roles. While women exhibit diversity in their beliefs and practices, what is important to recognize is that women in new religious movements represent an expression of dissatisfaction with the status quo in society and an attempt to repair its ills through religion. Sadly, in the case of Hindu nationalist women, repairing the ills of their society often comes at the expense of the dignity and human rights of their Muslim sisters.

Varieties of "Fundamentalism" and Women's Human Rights. At the end of the twentieth century, the world witnessed a resurgence of political activism motivated by religious beliefs. Western discourse has tended to label such ideas and actions as "fundamentalism" and applied the term primarily to events, actors, and movements in the Global South, especially in the context of Islam and Middle Eastern countries. Western discourse has erroneously labeled Islam as fundamentalist and highlighted only the extreme forms found in Afghanistan, Saudi Arabia, and Iran. The tendency in the West has been to point out the Taliban refusal to let girls go to school or to work, the imposition of the burqa on Afghan females, and laws prohibiting women from driving in Saudi Arabia as evidence of the lack of human rights for women in Islamic countries and their second-class status in their societies. But the word "fundamentalism" was originally a term certain U.S. conservative Christian reformers applied to themselves (Hawley, 1994); it has now come to be applied to other religious movements. At the root of conservative or "fundamentalist" movements is found a disappointment with modernity and a fear that modernity with its emphasis on secularism has pushed religion to the sidelines of modern society (Armstrong, 2001). In the Global South, modernity, often imposed through the expansion of imperialism, colonialism, and globalization, often denigrated and undermined non-Western traditions and cultures. In the Global North, the rise of conservatism results from a fear of losing social, political, economic power, and control, therefore, being unable to influence social and economic forces (Boden, 2007). In response, conservative religious groups and individuals have challenged secularist ideals and practices such as the separation of church and state and the belief in the right of people to be free of state religion, ideas that have become embedded in modern democratic societies. Rather than being a relic of some historical past, "fundamentalism" represents the flipside of modernity (Armstrong, 2001). The conservatively religious reject some, if not all, aspects of feminist ideology and emphasize conventional roles for women. In the Global North, conservative religious groups oppose abortion and contraceptive rights for women, same-sex marriage, and female sexual autonomy (Wald and Calhoun-Brown, 2007). In the United States in the 1970s, Christian conservative groups spearheaded and eventually defeated the Equal Rights Amendment that would have enshrined equal rights for women in the U.S. Constitution (Young, 2008).

Transnationally, conservative organizations have joined forces with their conservative counterparts in the Global South to develop a transnational conservative counternetwork to undermine transnational feminist efforts to improve women's rights globally. In a number of United Nations conferences pertaining to women, population, and human rights, a transnational conservative network coordinated their efforts to weaken women's rights on issues involving sexuality, equality, and gender. This transnational conservative network was comprised of organizations such as the Organization of the Islamic Conference, the Catholic Family and Rights Institute, the National Right to Life Committee, along with the Vatican, and supported by conservative governments (Iran, Morocco, Nicaragua, Argentina, and Iran) (Chappell, 2006).

Fundamentalist or conservative values are not found only among the religious. Conservativism or fundamentalism exists among secularists. While secular societies often portray themselves as liberal, tolerant, and upholding the human rights of women and men, recently the rise of secular conservatism in Western societies has been accompanied by ideas, policies, and actions that can be considered illiberal, intolerant, and a violation of women's human rights. In 2004 the French Parliament passed a law prohibiting the wearing of headscarves to schools, a law primarily affecting Muslim girls. Recently, France's lower house of Parliament overwhelmingly approved a bill that would ban wearing the full Islamic veil in public (Fraser, 2010). Justice Minister Michele Alliot-Marie said it was a victory for democracy and added that, "[v]alues of freedom [are] against all the oppressions which try to humiliate individuals, equality between men and women, against those who push for inequality and justice." This was a significant vote as it identified the religious dress (burka and/or niquab) to be an outward sign of religious persecution against women. On the other hand, such bans deny women the right to make their own decisions about their lives, forces women to choose between their religious beliefs and whether they can work or go to school, and denies women their right to self-expression and religious freedom (Najmabadi, 2006; Sunderland, 2012). Scott opines that the headscarf ban gives the appearance of gender equality in France but masks and ignores the continued denial of formal equality to women in the areas of jobs, wage discrimination, and domestic violence (2007: 172).

Secular efforts to overturn the "oppression" of Muslim women were woven into the justifications for the overthrow of the Iraqi government and the Taliban in Afghanistan. Abu-Lughod explores the issue of the salvation rhetoric (saving Muslim women from their culture and religion) and how it is used to justify intervention, the war on terrorism, and the installation of regimes more sympathetic to the West, and asks whether "Muslim women really need saving" (Abu-Lughod, 2002). Secular regimes' efforts to use Islam as a hammer to engage in interventionist and imperialist practices has been questioned by Toor, who argues that often Western discourse on Islam essentializes Islamic societies (Toor, 2011; Akbar and Oza, 2013). Citing examples from Pakistan, Toor's research demonstrates the fluidity of Islamic practice and how the political and social elites ignore Islamic law when it is inconvenient or deploy it when it is useful for their social and political goals. Religion and culture are merely toolboxes used when they are convenient for societies and communities to uphold the moral, cultural, social, and political order (Toor, 2011).

The issue of human rights, specifically women's human rights, lies at the center of the debate about conservative religious movements (Howland, 1999; Boden, 2007). On the one hand, it seems obvious that certain international agreements concerning the rights of all people to a basic education, control over their bodies, and freedom to choose a mate or a job or a form of religious expression are violated by a denial of these rights to women. On the other hand, multiculturalist societies often advocate respect for religious diversity and tolerance of religious practices which differ from one's own, and especially from those of the majority, but they have not always supported female religious minorities' rights to self-expression. As Boden argues, the choice between "authentic religion or human rights" is a false one. Religion and human rights address our human desire for justice, and the task remains to determine how communities of women can learn from each other (Boden, 2007).

Women as Religious Leaders

Today, disparity continues in the practice of male-centered church leadership. In the Roman Catholic Church, priests, bishops, archbishops—and of course the Pope himself—are all males, and females are strictly prohibited in from receiving the sacrament of Holy Orders, which confirms the person into life of holy service. Women can become nuns or sisters, but the true power in the Catholic Church lies in the priesthood. Although the reasons for this are stated to date back to the Apostles, the 12 male followers of Jesus Christ, little factual information regarding the prohibition of women into the priesthood is offered. In 2006, Fr. Roy Bourgeois, a Maryknoll priest, participated in the ordination of a woman priest, Janice Sevre-Duszynska. The Vatican told Fr. Bourgeois to recant his support of women priests, and this ordination was never officially recognized. He later was informed that he would be excommunicated if he did not recant, which he did not do. The Vatican Congregation for the Doctrine of Faith issued a penalty of excommunication on May 29,

2008, stating that those who supported the ordination of women priests in the Roman Catholic Church, as well as the organization of Roman Catholic Womenpriests (which was the organization which these women formed), would be excommunicated. Fr. Roy Bourgeois still advocates for the rights of women, stating that he believes the dismissal of women priests is committing a sexist act, which is a sin (Bourgeois, 2011). Despite the Vatican's stance, Sevre-Duszynska is among 100 female priests and 11 female bishops to claim ordination from increasingly vocal priests and groups supporting the ordination of women. Recent research questions the continued stance of the Vatican. Some scholars of early Christian history believe that Mary Magdalene and other women may have been apostles and that Jesus had a wife. Karen L. King, an authority on women's roles in early Christian history, recently discovered a papyrus scrap suggesting that Jesus had a wife and a female apostle (Levitt, 2012).

The most highly organized religions welcome women clergy the least. Thus, in Catholicism, the clergy has been restricted to not only men, but celibate men, since the eleventh century. Eastern Christianity (the Greek and Russian Orthodox churches) allows women to marry priests but not to be ordained. In some of the larger, institutionalized Protestant churches a growing number of women have been ordained, including the Rev. Susan Andres (Presbyterian), Bishop Katharine Jefferts Schori (Episcopal), and Bishop Vashti McKenzie (African Methodist Episcopal) (Fiedler, 2010). In the twenty-first century, more women are breaking through the "stained glass ceiling," but they typically

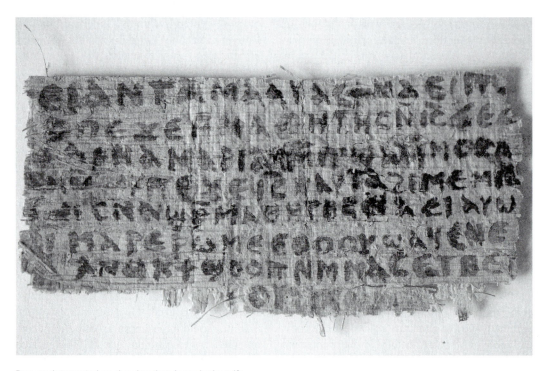

Papyrus interpreted as showing that Jesus had a wife.

are found in associate positions and earn less pay and benefits than male religious leaders.

Women tend to emerge as ministers in sects that do not control their clergy and that depend on genuine spontaneous religious emotion, as opposed to a weighty establishment supported by endowments and state cooperation. Thus, the loosely organized Pentecostal or evangelical sects are frequently ministered by women.

Since Jewish girls are not required by religious law to study the Scriptures and sacred texts as boys are, it has only been the exceptional Jewish woman who has qualified, in the past, for the specialized learning of the rabbi. However, Judaism, like Protestant Christianity, lacks a single central hierarchy, so it allows for a proliferation of congregations of varying opinions on matters of administration and discipline. In Conservative and Reform Judaism, the predominant forms in the United States, female rabbis are now ordained. Islam, like Judaism, has no formal clergy and no "church" hierarchy. Professional mullahs and ayatollahs in the Shiite branch along with other teachers and prayer leaders serve many of the functions of clergy, such as officiating at marriage and funeral rites and interpreting customary law. Women are not numbered among these revered individuals. The conventions of *purdah* (segregation of women) and veiling severely restrict Muslim women from participating in services and prayers with men, not to mention leading them. These same conventions have in some places given rise to a class of female mullahs whose job is to minister to women, to teach the rudiments of the Qur'an, and to conduct rituals with women at home. A few female adherents of Islam have led prayers to mix-sexed congregations in the United States, Canada, South Africa, and Great Britain, but such acts remain highly controversial and opposed by most Muslims both male and female (Fiedler, 2010).

In July 2010, the Church of England's ruling body, after recognizing women deacons and priests for several years, decided to allow women to be ordained as bishops, a decision accompanied by controversy (BBC News, 2010). Conservatives wanted to ensure that parishes unwilling to be served by a woman bishop could call upon the oversight of a male alternative, making clear how polarizing the issue of women and religious leadership can still be.

Healers

In folk traditions around the world, both in cities and in the countryside, women have served their communities as healers and midwives. These traditional arts are generally thought to have a supernatural or spiritual component as well as a practical one. Both illness and childbirth are widely viewed as spiritually dangerous states. Curers, sometimes termed "shamans," are active in societies where it is believed that illness—or certain types of illness—is caused by supernatural agency. Both curers and midwives are thought to have esoteric knowledge about how to fend off or appease threatening supernatural beings. Traditional curers of this sort need not be exclusively female but often are, and midwifery almost everywhere is a women's profession.

Among Native Americans, women healers perform cures, lead hunting ceremonies, and create artifacts, such as baskets, ornaments, and talismans. They officiate at burials, births, child namings, and menstrual and pregnancy rituals. The healers perform these rites through dancing and chanting as well as songs they sing and stories they tell. Native American women writers reflect in fiction and poetry the woman healer's connection to the spirit world (Allen, 1988). One such work is the novel *The Woman Who Owned the Shadows* by Paula Gunn Allen (1983), and another is *Ceremony* by Leslie Marmon Silko (1977).

Box 11.4   **"WITHOUT A HUSBAND I SHALL LIVE HAPPILY"**

According to folk tales dating to the early seventeenth century, the Nishan Shaman was a young widow who dutifully took care of her mother-in-law and her domestic duties. But she had a far-reaching reputation for her ability to communicate with the dead and bring them back to life. She had a lover who assisted her in her seances. On one ghostly journey, she met her deceased husband who begged her for resurrection. She refused, saying:

Without a husband
I shall live happily.
Without a man
  I shall live proudly.
  Among mother's relatives
I shall live enjoyably.
  Facing the years
  I shall live cheerfully.
Without children
  I shall live on.
Without a family
  I shall live lovingly.
Pursuing my own youth,
I shall live as a guest.

Source: From "The Nishan Shaman Caught in Cultural Contradictions" by Stephen Durrant, *Signs* 5 (1979): 345–6. Copyright © 1979, by The University of Chicago Press. Reprinted by permission of the University of Chicago Press.

Missionaries and Martyrs

The large-scale religions of the world reflect the institutionalized worlds of men. However, they started as popular religions, often as sects of rebels against a greater system, as the Christians within the Roman Empire or the Buddhists in India. All have known periods of danger and persecution; all have entered into periods of struggle to win recognition for themselves. During these times, women often played significant roles.

While the role of a missionary is dangerous and often results in death, women have found favorable conditions for the expression of their zeal and spirit of adventure. Women were welcomed into the original Buddhist fellowships for their missionary contributions but later restricted as the religion became established and more secure (Carmody, 1979). Likewise, women have enjoyed a long and honorable history in Christian missions. The Samaritan woman Jesus sent to spread news of his coming among her people might be called the first of all Christian missionaries (McNamara, 1996). In the conversion of Europe, Christian queens opened the way for priests and monks by marrying pagan kings and converting them; the most famous of these was Clotilda, wife of Clovis, king of the Franks at the beginning of the sixth century C.E. (McNamara, 1996). Modern Christian missionary women tend to fall under the control and supervision of men: Catholic nuns by supervisory priests and Protestant missionaries by husbands, male relatives, or male mission heads.

Mother Teresa, a Catholic nun and missionary, was a great leader. After experiencing a mystical vision she established a new religious society of nuns to care for the poor, sick, and dying young children. While she believed that this calling was chosen for her by God, she had to deal with many people doubting her sanity, but she continuously maintained a radiant and joyous persona. During her career, most of her mentors and confidants were men, including priests and bishops. Throughout her life she helped thousands of people in need and received the Nobel Peace Prize for her work in 1979, becoming the sixth woman to receive this award (Murray, 2008).

Religious Rebels

In the early centuries of Christianity, women were active in heretical movements such as Montanism and Gnosticism. Women's participation in these movements arose from social rather than intellectual motives. Women saw in early Christianity a vehicle for liberation, for activity on a broader scale than was offered by the traditional home-bound destiny. Some rebelled against versions of Christianity that imposed restrictions on women (McNamara, 1983).

In the major religious rebellions in Europe in the sixteenth century, Protestant churches freed themselves from the authority of the pope and his orthodox establishment. In the process, women again took an active part as defenders and preachers of both new and old religions. However, Catholics and Protestants alike were alarmed by the apparent assumption on the part of women that the new conditions would offer them a broader field of activity. Both acted to put an end to the threat. Catholic women like Angela Merici (1474–1540) and Mary Ward (1585–1645),

who championed a more active public role for nuns, were severely disciplined. Protestant women like Anne Askew (1521–1546) were executed for thinking that the priesthood of all believers urged by Luther and his contemporaries included women (Dickens, 1964).

The late medieval period in Europe had also been a time of great social upheaval. From the fifteenth century on, women were perceived to behave in a variety of eccentric and unconventional ways. An example from the early fifteenth century (c. 1412–31) was Joan of Arc, who led troops of French soldiers against the invading English armies. The English burned her at the stake as a heretic and witch; however, the French supported her memory as a martyr, and she was finally canonized by the Catholic Church (see Box 11.5).

Historians have recently been reinterpreting the great witch hunt in western Europe in light of the work of anthropologists on witchcraft in other cultures. The accused witches in eastern England, southwestern Germany, and Switzerland, for example, seem to have been the same sort of women accused in Africa and elsewhere outside Europe: old women, deprived of the protection of husbands or sons, living on the risky margins of society. These were the women who irritated and angered neighbors with efforts to gain assistance and ill-tempered cursing of the ungenerous.

During the medieval era, Europe, alongside the church, was a world of popular religion (Simpson, 1994). Wise women devoted to healing and prophesying flourished, not unlike the female curers found in Catholic countries in Latin America today. Medieval popular religion was full of vestiges of paganism, rituals, incantations, herbalism, and magic, both beneficial and malevolent. The medieval church systematically dealt with that religion in a successful manner. The harmless and beneficial practices of the country people were "Christianized;" for example, incantations to old goddesses were retained, with the

---

Box 11.5   THE TRIAL OF JOAN OF ARC

Joan of Arc, at the instigation of "voices" sent by God, took up arms against the English occupation of France in 1428. Her military victories against the English began the process of ultimate French victory in the Hundred Years' War (1337–1453). She was captured by the English and tried. Her prosecutors dwelt particularly on her insistence on wearing male clothing:

You have said that, by God's command, you have continually worn man's dress . . . that you have also worn your hair short, cut en rond [a "bowl" cut] above your ears, with nothing left that could show you to be a woman; and that on many occasions you received the Body of our Lord dressed in this fashion, although you have been frequently admonished to leave it off, which you have refused to do, saying that you would rather die than leave it off, save by God's command. And you said further that if you were still so dressed and with the king and those of his party, it would be one of the greatest blessings for the kingdom of France; and you have said that not for anything would you take an oath not to wear this dress or carry arms; and concerning all these matters you have said that you did well, and obediently to God's command.

Source: From W. S. Scott, editor and translator. *Trial of Joan of Arc*. London: Folio Society, 1968:156. © The Folio Society, 1956. Reprinted by permission of the Folio Society.

---

names of Christian saints substituted. The demons of hell were reduced to mischief makers of limited intelligence and minimal power.

Another set of theories associates witchcraft with heresy. In this view, the sixteenth-century belief in demon worshipers and witch churches with covens, sabbaths, "black masses," and other paraphernalia of witchcraft developed as a result of the mentality of the Catholic Inquisition and the fear of women that the Protestant Reformation awoke.

There may indeed have been witch cults. One or two such groups have been uncovered. The women may have been religious visionaries or sexual nonconformists, antisocial rebels of one sort or another. These witches may have been women who had seized upon the illusion of religious and moral freedom that the Reformation seemed to offer, only to learn that the leaders of the new churches were no more welcoming than had been those of the old.

Religious Expression

The Religious Experiences of Women

Contemporary feminists argue that established world religions reflect and enhance profoundly sexist values prevailing in the societies in which they are found. They have not only denied women a place in leadership but have promulgated ideas that devalue women in general (see Chapters 1 and 2). Why, then, are women in great numbers the world over devoted members of religions?

Women's personal experiences of religion suggest that they see and feel something beyond and apart from the negative messages that male clergy, ritual, and teaching convey. Women often make aspects of religion that are underplayed by the male hierarchy the essence of their own belief. For example, many Christian women have concentrated on Mary, on Christ as healer and nurturer, or on a loving, benevolent, even maternal God (Bynum,

1982). Many Roman Catholic women primarily focus their worship on the Virgin Mary or other female saints, and many feast days are devoted to them (Stuckey, 2010).

While the major religions have produced formal codes, the great masses of their adherents have developed their own versions of belief and practice. Catholic women are everywhere excluded from the clerical hierarchy of Catholicism, so they have developed their own folk practices. In belief and practice, rural Italian Catholic women may well resemble rural Mexican, Irish, or Peruvian Catholic women more closely than they do the urban Roman priest. Indeed, in some respects, rural Catholic women may have in common certain religious attitudes and interests with their rural Islamic and Hindu sisters that neither shares with the men who dominate their systems of codified knowledge. The popular versions of the religions of the world have often provided a scope for women's activities denied them by the male governing elite in the formalized versions of these religions. For the majority of religious women in the past, this standing appears to have been enough. For a few, as we shall see, it was not; and today numbers of women are demanding an equal place "at the top."

We have seen that women have made many dramatic and effective accommodations to the restraints placed on them by organized religion, even if their participation is viewed by men as marginal. Religion is simply one of the most universal and distinctive of human activities, and women are human in every way, subject to all the multiplicity of impulses, emotions, and inquiries that lead men to faith. In this sense, religion is necessary to many women for reasons of pure individual satisfaction. For Marta Morena Vega (2000), a Santería priestess, religious practice has enabled her to fulfill her mission in life. Some women, particularly in patriarchal monotheistic religions, seek individual fulfillment in a greater union with God by means of a life of prayer and meditation (Mahmood, 2005). These women seem to compensate for their exclusion from the religious hierarchy and their ignorance of elite languages and rituals by developing a more personal, idiosyncratic approach to religion (Gross, 1996).

One Yemenite Jewish woman said her mother never suffered from not learning Hebrew: "My mother says what she wants to God." Similarly, the Muslim saint Leila Mimouna, illiterate like most of her sisters, said "Mimouna knows God and God knows Mimouna" (Fernea and Bezirgan, 1977: 197). Barred from the study of theology even after Protestantism had made the Scriptures available in the languages of its adherents, women

The Penitent Magdalene (c. 1560) by Titian. The painting presents a picture of a beautiful woman, representing Mary Magdalene, depicted in the Christian Bible as a fallen woman redeemed by Jesus. Versions of the biblical story include her as a close companion and disciple of Jesus. She has remained a popular image for Roman Catholicism.

Box 11.6 A MOROCCAN STORY

One day two old ladies decided to invoke the Devil and persuade him to part with some of his magic secrets. So they pretended to quarrel, for it is well known that the devil appears whenever there is a dispute. "I am sure that the Devil must be dead," said one old woman. "And I am sure that he is not; what makes you say such a silly thing?" retorted the other, and they went on arguing furiously. The Devil was very flattered to be the subject of their argument and he decided to make himself visible. "Indeed, I am very much alive—here I am!" he said, appearing before the two old ladies. "How can we be sure that you are really the Devil?" asked one shrewdly. "You must prove it to us by doing something extraordinary. Let's see you squeeze yourself into a sugar bowl," added the other. "Easy!" said the Devil and he slipped into the bowl. As soon as he was inside the old ladies put the lid on and held it down firmly. "Let me out and I will do you a good turn," begged the Devil. "How can you do that, Father of Evil?" demanded the old women. "I shall teach you how to dominate men," he replied, and so he did. And that is why witches are feared everywhere to this day, especially by men.

Source: Epton, 1958, p. 44.

---

used vehicles such as the novel, poetry, or the popular hymn to make religious statements. Contemporary artists have imaginatively interpreted biblical texts, as in Judith Kates and Gail Twersky Reimer's collection of writings by many distinguished authors inspired by the biblical book of Ruth (1994).

Women and Possession

The popular religions of the poor, marginal, and alienated make their mystics the visionaries of ecstasy cults and the mediums of "possession" sects. Women believed to be possessed by spirits may be regarded as holy or unclean, depending on the circumstances. Possessed women may become healers or be thought of as diseased or infected by a spirit whose purpose is malicious, a spirit that is an enemy of the recognized deities of the group. Women who are thus possessed often have reason to complain of their circumstances in the first place. They are frequently the victims of an exogamous marital situation, vulnerable to hostile charges of witchcraft when misfortune strikes any member of the husband's kin, as well as vulnerable to repudiation, isolation, and lack of support.

Possession has been found, sometimes in mass outbreaks, among women in every area of the world. Possession tends to afflict alienated people who are responding to the strains of oppression or social stress of other kinds. It is an experience that is guaranteed to gain attention for a discontented woman, and it provides a vehicle for revenge against an oppressive husband, co-wife, mother-in-law, or, in the case of nuns, father confessor (Simpson, 1978).

Possession serves a variety of purposes for the possessed. First of all, it frees women from the guilt associated with rebellion and from responsibility for antisocial behavior. Women can say and do things that would never be permitted if they were in control of themselves. Where the religious structure is not too rigid or highly controlled, possession gives women access to real cultic power. Many possessed women are believed to gain sufficient control over spirits to have the ability to work healing magic, divination, or other powerful spells. Such women are particularly useful in curing similarly afflicted women. Throughout China, Taiwan, and Malaysia, female mediums belonging to the cult of Chen Jinggu perform rituals to ensure that female supplicants become pregnant and safely deliver their babies. In addition, Chen Jinggu's mediums protect children from harm and may even be called upon to rescue children inflicted by harmful spirits (Baptandier, 2008). For many women, possession, like mysticism, has proven to be the first stage of a liberating experience that culminated in a more active life of social service and reform (Simpson, 1978; Hoehler-Fatton, 1996).

The male establishment tends carefully to control possessed behavior. The mechanics of exorcism, for example, often involve much physical abuse of the possessed women (to guard against faking). The saint is never far from accusations of malicious witchcraft or heresy. Like Joan of Arc, saints will be allowed to obey "voices" only up to the point where established authorities are not discomfited. However, the dominating powers are generally willing to allow some latitude to these strong spirits to avert a more general social disruption. Thus, female cults, like some of the more expressive churches organized by black prophets in America, are often on the edge between the socially acceptable role of releasing strong emotions and the socially unacceptable role of revolution.

Women and Religion in the United States

The formal separation between church and state in the United States has not prevented special forms of dialogue between religious organizations and the government. Religious groups committed to major social reforms have spearheaded important political and legal changes; other religious groups, more conservative in orientation, have provided focal points for resistance and reaction. It has been largely through their participation in religious groups, rather than in government itself, that women have had a strong voice in political processes. In particular, feminism, with its call for women's rights and its role in other legislative reforms (most notably abolition of slavery and suffrage), has had a significant impact on the history of religion in America.

Leadership by Women

Protestant Denominations. Women emerged as religious leaders and reformers early in American history in the notoriously intolerant context of colonial New England. Anne Hutchinson, a Puritan woman from the Massachusetts Bay Colony, was banished for her refusal to stop preaching to mixed-sex groups. In 1638, she was driven out of Massachusetts with her husband and children and excommunicated from the Puritan community in Boston. She led her followers to Rhode Island, where she helped to establish a new colony and pursued her evangelical ministry. Her friend Mary Dyer, who supported her throughout her trials in Massachusetts, died on the gallows in 1660 for defending the Quakers who had begun to preach in the colony and for refusing to accept banishment (Dunn, 1979).

The Quakers, or Society of Friends, believed in the equality of all people, including the equality of women and men. They opposed settlement on lands claimed by Native Americans and particularly opposed the institution of slavery. Despite the hostility of the colonies to Quakerism, the movement spread. Nearly half the Quaker missionaries were women, mostly traveling without husbands and often with other women. They

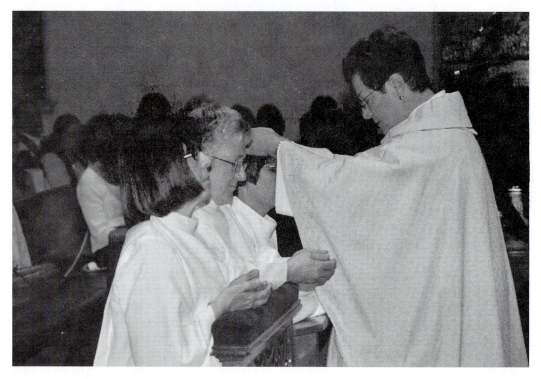

Bishop Andrea M. Johnson (right), Roman Catholic Womanpriest (RCWP-USA), ordained as a Roman Catholic bishop in 2009.

continued to travel and do missionary work through the seventeenth century. In these early years, while numbers of women's "meetings" (congregations) were established, there was some difference of opinion on how strong they should be or even how legitimate they were. Some women's meetings deferred to men; others were quite assertive of their autonomy and conducted their own affairs (Dunn, 1979).

Quaker women's experience in the organization of religious meetings provided training in the public arena that few women of colonial or postcolonial times had an opportunity to gain. The "Friends" became accustomed to public speaking, to creating organizational structures and to feeling equal to others. Quakers were disproportionately represented among American women abolitionists, feminists, and suffragists (Dunn, 1979). Sarah Grimké (1792–1873), Angelina Grimké Weld (1805–1879), and Lucretia Coffin Mott 1793–1880) are among the most famous of these women in the nineteenth century.

Although Lucretia Mott grew up as a Quaker, she held her own convictions on social reforms, not limited by the views of more traditional Quakers. For example, she was a radical abolitionist, whereas many Quakers preferred gradual emancipation. Delivering sermons at the Quaker Meeting House, Mott preached to male-dominated audiences, asking them them to question organized religion and to defy social norms and religious traditions. Mott fought for sexual and racial equality, peace, temperance, prison reform, religious freedom, and Native American rights. She considered herself a religious radical, supporting liberal religions, particularly those in favor of female involvement. Mott's reformist views particularly influenced and shaped the abolitionist and feminist movements in America. She began to form her views when she attended the World Anti-Slavery Convention in London in 1840 together with Elizabeth Cady Stanton (Buhle and Buhle, 1978). When Mott and Stanton returned to America, they brought a firm objective: to continue to work for both the abolition of African American slavery and an end to women's inferior property and family rights. Eight years later, under their leadership, the Women's Rights Convention took place in July 1848 at Seneca Falls, New York. The convention is considered the official beginning of the women's rights movement in the United States (Seneca Falls is now the site of a national museum). Mott understood women's rights as a part of the universal principles of liberty and equality (Faulkner, 2011).

Christian Science, a late nineteenth-century sectarian religion, also supported women's rights. Its founder, Mary Baker Eddy (1821–1910), believed and preached that God is both masculine and feminine. She frequently referred to God in her writings as "Father–Mother God." Christian Science has a very successful and extensive establishment today, including its widely read newspaper the *Christian Science Monitor*, published in Boston, and free reading rooms in towns and cities throughout the world.

Seventh-Day Adventism, an evangelical religion, was guided by Ellen Harmon White (1827–1915) from its beginning in Battle Creek, Michigan, in 1860 (Zikmund, 1979). She emphasized temperance, education, and health, particularly in diet. Her hegemony over Adventism lasted 50 years and was responsible for much of its influence and growth.

Many other U.S. women, black and white, rose to prominence and leadership in evangelical and revivalist movements in the nineteenth and twentieth centuries (Gilkes, 1985; Blackwell, 2001). Today, Holiness denominations are still working to keep women in clerical positions, drawing motivation from the strong presence of women in positions of leadership in their history (Teegarden, 2011). Like Quakerism, the evangelical and revivalist movements have been a training ground for women activists, providing them with unique opportunities for public speaking and group organizing. Religious activity was practically the only important extrafamilial activity permitted to most women in the nineteenth and much of the twentieth centuries. Today there are societal forces that continue to encourage women to keep their main focus on religion, but women have been accepted as teachers in evangelical schools even in some more orthodox communities. Nevertheless, controversy and resistance still exist when a woman is thought to speak or teach with a certain amount of "authority" (Creegan and Pohl, 2005).

Religious organizing has been pivotal to African American women, who played a key role in creating and fostering the development of churches, missionary societies, national organizations, and women's conventions. These religious endeavors also provided a platform for black women to participate in social and political activism. Such involvement not only taught women effective ways of organizing but also led to a growing national black feminist awareness. Organizations like the National Association of Colored Women, the National League of Colored Republican Women, and the National Council of Negro Women tackled critical issues of the times, ranging from discrimination, to segregation, lynching, suffrage, colonialism, and imperialism (Collier-Thomas, 2010).

Box 11.7   PHILLIS WHEATLEY: THOUGHTS ON THE WORKS OF PROVIDENCE

Arise, my soul, on wings enraptur'd, rise
To praise the monarch of the earth and skies...
Creation smiles in various beauty gay,
While day to night, and night succeeds to day:
That *Wisdom*, which attends *Jehovah's* ways,
Shines most conspicuous in the solar rays:
Without them, destitute of heat and light,
This world would be the reign of endless night:
In their excess how would our race complain,
Abhorring life! how hate its length'ned chain!
From air adust what num'rous ills would rise?
What dire contagion taint the burning skies?
What pestilential vapours, fraught with death,
Would rise, and overspread the lands beneath?
Hail, smiling morn, that from the orient main
Ascending dost adorn the heav'nly plain!
So rich, so various are thy beauteous dies,
That spread through all the circuit of the skies,
That, full of thee, my soul in rapture soars,
And thy great God, the cause of all adores....
Infinite *Love* where'er we turn our eyes
Appears: this ev'ry creature's wants supplies;
This most is heard in *Nature's* constant voice,
This makes the morn, and this the eve rejoice;
This bids the fost'ring rains and dews descend
To nourish all, to serve one gen'ral end,
The good of man: yet man ungrateful pays
But little homage, and but little praise.
To him, whose works array'd with mercy shine.
What songs should rise, how constant, how divine!

Source: From John C. Shields, editor, *The Collected Works of Phillis Wheatley*, pp. 43–50. The Schomburg Library of Nineteenth-Century Black Women Writers, Henry Louis Gates, Jr., editor. New York: Oxford University Press, 1988.

Jewish Denominations. American Jewish women contribute to religious life as professionals and through domestic activities. The heart of Judaism since the diaspora (exile from the Holy Land) has been the ritual of hearth and home. Of major importance to Jewish self-definition is kashrut, or purity, particularly of diet. It is the responsibility of religious Jewish women to keep kitchens *kosher*, to see that meat and milk are not mixed and that the family consumes no "unclean" foods such as pork or shellfish or improperly butchered meats. Women prepare the festive foods for holidays and most particularly

Box 11.8 GWENDOLYN BROOKS: THE PREACHER RUMINATES BEHIND THE SERMON

I think it must be lonely to be God.
Nobody loves a master. No. Despite
The bright hosannas, bright dear-Lords, and bright
Determined reverence of Sunday eyes.

Picture Jehovah striding through the hall
Of His importance, creatures running out
From servant-corners to acclaim, to shout
Appreciation of His merit's glare.

But who walks with Him?—dares to take His arm,
To slap Him on the shoulder, tweak His ear,
Buy Him a Coca-Cola or a beer,
Pooh-pooh His politics, call Him a fool?

Perhaps—who knows?—He tires of looking down.
Those eyes are never lifted. Never straight.
Perhaps sometimes He tires of being great
In solitude. Without a hand to hold.

Source: From Gwendolyn Brooks, *Selected Poems*. New York: Harper & Row, 1963. Reprinted By Consent of Brooks Permissions.

for the celebration each week of the Sabbath. The conduct of traditional Jewish life is completely dependent on women's perpetuation of religious traditions in the home.

In 1988, Conservative Judaism moved women to the focal point by declaring that the home was the center of Jewish religious life. Various Jewish women's groups, particularly charity organizations, provide an arena for major public activities. Prominent among these is Hadassah, founded in 1912 under the leadership of an American woman, Henrietta Szold (1860–1945). In 1893, Hannah Greenbaum Solomon (1858–1942) initiated the National Council of Jewish Women, dedicated to education, social reform, and issues concerning women. These organizations and others like them provide vehicles for women to learn how to organize, how to manage money, and how to raise funds; they raise and distribute millions of dollars in the causes they espouse.

Some women have turned to Kabbalah, a mystical offshoot of Rabbinic Judaism, to find a woman-centered approach to spirituality. Traditional kabbalistic beliefs posit that God has both male and female aspects and that the female divine element, the *shekhina*, plays a crucial role. Perle Besserman, a scholar of Jewish mysticism, has written and taught about a feminine God for twenty-first-century women. While the prevalent understanding of God is synonymous with "male" and "power," the Torah includes descriptions of God as a mother caring for *his* children, and Isaiah describes God as a "midwife," "nurse,"

The Reverend Ellen Barrett, the first declared lesbian to be ordained an Episcopal priest, January 10, 1977.

and "protective mother eagle." Besserman has been a leader in emphasizing this Jewish feminist notion of God, which centers on women's power to create a strong sense of self, to destroy feelings of inferiority, and to transform the self. This women's approach to Kabbalah attempts to address the conflicts of contemporary Jewish women through a more balanced spiritual practice (Besserman, 2005).

Catholicism. Catholic women, in contrast to Jewish women, have had the option of following a "vocation" in religion by becoming nuns. As nuns, American women have played a number of influential roles in American life, particularly in education and nursing. Today, nuns may be women in street clothes who may or may not wear symbolic head coverings and crosses. They are no longer found only in the shadows of a cloister but also in public places. Since medieval times, nuns have held

professional responsibilities in education and attending the sick and elderly, but today they are also found in executive positions, managing self-supporting philanthropic or educational institutions and projects.

The decision to join a convent and become a nun may be prompted by expectations for the future that have nothing to do with religion. For a poor Catholic girl, convent life has long meant moving to another class with privileges that she may not have if she remained in secular life. She might be seeking an orderly and secure life where education is offered, friendship of sisters is promised, and marriage and children are prohibited. Organized religions do offer spiritual security and, above all, ethical and moral codes that are time-tested. Catholic women have choices to make and require the freedom to follow their sincere beliefs.

Collectively, nuns in the United States have challenged the male hierarchical model of leadership within the Catholic Church. The Leadership Conference of Women Religious, an organization comprising more than three fourths of all U.S. Catholic nuns, has called on the Church to engage in dialogue on issues such as artificial birth control and the ordination of females. Their desire to make Catholicism more inclusive of secular and religious women has placed them in conflict with the Church. In response to their request for dialogue on these matters, the Vatican has accused the nuns of taking positions different from those of the Church and has decided to take over and reorganize the nuns' organization (Birnbaum, 2012). In response to the Vatican critique of American nuns as being too outspoken on social justice issues and insufficiently supportive of the church's teachings on abortion and same-sex marriage, Network, a Catholic social justice lobby group, organized the "Nuns on the Bus" tour in the summer of 2012, traveling from Iowa to Virginia mobilizing support for the efforts of Catholic nuns to take care of the poor and to highlight their concerns about the government's declining support of the safety net for poor Americans.

In following Christian beliefs, Native American women often find themselves in conflict: some of their ancestral traditions are at opposite ends of the monotheistic/patriarchal scriptures of Judeo-Christianity. The Native American (Laguna Pueblo) scholar Paula Gunn Allen (1939–2008) asserted that "[t]raditional tribal lifestyles are more often gynocratic than not, and they are never patriarchal" (Allen, 1988: 2). One can begin to judge the basic conflicts that arose when Native Americans were gradually converted to Christianity by missionaries and conquerors. The work of Mary TallMountain (1918–1994, Athabascan) demonstrates the "difficult and uneasy alliance between the pagan awareness that characterized tribal thought and the less earthy, more judgmental view of medieval Christianity" (Allen, 1988: 172). TallMountain was a devout Roman Catholic, and her poetry reveals the conflict between her faith and her tribal awareness (TallMountain, 1981).

Feminist Contributions to Religious Change

Religious change comes from many different sources and in many different forms. The spokeswomen for the numerous sectarian branches of religion in the United States mentioned here all sought changes in established practice and belief. Elizabeth Cady Stanton, one of the presidents of the National Woman Suffrage Association and cofounder in 1868 with Susan B. Anthony of the radical magazine *The Revolution*, went further than most of her colleagues and even today's feminists in confronting the sexist language of the Scriptures. Maintaining that the Bible contributed to the low self-image of women, she attempted twice to organize a group to write commentaries on passages from the Old and New Testaments dealing with women. Eventually, between 1895 and 1898, she succeeded in publishing *The Woman's Bible*, parts I and II, and an appendix (see Stanton, [1895–98] 1972).

This work is the result of Stanton's belief that the language and interpretations of

---

Box 11.9   FEMINIST GODDESS WORSHIP TODAY

What often began as more "secular" consciousness-raising groups turned into ritual circles creating a spiritual practice unique to each group. The rites conducted within these ritual circles are usually focused on the everyday experiences of women. Often, reproductive activities are highlighted: celebrations of menarche, menstruation, birthing and menopause. But other events such as divorce, abortion, and recovery from rape are ritually recognized often through rites of healing and renewal…Small, non-hierarchical groups are the ideal of these ritual circles so that all women can be intimately involved in the ritual procedure (as opposed to the model of priest and congregation). The non-hierarchical model also allows each woman to form her own belief system rather than be told what to believe; in Feminist Goddess Worship, every woman is her own priestess.

Source: From Chris Klassen, *Storied Selves: Shaping Identity in Feminist Witchcraft.* Lanham: Lexington Books, 2008, pp. 17–18.

passages dealing with women in the Bible were a major source of women's inferior status because women turned to the Bible so much for comfort and inspiration. She maintained that the language of the Scriptures had to be rendered in such a way that it would not center only on man, celebrate man as the superior creation, or allow man to dominate woman. Certain passages in the Bible, Stanton believed, could be interpreted to conform to women's experiences as humans as well as men's experiences.

Stanton's attempts were not well received by the majority of suffragists, and the National American Woman Suffrage Association disclaimed any official connection with *The Woman's Bible* in 1895. The organization feared a backlash from society at large on purely religious issues, a reaction that could have halted the political and social changes being sought.

Rabbi Sally Priesand, the first woman to be ordained a rabbi, June 2, 1972.

The decision was based on the view that it was possible to separate political and secular issues from religious ones. Stanton, on the other hand, saw the traditions of religious belief as an important cause of women's subordination. Nowadays, some biblical historians criticize Stanton for expressing anti-Jewish views in *The Woman's Bible*. They urge caution about belief in unsubstantiated theories concerning the history of the Israelites that result in blaming Judaism for the existence of patriarchy (Plaskow, 1979; Bird, 1989).

In addition to changing the language of devotion, feminists in the United States developed new versions of traditional rituals. They have taken out the sexist bases of general rituals and added new rituals for women to complement those specifically intended for men. For example, some Jewish women have written a complement to the boy's *brit milah* to bring their daughters into the covenant (Plaskow, 1979). Aviva Cantor (1979) composed a woman's *Haggadah*, a version of the Jewish Passover text that traditionally celebrates freedom from slavery and oppression, while others have developed Sabbath prayers for women (Janowitz and Wenig, 1979).

Feminist theologians and philosophers address the deeper issues of belief and practice in all the world religions, including Buddhism (Gross, 1999; Peach, 2002), Confucianism (Woo, 1999; Heisook, 2009), and Islam (Hassan, 1999; Helie-Lucas, 1999; Badawi, 2003), as well as Judaism and Christianity. For some religious feminists, the old traditions are insufficient, even when revised. Some second-wave feminists continue to dismiss spirituality as irrevocably flawed in its patriarchal ideology. There are feminist sects within Judaism, Christianity, and Islam trying to bring about change, although this pursuit is often met with contention and hostility. Some feminists have chosen to blaze their own trail, cultivating a history and practices of feminist goddess worship (Stuckey, 2010).

Others, while looking for spiritual growth and healing, and finding the established religions outmoded and meaningless, look to mysticism, paganism, and other sources to create new religions. They believe that "the margin may also be the leading edge, whose experiments create the future" (Puttick, 1997: 2). They may, in fact, have had an impact in some areas, most discernibly in the incorporation of respect for the environment into religious doctrines as well as the promotion of alternative medicine and health approaches.

Summary

Religion and society affect each other. As societies become more complex and hierarchical, so do their religious institutions. In societies that deny leadership roles to women, religious institutions do so too. Religious beliefs about what is "good behavior" influence societies.

Despite their devalued status in religion, women have been active participants in religions throughout history. Many women focus on certain aspects of religion (such as the healing Christ or the Virgin Mary) that appeal to their concerns and evolve from their beliefs and practices. "Popular" versions of traditional religions often provide scope for women's activities.

Some ancient religions included goddess worship and gave priestesses status. The origin myths of many of the major religions support the dominant religious and social roles of men. Most religions have conceptions of supernatural beings, and females are featured among them. These beings may be souls, saints, ghosts, and goddesses. The goddess is often envisaged as a threatening being who is tamed and controlled by being linked to a male god. As monotheism entered religious belief, the goddesses of ancient religions were dropped in favor of a single male God. Some feminists believe that worship of a female God would enhance women's social position.

Religious codes govern human conduct and exert social controls. Life-cycle rituals for men enhance their power and status in the community, but the wedding ceremony, the most important ritual for women in patrilineal societies, serves only to shift control over women from father to husband.

Religious leaders in many societies attempt to control female sexuality by urging women to stay within the home and to be modest and decorous. Many religious laws require women and men to be separate during the menstrual period. Religious codes also protect women and promote family life and procreation.

In public worship, women are subject to a number of controls. They are frequently prohibited from lay participation in rituals and sometimes segregated from men. Even so, it is women who spend the most hours of devotion in organized religion.

The most highly organized religions are the least welcoming to women as clergy. Many women find that they can play far more active roles in the religions that are on the fringes of or in conflict with "established" religion. Often, women emerge as preachers or leaders of these sects.

Women excel at ritual and spiritual services connected with nurturance and healing. That is why so many women are numbered among the healers of societies. Women have also served the various religions as missionaries and martyrs.

Women have also been active as rebels in religious movements, probably because they have often seen rebellion as the only means of winning more liberation for themselves. During the Reformation, women heretics were frequently accused of being witches. Some women have found fulfillment in religions through an idiosyncratic approach. Mysticism and possession by spirits are both highly personal expressions of religion.

Women, especially Quakers, were among the early religious leaders and reformers in U.S. history. In the nineteenth century, women had important parts to play in the founding and organization of the Shakers, Christian Scientists, Seventh-Day Adventists, and a number of evangelical movements. Jewish women have been responsible for maintaining religious traditions in the home and are active in the public arena by means of various Jewish women's groups. American nuns have played influential roles in education and nursing in the United States.

Feminists have contributed to religious change. Elizabeth Cady Stanton wrote a commentary on the Bible, *The Woman's Bible*, while feminists today are developing new versions of traditional rituals and adding new rituals for women.

Discussion Questions

1. Nearly everyone receives some religious education—in the home, in school, in church or other formal religious institution, in the community at large—on both a conscious and an unconscious level. If this includes you, what do you think you learned about relations between women and men from this background? What were the sources of what you learned (the Bible, ritual, prayer, your parents)?
2. Religious movements challenge the status quo, looking to the past as well as the future. Select one—fundamentalist, evangelist, or a new movement—and examine how the roles assigned to women relate to its vision of the world.
3. What have been the arguments concerning the gender of God? Do you have an opinion? If so, what is your view and why?
4. When you read the two poems in Boxes 11.7 and 11.8, what seems to you to be the different conceptions of God described by Wheatley and Brooks? Do you have a

personal conception of God? If so, how would you describe it?

Recommended Readings

Boden, Alison L. *Women's Rights and Religious Practice: Claims in Conflict.* Basingstoke: Palgrave Macmillan, 2007. The author discusses the conflict between human's rights and religious practices and how they can be reconciled to ensure the human rights of women.

Fiedler, Maureen E., editor. *Breaking Through the Stained Glass Ceiling: Women Religious Leaders in Their Own Words.* New York: Seabury Books, 2010. The author interviews a variety of female religious leaders, theological scholars, religious feminist activists, spiritualists, and religious women in the social justice, peace, and ecology movements. The women interviewed represent the major religious and spiritual faiths: Islam, Christianity, Judaism, Hinduism, Buddhism, Bahaism, Native American, Wiccan/Goddess, and Womanist.

Franzmann, Majella. *Women and Religion.* New York: Oxford University Press, 2000. Provides case examples of women's experiences in each of the five major world religions. Major themes and issues are explored within the cultures and traditions of these religions.

Stuckey, Johanna H. *Women's Spirituality: Contemporary Feminist Approaches to Judaism, Christianity, Islam and Goddess Worship.* Toronto, Canada: Inanna Publications and Education Inc., 2010. Examines the religious traditions around the world and sheds light on the role of women's spirituality within these religions. It also speaks to the history and experiences of the marginalization of women in the context of mainstream religion and feminists' role in overcoming these forces.

chapter **12**

Women and Work

Human societies generally organize the work needed for survival by dividing tasks among their members. Individual work assignments are decided in a variety of ways. Strength and skill are obvious and basic determinants. Status and value also influence work patterns, and some tasks are thought to merit higher rewards than others. All known societies have used gender as a criterion for work assignments; these are largely arbitrary, however, because the content of roles varies from culture to culture and time to time. Yet a gendered division of labor exists.

Gender affects who is assigned which tasks, but class and race/ethnicity further intervene so that women of color and poor women are usually found in the most undervalued work. These class, caste, and racial/ethnic divisions among women are reinforced by *globalization*, an economic, social, political, and cultural process in which industries operate on a worldwide scale to take advantage of cheap labor costs to enhance their profits.Many societies judge the value of work in terms of economic rewards. "Do you work?" means, for many people, "Do you earn money?" That is why the idea that a homemaker does not "work" is so common. Although housekeeping services can be bought and sold, when this labor is performed for "free" it is not considered "work" (see Chapter 7). Many feminists have challenged the basic assumptions that most people hold about the nature and definition of "work" itself.Unpaid labor often contributes enormously to the goods and services that keep a society well and functioning. Masking the economic value of women's unpaid labor serves the interests of those who have property and power. Statistics indicate that women complete more than two thirds of the world's unpaid work, and this labor is estimated to be worth 50% of the world GDP, or almost $11 trillion (United Nations Development Fund for Women, 2007). Failing to acknowledge the value of such work in economic terms distorts an accurate assessment of a country's gross national product and keeps in place a system that undervalues both the producers of this labor, women, and their work.

Many theories hold that relationships between people are fundamentally based on economic power. The economic inequality between women and men has contributed to a widely held stereotype of women as dependent. A vicious cycle develops in which women's dependence is cited as the reason for their economic inequality. Hence, social inequalities between women and men are often the result of economic inequalities. This chapter examines some of these ideas in order to understand women's roles in reproduction and production and the impact of economic change on women's roles within and outside the family. It considers various types of work that women perform and the obstacles they face as workers. Finally, the chapter examines the roles played by support groups, government, and the women's movement in influencing women's opportunities for paid work.

The Labor of Women

Division of Labor by Gender

Every known society has had some sort of division of labor by gender, but the work done by women and men has varied by geographical region, by historical era, and from society to society. While clerical work is typical for women in developed Western countries and in many developing countries in the Asia/Pacific region, employed women in the Middle East/North Africa are found predominantly in the professional/technical occupations. Women in other developing countries are concentrated in agriculture or the service sector (Ernst and Kapos, 2012). The Asia/Pacific region has the lowest concentration of occupational sex segregation; the Middle East/North Africa region has the highest level. Table 12.1 indicates the extent to which occupational sex segregation (defined as an occupation in which one gender accounts for 80% of the workforce) is an enduring feature within societies. In the past three decades there have been changes in the gender division of labor. Women have entered some occupations previously held by men—architects/engineers, legislative and government officials, managers, and buyers—as Table 12.1 illustrates. However, the other four predominantly male occupations—protective services such as policemen and firefighters; production supervisors and foremen; blacksmiths and toolmakers; and bricklayers, carpenters, and construction workers—remain strongly male-identified. Women who have entered traditionally male occupations find that advancement is very difficult, and they typically remain at the lowest levels. Men, on the other hand, have always found work in "female" occupations, such as nursing or social work, and they continue to do so. Once employed in a typically female occupation, men also move quickly into higher-level administrative or supervisory positions in these occupations (Kimmel, 2000).

The division of labor by gender has often been related to the differences in the reproductive roles assigned to women and men. Since women necessarily bear, and until recent times have necessarily nursed, infants, they have always been assigned the additional social role of child care, even though this assignment is not necessitated by either function. Yet the physical burdens women bear while pregnant and nursing are often assumed to place some limitation on their ability to participate fully in the productive economy (see Chapter 7). An examination of women's roles in a variety of preindustrial and developing societies, however, shows that they do

TABLE 12.1 The Eight Most Typical Occupations for Women and Men Globally and the Percentage of the Dominant Sex in the Occupation

Eight Typical Female Occupations	%	Eight Typical Male Occupations	%
Maids, housekeepers, domestics	85	Protective services	96
Typists	85	Bricklayers, carpenters, construction	95
Nurses	82	Production supervisors, foremen	95
Tailors, dressmakers	64	Blacksmiths, toolmakers	95
Hairdressers, beauticians	60	Managers	86
Cashiers, bookkeepers	52	Legislators, government officials	84
Teachers	50	Sales supervisors, buyers	83
Salespersons, shop assistants	50	Architects, engineers	79

Source: Richard Anker, *Gender and Jobs: Sex Segregation of Occupations in the World*, p. 265. Geneva: ILO, 1998. Copyright © 1998 International Labour Organization.

Box 12.1   THE LIVES OF FEMALE SILK WORKERS IN CHINA

Pei's days at the silk factory were very long. The girls arrived every morning at five thirty. When the horn wailed its low cry for them to stop working at seven thirty each evening, they left the factory wilted and drained from the wet heat. Most of the time they were given half an hour for lunch and ten minutes off for every three hours they worked. Sometimes, if they were behind their quota, these breaks never came. The male managers hired by the owner, Chung, waved their sticks and shouted, "Keep working!" The girls reluctantly obeyed.

Many of the girls argued and complained bitterly among themselves. "We are here before the sun rises," said one girl.

…"Let's see how they feel standing all day in this heat!" another voice said.

…Pei slowly began to feel comfortable working in the silk factory and living at the girls' house. Everything was new and exciting. She saw and felt things she had never dreamed of. Every other month, Lin took Pei to the theater, where a traveling troupe of actors would…portray both the men and women in an opera…Pei sat…completely still, captivated by the splendor of light and music.

Source: Gail Tsukiyama, *Women of the Silk*. New York: St. Martin's Press, 1991. © 1991 by Gail Tsukiyama. Reprinted by permission of St. Martin's Press, LLC. All rights reserved.

---

engage in fairly strenuous economic activities even while pregnant and nursing.

The labor involved in reproduction itself is essential for any society. With the exception of those employed to care for the young, most women receive no economic compensation for mothering, even though societies could not exist without the work involved. Using the Department of Labor's figures for the hourly wages paid for certain types of work, Table 12.2 estimates what women in the United States would earn if they were paid for their unpaid labor.

Maintenance of the Domestic Unit

To the extent that women are involved in child care—and this extent varies historically and cross-culturally—the other work they do must be carried out at the same time. "Housework," such as cooking and cleaning, generally falls into this category. As with

reproduction, this work serves an important function: it "services" the male worker so that he can return, fed and refreshed, to the workplace the next day. However, the housewife is not compensated for this work either.

In most parts of the world for most of human history, virtually all women's productive labor was domestic, performed without compensation for the benefit of family members. Under these conditions, the labor done by women and men, although often differentiated, was viewed as making equivalent contributions. *Social labor*, labor done for the good of the larger community beyond the family, did have value, earning esteem for the laborer beyond family rewards. As the social labor sector grew with increasing urbanization and capitalism, it became a larger component of the whole economy. With this change, women began to lose ground. That women's domestic work was essential to the total economy but deemed lacking

Indian women carrying water.

TABLE 12.2 What Women in the United States Would Earn if They Were Paid for Their Unpaid Labor

Role	Number of Hours per Week	Hourly Rate ($)	Dollar Amount ($)
Food preparer	18	10.05	180
Cleaner	6	9.45	57
Washer	3	9.02	27
Ironer	3	9.45	28
Chauffeur	10	12.57	125
Social secretary	18	15.40	277
Psychologist	10	150.00	1,500
Child-care worker	51	9.90	504
Health-care worker	1	11.65	11
Repairer	2	18.00	36
Total			$2,745

Source: Calculations are based on data found in U.S. Department of Labor, Bureau of Labor Statistics, 2009.

in economic or social value also diminished women's opportunities to participate in valued social labor outside the home (Dalla Costa and James, 1975).

Feminists have challenged such traditional conceptions of the separate "private" and "domestic" spheres of life as misleading and damaging to women. Women combine many sorts of work with child care. Work such as weaving and making pottery and running businesses, such as beauty parlors and family grocery stores, can be carried out in or near the home. Alternatively, societies may take responsibility for making child-care facilities available so that both parents can work at other jobs.

Women's Work in the Marketplace

Despite women's assigned responsibilities in the domestic sphere, many have managed to sell some of their labor, and larger numbers are continuing to do so. Women find more restrictions in their job choices than men, men rarely take the jobs largely filled by women, and women's jobs are stereotyped in the workplace just as they are in the home. An activity that is highly regarded in one society when done by men may be considered unimportant in another society when done by women. A more insidious pattern of integrating women into the labor market is illustrated by an early twentieth-century example. This pattern encouraged women's entry into bookkeeping, which had been formerly occupied by men. Compensation was then lowered and office management, the traditional authority associated with the position, was eliminated. A new office position, accountant, was established, with higher prestige and pay, and became a male-identified occupation (Machung, 1988). When work is divided along gender lines, it is not the work itself that determines its value but the gender of the person doing it.

The Contribution of Women to Economic Development

As long as women are expected to be the primary caretakers of their children, they will be forced to choose between child care, wage labor, or, as a compromise, part-time work. In Western societies, part-time work as a solution to problems associated with the lack of day care penalizes the female wage earner. Employers typically pay part-time workers lower hourly wages and provide few, if any, benefits compared to full-time workers in the same job. For those who must work for wages or who choose to do so, the problems of arranging for adequate child care may be severe, especially if fathers continue to maintain that these are the mothers' problems. Even in dual-career households, women, whether employed full-time or part-time, often have a "second shift": they assume the major share of household and child responsibilities after a "work day." This inequality strains marital relations and women's health and life satisfaction (Hochschild and Machung, 2003).

Many strides have been made in fathers' participation in domestic responsibilities. Previously when women joined the work force this was seen as a strain on marriage or as a contributor to divorce. Today this is not the case, and well-educated working women are no longer more likely to go through a divorce—in many cases, they are less likely. In fact, men now find educated women, and career women, more attractive as marriage partners. Educated couples, with egalitarian gender views, report the highest rates of marital satisfaction. Men now contribute more to housework than ever before, and divorce rates are on the decline (Coontz, 2009).

However, there are still barriers to overcome and mindsets that continue to contribute to inequality. One has been termed the "masculine mystique." This is the belief of some men that women's work commitments and earning successes are threatening and the consequent resistance to sharing in household chores by men. Another, the "career mystique," is the belief that a successful career requires all of one's time and energy and that child care and household tasks should be delegated to others. Such an extreme stance in the direction of career responsibilities does not acknowledge the possibility of the creative integration of work and family responsibilities by both partners (Coontz, 2009).

In contemporary developing countries, models of economic growth and change have tended to follow patterns set by Western industrialism. Where women were once heavily involved in small-scale agriculture based on intensive labor and simple technology, there is now a tendency to consolidate land holdings, to use industrial machinery, and to emphasize production for the market rather than for the home. It has consistently been men who have been taught to use the new machinery (such as tractors) and given the means to acquire it. As a result of being excluded from modernized agricultural production, women in developing countries have lost their influence over the deployment of resources, even within the home.

When men lose their jobs through the shift from labor-intensive to capital-intensive production, they are viewed as unemployed. Because what women do outside the home has been considered by societies to be economically negligible, women similarly "unemployed" often are not considered an economic casualty; since women's uncompensated work is not figured into the GDP, their lack of employment outside the home is not factored into unemployment numbers. Feminists question this standard interpretation of economic "development" and women's invisibility in it (Boserup, 1970; Acosta-Belén and Bose, 1990).

The latest U.S. census from the Bureau of Labor Statistics has revealed that the U.S. workforce is now composed of almost 50% women. Women are now making more money management decisions and the majority of the buying decisions, substantially affecting global economies. This phenomenon has been termed "sheconomy." Although most women still earn less than men, single women living in urban areas and without children are actually out-earning men. This shift has a lot to do with women's increased education. There are now more women in their late twenties holding a bachelor's degree than men. Since money management has shifted to women to such a great extent, many companies have begun specifically targeting women clientele with their marketing campaigns and service delivery (Luscombe, 2010).

The Domestic Mode of Production

Anthropologists use the phrase *domestic mode of production* to describe the organization of economic systems such as hunting–gathering, small-scale, frontier, and peasant economies. In such systems, the economic roles of women and men are integrated into other domestic roles within the household, which serves as the basic unit of both production and consumption. The division of labor is by age and gender, with relatively little specialization within these two categories. Women's contributions in these economies are variable in type and extent.

Food Production

Although women's roles in food production (subsistence) are quite variable, some general patterns can be found. In hunting–gathering societies, women are primarily responsible for the collection and processing of plant foods; in some cases, they do the fishing. Men were responsible for hunting large animals, an important but much less reliable form of protein. In horticultural societies that depend on cultivated plants, women tend to be mostly responsible for planting, weeding, and harvesting; men are often assigned the more sporadic tasks of clearing the forest for new gardens and the like. In pastoral societies that depend on herding large animals (sheep, goats, cattle, yak, horses, llamas, alpacas, reindeer), women are often associated with milking, preparing butter and cheese, and care of young herd animals, while men are in charge of protection of the herd from raiders and predators. Yet, in certain societies herding is women's work, and in others farming is men's work.

Increased technology curtails to some extent the participation of women in those traditional activities. For example, women in herding societies are rarely directly involved in ranching operations, which are oriented toward markets rather than household consumption. When agricultural production is intensified by the use of plow and oxen, men assume the tasks of cultivation. Although the digging stick is often a woman's tool, the plow rarely is. Women are generally credited with inventing most of the techniques of agriculture and storage (pottery and baskets). Further, it is probable that women were the inventors of spinning (and later of the spinning wheel), weaving, and other techniques of cloth production. However, as with so many of the genuinely creative people in world history, women's names and records have been forgotten while the records of military adventures and the activity of men and their inventions survive.

Maintenance

Simply producing food by gathering, cultivating, fishing, or herding is not enough to provide for family needs. Researchers who attempt to find a relationship between subsistence activities (food production) and women's status often overlook this point. Food processing, for example, may be a critical task in subsistence. While Mexican peasant men are primarily responsible for growing their food staple, corn, Mexican peasant women spend considerable amounts of time and energy turning corn into food—husking and shelling it, grinding it, and forming and cooking tortillas. Food preservation and storage are critical tasks. Fish and meat may be dried or smoked or preserved in oil. Such tasks often are assigned to women.

Women farmers in low-income countries have begun to get more recognition and patronage internationally. Since food prices increased in 2007 and 2008, the United Nations World Food Program has turned to locally grown agriculture to feed the hungry. Women produce 60–80% of the food in poorer countries, but it is usually through small-scale agricultural businesses. The United Nations commitment to working with women farmers has led them to gather data about gender disparities in agriculture, which can influence policy makers and provide material help for women. Helping female farmers is beginning to be seen as an investment in a country's future, both supporting their capacity for production as well as their ability to provide for their families (Harshbarger, 2010).

Women also tend to take on the tasks of making clothing. The Inuit (Eskimo) men who hunt for sea mammals and caribou could not do so unless provided with warm parkas, leggings, and boots made by women. In societies that use plant or animal fibers for clothing, women generally do the spinning, weaving, and sewing. Women also construct tents and houses in many societies. They also have considerable responsibility for the care and health of their families. In many societies, women play important roles as healers of the sick, midwives, and "morticians" (laying out the dead) (see Chapter 11).

Inuit woman preparing animal skins for clothing.

Exchange and Marketing

Although economies based on the domestic mode of production are geared toward production for household use, some wares become commodities, exchanged to obtain goods and services not produced in the household. In some societies, like those in West Africa and the Caribbean, women play a significant role as traders, merchants, and brokers. Their participation in the market has tended (though not invariably) to be limited to short-distance trade in necessities, such as food and utensils, rather than long-distance "luxury" items, such as precious metals, gems, and ivory. Where women do engage in mercantile activities, they tend to retain considerable control over their income, enhancing their autonomy and status.

The Capitalist Mode of Production

Urbanization and Class Distinctions

The development of *social stratification*, socially constructed layers of classes that commanded vastly different shares of the economic resources of the community, was one of the by-products of the development of civilization. Urbanization and capitalism

accelerated that process. Cities provide a wide range of socioeconomic and cultural opportunities and depend on migrants for population growth and maintenance. Younger daughters and sons of the rural population come to the city with the hope of finding employment and social mobility.

Until recently, women migrating to a city rarely found a dazzling array of choices open to them. Previously, they usually entered into the class structure as the appendages of fathers or husbands. If totally on their own, they probably most readily found work as servants or entered the ranks of "unskilled" laborers. Such women were paid little, transient, and obliged by the discrimination of most societies against working women to supplement their meager incomes with sex work. For women who lack skills, education, and social networks, this situation has not changed dramatically even today.

Working for Wages: Its Organizational Prerequisites

In order to "free" labor from the household, which requires work to sustain itself, certain basic arrangements must be made. One kind of arrangement involves a division of labor in the social sphere whereby some workers provide, on a regular basis, goods and services once produced only in the home for family consumption.

Labor directed strictly to household use, for example, the weaving of cloth for clothing, benefits only the family. When the same labor is sold in specialized production, the owner of the resources, tools, and products takes part of the value (after costs) produced by labor and allows the worker to take only a small share back to the family in the form of wages. The profit taken by the owner is accumulated and reinvested in more materials, tools, and products to increase future profits and personal wealth.

Women's Work

Slaves and Serfs. In some economic systems, slaves, who were not paid at all for working, were the lowest level of worker. Prior to the U.S. Civil War, enslaved black people were worked to obtain the maximum amount of labor possible, generally by means of coercion. In addition to the work performed for their masters, female slaves cooked and cared for their own families and produced more slaves for their owners. Unlike other women in this era, slave women were defined first as workers (Jones, 1985; White, 1985; Branch, 2011).

In Europe, after the slave-based economic system of the Roman Empire was overturned in the fifth century and replaced by small-scale economies of free and slave labor, there developed a system of serfdom which existed for centuries that bound female and male workers to the soil. Serfdom gradually gave way to economic systems based on "free" wage labor. "Free" labor has been the most effective source of work in western European economies since the fourteenth century. The broad base of most contemporary economies is the "working class." With the development of industrial capitalism, the vast majorities of workers outside the home sell their labor for wages and cannot exist without doing so. They are "free" to accept what work they can find but are not free to withhold selling their labor for wages if they are to survive economically.

Sex Work. Sex work is defined as the sale of sexual services. In the United States historically, sex work has primarily been organized into relationships of economic dependence, very often with third parties as the employers or "bosses," as in the case of procurers, pimps, or madams. Men, but also women (parents, spouses, lovers, employers, brothel owners), play these intermediary roles, and both gain by the dependent relationship involved (Hirata, 1979; Rosen, 1982; Butler, 1985). Most women do not intend or aspire to become sex workers; rather, in certain circumstances, sex work may provide the only means of generating an income. Poor females, both women and children, are the most vulnerable group (Bertone, 2000; Brennan, 2002). It is not uncommon for poor women across the globe to be trapped in international sexual slavery rings, lured by false promises of good wages for working as "entertainers." Often shunned by other women, female sex workers are vulnerable to crime and diseases such as syphilis and AIDS; are brutalized by pimps, madams, and clients; and do not control the remuneration for their services.

Although most people in the general public are unaware, human trafficking is the fastest-growing criminal enterprise in the world. Kevin Bales, president and cofounder of Free the Slaves, states, "there are more people in slavery today than at any other time in human history." Currently, there are approximately 27 million victims worldwide, throughout 47 nations (Choi-Fitzpatrick, 2008). The United States alone has approximately 15,750 men, women, and children trafficked each year (Choi-Fitzpatrick, 2008). Rates of human trafficking in India and Asia are estimated to be in the millions. These individuals face horrific circumstances—forced into sexual slavery, held captive, brainwashed, often drugged, and threatened with physical harm to themselves and their families' lives. Fortunately, organizations in the United States like the Immigration and Customs Enforcement and the Coalition to Abolish Slavery & Trafficking and international organizations such as the United Nations are working to build public awareness and end this underrecognized form of slavery (Fischer, 2010).

Working-Class Women: Skilled Labor. Production was generally a household enterprise until the development of the factory system and workplaces designed to fit the industrial model. In small-scale craft enterprises, it was commonplace for the man to work at the craft, producing goods, while his wife ran the shop, sold the goods, and kept the books. In Europe, where this division of labor was most pronounced, the more elite, urban professions and crafts had organized themselves into guilds by the thirteenth century. However, women were barred as members (except, in some cases, as widows) from the most skilled and lucrative occupations, and the knowledge of crafts was a "mystery" to them, opened for the most part to licensed male apprentices.

In some guilds, women did participate as independent and active working members. Out of several hundred crafts registered in thirteenth-century Paris, six were composed exclusively of women: silk spinners, wool spinners, silk weavers, silk-train makers, milliners of gold-braided caps, and makers of alms purses. In England, fourteenth-century guilds listed women as brewers, bakers, corders, and spinners and as working in wool, linen, and silk. It is likely that these guilds were organized by employers or civil authorities for the purpose of placing women under surveillance to prevent them from pilfering materials (Shahar, 1983).

Working-Class Women: Domestic Wage Labor.

A vast proportion of wage-earning women have worked as domestic laborers: maids, cooks, and nursemaids. They have contributed to the maintenance of a distinctive standard of living for women and men of the middle and upper classes, enabling them to occupy large, sometimes sumptuous, residences and to enjoy elaborate lifestyles.

Today, in industrially developed nations, many of the former tasks of female domestics are provided by service industries such as hospitals, day-care centers, hotels, and restaurants or by machinery in the home, such as washing machines. However, were it not for the availability of relatively cheap domestic labor, filled largely by immigrant women,

many middle-class professional women would be obliged to stay at home to care for their families since few men are willing to do so or to share parenting responsibilities equally. Many women acknowledge their dependence on child-care workers, but the lack of affordable, flexible, high-quality, and well-paying childcare centers reduces all women's options in combining paid work and care for their children. In some areas, domestic workers have begun to form associations to enforce minimum-wage levels.

Working-Class Women: Factory Workers.

The proportion of women in the U.S. labor force has increased steadily since 1900 (Table 12.3), beginning with a major influx of European immigrants, many with previous experience in the needle trade and garment factories. Female factory workers were not new to the U.S. economy in 1900. In the 1820s and 1830s, single women were employed in textile mills throughout New England. They labored 12–13 hours a day, 6 days a week, and were paid half or less the pay of men. Most were young daughters of farmers who worked for a short period before marriage to help support their families and themselves. At the new model factory at Lowell, Massachusetts, they lived in company housing and their lives were closely supervised. In China, the female children of poor rural families helped their families survive by working in silk factories. Gail Tsukiyama's novel *Women of the Silk* describes the life of such a young girl who leaves her rural home to work in the Chinese silk industry in the 1920s (Tsukiyama, 1991). Like their sisters in New England mills, Tsukiyama's novel depicts these young girls working long hours for very little pay (see Box 12.1).

From time to time, the women workers resisted their situation. However, their efforts to improve working conditions through protest, strikes, organizations, and alliances with men's groups met with little success. By the

TABLE 12.3 Women in the U.S. Labor Force: Selected Years

Women in the Labor Force		Women as a Percent of the Labor Force
Year	(Thousands)	
1900	4,999	18.1
1910	8,076	21.2
1920	8,229	20.4
1930	10,396	21.9
1940	13,007	24.6
1950	18,412	28.8
1960	23,272	32.3
1970	31,560	36.7
1980	41,283	44.2
1990	56,554	45.3
2001	57,933	47.9
2009	66,000	46.8

Source: U.S. Department of Labor, Bureau of Labor Statistics, selected years.

Women strikers from the early 20th century.

mid-twentieth century, poorer immigrant women, initially Irish, rapidly outnumbered native-born female factory workers and took over the struggle to organize and protect factory workers. Out of these struggles emerged leaders like Mary Harris ("Mother") Jones (1830–1930) and Elizabeth Gurley Flynn (1890–1964), who were central to the victories of the labor movement.

Immigrant women worked in a wide variety of industries but were predominant in the garment industry—and still are. It was in this industry that their union activities had the greatest impact. A strike of women shirtwaist workers in New York City in 1909 brought tens of thousands of members to the International Ladies' Garment Workers Union (ILGWU). Although beaten by hired thugs, the picketing women managed to win an increase in wages. Another goal, recognition for the union, was not achieved until 1913. While 80% of the garment workers were women, the ILGWU was dominated by men; not surprisingly, it classified the male-dominated crafts of cutting and pressing as highly paid skilled labor and the female-dominated tasks of joining,

draping, and trimming as unskilled, with women being paid accordingly. The union leaders did not press for the safety regulations demanded by the women in 1909, and many women perished in the Triangle Shirtwaist Factory fire in 1911 (Kennedy, 1979).

Beginning in the 1970s, the garment sweatshop was revitalized in cities like New York, Miami, and Los Angeles, utilizing a new immigrant force—women from East Asia, Latin America, and the Caribbean. Part of a global workforce in the apparel industry, immigrant women's exploitation and their resistance to it has remained largely unchanged over the decades (Louie, 2001).

Working women have had to contend with society's view of the proper role of females. During the Great Depression of the 1930s, employed women were told they were taking jobs from men. This propaganda ignored the fact that most of the jobs women held were low-paid, traditionally female ones, which men had not previously performed. After World War II, they were told that to work away from home was unfeminine and harmful to their families. Women who had worked in heavy industry during both wars to help the nation and support their families were made unwelcome there when the men came home. Women lacked the power to fight for their interests, to resist layoffs, and to hold on to their high wages. *Rosie the Riveter*, a documentary film, depicts the history of women's incorporation into and removal from manufacturing work in the 1940s.

In the 1970s, a few women began to obtain high-paying heavy industrial jobs at twice the wages they could earn as secretaries. Many women have fought for legal reforms to ban gender discrimination in hiring and promotion but remain rare in technical, industrial, and "skilled" trades. To increase women's participation in the skilled trades, the U.S. Department of Labor in 1978 established regulations that required companies receiving any federal funding to adhere to goals and timetables and to set aside apprenticeships for women. Those few women who have entered the nontraditional trades report job isolation and sexual harassment, despite Department of Labor regulations against such activities, with the effect of further reducing women's participation in the skilled trades.

More recently, the Obama administration has made strides in focusing policy on women's equality. The White House Council on Women and Girls was created to provide leadership in the areas of women's and girls' health, empowerment, and human rights. The Obama administration has also worked with the National Economic Council on policies promoting women's economic security (Lieberman, 2010).

With global competition, employers face more demands to keep costs down. One solution has always been to turn to women because their labor can be purchased at a lower rate than that of men. In the Midwest since the 1980s, for example, immigrant Mexican, Laotian, and Vietnamese women have worked in various capacities in the meatpacking industry, now no longer a male domain (Broadway, 1994).

The Service Sector Worker. Women today predominate in clerical work, sales, and services. Although both women and men work as salespeople, they sell different things. Men generally sell cars and insurance; women sell cosmetics and women's clothing. In the United States, most women who work do so in the service sector, which involves the sale and distribution of goods and services themselves. In the past these exclusively female jobs were called *pink-collar* work to distinguish them from male *blue-collar* work.

Office workers are the largest occupational category for women today. Women occupy administrative support positions, while men primarily hold the management positions (Bravo, 2003). In part, the gender segregation of office workers is something of an illusion, a product of labeling the things done by women and men differently. For example, men might be hired as administrative "analysts" and women as administrative "assistants," though they end up doing the same job. By giving the same job two different titles, one for men and one for women, companies can classify the title used for women at a lower wage rate.

Clerical and secretarial work became available to women late in the nineteenth century, especially with the introduction of the typewriter. Computers and other new technologies have further changed the nature and conditions of office work. The lowest-level clerical jobs, which have served as entry points for women, are disappearing. New technology with electronic surveillance capabilities— for example, the timing of customer-service calls—has enabled employers and supervisors to more closely monitor a woman's work, contributing to a loss of her sense of security and control. In other cases, jobs are being "outsourced" to "cheaper" labor markets overseas as corporations compete globally, drawing women in other parts of the world into automated office work. Although the new technologies do provide new opportunities for women, they also reinforce gender and economic inequalities worldwide (Bravo, 2003; Scott-Dixon, 2004).

Many women have also begun to work in the hospitality services, although getting a management position as a woman is rare. In Turkey, women working in hotel services generally enjoy working in tourism and tend to have formal training and education in this area. However, maintaining a work–life balance is difficult, wages are low, and promotions are hard to come by (Okumus et al., 2010). Only 7% of the general managers in Middle Eastern hotels are women, and those reaching higher positions have had to work much harder and longer for it than their male counterparts (Warnock, 2009). In the United States, women in the hospitality industry are outnumbered as well, and at times women find it hard to gain respect (Lennox, 2008). Women on the retail end of hospitality services also face a glass ceiling. More than 1 million female employees at Wal-Mart filed the largest class action suit against the company accusing the company of engaging in compensation and promotion policies and practices prone to gender bias (Cohen, 2010). In 2011 the U.S. Supreme Court dismissed the class action suit, stating that such a large number of diverse women did not constitute a class.

U.S. women working full time and year-round earn about 70% of what men earn. Latinas and African American women earn 52% and 61% of male earnings, respectively (Table 12.4). The differential has improved only slightly in some 30 years, although women are entering the workforce in increased numbers and are working in jobs formerly held only by men. In some countries, the pay differential between women and men is even greater. The International Labour Organization reports that the highest wage gaps between women and men are found in Korea, Thailand, Lithuania, and Kazakstan

TABLE 12.4 Median Weekly Earnings of Women and Men, 2008 (All Workers, 16 Years and Over $722)

	Females ($)	Males ($)
Age 16 and over	636	798
Race		
White	654	825
Black	554	620
Hispanic	501	559
Asian	753	966
Educational attainment		
Less than high school diploma	378	497
High school diploma	520	709
College graduate (BA)	878	1172
Occupation		
Agriculture	436	469
Construction	672	719
Manufacturing	601	811
Wholesale/Retail trade	510	683
Information	761	999
Financial services	712	1015
Education/Health services	690	910

Source: U.S. Department of Labor, Bureau of Labor Statistics, 2009.

(ILO, 2010). One argument made to explain this discrepancy is that the pay differential results from women having less experience than men, which ignores the impact of gender discrimination. To test this argument, economists have held constant the variables of age, experience, and duration of the job and have found that women still get paid less than men and are still promoted more slowly (Rotella, 1980; ILO, 2010).

The Contingent Worker. Contingent workers include part-time, temporary, and freelance workers. They comprise a "flexible" workforce and are increasingly prevalent. Employers rely on these workers when they perceive a need and release them when there is no future need. Some contingent workers are voluntary, preferring this particular work arrangement, while others are involuntary and are looking for full-time, regular employment.

Home workers and independent contractors are another part of the flexible workforce. Most home-based white-collar workers are self-employed (75%) and married women (75%). Home workers list four major reasons to work at home: (1) family responsibilities; (2) control over work hours and setting; (3) elimination of the expense of traveling and of office politics; and (4) the need to earn extra money (Christensen, 1988). Women performing home work report stress in trying to balance work at home with household responsibilities.

Contingent work raises disturbing issues concerning the development of a new workforce of women dependent on the capricious demands of employers. Contingent workers rarely receive the benefits and security associated with full-time employment. Employers feel less need to provide training and occupational advancement. On average, home workers receive lower wages than on-site employees. Yet, for many women, a contingent job with a weak attachment to an employer is the only solution to the problems of inadequate child care, partial retirement, and continuing education.

Like women in the United States, approximately one third of European women work part time, which allows them to combine earning an income and keep up their family responsibilities. Part-time female European workers also earn lower pay, have few benefits, and lack representation and voice in the workplace (ILO, 2010). To overcome these disadvantages, the Netherlands provides part-time employees the same benefits (pensions, vacation, and sick pay) as full-time workers.

The Military. Women are increasingly serving active duty in the military, involved in the front lines of battle. In addition to their strong sense of responsibility to their country, many of these women also balance the responsibilities of a family and child care. They also want money and benefits for their families. While women in the military with and without children do not always show significant discrepancies between their levels of stress, role strain, health, and military career aspirations (Hopkins-Chadwick, 2009), there are specific challenges for some mothers. Some of the challenges of mothers in the military have been highlighted by mothers of special needs children who are also enlisted in active duty positions.

One investigation into the lives of low-income women soldiers found that the demands of military life were incompatible with successfully mothering a child with disabilities. Several conflicts arose for these women that made their situation more challenging. For one, the women perceived mixed messages about prioritizing family life and military mission. Often they felt they were seen as being slackers when they needed to take time out to address their children's medical needs. The low-cost day care much needed by these mothers was not readily accessible due to long waiting lists. Many women have discovered that serving active duty was too demanding to balance successfully with the

Female soldier in uniform.

care of a child with special needs (Taylor et al., 2005).

More recently, the repeal of the don't ask, don't tell policy that forced LGBTQ servicepeople into the closet or out of military service has meant that women may now serve openly as lesbian or bisexual, rather than risk a dishonorable discharge.

The Professions. The professions include the arts, law, medicine, teaching, and management. They often require more training and education than other kinds of work. Most of the professions set their own standards for qualifications and performance and generally pay more than blue- and pink-collar work. Work in the professions is highly segregated by gender. Most fall into one of two categories: those that society deems "female" and those that society deems "male." For example, in the United States, nursing, elementary and secondary teaching, social work, and library work are considered women's professions and women outnumber men in them. Women are underrepresented in most other (men's) professions, especially in medicine, science, engineering, and higher management and as stockbrokers.

Within the "women's professions" there is gender segregation that places men at the highest levels. More men than women, for example, are principals, superintendents, chief officers, and faculty and administrators of professional schools. For the most part, these female professions offer limited career mobility to women; they are the lowest-paying and least prestigious of the professions. Yet, they are enormously important to society. They provide large numbers of women with the opportunity to pursue gratifying careers, although society has not elected to reward them with high pay or status. It is likely that women are poorly paid and even sometimes belittled *because* they are in women's professions.

Some governments have made the connection between women's low pay and high child poverty rates and have attempted to make changes for this reason. The United Kingdom planned to halve child poverty by 2010 and proposed an Equality Bill to improve maternity pay and allow for affordable child care, among other assistance. It was found that half the poor children in the United Kingdom lived in working households, but the mothers were stuck in part-time, low-paid jobs (BBC News, 2008). Bridget Bodman found that when she switched jobs, the man who took her old job was paid significantly more, so she took legal action and won the case. She says, "I just wanted to equalize things. I wanted to get the money that the man after me and the man before me had got. I wasn't a hell raiser and it wasn't just about principle....I did equal work" (Sugden, 2009).

Although many women have been trained and are active in the arts, few have held top-ranking positions in architecture or design or as producers or directors in theater or film. Women have also experienced systematic discrimination as artists, so it is harder for them than for men to gain recognition and to make a living in the arts. In recent years, thanks in part to the women's movement and in part to antidiscrimination laws, increasing numbers of women have entered and achieved success in professions formerly reserved for men. Today, more women gain employment in professions such as accounting, informational technology, financial management, optometry, dermatology, forensic pathology, and veterinarian medicine (Rosin, 2010).

Women in "male professions" often encounter serious obstacles. Not only will they be in the minority among their peers, but their subordinates, whether female or male, may have difficulty relating to them and vice versa. Research on perceptions of women in the workplace indicates that female candidates are often subject to prejudice, except when they are applying within an industry that is congruent with female gender roles (Garcia-Retamero and Lopez-Zafra, 2006).

Gender segregation is evident within "male professions" as well: female physicians tend to go into pediatrics, female lawyers into probate (dealing with wills and property dispositions to widows and offspring), and female professors into the humanities and social sciences rather than the physical sciences. Gender segregation between and within the professions is in part the result of gender discrimination in education (see Chapter 9). For female professionals who pursue both career and family, there are many role conflicts since both jobs and families make demands on a woman's time and energy. The male model of professional development is especially problematic for women who are raising a family. Many professions and employers within the professions, especially male-dominated ones, assume that individuals dedicate most of their time and energies to work. Some women choose not to follow the male model of professonal development. In India, professional women in the information technology sector forgo promotions and advancement in their companies so as not to neglect their family responsibilities (Radhakrishnan, 2009). In the United States some professional women now in their thirties and forties are "choosing" to leave careers that had been closed to their mother's generation and previous generations of women, albeit perhaps only temporarily. Having experienced the fast track to a law partnership or corporate management, for example, they have found the male-defined work conditions enormously dissatisfying. Although this option is open primarily to the wealthy or those with high income–earning spouses, their decision to "opt out" goes beyond the issue of balancing work and family to questioning the place and satisfaction of work itself in life (Belkin, 2003).

Women in academia would benefit from more generous family policies, as the turnover rate is high (see Chapter 9). Family policies become a significant factor in advancement and retention, and women need better representation (Audrey and Tikka, 2008). Family-friendly policies could be helpful to faculty with caregiving responsibilities; however, the structure and culture of academia often make it hard for women to balance work and family. For example, the way the tenure system is set up makes it hard for women because the six or seven years necessary to focus on tenure in one's early career often coincide with the optimal years for having children. It is found that men receiving tenure are more likely to be married with children than women receiving tenure. Women often feel they have to choose between work and family life. Certain policies have been proposed by individual universities that would make it easier for a woman to attain that balance. The University of California, Berkeley, has proposed a right to a one-semester relief from teaching duty for parents with young children, a right to one year of pausing the tenure clock for child- or adult-dependent care responsibilities, a right to request unpaid leave for the care of a sick family member, high-quality child and infant-care availability, spousal employment assistance, and more part-time options for faculty with family caregiving responsibilities (Cockrell, 2003).

Other universities, finding that faculty want more balanced lives, have put in their own family-friendly and flexible workplace policies. Some schools have tried flexible work schedules, lactation stations, parenting seminars, eldercare, and "new mom" support groups to achieve more work–life balance. Universities must also make an effort to reduce the stigma involved in requesting utilization of these policies. Universities benefit from creating a balanced environment as much as the faculty do because employees work harder when they have more flexible, supportive working conditions (Novotney, 2010).

Women who attempt to balance both professional careers and family life face obstacles to success that vary by occupation, although there are some common barriers. In the United Kingdom, civil engineering, with its dominant male culture, prioritizes work and long hours as the norm with personal interests and family life taking the back seat. They value presenteeism, so even when there is no significant work to be done, one shows commitment by staying late and working long hours (Watts, 2007).

Women engineers have developed various strategies to maintain a work–life balance, such as creating firm boundaries between work and personal life, cutting back on extracurricular work activities, or employing cleaners to free up some of their personal time. Unfortunately, these women engineers are often inhibited from speaking out against the practices of being overworked as they are culturally implicit within the occupation's culture (Watts, 2007).

The manner in which men and women view and navigate the home–work balance differs by gender across one's life span. A study of mid-life men and women in Scotland between the ages of 50 and 52 years found gender to have a large impact on how home and work life was handled. Men tended to view the struggle of home–work life balance as a conflict of the past, when their children were younger (most of their children were now adolescents). Women, on the other hand, were still struggling with this conflict in the form of balancing paid work, adolescent/adult children, and aging parent responsibilities. Women also tended to have weaker boundaries between home and work responsibilities, which was often more acceptable in predominantly female careers that also placed value on caring. Men's careers that valued pragmatic qualities

in their workers often fostered stronger boundaries between work and home life (Emslie and Hunt, 2009).

Some conceptualize the care of others as being a matter of ethical responsibility. A comprehensive approach to viewing ethics includes everyday decisions of caring for oneself and others as integral to the idea of "ethics." This brings back more the original essence of the word ethics, previously referring to knowledge about how to live a good life (Tronto, 2001). This is certainly applicable to women with the extensive time they spend engaged in child and eldercare.

Corporate Management at the Highest Levels.

In the United States, affirmative action suits, affirmative action policies of companies, and the women's movement have called attention to the gender gap in the corporate ladder. More women are reaching middle-management ranks, but few are senior managers, being skipped over while male peers or juniors are chosen for these positions. Not surprisingly, women executives continue to be compensated at a lower rate than male executives. In 2011, only 3.6% of Fortune 500 companies had female CEOs, and in 2009 women held only 15.2% of Fortune 500 board seats (Catalyst, 2012)—very low percentages indeed. Yet one study found that gender diversity in business is associated with increased sales revenue, increased profits, and a greater market share (Herring, 2009; Kay, 2010).

Women who have achieved leadership positions have developed tactics to excel in both their home and work responsibilities. An interview with some of the top women leaders in Eastern and Western countries found similarities between the women contributing to their success both at work and at home. These women were able to combine work and family as a result of flexible working conditions and family support. They also prioritized integrating different life domains. These women tended to display transformational leadership qualities at work, including an emphasis on interconnectedness, which gave them social support, contributing to their ability to balance their personal and professional lives. They excelled at optimization strategies, such as scheduling time and multitasking, and compensation strategies, such as outsourcing basic duties when resources were limited. These tactics contributed to their ability to successfully balance their lives (Cheung and Halpern, 2010).

In the twenty-first century, some businesses are beginning to value those management styles, often identified with female leadership styles, which stress teamwork, flexibility, and collaboration in problem solving as making them better able to adapt to the current global economic environment characterized by uncertainty and the need to constantly evolve. Increasingly companies in both the Global North and Global South are choosing women to lead their businesses (Box 12.2).

Whether women earn high salaries as professionals or low wages as caregivers, salesclerks, or sex workers, discrimination against them is found at all levels and categories of work. Women experience the "glass ceiling," which keeps them from reaching the highest levels of corporate and public responsibility; the "sticky floor" keeps the vast majority of the world's women stuck in low-paid jobs, the "glass wall" concentrates women in female-dominated jobs, and the "glass cliff" refers to the tenuous nature of women's leadership positions (Albeda and Tilly, 1997; Kimmel, 2000; Barretto, Ryan, and Schmitt, 2009).

Box 12.2   WOMEN AT THE TOP

Around the world women are breaking the glass ceiling and taking positions at the head of companies.

Sheryl Sandberg (US), COO of Facebook (technology)
Indra Nooyi (US), Chair and CEO of PepsiCo (food)
Maria das Graças Silva Foster (Brazil), CEO of Petrobas (oil)
Ursula Burns (US), Chair and CEO of XEROX (technology)
Marissa Mayer (US), CEO of Yahoo (technology)
Zhang Xin (China), Co-founder and CEO, Soho China, Ltd. (real estate)
Safra Catz, (US), President and CFO of Oracle (technology)
Cher Wang (Taiwan), Co-founder and Chair of HTC (technology)
Chandra Kochhar (India), Managing Director and CEO of ICICI Bank (financial)
Chua Sock Koong (Singapore), CEO of SingTel (technology)
Shaikha Al-Bahar (Kuwait), CEO of National Bank of Kuwait (financial)
Guler Sabanci (Turkey), Chair and Managing Director, Sabanci Holding (diversified)

Source: www.forbes.com/power-women/list/. Retrieved October 4, 2012.

Globalization and the Transformation of Work

Today, globalizing forces have profoundly altered national economies and the workplace. Globalization entails "the internationalization of the capitalist economy in which states, markets, and civil society are restructured to facilitate the spread of global capital" (Peterson and Runyan, 2010: 193). Since the conclusion of World War II, capitalism has integrated the world's countries into a single global economy, a process that accelerated with the end of colonialism and the collapse of communism in Russia and Eastern Europe in the late 1980s. This led to the migration of jobs from industrial centers in Europe and the United States to countries in which manufacturers could pay lower wages to nonunionized workers, reorganizing the global economy and powerfully affecting former industrial workers (Box 12.3).

Globalization touches the lives of women and men in developing countries. As manufacturing industries have relocated to low-wage countries in search of cheap, docile labor, many women in developing countries have joined the global assembly line in industries as diverse as clothing, food production, and electronics. The governments in the Caribbean and Latin America, eastern Europe, and many countries of Asia advertise the availability of a large supply of female labor. Work in multinational corporation factories compromises workers' health and life expectancy; women perform repetitive tasks and are exposed to dangerous chemicals. However, the women in these countries face extreme poverty and need even the lowest wages for survival; they have almost no possibility of resisting exploitation.

As economic conditions in developing countries worsened over the past four decades, governments were forced to implement specific policies of international financial institutions like the International Monetary Fund, the World Bank, and the World Trade Organization. These policies benefited the global economy as determined by the advanced industrialized countries. In exchange for loans and aid, developing countries have had to agree to cut government spending on health, education, and welfare; reduce the number of government jobs; sell off government-owned and -operated businesses; and open their economies to foreign investors. These structural adjustment programs have caused enormous hardships (Wichterich, 1998; Dickinson and Schaeffer, 2001). Migration becomes an economic strategy for family survival in developing countries; women often lead the way.

Those women who cannot find work in their own country migrate to developed countries or wealthier developing countries. They find jobs performing traditional women's tasks. The less educated often work as nannies, maids, and sex workers and send remittances back home to feed, clothe, house, and educate their families there. For example, Sri Lanka women are recruited to the Middle East and Filipinas to Hong Kong to work in households (Constable, 2007). They make it possible for women in industrialized countries to go out and work with the knowledge that their child will be looked after, their homes cleaned, and their elderly relatives attended. These immigrant workers are poorly paid, have little or no rights in the host country, are often subject to emotional and physical abuse, and, in the case of sex workers, run the risk of contracting HIV/AIDS and other sexually transmitted diseases. For the small numbers of educated and skilled women from developing countries who seek to continue their professions in the developed countries, their experiences have generally been of downward mobility, that is, starting over again (for example, by taking licensing exams) and getting little or no credit for their skills and years of experience.

Self-Employment

Historically, few women have been self-employed due, in part, to the different socialization of girls and boys. Girls tend not to be taught to take the initiative or to

Box 12.3   PAULINE LEARNS TO SEW

When I come back from having babies.
they put me on sewing.
I could no more sew a straight line
than I could milk a chicken
but the other ladies helped me,
showed me how to set the need
line the cloth to make a turn,
pull my thread to the side
so it wouldn't jam up in the bobbin.
I won't say I ever was much good at it,
but nobody'd accuse me a not trying.
A lifetime, it seems. Husband,
three kids growed. Mama passed.
Went from T-shirts and boxers to
sweat shirts then collars then elastic.
One day, outta the blue, they unbolted
the machines, loaded them in trucks,
hauled 'em down to Mexico or someplace.
Nothing left on second floor
but concrete and empty bolt holes.
We was like family, us sewers.
You'd a thought we lost a brother or sister,
the weight we felt, grief tangling up among us.
You'd find broke needles in corners
for a while after, lengths a thread.
Ladies getting old by then just retired.
Young ones, they got on
somewhere else in the mill, some
other machine. Didn't lose nobody from it,
not really. Took our spirit, that's all.
You can work a 8-hour shift without spirit,
but it ain't half worth it, you know?

Source: Barbara Presnell, *Piece Work*. Cleveland, OH: Cleveland State University Poetry Center, 2007. Copyright © 2007 by Barbara Presnell. Used by permission of The Permissions Company, Inc., on behalf of the Cleveland State UniversityPoetry Center www.csuohio.edu/poetrycenter/

be assertive or independent. When girls do show these qualities, which underlie successful self-employment, they often receive fewer rewards than boys or even negative sanctions.

Financial institutions globally have long maintained discriminatory practices, denying loans and credit that could enable women to start or run a business simply on the basis of gender. As women in the industrialized countries campaign to legislate against such discrimination, it is not easy to end traditional attitudes translated into business practices.

Madame C. J. Walker.

Despite the obstacles, quite a few ambitious women have managed to overcome many of the financial barriers to self-employment. Madame C. J. Walker (born Sarah Breedlove, 1867–1919), for example, was an early African American inventor and entrepreneur who in 1905 developed and sold hair products for black women. With her wealth, she became an activist against lynching and a philanthropist (Bundles, 2001). In the twentieth and twenty-first centuries, highly successful women are primarily found in the entertainment, cosmetics, and clothing industries: they include Lady Gaga, Oprah Winfrey, Estee Lauder, Donna Karan, Vera Wang, and Bobbi Brown.

The factors that propel women to become self-employed vary. In the Global North, self-employed women include those who previously worked in major corporations but left to start their own enterprises because of dissatisfaction over gender inequities in pay, power, and promotion (Wirth, 2001). However, the vast majority of self-employed women in the world choose self-employment for other reasons. For many women who must combine work and family responsibilities, self-employment allows them to earn needed income and to take care of their families at the same time. Some female entrepreneurs in Africa have started their own businesses in nontraditional fields such as construction and information technology (Kigozi, 2007).

Globally, self-employed women have some commonalities: they tend to work out of their homes; they are found in enterprises at the lower end of economic productive activities, particularly those with little barriers to entry (food, child care, and craft production); and they start enterprises that allow them to use their traditional skills and knowledge. In developed countries, more self-employed women are engaged in commerce and services than in developing countries, where self-employed women typically establish businesses involving artisan crafts and agriculture (United Nations, 2000).

Unemployment

Most countries recognize the responsibility to provide jobs to those who cannot find them, even though many governments may fail to avoid high levels of unemployment. The United States is almost alone in denying this obligation. Governmental attempts to encourage or stimulate private sector employment are often unsuccessful, especially for women, the working class, and minorities, who are routinely "last hired and first fired." It has been argued that the right of an individual to employment, provided by the government if not available otherwise, should be recognized as a human right (Nickel, 1978–79; Sen, 2001).

Unemployment rates have almost always been higher for women than for men, and young women experience more unemployment and longer periods of unemployment than young men (United Nations, 2000). Given the high unemployment rates and outsourcing of jobs in the United States today, there are more jobs available in the service sector but fewer available in manufacturing. For this reason, the job market has opened up for women. If women are to be able to lead decent, productive lives, among the first priorities must be the assurance that when they seek employment, jobs will be available. To be able to compete on equal terms with men for an inadequate number of actual jobs will not be enough.

The Politics of Work: Barriers and Strategies

Sexual and Gender Harassment

Sexual and gender harassment has only recently come under legal scrutiny. This pervasive problem for women workers is very much underreported, though the testimony given by attorney Anita Hill in 1991 against Supreme Court nominee Clarence Thomas encouraged more women to come forward about their experiences (Morrison, 1992).

In the workplace, sexual harassment occurs when an employer or supervisor demands sexual favors from an employee under threat of dismissal or other reprisal, often not made explicit, or when an employee is subjected to persistent unwelcome sexual advances or innuendoes (see Box 12.4). It includes not only the harassment of females by males but also the harassment by customers of women whose job requires that they wear sexually provocative clothing, male employees by female supervisors, and homosexual advances (Christensen, 1988). Studies have found that many men view certain sexual behaviors (sexual advances or solicitation of sex in exchange for a reward) as flattering to women. These behaviors contribute to a hostile work environment and may inflict great harm upon a victim. Sexual harassment is costly to both the private and public sectors. Sexual harassment costs the United States government an estimated $189 million annually due to the high turnover of female employees, absenteeism, and productivity declines that result (Kimmel, 2000).

In the past, women who were victimized by sexual harassment were unlikely to complain. They felt that speaking up or confronting a harasser would make no difference. However, as more workplaces establish codes of conduct to regulate such offensive behaviors (Box 12.5), women are increasingly seeking redress at their workplace and in the courts.

Countries as diverse as Argentina, Canada, Costa Rica, Japan, New Zealand, the Philippines, South Africa, the United States,

---

Box 12.4   LEVELS OF SEXUAL HARASSMENT

- Gender harassment: generalized sexist statements and behavior not designed to elicit sexual cooperation but to convey insulting, degrading, and/or sexist attitudes toward women or homosexual people.
- Seductive behavior: unwanted, inappropriate, and offensive physical or verbal sexual advances.
- Sexual bribery: solicitation of sexual activity or other sex-linked behavior by promise of reward.
- Sexual coercion: coercion of sexual activity or other sex-linked behavior by promise of reward.
- Sexual assault: physical assault and/or rape.

Source: From S. R. Zalk, "Harrassment on the Job: What Everyone Ought to Know," *Dental Teamwork* (May–June 1991): 13. Copyright © 1991 American Dental Association. All rights reserved. Reprinted by permission.

and the members of the European Union have defined sexual harassment as a legal wrong that merits sanctions and remedies.

Social Support for Working Women

Unions. The labor union is the principal organized support group for working people outside the family. In the past, unions have not always been particularly supportive of women workers. It is noteworthy that many primary fields of women's employment, whether blue-collar, pink-collar, or professional, are not unionized.

The conditions militating against women's participation in trade union activity today are much the same as they were over a century ago. Women are seen as dependents, whose primary role is in the home. The demands of domestic responsibility leave women little time to devote to union activities. Women traditionally lack training and experience in public speaking and self-assertion, important aspects of union activity. As the least skilled and lowest-paid workers, they have had little bargaining leverage with employers. Women have also faced considerable hostility from working men, who often view female colleagues as direct competitors for jobs or union positions and are made uneasy at home by wives who are too "independent" (Kennedy, 1979).

Unionization has proven beneficial to working women, and existing unions are gradually becoming more aware of women's issues. The United Auto Workers, for example, has endorsed equal pay, gender-integrated seniority lists, day care, and the Equal Rights Amendment. Despite unions' growing awareness of the importance of organizing for working women's rights, most women do not join unions. In the United States, only 7 million out of a total of 58 million working women (11%) belong to unions or professional associations. To improve the status of all working women, 3,000 women representing 58 trade unions formed the Coalition of Labor Union Women (CLUW) in 1974. During the past

Women on the salad dressing filling machine assembly line in 1927.

decade, a number of significant efforts have been made to organize clerical women workers and to negotiate contracts that would address their interests.

The CLUW is America's only national organization for union women and now has over 40 chapters. The goal of CLUW is to determine common problems and develop action programs to deal effectively with these concerns. Other basic goals of the organization include promoting affirmative action, strengthening the role of women in unions, organizing unorganized women (especially younger members), and increasing the involvement of women in the political and legislative process. Some of their activities include speaking out on specific issues such as equal pay, child and elder care benefits, job security, safe workplaces, affordable healthcare, contraceptive equality, and protection from sexual harassment and violence in the workplace (CLUW.org, 2009).

Women in Lesotho, a country in southern Africa. These women are accomplishing the kind of heavy work, requiring great physical strength, that has traditionally been associated with men.

One model for a trade union association sensitive to the productive and reproductive needs of women is the Self-Employed Women's Association (SEWA) in India. Formed in 1972, SEWA is a trade union of women who work as petty vendors and home-based producers. The union establishes savings and credit cooperatives to provide working capital to its members. Its producer cooperatives help women secure a higher price for their goods, enhancing their income. Through SEWA, members have been able to learn about plumbing, carpentry, radio repair, accounting, and management, thereby upgrading their skills. SEWA also provides legal services, which assist members in obtaining the benefits of labor legislation enacted by the Indian government, and welfare services, such as maternal protection schemes, widows' benefits, child care, and training of midwives (Self-Employed Women's Association, 2008).

In the United States, domestic workers (including nannies, housecleaners, and elder aides) have revitalized the labor movement, joining together in the National Domestic Workers Alliance (see Box 12.6). In 2010, New York State passed a Domestic Workers Bill of Rights, with significant input from the NDWA, which mandated minimum wage, overtime, and paid sick and personal days for domestic workers.

Professional Organizations. Since women have not been well represented in the professions in the past, they have not been prominent in the leadership of professional organizations. Beginning in 1969, groups of professional women began to take responsibility for raising the consciousness of the members of professional organizations about the problems and rights of women and the need to include women in leadership positions. One of the authors of this text, Florence Denmark, helped develop a section on the psychology of women for the American Psychological Association and became its president (1980–81). Many other professional organizations, such as the American Historical Association, the American Philosophical Association, the American Anthropological Association, and the American Political Science Association, have experienced the development of women's caucuses. As a result, women are playing a greater role than in the past in keeping these groups alert to the problems of women professionals and to the need to include gender in the curriculum of these disciplines.

Networks. The family, the union, and the professional association are formal organizations that have a legal standing. Networks are loose connections among individuals who know one another (or of one another) and support one another; they are informal and have no legal standing. They are, for many, the most significant support group in the workplace. Networks are at once powerful and "invisible," operating to influence career opportunities and the workings of the business and professional worlds but not legally liable or open to attack.

Men in power have always relied on networks. The "old boys' network" often begins in school, especially private schools, or at colleges, where young men get to know others who share their interests. These acquaintances are often kept up through a lifetime and broadened and shaped through other associations: clubs, civic groups, and special membership organizations. Networks provide their members with access to important information and resources.

Women who share experiences and interests have developed their own groups and relationships for mutual aid, sometimes on a formal but more often on an informal basis (Hunt et al., 2009). The women's movement has created a supportive climate for the formation of women's networks by keeping women aware of their need for one another and by encouraging women's mutual support. Women use professional caucuses, newsletters, and regular meetings as more or less formal networking instruments.

Laws against Sexist Job Discrimination

Although there is no U.S. constitutional amendment that guarantees to its female citizens equality under law, two federal statutes enacted in the 1960s provide the legal basis for women's equality in the workplace. Title VII of the Civil Rights Act of 1964, particularly Section 703(a), prohibits discrimination on the basis of sex in hiring or discharging individuals and in terms of compensation and conditions of work. It also prohibits classifying (on the basis of sex) either applicants or employees to avoid adversely affecting women's opportunities. The Equal Pay Act of 1963, amended by the Education Amendments of 1972 (Higher Education Act), guarantees to women equal pay for work equal to that of male employees. The 1972 amendments extended coverage of both acts to executive, professional, and other job categories.

Affirmative action requires that employers who have discriminated against women and minorities set goals for reducing or ending such discrimination. For instance, if it can be shown on the basis of population figures or numbers of qualified applicants that a nondiscriminatory hiring policy would have resulted in about a quarter of the workers in a given category being women, an employer may be required to set a goal of 25% women employees in that category. Preference has often been given to groups, such as veterans, to compensate for their previous personal sacrifices in the national interest (though many individual

---

Box 12.5   U.S. GUIDELINES FOR EMPLOYERS ON SEXUAL HARASSMENT

The U.S. government has adopted guidelines for employers to eliminate sexual harassment in the workplace. Here is an excerpt:

Prevention is the best tool for the elimination of sexual harassment. An employer should take all steps necessary to prevent sexual harassment from occurring. They should clearly communicate to employees that sexual harassment will not be tolerated. They can do so by establishing an effective complaint or grievance process and taking immediate and appropriate action when an employee complains.

Source: www.eeoc.gov/facts/fs-sex.html. Retrieved September 11, 2013.

Box 12.6   FINDINGS OF THE NATIONAL DOMESTIC WORKERS ALLIANCE SURVEY

Low pay is a systemic problem in the domestic work industry.

- 23 percent of workers surveyed are paid below the state minimum wage.
- 70 percent are paid less than $13 an hour.
- 67 percent of live-in workers are paid below the state minimum wage, and the median hourly wage of these workers is $6.15.

Using a conservative measure of income adequacy, 48 percent of workers are paid an hourly wage in their primary job that is below the level needed to adequately support a family.

Source: National Domestic Workers Alliance and the Center for Urban Economic Development, University of Illinois at Chicago, 2011–2012.

veterans suffered little). Affirmative action is an effort to compensate for past (and present) wrongs done by employers, both public and private, to women and members of minority groups.

Many of the gains women achieved during the late 1960s and 1970s were reversed in the next decades, beginning with the Reagan administration, which came into office with the support of various groups bitterly opposed to affirmative action. During the Reagan administration, both the Equal Employment Opportunity Commission and the Civil Rights Commission rejected the concept of comparable worth (see below). In the 1990s and up to the present, a more conservative Supreme Court has adopted a less supportive approach to women's equal rights on affirmative action grounds. For example, in 2007 the U.S. Supreme Court ruled that Lilly Ledbetter, a female supervisor at a Goodyear plant in Alabama, was not entitled to compensation under Title VII of the Civil Rights Act because she had filed her discrimination case more than 180 days after her company began to pay her lower wages compared to male supervisors. To rectify the statute of limitation clause regarding discrimination, in 2009 the U.S. Congress passed a law amending the Civil Rights Act and extended the timeline for filing a discrimination case. The Lilly Ledbetter Fair Pay Act of 2009 grants a woman the right to file discrimination suits against an employer as long as she is affected by that discriminatory decision in terms of paychecks, pension, and other benefits. Because of the Lilly Ledbetter Fair Pay Act, more women have been able to file discrimination lawsuits and win damages.

Within the European Union, the European Court of Justice has ruled favorably on affirmative action cases for women. Its rulings in the 1990s allow employers to take into consideration the fact that women competing with men for jobs may have had breaks in their careers in order to meet their family responsibilities. The development of European law with respect to women, work, and equality has led to the advancement of women's rights on issues related to pay, pensions, part-time work, night work, and work in the armed services. The European Court of Justice has ordered member states of the European Union to end discriminatory treatment of women in the workplace. As a result, national laws that discriminate against women in the workplace have been overturned. Throughout Latin America, the majority of countries have constitutional guarantees or laws requiring equal pay for equal work. Chile has strengthened this right by allowing women the right to submit formal complaints or file court cases if they are the victims of wage discrimination (Berger, 2012).

Many women experience job discrimination due to pregnancy and maternity leave. The United States does not require that employers provide any paid maternity leave, although many companies are required to give up to three months of unpaid leave. Europe tends to be more generous with maternity leave. Britain offers the longest maternity leave, providing 52 weeks leave with a partial salary. Germany, France, and Belgium offer closer to four months leave (see Chapter 7, Box 7.7). Currently in the works in Europe is a proposal requiring fully paid maternity leave for five months and paternity leave for two weeks. The proposal was passed by the European Union Parliament and will go before the European Union states for review. Some governments feel that if passed, this will hurt the economy and deter employers from hiring women (Lieberman, 2010). On the other hand, several studies have found that family-friendly policies may benefit companies in the long run because employees' productivity, commitment, and job satisfaction increase as a result (Sabattini and Crosby, 2009).

Equal Pay–Comparable Worth

Those who have enforced laws against discrimination in the past have applied them only to persons doing the same work. It was illegal for an employer to pay a man more than a woman for the same job with the same job specifications. This interpretation may be in the process of changing. Only if it does will a real attack on the inequities faced by women in the labor force be possible, for few women do the same work as men. "Women's work" is generally compensated at rates substantially lower than what men get for work of comparable value. Discrimination against women begins with initial gender segregation of tasks and persists into the sphere of remuneration.

Juanita Kreps, the secretary of labor in the Carter administration (1977–81), has pointed out "that many of the occupational groups in which women are concentrated pay low wages while requiring higher than average educational achievement....These higher levels of education do not pay off for either men or women in these 'female' occupations" (Kreps, 1971: 40). Demands have developed for "equal pay for work of comparable value." Comparable worth proceeds beyond equal pay for women and men in the same job, as women and men are rarely found in the same job category. Instead, the theory of comparable worth states that wages reflect the skills, training, and conditions of the work, with women and men receiving equal pay for positions assessed as having equivalent value.

To date, the U.S. Supreme Court has been unwilling to rule on comparable worth. However, if it can be proved that an employer intentionally discriminates in pay rates between women and men performing similar jobs, the courts will rule that violation of Title VII has occurred. In contrast to the United States, the European Union, in both judicial rulings and legislative action, has contributed to growing support and respect for the principle of equal pay for work of equal value. In a case involving pay differentials between mostly (male) pharmacists and mostly (female) speech therapists, the court ruled that the employer (the British National Health Service) was obligated to abide by the principle of equal pay for work of equal value (Heide, 2001).

The Impact of the Women's Movement

Many feminist organizations have demanded recognition of a woman's right to engage in useful, meaningful, and rewarding work. It has also stood for equal pay and respect for women in the workplace, equal opportunity in job and career advancement, and improvement in opportunity, pay, and recognition for women of color.

Practical arrangements to relieve the burdens of women who work outside the home have been few and far between. The number of day-care centers has increased but not nearly enough to accommodate all working mothers, and they are still too costly. A few work organizations have experimented with *flextime*, instituting a system of flexible work hours so that women and men can carry out home and family responsibilities during the day and work as well. However, such arrangements are still unusual, and not always actually flexible: ever-present mobile devices, laptop computers, and the expectation of constant availability pressure women and men at home with children to keep working even on their off-hours.

One of the most important developments within the U.S. women's movement in recent years is the growing recognition that deeper and more fundamental changes than these are needed in the economy. Women cannot achieve feminist objectives without a substantial breakdown of the class differ-ences that pit the interests of advantaged women against those of disadvantaged women. An equal opportunity to exploit the weak is not the aim of the women's move-ment. More humane and less hierarchical organizations of work are needed, along with a concern on the part of society with what work is for, what investments shall be made, and what products shall be made. Work that serves human needs and interests while respecting the environment is better for both women and men than work for increased profits. Progress toward these objectives will require fundamental changes in the way the work of both women and men is organized and conducted.

Summary

Every known society has assigned work by gender, and the work done by women has tra-ditionally been valued less than that done by men. Women's reproductive functions have been used as an excuse for the division of labor by gender. Although the labor involved in reproduction and childrearing is essential for any society, often it is not recognized and almost always unpaid.

Maintaining the domestic unit is essential to the functioning of society and the econ-omy, but it has been given neither economic nor social value. Women who sell their labor in the marketplace find their jobs devalued; they are restricted in their job choices and paid less than men.

When a society's economy is based on a sim-ple domestic mode of production, economic and domestic roles tend to be integrated for both women and men. As a society mod-ernizes and work becomes capital-intensive rather than labor-intensive, women tend to be phased out of the economy and confined to the domestic sphere. Women "subsidize" capitalist enterprises by servicing workers for free, producing and caring for the next gener-ation of workers, and providing a cheap pool of labor when needed.

As slavery and serfdom gave way to "free" wage labor, a working class evolved. Within this class, women have been barred from most trades of skilled labor by guilds and craft orga-nizations. Most working-class women have been employed as domestic wage labor. In past centuries in the United States, increasing numbers of women, particularly immigrants, have found work in factories. Today's immi-grants, pushed by the forces of globalization, find work in the service sector as nannies, maids, and sex workers. Most women today are employed as pink-collar workers in cleri-cal work, sales, and services, jobs considered "female." A growing economic trend is the use of contingent workers, who do not receive the benefits, security, or earnings of full-time workers.

The professions are also segregated by gender. Within the "female professions," men hold most top-level jobs. Women sometimes find it difficult to enter a "male profession," much less to rise within it, but some gains are evident. A few professional women are choos-ing to "opt out" of their careers, question-ing the male-defined conditions of the work itself.

Economic competition between companies and countries has intensified as a result of glo-balization. Multinational corporations move their operations to regions where the labor costs are cheaper. Some women in develop-ing countries migrate to developed countries or wealthier developing countries, where their labor often benefits middle-class and upper-class households, including allowing many professional women to advance their careers.

Women find it difficult to compete with men for jobs because their interests are not entirely separate from those of the men to whom they are in some way related. Many men do not support women's attempt to gain economic equality because they believe this would threaten their superior status in the job market and at home.

Women on the job may be subject to sexual or gender harassment. Women who work can find social support in formal organizations, such as unions and professional organizations. Women's informal networks are especially important for mutual aid and information and resource sharing.

More countries are passing laws to lessen job discrimination. The Equal Opportunity Act and Equal Pay Act help U.S. women challenge job discrimination. Affirmative action programs attempt to improve the opportunities of those who have suffered from discrimination. Many women today are calling for laws that will require equal pay for work of comparable value.

The women's movement has raised women's aspirations and brought about some changes in attitude. However, it appears that feminist objectives will not be achieved without structural changes in the economy and society.

Discussion Questions

1. Think about women you know and the work that they do. How does what you have learned in this chapter help you understand their work experiences? You could even interview women you know and compare their work lives.

2. Select a place of work—a hospital, a business firm, a school—to which you have access. List all the positions and who holds them by gender. Are particular types of work done mainly or exclusively by women? Are women found mainly at some levels and not at others?

3. Many women feel that family obligations pose special problems for them as they pursue careers. In what ways does our society provide "relief" for women who work or study outside the home? To what extent are these services satisfactory or unsatisfactory? What are some alternative means for alleviating this problem?

4. Research the experiences of working women in another country or region of the world. What kinds of work do these women do? What child-care options do they have? How do they balance family and work responsibilities? What are the similarities and differences between women in your society and the one you chose to study?

5. If you have a particular career goal, study the roles of women in that career or profession in the past and at present. What proportion of people in the field is female? If there are obstacles to women's success in this field, might they be overcome?

Recommended Readings

Ehrenreich, Barbara, and Arlie Russell Hochschild, editors. *Global Woman: Nannies, Maids, and Sex Workers in the New Economy.* New York: Henry Holt, 2002. This book examines the impact and consequences of globalization on women around the world. The lives of women migrants from the Dominican Republic, Taiwan, Vietnam, Mexico, Thailand, Sri Lanka, and the Philippines are analyzed.

Kessler-Harris, Alice. *Out to Work: A History of Wage-Earning Women in the United States,* 20th ed. Oxford: Oxford University Press, 2003. This history of working women from the colonial period to the end of the twentieth century looks at the interrelationships of work, family, and ideas about work and family.

Pearson, Allison. *I Don't Know How She Does It: The Life of Kate Reddy, Working Mother.* New York: Knopf, 2002. In this novel, a woman attempts to balance her successful and challenging career as a hedge-fund investment manager with the demands of her husband and two small children.

Shriver, M. *The Shriver Report: A Woman's Nation Changes Everything.* Washington, DC: The Center for American Progress, 2009. Now that women compose half of the U.S. workforce, this report carefully considers the effect on and implications for family life, as well as for American culture at large.

Feminism and Politics

The very act of being an advocate for justice is…fueled by a belief in political and social change, a belief in the idea that we can make a better world. As an activist, you have got to believe. This belief in the possibility of social change not only fuels people's willingness to engage in activism, but it is, in itself, the first lesson for social activists of any kind.

URVASHI VAID, 2012

What is the moral meaning of who we are? What do we take personally? How do perceived issues propel or diffuse our political commitments? I think these questions can only be answered again and again with difficulty.

JUNE JORDAN, 1998

(Clockwise from top left) Hillary Clinton, former secretary of state 2008–2012; Angela Dorothea Merkel, Chancellor of Germany; Ellen Johnson Sirleaf, President of Liberia; Aung San Suu Kyi, chairperson of the National League for Democracy in Myanmmar. Former political prisoner from1989 until her release in 2010.

Politics encompasses more than just voting and running for office—the public sphere. Politics is also that which influences the choices we make and the lives we live in our most intimate moments—the private sphere. Consider the following statement made in 2012 by Todd Akin, a contender for a U.S. Senate seat representing Missouri. Responding to a question about whether he would support a woman's right to an abortion in the event of rape, he answered: "It seems to me, from what I understand from doctors, that's really rare. If it's a legitimate rape, the female body has ways to shut that whole thing down." Implicit in Akin's statement is the idea that if a rape results in pregnancy, then it's the woman's fault and therefore her choices about what to do about that pregnancy must be circumscribed by law and policy. In reality, more than 32,000 women who are raped each year will become pregnant (Geiger, 2012).

Now consider another view, that of Nobel Peace Laureate Leymah Gbowee. In her Nobel lecture, she argued that "[r]ape and abuse is the result of a larger problem, and that problem is the absence of women in the decision-making space. If more women were part of decision-making in most societies, there would be less exclusive policies and laws that are blind to abuses women endure" (Gbowee, 2011). Gbowee, who experienced the horrors of war in her country, Liberia, and its devastating impact on women, understands that rape and abuse under any circumstance reflect the gendered hierarchies and dichotomies pervasive in all societies (Peterson and Runyan, 2010).

These two contrary views show that violence against women, whether in the form of active violence (rape, sexual assault, domestic abuse, enforced sterilization, coerced heterosexuality, honor killings) or structural violence (women's unpaid and low-paid work, poverty, lack of access to capital and credit, pension and social security benefits, employment discrimination, lack of reproductive rights, and educational opportunities) all involve political and legal choices and decisions made by (mostly)

men in both the private and public spheres. As the 1970s feminist phrase put it: "The personal is political." Gender hierarchies and structural inequalities shape our realities daily and affect us all day long: at home, in the office, and in the public square. This chapter examines these hierarchies and inequalities by focusing on the gender politics through which public laws and policies are created. Just as importantly, it examines how feminist scholars and activists—past and present, nationally and globally—have participated in the political process, often seeking to redress asymmetries of power. In this sense, politics is about our morals, our commitments, and, indeed, our desire and ability to effect social change.

Public laws, made and enforced largely by men, have determined women's sexual and reproductive rights by defining marriage, when sexual relations are or are not legal, and whether a woman must continue a pregnancy. Until recently domestic violence was largely ignored by law enforcement and the seriousness of rape minimized, except when it was the rape of "our" women by men belonging to a subordinate minority. Also, the rights of women were not understood to be human rights, to be included on the agendas of those working to promote the international recognition of human rights (Tickner, 2001).

Public policy determines the effective rights and obligations of women to their children and their ability to carry out their wishes with regard to their children's care, education, and safety. Public policy also restricts and shapes women's rights and capacities to select ways to support themselves and determines the conditions under which they work. Politics has served as a means for men to control women's lives.

Feminists have advocated that women increase their formal political participation, in part to change the male-centered and male-dominated construction of politics, policies, and laws. At the same time, they have argued that political and social life ought to better reflect women's values of caring and concern for others (Tronto, 1993; Harrington, 1999; Held, 2006).

Feminist political scientists have explored the roles women play in formal and grassroots or community-level organizations, their leadership styles, intraparty roles, and power, and how they organize on issues they consider important (Bookman and Morgen, 1988; Hawkesworth, 2012). In recent years, women have often voted quite differently from men, forcing candidates and political parties to pay attention to the "women's vote." Also, women have been gaining political power around the world. Feminist political scientists have studied the rise of women to elective legislative and executive offices and ask whether having more women in positions of political power leads to more progressive policies and laws in relation to gender.

Political Power

What Is Power?

Power is the capacity to get something done, whether directly or indirectly. Women may exercise power in the domestic sphere in terms of their influence within their families. Men's power, in contrast, is "more co-ordinated and structured within an institutionalized framework" (Ridd and Callaway, 1987: 3). Political power is usually exercised by means of institutionalized structures, including the military, the government, the economy, and religious, educational, and legal systems. Such structures protect those who wield power and enable them to disperse their power more widely (Hartsock, 1983; Ridd and Callaway, 1987).

The power that individuals or groups possess involves "a social relationship between groups that determines access to, use of, and control over the basic material and ideological resources in society" (Bookman and Morgen, 1988: 4). Except in small-scale societies (Sanday, 1981, 2002), men generally have greater access to and control over resources. Power over others fosters relationships of social distance and subordination.

Power is also the capacity to not do something—to not marry, not bear or be responsible for a child, not engage in physical labor, and not have sexual intercourse when another demands it. Only those who have sufficient power to protect themselves from the aggression of others can ensure they will not be coerced to the will of others.

Feminists have pointed out that power need not imply dominance. Power to get things done can be shared and distributed evenly. This is the notion behind the organizations of most feminist utopias. The sharing of power has been attempted on a small scale in communes and simple societies throughout the world. In a complex industrial society, the sharing of power has been difficult even to imagine. Feminists seek, at the very least, to reduce the extent to which society is organized hierarchically, with vast disparities of power between those who command and those who must obey.

Some individuals conclude that because men have such power over women, women are powerless, but this is not quite true: power is a social relationship. Power can be wielded by the "powerless" despite the fact that they possess fewer resources and must often organize in larger numbers to offset their "powerlessness." As long as the analysis of power and politics is confined to the study of institutions in which fewer female faces are present—courts, bureaucracies, legislatures, and executive levels—women will be perceived as more powerless than they are. A more fruitful approach to a better understanding of women and politics would be to look at arenas where women can be found—neighborhoods, schools, associations, and organizations (Moser and Peake, 1987; Bookman and Morgen, 1988; Dalley, 1988; Cott, 1990).

Power and Authority

There is an important distinction between *power* and *authority*. Those with authority are accepted as being justified in having and using

---

Box 13.1   WOMEN DO NOT BELONG IN THE PUBLIC SPHERE

In the nineteenth century women were told:

The civil law, as well as nature herself, has always recognized a wide difference in the respective spheres and destinies of man and woman. Man is or should be woman's protector and defender. The natural and proper timidity and delicacy which belongs to the female sex evidently unfits it for many of the occupations of civil life. The constitution of the family organization, which is founded in the divine ordinance, as well as in the nature of things, indicates the domestic sphere as that which properly belongs to the domain and functions of womanhood. The harmony, not to say identity, of interests and views which belong or should belong to the family institution, is repugnant to the idea of a woman adopting a distinct and independent career from that of her husband....

...It is true many women are unmarried and not affected by any other duties, complications, and incapacities arising out of the married state, but these are exceptions to the general rule. The paramount destiny and mission of women are to fulfill the noble and benign offices of wife and mother.... And the rules of civil society must be adapted to the general constitution of things, and cannot be based upon exceptional cases.

...In my opinion, in view of the peculiar characteristics, destiny, and mission of women, it is within the province of the legislature to ordain what offices, positions, and callings shall be filled and discharged by men and shall receive the benefit of those energies and responsibilities, and that decision and firmness which are presumed to predominate in the sterner sex.

And in the twentieth century women were told:

And if a woman wants to run for political office in the constituency in which she was born she is told, "You left long ago. Go run somewhere else." And if she wants to run in her husband's constituency, she is told, "You didn't come here to rule; you came here to marry."

Sources: Bradwell v. *Illinois,* 1873; Justice Bradley quoted in Goldstein, 1979, pp. 49–51; Miria-R-K-Matembe, member of the Uganda Constituent Assembly at the USAID Gender and Democracy in Africa Workshop, Washington, DC, July 27, 1995. From *African Voices* (Fall 1995), http:// www.usaid. gov/regions/afr/abic/avoices/avfal95.htm#workshop accessed 1998.

---

power. People who seize power need eventually to find a way of legitimizing it in order to command obedience to decisions without resorting to the continued use or threat of force. Economic power and authority are the ability and accepted right to control the production and distribution of resources; political power and authority are the ability and accepted right to control or influence decisions about war and peace, legal protection and punishment, and group decision making in general, including the assignment of leadership roles. In complex societies, political power usually includes a great deal of economic power, but political and economic power can and do operate separately. Sometimes they function in a complementary way; at other times, they are at odds.

Although power and authority are often exercised by the same person, they are distinct, and each may be exercised without the other. Women have from time to time exercised

Box 13.2   SULTANA'S DREAM (1905)

I became very curious to know where the men were. I met more than a hundred women while walking there, but not a single man.

"Where are the men?" I asked her.

"In their proper places, where they ought to be."

"Pray let me know what you mean by 'their proper places.'"

"Oh, I see my mistake, you cannot know our customs, as you were never here before. We shut our men indoors."

"Just as we are kept in the *zenana*?"*

"Exactly so."

"How funny." I burst into a laugh. Sister Sara laughed too.

"But, dear Sultana, how unfair it is to shut in the harmless women and let loose the men."

"Why? It is not safe for us to come out of the *zenana*, as we are naturally weak."

"Yes, it is not safe so long as there are men about the streets, nor is it so when a wild animal enters a marketplace."

"Of course not."

"Suppose some lunatics escape from the asylum and begin to do all sorts of mischief to men, horses, and other creatures: in that case what will your countrymen do?"

"They will try to capture them and put them back into their asylum."

"Thank you! And you do not think it wise to keep sane people inside an asylum and let loose the insane?"

"Of course not!" said I, laughing lightly.

"As a matter of fact, in your country this very thing is done! Men, who do or at least are capable of doing no end of mischief, are let loose and the innocent women shut up in the *zenana*! How can you trust those untrained men out of doors?"

"We have no hand or management of our social affairs. In India man is lord and master. He has taken to himself all powers and privileges and shut up women in the *zenana*."

"Why do you allow yourselves to be shut up?"

"Because it cannot be helped as they are stronger than women."

"A lion is stronger than a man, but it does not enable him to dominate the human race. You have neglected the duty you owe yourselves, and you have lost your natural rights by shutting your eyes to your own interests."

"But my dear Sister Sara, if we do everything by ourselves, what will the men do then?"

"They should not do anything, excuse men; they are fit for nothing. Only catch them and put them into the *zenana*."

"But it would be very easy to catch and put them inside the four walls?" said I. "And even if this were done, would all their business—political and commercial—also go with them into the *zenana*?"

Sister Sara made no reply. She only smiled sweetly. Perhaps she thought it was useless to argue with one who was no better than a frog in a well.

---

power (the ability to get someone to do something) but often have not held authority, due to cultural beliefs that women do not possess a legitimate right to power (O'Barr, 1984). Women exercising power are often accused of "manipulating" others because they are not acknowledged as rightfully powerful.

History provides many examples of women who held power by virtue of their relationships with powerful men. Royal mistresses in the courts of European kings even had official status. In the United States in the twentieth and twenty-first centuries, women married to presidents have occasionally exercised notable political power. When Woodrow Wilson collapsed in office in 1919, his wife Edith Axson Wilson played a crucial role in helping him

Hillary Clinton represents a new kind of feminist leadership in the United States today.

maintain the presidency. Eleanor Roosevelt was able to undertake major humanitarian programs because of her influence with her husband, Franklin Delano Roosevelt, and his associates. When some of her ideas were not endorsed by the president, she pursued them through women's networks (Cook, 1992). Hillary Rodham Clinton was the first first lady to have a visible role in political appointments but was often criticized for wielding illegitimate power. She was later elected senator from New York and, not long after, became secretary of state. In these latter capacities, she could exercise power in her own right.

The exercise of power based on unofficial influence is difficult to establish or assess. Reference to the power of the "women behind the throne" has often been used by those who wish to justify a status quo in which women have little direct power—or authority—of their own. More than ever women are challenging traditional notions that women lack power and authority. As women fought to gain political power throughout the twentieth and twenty-first centuries, we have seen the rise of women presidents and prime ministers. Unlike in previous eras, today it is more common to see women serve as presidents, prime ministers, or queen regnant of their countries, commanding considerable power and/or authority.

Types of Government

As societies have become larger and more complex, forms of government have become more specialized and exclusionary. Full participation occurs only in the smallest, simplest societies, such as hunting-and-gathering bands, where political decisions are made by public discussion and consensus. There are no government specialists, and leaders arise in particular situations according to need and skills. An older woman with experience and skill might organize and direct others in food gathering. A good public speaker might assume responsibility for expressing the will of the community.

Similar principles apply in slightly larger and more complex societies but on a more restricted basis. Some persons hold positions of authority as "chief" or "war leader" or "council member." In these societies, women tend to be more segregated as a group. If women do play a role in political processes, they tend to do so as "women," not as ordinary and equal group members. Among the Iroquois in North America, certain women, and not men, were entitled to select male group leaders. Men, on the other hand, were entitled to hold the leadership positions; women were not (Sanday, 1981).

The most complex forms of government are national states, which exclude most members of society from direct participation in making governmental decisions, though to qualify as democratic they must have periodic elections. At the higher levels of a hierarchical structure, few can participate; but on the local level, small communities can conduct much of their business themselves. Here, participatory democracy may be possible even in a large, complex state. It is at the local level that women's voices are most likely to be heard. For example, more women are found in China on public councils in rural communities and in the United States on school boards and town councils and in greater numbers in state legislatures than at the federal level.

Women's Political Power in the Past

Women have occasionally exercised authority and political power in the past, both in dynastic states in Europe and in some preindustrial societies (Schiff, 2010). Such power often derived from their kinship positions as daughters, sisters, wives, and mothers. In the early Middle Ages in Europe, when a ruler's officials were actually royal household servants (and the head of the household governed the domestic affairs of the royal estate, which was the kingdom), it was considered perfectly natural to place the ruler's wife, or queen, at the head of these servants. When Henry II of England went to war (which was a great deal of the time) he left his queen, Eleanor of Aquitaine (c. 1122–1204), in charge of his kingdom. All his officials were ordered to report to her whenever he was away. As regents for their husbands or sons, queens could wield significant political power. Only when Henry II began to suspect that his queen favored their sons over him did he discontinue making her England's ruler in his absence (Kelly, 1957).

Historically, the rules of primogeniture limited the power wielded by royal women. In Great Britain such laws of primogeniture date back to the seventeenth century and gave male children the right to succession to the throne before their sisters. In an effort to modernize the British monarchy, this law was finally repealed in 2011, and as a result the new rules allow a firstborn daughter to precede a son to the throne.

As the governments of Europe and elsewhere became more bureaucratically organized, women were less likely to share in political power. The recognized offices that might have been delegated to the queen gradually shifted to ministers, judges, councilors, and other functionaries, who were never women. Even in the reign of Queen Elizabeth I (1558–1603), who governed by virtue of inherited right, not a single woman was ever appointed to a ministerial post (Neale, 1957).

Similarly, European colonial rule precipitated erosion of women's power where it had existed. Among the Iroquois of North America, for example, both women and men participated in village decision making. Women appointed men to official positions in the League of the Iroquois and could veto their decisions, although men controlled league deliberations. Iroquois women and men exercised separate but equal political power during the height of the Iroquois confederacy (Sanday, 1981; Mann 2000). After a steady encroachment on their power by British and French colonizers, the Iroquois became unable to sustain themselves economically. English Quakers, who intended to preserve the Iroquoian culture, suggested solutions that fundamentally restructured Iroquois gender relationships. Quaker missionaries insisted on husband–wife nuclear family relationships, which shut out the traditional power of the wife's mother in the family. In imposing their own cultural assumptions, the Quakers helped develop a new pattern of male dominance where it had not existed before (Sanday, 1981).

Another example of the erosion of women's political power under colonial rule is that of the Igbo of southern Nigeria, where precolonial social arrangements included women's councils. By tradition, these councils exercised peacekeeping powers, including the corporal punishment and public humiliation of the offender and the destruction of the offender's property (Sanday, 1981). British colonial rule in the late nineteenth century disrupted these cultural practices, which had afforded women real power. British authorities created new "warrant" chiefs where none had existed before, giving the position to local men (Falola and Aderinto, 2010).

Patterns of Male Dominance

Anthropologist Ernestine Friedl has defined *male dominance* as a pattern in which men have better access, if not exclusive rights, to those activities to which society accords the greatest value and by which control and influence are exercised over others (Sanday, 1981). Thus, male dominance means excluding women from political and economic decision making and includes aggression against women.

Male dominance occurs in various kinds of social relationship. It may consist of cultural assumptions about natural male aggressiveness, about being "tough" and "brave." It may involve designating specific places where only males may congregate, like men's clubs and bars, street corners, legislative chambers, courts, or boardrooms. It may involve wife beating and battering (Gordon, 1988). It may result in murder, as in India where "bride burning" occurs when husbands seek to remarry and to acquire another dowry (for a fuller explanation, see Oldenburg, 2002). Another form of male control of women was seen during and after the 2011 "Arab Spring" in Egypt. Many female activists took to the streets and slept in Tahrir Square, encouraged by men to support the uprising that removed Hosni Mubarak from power. While most Egyptian women admit to being sexually harassed when they are in Cairo's public spaces, they noted that they were not sexually harassed in Tahrir Square. But outside of the Square security forces punished women activists by forcing them to endure sexual assaults and virginity tests. Female activists continue to experience these tactics at the hands of the Egyptian security forces. Repulsed by such treatment and the everyday sexual harassment they experience, thousands of Egyptian women marched in December 2011 to demonstrate against state security forces caught on video in the act of attacking, beating, and stripping female demonstrators in Tahrir Square. To carry out the march, women had to depend upon men to protect them (Kirkpatrick, 2012). This kind of control reminds us that although women may wield some political power and authority, they often do so only with the support and protection of men.

Women as Political Leaders

History provides several examples of women political leaders. In modern times, powerful female political figures have included Margaret Thatcher (United Kingdom), Indira Gandhi (India), Corazon Aquino (Philippines), Golda Meir (Israel), Benazir Bhutto (Pakistan), Megawati Sukarnoputri (Indonesia), Eva Perón (Argentina), Angela Merkel (Germany), Michelle Bachelet (Chile), Dilma Rousseff (Brazil),and Ellen Johnson-Sirleaf (Liberia). In 2012, women functioned at the highest levels of political power in 22 countries, including Argentina, Brazil, Germany, India, Liberia, Slovakia, and Thailand. Today, more women serve as presidents and prime ministers, but even more women are winning political office as parliamentarians, state legislators, and local councilwomen.

Generally, there is an inverse relationship between higher political offices and the presence of women in them. Universally, there are many more women in lower-level political offices than in high ones. On average, in 2012 women comprised 19% of national legislators and 7% of executive cabinet ministers worldwide. Table 13.1 shows that the most promising picture comes from the Scandinavian countries, with their mixed economies and their concern for both social welfare and social justice. Socialist states have made great efforts to recruit women into national legislatures, but in most of the states of the former Soviet bloc, the number of women in political office declined when tradition and capitalism became more influential than communism. Since China's transition to state capitalism, the government has lifted gender quotas for women at

TABLE 13.1 Women In National Legislative Offices, 2011

Country	Percentage of Women in National Legislature		
Europe		East Asia	
Austria	28	China	21
Denmark	38	Indonesia	18
France	19	Japan	11
Germany	33	Philippines	22
Greece	17	Africa	
Hungary	9	Algeria	8
Norway	40	Ghana	8
Poland	20	Kenya	10
Russia	14	Mozambique	39
Sweden	45	Nigeria	4
United Kingdom	22	South Africa	45
Middle East		North America	
Afghanistan	28	Canada	25
Iraq	25	United States	17
Israel	19	Central/South America	
Saudi Arabia	0	Argentina	39
South Asia		Bolivia	25
Bangladesh	19	Brazil	9
India	11	Cuba	43
Nepal	33	Ecuador	32
Pakistan	22	Venezuela	17

Source: Inter-Parliamentary Union, "Women in Parliaments", situation as of 31 August 2011, (http://www.ipu.org/wmn-e/classif.htm).

the local governmental and administrative levels. Consequently, fewer women occupy seats in the National People's Congress and the Communist Party Committee (Edwards, 2007). In Latin America many women are winning elections to provincial and national legislatures (Schwindt-Bayer, 2011). In the Middle East, South Asia, and Africa, women are least likely to be found in high-level political positions.

In the past women who held cabinet-level positions found themselves ghettoized in ministries reserved for women—health and welfare, education, culture, the family, and consumer affairs (Randall, 1987). But today throughout the world, more women serve in high cabinet positions in once-considered male-dominated areas such as defense, treasury, and foreign affairs. Condoleezza Rice served as the national security advisor during the first administration of George W. Bush. Madeleine Albright (in the Clinton administration) and Hillary Rodham Clinton (in the Obama administration) have demonstrated that women can handle the challenges of foreign affairs during turbulent times. In France, Michèle Alliot-Marie served as the minister of defense from 2002 to 2007 in the Chirac government. Christine Lagarde, the noted French economist, as managing director of the International Monetary Fund, oversees the global economy.

Recent Political Gains of Women in the United States

In view of the gender socialization women undergo, the effects of the contemporary women's movement on the pattern of female office holding are striking. Women's increased political participation in the United States after the 1990s was largely a result of women deciding it was time to change the face of the U.S. Congress and the state legislatures (Maloney, 2008). National attention was given to the dominance of white males in Congress and their male bias during the senate hearings to confirm Clarence Thomas as nominee to the U.S. Supreme Court in 1991. Anita Hill, a former assistant to Thomas, had been called on to testify. In her public testimony, Hill testified that Thomas, her supervisor when she worked at the U.S. Equal Employment Opportunity Commission, had sexually harassed her. During the Thomas hearings, Hill was belittled and ridiculed by the all-white male members of the Senate Judiciary Committee. Angered by the insensitive treatment of both Hill and the issue of sexual harassment by the Senate committee, women entered the political arena with a new energy. Many more women decided to run for office. Many more made financial contributions. In addition, women feared the further erosion of specific rights, such as those governing their reproductive choices.

In the 1980s an important political "gender gap" emerged. It was after the 1980 election that analysts began to note significant differences between women and men in political viewpoints, party identification, and voting decisions. U.S. men, to a greater extent than women, aligned their party identification and voting behavior with parties and candidates that were conservative on social welfare issues and more in favor of expenditures on defense. Women, to a greater extent than men, supported parties and candidates that expressed concern for social welfare issues and increased spending on education (Kaufmann and Petrocik, 1999). These tendencies have continued: women are more inclined to favor public policies that support the protection of the environment, fewer militaristic resolutions to disputes, and programs for quality healthcare, racial equality, and family support.

Table 13.2 displays the increased representation of women as candidates and winners for Congress in the period 1970–2011. While the increase in the number of women is significant—especially in view of the 2012 election—as of 2011 women held only 17% of the seats in the U.S. Senate and 16.8% of the seats in the U.S. House of Representatives. Women have been even more successful in state legislatures, where their presence has increased fivefold over the past two decades. From 301 legislators in 1969, or 4% of the total, women have grown to 1,742, or 23.6% of the legislators from the 50 states. It is not enough for women to be elected or appointed to political office for women's concerns to be heard. Women have far less economic power than men and are hardly represented at all in the upper reaches of the corporate world. The more that economic power and corporate influence affect politics—and the extent of this is enormous in the United States—the less will women's voices be effective.

Political Gains of Women in Office around the Globe

U.S. women have gained access to higher office, and so, too, have their peers around the world. Globally, the United States ranks 70th in the percentage of women it elects to high political office, falling behind many Western democratic and Global South countries (McDonagh, 2009). How can countries elect more women to national legislative bodies? In many countries, gender quotas help more women get elected to office. In India, a 1993 constitutional amendment created the Panchayat Raj Act, which allocates 33% of seats at the village and district levels to women. As a result of this act, close to 6 million women have been elected to village- and district-level office. In South Africa, the post-apartheid African National Congress government adopted a law to require a 30% quota for women candidates. Today, women hold 44.5% of the lower legislative seats in South Africa. The Nordic countries have made tremendous gains in getting women elected to higher office. Women in Sweden and Norway occupy 45% and 39.6%, respectively, of parliamentary seats. There are 26 countries in which women account for 30% or more of their national parliaments. Although more and more women are gaining political office in some countries, Belize, Oman, Qatar, and Saudi Arabia have no women sitting in parliament as representatives (Inter-Parliamentary Union, 2011).

TABLE 13.2 Women Candidates for the U.S. Congress, 1970–2012 (Party and Seat Summary for Democratic and Republican Party Nominees)*

	Senate		House of Representatives	
	Candidates	*Winners*	*Candidates*	*Winners*
1970	1 (1R)	0	25 (15D, 10R)	12 (9D, 3R)
1980	5 (2D, 3R)	0	52 (27D, 25R)	19 (10D, 9R)
1990	8 (2D, 6R)	1 (1D)	69[†] (39D, 30R)	28[†] (35D, 12R)
2000	6 (4D, 2R)	6 (4D, 2R)	122[†] (80D, 42R)	59[†] (41D, 18R)
2010	36 (19D, 17R)	15 (9D, 6R)	262 (134D, 128R)	138 (91D, 47R)
2012	36 (20D, 16R)	18 (12D, 6R)	298 (190D, 108R)	166 (118D, 48R)

*Includes major party nominees for the general elections, not those running in special elections.

[†]Does not include two (1D, 1R) candidates—one incumbent who won her race and one challenger for nonvoting delegate of Washington, D.C.

Source: Center for the American Woman and Politics (CAWP), Eagleton Institute of Politics, Rutgers, The State University of New Jersey, 2012. www.cawp.rutgers.edu/index.php. Retrieved November 19, 2012.

Do Women in Office Make a Difference?

If women in political office make a difference, what kind of difference do they make? What is the link between women's participation in political office and the advancement of public policy supportive of women's needs? Indeed, women heads of state can make a difference by appointing more women to cabinet positions, establishing policies that support working women and women's reproductive rights, and criminalizing practices harmful to women's integrity as Jóhanna Siguroardóttir of Iceland, Michele Bachelet of Chile, and Dilma Rousseff of Brazil have done (Hawkesworth, 2012). But it takes more than having a female head of state to achieve policies and programs that address the needs and interests of women.

Some scholars have noted a critical threshold of 30%; that is, when women make up 30% of political institutions, they are able to influence policy outcomes. In the Nordic countries, where women account for at least 30% of the parliamentary seats, public policy has addressed women's needs. In Norway, the government provides opportunities for women to combine their child-care and employment demands. Women- and family-centered public policies include expanding child-care services; offering flexible work hours; improving pension rights for unpaid care work; and increasing child benefits for families that do not use public child-care services. In South Africa, where government quotas reserve 30% of parliamentary and 50% of local government candidacies for women, the impact has made a difference in women's lives. In 1995, the South African parliament passed the Convention on the Elimination of All Forms of Discrimination Against Women without reservations, and it has introduced "the women's budget process," which analyzes the gender impact of the government's budget (Women's Environment and Development Organization, 2001). Studies of

village female representatives in India document that they possessed a better understanding of their constituents' needs than did their male counterparts (Lindgren, Inkinen, and Widmalm, 2009).

Even in countries that have not attained the 30% threshold, women officeholders generally, regardless of political party or label, take more feminist positions on women's issues than their male colleagues. Studies conducted of women parliamentarians in Europe support this view (Randall, 1987; Leyenaar, 2008). In Malaysia, though females only make up 10% of the national parliament, they successfully pushed through legislation that concerned childcare, crimes related to children, and improving the lives of disabled children (Zakuan, 2010). There is also sufficient evidence that in the U.S. Congress "in addition to advocating for their districts, female legislators do exhibit a profound commitment to the pursuit of policies for women, children, and families" (Swers, 2002: 132). Women officeholders are more open and inclusive than their male counterparts. In place of carrying out business behind closed doors, women favor involving the general public in the political process and providing increased access to constituent groups often left out of policy making (Center for the American Woman and Politics, 1991; Kathlene, 1992; Dolan, 2001; Women's Environment and Development Organization, 2001). Women legislators also willingly work collectively across party lines to accomplish specific goals (Waylen, 2010). Former New York congresswoman the late Bella Abzug found greater support among her female colleagues, both Democrats and Republicans, than from the male members of her own party on issues of concern to women (Abzug, 1984).

Other scholars question the "critical mass" argument and point out that not all women elected to office can be counted on to represent women's interests (Chowdhury, 2008; Childs and Krook, 2009). Women do not constitute a monolithic group; they are divided by political ideology, class background, race, and religious beliefs, which influence their attitudes and beliefs about women's place in society. Even women who are very supportive of women's rights differ over what strategies and policies can best improve women's lives. Molyneux argues that women divide between those who argue for practical gender interests and others who support strategic gender interests (Molyneux, 1998). In other words, some women in office are more concerned about meeting the short-term basic needs of women such as providing equality in the areas of education and employment; others are concerned with transformational politics and seek to implement policies that tackle the division of labor and reproductive issues. The former group accepts gender inequality and male authority as a given; the latter want to undermine or transform gender inequalities and the structures that render women subordinate to men (Molyneux, 1998). Conflicts over which policies and laws best improve the lives of women drive a wedge in the unity of women.

Perhaps an indication of the importance and success of women in the political arena has been the emergence of the ultra-conservative right and its anti-feminist platform. The values of cultural and religious ultra-conservatives (fundamentalist Christians, Jewish, and Islamic groups and individuals as well as nongovernmental organizations such as Concerned Women of America and the Eagle Forum) are shaped by a belief that women are subordinate to men. Strongly committed to traditional family values, they believe that women should confine themselves to the private sphere of the home and men should be the breadwinners and active in the public sphere. Such beliefs lead ultra-conservative groups and individuals to oppose gender equality, sexual reproductive rights, and sexual equality rights for women and men who challenge conventional norms

(Chappell, 2006). The rise of female conservative politicians challenges the notion that a critical mass of female politicians will deliver the appropriate gender goods to their female constituents. Childs and Krook (2009) argue against excessive reliance on a critical mass of women in public office; rather, it is more effective to find "critical actors"—women and men willing to propose and support legislation that addresses women's human rights and needs. Other scholars have added that it's not enough to have men and women politicians actively promoting women's rights. Without an effective and strong women's movement outside of government helping to promote a feminist legislative agenda and pushing to hold politicians accountable, gender-friendly legislation and policies will not result (Gouws, 2008; Leyenaar, 2008).

Right-Wing Women

Backlash against women's rights has not only come from governments and corporate interests, but also from right-wing women and transnational conservative activists and organizations (Chappell, 2006). Throughout history, women have not only organized in support of equality and justice, but have been part of fascist movements. Claudia Koonz (1987), for instance, has written about the history of women's involvement in Nazi Germany. Kathleen Blee (1991) has written about women in the Ku Klux Klan. She writes that "[o]ne of the largest and most influential right-wing women's organizations of the immediate post suffrage period was the Women of the Ku Klux Klan [WKKK]. From 1923 to 1930, women poured into the Klan movement to oppose immigration, racial equality, Jewish-owned businesses, parochial schools, and 'moral decay.'" Women's involvement in right-wing movements has a long history and is in evidence from across the world. For instance, women participated in the destruction of the Babri Masjid (a sixteenth-century mosque destroyed by Hindu mobs in 1992 in India) and the systematic violence against Muslims in Gujarat in 2002. Women were part of Italian fascist movements and also actively participated in Latin American dictatorships. Women's participation in racist and fascist movements underscores that women's political organizing, while overwhelmingly marked by a quest for justice and equality, is not an "essential" calling, that is, women are not innately more prone to justice and, as their participation in right-wing movements demonstrates, can be just as racist as their male counterparts.

Yet history shows that women have come together to elect representatives and influence governmental decisions supportive of social justice and equality for all and can promote policies and practices that attend to women's issues. Increasingly, women realize that they have to become the change they wish to see, and they often do this by running for office and seeking appointments themselves. Can women build together significant political forces to oppose further incursions on the gains made and make further progress? Have women developed the networks, the organizations, the ways of offering support to one another to marshal their forces, get their opinions heard, and make their presence felt in political processes? The answer depends on women.

Obstacles Facing Women in Politics

Scholars identify three theoretical explanations for why more women are not elected to public office. The sociological theory attributes the low level of women officeholders to culture. Patriarchal cultures socialize their citizens to think in terms of a public/private dichotomy that locates women in the domestic sphere (Hang, 2012). Women are not expected to hold political decision-making positions. The question raised about female, but not male, candidates is: Who is taking care of the family? As a result, social norms and expectations about women's proper roles act as a brake to recruitment into politics and to political advancement. Women's usual work roles of teacher, clerk, and nurse are not the professions that typically recruit or train people for higher political office. Even when women are as qualified as men to run for office, they are more likely to believe that they are not as qualified and also less likely to believe that they can actually win office. Men, on the other hand, are more likely to overestimate their qualifications for running for office and winning (Krook, 2010). In addition, when women have the education and the occupational experience for holding higher political office, their fellow citizens must be willing to vote for them. Opinion polls indicate that though the public is more willing than in the past to elect women to higher political office, about 25% of Americans are unwilling to vote for a woman for president (Conway, 2001). The 2008 U.S. presidential primary elections demonstrate the continued voter reluctance to support female candidates. Though Hillary Clinton won 18 million votes for the Democratic nomination, she still lost to Barack Obama (Collins, 2009). Opinion polls taken of voters in countries such as Japan and Nigeria find that voters remain unfavorably disposed to electing a female to political office. And a majority of Nigerian men indicated they would not let their wives participate in politics (Arowolo and Aluko, 2010; Eto, 2010).

A second explanation for the low rates of women in elected office points to their involvement in nonpolitical activities. Household, child-care, and work responsibilities, with which women are still disproportionately saddled, leave them little time to engage in the political process (Conway, 2001; Peterson and Runyan, 2010).

A third explanation has to do with institutional impediments. Gatekeepers such as party leaders, interest group leaders, and campaign fundraisers often discourage women from running for office (Conway, 2001; Krook, 2010; Hawkesworth, 2012). In Latin American countries, political parties' procedures and rules for the selection of candidates make it more difficult to attract women to run for office (Hinojosa, 2012). Many political parties, dominated by men, tend to recruit men, whom they view as more likely to win elections. In many countries, male candidates are recruited in male-dominated clubs and meeting (Arowolo and Aluko, 2010), or political activities take place in the evenings and until late at night when women are expected to be home taking care of their families (Krook, 2010). Voters judge more negatively a woman who sacrifices her family to run for political office. Traditionally, male politicians have sought campaign funds from business and community leaders who are interested in backing candidates as a way of establishing future access to them. Women candidates often face difficulties in finding backers, raising funds, and creating large-scale organizations of devoted followers who see possible benefits in their election. The fundraising success of Hillary Rodham Clinton in her races for the Senate and the presidential primary were exceptions.

In part to overcome this obstacle, EMILY (Early Money Is Like Yeast) was founded in 1982 to support pro-choice Democratic women candidates through raising money to launch campaigns in the first stages. EMILY's List is a network of donors and has been one of the largest contributors to female candidates. For pro-choice Republican women candidates, WISH (Women in the Senate and House) offers financial support. If traditional financial backers do not take women seriously as political candidates, women are showing that they can fund themselves.

Another institutional impediment to the selection of women to run for office concerns the election procedure. Studies document that gatekeepers are more willing to endorse and promote women candidates running in multimember, rather than single-member, electoral districts. Electoral systems that use some form of proportional representation (with more than one candidate representing an electoral district) have had greater success in getting women to run for and win elections. Proportional representation electoral systems exist in the Nordic countries and elsewhere, but not in the United States.

The 2008 and 2012 U.S. Presidential Elections

The historic 2008 electoral campaigns of Hillary Clinton running as a presidential contender in the Democratic Party primary and Sarah Palin as the vice-presidential nominee on the Republican Party ticket demonstrate the challenges facing American women running for the highest office. Both candidates played the "masculine mystique" card in order to appeal to the electorate, doing so in different ways (Sklar, 2008). Clinton campaigned as a competent woman able to handle such "masculine" issues as being tough on defense through her service on the Senate Armed Services Committee and her support of the 2003 war against Iraq (Carroll, 2009). Palin's appeal to voters was based on her ability to engage in "masculine" activities such as hunting and fishing. Palin also went to great lengths to prove to the electorate that she could balance her roles as wife and mother of five children while serving as an elected official. Both candidates faced the double bind of women: Clinton's competence was negated by the public's perception of her as being less than feminine; while Palin's femininity left many voters judging her as less than competent (Carlin and Winfrey, 2009). Neither candidate was able to build a campaign that united voters across the gender, generational, class, and racial divide (Sklar, 2008; Lind, 2009).

Gender and race played a very different role in the 2012 national elections. Unlike the 2008 elections, where women were part of the presidential and vice presidential races, in 2012 the focus was on women voters as well as some key Senate races, which were won by women. In a tightly contested race, incumbent President Barack Obama sought re-election; he was challenged by Republican Mitt Romney. Obama's ultimate win has been widely credited to women voters as well as black, Latino, and Asian voters. Consider the following: 93% of blacks, 71% of Latinos, and 73% of Asian Americans voted for Obama. In addition to people of color overwhelmingly voting for Obama, according to CNN exit polls, 55% of women voted for Obama while only 44% voted for Romney. In contrast to the people of color and women who voted for Obama, Republican candidate Romney got 59% of the white vote, which represented a 20-point margin over Obama. However, if we were to look at the election results by intersections of race and gender, then 56% of white women voted for Romney. In fact, election results between 1980 and 2012 show that the majority of white women voted for Republican candidates in every election, except during the 1992, 1996, and 2000 elections (Junn, 2012). Therefore, Obama's win cannot be credited entirely to women, devoid of race and class factors. Rather, it was the combination of women and people of color votes that returned him to office. Furthermore, the victory of women's issues in the 2012 election is credited to particular Senate races in which women won against deeply conservative men who were advocating against women's reproductive choice. For instance, Democrat Claire McCaskill defeated Missouri's Republican candidate, Todd Akin,

whose infamous comments about "legitimate rape" were discussed earlier. The other major victory was in the election of Elizabeth Warren from Massachusetts, who defeated Scott Brown. The 2012 election ushered in yet other victories in the realms of gender and sexual identity. Tammy Baldwin of Wisconsin became the first openly gay person ever elected to the U.S. Senate, and Stacie Laughton, who was elected to the New Hampshire house of representatives, became the first transgender person elected to any state legislature.

Women as Citizens

Women's relationship to the nation has always been fraught. In this section, we examine how both women and men are important to nation building, but in different ways. In order to understand how women and men's relationship to the nation differs, first we need to look closely at the nation itself. Nations are not pregiven or "natural" formations. That is, all nations were created or invented at particular moments in history. By "invented" we do not mean that they are fictitious but that they are constantly being created. From the smallest and the most mundane actions, such as buying postage stamps depicting a national flag, to spectacular performances such as viewing national Independence Day parades, we are constantly generating a sense of "our" common identity through notions of a common past and collective destiny. Most nations depend on a sense of territorial integrity, a belief that everyone in the country is—or should be—part of the "imagined community" and possesses a common culture (Anderson, 1991). Such a belief is called nationalism, a dynamic and highly ideological phenomenon—one that changes over time and is often highly contested. Ann McClintock famously stated, "All nationalisms are gendered, all are invented, and all are dangerous" (McClintock, 1996: 104).

So what does it mean to say that nations are profoundly gendered entities? Consider for instance the way we call nations "fatherland" or "motherland," two terms that evoke distinct sentiments. "The motherland provides a passive, receptive, and vulnerable image in contrast to the active image of the fatherland, which is the force behind government and military action—invasion, conquest, and defense" (Ivekovic and Mostov, 2006: 11). During war and invasion, the occupied nation is described in feminized terms while the invading army is masculinized. In addition to being gendered, nations are also "raced." That is, nations are imagined as a collective of particular races. The racial construction of nations is most acutely evidenced during conflict when women from one nation or community are raped by another in order to emasculate its men, shame the community, and impregnate its women by the "seed of the enemy." Much of the literature on nations and nationalism does not examine gender closely (Yuval-Davis, 1997). Nira Yuval-Davis and Flora Anthias (1989) suggest five different ways in which to understand this relationship:

1. Women are thought to be biological reproducers of the nation. That is, they give birth to the nation's citizens, to its heroes and martyrs.
2. Women are symbolic signifiers of the nation. They represent the female nation such as "mother India" that needs to be both protected even while being a source of fierce power. Symbolically they are cherished for the sacrifices they make for their children as well as for the nation. Since women are both a source of pleasure and sacrifice, they are also potential enemies and traitors to the nation.
3. Women are considered the boundaries of the nation. Women's bodies serve as territorial markers of the nation. Being symbolic

of nation and community, women's bodies invite both protection and violation, facilitating both nation-building endeavors and acts of war. Thus an enemy's "rape and violation of individual women becomes symbolically significant in nationalist discourse and the politics of national identity as a violation of the nation and an act against the collective men of the enemy nation" (Ivekovic and Mostov, 2006: 11).
4. Women are made into repositories of national culture. Women are responsible for transmitting "appropriate and correct culture" to children and for safeguarding cultural boundaries intergenerationally.
5. Women actively participate in the political, economic, and militaristic enterprises of the nation. Women are part of formal and informal governance of the nation; they contribute to its economy through both waged and unwaged labor; and they are also part of the nation's military apparatus. While historically women were not admitted into combat units, since the 1970s many countries have begun to allow women to engage in active combat. Yet women's participation in a country's military is not limited to their direct participation. Rather, as Cynthia Enloe explains, we need to understand the militarization as "a step-by-step process by which a person or a thing gradually comes to be controlled by the military *or* comes to depend for its well-being on militaristic ideas" (Enloe, 2000: 3).

The dominant model of "citizen" is often based on the image of the male warrior-hero (Hartsock, 1983). Consequently, even though the concept of citizenship implies an equality of rights and obligations of all members within the nation-state, it is rarely so. In fact there are tremendous disparities in the privileges and penalties of citizens among different races, classes, sexualities and genders. In the United States, heterosexual, white, upper-class men are "ideal" citizens while women have had to inhabit correspondingly circumscribed positions. Niral Yuval-Davis wrote that "in Britain women lost their citizenship during Victorian times, when they got married; they continued to lose it if they got married to 'foreigners' until 1948, and it was not until 1981 that they got independent right to transfer their citizenship to their children" (Yuval-Davis, 1997: 12). While voting alone does not encapsulate the rights conferred through citizenship, it is one of its most visible markers. In the United States and elsewhere, one of the ways in which women demanded that the state acknowledge their citizenship was through the right to vote.

The Struggle for the Vote

The Thirteenth Amendment brought an end to slavery in the United States in 1865. When women attempted to eliminate the word *male* in the proposed Fourteenth Amendment,

which would ensure the "rights, privileges, and immunities of citizens" to freed slaves, they were advised by male abolitionists that it was not yet their turn. After decades of unceasing work in the cause of black emancipation, women found that they could count on little support from their male colleagues when the matter concerned women's rights, in this case the right to vote.

In 1869, Susan B. Anthony (1820–1906) and Elizabeth Cady Stanton (1815–1902) organized the National Woman Suffrage Association, devoted to achieving national suffrage through a state-by-state effort to change the law. In 1875, the Supreme Court ruled unanimously that the St. Louis registrar of voters could not be compelled to register Virginia Minor as a voter just because she was a citizen. This court ruling made it clear that only a constitutional amendment could achieve the vote for women. By 1878, the Stanton amendment was introduced into Congress: it was this proposal that would be ratified more than 40 years later as the Nineteenth Amendment. In 1890, the National American Woman Suffrage Association was formed (Kerber, 1998).

Alice Paul was a militant suffragette who worked tirelessly for the enfranchisement of women in both the United States and England. She was imprisoned many times and often suffered torture in jail. While on a hunger strike, for example, she was tied to a chair and force-fed to the point of vomiting. President Woodrow Wilson tried to have her declared insane.

Helena Hill Weed of Norwalk, Connecticut, was imprisoned for three days for carrying a banner that read "Governments derive their just powers from the consent of the governed."

To dramatize the hypocrisy of Woodrow Wilson's words when he led the United States into World War I "to make the world safe for democracy," Alice Paul's (1885–1977) suffrage group organized a silent picket in front of the White House in 1916. After several months, demonstrators were forcibly removed by the police for obstructing the public way, and 218 women from 26 states were arrested in 1917. In prison, they went on a hunger strike. The courts ordered their release several months later on the grounds that both arrests and convictions were illegal. Despite last-minute efforts by anti-suffrage groups after the war, proclaiming that enfranchising women would open up a Pandora's box of evils, the Nineteenth Amendment was passed by Congress in 1918 and ratified by three fourths of the state governments by August 26, 1920. Finally, American women could vote.

By the time women gained the right to vote in the United States, they could already do so in 10 other countries. The first country to grant women's suffrage was New Zealand, in 1893. Women's suffrage was achieved in England after an equally long but far more militant struggle: women aged 30 and above were allowed to vote in 1918, and women under 30 were given the vote in 1928. Women gained the right to vote in Ecuador in 1929, in Turkey in 1930, while in France they had to wait until 1944. After World War II, women in South Korea, Japan, Greece, and Italy were allowed to vote, but it was not until 1971 that most women in Switzerland won this right (only in 1990 did all cantons permit it).

Equal Rights Amendment

While the right to vote offered women participation as citizens in electoral democracy, it did not necessarily guarantee equal rights. In the United States the National Women's Party first proposed the Equal Rights Amendment (ERA) at the seventy-fifth anniversary

conference of the Seneca Falls Convention in 1923. It was introduced into Congress that year and repeatedly for the next 40 years. The Citizen's Advisory Council on the Status of Women recommended passage of the ERA in 1970. Hearings were held by the Senate Judiciary Committee after pressure from the National Organization for Women. Seriously debated by Congress for the first time in 1971, the ERA was finally adopted on March 22, 1972. However, it still required ratification by 38 states—three fourths of the state legislatures—before becoming law.

After the first 30 states ratified the ERA, the process began to slow down as opponents painted the ERA as a threat to personal, social, and religious values (Newland, 1979). By 1980, a more conservative political environment throughout the country made it impossible for the amendment to pass state legislative scrutiny and votes. Time ran out for its ratification by the end of June 1982 (Mansbridge, 1986). Efforts to achieve the legal equality the amendment would have hastened have, however, continued, often with greater resolve.

Women and the Law

Women's attempts to get legal equality and recognition have a long history and a contentious relationship with the law. Laws are the governing rules of society. They develop from several sources: ancient custom, legislative bodies, judicial decisions, and administrative agencies. Feminists, however, pose critical questions about the gendering of law in society. Feminist legal theorists note that "ostensibly 'objective' legal rules rest on the perspectives of 'the reasonable man'" (Martin and Jurik, 2007: 154). Moreover, "the law sees and treats women the way men treat women" (MacKinnon, 1991: 186). Critical race theorists take these understandings a step further, arguing that it is not simply men who are the subject of law but specifically heterosexual white men. Such theorists seek a jurisprudential method that would incorporate a "multiple consciousness" to give voice to those historically rendered silent and invisible in the law because of race, sex, class, sexual orientation, or physical abilities (Matsuda, 1989). As historian Linda Kerber (1998: 309) puts it, "whether one is male or female, racially marked in a system that treats Caucasians as 'normal,' married or single, heterosexual or homosexual, continues to have implications for how we experience the equal obligations of citizenship."

In its regulation of the family, the law's concern has traditionally been to create a space in which the male head of household can exercise power and authority (O'Donovan, 1981). By viewing women as belonging to the "private" domestic sphere, the men who make and interpret laws, like the men who theorize about political power, act on assumptions that make women less than full legal citizens and political beings. These assumptions about women's rightful place are intimately linked to the patriarchal political philosophies that underpin democratic societies (Okin, 1979). For example, laws have explicitly commanded husbands and fathers to control their families. Colonial Americans used ducking stools, stocks, and other instruments of humiliation and torture to correct women found guilty of scolding, nagging, or disturbing the peace. When women are thus classified as a group and subjected to gender-based social policies, their social roles are often reinforced by political and legal sanctions.

Traditional moral codes have been based on a sexual double standard for women and men that has affected criminal law and a large amount of civil law, especially family law. Moreover, a society's laws, moral code, and popular conceptions of social norms reinforce each other. Lawmakers and those who enforce the law start from an idea of what the "normal"

family is. They act on the basis of their notions of what women are like and ought to do and their unexamined assumptions about what women need and want. Anyone who does not conform to their assumptions is either treated as invisible (as battered wives, incest victims, and working female heads of households have tended to be) or sought out and made the object of pressure to conform (as are lesbians and "welfare mothers").

In studying the lives of young working-class and poor African American women, sociologist Joyce Ladner (1972) pointed out that their lives were in large part governed by laws, customs, and restrictions based on a white middle-class male perception of what is "normal" and what is "deviant." For example, until recently, white middle-class male norms associated "working mothers" with deviance, though it was very common for African American mothers to hold jobs (see Chapter 8). Women of color then, face "intersecting" sets of subordination. That is, they have to deal with their racial and gender subordination simultaneously within structures that assumes white and male as normative.

Women of color's intersecting subordinations were most visibly illustrated in the case surrounding Anita Hill and Clarence Thomas. In 1991 when Thurgood Marshall, the first African American U.S. Supreme court justice decided to retire, Clarence Thomas was selected by then-president George H. W. Bush to replace him. Anita Hill, a professor at the University of Oklahoma, alleged that Thomas had sexually harassed her when she worked for him a few years earlier at the Equal Employment Opportunities commission, challenging Thomas's nomination to the Supreme Court. The hearings resulted in a huge media spectacle. Thomas eventually won the case and was nominated to the bench. However, the case created an unprecedented awareness of sexual harassment in the workplace. Indeed, sexual harassment complaints more than doubled after the hearings. The case highlighted the manner in which Anita Hill could only be understood within the legal contours of the hearings as either a "white woman" or "a black man." Crenshaw (1992: 404) explains that this inability is understood "[i]n legal doctrine…in terms of doctrinal exclusion, that is, the ways in which the specific forms of domination, to which black females are subject sometimes falls between the existing legal categories for recognizing injury…[so that] racial and gender discrimination law require that we mold our experience into that of either a white woman or black men in order to be legally recognized."

Feminist scholars have also pointed to the conflict within legal cases between equality and difference (Scott, 1988). The conflict arises in anti-discrimination law that recognizes that women must get equal pay for equal work. At the same time feminist scholars and others have argued for recognizing that there are important differences among women. Yet the law does not have the capacity to simultaneously deal with women as a "class" while recognizing their internal differences. This quandary was evident in a recently resolved case brought on by large groups of women against the mega chain Wal-Mart. In what was the largest civil rights class action suit in U.S. history, Betty Dukes filed a sexual discrimination suit against her employer, Wal-Mart. Representing 1.6 million women workers, the case began in 2000 and continued for over a decade. In 2011 the Supreme Court ruled in Wal-Mart's favor, claiming that the differences among women prevented them from being constituted as a class. The case demonstrates juridical constraints in recognizing gender and race subordination simultaneously.

Other contexts of legal bias have included a double standard of sexual morality in which laws treat female prostitutes as "deviant," labeling them "criminals," but consider their male customers to be "normal" men indulging a natural appetite. Laws have customarily treated adultery as a serious crime when committed by women, while often disregarding it when committed by men. The prejudice in favor of the "unwritten law" that excuses husbands who murder adulterous wives is still not entirely eradicated from society's practice of law.

Although many more U.S. women are entering the legal profession and media images suggest that women are often judges, attorneys, and police officers, the law still treats women unfairly in many ways. Lawmakers determine governmental budgets and the respective priorities of health services, day-care centers, education, job creation, and expenditures on weapons and defense. The government shapes welfare regulations that determine the legal obligations of mothers and that fail to recognize unpaid caring for children or others as work.

Women's Political Participation

Even though women's role in the nation-state, law, and citizenship has been curtailed, diminished, or denied because of male bias, women have historically challenged these practices and priorities of the state and its laws by formally and informally organizing. Prior to achieving the vote for women in the United States, women's primary form of political participation was the voluntary association. Women had, in fact, little choice if they wanted to effect change in political and social arenas. Women's organizations lobbied the government and other institutions, effectively innovating the strategy of pressure-group politics, now a commonly recognized political practice in the United States (Cott, 1990; Lebsock, 1990; Scott, 1991). Women continue to participate in voluntary associations in large numbers.

Ruth Bader Ginsburg was appointed to the U.S. Supreme Court in 1993 by President Clinton. In 1972, Ginsburg was the first woman to be hired with tenure at Columbia Law School, arguing a total of six cases involving women's rights before the Supreme Court.

Sandra Day O'Connor, the first woman to sit on the U.S. Supreme Court, was appointed in 1981 by President Reagan. Her appointment broke an all-male tradition that dated to the founding of the country. She has written about her experiences in *The Majesty of the Law* (2003).

In the 1790s, women organized societies to assist the poor. In the period before the Civil War, women organized against the evils of alcohol, the most notable organization being the Women's Christian Temperance Union. Women called for the abolition of slavery, educational opportunities for women, better working conditions, and help for "fallen" women. Beginning in the 1860s, women developed the club movement, culminating in such national organizations as the National Council of Jewish Women, 1893; the National Association of Colored Women, 1896; the National Association of Collegiate Women, 1896; and the National Congress of Mothers, 1897, which later became the Parent–Teacher Association (PTA) (Cott, 1990; Lebsock, 1990; Scott, 1991).

In the twentieth century, led by Emma Goldman (1869–1940) and Elizabeth Gurley Flynn (1890–1964), radical women became pacifists and socialists. They supported Margaret Sanger (1879–1966) in her campaign for legalizing birth control. When the labor movement resisted women's participation, women formed the National Women's Trade Union League (NWTUL) in 1903. The NWTUL supported the women's suffrage campaign, whose numbers swelled to 2 million members by the time the National American Woman Suffrage Association (NAWSA) was formed in 1890. Women organized to reform the city, alleviate the evils of industrialization, and prevent the exploitation of children, working women, and immigrants. In this way they helped lay the foundation for the modern welfare state (Lebsock, 1990), which has been steadily dismantled over the last 20 years.

Elena Kagan, the fourth woman to serve on the U.S. Supreme Court, was appointed in 2010. Nominated by President Obama, Kagan was previously a professor at the University of Chicago Law School and the first female dean of Harvard Law School. In 2009 she left Harvard when she was nominated by President Obama to be the U.S. Solicitor General.

Sonia Sotomayor, the third woman and first Latina to serve on the U.S. Supreme Court, was appointed by President Obama. She was raised in a New York housing project by parents who had little formal schooling but stressed the importance of education. Sotomayor excelled in school, graduating from Yale Law School and going on to have an impressive legal career in both public and private law.

Box 13.3   CARRIE CHAPMAN CATT REMEMBERS

To get the word "male" in effect out of the constitution cost the women of the country 52 years of pauseless campaign…during that time they were forced to conduct 56 campaigns of referenda to male voters; 480 campaigns to get [state] legislatures to submit suffrage amendments to voters; 47 campaigns to get state constitutional conventions to write woman suffrage into state constitutions; 277 campaigns to get state party conventions to include woman suffrage planks; 30 campaigns to get presidential party conventions to adopt woman suffrage planks in party platforms, and 19 campaigns with 19 successive Congresses.

Source: Goldstein, 1979, p. 62.

Box 13.4 SISTERS IN STRUGGLE: AFRICAN AMERICAN WOMEN CIVIL RIGHTS LEADERS

Black women in their homes, churches, social clubs, organizations, and communities throughout the South performed valuable leadership roles during the modern civil rights movement in the United States. Although race, gender, and class constraints generally prohibited their being the recognized articulators, spokespersons, and media favorites, these women did perform a multiplicity of significant leadership roles, such as the initiation and organization of action, the formulation of tactics, and the provision of crucial resources (e.g., money, communication channels, personnel) necessary to sustain the movement. Sisters in struggle, they were empowered through their activism.

...In countless ways, Black women who lived and worked in the South in the 1950s and 1960s led the way in the fight against oppression, in spite of and because of their race, gender, and class. The blood, sweat, and tears that they shed generated protest and activism by other disadvantaged groups—women, farm workers, gays and lesbians, the handicapped, welfare rights activists—all of whom have been in profound ways the beneficiaries of the civil rights movement. The roles that they performed, whether at the grass-roots level or behind the scenes, represent profiles in courage and suggest that they were *leaders* in their communities, *leaders* in the day-to-day fight against various forms of oppression, and *leaders* in the modern civil rights movement.

Source: From Bernice McNair Barnett, "Invisible Southern Black Women Leaders in the Civil Rights Movement: The Triple Constraints of Gender, Race, and Class," in *Gender and Society* 7, 2 (1993): 177, copyright © 1993 by Sage Publications, Inc. Reprinted by permission of Sage Publications, Inc.

Women and Peace Movements

A significant proportion of women's movements have expressed their political disagreement with many men about the excessive use of force, the priority given to militarism versus social agendas, and the effects of nuclear weapons on societies. This is not to suggest that there is something "essential" or innate about women in their call for peace; indeed, women have also participated in armed struggles. Rather, because women disproportionately suffer the political, economic, and social consequences of militarism, it is in that context that women have agitated against armed conflict. Women have historically worked for peace through voluntary associations.

In the last two centuries, especially in Europe and the United States, women have organized a number of national and international peace societies. In the late nineteenth century, international socialist leaders Clara Zetkin (1857–1933) and Rosa Luxemburg (1870–1919) were committed to breaking down national borders and ending military competition between nations, positions that were not always taken by their male colleagues. An Austrian woman, Bertha von Suttner (1843–1914), wrote a major book about disarmament, *Lay Down Your Arms* (1889), and suggested the creation of the Nobel Peace Prize. She received it herself in 1905 (Boulding, 1977). Other significant women recipients have been Alva Myrdal in 1982 for

---

Box 13.5   NATIONAL ORGANIZATION FOR WOMEN (NOW) STATEMENT OF PURPOSE, 1966

To take action to bring women into full participation in the mainstream of American society now, exercising all the privileges and responsibilities thereof in truly equal partnership with men.

…We do not accept the traditional assumption that a woman has to choose between marriage and motherhood, on the one hand, and serious participation in industry or the professions on the other.

Source: The National Organization for Women Statement of Purpose (1966), reprinted by permission. This is a historical document and may reflect the current language and priorities of the organization.

---

her work to further disarmament and peace in international organizations (Bok, 1991) and Rigoberta Menchú Tum in 1992 for her opposition to the cultural genocide of the Indian peoples of Guatemala (Burgos-Debray, 1984). Shirin Ebadi, an Iranian human rights lawyer, received the Nobel Peace Prize in 2004 for her work in promoting women's human rights in Iran. The following year Wangari Muta Maathai from Kenya was award the Nobel Peace Prize for her work in "sustainable development, democracy, and peace." And in 2011 Ellen Johnson Sirleaf of Liberia, the first woman to be elected president in modern Africa, received the Nobel Peace Prize along with Leymah Gbowee and Tawakkol Karman of Yemen for their efforts in promoting peace and democracy in their countries.

World War I (1914–18) galvanized individual women, particularly suffragists, into forming peace organizations. Jane Addams, founder of the first settlement house in the Chicago slums in the 1890s, became a leader in the women's international peace movement during this war. A cofounder of the Women's International League for Peace and Freedom, Addams called for a women's peace conference in 1915 and helped to form the Woman's

Peace Party (WPP) (Steinson, 1980; Rupp, 1997). Mary Church Terrell, a founder of the National Association of Colored Women and of the NAACP, became a member of the WPP's executive committee in 1915 (Alonso, 1993).

During the 1960s, Women Strike for Peace and Another Mother for Peace (now defunct) were founded in response to threats to the world's atmosphere from nuclear testing and to protest the U.S. pursuit of the war in Vietnam. One founder of Women Strike for Peace, Bella Abzug, became a congresswoman. Many women who became involved in feminist consciousness-raising in the contemporary women's liberation movement were first active in peace efforts. In the 1970s, Women for Racial and Economic Equality linked the concerns of women of color and the poor, including racism, welfare reform, reproductive rights, employment, housing, healthcare, and others, to peace and the conversion of military expenditures to social ones (Swerdlow, 1982; Alonso, 1993).

The peace movement has been global. In the early twentieth century, peace was a concern of women's suffrage and internationalist socialist movements worldwide, including the Pan Pacific and Southeast Asia Women's Association and, after World War II, the All African Women's Conference and the Federation of Asian Women's Associations (Boulding, 1977). And women's peace organizations were active in the United Nations Decade for Women (1975–85).

In 1981, women organized the first peace encampment at Greenham Common to protest the placement of U.S. cruise missiles in England (Snitow, 1985); Nordic women sponsored a peace march across Europe; and women of the Pacific Islands campaigned against the nuclear testing in the Pacific that contributes to the high incidence of birth defects and miscarriages among women in the region. In 2000, women from all over the United States met in Washington on Mother's Day to participate in the Million Mom March in opposition to gun violence. A year later, women came together after the attacks on September 11, 2001, to condemn the violence and call for peace. One of the earliest attempts to bring together the voices of women from around the world was by Susan Hawthorne and Bronwyn Winter in their book *September 11, 2001: Feminist Perspectives.* In it they attempt both a testimonial as well as a documentation of the different voices of women over and against the "masculinist politics of war."

Around the world and across historical time, women have always organized; they have organized against colonialism, formed trade unions, and protested against socially destructive practices within their own communities, such as in the pervasiveness of alcoholism. The latter can be seen in the anti-arrack movement in the southern state of Andhra Pradesh, India. Political organizing by women has not been limited to urban educated arenas but has also been evident among women from rural and peasant classes. For, contrary to the dominant way in which such histories are narrated, feminist historians highlight the ways

in which peasant men and women organized collectively during Chile's agrarian reform. Women's involvement in these struggles helped shape both agrarian as well as national politics (Tinsman, 2002). Formal histories have also tended to ignore the importance of grassroots activism and of women's place within it. Filling this gap, Patricia Hill Collins has written about definitions of power and

Like Dr. Martin Luther King Jr., Mahatma Gandhi, and the Dalai Lama, Aung San Suu Kyi has become an international symbol of struggle against repression and brutality. The daughter of a Burmese military hero, a wife, and a mother, she became the spokesperson for her country's beleaguered democracy movement. Aung San Suu Kyi spent nearly 20 years under house arrest until she was finally freed in 2010. In April 2012 she was elected to the Burmese parliament. Her 1991 Nobel Peace Prize is only one of many international awards that she has earned for her courageous leadership of the Burmese people in their battle against authoritarian rule.

resistance and of the activist traditions in the African American community. She emphasizes the individual and group actions "that directly challenge the legal and customary rules governing African-American women's subordination…" (Collins, 2000: 142). Many ordinary African American women in the South contributed to the civil rights movement of the 1950s and 1960s; feminist historians search out these largely unsung heroines by looking beyond the actions of men (and women) whose names are usually singled out (Barnett, 1993).

Global Feminism and Human Rights

Today, networks of global feminist organizations engaged in grassroots activism challenge and influence governments and their policies through the World Wide Web, the Internet, fax machines, and other telecommunications media (Hawkesworth, 2012). Lori Wallach, director of Public Citizen's Global Trade Watch, organized successful protests against the World Trade Organization (WTO) at its meeting in Seattle in 1999. Effectively protesting the potential consequences of globalization (see Chapter 12) on women and the poor, grassroots activism contributed to the collapse of the WTO meeting. Women's grassroots activism in the United States has been critical in promoting educational opportunities for girls in school, has led to the passage of the federal Violence Against Women Act in 1994, and has mobilized women to ensure their continued access to reproductive health care (Palley, 2001).

In the uprisings across north Africa that came to be known as "Arab Spring," women leaders of the uprisings were able to effectively use telecommunications media to spread word about their protests. In Tunisia, for instance, where the uprisings first began to remove President Zine el Abidine Ben Ali, it was Lina Ben Mhenni who would broadcast information about the street protests unfolding throughout Tunisia via her blog and her Facebook and Twitter accounts. And she took the very unusual step of using her real name. The Egyptian protests in Tahrir Square that inspired many other protests around the world, including those in New York City's occupation of Zuccotti Park, were initiated by a 26-year-old woman, Asmaa Mahfouz, when she uploaded a video asking people to join her on January 25 to protest the regime of President Mubarak. The video went viral across the Internet, inspiring thousands to join her. Analagous protests in Yemen were sparked by the arrest of Tawakkol Karman, the head of Women Journalists Without Chains. She was award the Nobel Peace Prize for her efforts in 2011 along with Leymah Gbowee and Ellen Johnson Sirleaf. In several other countries in the region, women have been central in sparking, coordinating, and generating the uprisings. The extent to which the participation of thousands of women across these movements has necessarily advanced a feminist agenda—whatever might be meant by that term—is still a matter of debate. It is important to acknowledge, though, that feminism looks different in different places, and it would be a fallacy to judge the movements in other parts of the world on the basis of the feminist movements in North America.

The movements in North Africa generated solidarity from across the world, including from the global women's movement. This movement was initiated in the 1970s with the development of feminist consciousness and women's increased participation in nation building, which led individuals and groups to place pressure on the United Nations to take up a year of intensive discussion on the position of women worldwide. Delegates reached agreement on a UN-sponsored examination of the status of women. The first UN-sponsored world conference on women took place in 1975 in Mexico City. The themes of the UN women's conference as well as those of the second (held in Copenhagen in 1980) and the third (in Nairobi in 1985) were equality, peace, and development. The Fourth World Conference on Women, in Beijing in 1995, assessed global progress toward improving the lives of women and girls, as well as identifying the factors that hinder such progress. A special session of the UN General Assembly, designated Beijing+5, was held in 2000 to consider how the platform for action resulting from the Beijing Conference had been implemented.

An important outcome of the first UN conference on women was the creation of a major international treaty concerned with women's rights—the Convention on the Elimination of All Forms of Discrimination Against Women (CEDAW)—which became effective in 1979. To date, 170 countries have ratified CEDAW, though many have attached reservations that weaken it. While most of the world's governments have ratified the CEDAW treaty, the United States and Afghanistan have yet to do so.

These four UN-sponsored world conferences enabled women from all over the globe to share experiences and views. The official UN conferences brought together government representatives (some of whom were men) and the members of many nongovernmental groups, which met in unofficial sessions. At the end of these conferences, global blueprints of action were approved by the UN General Assembly, calling upon governments and communities to eliminate all forms of discrimination against women and to work to improve the lives of women worldwide. At the Fourth World Conference on Women, governments agreed to the idea that women's rights are human rights; recognized the right of women to have control over and to decide on matters relating to their sexuality; adopted language that recognized the family "in its various forms"; and agreed to end female

genital cutting and prenatal sex selection, to eradicate violence against women and girls, to secure girls' education free of discrimination in schools, and to mainstream international feminism.

In addition to the UN-sponsored world conferences on women, other major UN conferences have benefited from the contributions of feminist thinkers and activists working throughout the 1980s and 1990s. The 1992 UN Earth Summit in Rio de Janeiro successfully incorporated women's issues related to the environment and sustainable development. The 1993 World Conference on Human Rights in Vienna accepted the principle that "women's rights are human rights." The Vienna Plan of Action called for the eradication of violence against women in both the public and private spheres. The 1994 Conference on Population and Development in Cairo acknowledged that the empowerment and education of women are means of improving women's health and that such efforts serve as the best methods to reduce population growth rates.

Global feminist organizing has been very effective at highlighting the issue of violence against women, which affects women globally and cuts across lines of class, race, educational attainment, ethnicity, region, religion, and language. Women experience violence in various forms: in the home, in refugee camps, in prisons, during armed conflict and civil war, and in international sex trafficking operations. The most far-reaching international treaty to work toward the eradication of violence against women is the Inter-American Convention on Violence against Women (ICVW), which went into effect in 1995. The convention defines violence against women as "any act or conduct, based on gender, which causes death or physical, sexual or psychological harm or suffering to women." The ICVW requires states to take immediate action "to prevent, investigate and impose penalties for violence against women" as well as to "modify legal or customary practices that sustain violence" (Meyer, 1999; O'Hare, 1999).

Violence against women remains an enormous problem, and women are far from actually attaining equal rights. However, internationally, women have made great progress in gaining recognition of these problems and have had an impact on global issues affecting them. Conferences and meetings have served as a consciousness-raising process as women from around the world have gained new insights on the varieties of patriarchal oppression and have developed a healthy respect for the differences among themselves. In the process, women have changed how gender is understood and lived worldwide.

More progress toward feminist goals has been made in the past 30 years than in any other period of modern history. Such success has set off a strong reaction within the United States and elsewhere. For instance, during the 2012 presidential elections, women's right to safe abortions as well as the Lilly Ledbetter Fair Pay act featured prominently as dividing issues between the Republican and Democrat parties. Thus, efforts of various U.S. political candidates, presidents, and their administrations to dismantle and discredit legislative, judicial, and economic gains made over previous decades present new challenges to feminists of every kind. The elimination of the right of abortion for Medicaid recipients and abortion counseling for women globally has threatened women's rights. Making abortions difficult for some women (especially poor women) to obtain makes it easier down the road to eliminate reproductive rights for all women. The government's opposition to reproductive rights in the 1980s, the 1990s, and the current millennium has contributed to dividing women in the United States who are supportive of many feminist concerns but, for religious and political reasons, oppose government funding of abortion. Even President Clinton (1992–2000), viewed as supportive of women's rights, helped to divide women by setting welfare term limits for poor women and undercutting the recognition that all persons should have, by right, enough resources to stay alive.

Summary

Women have been far less visible than men in formal political activity. The women's movement has challenged women's exclusion from the "public" sphere. Power is distinct from authority. Women have seldom exercised either power or authority.

As societies become more complex, governmental power tends to be exercised by the few on behalf of the many. Women tend to be segregated as a group and excluded from political power, along with subordinated racial, ethnic, and religious groups. Women who do participate in government tend to do so on the local level.

In the past, some women exercised political power in their own right in dynastic states and in precolonial African societies. As government became more bureaucratic and as colonial powers altered these societies, the power of these women leaders eroded.

Male dominance is associated with the increasing complexity of societies and societal responses to stress and change. It is manifested in the exclusion of women from economic and political decision making and in violence against women.

The women's movement has encouraged increasing numbers of women to seek public office. Studies show that regardless of party label or level of office, women officeholders tend to take more feminist positions on women's issues than do men. Nonetheless, women still face opposition, some of which they are attempting to overcome through such methods as raising their own funds to support candidates with feminist viewpoints. In various other countries, women have been able to win political office in greater percentages than in the United States.

Laws tend to have a sexist bias because they are based on male-defined norms. Many laws and moral codes are based on a double standard. Family law often coerces women into traditional roles. Laws designed to "protect" women often have the effect of restricting women's choices and activities. Women who break the law are subjected to laws made by male legislators, enforced by male police officers, and interpreted by male judges.

Marginalized from "politics" as men define it, women have sought to achieve their objectives through a wide range of voluntary associations. Women's involvement in peace movements testifies to their political opposition to many of men's wars. While women may tend to be more "pacific" than men, this does not mean that they cannot be motivated to fight.

Women's chief struggle at the beginning of the twentieth century was to obtain the right to vote. The modern women's liberation movement developed from two sources: organizations formed to work for women's equality and a younger, more radical group involved in the civil rights, New Left, and anti–Vietnam War movements and concerned with liberation from male oppression.

In the 1980s, a global feminism emerged with the aid of the UN conferences on women, human rights, the environment, and sustainable development. These global conferences brought together women worldwide to share experiences and to develop strategies to eliminate global patriarchy and improve the lives of women.

Feminist unity is made more difficult by the fact that women have different ethnic, national, religious, class, and racial backgrounds, as well as different sexual orientations, and thus have different priorities. Some women carry a double burden in having to deal with both sexism and racism. The need for all women to engage in the political process and to focus clearly on necessary goals is paramount if they are to ensure that recent gains will not be lost and that new gains will be won. Women's unity will benefit from understanding the differences among women.

Women have demonstrated their power to mobilize themselves and others to elect legislators and promote policies supportive of women's issues. Future progress in all areas of women's rights and liberation depends to a large part on women themselves.

Discussion Questions

1. Document the life of a woman political leader of your choice. How did she manage to succeed, given the obstacles to women's political leadership?

2. Find out which women hold political offices or leadership positions in your town, county, or congressional district. On the basis of what you have read in this chapter, design a questionnaire to find out what positions these women hold on a variety of feminist issues.

3. Do an oral-history interview with women in your own family on their role in and views on key aspects of the women's movement. Were members of your family suffragists? Did any participate in the social movements of the 1960s? How many have been involved in voluntary organizations? Which ones? Have any participated in electoral politics? If not, why not?

4. What kinds of organization exist in your locality to deal with issues concerning women, violence, and the law (such as a rape crisis center, a battered wife center, or a group concerned with women in prison)?

5. How do women from different racial or ethnic groups or economic classes differ in their perceptions and attitudes on feminist issues? Select one issue as a

"problem" and suggest "solutions." How might women from two groups argue from the perspectives of their different backgrounds?

Recommended Readings

Freeman, Jo. *We Will Be Heard: Women's Struggles for Political Power in the United States*. Lanham, MD: Rowman & Littlefield, 2008. The feminist activist and scholar traces the history of American women in politics and the struggles of women to promote laws and policies favorable to women's interests.

Hawkesworth, Mary. *Political Worlds of Women*. Boulder, CO: Westview Press, 2012. An analysis of women's activism in informal and formal political institutions and the challenges facing women's effort to achieve justice locally, nationally, and globally.

McDonagh, Eileen. *The Motherless State: Women's Political Leadership and American Democracy*. Chicago: University of Chicago Press, 2009. An analysis of why the United States elects fewer women to political office compared to other Western liberal democracies

Schiff, Stacy. *Cleopatra: A Life*. New York: Little, Brown & Company, 2010. A biography of the last great Egyptian monarch. Often judged harshly by others, Schiff portrays Cleopatra as a brilliant woman and effective ruler of her country, a political realist who was fiercely devoted to her country and people.

Vaid, Urvashi. *Irresistable Revolution: Confronting Race, Class and the Assumptions of LGBT Politics*. New York: Magnus Books, 2012. A book of essays that uses an intersectional analysis to argue for a feminist and a race- and class-conscious political agenda for LGBT activism.

REFERENCES

AARP. "A Profile of Older Americans." Washington, DC: AARP, 1999.

———. "Lifestyles, Dating and Romance: A Study of Midlife Singles." Washington, DC: AARP, 2003.

Abu-Lughod, Lila. *Remaking Women: Feminism and Modernity in the Middle East*. Princeton, NJ: Princeton University Press, 1998.

———. "Do Muslim Women Really Need Saving? Anthropological Reflections on Cultural Relativism and Its Others." *American Anthropologist* 104 (2002): 783–90.

Abzug, Bella, and Mim Kelber. *Gender Gap*. Boston: Houghton Mifflin, 1984.

Acocella, J. "Mother's Helpers." *New Yorker*, May 5, 2003.

Acosta-Belén, Edna, and Christine Bose. "From Structural Subordination to Empowerment: Women and Development in Third World Contexts." *Gender and Society* 4, 3 (1990): 299–320.

Adler, Nancy E. "Commentary: When Separate Is More Equal." *JAMA* 304, 24 (2010): 2738–9.

Adler, Roy D. "Women in the Executive Suite Correlate to High Profits." *Harvard Business Review*, Nov. 16, 2001.

Aeberhard, Jane Hodges. "Sexual Harassment in Employment: Recent Judicial and Arbitral Trends." In *Women, Gender, and Work*, edited by Martha Fetherolf Loutfi. Geneva: International Labour Office, 2001.

Agosin, Marjorie, editor. *Women, Gender, and Human Rights: A Global Perspective*. New Brunswick, NJ: Rutgers University Press, 2001.

Ahmadu, Fuambai. "Rites and Wrongs: An Insider/Outsider Reflects on Power and Excision." In *Female 'Circumcision' in Africa: Culture, Controversy, and Change*, edited by Bettina Shell-Duncan and Ylva Hernlund. London: Lynne Rienner, 2000.

Ahmed, Leila. *Women and Gender in Islam: Historical Roots of a Modern Debate*. New Haven, CT: Yale University Press, 1992.

———. *A Border Passage*. New York: Farrar, Straus and Giroux, 1999.

Aiken, Susan Hardy, Karen Anderson, Myra Dinnerstein, et al., editors. *Changing Our Minds: Feminist Transformations of Knowledge*. Albany, NY: SUNY Press, 1988.

Aizley, Hailyn. *Confessions of the Other Mother: Non-Biological Lesbian Moms Tell All*. Boston: Beacon Press, 2006.

Akbar, Amna, and Rupal Oza. "'Muslim Fundamentalism' and Human Rights in the Age of Terror and Empire." In *Gender, National Security and Counter-Terrorism: Human Rights Perspectives*, edited by Margaret Satterthwaite and Jayne Huckerby. New York: Routledge, 2013.

Albeda, Rany, and Chris Tilly. *Glass Ceilings and Bottomless Pits: Women's Work, Women's Poverty*. Boston: South End Press, 1997.

Alcoff, Linda. "Cultural Feminism versus Post-structuralism: The Identity Crisis in Feminist Theory." *Signs* 13, 3 (1988): 405–36.

———. "The Politics of Postmodern Feminism, Revisited." *Cultural Critique* 36 (Spring 1997): 5–27.

———. *Visible Identities: Race, Gender and the Self*. New York: Oxford University Press, 2006.

———. "Epistemic Identities." *Hypatia* 7 (2010): 138–147.

Alcoff, Linda, and Elizabeth Potter, editors. *Feminist Epistomologies*. New York: Routledge, 1993.

Alcott, Louisa M. *Little Women*. New York: Western, 1873.

Ali, Ayaan Hirsi. *Infidel*. New York: Simon & Schuster, 2007.

Allen, Paula Gunn. *The Woman Who Owned the Shadows*. San Francisco: Spinsters Ink, 1983.

———. *The Sacred Hoop: Recovering the Feminine in American Indian Traditions*. Boston: Beacon Press, 1988.

Almeida, Deidre A. "The Hidden Half: A History of Native American Women's Education." *Harvard Education Review* 67, 4 (1997): 757–71.

Alonso, Harriet Hyman. *Peace as a Women's Issue*. Syracuse, NY: Syracuse University Press, 1993.

Amato, Paul R. "Research on Divorce: Continuing Trends and New Developments." *Journal of Marriage and Family* 72, 3 (2010): 650–66.

Ambrose, Susan A., Kristin L. Dunkle, Barbara L. Lazarus, et al. "Women, Science, Engineering, and Technology through the Ages." In *Journeys of Women in Science and Engineering: No Universal Constants*, edited by Susan A. Ambrose, Kristin L. Dunkle, Barbara L. Lazarus, et al. Philadelphia: Temple University Press, 1997.

American Association of University Women. *AAUW Report: How Schools Shortchange Girls*. Washington, DC: American Association of University Women, 1992.

Ammot, Teresa L., and Julie A. Matthaei. *Race, Gender, and Work*. Boston: South End Press, 1991.

Amnesty International. *Deadly Delivery: The Maternal Health Care Crisis in the USA*. Amnesty International USA, 2010.

Amt, Emilie, editor. *Women's Lives in Medieval Europe: A Sourcebook*. London: Routledge, 1993.

Anantnarayan, Lakshmi. "Why Are US Doctors Allowing Female Genital Mutilation?" *The Guardian*, May 11, 2010. http://www.guardian.co.uk/commentisfree/2010/may/11/female-genital-mutilation-us-nicking.

Anderson, Benedict, *Imagined Communities: Reflections on the Origin and Spread of Nationalism*. New York: Verso, 1993.

Anderson/Sankofa, David A. *The Origin of Life on Earth: An African Creation Myth*: Mt. Airy, MA: Sights Productions, 1991.

Anderson, Elizabeth. "Uses of Value Judgments in Feminist Social Science: A Case Study of Research on Divorce." *Hypatia* 19 (2004): 1–24.

Anderson, Leona M., and Pamela Dickey Young, editors. *Women and Religious Traditions*, 2nd ed. Ontario: Oxford University Press, 2010.

Anderson, Nickela, and Karen D. Hughes. "The Business of Caring: Women's Self-Employment and the Marketization of Care." *Gender, Work & Organization* 3 (2009).

Angelou, Maya. *I Know Why the Caged Bird Sings*. New York: Knopf, 1969.

Angier, N. "The Importance of Grandma." *New York Times*, November 5, 2002, D1, D4.

Anker, Richard. *Gender and Jobs: Sex Segregation of Occupations in the World*. Geneva: International Labour Office, 1998.

Anzaldúa, Gloria. *Borderlands/La Frontera: The New Mestiza*. San Francisco: Aunt Lute Books, 1987.

———, editor. *Making Face, Making Soul—Haciendo Caras: Creative and Critical Perspectives by Women of Color*. San Francisco: Aunt Lute Books, 1990.

———. *Interviews/Entrevistas*, edited by AnaLouis Keating. New York: Routledge, 2000.

Applebaum, Susan. "Daughters and Mothers." In *Girlhood in America: An Encyclopedia*, edited by Miriam Forman-Brunell. Santa Barbara, CA: ABC-CLIO, 2001.

Archer, C. J. "Children's Attitudes toward Sex Role Division in Adult Occupational Roles." *Sex Roles* 10 (1984): 1–10.

Arextaga, Begoña. *Shattering Silence: Women, Nationalism, and Political Subjectivity in Northern Ireland*. Princeton, NJ: Princeton University Press, 1997.

Arias, E. "United States Life Tables, 2002." *National Vital Statistics Reports: From the Centers for Disease Control and Prevention, National Center for Health Statistics, National Vital Statistics System* 53, 6 (2004): 1–38.

Aristotle. *The Generation of Animals*, vols. 1 and 4, translated by A. L. Peck. Cambridge, MA: Harvard University Press, 1943.

Armstrong, Karen. *Islam: A Short History*. New York: Modern Library 2001.

Armstrong, M. J. "Ethnic Minority Women as They Age." In *Women as They Age*, 2nd ed., edited by J. D. Garner and S. O. Mercer. New York: Haworth, 2001.

Arowolo, Dare, and Folorunso Aluko. "Women and Political Participation in Nigeria." *European Journal of Social Sciences* 144, 4 (2010): 581–93.

Arthur, Kathryn Weedman. "Feminine Knowledge and Skill Reconsidered: Women and Flaked Stone Tools." *American Anthropologist* 112, 2 (2010): 228–43.

Associated Press, The. "Commander to Rescind a Provision on Pregnancy." *The New York Times*, December 2009. Accessed November 1, 2010 from http://www.nytimes.com/2009/12/26/us/26military.html.

Astrid, Henry. *Not My Mother's Sister: Generational Conflict and Third-Wave Feminism*. Bloomington: Indiana University Press, 2004.

Atwood, Margaret. *The Handmaiden's Tale*. Boston: Houghton Mifflin, 1986.

Austen, Jane. *Pride and Prejudice*. New York: Dell, 1959.

Axelrod, J. G. "Who's the Boss? Employee Leasing and the Joint Employer Relationship." *Labor Lawyer* 3 (1987): 853–72.

Ayubi-Moak, I., and B. L. Parry. "Psychiatric Aspects of Menopause: Depression." In *Women's Mental Health: A Comprehensive Textbook*, edited by Susan G. Kornstein and Anita H. Clayton. New York: Guilford Press, 2002.

Ba, Mariama. *So Long a Letter*, translated by Modope Bode-Thomas. London: Heinemann, [1980] 1981.

Bacchetta, Paola. *Gender in the Hindu Nation: RSS Women as Ideologues*. New Delhi: Women Unlimited, 2004.

Badawi, Jamal. *Gender Equity in Islam: Basic Principles*. Plainfield, IL: American Trust Publications, 2003.

Bakalar, Nicholas. "Despite Advice, Many Fail to Breast-Feed." *New York Times*, April 19, 2010.

Baker, Christina Looper, and Christina Baker Kline. *The Conversation Begins: Mothers and Daughters Talk About Living Feminism*. New York: Bantam Books, 1996.

Balli, Cecilia. "Thirty-Eight" In *Colonize This!: Young Women of Color on Today's Feminism*, edited by Daisy Hernández and Bushra Rehman. Berkeley, CA: Seal Press, 2002.

Bambara, Toni Cade. *The Salt Eaters*. New York: Random House, 1980.

Bandura, Albert. "Influence of Models' Reinforcement Contingencies on the Acquisition of Imitative Responses." *Journal of Personality and Social Psychology* 1 (1965): 589–95.

Bao, Xiaolan. "Politicizing Motherhood: The Chinese Garment Workers' Campaign for Daycare Centers in New York City, 1977–1982." In *Asian/Pacific Islander American Women: A Historical Anthology*, edited by Shirley Hune and Gail M. Nomura. New York: New York University Press, 2003.

Baptandier, Brigitte. *The Lady of Linshui: A Chinese Female Cult*, translated by Kristin Ingrid Fryklund. Stanford, CA: Stanford University Press, 2008.

Barjatya, Sooraj, director. *Hum Aapke Hain Koun!* Rajshri Productions, 1994.

Barker-Benfield, G. J. "Sexual Surgery in Late Nineteenth-Century America." In *Seizing Our Bodies: The Politics of Women's Health*, edited by Claudia Dreifus. New York: Vintage Books, 1977.

Barnett, Bernice McNair. "Invisible Southern Black Women Leaders in the Civil Rights Movement: The Triple Constraints of Gender, Race, and Class." *Gender and Society* 7, 2 (1993): 162–82.

Baron-Cohen, Simon. *The Essential Difference: Men, Women and the Extreme Male Brain*. London: Allen Lane, 2003.

Baron, Beth. *Egypt as a Woman: Nationalism, Gender, and Politics*. Berkeley: University of California Press, 2005.

Baruch, Elaine Hoffman. *Women and Power: Literary and Psychoanalytic Perspectives*. New York: New York University Press, 1991.

Basu, Amrita. "Feminism Inverted: The Real Women and Gendered Imagery of Hindu Nationalism." *Bulletin of Concerned Asian Scholars* 25 (1993): 25–36.

Bauer, Nancy. "Lady Power." Opinionator, *NY Times* online, June 20, 2010. http://opinionator.blogs.nytimes.com/2010/06/20/lady-power/. Accessed December 20, 2012.

Baumgardner, Jennifer, and Amy Richards. *ManifestA: Young Women, Feminism, and the Future*. New York. Farrar, Straus and Giroux, 2000.

Baydar, Nazli, and Jeanne Brooks-Gunn. "Profiles of Grandmothers Who Help Care for Their Grandchildren in the United States." *Family Relations* 47, 4 (1998): 385–93.

BBC News. *Women Bishops Should Be Allowed, General Synod Rules*. July 12, 2010. http://www.bbc.co.uk/news/10603968.

BBC News. "Women's Low Pay 'Behind Poverty.'" June 2008. Accessed November 1, 2010, from http://news.bbc.co.uk/go/pr/fr/-/2/hi/business/7465136.stm.

Bechdel, Alison. *The Indelible Alison Bechdel: Confessions, Comix, and Miscellaneous Dykes to Watch Out For*. Ithaca, NY: Firebrand Books, 1998.

———. *Fun Home: A Family Tragicomic*. New York: Houghton Mifflin, 2006.

———. *Are You My Mother? A Comic Drama*. New York: Houghton Mifflin, 2012.

Beck, M. "Trading Places." *Newsweek*, July 16, 1990.

Belkin, Lisa. "The Opt-out Revolution." *New York Times Magazine*, Oct. 26, 2003, 42–7, 58, 85–6.

Bell, Linda, editor. *Visions of Women*. Clifton, NJ: Humana Press, 1983.

Beltran, Mary C. "The Hollywood Latina Body as Site of Social Struggle: Media Constructions of Stardom and Jennifer Lopez's 'Cross-Over Butt.'" *Quarterly Review of Film and Video* 19 (2002): 71–86.

Bem, Sandra L. "Gender Schema Theory: A Cognitive Account of Sex Typing." *Psychological Review* 88 (1981): 354–64.

———. "Gender Schema Theory and Its Implications for Child Development: Raising Gender-Aschematic Children in a Gender-Schematic Society." *Signs* 8 (1983): 598–616.

———. "Androgyny and Gender Schema Theory: A Conceptual and Empirical Integration." In *Nebraska Symposium on Motivation, 1984: Psychology and Gender*, edited by T. B. Sonderegger. Lincoln: University of Nebraska Press, 1985.

Beneria, Lourdes, and Gita Sen. "Class and Gender Inequalities and Women's Role in Economic Development—Theoretical and Practical Implications." *Feminist Studies* 8, 1 (1982): 157–75.

Bennett, Rosemary. "Growing up with a Sister Makes People More Balanced." In *The Times*, April 2, 2009. http://www.thetimes.co.uk/tto/life/families/article1758377.ece.

Beoku-Betts, Josephine. "African Women Pursuing Graduate Studies in the Sciences: Racism, Gender Bias, and Third World Marginality." In *Removing Barriers: Women in Academic Science, Technology, Engineering, and Mathematics*, edited by Jill M. Bystydzienski and Sharon R. Bird. Bloomington: Indiana University Press, 2006.

Berger, Iris. Women in East and Southern Africa. In *Women in Sub-Saharan Africa: Restoring Women to History*, edited by Iris Berger and E. Frances White. Bloomington: Indiana University Press, 1999.

Berger, Iris, and E. Frances White, editors. *Women in Sub-Saharan Africa: Restoring Women to History*. Bloomington: Indiana University Press, 1999.

Berger, Ryan. "Equal Access/Equal Pay." *Americas Quarterly* 6, 3 (2012): 77.

Bertone, Andrea Marie. "Sexual Trafficking in Women: International Political Economy and the Politics of Sex." *Gender Issues* 18, 1 (2000): 4–22.

Besserman, Perle. *A New Kabbalah for Women*. New York: Palgrave MacMillan, 2005.

Bethell, T. N. "The Gender Gap." Washington, DC: AARP, 2005.

Bhatia, Krishan. *Indira: A Biography of Prime Minister Gandhi*. New York: Praeger, 1974.

Bhattacharya, Priyanka. "Indian Men Seeking Male-Specific Skin Care." *GCI Magazine* online, September 5, 2008. http://www.gcimagazine.com/marketstrends/regions/bric/27921834.html. Accessed November 30, 2012.

Bianchi, Suzanne M. "Mothers and Daughters 'Do,' Fathers 'Don't Do' Family: Gender and

Generational Bonds." *Journal of Marriage and Family* 68, 4 (2006): 812–16.

Bianchi, Suzanne M., and Lynne M. Casper. "American Families." *Population Bulletin* 55, 4 (2000).

Biegel, Stuart, and Shiela James Kuehl. *Safe at School: Addressing the School Environment and LGBT Safety through Policy and Legislation.* Los Angeles: Great Lakes Center for Education Research and Practice, National Education Policy Center and the Williams Institute in the UCLA Law School, 2010.

Bienstock, Beverly Gray. "The Changing Image of the American Jewish Mother." In *Changing Images of the Family*, edited by Virginia Tufte and Barbara Myerhoff. New Haven, CT: Yale University Press, 1979.

Bird, Phyllis. "Women's Religion in Ancient Israel." In *Women's Earliest Records: From Ancient Egypt and Western Asia*, edited by Barbara S. Lesko. Atlanta: Scholars Press, 1989.

Birnbaum, Norman. "The Vatican's Latest Target in the War on Women: Nuns." *The Nation*, April 24, 2012.

Bishop, Sharon, and Marjorie Weinzweig, editors. "Preferential Treatment." In *Philosophy and Women*. Belmont, CA: Wadsworth, 1979.

Blackwell, Marilyn S. "Surrogate Ministers: Women, Revivalism and Maternal Associations in Vermont." *Vermont History* (2001): 69.

Blackwood, Evelyn. "Mothers to Daughters: Social Change and Matrilineal Kinship in a Minangkabau Village." In *Globalization and Change in Fifteen Cultures: Born in One World, Living in Another*, edited by George Dearborn Spindler and Janice E. Stockard. Belmont, CA: Wadsworth, 2006.

———. *Falling into the Lesbi World: Desire and Difference in Indonesia.* Honolulu: University of Hawaii Press, 2010.

Blee, Kathleen M. "Women in the 1920's Ku Klux Klan." *Feminist Studies* 17, 1 (1991).

Blount, Marcellus, and George P. Cunningham, editors. *Representing Black Men.* New York: Routledge, 1989.

Blum, Linda M. *Between Feminism and Labor: The Significance of the Comparable Worth Debate.* Berkeley, CA: University of California Press, 1991.

Boden, Alison. *Women's Rights and Religious Practice: Claims in Conflict.* Basingstoke, UK: Palgrave Macmillan, 2007.

Bok, Sissela. *Alva Myrdal.* Reading, MA: Addison Wesley, 1991.

Bollé, Patrick. "Part-Time Work: Solution or Trap?" In *Women, Gender, and Work*, edited by Martha Fetherolf Loutfi. Geneva: International Labour Office, 2001.

Bongaarts, J., and Z. Zimmer. "Living Arrangements of Older Adults in the Developing World: An Analysis of Demographic and Health Survey Household Surveys." *The Journals of Gerontology. Series B, Psychological Sciences and Social Sciences* 57, 3 (2002): 145–57.

Bonomi, Patricia U. *The Lord Cornbury Scandal: The Politics of Reputation in British America.* Chapel Hill: University of North Carolina Press, 2000.

Bookman, Ann, and Sandra Morgen, editors. *Women and the Politics of Empowerment.* Philadelphia: Temple University Press, 1988.

Boos, Florence S. "Catherine Macaulay's *Letters on Education* (1790): An Early Feminist Polemic." *University of Michigan Papers in Women's Studies* 2 (1976): 64–78.

Bordo, Susan. *Unbearable Weight: Feminism, Western Culture, and the Body.* Berkeley: University of California Press, 1993.

Bornstein, Kate. *Gender Outlaw. On Men, Women and the Rest of Us.* New York: Routledge Press, 1994.

Boserup, Esther. *Women's Role in Economic Development.* New York: St. Martin's Press, 1970.

Boston Women's Health Book Collective. *Our Bodies, Ourselves.* New York: Simon & Schuster, [1971] 2011.

———. *Our Bodies, Ourselves: Menopause.* New York: Simon & Schuster, 2006.

———. *Our Bodies, Ourselves: Pregnancy and Birth.* New York: Simon & Schuster, 2008.

Boulding, Elise. *Women in the Twentieth Century World.* New York: Wiley, 1977.

Bourgeois, Fr Roy. "Father Roy Bourgeois Responds to Second Canonical Warning." Letter from Father Bourgeois to the Maryknoll Community and Superior

General Rev. Edward Dougherty, August 8, 2011. www.womensordination.org/contnt/view/366/42/. Accessed April 5, 2013.

Boxer, Marilyn. *When Women Asked the Questions: Creating Women's Studies in America.* Baltimore: Johns Hopkins University Press, 1998.

Boxer, Marilyn, and Jean H. Quataert. "Women in the Early Modern Era: Religious Upheaval, Political Centralization, and Colonial Conquest." In *Connecting Spheres: Women in the Western World, 1500 to the Present,* edited by Marilyn J., Boxer and Jean H. Quataert. New York: Oxford University Press, 2000.

Boylan, Esther. *Women and Disability.* Atlantic Highlands, NJ: Zed Books, 1991.

Bradsher, J. E. "Older Women and Widowhood." In *Handbook on Women and Aging,* edited by J. M. Coyle. Westport, CT: Greenwood, 2001.

Braithwaite, Ronald L., Kimberly Jacob Arriola, and Cassandra Newkirk, editors. *Health Issues among Incarcerated Women.* New Brunswick, NJ: Rutgers University Press, 2006.

Branch, Enobong Hannah. *Opportunity Denied: Limiting Black Women to Devalued Work.* New Brunswick, NJ: Rutgers University Press, 2011.

Bravo, Ellen. "The Clerical Proletariat." In *Sisterhood Is Forever,* edited by Robin Morgan. New York: Washington Square Press, 2003.

Brennan, Denise. "Selling Sex For Visas: Sex Tourism as a Stepping-Stone to International Migration." In *Global Women: Nannies, Maids, and Sex Workers in the New Economy,* edited by Barbara Ehrenreich and Arlie Russell Hochschild. New York: Metropolitan Books, 2002.

Bright, Susie. *Susie Bright's Sexual Reality: A Virtual Sex Reader.* Seattle: Cleis Press, 1992.

Brizendine, Louanne. *The Female Brain.* New York: Morgan Road Books, 2006.

Broadway, Michael. "Beef Stew: Cattle, Immigrants, and Established Residents in a Kansas Beefpacking Town." In *Newcomers in the Workplace,* edited by Louise Lamphere, Alex Stepick, and Guillermo Grenier.

Philadelphia: Temple University Press, 1994.

Brody, J. E. "The Risks and Demands of Pregnancy after 20." *New York Times,* May 11, 2004, D8.

Bronstein, Phyllis. "The Family Environment: Where Gender Role Socialization Begins." In *Handbook of Girls' and Women's Psychological Health,* edited by Judith Worell and Carol D. Goodheart. New York: Oxford University Press, 2006.

Brooks, Gwendolyn. *Selected Poems.* New York: Harper & Row, 1963.

Brooks, Rosa. "No Escaping Sexualization of Young Girls." *Los Angeles Times,* August 25, 2006. http://www.commondreams.org/views06/0825–33.htm. Accessed December 21, 2012.

Brown, Elicia. "Immersed in a Dilemma." *Jewish Week,* Nov. 14, 2003, 62.

Brown, Helen Gurley. *Sex and the Single Girl.* New York: Random House, 1962.

Brown, Karen McCarthy. "Fundamentalism and the Control of Women." In *Fundamentalism and Gender,* edited by John Stratton Hawley. Oxford: Oxford University Press, 1994.

Brown, Lyn Mikel. "The 'Girls' in Girls' Studies." *Girlhood Studies* 1, 1 (2008): 1–12.

Brown, Lyn Mikel, and Carol Gilligan. *Meeting at the Crossroads: Women's Psychology and Girls' Development.* Cambridge, MA: Harvard University Press, 1992.

Browne, A. "Violence against Women by Male Partners: Prevalence, Outcomes, and Policy Implications." *American Psychologist* 48 (1993): 1077–87.

Brumberg, Joan J. *The Body Project: An Intimate History of American Girls.* New York: Random House, 1997.

Brunsdon, Charlotte, Julie D'Acci, and Lynn Spigel, editors. *Feminist Television Criticism: A Reader.* Oxford: Oxford University Press, 1997.

Brydon, Anne, and Sandra Niessen. *Consuming Fashion: Adorning the Transnational Body.* Oxford, UK: Berg, 1998.

Buhle, Mari Jo. "Introduction." In *The Politics of Women's Studies: Testimony from Thirty Founding Mothers,* edited by Florence Howe. New York: Feminist Press, 2000.

Buhle, Mari Jo, and Paul Buhle, editors. *The Concise History of Woman Suffrage: Selections from the Classic Work of Stanton, Anthony, Gage, and Harper.* Urbana: University of Illinois Press, 1978.

Buirski, Nancy, director. *The Loving Story.* New York: HBO Documentary, 2011.

Bunch, Charlotte. "Lesbians in Revolt." In *Lesbianism and the Women's Movement,* edited by Nancy Myron and Charlotte Bunch. Baltimore: Diana Press, 1975.

Bundles, A'Lelia Perry. *On Her Own Ground: The Life and Times of Madame C. J. Walker.* New York: Scribner, 2001.

Bureau of Labor Statistics. "Women in the Labor Force: A Databook." 2011(A). http://www.bls.gov/cps/wlf-databook-2011.pdf. Accessed November 23, 2012.

———. "Women at Work." March 2011(B). http://www.bls.gov/spotlight/2011/women/. Accessed November 23, 2012.

———. *Labor Force Statistics from the Current Population Survey: Employed Persons by Occupation, Race, Hispanic or Latino Ethnicity, and Sex,* 2012. Accessed from http://www.bls.gov/cps/cpsaat10.htm.

Bureau of Population Research. "Analysis of Data from the U.S. Census Bureau, Census 2000 Supplementary Survey, 2001 Supplementary Survey and 2002 through 2010 American Community Survey (ACS)." Washington, DC: Bureau of the Census, 2010.

Burgess, E. O. "Sexuality in Midlife and Later Life Couples." In *The Handbook of Sexuality in Close Relationships,* edited by John H. Harvey, Amy Wenzel and Susan Sprecher. Mahwah, NJ: Lawrence Erlbaum, 2004.

Burgos-Debray, Elizabeth, editor. *I, Rigoberta Menchu.* London: Verso, 1984.

Burke, Carole. *Camp All-American, Hanoi Jane, and the High-and-Tight: Gender, Folklore, and Changing Military Culture.* Boston: Beacon Press, 2004.

Burns, Ken, Sarah Burns, and David McMahon, directors. *The Central Park Five,* 2012.

Burstyn, Varda, editor. *Women against Censorship.* Vancouver: Douglas and McIntyre, 1985.

Burton, Antoinette. *At the Heart of the Empire: Indians and the Colonial Encounter in Later Victorian England.* Berkeley: University of California Press, 1998.

Butler, Anne M. *Daughters of Joy, Sisters of Misery: Prostitutes in the American West, 1865–90.* Urbana: University of Illinois Press, 1985.

Butler, Judith. "Critically Queer." *GLQ -New York* 1, 1 (1993): 17–32.

Butler, Judith. *Gender Trouble: Feminism and the Subversion of Identity.* New York: Routledge, 1990.

———. *Bodies That Matter: On the Discursive Limits of "Sex."* New York: Routledge, 1993.

———. *Undoing Gender.* New York: Routledge, 2004.

Bynum, Caroline Walker. *Jesus as Mother: Studies in the Spirituality of the High Middle Ages.* Los Angeles: University of California Press, 1982.

Bystydzienski, Jill M., and Sharon R. Bird. "Introduction." In *Removing Barriers: Women in Academic Science, Technology, Engineering, and Mathematics,* edited by Jill M. Bystydzienski and Sharon R. Bird. Bloomington: Indiana University Press, 2006.

Caldwell, Sarah. *Oh Terrifying Mother: Sexuality, Violence and Worship of the Goddess Kali.* New York: Oxford University Press, 2000.

Calhoun, Cheshire. *Feminism, the Family, and the Politics of the Closet: Lesbian and Gay Displacement.* New York: Oxford University Press, 2003.

Califia, Pat. *Sapphistry: The Book of Lesbian Sexuality.* Tallahassee, FL: Naiad Press, 1988.

Callan, Hilary, and Shirley Ardener, editors. *The Incorporated Wife.* London: Croom Helm, 1984.

Campbell, Rebecca, Tracy Sefl, and Courtney E. Ahrens. "The Physical Health Consequences of Rape: Assessing Survivors' Somatic Symptoms in a Racially Diverse Population." *Women's Studies Quarterly* 31 (2003):90–7.

Campbell, Sister Simone. Interviewed by Bill Moyers, June 27 and August 24, 2012. www.billmoyers.com/episode/full-show-nuns-faith-and politics/. http://billmoyers.com/episode/full-show-nuns-faith-and-politics/. Accessed November 17, 2012.

Canetto, S. S. "Older Adult Women: Issues, Resources, and Challenges." In *Handbook of the Psychology of Women and Gender*, edited by R. K. Unger. New York: Wiley, 2001.

———. "Older Adulthood." In *The Complete Guide to Mental Health for Women*, edited by L. Slater, J. H. Daniel, and A.E. Banks. Boston: Beacon Press, 2003.

Cantor, Aviva. "Jewish Women's Haggadah." In *Womanspirit Rising: A Feminist Reader in Religion*, edited by Carol P. Christ and Judith Plaskow. San Francisco: Harper & Row, 1979.

Carby, Hazel. *Reconstructing Womanhood: The Emergence of the Afro-American Woman Novelist*. New York: Oxford University Press, 1987.

Card, Claudia , editor. *Feminist Ethics*. Lawrence, KS: University Press of Kansas, 1991.

———. *Lesbian Choices*. New York: Columbia University Press, 1995.

———. "Rape as a Weapon of War." *Hypatia* 11, 4 (1996): 5–18.

Carlin, Diana B., and Kelly L. Winfrey. "Have You Come a Long Way, Baby? Hillary Clinton, Sarah Palin, and Sexism in 2008 Campaign Coverage." *Communication Studies* 60, 4 (2009): 426–343.

Carmody, Denise. *Women and World Religions*. Nashville, TN: Abingdon, 1979.

Carnoy, Martin. "The Family, Flexible Work and Social Cohesion at Risk." In *Women, Gender, and Work*, edited by Martha Fetherolf Loutfi. Geneva: International Labour Office, 2001.

Caroli, Betty. *First Ladies: From Martha Washington to Michelle Obama*, 4th ed. New York: Oxford University Press, 2010.

Carr, C. *On Edge: Performance at the End of the Twentieth Century*. Middletown, CT: Wesleyan University Press, 2006.

Carroll, Susan J. "Reflections on Gender and Hillary Clinton's Presidential Campaign: The Good, the Bad, and the Misogynic." *Politics & Gender* 5, 1 (2009): 1–20.

Carson, Rachel. *Silent Spring*. Boston: Houghton Mifflin Harcourt, [1962] 2002.

Catalyst, 2012. *Women CEOs of the Fortune 1000*. Accessed from http://www.catalyst.org/ publication/ 271/women-ceos-of-the-fortune-1000.

Catalyst. *Women in Medicine: Quick Takes*. Accessed 10/10/12. www.catalyst.org/publication/208/women-in-medicine. April 2012.

Center for the American Woman and Politics. *The Impact of Women in Public Office: An Overview*. New Brunswick, NJ: Eagleton Institute of Politics, Rutgers University, 1991.

———. *Women Candidates for Congress 1970–2012. Fact Sheet*. New Brunswick, NJ: Eagleton Institute of Politics, Rutgers University, 2012.

Centers for Disease Control and Prevention (CDC). *HIV Prevention and Strategic Plan through 2005*. Atlanta: CDC, 2001.

———. *Women's Reproductive Health: Hysterectomy Fact Sheet. Hysterectomy in the U.S. 2000–2004*, 2005. Accessed from www.cdc.gov/ reproductivehealth/womensrh/00–04-FS_ Hysterectomy.htm.

———. *HIV in the United States: An Overview*. Atlanta: CDC, 2009. Accessed from www .cdc.gov/topics/survillance/resources/fact-sheets/us_overview.htm.

———. *Chlamydia*. Accessed from www.cdc.gov/ std/stats10/chlamydia.htm. Atlanta: CDC, 2010.

———. *STD Trends in the United States: 2010 National Data for Gonorrhea, Chlamydia, and Syphilis*. Atlanta: CDC, 2010. Accessed from www.cdc.std/stats10/trends.htm.

———. *Special Features on Socioeconomic Status and Health*. Atlanta: CDC, 2011. Accessed from www.cdc.gov/nchs/hus.htm.

———. *HPV Vaccine Information for Young Women—Fact Sheet*. Atlanta: CDC, 2012. Accessed from www.cdc.gov/std/hpv/stdfact-hpv-vaccine-young-women.htm.

———. *Women's Safety and Health Issues at Work*. Atlanta: CDC, 2012. Accessed from www .cdc.gov/niosh/topics/women.

——— and National Center for Injury Prevention and Control et al. *The National Intimate Partner and Sexual Violence Survey: 2010 Summary Report*. Atlanta: CDC, 2012.

Chabram-Dernersesian, Angie, and Adela de la Torre, editors. *Speaking From the Body: Latinas on Health and Culture.* Tucson, AZ: The University of Arizona Press, 2008.

Chadha, Gurinder, director. *Bride and Prejudice.* Miramax Films, 2004.

Chadwick, Whitney. *Women, Art, and Society.* London: Thames and Hudson, 1990.

Chakravarty, Sumita. *National Identity and Indian Popular Cinema, 1947–1987.* Austin: University of Texas Press, 1993.

Chamberlain, Mariam K., editor. *Women in Academe: Progress and Prospects.* New York: Russell Sage Foundation, 1988.

Chappell, Louise. "Contesting Women's Rights: Charting the Emergence of a Transnational Conservative Counter-network." *Global Society* 20, 4 (2006): 491–520.

Chase, Susan E., and Mary F. Rogers, editors. *Mothers and Children: Feminist Analyses and Personal Narratives.* New Brunswick, NJ: Rutgers University Press, 2001.

Chatterjee, Partha. *The Nation and Its Fragments: Colonial and Postcolonial Histories.* Princeton, NJ: Princeton University Press, 1993.

Chavkin, Wendy, and Ellen Chesler, editors. *Where Human Rights Begin: Health, Sexuality, and Women in the New Millennium.* New Brunswick, NJ: Rutgers University Press, 2005.

Cherlin, Andrew J. "American Marriage in the Early Twenty-First Century." *The Future of Children* 15, 2 (2005): 33–55.

———. "Demographic Trends in the United States: A Review of Research in the 2000s." *Journal of Marriage and Family* 72, 3 (2010): 403–19.

Chesler, Phyllis. *Women and Madness.* Garden City, NY: Doubleday, 1972.

Cheung, Fanny M., and Diane F. Halpern. "Women at the Top: Powerful Leaders Define Success as Work + Family in a Culture of Gender." *American Psychologist* 65, 3 (2010): 182–93.

Childs, Sarah, and Mona Lena Krook. "Analysing Women's Substantive Representation: From Critical Mass to Critical Actors." *Government and Opposition* 44, 2 (2009): 125–45.

Chodorow, Nancy. *The Reproduction of Mothering: Psychoanalysis and the Sociology of Gender.* Berkeley: University of California Press, 1978.

Choi-Fitzpatrick, Austin. *Slavery Still Exists and It Could Be in Your Backyard: A Community Members' Guide to Fighting Human Trafficking and Slavery.* Washington, DC: Free the Slaves, 2008.

Chowdhury, Najma. "Lessons on Women's Political Leadership from Bangladesh." *Signs* 34, 1 (2008): 8–15.

Christ, Carol P. "Why Women Need the Goddess: Phenomenological, Psychological, and Political Reflections." In *Womanspirit Rising: A Feminist Reader in Religion,* edited by Carol P. Christ and Judith Plaskow. San Francisco: Harper & Row, 1979.

———. *Laughter of Aphrodite: Reflections on a Journey to the Goddess.* New York: Harper & Row, 1987.

Christensen, A. S. "Sex Discrimination and the Law." In *Women Working: Theories and Facts in Perspective,* edited by Ann H. Stromberg and Shirley Harkness. Mountain View, CA: Mayfield, 1988.

Chusmir, Leonard H., and Barbara Parker. "Dimensions of Need for Power: Personalized vs. Socialized Power in Female and Male Managers." *Sex Roles* 11 (1984): 759–69.

Cifcili S. Y., M. Akman, A. Demirkol, et al. "'I Should Live and Finish It': A Qualitative Inquiry into Turkish Women's Menopause Experience." *BMC Family Practice* 10, 2 (2009).

Cixous, Hélène. "The Laugh of the Medusa." In *New French Feminisms,* edited by Elaine Marks and Isabelle de Courtivron. New York: Schocken, 1981. (Originally published as "Le rire de la meduse," *Signs* 1 (1976): 875–93.)

Claes, Marie-Thérèse. "Women, Men and Management Styles." In *Women, Gender, and Work,* edited by Martha Fetherolf Loutfi. Geneva: International Labour Office, 2001.

Clark, Veve, Shirley Nelson Ganer, Margaret Higonnet, et al., editors. *Antifeminism in the Academy.* New York: Routlege, 1996.

Clarke, Cheryl. "The Failure to Transform: Homophobia in the Black Community." In *Home Girls: A Black Feminist Anthology*, edited by Barbara Smith. New York: Kitchen Table Women of Color Press, 1983.

Clement, Grace. *Care, Autonomy, and Justice*. Boulder, CO: Westview Press, 1996.

Clifton, Donna, and Charlotte Feldman-Jacobs. *Current Status of the World's Women and Girls*. Washington, DC: Population Reference Bureau, 2011.

Clifton, Lucille. "Wishes for Sons." In *Quilting: Poems 1987–1990*. Rochester, NY: BOA Editions, 1991.

Clinton, Hillary Rodham. "In France, Day Care Is Every Child's Right." *The New York Times*, April 7, 1990.

CLUW. "CLUW Mission Statement." *Coalition of Labor Union Women*. November, 2009. Accessed November 1, 2010 from http://www.cluw.org/about.html.

Cockrell, C. "Making Academia More Family-Friendly." *Berkeleyan*, April, 2003. Accessed November 1, 2010, from http://Berkeley.edu/news/berkeleyan/2003/04/30_facfam.shtml.

Cohen, P. N. "Working Women of Wal-Mart United." *Huffington Post*, April, 2010. Accessed November 1, 2010 from http://www.huffingtonpost.com/phillip-n-cohen/working-women-of-wal-mart_b_552942.html.

Cohn, Carol. *Women and Wars*. Cambridge, UK: Polity Press, 2013.

Coleman, Emily. "Infanticide in the Early Middle Ages." In *Women in Medieval Society*, edited by Susan Mosher Stuard. Philadelphia: University of Pennsylvania Press, 1976.

Colette, Sidonie-Gabrielle. *My Mother's House, and Sido*, translated by Una Vincenzo and Enid McLead. New York: Farrar, Straus and Giroux, 1953.

College Board, The. *The Educational Crisis Facing Young Men of Color*. New York: The College Board, 2010.

Collier-Thomas, Bettye. *Jesus, Jobs, and Justice: African American Women and Religion*. New York: Random House, 2010.

Collins, Alicia C. "Black Women in the Academy." In *Sisters of the Academy*, edited by Reitumetse Obakeng Mabokela and Ann L. Green. Sterling, VA: Stylus, 2001.

Collins, Gail. *When Everything Changed: The Amazing Journey of American Women From 1960 to the Present*. Boston: Little Brown, 2009.

Collins, Patricia Hill. *Black Feminist Thought: Knowledge, Consciousness, and the Politics of Empowerment*. New York: Routledge, Chapman, and Hall, 1990.

———. "It's All in the Family: Intersections of Gender, Race, and Nation." *Hypatia* 13, 3 (1998): 62–82.

———. *Black Feminist Thought: Knowledge, Consciousness, and the Politics of Empowerment*, 2nd ed. New York: Routledge, 2000.

———. "The Meaning of Motherhood in Black Culture and Black Mother–Daughter Relationships." In *Double Stitch: Black Women Write About Mothers & Daughters*, edited by Patricia Bell-Scott, Beverly Guy-Sheftall, Jacqueline Jones Royster, et al. Boston: Beacon Press, 2000.

Collins, Suzanne. *The Hunger Games*. New York: Scholastic Press, 2008.

Colwill, Nina L. *The New Partnership: Women and Men in Organizations*. Palo Alto, CA: Mayfield, 1982.

Colyar, Julia. "Communities of Exclusion: Women Student Experiences in Information Technology Classrooms." *Journal about Women in Higher Education* 1, 1 (2008):123–42.

Combahee River Collective. "A Black Feminist Statement." In *Capitalist Patriarchy and the Case for Socialist Feminism*, edited by Zillah Eisenstein. New York: Monthly Review Press, 1979.

Conboy, Katie, Nadia Median, and Sarah Stanbury, editors. *Writing on the Body*. New York: Columbia University Press, 1997.

Constable, Nicole. *Cross-Border Marriages: Gender and Mobility in Transnational Asia*. Philadelphia: University of Pennsylvania Press, 2005.

———. *Maid to Order in Hong Kong: Stories of Migrant Workers*. Ithaca, NY: Cornell University Press, 2007.

Conway, M. Margaret. "Women and Political Participation." *PS: Political Science and Politics* 25, 2 (2001): 231–3.

Cook, Blanche Wiesen. *Eleanor Roosevelt*, vol. 1. New York: Penguin, 1992.

Cook, Daniel Thomas, and Susan B. Kaiser. "Betwixt and Between: Age Ambiguity and the Sexualization of the Female Consuming Subject." *Journal of Consumer Culture* 4 (2004): 203–27.

Cooke, Lynn Prince, and Janeen Baxter. "'Families' in International Context: Comparing Institutional Effects across Western Societies." *Journal of Marriage and Family* 71 (2010): 516–36.

Cookson, Shari, director. "Living Dolls: The Making of a Child Beauty Queen." In L. Otto (producer), *American Undercover*, HBO documentary, 2001. New York: Home Box Office.

Coontz, Stephanie. "Sharing the Load: Quality Marriages Today Depend on Couples Sharing Domestic Work." In *The Shriver Report: A Woman's Nation Changes Everything*. Washington, DC: Center for American Progress, 2009.

———. *A Strange Stirring: The Feminine Mystique and American Women at the Dawn of the 1960s*. New York: Basic Books, 2011.

———. "The Myth of Male Decline." *New York Times* Sunday Book Review, September 30, 2012, 1.

Cooper, Anna Julia. *A Voice from the South*. New York: Oxford University Press, [1892] 1998.

Corbett, Christianne, Catherine Hill, and Andresse St. Rose. *Why So Few? Women in Science, Technology, Engineering and Mathematics*. Washington, DC: AAUW, 2010.

Corder, Judy, and Cookie W. Stephen. "Females' Combination of Work and Family Roles: Adolescents' Aspirations." *Journal of Marriage and the Family* 46 (1984): 391–402.

Cornelisen, Ann. *Women of the Shadows: The Wives and Mothers of Southern Italy*. Boston: Little, Brown, 1976.

Cott, Nancy F. *The Bonds of Womanhood: "Woman's Sphere" in New England, 1780–1835*. New Haven, CT: Yale University Press, 1977.

———. *The Grounding of Modern Feminism*. New Haven, CT: Yale University Press, 1987.

———. "Across the Great Divide: Women in Politics before and after 1920." In *Women, Politics and Change*, edited by Louise A. Tilly

and Patricia Gurin. New York: Russell Sage Foundation, 1990.

Courtois, C. "The Aftermath of Child Sexual Abuse: The Treatment of Complex Post-Traumatic Stress Reactions." In *Psychological Perspectives on Human Sexuality*, edited by L. Szuchman and Frank Muscarella. New York: Wiley, 2000.

Creegan, Nicola Hoggard, and Christine D. Pohl. *Living on the Boundaries: Evangelical Women, Feminism, and the Theological Academy*. Downers Grove, IL: InterVarsity Press, 2005.

Crenshaw, Kimberlé. "Demarginalizing the Intersection of Race and Sex: A Black Feminist Critique of Antidiscrimination Doctrine, Feminist Theory, and Antiracist Politics." *The University of Chicago Legal Forum* (1989):139–67.

———. "Mapping the Margins: Intersectionality, Identity Politics, and Violence against Women of Color." *Stanford Law Review* 43, 6 (1991): 1241–99.

———. "Whose Story Is It Anyway?: Feminist and Antiracist Appropriations of Anita Hill." In *Race-ing Justice, En-gendering Power: Essays on Anita Hill, Clarence Thomas, and the Construction of Social Reality*, edited by Toni Morrison. New York: Pantheon, 1992.

Crimmins, Eileen, Jung Ki Kim, and Aaron Hagedorn. "Life with and without Disease: Women Experience More of Both." *Journal of Women & Aging* 14, 1–2 (2002): 47–59.

Crittendon, Ann. *The Price of Motherhood*. New York: Henry Holt, 2001.

Cueller, Alison, Adelle Simmions, and Kenneth Finegold. *The Affordable Care Act and Women, 2012*. www.aspe.hhs.gov/health/2012/ACA&Women/rb.shtml.

Currah, Paisley, Richard M. Juang, and Shannon Price Minter. "Introduction." In their *Transgender Rights*. Minneapolis: University of Minnesota Press, 2006.

Cusk, Rachel. *A Life's Work: On Becoming a Mother*. New York: Picador, 2002.

D'Emilio, John. *Sexual Politics, Sexual Communities: The Making of a Homosexual Minority in the United States, 1940–1970*. Chicago: University of Chicago Press, 1983.

Dalla Costa, Mariarosa, and Selma James. *The Power of Women and Subversion of the Community*. Bristol, CT: Falling Wall Press, 1975.

Dalley, Gillian. *Ideologies of Caring: Rethinking Community and Collectivism*. London: Macmillan Education, 1988.

Daly, Mary. *Beyond God the Father: Toward a Philosophy of Women's Liberation*. Boston: Beacon, 1973.

———. *Gyn-Ecology: The Metaethics of Radical Feminism*. Boston: Beacon Press, 1978.

Danforth, Loring M. *The Death Rituals of Rural Greece*. Princeton, NJ: Princeton University Press, 1982.

Darroch, Jacqueline, Gilda Sedgh, and Haley Ball. *Contraceptive Technologies: Responding to Women's Needs*. New York: Guttmacher Institute, 2011.

Das Gupta, Monica. "Family Systems, Political Systems, and Asia's 'Missing Girls': The Construction of Son Preference and Its Unraveling." Washington, DC: The World Bank, 2009. http://proxy.library.carleton.ca/login?url=http://elibrary.worldbank.org/content/workingpaper/10.1596/1813–9450-5148.

Davies, Anita A., Rosilyne Borland, Carolyn Blake, et al. "The Dynamics of Health and Return Migration." *PLOS [Public Library of Science] Medicine* 8, 6 (2011).

Davies, Carole Boyce. "Black/Female/Bodies Carnivalized in Spectacle and Space." In *Black Venus 2010: They Called Her "Hottentot,"* edited by Deborah Willis. Philadelphia: Temple University Press, 2010.

Davis, Angela. "Reflections on the Black Woman's Role in the Community of Slaves." *Black Scholar* 3 (1971): 2–15.

———. *Women, Race, and Class*. New York: Random House, 1983.

———. *The Angela Davis Reader*, edited by Joy James. Malden, MA: Blackwell, 1998.

Davis, Flora. *Moving the Mountain: The Women's Movement in America since 1960*. New York: Simon & Shuster, 1991.

Davis, Kathy. *The Making of Our Bodies, Ourselves. How Feminism Travels Across Borders*. Durham, NC: Duke University Press, 2007.

Dawkins, Richard. *The Selfish Gene*. New York: Oxford University Press, 1976.

Daymond, M. J., Dorothy Driver, Sheila Meintjes, et al., editors. *Women Writing Africa I: The Southern Region*. New York: Feminist Press, 2003.

De Beauvoir, Simone. *The Second Sex*, translated by H. M. Parshley. New York: Knopf, 1953.

———. *Force of Circumstance*, translated by Richard Howard. New York: Putnam, 1964.

———. *The Second Sex*, translated by Constance Borde and Sheila Malovany-Chevallier. New York: Vintage, [1949] 2011.

De Pillis, Emmeline, and Lisette de Pillis. "Are Engineering Schools Masculine and Authoritarian? The Mission Statements Say Yes." *Journal of Diversity in Higher Education* 1, 1 (2008): 33–44.

De Veaux, Alexis. *Warrior Poet: A Biography of Audre Lorde*. New York: W. W. Norton and Company, 2006.

Dean-Jones, L. *Women's Bodies in Classical Greek Science*. Oxford: Clarendon, 1994.

Deaux, Kay, and Brenda Major. "Putting Gender into Context: An Interactive Model of Gender-Related Behavior." *Psychological Review* 94 (1987): 369–89.

Delaney, Janice, Mary J. Lupton, and Emily Toth, editors. *The Curse: A Cultural History of Menstruation*. New York: New American Library, 1976.

Delany, Samuel R. *The Tales of Nevèrÿon*. Hanover, NH: University Press of New England/Wesleyan University Press, 1993.

Delany, Sarah Louise, Annie Elizabeth Delany, and Amy Hill Hearth. *Having Our Say: The Delany Sisters' First 100 Years*. New York: Kodansha International, 1993.

DeMello, Margo. *Bodies of Inscription: A Cultural History of the Tattoo*. Durham, NC: Duke University Press, 2000.

DeNavas-Walt, Carmen, Bernadette D. Proctor, and Jessica C. Smith. *Income, Poverty, and Health Insurance Coverage in the United States: 2010*. U.S. Census Bureau, Current Population Reports, P60–239. Washington, DC: U.S. Government Printing Office, 2011.

Denmark, Florence L. "What Sigmund Freud Didn't Know about Women." Convocation address, St. Olaf's College, Northfield, MN, January 1977.

———. "The Myths of Aging," *Eye on Psi Chi* 7, 1 (2002): 14–21.

Denmark, Flornece, Vita Carulli Rabinowitz, and Jeri A. Sechzer. *Engendering Psychology: Women and Gender Revisited.* Boston: Pearson Allyn and Bacon, 2005.

Denmark, Florence, and Marcia Guttentag. "Dissonance in the Self-Concepts and Educational Concepts of College and Non-college-oriented Women." *Journal of Counseling Psychology* 14 (1967): 113–15.

Denmark, Florence L., V. C. Rabinowitz, and J. A. Sechzer. *Engendering Psychology: Women and Gender Revisited*, 2nd ed. Boston: Pearson Education, 2005.

Derrida, Jacques. *Writing and Difference*, translated by Alan Bass. London: Routlege, 1978.

Des Jardins, Julie. *The Madame Curie Complex: The Hidden History of Women in Science.* New York: Feminist Press, 2010.

Deutsch, Nancy L., and Barbara Schmertz. "'Starting from Ground Zero:' Constraints and Experiences of Adult Women Returning to College." *The Review of Higher Education* 34, 3 (2011): 477–504.

Devlin, Rachel. "Daughters and Fathers." In *Girlhood in America: An Encyclopedia*, edited by Miriam Forman-Brunell. Santa Barbara, CA: ABC-CLIO, 2001.

Dickens, Arthur G. *The English Reformation.* New York: Schocken, 1964.

Dickie, Margaret, and Thomas Travisano, editors. *Gendered Modernisms: American Women Poets and Their Readers.* Philadelphia: University of Pennsylvania Press, 1996.

Dickinson, Torry D., and Robert K. Schaeffer. *Fast Forward: Work, Gender, and Protest in a Changing World.* Lanham, MD: Rowman & Littlefield, 2001.

Didion, Joan. *The Year of Magical Thinking.* New York: Vintage Books, 2006.

Dinnerstein, Dorothy. *The Mermaid and the Minotaur: Sexual Arrangements and Human Malaise.* New York: Harper Collins, 1977.

Disney, Jennifer. *Women's Activism and Feminist Agency in Mozambique and Nicaragua.* Philadelphia: Temple University Press, 2008.

Divale, William Tulio, and Marvin Harris. "Population, Warfare, and the Male Supremacist Complex." *American Anthropologist* 78, 3 (1976): 521–38.

Dolan, Julie. "Political Appointees in the United States: Does Gender Make a Difference?" *PS: Political Science and Politics* 25, 2 (2001): 213–16.

Donoghue, Glenda D, editor. *Women's Health in the Curriculum: A Resource Guide for Faculty.* Philadelphia: National Academy on Women's Health Medical Education, 1996.

Doress, Paula Brown, and Diana Laskin Siegal. *Ourselves, Growing Older: Women Aging with Knowledge and Power.* New York: Simon & Schuster, 1987.

———. *The New Ourselves Growing Older.* New York: Simon & Schuster, 1994.

Dorfman, Lorraine, and Linda Rubenstein. "Paid and Unpaid Activities and Retirement Satisfaction among Rural Seniors." *Physical & Occupational Therapy in Geriatrics* 12, 1 (1994): 45–63.

Douglas, Susan J., and Meredith W. Michaels. *The Mommy Myth: The Idealization of Motherhood and How It Has Undermined All Women.* New York: The Free Press, 2004.

Douthat, Ross. "Red Family, Blue Family." *New York Times*, May 10, 2010, A23.

Dowd Hall, Jacqueline. "'The Mind That Burns in Each Body': Women, Rape, and Racial Violence." In *Powers of Desire: The Politics of Sexuality*, edited by Ann Snitow, Christine Stansell, and Sharon Thompson. New York: Monthly Review Press, 1983.

Dreby, Joanna. "Negotiating Work and Parenting over the Life Course: Mexican Family Dynamics in a Binational Context." In *Across Generations: Immigrant Families in America*, edited by Nancy Foner. New York: New York University Press, 2009.

Dreifus, Claudia. "Chloe Wofford Talks about Toni Morrison." *New York Times Magazine*, Sept. 11, 1994.

Driscoll, Catherine. "Girls Today, Girls, Girl Culture and Girl Studies." *Girlhood Studies* 1, 1 (2008): 13–32.

Duenwald, M., and B. Stamler. "On Their Own, in the Same Boat." *New York Times*, April 13 2004, E1, E13.

Duggan, Lisa, and Nan Hunter. *Sex Wars: Sexual Dissent and Political Culture*. New York: Routledge, 1995.

Duncan, Carol. "Happy Mothers and Other New Ideas in French Art." *Art Bulletin* 55 (1973): 570–83.

Dunn, Mary Maples. "Woman of Light." In *Women of America: A History*, edited by Carol Ruth Berkin and Mary Beth Norton. Boston: Houghton Mifflin, 1979.

Durham, Meenakshi Gigi. "Sex in the Transnational City: Discourses of Gender, Body and Nation in the 'New Bollywood." In *Cinema, Law and the State in Asia*, edited by Corey Creekmur and Mark Sidel. New York: Palgrave Macmillan, 2007.

Durrant, Stephen. "The Nisan Shaman Caught in Cultural Contradictions." *Signs* 5 (1979): 338–47.

Dworkin, Andrea. *Pornography: Men Possessing Women*. New York: G. P. Putnam, 1979.

Eagly, Alice H. *Sex Differences in Social Behavior: A Social-Role Interpretation*. Hillsdale, NJ: Erlbaum, 1987.

Edwards, Louise. "Strategizing for Politics: Chinese Women's Participation the One-Party State." *Women's Studies International Forum* 30, 5 (2007): 380–390.

Edwards, Louise, and Mina Roces, editors. *Women in Asia*. Ann Arbor: University of Michigan Press, 2000.

Ehrenreich, Barbara. *Nickel and Dimed: On (Not) Getting by in America*. New York: Henry Holt, 2001.

———. "Feminism's Assumptions Upended." *Los Angeles Times*, May 16, 2004.

———, and Deirdre English. *Witches, Midwives, and Nurses: A History of Women Healers*. New York: Feminist Press, 1973.

———, and Deirdre English. "Complaints and Disorders: The Sexual Politics of Sickness." In *Seizing Our Bodies: The Politics of Women's Health*, edited by Claudia Dreifus. New York: Vintage Books, 1977.

———, and Arlie Russell Hochschild, editors. *Global Women: Nannies, Maids and Sex Workers in the New Economy*. New York: Metropolitan Books, 2002.

Eisenhart, Margaret A., and Elizabeth Finkel. *Women's Science: Learning and Succeeding from the Margins*. Chicago: University of Chicago Press, 1998.

Eisenstein, Zillah. *The Radical Future of Liberal Feminism*. New York: Longman, 1981.

———. *Against Empire: Feminisms, Racism and the West*. London: Zed Books, 2004.

Eisler, Benita, editor. *The Lowell Offering: Writings by New England Mill Women*. New York: Harper & Row, 1977.

El-Zanaty, Fatma, and Ann Way. *Egypt Demographic and Health Survey 2008*. Cairo, Egypt: Ministry of Health, 2009.

Ellin, Abby. *More Women Look Over the Counter for a Libido Fix*. 2012. Accessed from http://www.nytimes.com/2012/07/03/health/more-women-seek-over-the-counter-sexual-reme dies.html?pagewanted=all&_r=0.

Ellis, Kate, Nan D. Hunter, Beth Jaker, et al., editors. *Caught Looking: Feminism, Pornography and Censorship*. New York: Caught Looking, 1986.

Ellis, Pat, editor. *Women of the Caribbean*. London: Zed Books, 1986.

Ember, Carol R. "Feminine Task Assignment and the Social Behavior of Boys." *Ethos* 1, 4 (1973): 424–39.

Emslie, C., and K. Hunt. "'Live to Work' or 'Work to Live'? A Qualitative Study of Gender and Work–Life Balance among Men and Women in Mid-life." *Gender, Work and Organization* 16, 1 (2009): 151–72.

Engels, Friedrich. *The Origin of the Family, Private Property and the State*, translated by Alec West, edited by Eleanor Burke Leacock. New York: International Publishers, [1884] 1972.

Engle, Karen. "Feminism and Its (Dis)Contents: Criminalizing Wartime Rape in Bosnia and Herzegovina." *American Journal of International Law* 99, 4 (2005): 778–816.

Enloe, Cynthia. *Maneuvers: The International Politics of Militarizing Women's Lives.* Berkeley: University of California Press, 2000.

——. *Globalization and Militarism: Feminists Make the Link.* New York: Rowman and Littlefield, 2007.

Epstein, Cynthia. "Great Divides: The Cultural, Cognitive and Social Bases of the Global Subordination of Women." *American Sociological Review* 72 (February 2007): 1–22.

Epstein, Randi Hutter. *Get Me Out of Here: The History of Childbirth From the Garden of Eden to the Sperm Bank.* New York: W.W. Norton, 2010.

Epton, Nina. *Saints and Sorcerers: A Moroccan Journey.* London: Cassell, 1958.

Erikson, Erik. *Childhood and Society.* New York: Norton, 1963.

Ernst, E., and S. Kapos. *Global Employment Trends 2012: Preventing a Deeper Job Crisis.* Geneva: International Labour Office, 2012.

Etaugh, Claire. "Women in the Middle and Later Years." In *Psychology of Women: A Handbook of Issues and Theories*, edited by Florence Denmark and Michele Antoinette Paludi. Westport, CT: Greenwood Press, 2008.

Etaugh, Claire, and Judith S. Bridges. *Women's Lives: A Topical Approach.* Boston: Pearson Allyn and Bacon, 2006.

Eto, Makiko. "Women and Representation in Japan: The Causes of Political Inequality." *International Feminist Journal of Politics* 12, 2 (2010): 177–201.

Evans, Sara. *Personal Politics: The Roots of Women's Liberation in the Civil Rights Movement and the New Left.* New York: Vintage, 1980.

Fabian, Ann. *The Skull Collectors: Race, Science, and America's Unburied Dead.* Chicago: University of Chicago Press, 2010.

Falk, Nancy Auer. *Unspoken Worlds: Women's Religious Lives in Non-Western Cultures.* New York: Harper Collins, 1980.

Falola, Toyin, and Saheed Aderinto. *Nigeria, Nationalism, and Writing History.* Rochester, NY: University of Rochester Press, 2010.

Faulkner, Carol. *Lucretia Mott's Heresy: Abolition and Women's Rights in Nineteenth-Century America.* Philadelphia: University of Pennsylvania Press, 2011.

Fausto-Sterling, Anne. *Sexing the Body: Gender Politics and the Construction of Sexuality.* New York: Basic Books, 2000.

Feaver, Vicki. "Mothers and Daughters." *Times Literary Supplement*, February 29, 1980.

Federbush, Marsha. "The Sex Problems of School Math Books." In *And Jill Came Tumbling After: Sexism in American Education*, edited by Judith Stacey, Susan Béreaud, and Joan Daniels. New York: Dell, 1974.

Feinberg, Leslie. *Transgender Warriors: Making History from Joan of Arc to RuPaul.* Boston: Beacon Books, 1996.

Fernandes, Leela. "Unsettling 'Third Wave Feminism': Feminist Waves, Intersectionality, and Identity Politics in Retrospect." In *No Permanent Waves: Recasting Histories of U.S. Feminism*, edited by Nancy Hewitt. New Brunswick, NJ: Rutgers University Press, 2010.

Fernea, Elizabeth W., and Basima Q. Bezirgan, editors. *Middle Eastern Muslim Women Speak.* Austin: University of Texas Press, 1977.

Fernea, Robert A., and Elizabeth W. Fernea. "Variation in Religious Observance among Islamic Women." In *Scholars, Saints, and Sufis: Muslim Religious Institutions Since 1500*, edited by Nikki R. Keddie. Berkeley: University of California Press, 1972.

Fett, Sharla M. *Healing, Health, and Power on Southern Slave Plantations.* Chapel Hill, NC: University of North Carolina Press, 2002.

Fiedler, Maureen E., editor. *Breaking Through the Stained Glass Ceiling: Women Religious Leaders in Their Own Words.* New York: Seabury Books, 2010.

Field, Connie, director. *The Life and Times of Rosie the Riveter.* Clarity Films, 1980.

Fine, Cordelia. *Delusions of Gender: How our Minds, Society, and Nuerosexism Create Difference.* New York: W.W. Norton, 2010.

Finney, Nikki. *Head Off and Split.* Chicago: TriQuarterly Books/Northwestern University Press, 2011.

Fiol-Matta, Lisa, and Mariam K. Chamberlain. *Women of Color and the Multicultural Curriculum: Transforming the College Classroom.* New York: Feminist Press, 1994.

Fiorenza, Elisabeth Schussler. "Word, Spirit, and Power: Women in Early Christian Communities." In *Women of Spirit: Female Leadership in the Jewish and Christian Traditions*, edited by Rosemary Ruether and Eleanor McLaughlin. New York: Simon & Schuster, 1979.

———. *In Memory of Her: A Feminist Theological Reconstruction of Christian Origins*. New York: Crossroad, 1983.

Firestone, Shulamith. "The Women's Rights Movement in the U.S.A.: New View." In *Notes From the First Year*. New York: The New York Radical Women, 1968.

———. *The Dialectic of Sex*. New York: Morrow, 1970.

———. *The Dialectic of Sex: The Case for Feminist Revolution*. New York: Farrar, Straus and Giroux, [1970] 2003.

Fischer, M. A. "Freedom Fighter." *Readers Digest* (2010):128–41.

Fisher, Elizabeth. "Children's Books: The Second Sex, Junior Division." In *And Jill Came Tumbling After: Sexism in American Education*, edited by Judith Stacey, Susan Béreaud, and Joan Daniels. New York: Dell, 1974.

Fitzpatrick, Tanya R., and Barbara Vinick. "The Impact of Husbands' Retirement on Wives' Marital Quality." *Journal of Family Social Work* 7, 1 (2003): 83–100.

Flaubert, Gustave. *Madam Bovary*, translated by Geoffrey Wall. London: Penguin Books, [1857] 2003.

Flax, Jane "Forgotten Forms of Close Combat: Mothers and Daughters Revisited." In *Toward a New Psychology of Gender*, edited by Mary M. Gergen and Sara N. Davis. New York: Routledge, 1997.

Fliegel, Zenia. "Half a Century Later: Current Status of Freud's Controversial Views of Women." Paper presented at the American Psychological Association Conference, Montreal, Canada, 1980.

Flores, William V. "Mujeres en huelga: Cultural Citizenship and Gender Empowerment in a Cannery Strike." In *Latino Cultural Citizenship*, edited by William V. Flores and Rina Benmayor. Boston: Beacon Press, 1997.

Foblets, Marie Claire S. F. G. "Family Disputes Involving Muslim Women in Contemporary Europe: Immigrant Women Caught between Islamic Family Law and Women's Rights." In *Religious Fundamentalisms and the Human Rights of Women*, edited by Courtney W. Howland. New York: St. Martin's Press, 1999.

Folbre, Nancy. *The Invisible Heart: Economics and Family Values*. New York: New Press, 2001.

———. "Reader Response: 'Womanly' Jobs and Low Pay." *The New York Times*, August 2010. Accessed November 1, 2010, from http://economix.blogs.nytimes.com/2010/08/18/reader-response-womanly-jobs-and-low-pay.

Forman-Brunell, Miriam. *Girlhood in America: An Encyclopedia*. Santa Barbara, CA: ABC-CLIO, 2001.

Foucault, Michel. *The History of Sexuality. An Introduction*, vol. 1, translated by Robert Hurley. New York: Pantheon, 1978.

———. *The History of Sexuality*. New York: Vintage Books, 1980.

Fox Keller, Evelyn. *The Mirage of a Space between Nature and Nurture*. Durham, NC: Duke University Press, 2010.

Fox, Margalit. "Betty Friedan, Who Ignited Cause in 'Feminine Mystique,' Dies at 85." *New York Times*, February 5, 2006. http://www.nytimes.com/2006/02/04/national/05cnd-friedan.html?pagewanted=all. Accessed November 25, 2012.

Fox, Mary Frank. "Women, Science, and Academia: Graduate Education and Careers." *Gender & Society* 15, 5 (2001): 654–66.

Francis, Richard C. *Epigenetics: The Ultimate Mystery of Inheritance*. New York: W.W. Norton, 2011.

Fraser, Arvonne S., and Irene Tinker, editors. *Developing Power: How Women Transformed International Development*. New York: Feminist Press, 2004.

Fraser, C. "French MPs Vote to Ban Islamic Full Veil in Public." BBC, July 13, 2010. Accessed at www.bbc.co.uk.

Fray, Janet, Nancy Evans, Brynn Taylor, et al. "State of the Evidence: The Connection between Breast Cancer and the

Environment." *International Journal of Occupational and Environmental Health* 15, 1 (2009): 43–78.

Freeman, James M. "The Ladies of Lord Krishna." In *Unspoken Worlds: Women's Religious Lives in Non-Western Cultures*, edited by Nancy Falk and Rita Gross. New York: Harper & Row, 1980.

Freixas, A., B. Luque, and A. Reina. "Critical Feminist Gerontology: In the Back Room of Research." *Journal of Women and Aging* 24, 1 (2012): 44–58.

Freud, Sigmund. "Some Psychological Consequences of the Anatomical Distinction between The Sexes." *International Journal of Psychoanalysis* 8 (1925): 133–43.

Fried, L. P., C. M. Tangen, J. Walston, et al. "Frailty in Older Adults: Evidence for a Phenotype." *Journal of Gerontology* 56A, 3 (2001): M146–56.

Friedan, Betty. *The Feminine Mystique*. New York: Dell, 1963.

Fry, Richard, and D'Vera Cohn. *Women, Men and the New Economics of Marriage*. Washington, DC: Pew Research Center, 2010.

Gakidou, E., Cowling, K., Lozano, R., et al. "Increased Educational Attainment and Its Effect on Child Mortality in 175 Countries between 1970 and 2009: A Systematic Analysis." *Lancet* 376 (2010): 959–74.

Gallagher, Catherine, and Thomas Laqueur, editors. *The Making of the Modern Body: Sexuality and Society in the Nineteenth Century*. Berkeley: The University of California Press, 1987.

Galsworthy, Theresa D. "Osteoporosis: Statistics, Intervention, and Prevention." *Annals of the New York Academy of Sciences* 736 (1994):158–64.

Gangoli, Geetanjali. "Sexuality, Sensuality and Belonging: Representations of the 'Anglo-Indian' and the 'Western' Woman in Hindi Cinema." In *Bollyworld: Popular Indian Cinema through a Transnational Lens*, edited by Raminder Kaur and A. J. Sinha. Thousand Oaks, CA: Sage, 2005.

Garcia-Retamero, R., and E. Lopez-Zafra. "Prejudice against Women in Male-Congenial Environments: Perceptions of Gender Role Congruity in Leadership." *Sex Roles* 55, 1–2 (2006): 51–61.

Garland, Howard, Karen F. Hale, and Michael Burnson. "Attributes for the Success and Failure of Female Managers: A Replication and Extension." *Psychology of Women Quarterly* 7 (1982): 155–62.

Garland-Thomson, Rosemarie. "Feminist Disability Studies." *Signs* 30, 2 (2005): 1557–87.

Garner, J. Dianne, and Susan O. Mercer. *Women as They Age*. New York: Haworth Press, 2001.

Garry, Ann. "Intersectionality, Metaphors, and the Multiplicity of Gender." *Hypatia* 26, 4 (2011): 826–50.

Gaskell, Elizabeth. *North and South*, edited by Angus Easson. New York: Oxford World's Classics, [1855] 2008.

Gaylord, S. "Women and Aging: A Psychological Perspective." In *Women as They Age*, edited by J. D. Garner and S. O. Mercer. New York: Haworth, 2001.

Geiger, Kim. "Statistics on Rape and Pregnancy Are Complicated." *Los Angeles Times*, August 23, 2012. http://latimes.com/2012/Aug/23/news/la-pn-statistics-on-rape-and-pregnancy-are-complicated. Accessed October 11, 2012.

Germon, Jennifer. *Gender: A Genealogy of an Idea*. New York: Palgrave Macmillan, 2009.

Gerson, Kathleen. "Work without Worry." *New York Times*, May 11, 2003, A15.

Gibbons, C., and T. C. Jones. "Kinship Care: Health Profiles of Grandparents Raising Their Grandchildren." *Journal of Family Social Work* 7, 1 (2003): 1–14.

Giddings, Paula. *When and Where I Enter: The Impact of Black Women on Race and Sex in America*. New York: Bantam Books, 1984.

———. *Ida, a Sword Among Lions: Ida B. Wells and the Campaign Against Lynching*. New York: Harper, 2009.

Gilchrist, Roberta. Gender and Material Culture: The Archaeology of Religious Women. London and New York: Routledge, 1994.

Gilkes, Cheryl Townsend. "'Together and in Harness': Women's Traditions in the Sanctified Church." *Signs* 10 (1985): 687–99.

Gillick, M. "Pinning down Frailty." *Journal of Gerontology* 56A, 3 (2001): M134–5.

Gilligan, Carol. *In a Different Voice: Psychological Theory and Women's Development.* Cambridge, MA: Harvard University Press, 1982.

———. *In a Different Voice.* Cambridge, MA: Harvard University Press, 1993.

Gilligan, Carol, Nona P. Lyons, and Trudy J. Hanmer, editors. *Making Connections: The Relational Worlds of Adolescent Girls at Emma Willard School.* Cambridge, MA: Harvard University Press, 1990.

Gilman, Charlotte Perkins. *Women and Economics.* Reprint. Edited by Carl Degler. New York: Harper Torchbooks, [1898] 1966.

———. *The Yellow Wall-Paper.* Reprint, with an afterword by Elaine R. Hedges. New York: Feminist Press at CUNY, [1899] 1973.

———. *Herland.* New York: Pantheon, [1915] 1979.

Gilman, Sander. *Difference and Pathology: Stereotypes of Sexuality, Race, and Madness.* Ithaca, NY: Cornell University Press, 1985.

Gines, Kathryn T. "Black Feminism and Intersectional Analyses: A Defense of Intersectionality." *Philosophy Today* 36, SPEP Supplement (2011): 275–84.

Glasman, Lynn. "Mother 'There for' Me: Female-Identity Development in the Context of the Mother-Daughter Relationship: A Qualitative Study." *Dissertation Abstracts International Section B: The Sciences and Engineering* 62 (7-B), 3377, 2002.

Glassgold, Judith M., and Suzanne Iasenza, editors. *Lesbians and Psychoanalysis: Revolution in Theory and Practice.* New York: Free Press, [1995] 2000.

Glickman, Rose L. *Daughters of Feminists.* New York: St. Martin's Press, 1993.

Gokulsing, K. Moti, and Wimal Dissanayake. *Indian Popular Cinema: A Narrative of Cultural Change.* Stoke on Trent, UK: Trentham Books, 2004.

Goldenberg, Naomi. *Changing of the Gods: Feminism and the End of Traditional Religions.* Boston: Beacon, 1979.

Goldman, Emma. "The Traffic in Women," and "Marriage and Love" In *Red Emma Speaks: An Emma Goldman Reader* 3rd ed. Compiled and edited by Alix Kates Shulman. New York: Humanity Books, [1911] 1996.

Goldstein, Leslie Friedman. *The Constitutional Rights of Women: Cases in Law and Social Change.* New York: Longman, 1979.

Gonzalez, R. G. "American Indian Students." In *Women in Higher Education: An Encyclopedia*, edited by A. M. M. Aleman and K. A. Renn. Santa Barbara, CA: ABC-CLIO, 2002.

Goody, Jack. *Production and Reproduction: A Comparative Study of the Domestic Domain.* Cambridge: Cambridge University Press, 1976.

Gopinath, Gayatri. "Bollywood Spectacles: Queer Diasporic Critique in the Aftermath of 9/11." *Social Text* 23, 3–4 (Fall-Winter 2005): 157–69.

———. *Impossible Desires: Queer Diasporas and South Asian Cultures.* Durham, NC: Duke University Press, 2005.

Gordon-Reed, Annette. *The Hemingses of Monticello: An American Family.* New York: W.W. Norton, 2008.

Gordon, Linda. *Woman's Body, Woman's Right: A Social History of Birth Control in America.* New York: Grossman, 1976.

———. *Heroes of Their Own Lives.* New York: Penguin, 1988.

Gottlieb, N. "Families, Work and the Lives of Older Women." In *Women as They Age: Challenge, Opportunity, and Triumph*, edited by J. Dianne Garner and Susan O. Mercer. New York: Haworth Press, 1989.

Gouws, Amanda. "Obstacles for Women in Leadership Positions: The Case of South Africa." *Signs* 34, 1 (2008): 21–7.

Govindan, Padma P., and Bisakha Dutta. "'From Villain to Traditional Housewife!' The Politics of Globalization and Women's Sexuality in the 'New' Indian Media." In *Global Bollywood*, edited by Anandam P. Kavoori and Aswin Punathambekar. New York: New York University Press, 2008.

Grady, Denise. "Maternal Deaths in Sharp Decline across the Globe." *New York Times*, April 14, 2010, A1, 11.

Graff, Gerald. *Curriculum Reform and the Culture Wars.* New York: Garland, 1994.

Grant, Therese M., Dana C. Jack, and Annette L. Fitzpatrick, "Carrying the Burdens of Poverty, Parenting, and Addiction: Depression

Symptoms and Self-Silencing among Ethnically Diverse Women." *Community Mental Health* Journal 47, 1 (2011): 90–8.

Gray, Janet. *State of the Evidence: The Connection between Breast Cancer and the Environment*, 5th ed. San Francisco: Breast Cancer Fund, 2008.

Green, Monica H., editor and translator. *The "Trotula": A Medieval Compendium of Women's Medicine*. Philadelphia: University of Pennsylvania Press, 2001.

Green, Rayna. *Women in American Indian Society*. Philadelphia: Chelsea House, 1992.

Greenberg, Julie A. "The Roads Less Traveled: The Problem with Binary Sex Characteristics." In *Transgender Rights*, edited by Paisley Currah et al. Minneapolis: University of Minnesota Press, 2006.

Greene, Beverly. "Psychotherapy with African-American Women: Integrating Feminist and Psychodynamic Models." *Journal of Training and Practice in Professional Psychology* 7, 1 (1993): 49–66.

Greenwald, Maurine Weiner. *Women, War, and Work: The Impact of World War I on Women Workers in the United States*. Westport, CT: Greenwood Press, 1980.

Greer, Germain. *The Female Eunuch*. London: MacGibon and Kee, 1970.

Grewal, Inderpal, and Caren Kaplan, editors. *Scattered Hegemonies: Postmodernity and Transnational Feminist Practices*. Minneapolis: University of Minnesota Press, 1994.

Griffin, Susan. "Rape: The All-American Crime." *Ramparts* 10, 3 (September 1971): 26–35.

Gross, Rita. *Feminism and Religion: An Introduction*. Boston: Beacon, 1996.

———. "Strategies for a Feminist Revalorization of Buddhism." In *Feminism and World Religions*, edited by Courtney W. Howland. Albany, NY: SUNY Press, 1999.

Grosz, Elisabeth. *Volatile Bodies; Toward a Corporeal Feminism*. Bloomington: Indiana University Press, 1994.

Grubow, Liz. "The Mystique of Mainstream Middle Eastern Beauty." *GCI Magazine*. November 5, 2010.

Gupta, Sanjay. "Those Fragile Hearts." *Time*, February 10, 2003, 84.

Gutek, Barbara A., and Tora K. Bikson. "Differential Experiences of Men and Women in Computerized Offices." *Sex Roles* 13 (1985):123–36.

Gutgold, Nichola. *Seen and Heard: The Women of Television News*. Plymouth, UK: Lexington Books, 2008.

Guttmacher Institute. *Worldwide Abortion: Legality, Incidence and Safety*. New York: Guttmacher Institute, 2008.

———. *Making Abortion Services Accessible in the Wake of Legal Reforms*. New York: Guttmacher Institute, 2012.

Guy-Sheftall, Beverley, editor. *Words of Fire: An Anthology of African American Feminist Thought*. New York: New Press, 1995.

Gwobee, Leymah. Nobel lecture, delivered December 10, 2011. http://www.nobelprize.org/nobel_prizes/peace/laureates/2011/gbowee-lecture_en.html. Accessed December 19, 2012.

Haberman, Clyde. "On 5th Ave., a Grandmothers' Protest as Endless as the Wars." *New York Times*, May 7, 2010, A20.

Halberstam, J. Jack *Gaga Feminism: Sex, Gender, and the End of Normal*. Boston: Beacon Press, 2012.

Hall, Kim. *Feminist Disability Studies*. Bloomington: Indiana University Press, 2011.

Hall, Roberta M., and Bernice R. Sandler. *The Classroom Climate: A Chilly One for Women?* Washington, DC: Association of American Colleges, 1982.

Hall, Stuart. "Cultural Identity and Diaspora." In *Identity: Community, Culture, Difference*, edited by Jonathan Rutherford. London: Lawrence and Wishart, 1990.

Halliwell, Emma, and Helga Dittmar. "A Qualitative Investigation of Women's and Men's Body Image Concerns and Their Attitudes toward Aging." *Sex Roles* 49, 11–12 (2003): 675–84.

Hamberger, L. K., B. Ambuel, A. Marbella, et al. "Physician Interaction with Battered Women." *Journal of the American Medical Association* 7 (1998): 575–82.

Hang, Truong Thi Thuy. "Women's Leadership in Vietnam: Opportunities and Challenges." *Signs* 34, 1 (2008):16–21.

Haraway, Donna. *Primate Visions: Gender, Race, and Nature in the World of Modern Science*. New York: Routledge, 1989.

Harding, Sandra, editor. *Feminism and Methodology: Social Science Issues*. Bloomington: Indiana University Press, 1987.

Harding, Sandra. *Whose Science? Whose Knowledge? Thinking from Women's Lives*. Ithaca, NY: Cornell University Press, 1991.

———. *The Feminist Standpoint Theory Reader*. New York: Routledge, 2004.

Harrell, Jules P., Sadiki Hall, and James Taliaferro. "Physiological Responses to Racism and Discrimination: An Assessment of the Evidence." *AJPH* 93, 2 (2003): 243–8.

Harrell, Steven. "Men, Women, and Ghosts in Taiwanese Folk Religion." In *Gender and Religion: On the Complexity of Symbols*, edited by Caroline Walker Bynum, Steven Harrell, and Paula Richman. Boston: Beacon, 1986.

Harrington, Mona. *Care and Equality: Inventing a New Family Politics*. New York: Routledge, 2000.

Harris, Ann Sutherland, and Linda Nochlin. *Women Artists 1550–1950*. New York: Knopf, 1977.

Harris, Cheryl I. "Myths of Race and Gender in the Trials of O.J. Simpson and Susan Smith—Spectacles of our Times." *Washburn Law Journal* 35, 2 (1996): 231.

Harrison, Cynthia. *On Account of Sex: The Politics of Women's Issues, 1945–1968*. Berkeley: University of California Press, 1988.

Harshbarger, Rebecca. "Status of Female Farmers Rises during Food Crisis." *Women's eNews*, August 11, 2010. Accessed August 11, 2010 from: http://www.womensenews.org.

Hartmann, Heidi. "The Unhappy Marriage of Marxism and Feminism." In *Women and Revolution*, edited by Lydia Sargent. Boston: South End Press, 1981.

Hartog, Hendrik. *Man and Wife in America: A History*. Cambridge, MA: Harvard University Press, 2000.

Hartsock, Nancy C. M. *Money, Sex, and Power*. New York: Longman, 1983.

———. *The Feminist Standpoint Revisited and Other Essays*. Boulder, CO: Westview Press, 1998.

Harvey, William B. *Minorities in Higher Education 2002–2003*. Washington, DC: American Council on Education, 2003.

Hass, Nancy. "Hey Dads, Thanks for the Love and Support (and the Credit Card)." *The New York Times*, June 16, 2002, 1–2.

Hassan, Riffat. "Feminism in Islam." In *Feminism and World Religions*, edited by Courtney W. Howland. Albany, NY: SUNY Press, 1999.

Hawkesworth, Mary. *Political Worlds of Women*. Boulder, CO: Westview Press, 2012.

Hawley, John Stratton, editor. *Fundamentalism and Gender*. Oxford: Oxford University Press, 1994.

———. "Fundamentalism." In *Religious Fundamentalisms and the Human Rights of Women*, edited by Courtney W. Howland. New York: St. Martin's Press, 1999.

Hawthorne, Susan, and Bronwyn Winter, editors. *September 11, 2001: Feminist Perspectives*. North Melbourne, Australia: Spinifex Press, 2002.

Hebald, Carol. *The Heart Too Long Suppressed: A Chronicle of Mental Illness*. Boston: Northeastern University Press, 2001.

Heide, Ingeborg. "Supranational Action against Sex Discrimination: Equal Pay and Equal Treatment in the European Union." In *Women, Gender, and Work*, edited by Martha Fetherolf Loutfi. Geneva: International Labour Office, 2001.

Heisook, Kim. "Feminist Philosophy in Korea: Subjectivity of Korean Women." *Signs* 34 (2009): 247–51.

Held, Virginia. "The Equal Obligations of Mothers and Fathers." In *Having Children: Philosophical and Legal Reflections on Parenthood*, edited by Onora O'Neill and William Ruddick. New York: Oxford University Press, 1979.

———. *Feminist Morality: Transforming Culture, Society, and Politics*. Chicago: University of Chicago Press, 1993.

———, editor. *Justice and Care: Essential Readings in Feminist Ethics*. Boulder, CO: Westview Press, 1995.

———. *The Ethics of Care: Personal, Political, and Global*. New York: Oxford University Press, 2006.

Helie-Lucas, Marie-Aimee. "What Is Your Tribe: Women's Struggles and the Construction of Muslimness." In *Religious Fundamentalisms and the Human Rights of Women*, edited by Courtney W. Howland. New York: St. Martin's Press, 1999.

Heller, Nancy G., Susan Fisher Sterling, Jordana Pomeroy, et al. *Women Artists: Works from the National Museum of Women in the Arts*. Washington, DC: National Museum of Women in the Arts, 1980.

Helly, Dorothy O., and Susan M. Reverby, editors. *Gendered Domains: Rethinking Public and Private in Women's History* (*Essays from the Seventh Berkshire Conference on the History of Women*). Ithaca, NY: Cornell University Press, 1992.

Hennig, Margaret, and Anne Jardim. *The Managerial Woman*. Garden City, NY: Anchor Press/Doubleday, 1977.

Henry, Astrid. *Not My Mother's Sister: Generational Conflict and Third Wave Feminism*. Bloomington: Indiana University Press, 2004.

Herdt, Gilbert. *Sambia Sexual Culture: Essays from the Field*. Chicago: University of Chicago Press, 1999.

Herman, Rebecca, and Kay Wallen. "Cognitive Performance in Rhesus Monkeys Varies by Sex and Prenatal Androgen Exposure." *Hormones and Behavior* 51, 4 (2007): 496–507.

Herring, C. "Does Diversity Pay? Race, Gender, and the Business Case for Diversity." *American Sociological Review* 74 (2009): 208–24.

Hersh, Seymour M. *The Road to Abu Ghraib*. New York: Harper Collins, 2004.

Hertz, Rosanna. *Single by Chance, Mothers by Choice. How Women Are Choosing Parenthood Without Marriage and Creating the New American Family*. New York: Oxford University Press, 2006.

Herzig, Abbe H. "Becoming Mathematicians: Women and Students of Color Choosing and Leaving Doctoral Mathematics." *Review of Education Research* 74, 2 (2004): 171–214.

Hetherington, E. Mavis, and John Kelly. *For Better or for Worse: Divorce Reconsidered*. New York: W.W. Norton, 2002.

Heywood, Leslie, and Jennifer Drake, editors. *Third Wave Agenda: Being Feminist, Doing Feminism*. Minneapolis: University of Minnesota Press, 1997.

Hill Collins, Patricia. *Black Feminist Thought: Knowledge, Consciousness and the Politics of Empowerment*. Boston: Unwin Hyman, 1990.

Hill, Bridget, editor. *The First English Feminist: Reflections Upon Marriage and Other Writings by Mary Astell*. Aldershot, UK: Gower/Maurice Temple Smith, 1986.

Hill, Catherine, and Elena Silva. *Drawing the Line: Sexual Harassment on Campus*. Washington, DC: American Association of University Women Educational Foundation, 2005.

Hinkle, Yvonne, Ernest Johnson, Douglas Gilbert, et al. "African-American Women Who Always Use Condoms: Attitudes, Knowledge about AIDS, and Sexual Behavior." *Journal of American Medical Women's Association* 47, 6 (1992): 230–7.

Hinojosa, Magda. *Selecting Women, Electing Women: Political Representation and Candidate Selection in Latin America*. Philadelphia: Temple University Press, 2012.

Hirata, Lucie Cheng. "Free, Enslaved, and Indentured Workers in Nineteenth-Century Chinese Prostitution." *Signs* 5 (1979): 3–29.

Hirji, Faiza. "Ranis Making Rotis: Dreams of the Good South Asian Girl." *Topia* 26 (Fall 2011): 145–63.

Hochschild, Arlie Russell, with Anne Machung. *The Second Shift*. New York: Penguin, 2003.

Hoebel, E. Adamson. *The Cheyennes: Indians of the Great Plains*. New York: Holt, Rinehart & Winston, 1960.

Hoehler-Fatton, Cynthia. *Women of Fire and Spirit: History, Faith, and Gender in Roho Religion in Western Kenya*. New York: Oxford University Press, 1996.

Hoffman, Walter James. *Mythology of the Menomoni Indians*. Washington, DC: Judd and Detweiler, 1890.

Holmgren, Janet L. "The Compelling Case for Women's Colleges." *The San Jose Mercury News*, October 11, 2006.

Holmstrom, Nancy, editor. *The Socialist Feminist Project*. New York: Monthly Review, 2002.

hooks, bell. *Feminist Theory: From Margin to Center*. Boston: South End Press, 1984.

Hopkins-Chadwick, D. L. "Stress in Junior Enlisted Air Force Women with and without Children." *Western Journal of Nursing Research* 31, 3 (2009): 409–27.

Horney, Karen. "Flight from Womanhood: The Masculinity Complex in Women." *International Journal of Psychoanalysis* 7 (1926): 324–39.

———. *New Ways in Psychoanalysis*. New York: Norton, 1939.

———. "On the Genesis of Castration Complex in Women." In *Psychoanalysis and Women* edited by Jean Baker Miller. New York: Brunner/Mazei, 1973.

Hoskins, Janet. "Blood Mysteries: Beyond Menstruation as Pollution." *Ethnology* 4, 4 (2002): 299–301.

Hossain, Rokeya Sakhawat. *Sultana's Dream and Selections from the Secluded Ones*, edited and translated by Roushan Jahan. New York: Feminist Press, 1988.

Howe, Florence, editor. *The Politics of Women's Studies. Testimony from 30 Founding Mothers.* New York: Feminist Press, 2000.

Howe, Louise Kapp. *Pink Collar Workers*. New York: Avon Books, 1978.

Howland, Courtney W., editor. *Religious Fundamentalisms and the Human Rights of Women*. New York: St. Martin's Press, 1999.

Hoyert, D. L., H. C. Kung, and B. L. Smith. "Deaths: Preliminary Data for 2003." *National Vital Statistics Reports: From the Centers for Disease Control and Prevention, National Center for Health Statistics, National Vital Statistics System* 53, 15 (2005): 1–48.

Htun, Mala, and S. Laurel Weldon. "State Power, Religion, and Women's Rights: A Comparative Analysis of Family Law." *Indiana Journal of Global Legal Studies* 18, 1 (2011): 145–65.

Hulbert, Ann. *Raising America: Experts, Parents, and a Century of Advice about Children*. New York: Knopf, 2003.

Hull, Gloria T., Patricia Bell Scott, and Barbara Smith, editors. *All the Women Are White, All the Blacks Are Men, but Some of Us Are Brave: Black Women's Studies*. New York: Feminist Press, 1982.

Hune, Shirley. *Asian Pacific American Women in Higher Education: Claiming Visibility and Voice*. Washington, DC: Association of American Colleges and Universities, 1998.

———. "Asian Pacific American Women and Men in Higher Education: The Contested Spaces of Their Participation, Persistence, and Challenges as Students, Faculty, and Administrators." In *"Strangers" of the Academy: Asian Women Scholars in Higher Education*, edited by Guofang Li and Gulbahar H. Beckett. Sterling, VA: Stylus Publishing, 2006.

———. "Asian American Women Faculty and the Contested Space of the Classroom." In *Women of Color in Higher Education: Turbulent Past, Promising Future*, edited by G. Jean-Marie and B. Lloyd-Jones. Bingley, UK: Emerald Group Publishing, 2011.

Hunt, Arthur S., and C. C. Edgar. *Select Papyri. 1, Non-Literary Papyri, Private Affairs* [in Greek text with English parallel translation, introduction and notes]. London: Heinemann; Cambridge, MA: Harvard University Press, 1932.

Hunt, Laurie, Gina LaRoche, Stacy Blake-Beard, et al. "Cross-Cultural Connections: Leveraging Social Networks for Women's Advancement." In *The Glass Ceiling in the 21st Century*, edited by Manuela Barreto, Michelle K. Ryan, and Michael T. Schmitt. Washington, DC: American Psychological Association, 2009.

Hunter, Erica. "Change and Continuity in American Marriage." In *Introducing the New Sexuality Studies*, 2nd ed., edited by S. Seidman, N. Fischer, and C. Meeks. London: Routledge, 2011.

Huston, Perdita. *Families as We Are: Conversations from Around the World*. New York: Feminist Press, 2001.

Huxley, Rachel R., and Mark Woodward. "Cigarette Smoking as a Risk Factor for Coronary Heart Disease in Women Compared with Men: A Systematic Review and Meta-Analysis of Prospective Cohort Studies." *Lancet* 378, 9799 (2011): 1297–305.

Hvas, L. "Positive Aspects of Menopause: A Qualitative Study." *Maturitas* 39, no. 1 (2001): 11–17.

Hymowitz, Kay S. *Manning Up: How the Rise of Women Has Turned Men into Boys*. New York: Basic Books, 2012.

Ihle, Elizabeth L. *History of Black Women's Education in the South, 1865–Present: Instruction Modules for Educators*, 4 vols. Washington, DC: U.S. Department of Education, 1986.

Institute of Medicine. *The Hidden Epidemic: Confronting Sexually Transmitted Diseases*, edited by Thomas R. Eng and William T. Butler. Washington, DC: National Academy Press, 1997.

Institute of Medicine. *Women's Health Research: Progress Pitfalls, and Promise*. Washington, DC: National Academies Press, 2010.

International Labour Organization. *Women in Labour Markets: Measuring Progress and Identifying Challenges*. Geneva: ILO, 2010.

Inter-Parliamentary Union. *Women in National Parliaments*. http://www.ipu.org/wmn-e/classif.htm, 2012. Accessed November 23, 2012.

International Rescue Committee (IRC). *Mortality in the Democratic Republic of Congo: An Ongoing Crisis*. New York: International Rescue Committee, 2008.

Ions, Virginia. *Egyptian Mythology*. New York: Peter Bedrick Books, 1991.

Irigaray, Luce. *Speculum of the Other Woman*, translated by Gillian C. Gill. Ithaca, NY: Cornell University Press, [1974] 1985.

———. *This Sex Which Is Not One*, translated by Catherine Porter. Ithaca, NY: Cornell University Press, 1985.

Ivekovic, Rada, and Julie Mostov, editors. *From Gender to Nation*. New Delhi: Zubaan, 2006.

Iverson, Torben, and Frances Rosenbluth. *Women, Work, and Politics*. New Haven, CT: Yale University Press, 2010.

Iyer, Aarti. "Increasing the Representation and Status of Women in Employment: The Effectiveness of Affirmative Action." In *The Glass Ceiling in the 21st Century*, edited by Manuela Barreto, Michelle K. Ryan, and Michael T. Schmitt. Washington, DC: American Psychological Association, 2009.

Jackson, Stevi, Jane Prince, and Pauline Young. "Introduction to Science, Medicine and Reproductive Technology." In *Women's Studies: Essential Readings*, edited by Stevi Jackson. New York: New York University Press, 1993.

Jacobs, Sue-Ellen, Wesley Thomas, and Sabine Lang, editors. *Two-Spirit People: Native American Gender Identity, Sexuality, and Spirituality*. Urbana: University of Illinois Press, 1997.

Jaggar, Alison. *Feminist Politics and Human Nature*. Totowa, NJ: Rowman and Allanheld, 1983.

Jagose, Annmarie. "Feminism's Queer Theory." *Feminism and Psychology* 19, 2 (2009): 157–74.

James, Victoria, and Ishmael Mafundiwa. *Best Practice Documentation of "Changing the River's Flow" Programmes in Namibia*. Harare: SafAIDS, 2011.

Janowitz, Naomi, and Maggie Wenig. "Sabbath Prayers for Women." In *Womanspirit Rising: A Feminist Reader in Religion*, edited by Carol P. Christ and Judith Plaskow. San Francisco: Harper & Row, 1979.

Jardanova, Ludmilla. "Natural Facts: An Historical Perspective on Science and Sexuality." In *Women's Studies: Essential Readings*, edited by Stevi Jackson. New York: New York University Press, 1993.

Jaskoski, Helen. "'My Heart Will Go Out': Healing Songs of Native American Women." *International Journal of Women's Studies* 4, 2 (1981):118–34.

Jay, Karla, and Allen Young. *Out of the Closets: Voices of Gay Liberation*, 20th anniversary edition. New York: New York University Press, 1992.

Jayawardena, Kumari. *Feminism and Nationalism in the Third World*. London: Zed Books, 1986.

Jayson, Sharon. "Getting Reliable Data on Infidelity Isn't Easy." *USA Today*, November 17, 2008.

Jean-Marie, Gaetane, and Brenda Lloyd-Jones, *Women of Color in Higher Education: Changing Directions and New Perspectives*. Bingley, UK: Emerald Group Publishing, 2011a.

———. *Women of Color in Higher Education: Turbulent Past, Promising Future*. Bingley, UK: Emerald Group Publishing, 2011b.

Jemal, Ahmedin, Rebecca Siegel, Elizabeth Ward, et al. "Cancer Statistics, 2008." *CA: A Cancer Journal for Clinicians* 58, 2 (2008): 71–96.

Jenkins, C. L. "Introduction: Widows and Divorcees in Later Life." *Journal of Women & Aging* 15, 2–3 (2003): 1–6.

Jessup, Martha A., Janice C. Humphreys, Claire D. Brindis, et al. "Extrinsic Barriers to Substance Abuse Treatment among Pregnant Drug Dependent Women." *Journal of Drug Issues* 33, 2 (2003): 285–304.

John, R., P. H. Blanchard, and C. H. Hennessy. "Hidden Lives: Aging and Contemporary American Indian Women." In *Handbook on Women and Aging*, edited by Jean M. Coyle. Westport, CT: Greenwood Press, 1997.

Johnson, Merri Lisa. *Jane Sexes It Up: True Confessions of Feminist Desire*. New York: Seal Press, 2002.

Johnston, Heidi Bart, Elizabeth Oliveras, Shamima Akhter, et al. "Health System Costs of Menstrual Regulation and Care for Abortion Complications in Bangladesh." *International Perspectives on Sexual & Reproductive Health* 36, 4 (2010): 196–200.

Jones, Geoffrey. *Beauty Imagined: A History of the Global Beauty Industry*. Oxford: Oxford University Press, 2010.

Jones, Jacqueline. *Labor of Love, Labor of Sorrow: Black Women, Work, and the Family from Slavery to the Present*. New York: Basic Books, 1985.

Jones, James H. *Bad Blood: The Tuskegee Syphilis Experiment*, new and expanded Edition. New York: Free Press, 1993.

Jones, Landon Y. *The Essential Lewis and Clark*. New York: HarperCollins, 2000.

Jordan-Young, Rebecca. *Brainstorm: The Flaws in the Science of Sex Differences*. Cambridge, MA: Harvard University Press, 2010.

Jordan, June. *Affirmative Acts: Political Essays*. New York: Anchor Books, 1998.

Joseph, Gloria. "Black Mothers and Daughters: Their Roles and Functions in American Society." In *Common Differences: Conflicts in Black and White Feminist Perspectives*, edited by Gloria I. Joseph and Jill Lewis. New York: Anchor Press/Doubleday, 1981.

———. "Black Mothers and Daughters: Traditional and New Perspectives." In *Double Stitch: Black Women Write About Mothers & Daughters*, edited by Patricia Bell-Scott et al. Boston: Beacon Press, 1991.

Junn, Jane. "What's Revolutionary about the Gender Gap in Voting?" Plenary Session on Revolutionary Futures. National Women's Studies Association Annual Conference, 2012.

Kinsella, K., and V. A. Velkoff. "An Aging World: 2001" [in French]. *Population Paris* 57 (2002): 928–9.

Kaiser Family Foundation (KFF). *HIV/AIDS Policy Fact Sheet*. Washington, DC, 2006.

———. *Maternal Health Deaths Drop by Nearly Half Worldwide over 20 Years; Greater Progress Still Needed*. U.N. Reports, 2012.

Kanter, Rosabeth M. *Men and Women of the Corporation*. New York: Basic Books, 1977.

Karkazais, Katrina. *Fixing Sex: Intersex, Medical Authority, and Lived Experience*. Durham, NC: Duke University Press, 2008.

Karmel, Marjorie. *Thank You, Dr. Lamaze*. New York: Dolphin, 1965.

Kates, Judith, and Gail Twersky Reimer, editors. *Reading Ruth: Contemporary Women Reclaim a Sacred Story*. New York: Ballantine, 1994.

Kathlene, Lyn. "Studying the New Voice of Women in Politics." *Chronicle of Higher Education*, Nov. 18, 1992, B1–2.

Katz, S. J., M. Kabeto, and K. M. Langa. "Gender Disparities in the Receipt of Home Care for Elderly People with Disability in the United States." *JAMA* 284, 23 (2000): 3022–7.

Kaufman, Polly Welts. *Women Teachers on the Frontier*. New Haven, CT: Yale University Press, 1984.

Kaufmann, Karen M., and John R. Petrocik. "The Changing Politics of American Men: Understanding the Sources of the Gender Gap." *American Journal of Political Science* 43, 3 (1999): 864–87.

Kay, Kathy. "She-Power: The Impact of Women in Society." *Foreign Policy* 181 Special Section (2010): 12–13.

Kaya, B. *Census Bureau Reports Women-Owned Firms Numbered 7.8 Million in 2007, Generated Receipted of $1.2 Trillion*. (Report No. CB10–184), 2007. Accessed from U.S. Census Bureau website: http://www.census.gov/newsroom/releases/archives/business_ownership/cb10–184.html.

Keaton, Trica. "Arrogant Assimilationism: National Identity Politics and African-Origin Muslim Girls in the Other France." *Anthropology and Education Quarterly* 36, 4 (2005): 405–23.

Kehily, Mary Jane. "Taking Centre Stage? Girlhood and the Contradictions of Femininity across Three Generations." *Girlhood Studies* 1, 2 (2008): 51–71.

Keller, Evelyn Fox. *Reflections on Gender and Science.* New Haven, CT: Yale University Press, 1985.

Kelly-Gadol, Joan. "Did Women Have a Renaissance?" In *Becoming Visible: Women in European History*, edited by Renate Bridenthal and Claudia Koonz. Boston: Houghton Mifflin, 1977.

Kelly, Amy. *Eleanor of Aquitaine and the Four Kings.* New York: Vintage, 1957.

Kelly, Joan. "Did Women Have a Renaissance?" In *Becoming Visible: Women in European History*, 2nd ed., edited by Renate Bridenthal, Claudia Koonz, and Susan Stuard. Boston: Houghton Mifflin, 1987.

Kennedy, Elizabeth Lapovsky, and Madeline D. Davis. *Boots of Leather, Slippers of Gold: The History of a Lesbian Community.* New York: Penguin Books, 1993.

Kennedy, Susan Estabrook. *If All We Did Was to Weep at Home: A History of White Working Class Women in America.* Bloomington: Indiana University Press, 1979.

Keohane, Nannerl O. "'But for her sex…': The Domestication of Sophie." *University of Ottawa Quarterly* 49 (1980): 390–400.

Kerber, Linda K. *Women of the Republic: Intellect and Ideology in Revolutionary America.* Chapel Hill: University of North Carolina Press, 1980.

———. *No Constitutional Right to Be Ladies: Women and the Obligations of Citizenship.* New York: Hill and Wang, 1998.

Kessler-Harris, Alice. *Out to Work*, 20th ed. Oxford: Oxford University Press, 2003.

Khademi, S., and Cooke, M.S. "Comparing the Attitudes of Urban and Rural Iranian Women toward Menopause." *Maturitas* 46 (2003): 113–21.

Khan, Mehboob , director. *Aurat.* National Studios, 1940.

———, director. *Mother India.* Mehboob Productions, 1957.

Kibria, Nazli. "'Marry into a Good Family': Transnational Reproduction and Intergenerational Relations in Bangladeshi American Families." In *Across Generations: Immigrant Families in America*, edited by Nancy Foner. New York: New York University Press, 2009.

Kigozi, Margaret. "Women as Wealth Creators and Managers in Uganda." In *Unpacking Globalization: Markets, Gender, and Work*, edited by Linda C. Lucas. Lanham, MD: Lexington Books, 2007.

Kimmel, Michael S. *The Gendered Society.* New York: Oxford University Press, 2000.

King, Jacqueline E. *Equity in Higher Education, 2010.* Washington, DC: American Council on Education, 2010.

King, Margaret L. "Book-Lined Cells: Women and Humanism in the Early Italian Renaissance." In *Beyond Their Sex*, edited by Patricia H. Labalme. New York: New York University Press, 1980.

King, Ynestra. "Engendering a Peaceful Planet: Ecology, Economy, and Eco-Feminism in Contemporary Context." *Women's Studies Quarterly* 23 (Fall–Winter 1995).

Kingston, Maxine Hong. *The Woman Warrior.* New York: Knopf, 1976.

Kinnaird, Joan K. "Mary Astell and the Conservative Contribution to English Feminism." *Journal of British Studies* 19 (1979): 53–75.

Kinsella, K., and V. Velkoff. *An Aging World.* U.S. Cenus Bureau. Series P95/01–1. Washington, DC: GPO, 2001.

Kinsey, Alfred C. *Sexual Behavior in the Human Female.* Philadelphia: W. B. Saunders; Bloomington: Indiana University Press, 1953.

———, et al. *Sexual Behavior in the Human Male.* Philadelphia: W. B. Saunders; Bloomington: Indiana University Press, 1948.

Kirkpatrick, David D. "Egypt's Women Find Power Still Hinges on Men." *The New York Times*, January 10, 2012.

Kittay, Eva Feder. *Love's Labor: Essays on Women, Equality, and Dependency.* New York: Routledge, 1999.

———, and Diana T. Meyers, editors. *Women and Moral Theory*. Totowa, NJ: Rowman and Allanheld, 1987.

Kleinfeld, Judith. "No Map to Manhood: Male and Female Mindsets Behind the College Gender Gap." *Gender Issues* 26 (2009a): 171–82.

———. "The State of American Boyhood." *Gender Issues* 26 (2009b): 113–29.

Kliff, Sarah, and Lena H. Sun. "Planned Parenthood says Komen Decision Causes Donation Spike." *The Washington Post*, February 1, 2012. http://www.washington post.com/national/health-science/planned-parenthood-says-komen-decision-causes-d onation-spike/2012/02/01/gIQAGLsxiQ_ story.html?wpisrc=nl_headlines. Accessed November 25, 2012.

Klinenberg, Eric. *Going Solo*. New York: Penguin Press, 2012.

Klonoff, E. A., and H. Landrine. "The Schedule of Sexist Events: A Measure of Lifetime and Recent Sexist Discrimination in Women's Lives." *Psychology of Women Quarterly* 19 (1995): 439–72.

Kohlberg, Lawrence. A Cognitive-Developmental Analysis of Children's Sex-Role Concepts and Attitudes. In *The Development of Sex Differences*, edited by E. E. Maccoby. Stanford, CA: Stanford University Press, 1966.

———, and Dora Z. Ullian. Stages in the Development of Psychosexual Concepts and Attitudes. In *Sex Differences in Behavior*, edited by R. C. Friedman, R. M. Richard, and R. L. Vande Wiele. New York: Wiley, 1974.

———, and Edward Zigler. "The Impact of Cognitive Maturity on the Development of Sex-Role Attitudes in the Years 4–8." *Genetic Psychology Monographs* 75 (1967): 89–165.

Kohlstedt, Sally Gregory. "Sustaining Gains: Reflections on Women in Science and Technology in 20th-Century United States." *NWSA Journal* 16, 1 (2004): 1–26.

Kolb, Deborah M., and Debra Meyerson. Keeping Gender in the Plot: A Case Study of the Body Shop. In *Gender at Work: Organizational Change for Equity*, edited by Aruna Rao,

Rieky Stuart, and David Kelleher. West Hartford, CT: Kumarian Press, 1999.

Kollontai, Alexandra. *Sexual Relations and Class Struggle: Love and the New Morality*, translated and introduced by Alix Holt. Bristol, UK: The Falling Wall Press, [1911] 1972.

Komarovksy, Mirra. *Blue-Collar Marriage*. New Haven, CT: Vintage, 1962.

Konigsberg, Ruth Davis. "Chore Wars." *Time*, August 8, 2011, 45–9.

Koonz, Claudia. *Mothers in the Fatherland: Women, the Family, and Nazi Politics*. New York: St. Martin's Press, 1987.

Korn/Ferry International. *Executive Profile 1990: A Survey of Corporate Leaders*. New York: Korn/Ferry International, 1990.

Kramarae, Cheris. *The Third Shift: Women Learning Online*. Washington, DC: American Association of University Women Educational Foundation, 2001.

Kreider, Rose M., and Diana B. Elliott. *America's Families and Living Arrangements: 2007*. Washington, DC: U.S. Census Bureau, September 2009.

———, Tavia Simmons, and U. S. Census Bureau. *Marital Status, 2000*. Washington, DC: U.S. Dept. of Commerce, Economics and Statistics Administration, U.S. Census Bureau, 2003.

Kreps, Juanita M. *Sex in the Marketplace: American Women at Work*. Baltimore: Johns Hopkins University Press, 1971.

Kristeva, Julia. *Desire in Language: A Semiotic Approach to Literature and Art*, edited by Leon Roudiez; translated by Thomas Gora, Alice Jardine, and Leon Roudiez. New York: Columbia University Press, 1980.

Kristof, Nicholas D., and Sheryl WuDunn, *Half the Sky: Turning Oppression into Opportunity for Women Worldwide*. New York: Alfred A. Knopf, 2009.

Krook, Mona Lena. "Why Are Fewer Women Than Men Elected? Gender and the Dynamics of Candidate Selection." *Political Studies Review* 8, 2 (2010): 155–68.

Kulick, Don. *Travesti: Sex, Gender, and Culture among Brazilian Transgendered Prostitutes*. Chicago: University of Chicago Press, 1998.

La Ferla, Ruth. "Underdressed and Hot: Dolls Moms Don't Love." *The New York Times*, Section 9, p. 1. http://www.nytimes.com/2003/10/26/style/noticed-underdressed-and-hot-dolls-moms-don-t-love.html?pagewanted=all&src=pm. Accessed December 21, 2012.

Ladner, Joyce A. *Tomorrow's Tomorrow: The Black Woman*. Garden City, NY: Doubleday, 1972.

Lamb, Sharon. *The Secret Lives of Girls: What Good Girls Really Do—Sex Play, Aggression, and Their Guilt*. New York: Free Press, 2001.

Lamott, Anne. *Operating Instructions. A Journal of My Son's First Year*. New York: Pantheon, 1993.

Larrieu, Julie A., Sherryl S. Heller, Anna T. Smyke, et al. "Predictors of Permanent Loss of Custody for Mothers of Infants and Toddlers in Foster Care." *Infant Mental Health Journal* 29, 1 (2008): 48–60.

Larsen, Nella. *Quicksand*. New York: Knopf, 1928.

———. *Passing*. New York: Knopf, 1929.

Leach, Fiona. "Negotiating, Constructing and Reconstructing Girlhoods." *Girlhood Studies* 3, 1 (2010): 3–8.

Leboucher, G. "Maternal Behavior in Normal and Androgenized Female Rates: Effect of Age and Experience." *Physiology and Behavior* 45, 2 (1989): 313–19.

Lebsock, Suzanne. "Women and American Politics, 1880–1920." In *Women, Politics and Change*, edited by Louise A. Tilly and Patricia Gurin. New York: Russell Sage Foundation, 1990.

Lee, Jonghyun. "Shamanism and Its Emancipatory Power for Korean Women." *Journal of Women and Social Work* 24 (2009): 186–98.

Lee, Vera. *The Reign of Women in Eighteenth-Century France*. Cambridge, MA: Schenckman, 1975.

Lees, Susan. "Motherhood in Feminist Utopias." In *Women in Search of Utopia*, edited by Elaine Baruch and Ruby Rohrlich-Levy. New York: Schocken Books. 1984.

Leman, Kevin. *The Birth Order Book: Why You Are the Way You Are*. Old Tappan, NJ: F.H. Revell, 1985.

Lennox, P. B. "In Her Own Words: Women in Hospitality Profile." *Women in Hospitality*, January, 2008. Accessed November 1, 2010, from http://www.womeninhospitality.com/article-library.

Leonhardt, David. "It's a Girl! (Will the Economy Suffer?)" *New York Times*, October 26, 2003, 1, 11.

Lerner, Gerda. *The Female Experience: An American Documentary*. New York: Oxford University Press, 1992.

Levey, Naomi N. "Life Expectancy of U.S. Women Slips in Some Regions." *Los Angeles Times*, June 15, 2011.

Lévi-Strauss, Claude. *Tristes tropiques*, translated by J. Russell. New York: Basic Books, [1958] 1963.

Levine, Ann D., and Naomi Neft. *Where Women Stand: An International Report on the Status of Women in Over 140 Countries, 1997–1998*. New York: Random House, 1997.

Levine, Lawrence. *The Opening of the American Mind: Canons, Culture, and History*. Boston: Beacon, 1997.

Levine, Nancy E., and Joan B. Silk. "Why Polyandry Fails: Sources of Instability in Polyandrous Marriages." *Current Anthropology* 38 (1997): 375–98.

Levison, Julie H., and Sandra P. Levison. "Women's Health and Human Rights." In *Women, Gender and Human Rights*, edited by Marjorie Agosin. New Brunswick, NJ: Rutgers University Press, 2001.

Levitt, Judith. "Women as Priests." *New York Times* September 30, 2012. www.nytimes.com/2012/09/30/opinion/Sunday/women-as-priests.html. Accessed October 13, 2012.

Levy, Ariel. "Raunchiness is powerful? C'mon, girls." *The Washington Post*, p. B5, Sept. 18, 2005.

Levy, Clifford. "Adoptions from Russia Continue, Official Says." *New York Times*, May 6, 2010, A6.

Levy, Darline Gay, and Harriet Branson Applewhite, editors. *Women in Revolutionary Paris, 1789–1795*. Urbana: University of Illinois, 1979.

Leyenaar, Monique. "Challenges to Women's Political Representation in Europe." *Signs: Journal of Women in Culture and Society* 34, 1 (2008): 1–7.

Lieberman, A. "EU Okays Moms Paid Leave; Women Not at Peace Tables." *WomensENews*, October, 2010. Accessed

October 23, 2010, from http:///www.wom ensenews.org.

Lihamba, Amandina, Fulata L. Moyo, Mugaybuso M. Mulokozi, et al. *Women Writing Africa III: The Eastern Region.* New York: Feminist Press, 2007.

Lind, JoEllen. "The Clinton/Palin Phenomenon and Young Women Voters." *Hamline Journal of Public Law & Policy* 30, 2 (2009): 513–47.

Lindgren, Karl-Oskar, Magdalena Inkinen, and Sten Widmalm. "Who Knows Best What the People Want: Women or Men? A Study of Political Representation in India." *Comparative Political Studies* 42, 1 (2009): 31–55.

Lindsay, Beverly, editor. *Comparative Perspectives of Third World Women: The Impact of Race, Sex, and Class.* New York: Praeger, 1980.

Linton, Simi. *Claiming Disability: Knowledge and Identity.* New York: New York University Press, 1997.

———. *My Body Politic: A Memoir.* Ann Arbor: University of Michigan Press, 2007.

Littleton, Christine. "Reconstructing Sexual Equality." *California Law Review* 25 (1987): 1279–337.

Livingston, Gretchen, and D'Vera Cohn. *Child-lessness Up among All Women; Down among Women with Advanced Degrees.* Washington, DC: Pew Research Center, 2010.

Livingston, Jennie. *Paris Is Burning.* Lionsgate, [1991] 2012.

Lloyd, Cynthia B., editor. *Growing Up Global: The Changing Transitions to Adulthood in Developing Countries.* Washington, DC: The National Academies Press, 2005.

Lloyd, Genevieve. *The Man of Reason: "Male" and "Female" in Western Philosophy.* Minneapolis: University of Minnesota Press, 1984.

Lockheed, Marlaine E. "The Double Disadvantage of Gender and Social Exclusion in Education." In *Girls' Education in the 21st Century,* edited by Mercy Tembon and Lucia Fort. Washington, DC: The International Bank for Reconstruction and Development/The World Bank, 2008.

Loewenberg, Bert James, and Ruth Bogin, editors. *Black Women in Nineteenth-Century Life:* *Their Words, Their Thoughts, Their Feelings.* University Park: Pennsylvania State University Press, 1976.

Longino, Helen. *Science as Social Knowledge: Values and Objectivity in Scientific Inquiry.* Princeton, NJ: Princeton University Press, 1990.

———, and R. Doell. "Body, Bias and Behavior: A Comparative Analysis of Reasoning in Two Areas of Biological Science." In *Sex and Scientific Inquiry,* edited by S. Harding and J. F. O'Barr. Chicago: University of Chicago Press, 1987.

Lopez, Iris. "Sterilization among Puerto Rican Women in New York City: Public Policy and Social Constraints." In *Cities of the United States,* edited by Leith Mullings. New York: Columbia University Press, 1987.

Lopez, S., A. Smith, B. Wolkenstein, et al. "Gender Bias in Clinical Judgment: An Assessment of the Analogue Method's Transparency and Social Desirability." *Sex Roles* 28 (1993): 35–45.

Lorber, Judith. *Gender Inequality: Feminist Theories and Politics,* 2nd ed. Los Angeles: Roxbury Publishing, 2001.

Lorde, Audre. *Sister Outsider.* Trumansberg, NY: Crossing Press, 1984.

———. "Uses of the Erotic: The Erotic as Power." In *Sister Outside: Essays and Speeches.* Freedom, CA: Crossing Press, 1984.

Lougee, Carolyn C. *Le Paradis des Femmes: Women, Salons, and Social Stratification in Seventeenth-Century France.* Princeton, NJ: Princeton University Press, 1976.

Louie, Miriam Ching Yoon. *Sweatshop Warriors: Immigrant Women Workers Take on the Global Factory.* Cambridge, MA: South End Press, 2001.

Love, Susan, and Karen Lindsey. *Dr. Susan Love's Breast Book.* Philadelphia: Da Capo Press, 2010.

Lubiano, Wahneema, editor. *The House That Race Built.* New York: Pantheon, 1997.

Lucas, Angela M. *Women in the Middle Ages: Religion, Marriage and Letters.* Brighton, UK: Harvester Press, 1983.

Lugones, Maria. *Pilgrimages/Peregrinajes: Theorizing Coalition against Multiple Oppressions.* Lanham, MD: Rowman and Littlefield, 2003.

————. "Heterosexualism and the Colonial/ Modern Gender System." *Hypatia* 22, 1 (2007): 186–209.

Luker, Kristin. *Abortion and the Politics of Motherhood*. Berkeley: University of California Press, 1984.

————. *Dubious Conceptions: The Policies of Teenage Pregnancy*. Cambridge, MA: Harvard University Press, 1996.

Luscombe, B. "The Rise of the Sheconomy: How Women Are Using Their Rapidly Increasing Spending Power to Impel Changes in the Way Companies Operate." *Time*, November 22, 2010, 58–61.

Lynch, Caitrin. *Juki Girls, Good Girls: Gender and Cultural Politics in Sri Lanka's Global Garment Industry*. Ithaca, NY: Cornell University Press, 2007.

Machung, Anne. *The Politics of Office Work*. Philadelphia: Temple University Press, 1988.

MacKenzie, Catriona, and Natalie Stoljar, editors. *Relational Autonomy: Feminist Perspectives on Autonomy, Agency, and the Social Self*. New York: Oxford University Press, 2000.

MacKinnon, Catharine A. "Feminism, Marxism, Method and the State: Toward Feminist Jurisprudence." In *Feminist Legal Theory*, edited by Katharine T. Bartlett and Rosanne Kennedy. Boulder, CO: Westview Press, 1991.

MacKinnon, Catharine A. *Feminism Unmodified: Discourses on Life and Law*. Cambridge, MA: Harvard University Press, 1987.

————. *Only Words*. Cambridge, MA: Harvard University Press, 1993.

Madera, Juan M., Michelle R. Hebl, and Randi C. Martin. "Gender and Letters of Recommendation for Academia: Agentic and Communal Differences." *Journal of Applied Psychology* 94, 6 (2009): 1591–9.

Mahmood, Saba. *Politics of Piety: The Islamic Revival and the Feminist Subject*. Princeton, NJ: Princeton University Press, 2005.

Mails, Thomas E. *The People Called Apache*. Englewood Cliffs, NJ: Prentice-Hall, 1974.

Maimonides. *The Code of Maimonides. Book 4: The Book of Women*, translated by Isaac Klein. New Haven, CT: Yale University Press (Judaica Series), 1972.

Mairs, Nancy. "Carnal Acts." In *Writing on the Body*, edited by Katie Conboy, Nadia Median, and Sarah Stanbury. New York: Columbia University Press, 1997.

Makwinja-Morara, Veronica. "Female Dropouts in Botswana Junior Secondary Schools." *Educational Studies* 45 (2009): 440–62.

Maloney, Carolyn B. *Rumors of Our Progress Have Been Greatly Exaggerated*. New York: Modern Times, 2008.

Mankekar, Purnima. "Brides Who Travel: Gender, Transnationalism, and Nationalism in Hindi Film." *Positions* 7, no. 3 (1999): 731–61.

Mankiller, Wilma, and Michael Wallis. *Mankiller: A Chief and Her People*. New York: St. Martin's Press, 1993.

Mann, Barbara Alice. *Iroquoian Women: The Gantowisas*. New York: Lang Press, 2000.

Mannathoko, Changu. "Promoting Education Quality through Gender-Friendly Schools." In *Girls' Education in the 21st Century*, edited by Mercy Tembon and Lucia Fort. Washington, DC: The International Bank for Reconstruction and Development/The World Bank, 2008.

Mansbridge, Jane J. *Why We Lost the ERA*. Chicago: University of Chicago Press, 1986.

Mansfield, Phyllis Kernoff, Patricia Barthalow Koch, and Ann M. Voda. "Qualities Midlife Women Desire in Their Sexual Relationships and Their Changing Sexual Response." *Psychology of Women Quarterly* 22, 2 (1998): 285–303.

Marchetti, Gina. *Romance and the "Yellow Peril": Race, Sex, and Discursive Strategies in Hollywood Fiction*. Berkeley: University of California Press, 1993.

Marieskind, Helen. "The Women's Health Movement: Past Roots." In *Seizing Our Bodies: The Politics of Women's Health*, edited by Claudia Dreifus. New York: Vintage Books, 1977.

Marlane, Judith. *Women in Television News Revisited: Into the Twenty-First Century*. Austin: University of Texas Press, 1999.

Marshall, Paule. *Brown Girl, Brownstones*. New York: Feminist Press, [1959] 1996.

Martin, Emily. *The Woman in the Body*. Boston: Beacon, 1987.

———. *The Woman in the Body: A Cultural Analysis of Reproduction.* Boston: Beacon Press, 1987.

———. *Flexible Bodies: Tracking Immunity in American Culture from the Days of Polio to the Age of AIDS.* Boston: Beacon Press, 1994.

Martin, Jane Roland. *Coming of Age in Academe: Rekindling Women's Hopes and Reforming the Academy.* New York: Routledge, 2000.

Martin, Susan Ehrlich, and Nancy C. Jurik. *Doing Justice, Doing Gender,* 2nd ed. Thousand Oaks, CA: Sage, 2006.

Mary Baker Eddy Library. *Science & Health with Key to the Scriptures.* Boston: The Mary Baker Eddy Library for the Betterment of Humanity, Inc. 2011. Accessed from http://www.marybakereddylibrary.org/mary-baker-eddy/writings/science-and-health.

Mascia-Lees, Frances E., and Patricia Sharpe. "The Anthropological Unconscious." *American Anthropologist* 96 (1994): 649–60.

———, and Nancy Johnson Black. *Gender and Anthropology.* Prospect Heights, IL: Waveland Press, 1999.

--------, Patricia Sharpe, and Colleen B. Cohen. "The Female Body in Postmodern Consumer Culture: A Study of Subjection and Agency." *Phoebe: An Interdisciplinary Journal of Feminist Scholarship, Theory and Aesthetics* 2 (1990): 29–50.

Mason, Mary Ann, and Marc Goulden. "Marriage and Baby Blues: Redefining Gender Equity in the Academy." *Annals, AAPSS* 596 (2004): 86–101.

Massey, Doreen. *Space, Place, and Gender.* Minneapolis: University of Minnesota Press, 1994.

Masters, William H., and Virginia E. Johnson. *Human Sexual Response.* Boston: Little, Brown, 1966.

Matsuda, Mari J. "When the First Quail Calls: Multiple Consciousness as Jurisprudential Method." *Women's Rights Law Reporter* 7 (1989): 9.

———. "Beside My Sister, Facing the Enemy: Legal Theory Out of Coalition." *Stanford Law Review* 43 (1991): 1189.

Matsui, Yayori. *Women's Asia.* London and Atlantic Highlands, NJ: Zed Books, 1989.

Matthews, Gareth. "Gender and Essence in Aristotle." *Australasian Journal of Philosophy* 64 suppl. (1986): 17–25.

May, Vivian. *Anna Julia Cooper, Visionary Black Feminist: A Critical Introduction.* New York: Routledge, 2007.

Mayer, A. L., and Tikka, P. M. "Family-Friendly Policies and Gender Bias in Academia." *Journal of Higher Education Policy and Management* 30, 4 (November 2008): 363–74.

Mayo, Katherine. *Mother India: Selections from the Controversial 1927 Text,* edited by Mrinalini Sinha. Ann Arbor: University of Michigan Press, [1927] 2000.

Mbilinyi, Marjorie. "'Women in Development': Ideology and the Marketplace." In *Competition: A Feminist Taboo?,* edited by Valerie Miner and Helen E. Longino. New York: Feminist Press, 1987.

McArdle, Elaine. "The Freedom to Say 'No.' Why Aren't There More Women in Science and Engineering? Controversial New Research Suggests: They Just Aren't Interested." *The Boston Globe,* May 18, 2008.

McCaffrey, Charlotte. "Wind Chill Factor." *Women's Studies Quarterly* 31, 1–2 (2003): 185–6.

McClintock, Ann. "'No Longer in a Future Heaven': Gender, Race and Nationalism." In *Becoming National: A Reader,* edited by Geoff Eley and Ronald Suny. New York: Oxford University Press, 1996.

McDougald, Elise Johnson. "The Struggle of Negro Women for Sex and Race Emancipation." In *Words of Fire: An Anthology of African American Feminist Thought,* edited by Beverley Guy-Sheftall. New York: New Press, 1995.

McGrath, Ellen, Gwendolyn Keita, Bonnie R. Strickland, et al., editors. "Women and Depression: Risk Factors and Treatment Issues." *Final Report of the American Psychological Association's Task Force on Women and Depression.* Washington, DC: American Psychological Association, 1990.

McNamara, Jo Ann Kay. *Sisters in Arms: Catholic Nuns through Two Millennia.* Cambridge, MA: Harvard University Press, 1996.

McNamara, Jo Ann. *A New Song: Celibate Women in the First Three Christian Centuries.* New York: Haworth, 1983.

———. *Sisters in Arms: Catholic Nuns through Two Millennia*. Cambridge, MA: Harvard University Press, 1996.

McWhorter, Ladelle. *Racism and Sexual Oppression in Anglo-America: A Genealogy.* Bloomington: Indiana University Press, 2009.

Mead, Margaret. *Sex and Temperament in Three Primitive Societies.* New York: Morrow, 1935.

———. *Male and Female: A Study of the Sexes in a Changing World.* New York: Dell, 1949.

Meadows, Susannah, and Mary Carmichael. "Meet the Gamma Girls." *Newsweek*, June 3, 2002.

Melkas, Hellinä. "Occupational Segregation by Sex in Nordic Countries: An Empirical Investigation." In *Women, Gender, and Work*, edited by Martha Fetherolf Loutfi. Geneva: International Labour Office, 2001.

Mendoza, Louis, and S. Shankar, editors. *Crossing into America: The New Literature of Immigration.* New York: The New Press, 2003.

Merchant, Carolyn. *The Death of Nature: Women, Ecology, and the Scientific Revolution.* San Francisco: Harper & Row, 1980.

Merrell, Susan Scarf. "Adoption's Dirty Secret." *The Daily Beast. Blogs & Stories*, April 17, 2010. http://www.thedailybeast.com/author/susan-scarf-merrell/.

Messer-Davidow, Ellen. *Disciplining Feminism: From Social Activism to Academic Discourse.* Durham, NC: Duke University Press, 2002.

Metcalfe, Amy Scott, and Sheila Slaughter. "The Differential Effects of Academic Capitalism on Women in the Academy." In *Unfinished Agendas: New and Continuing Gender Challenges in Higher Education*, edited by Judith Glazer-Raymo. Baltimore: The Johns Hopkins University Press, 2008.

MetLife. *The MetLife Study of Caregiving Costs to Working Caregivers: Double Jeopardy for Baby Boomers Caring for Their Parents.* Westport, CT: MetLife Mature Market Institute, 2011. http://www.metlife.com/assets/cao/mmi/publications/studies/2011/mmi-care-giving-costs-working-caregivers.pdf.

Meyer, Mary K. "Negotiating International Norms: The Inter-American Commission of Women and the Convention on Violence against Women." In *Gender Politics in Global Governance*, edited by Mary K. Meyer and Elisabeth Prügl. Lanham, MD: Rowman & Littlefield, 1999.

Meyers, Diana T., editor. *Feminists Rethink the Self.* Boulder, CO: Westview Press, 1997.

Milevsky, Avidan. *Sibling Relationships in Childhood and Adolescence: Predictors and Outcomes.* New York: Columbia University Press, 2011.

Mill, Harriet Taylor. "The Enfranchisement of Women." In *John Stuart Mill and Harriet Taylor Mill, Essays on Sex Equality*, edited by Alice S. Rossi. Chicago: University of Chicago Press, [1851] 1970.

Mill, James. "Government." In *Political Writings of James Mill*. Cambridge Texts in the History of Political Thought, edited by Terence Ball. Cambridge: Cambridge University Press, [1820] 1992.

Mill, John Stuart. "On the Subjection of Women." In *John Stuart Mill and Harriet Taylor Mill, Essays on Sex Equality*, edited by Alice S. Rossi. Chicago: University of Chicago Press, [1869] 1970.

Miller, Jean Baker. "The Development of Women's Sense of Self." In *Work in Progress*, Stone Center Working Paper Series 12. Wellesley, MA: Stone Center, 1984.

Miller, Virginia M., and Patricia J. M. Best. "Implications for Reproductive Medicine Sex Differences in Cardiovascular Disease." *Sexuality, Reproduction and Menopause* 9, 3 (2011): 21–8.

Millett, Kate. *Sexual Politics.* Garden City, NY: Doubleday, 1970.

Minh-ha, Trinh T. *Woman, Native, Other: Writing Postcoloniality and Feminism.* Bloomington: Indiana University Press, 1989.

Mishra, Vijay. *Bollywood Cinema: Temples of Desire.* New York: Routledge, 2002.

MIT Committee on Women Faculty. *A Study on the Status of Women Faculty in Science at MIT.* Cambridge, MA: MIT, 1999.

———. *A Report on the Status of Women Faculty in the Schools of Science and Engineering at MIT.* Cambridge, MA: MIT, 2011.

Mitchell, Juliet. *Woman's Estate.* New York: Vintage, 1973.

Moen, Phyllis, Jungmeen E. Kim, and Heather Hofmeister. "Couples' Work/Retirement Transitions, Gender, and Marital Quality." *Social Psychology Quarterly* 64, 1 (2001): 55.

Mohanty, Chandra Talpade. *Feminism without Borders: Decolonizing Theory, Practicing Solidarity*. Durham, NC: Duke University Press, 2003.

Molyneux, Maxine. "Analysing Women's Movements." *Development and Change* 29, 2 (1998): 219–45.

Monaghan, Patricia, editor. *Goddesses in World Culture*. 3 vols. Santa Barbara, CA: ABC-CLIO, 2011.

Monem, Nadine. *Riot Grrrl: Revolution Style Girl Now!* London: Black Dog Publishing, 2007.

Money, John, and Anke Ehrhardt. *A Man and Woman, Boy and Girl*. Baltimore: Johns Hopkins University Press, 1972.

Moraga, Cherrie, and Gloria Anzaldua, editors. *This Bridge Called My Back: Writings by Radical Women of Color*. New York: Kitchen Table/Women of Color Press, 1983.

Morello, Carole. "Old Terms for Blended Families Out of 'Step.'" *The Seattle Times*, January 20, 2011.

Morgan, Joan. "Hip-Hop Feminist." In *That's the Joint: The Hip-Hop Studies Reader*, 2nd ed., edited by Murray Forman and Mark Anthony Neal. New York: Routledge, 2012.

Morgan, Robin, editor. *Sisterhood Is Forever*. New York: Washington Square Press, 2003.

Morgan, Robin. *Sisterhood Is Powerful: An Anthology of Writings from the Women's Liberation Movement*. New York: Random House, 1970.

Morrison, Toni. *Playing in the Dark: Whiteness and the Literary Imagination*. Cambridge, MA: Harvard University Press, 1992a.

———, editor. *Race-ing Justice, En-gendering Power: Essays on Anita Hill, Clarence Thomas, and the Construction of Social Reality*. New York: Pantheon Books, 1992b.

Moser, Caroline O. N., and Peake, Linda. *Women, Human Settlements, and Housing*. London: Tavistock Publications, 1987.

Moses, Yolanda T. *Black Women in Academe: Issues and Strategies*. Washington, DC: Association of American Colleges, 1989.

Moynihan, Daniel Patrick. *The Negro Family: The Case for National Action*. Washington, DC: U.S. Department of Labor, 1965.

Moynihan, Ray. *Sex, Lies, and Pharmaceuticals: How Drug Companies Are Bankrolling the Next Big Medical Condition for Women*. Sydney, Australia: Allen & Unwin, 2010.

Mukherjee, Bharati. *Desirable Daughters*. New York: Hyperion, 2002.

Muley, Miriam. *The 85% Niche: The Power of Women of All Colors—Latina, Black and Asian*. Ithaca, NY: Paramount Market Publishing, 2009.

Muncy, Raymond L. *Sex and Marriage in Utopian Communities in 19th Century America*. Bloomington: Indiana University Press, 1973.

Mundy, Liza. *The Richer Sex: How the New Majority of Female Breadwinners Is Transforming Sex, Love, and Family*. New York: Simon & Schuster, 2012.

Murdock, George P. "Family Stability in Non-European Cultures." *Annals of the American Academy of Political and Social Science* 272 (1950): 175–201.

Murphy, Karen (now Talyaa Liera). "Public Says Children Better Off When Unhappy Parents Divorce, and Single Moms Suck." Babble Blog, September 20, 2007. http://www.babble.com/CS/blogs/strollerderby/archive/2007/09/20/public-says-children-better-off-when-unhappy-parents-divorce.aspx.

Murphy, Peter F., editor. *Feminism and Masculinities*. New York: Oxford University Press, 2004.

Murray, Paul. *I Loved Jesus in the Night: Teresa of Calcutta*. London: Paraclete Press, 2008.

Nagurney, Alexander J., John W. Reich, and Jason Newsom. "Gender Moderates the Effects of Independence and Dependence Desires during the Social Support Process." *Psychology and Aging* 19, 1 (2004): 215–18.

Najmabadi, Afsaneh. "Gender and Secularism of Modernity: How Can a Muslim Woman Be French?" *Feminist Studies* 32 (2006): 239–55.

Nanda, Serena. "The Hijras of India: Cultural and Individual Dimensions of an Institutionalized Third Gender Role." *Journal of Homosexuality* 11 (1986): 35–54.

Narayan, Uma. *Dis-locating Cultures: Identities, Traditions, and Third-World Feminism*. New York: Routledge, 1997.

Nash, Jennifer. "Re-thinking Intersectionality." *Feminist Review* 89 (2008): 1–15.

Nashat, Guity. "Women in the Middle East, 8,000 B.C.E.–C.E. 1800." In *Women in the Middle East and North Africa*, edited by Guity Nashat and Judith E. Tucker. Bloomington: Indiana University Press, 1999.

National Alliance for Caregiving, AARP, and Foundation Metropolitan Life. "Caregiving in the U.S. 2009." National Alliance for Caregiving, AARP. http://assets.aarp.org/rgcenter/il/caregiving_09_fr.pdf.

National Coalition for Women and Girls in Education. *Title IX at 35: Beyond the Headlines.* Washington, DC: AAUW, 2008.

National Council for Research on Women. *Balancing the Equation: Where Are Women and Girls in Science, Engineering and Technology?* New York: National Council for Research on Women, 2001.

National Eating Disorders Association. "Eating Disorders in Women of Color: Explanations and Implications," 2005. http://www.nationaleatingdisorders.org/nedaDir/files/documents/handouts/WomenCol.pdf. Accessed December 6, 2012.

National Institute of Allergy and Infectious Diseases, and National Institutes of Health. *Women's Health in the U.S.: Research on Health Issues Affecting Women.* Bethesda, MD: National Institute of Allergy and Infectious Diseases, U.S. Dept. of Health and Human Services, Public Health Service, National Institutes of Health, 2000.

National Institute of Mental Health. *Major Depressive Disorder Among Adults.* Bethesda, MD: NIMH, 2012.

National Women's Law Center. *Mothers Behind Bars.* Washington, DC: NWLC, 2012.

Neale, John E. *Queen Elizabeth I: A Biography* (1934). Garden City, NY: Doubleday, 1957.

Neel, Carol. "The Origins of the Beguines." *Signs* 14, 2 (Winter 1989): 321–41.

Negron-Mutaner, Frances. "Jennifer's Butt." *Aztlan: A Journal of Chicano Studies* 22, 2 (1997): 181–94.

Nemtsova, Anna. "Women and Higher Education Make Steady Progress in Afghanistan." *The Chronicle of Higher Education,* March 28, 2010. New York: Amnesty International USA, 2011.

Newbeck, Phyl. "Loving v. Virginia." In *Encyclopedia Virginia,* edited by Brendan Wolfe. Virginia Foundation for the Humanities, 2012. Accessed from www.encyclopediavirginia.org/Loving_v_Virginia_1967.

Newcomer, Mabel. *A Century of Higher Education for American Women.* New York: Harper, 1959.

Newland, Kathleen. *The Sisterhood of Man.* New York: Norton, 1979.

News Today, DOI: www.medical newstoday.com/releases/231300.php.

Nicholson, Linda. "Feminism in 'Waves': Useful Metaphor or Not?" *New Politics* 12, 4 (Winter 2010). http://newpol.org/node/173. Accessed November 30, 2012.

Nickel, James W. "Is There a Human Right to Employment?" *Philosophical Forum* 10 (1978–9): 149–70.

Nieto, Sonia. "Multicultural Education in the United States." In *The Routledge International Companion to Multicultural Education,* edited by James A. Banks, 79–95. New York: Routledge, 2009.

Ninian, Alex. "Bollywood." *Contemporary Review* 283, 1653 (2003): 235–40.

Noddings, Nel. *Caring: A Feminine Approach to Ethics and Moral Education.* Berkeley: University of California Press, 1984.

Nordberg, Jenny. "Where Boys Are Prized, Girls Live the Part: In Some Afghan Families, a Fake Son Is Considered Better Than None." *The New York Times,* September 21, 2012, A1, A10–11.

Novotney, A. "A More Family-Friendly Ivory Tower?" *APA Monitor* 41, 1 (January 2010): 54.

Nussbaum, Martha. *Sex and Social Justice.* New York: Oxford University Press, 1999.

NWSA (National Women's Studies Association). *A National Census of Women's and Gender Studies Programs in U.S. Institutions of Higher Education,* 2007. http://082511c.membershipsoftware.org/files/NWSA_CensusonWSProgs.pdf. Accessed November 23, 2012.

O'Barr, Jean. "African Women in Politics." In *African Women South of the Sahara,* edited by Margaret Jean Hay and Sharon Stichter. New York: Longman, 1984.

O'Donovan, Katherine. "Before and After: The Impact of Feminism on the Academic Discipline of Law." In *Men's Studies Modified: The Impact of Feminism on the Academic Disciplines*, edited by Dale Spender. New York: Pergamon, 1981.

O'Hare, Ursula A. "Realizing Human Rights for Women." *Human Rights Quarterly* 21, 2 (1999): 364–402.

OECD. *Education at a Glance 2010: OECD Indicators*. Organization for Economic Co-Operation and Development, 2010. Accessed from World Wide Web.

Okin, Susan Moller. *Women in Western Political Thought*. Princeton, NJ: Princeton University Press, 1979.

———. *Justice, Gender, and the Family*. New York: Basic Books, 1989.

———. *Is Multiculturalism Bad for Women?* Princeton, NJ: Princeton University Press, 1999.

Okumus, F., M. Sariisik, and S. Naipaul. "Understanding Why Women Work in Five-Star Hotels in a Developing Country and Their Work-Related Problems." *International Journal of Hospitality & Tourism Administration* 11, 1(January 2010): 76–105.

Oldenburg, Veena Talwar. *Dowry Murder: The Imperial Origins of a Cultural Crime*. New York: Oxford University Press, 2002.

Olujic, Maria B. "Embodiment of Terror: Gendered Violence in Peacetime and Wartime in Croatia and Bosnia-Herzegovina." *Medical Anthropology Quarterly* 12, 1 (1998): 31–50.

Orenstein, Peggy. *School Girls: Young Women, Self-Esteem, and the Confidence Gap*. New York: Anchor Books, 1994.

———. *Cinderella Ate My Daughter: Dispatches from the Front Lines of the New Girlie-Girl Culture*. New York: HarperCollins, 2011.

Orsi, Jennifer M., Helen Margellos-Anast, and Steven Whitman. "Black-White Health Disparities in the United States and Chicago: A 15-Year Progress Analysis." *American Journal of Public Health*. Online publication, December 17, 2009, e1–e8.

Oxford Latin Dictionary: Fascicle III. Oxford: Oxford University Press, 1971.

Padgett, Deborah. "Aging Minority Women: Issues in Research and Health Policy." In *Women in the Later Years: Health, Social and Cultural Perspectives*, edited by Lois Grau and Ida Susser. New York: Harrington Park Press, 1989.

Palley, Marian Lief. "Women's Policy Leadership in the United States." *PS: Political Science and Politics* 25, 2 (2001): 247–50.

Palmer, Susan Jean. *Moon Sisters, Krishna Mothers, Rajneesh Lovers: Women's Roles in New Religions*. Syracuse, NY: Syracuse University Press, 1994.

Palmieri, Patricia. "From Republican Motherhood to Race Suicide: Arguments on the Higher Education of Women in the United States, 1820–1920." In *Educating Men and Women Together: Co-education in a Changing World*, edited by Carol Lasser. Urbana: University of Illinois Press, 1987.

Paludi, Michele, editor. *Ivory Power*. Albany, NY: SUNY Press, 1990.

Park, Alice. "Study: Children of Lesbians May Do Better Than Their Peers." *Time Magazine Online*, http://www.time.com/time/health/article/0,8599,1994480,00.html.

Park, Lora E., Ariana F. Young, Jordan D. Troisi, et al. "Effects of Everyday Romantic Goal Pursuit on Women's Attitudes toward Math and Science." *Personality and Social Psychology Bulletin*, 37, 9 (2011): 1259–73.

Parker, Adam. "Women of the Cloth: Female Leadership Becoming Trend in Black Churches." *Post and Courier*, July, 2011, Accessed from http://www.postandcourier.com/news/2011/jul/24/women-of-the-cloth/.

Parker, Kim. "A Portrait of Stepfamilies." Washington, DC: Pew Research Center, 2011.

Parker, W. H., M. S. Broder, E. Chang, et al. "Ovarian Conservation at the Time of Hysterectomy and Long-Term Health Outcomes in the Nurses' Health Study." *Obstetric Gynecology* 113, 5 (2009): 1027–39.

Parker-Pope, Tara. "In a Married World, Singles Struggle for Attention." *The New York Times*, September 19, 2011.

Parreñas, Rhacel Salazar. *Children of Global Migration: Transnational Families and Gendered Woes*. Stanford, CA: Stanford University Press, 2005.

Paul, Annie Murphy. *Origins: How the Nine Months Before Birth Shape the Rest of Our Lives*. New York: Free Press, 2010.

Peach, Lucinda Joy. "Social Responsibility, Sex Change, and Salvation: Gender Justice in the Lotus Sutra." *Philosophy East & West*, 52 (2002): 50–74.

Peer, Basharat. "The Girl Who Wanted to Go to School." *The New Yorker*, October 10, 2012. http://www.newyorker.com/online/blogs/newsdesk/2012/10/the-girl-who-wanted-to-go-to-school.html#ixzz2GgScVG49.

Peiss, Kathy. *Hope in a Jar: The Making of America's Beauty Culture*. New York: Holt Paperbacks, 1999.

Peres, Judy. "In 50 Years, Kibbutz Movement Has Undergone Many Changes." *Chicago Tribune*, May 9 1998.

Pesquera, Beatriz M., and Denise A. Segura. "With Quill and Torch: A Chicana Perspective on the American Women's Movement and Feminist Theories." In *Chicanas/Chicanos at the Crossroads*, edited by David R. Maciel and Isidro D. Ortiz. Tucson: University of Arizona Press, 1996.

Petchesky, Rosalind P. "Human Rights, Reproductive Health, and Economic Justice: Why They Are Indivisible." In *The Socialist Feminist Project: A Contemporary Reader in Theory and Politics*, edited by Nancy Holmstrom. New York: Monthly Review Press, 2002.

Petchesky, Rosalind P., and Karen Judd. *Negotiating Reproductive Rights: Women's Perspectives across Countries and Cultures*. New York: Zed Books, 1998.

Petersen, Alan. *The Body in Question: A Socio-Cultural Approach*. New York: Routledge, 2007.

Petersen, Karen, and J. J. Wilson. *Women Artists: Recognition and Reappraisal from the Early Middle Ages to the Twentieth Century*. New York: Harper & Row, 1976.

Peterson, V. Spike, and Anne Sisson Runyan. *Global Gender Issues in the New Millennium*, 3rd ed. Boulder, CO: Westview Press, 2010.

Pew Forum on Religion & Public Life. "'Nones' on the Rise: One-in-Five Adults Have No Religious Affiliation," 2012. http://www.pewforum.org/unaffiliated/nones-on-the-rise.aspx. Accessed November 17, 2012. PEW Research Center, 2012.

Pharr, Suzanne. *Homophobia: A Weapon of Sexism*. Oakland, CA: Chardon Press, 1997.

Phelan, Shane. *Getting Specific: Postmodern Lesbian Politics*. Minneapolis: University of Minnesota Press, 1994.

Phillips, Susan. "The Social Context of Women's Health: Goals and Objectives for Medical Education." *Canadian Medical Association Journal* 152, 4 (1995): 507–11.

Piercy, Marge. *Woman on the Edge of Time*. New York: Knopf, 1976.

Pipher, Mary. *Reviving Ophelia: Saving the Selves of Adolescent Girls*. New York: Grosset/Putnam, 1994.

Planned Parenthood. *Mifepristone: Expanding Women's Options for Early Abortion in the United States*. New York: Katharine Dexter McCormick Library, 2010.

Plant, Judith, editor. *Healing the Wounds: The Promise of Eco-Feminism*. Philadelphia: New Society Publishers, 1989.

Plaskow, Judith. "Bringing a Daughter into the Covenant." In *Womanspirit Rising: A Feminist Reader in Religion*, edited by Carol P. Christ and Judith Plaskow. San Francisco: Harper & Row, 1979.

———. *Standing Again at Sinai: Judaism from a Feminist Perspective*. New York: Harper Collins, 1990.

Plato. *The Republic*, translated by Robin Waterfield. Oxford: Oxford University Press, 1998.

———. *The Collected Dialogues of Plato, including the Letters*, translated by Edith Hamilton, Huntington Cairns, and Lane Cooper. Princeton, NJ: Princeton University Press, 2005.

PLOS Medicine Editors. "Rape in War Is Common, Devastating, and Too Often Ignored." *PLOS Med* 6, 1 (2009): e1000021. doi:10.1371/journal.pmed.1000021.

Pollack, M. J. "Statement by Margaret J. Pollack, Acting Deputy Assistant Secretary of State for the Bureau of Population,

Refugees, and Migration, and Head of the United States Delegation to the United Nations Commission on Population and Development." *USUN Press Release #064.* New York: United Nations, March 31, 2009.

Pollet, Alison, and Page Hurwitz. "Strip til You Drop." *The Nation* (January 12, 2004): 20–1, 24–5.

Pomeroy, Sarah B. "Technicai Kai Mousikai: The Education of Women in the Fourth Century and in the Hellenistic Period." *American Journal of Ancient History* 2 (1977): 51–68.

Pomeroy, Sarah B. *Goddesses, Whores, Wives, and Slaves: Women in Classical Antiquity.* New York: Schocken, 1975.

Porter, Eduardo. "Motherhood Still a Cause of Pay Inequality." *New York Times*, June 13, 2012, B1.

Portes, Alejandro, and Alex Stepick. *City on the Edge: The Transformation of Miami.* Berkeley: University of California Press, 1993.

Porzelius, Linda Krug. "Physical Health Issues for Women." In *Issues in the Psychology of Women*, edited by Maryka Biaggio and Michel Hersen. New York: Kluwer Academic/Plenum, 2000.

Potash, Betty, editor. *Widows in African Societies: Choices and Constraints.* Stanford, CA: Stanford University Press, 1986.

Powell, B., and L. C. Steelman. "Testing an Undertested Comparison: Maternal Effects on Sons' and Daughters' Attitudes toward Women in the Labor Force." *Journal of Marriage and the Family* 44 (1982): 349–55.

Prasad, Madhava M. *Ideology of the Hindi Film: A Historical Construction.* Delhi: Oxford University Press, 1998.

Pratt, Minnie Bruce. "Identity: Skin Blood Heart." In *Yours in Struggle: Three Feminist Perspectives on Anti-Semitism and Racism*, edited by Elly Bulkin, Minnie Bruce Pratt, and Barbara Smith. Brooklyn, NY: Long Haul Press, 1984.

Prendergast, John, and Don Cheadle. *The Enough Moment: Fighting to End Africa's Worst Human Rights Crimes.* New York: Three Rivers Press, 2010.

Proust, Marcel. *Remembrance of Things Past: Swann's Way*, translated by C. K. Scott-Moncrieff. New York: Aeterna, [1913] 2011.

Puar, Jasbir. *Terrorist Assemblages: Homo-nationalism in Queer Times* Durham, NC: Duke University Press, 2007.

Pudasaini, Surabhi. "Filmi Feminism v Fraternity." *Himal: Southasian* online, August, 2009. http://www.himalmag.com/component/content/article/598-filmi-feminism-v-fraternity-women-in-indian-film-1-10-edited-by-nasreen-munni-kabir.html. Accessed November 25, 2012.

Pugliesi, Karen. "Women and Mental Health: Two Traditions of Feminist Research." *Women and Health* 19, 2–3 (1992): 43–68.

Putnam, Betsy Mennell. "Can Tribal Colleges Maintain Identity While Seeking Legitimacy?" *Tribal College Journal* 13, 1 (2001): 18–23.

Puttick, Elizabeth. *Women in New Religions: In Search of Community, Sexuality and Spiritual Power.* New York: St. Martin's Press, 1997.

Qin-Hilliard, Desirée Baolian. "Gendered Expectations and Gendered Experiences: Immigrant Students' Adaptation in Schools." *New Directions for Youth Development* 100 (2003): 91–109.

Radhakrishnan, Smitha. "Profession Women, Good Families: Respectable Feminisms and the Cultural Politics of a 'New' India." *Qualitative Sociology* 32 (2009): 195–212.

Rakow, Lana F., editor. *Women Making Meaning: New Feminist Directions in Communication.* New York: Routledge, 1992.

Randall, Vicky. *Women and Politics*, 2nd ed. Chicago: Chicago University Press, 1987.

Ranji, Usha, and Alina Salganicoff. *Women's Health Care Chartbook: Key Findings from Kaiser Women's Health Survey.* Menlo Park, CA: Henry J. Kaiser Family Foundation, 2011.

Ratcliff, Kathryn Strother. *Women and Health: Power, Technology, Inequality, and Conflict in a Gendered World.* Boston: Allyn and Bacon, 2002.

Rathus, Spencer A., Jeffery S. Nevid, and Lois Fincher-Rathus. *Human Sexuality in a World of Diversity*, 8th edition. Boston: Pearson College, 2011.

Ratner, Rochelle, editor. *Bearing Life: Women's Writings on Childlessness*. New York: Feminist Press, 2000.

Ray, Nicholas: *Lesbian, Gay, Bisexual, and Transgender Youth: An Epidemic of Homelessness*. Washington, DC: National Lesbian and Gay Task Force, 2006.

Raymond, Susan U., Henry M. Greenberg, and Stephen R. Leeder. "Beyond Reproduction: Women's Health in Today's Developing World." *International Journal of Epidemiology* 34, 5 (2005): 1144–8.

Rayor, Diane. *Sappho's Lyre. Archaic Lyric and Women Poets of Ancient Greece*. Berkeley: University of California Press, 1991.

Research, Office of Policy Planning and. "The Negro Family: The Case for National Action." Washington, DC: U.S. Department of Labor, 1965.

Reverby, Susan. "'Normal Exposure' and Inoculation Syphilis: A PHS 'Tuskegee Doctor' in Guatemala, 1946–48." *Journal of Policy History* 23, 1 (2011): 6–28.

Reverby, Susan. *Examining Tuskegee: The Infamous Syphilis Study and Its Legacy*. Chapel Hill: University of North Carolina Press, 2009.

Rexrode, K. M., and J. E. Manson. "Postmenopausal Hormone Therapy and Quality of Life: No Cause for Celebration." *JAMA* 287 (2002): 641–2.

Rhode, Deborah L. *Justice and Gender: Sex Discrimination and the Law*. Cambridge, MA: Harvard University Press, 1989.

Rich, Adrienne. *Of Woman Born: Motherhood as Experience and Institution*. New York: Norton, 1976.

———. "Compulsory Heterosexuality and Lesbian Existence." *Signs* 5, 4 (1980): 631–60.

Richards, Audrey I. *Chisungu: A Girls' Initiation Ceremony among the Bemba of Zambia*. London: Faber & Faber, 1956.

Ridd, Rosemary, and Helen Callaway. *Women and Political Conflict*. New York: New York University Press, 1987.

Rife, J. C. "Middle-Aged and Older Women in the Work Force." In *Handbook on Women and Aging*, edited by Jean M. Coyle. Westport, CT: Greenwood Press, 2001.

Rivera, Raquel Z. "'Butta Pecan Mamis: Tropicalized Mamis: Chocolate Caliente.'" In *That's the Joint: The Hip-Hop Studies Reader*, 2nd ed., edited by Murray Forman and Mark Anthony Neal. New York: Routledge, 2012.

Roberts, Dorothy. *Killing the Black Body: Race, Reproduction and the Meaning of Liberty*. New York: Vintage, 1998.

Robinson, Fiona. *Globalizing Care: Ethics, Feminist Morality, and International Relations*. Boulder, CO: Westview Press, 1999.

Robinson, Katy. *A Single Square Picture: A Korean Adoptee's Search for Her Roots*. New York: Berkley Books, 2002.

Rodriguez-Trias, Helen. Interview with Kathy Rolland, Eugene, Oregon, February 8, 1997.

Roosevelt, Eleanor. "Where, after All, Do Universal Human Rights Begin?" *Commission on Human Rights*. New York: United Nations, March 27, 1958.

Root, Maria P. P. *Love's Revolution: Interracial Marriage*. Philadelphia: Temple University Press, 2001.

Rosario, L. M. "The Self-Perception of Puerto Rican Women toward Their Societal Role." In *Work, Family and Health: Latina Women in Transition*, edited by R. E. Zambrana. New York: Hispanic Research Center, 1982.

Rosen, Ruth. *The Lost Sisterhood: Prostitution in America, 1900–1918*. Baltimore: Johns Hopkins Press, 1982.

Rosenberg, Tina. "The Daughter Deficit." *The New York Times Magazine*, August 23, 2009.

Rosenblatt, Roger, editor. *Consuming Desires: Consumption, Culture, and the Pursuit of Happiness*. Washington, DC: Shearwater, 1999.

Rosin, Hanna. "The Case against Breast-Feeding." *The Atlantic*, April 2009. http://www.the-atlantic.com/magazine/archive/2009/04/the-case-against-breast-feeding/7311/.

———. "The End of Men." *The Atlantic* (July–August 2010): 56–72.

———. *The End of Men: And the Rise of Women*. New York: Penguin, 2012.

———. "Who Wears the Pants in This Economy?" *The New York Times*, August 30, 2012. Accessed September 2, 2012 from http//nytimes.com/2012/09/02/magazine/who-wears-the-pants-in-this-economy.html.

Rossi, Alice S. "Equality between the Sexes: An Important Proposal." *Daedalus* 93 (1964): 607–52.

———. *The Feminist Papers: From Adams to de Beauvoir*. Lebanon, NH: Northeastern Press, 1988.

Rotella, Elyce J. "Women's Roles in Economic Life." In *Issues and Feminism: A First Course in Women's Studies*, edited by Sheila Ruth. Boston: Houghton Mifflin, 1980.

Roth, Benita. *Separate Roads to Feminism: Black, Chicana, and White Feminist Movements in America's Second Wave*. Cambridge: Cambridge University Press, 2003.

Rothblum, Esther, and Kathleen Brehony. *Boston Marriages: Romantic but Asexual Relationships among Contemporary Lesbians*. Amherst: University of Massachusetts Press, 1993.

Rousseau, Jean Jacques. *Émile*, translated by Barbara Foxley. New York: Dutton, [1762] 1966.

Roy, Arundhati. *The God of Small Things*. New York: Harper, 1997.

Rubin, Alissa J. "For Afghan Wives, a Desperate, Fiery Way Out." *The New York Times*, November 8, 2010.

Rubin, Gayle. "The Traffic in Women: Notes on the 'Political Economy' of Sex." In *Toward an Anthropology of Women*, edited by Rayna Reiter. New York: Monthly Review Press, 1975.

———. "Thinking Sex: Notes for a Radical Theory of the Politics of Sexuality." In *The Lesbian and Gay Studies Reader*. edited by Henry Abelove, Michele Aina Barale, and David M. Halperin. New York: Routledge, 1993.

Ruble, Thomas L. "Sex Stereotypes: Issues of Change in the 1970s." *Sex Roles*, 9 (1983): 397–402.

Ruddick, Sara. *Maternal Thinking: Toward a Politics of Peace*. Boston: Beacon Press, 1989.

Ruether, Rosmary Radfored, editor. *Feminist Theologies: Legacy and Prospect*. Philadelphia: Westminster Press, 2007.

Ruhl, Sarah. *In the Next Room: Or The Vibrator Play*. New York: Theatre Communications Group, 2010.

Ruiz, Vicki L. "A Promise Unfulfilled: Mexican Cannery Workers in Southern California." In *Unequal Sisters: A Multicultural Reader in U.S. Women's History*, edited by Ellen Carol DuBois and Vicki L. Ruiz. New York: Routledge, 1990.

Rupp, Leila J. *Worlds of Women*. Princeton, NJ: Princeton University Press, 1997.

Rushdie, Salman. *The Moor's Last Sigh*. New York: Random House, 1995.

Russ, Joanna. *The Female Man*. New York: Bantam Books, 1975.

Russell, Diana E. H. *The Secret Trauma: Incest in the Lives of Girls and Women*. New York: Basic Books, 1986.

———, editor. *Making Violence Sexy: Feminist Views on Pornography*. New York: Teacher's College Press, 1993.

Ruzek, Sheryl Burt. *The Women's Health Movement: Feminist Alternatives to Medical Control*. New York: Praeger, 1978.

Ryu, Mikyung. *Minorities in Higher Education 2010: Twenty-Fourth Status Report*. Washington, DC: American Council on Education, 2010.

Sabattini, Laura, and Faye J. Crosby, "Ceilings and Walls: Work-Life and 'Family-Friendly' Policies." In *The Glass Ceiling in the 21st Century*, edited by Manuela Barreto, Michelle K. Ryan, and Michael T. Schmitt. Washington, DC: American Psychological Association, 2009.

Sadigi, Fatima, Amira Nowira, Azza El Kholy, et al., editors. *Women Writing Africa IV: The Northern Region*. New York: Feminist Press, 2009.

Said, Edward. *Orientalism*. New York: Vintage. 1978.

Saldivar-Hull, Sonia. *Feminism on the Border: Contemporary Chicana Writers*. Berkeley: University of California Press, 1998.

———. *Feminism on the Border. Chicana Gender Politics and Literature*. Berkeley: University of California Press, 2000.

Sànchez Korrol, Virgina. "Women in Nineteenth- and Twentieth-Century Latin America and the Caribbean." In *Women in Latin America and the Caribbean*, edited by Marysa Navarro and Virginia Sànchez Korrol. Bloomington: Indiana University Press, 1999.

Sanchez-Hucles, J. V. "Intimate Relationships." In *The Complete Guide to Mental Health for Women*, edited by Lauren Slater, Jessica Henderson Daniel, and Amy Elizabeth Banks. Boston: Beacon Press, 2003.

Sanday, Peggy Reeves. *Female Power and Male Dominance: On the Origins of Sexual Inequality*. Cambridge: Cambridge University Press, 1981.

———. *Women at the Center: Life in a Modern Matriarchy*. Ithaca, NY: Cornell University Press, 2002.

Sandler, Bernice R., and Roberta M. Hall. *The Campus Climate Revisited: Chilly for Women Faculty, Administrators, and Graduate Students*. Washington, DC: Association of American Colleges, 1986.

———, Lisa A. Silverberg, and Roberta M. Hall. *The Chilly Classroom Climate: A Guide to Improve the Education of Women*. Washington, DC: National Association for Women in Education, 1996.

Sapiro, Virginia. *A Vindication of Political Virtue: The Political Theory of Mary Wollstonecraft*. Chicago: University of Chicago Press, 1992.

Saroca, Cleonicki. "Representing Rosalina and Annabel: Filipino Women, Violence, Media Representation and Contested Realities." *Kasarinlan: Phillipine Journal of Third World Studies* 22, 1 (2007): 32–60.

Satz, Debra. "Feminist Perspectives on Reproduction and the Family." In *The Stanford Encyclopedia of Philosophy*, edited by Edward N. Zalta, Summer 2011. Accessed from http://plato.stanford.edu/archives/sum2011/entries/feminism-family.

Sax, Linda J. *The Gender Gap in College*. San Francisco: Jossey-Bass, 2008.

Scanlon, Jennifer. *Bad Girls Go Everywhere: The Life of Helen Gurley Brown*. New York: Oxford University Press, 2009.

Schiff, Stacy. *Cleopatra: A Life*. New York: Little, Brown & Company, 2010.

Schmall, Emily. "Transgender Advocates Hail Law Easing Rules in Argentina." *New York Times*, March 25, 2012, A8.

Schulman, Sarah. *The Ties That Bind: Familial Homophobia and Its Consequences*. New York: The New Press, 2009.

Schwartz, Pepper. "Long-Distance Love." *AARP The Magazine*, November 2011.

Schwender, Martha. "A Life of Marital Bliss (Segregation Laws Aside)." *The New York Times*, January 27, 2002.

Schwindt-Bayer, Leslie A. "Women Who Win: Social Backgrounds, Paths to Power, and Political Ambition in Latin American Legislatures." *Politics & Gender* 7, 1 (2011): 1–33.

Scott-Dixon, Krista. *Doing IT: Women Working in Information Technology*. Toronto: Sumach Press, 2004.

Scott, Anne Firor. *Natural Allies: Women's Associations in American History*. Urbana: University of Illinois Press, 1991.

Scott, Joan Wallach. "Deconstructing Equality-versus-Difference: Or, the Uses of Poststructuralist Theory for Feminism." *Feminist Studies* 14 (Spring 1988): 33–50.

———. "Experience." In *Feminists Theorize the Political*, edited by Joan Scott and Judith Butler. New York: Routledge, 1992.

———. *Only Paradoxes to Offer: French Feminists and the Rights of Man*. Cambridge, MA: Harvard University Press, 1996.

———, editor. "Women's Studies on the Edge." *Differences* 9, 3 (1997).

———. *The Politics of the Veil*. Princeton, NJ: Princeton University Press, 2007.

Scott, W. S., editor and translator. *Trial of Joan of Arc*. London: Folio Society, 1968.

Seager, Joni. *The Penguin Atlas of Women in the World*, 4th ed. New York: Penguin, 2009.

Seaman, Barbara. "Women Speak Up and Take Control of Their Health." *Womens e-news*, February 19 2012. Accessed 05/03/2012. http://womensnews.org/story/health/120218/women-speak-and-take-control-their-health.

———, and Laura Eldridge, editors. *Voices of the Women's Health Movement*, vol. 1. New York: Seven Stories Press, 2012.

Sechzer, J. A. *Voices of the Women's Health Movement*, vol 2. New York: Seven Stories Press, 2012.

———, V. C. Rabinowitz, and F. L. Denmark. "Sex and Gender Bias in Animal and Human Research." In J. A. Sechzer, A. Griffin, and S. Pfafflin, editors. *Forging a Women's Health Research Agenda*. New York: New York Academy of Sciences, 1994.

Self-Employed Women's Association. *Annual Report 2008*. Accessed from Self-Employed Women's Association Web site: http://www.sewa.org/Annual_Report_2008-English.pdf.

Seligman, Linda J., editor. *Women Traders in Cross-Cultural Perspective: Mediating Identities, Marketing Wares*. Stanford, CA: Stanford University Press, 2001.

Sen, Amartya. "Work and Rights." In *Women, Gender, and Work*, edited by Martha Fetherolf Loutfi. Geneva: International Labour Office, 2001.

Sha`rawi, Hud·, and Margot Badran. *Harem Years: The Memoirs of an Egyptian Feminist (1879–1924)*. New York: Feminist Press, 1987.

Shahar, Shulamith. *The Fourth Estate: A History of Women in the Middle Ages*, translated by Chaya Galai. London: Methuen, 1983.

Sharma, Arvind, and Katherine K. Young, editors. *Feminism and World Religions*. Albany, NY: SUNY Press, 1999.

Sharpless, Rebecca. *Cooking in Other Women's Kitchens: Domestic Workers in the South, 1865–1960*. Chapel Hill: University of North Carolina Press, 2010.

Sheehy, Gail. *The Silent Passage: Menopause*. New York: Pocket Books, 1998.

Shernoff, M. "Gay Marriage and Gay Widowhood." *The Harvard Gay & Lesbian Review* 4, 4 (1997).

Sherwin, Susan. *No Longer Patient: Feminist Ethics and Health Care*. Philadelphia: Temple University Press, 1992.

Shiva, Vandana. *Staying Alive: Women, Ecology, and Development in India*. London: Zed Books, 1988.

Sicherman, Barbara. *Well-Read Lives: How Books Inspired a Generation of American Women*. Chapel Hill, NC: University of North Carolina Press, 2010.

Silko, Leslie Marmon. *Ceremony*. New York: Penguin Books, 1977.

Simmons, Christina. *Making Marriage Modern*. New York: Oxford University Press, 2009.

Simmons, Rachel. *Odd Girl Out: The Hidden Culture of Aggression in Girls*. New York: Harcourt, 2002.

Simpson, George E. *Black Religions in the New World*. New York: Columbia University Press, 1978.

Simpson, Jaqueline. "Margaret Murray: Who Believed Her and Why?" *Folklore* 105 (1994).

Simpson, Leigh Joe, et al. "Commentary: Gender Verification in the Olympics." *JAMA* 284 (2000): 1568–9.

Sinha, Mrinalina. "Gender and Nation." In *Women's History in Global Perspective*, vol. 1, edited by Bonnie Smith. Urbana: University of Illinois Press, 2004.

Sinnott, Megan J. *Toms and Dees: Transgender Identity and Female Same-Sex Relationships in Thailand*. Honolulu: University of Hawai'i Press, 2004.

Skelton, Karen, and Angela T. Geiger. *The Shriver Report: A Woman's Nation Takes on Alzheimer's*. New York: Simon & Schuster, 2010.

Sklar, Kathryn Kish. "A Women's Report Card on Hillary Rodham Clinton's Presidential Primary Campaign, 2008." *Feminist Studies* 34, 1–2 (2008): 315–22.

Slocum, Sally. "Woman the Gatherer: Male Bias in Anthropology." In *Toward an Anthropology of Women*, edited by Rayna R. Reiter. New York: Monthly Review Press, 1975.

Smith, Barbara, editor. *Home Girls: A Black Feminist Anthology*. New York: Kitchen Table Women of Color Press, 1983.

Smith, Patricia, editor. *Feminist Jurisprudence*. New York: Oxford University Press, 1993.

Smith, Valerie. *Not Just Race, Not Just Gender: Black Feminist Readings*. New York: Routledge, 1998.

Smith, Zadie. *White Teeth*. New York: Random House, 2000.

Smithson, Isaiah. "Introduction: Investigating Gender, Power, and Pedagogy." In *Gender in the Classroom: Power and Pedagogy*, edited by Susan L. Gabriel and Isaiah Smthson. Urbana: University of Illinois Press, 1990.

Snitow, Ann. "Holding the Line at Greenham Common: Being Joyously Political in Dangerous Times." *Mother Jones* (February/March 1985): 30–47.

Snyder, Jane McIntosh. *The Woman and the Lyre: Women Writers in Classical Greece and Rome*. Carbondale: Southern Illinois University Press, 1989.

Solinger, Rickie. *Pregnancy and Power: A Short History of Reproductive Politics in America*. New York: New York University Press, 2007.

Solomon, Miriam, "Standpoint and Creativity." *Hypatia* 24, 4 (2009): 226–37.

Sommer, B., N. Avis, P. Meyer, et al. "Attitudes toward Menopause and Aging across Ethnic/Racial Groups." *Psychosomatic Medicine* 61, 6 (1999).

Sontag, S. "The Double Standard of Aging." In *Psychology of Women: Selected Readings*, edited by Juanita H. Williams. New York: Norton, 1979.

Spelman, Elizabeth V. *Inessential Woman: Problems of Exclusion in Feminist Thought*. Boston: Beacon Press, 1988.

Spivak, Gayatri Chakravorty. "Can the Subaltern Speak?" In *Marxism and the Interpretation of Culture*, edited by Cary Nelson and Lawrence Grossberg. Urbana: University of Illinois Press, 1988.

Sprinkle, Annie. *Dr. Sprinkle's Spectacular Sex: Make Over Your Love life with One of the World's Greatest Sex Experts*. New York: Penguin, 2005

Stanton, Elizabeth Cady. *Eighty Years and More: Reminiscences 1815–1897*. New York: Schocken Books, [1898] 1971.

———. *The Woman's Bible* (1895–8), parts I, II, and appendix. New York: Arno, 1972.

Statistics, National Center for Education. "Bachelor's Degrees Conferred by Degree Granting Institutions, by Sex, Race/Ethnicity, and Field of Study, 2008–2009, Table 297." In *Digest of Education Statistics*, 2010–2011.

Stein, Elissa, and Susan Kim. *Flow: The Cultural Story of Menstruation*. New York: St. Martin Press, 2009.

Stein, Nan, Nancy L. Marshall, and Linda R. Tropp. *Secrets in Public: Sexual Harassment in Our Schools*. Center for Research on Women, Wellesley College and NOW Legal Defense and Education Fund. Wellesley, MA: Wellesley Centers for Women, 1993.

Steinem, Gloria. "Far from the Opposite Shore, or How to Survive Though a Feminist." *Ms* 7 (1978): 65–7, 90–4, 105.

Steinson, Barbara J. "The Mother Half of Humanity: American Women in the Peace and Preparedness Movements in World War I." In *Women, War and Revolution*, edited by Carol R. Berkin and Clara M. Lovett. New York: Homes & Meiers, 1980.

Stellman, Jeanne Mager, and Mary Sue Henifin. *Office Work Can Be Dangerous to Your Health*, rev. ed. New York: Ballantine-Fawcett, 1989.

Stephen, Cookie W., and Judy Corder. "The Effects of Dual-Career Families on Adolescents: Sex-Role Attitudes, Work and Family Plans, and Choices of Important Others." *Journal of Marriage and the Family* 47 (1985): 921–9.

Stern, Lori. "Conceptions of Separation and Connection in Female Adolescence." In *Making Connections: The Relational Worlds of Adolescent Girls at Emma Willard School*, edited by Carol Gilligan, Nona P. Lyons, and Trudy J. Hanmer. Cambridge, MA: Harvard University Press, 1990.

Stoppard, M. *HRT: Hormone Replacement Therapy*. New York: DK Publishing, 1999.

Strong, Bryan, Christine DeVault, and Theodore F. Cohen. *The Marriage and Family Experience*. Belmont, CA: Wadsworth, 2011.

Strout, Elizabeth. *Olive Kitteridge*. New York: Random House, 2008.

Stuckey, Johanna H. *Women's Spirituality: Contemporary Feminist Approaches to Judaism, Christianity, Islam and Goddess Worship*. Toronto: Inanna Publications, 2010.

Suárez-Orozco, Carola, Marcelo M. Suárez-Orozco, and Irina Todorova. *Learning a New Land: Immigrant Students in American Society*. Cambridge, MA: Harvard University Press, 2008.

Sugden, J. "Women Get Annoyed by Low Pay and Leave to Have Children." *The Times*, April 2009, 894646. Accessed November 1, 2010, from http://business.timesonline.co.uk/tol/business/law/article6157782.

Sunderland, Judith. "Damned If You Do, Damned If You Don't: Religious Dress and Women's Rights." In *The Unfinished Revolution: Voices from the Global Fight for Women's Rights*, edited by Minky Wordenm. New York: Seven Stories Press, 2012.

Surís, Alina, Lisa Lind, Michael Ashner, et al. "Sexual Assault in Women Veterans: An Examination of PTSD Risk, Health Care Utilization, and Cost of Care." *Psychosomatic Medicine* 66 (2004): 749–56.

Sutherland-Addy, Esi, and Aminata Diaw, editors. *Women Writing Africa II: West Africa and the Sahel*. New York: Feminist Press, 2005.

Sutton-Smith, Brian, and B. G. Rosenberg. *The Sibling*. New York: Holt, Rinehart and Winston, 1970.

Swerdlow, Amy. "Ladies' Day at the Capitol: Women Strike for Peace versus HUAC." *Feminist Studies* 8, 3 (1982): 493–520.

Swers, Michele L. *The Difference Women Make: The Policy Impact of Women in Congress*. Chicago: University of Chicago Press, 2002.

Tall Mountain, Mary. "There Is No Word for Goodbye." *Blue Cloud Quarterly* 9 (1981).

Tanaka, Yukiko. *Japan's Comfort Women: Sexual Slavery and Prostitution during World War II and the US Occupation*. London: Routledge, 2002.

———, and Elizabeth Hanson, translators and editors. *This Kind of Woman: Ten Stories by Japanese Women Writers, 1960–1976*. New York: Pedigree Books, 1982.

Tannen, Deborah. "Why Sisterly Chats Make People Happier." *The New York Times*, October 26, 2010.

Tanner, Nancy M. *On Becoming Human*. New York: Cambridge University Press, 1981.

Tasker, Yvonne, and Diane Negra, editors. *Interrogating Post-Feminism: Gender and the Politics of Popular Culture*. Durham, NC: Duke University Press, 2007.

Tavernise, Sabrina. "Life Spans Shrink for Least-Educated Whites in the U.S." *The New York Times*, September 21, 2012. Accessed from http://www.nytimes.com/2012/09/21/us/life-expectancy-for-less-educated-whites-in-us-is-shrinking.html.

Taylor, N. E., S. M. Wall, H. Liebow, et al. "Mother and Soldier: Raising a Child with a Disability in a Low-Income Military Family." *Council for Exceptional Children* 72, 1 (2005): 83–99.

Taylor, Paul, editor. *The Decline of Marriage and Rise of New Families*, Washington, DC: Pew Research Center, 2010a.

———. *The Return of the Multi-Generational Family Household*. Washington, DC: Pew Research Center, 2010b.

Taylor, Verta. "Social Movement Continuity: The Women's Movement in Abeyance." *American Sociological Review* 54, 5 (1989): 761–75.

Teegarden, Jessica. "'Come to the Water'" Inspires Holiness Movement in Women." Indianapolis: The Wesleyan Church Department of Communications, 2011. Accessed from http://www.wesleyan.org/doc/news_article?id=1456.

Tharu, Susi, and K. Lalita. *Women Writing in India*, 2 vols. New York: Feminist Press, 1993.

Thiébaux, Marcelle, editor. *The Writings of Medieval Women: An Anthology*, translated by Marcelle Thiébaux. New York: Garland, 1994.

Thompson, Clara. "Cultural Pressures in the Psychology of Women." *Psychiatry* 5 (1942): 331–9.

———. "Penis Envy in Women." *Psychiatry* 6 (1943): 123–5.

Tickner, J. Ann. *Gendering World Politics*. New York: Columbia University Press, 2001.

Tidball, M. Elizabeth. "Perspective on Academic Women and Affirmative Action." *Educational Record* 54 (1973): 130–5.

———. "Women's Colleges and Women Achievers Revisited." *Signs* 5 (1980): 504–17.

Tiefer, Lenore. "Sexology and the Pharmaceutical Industry: The Threat of Co-optation." *The Journal of Sex Research* 37 (2000): 273.

———. "In Pursuit of the Perfect Penis: The Medicalization of Male Sexuality." In *Readings in Gender and Culture in America*, edited by Nancy McKee and Linda Stone. Englewood Cliffs, NJ: Prentice Hall, 2002.

———. *Sex Is Not a Natural Act & Other Essays*. Boulder, CO: Westview Press, 2004.

Tinsman, Heidi. *Partners in Conflict: The Politics of Gender, Sexuality and Labor in the Chilean*

Agrarian Reform, 1950–1973. Durham, NC: Duke University Press, 2002.

Tolman, Deborah L. *Dilemmas of Desire: Teenage Girls Talk about Sexuality*. Cambridge, MA: Harvard University Press, 2002.

Tolstoy, Leo. *Anna Karenina*, translated by Richard Pevear and Larissa Volokhonsky. New York: Penguin Books, 2000.

Tomasello, Michael. "The Human Adaptation for Culture." *Annual Review of Anthropology* 28 (1999): 510.

Tong, Rosemarie, editor. *Globalizing Feminist Bioethics*. Boulder, CO: Westview Press, 2001.

Toor, Saadia. "Gender, Sexuality, and Islam under the Shadow of Empire." *The Scholar and Feminist Online* 9 (2011).

Townsend, Camilla. *Malintzin's Choices: An Indian Woman in the Conquest of Mexico*. Albuquerque: University of New Mexico Press, 2006.

Travis, C. B. *Women and Health Psychology: Mental Health Issues*. Hillsdale, NJ: Erlbaum, 1988.

Treblicot, Joyce, editor. *Mothering: Essays in Feminist Theory*. Totowa, NJ: Rowman & Allanheld, 1984.

Treiman, Donald J., and Heidi I. Hartmann. *Women, Work and Wages: Equal Pay for Jobs of Equal Value*. Washington, DC: National Academy Press, 1981.

Trexler, Richard C. "The Foundlings of Florence, 1395–1455." *History of Childhood Quarterly: The Journal of Psychohistory* 1, 2 (1973): 259–84.

Tronto, Joan C. *Moral Boundaries: A Political Argument for an Ethics of Care*. New York: Routledge, 1993.

———. "An Ethics of Care." In *Ethics in Community-Based Elder Care*, edited by Martha Holstein and Phyllis Mitzen. [Accessed from PsycINFO Database.] New York: Springer, 2001.

———. "Creating Caring Institutions: Politics, Plurality, and Purpose." *Ethics and Social Welfare* 4, 2 (2010): 158–71.

Tsukiyama, Gail. *Women of the Silk*. New York: St. Martin's Press, 1991.

U.S. Census Bureau. American Community Survey 3-Year Estimates, "B23001. Sex by Age by Employment Status for the Population 16 Years and Over," 2006–2008.

U.S. Census Bureau. "Grandparents Day 2004." Washington, DC: GPO, 2006.

U.S. Department of Defense. *Annual Report on Sexual Assault in the Military: Fiscal Year 2011*. Washington, DC: U.S. Department of Defense, 2012.

U.S. Department of Health and Human Services. *Women's Health in the U.S.: Research on Health Issues Affecting Women*. NIH Publication No. 04-4697, 2004.

———. *Healthy People 2020. Lesbian, Gay, Bisexual, and Transgender Health*. Washington, DC: U.S. Government Printing Office, 2010.

U.S. Department of Labor, Bureau of Labor Statistics. *Highlights of Women's Earnings in 2001*, report 960. Washington, D.C.: U.S. Department of Labor, 2002.

———. *Women in the Labor Force: A Databook (2011 Edition)*, report 1034. Washington, D.C.: U.S. Department of Labor, 2011. Accessed from http://www.bls.gov/cps/wlf-table15-2011.pdf.

———. *Employment and Earnings*. Washington, DC: U.S. Department of Labor, selected years.

U.S. Equal Employment Opportunity Commission. *Guidelines on Discrimination Because of Sex*. http://www.lectlaw.com/files/emp32.htm. Accessed October 7, 2004..

U.S. Preventive Services Task Force. *Screening for Breast Cancer*. Rockville, MD: USPSTF, 2009.

UCGS, University of Umeå. www.ucgs.umu.se/english/research/challenging-gender.

Uchendu, Victor. *The Igbo of South East Nigeria*. New York: Holt, Rinehart & Winston, 1965.

Udry, Richard. "The Biological Limits of Gender Construction." *American Sociological Review* 65, 3 (2000): 443–57.

UN AIDS. "Force for Change: World AIDS Campaign with Young People." In *World AIDS Campaign Briefing Paper*. Geneva: UN AIDS, 1998.

UN AIDS. *AIDS Epidemic Update*. New York: United Nations, 2001.

UN Women. "Progress of the World's Women: In Pursuit of Justice," 2011–2012. http://

progress.unwomen.org/pdfs/EN-Report-Progress.pdf. Accessed November 30, 2012.

UNAIDS. *UNAIDS Takes Action to Empower Women and Girls to Protect Themselves from HIV*, 2010. Accessed from http://www.unaids.org/en/knowlegdeCentre/resources/feature stories/archive/2010/20100302_women_HIV.ASP.

Unger, J. B., and T. E. Seeman. "Successful Aging." In *Women and Health*, edited by Marlene B. Goldman and Maureen Hatch. San Diego, CA: Academic Press, 2000.

United Nations Department of Economic and Social Affairs. *International Plan of Action on Aging*. New York: United Nations, 1998.

———. *The World's Women 2000: Trends and Statistics*. New York: United Nations, 2000.

———. *Women 2000*. New York: United Nations, 2001.

———. *Population and Vital Statistics Report*, series A, vol. LIV. New York: United Nations, 2002a.

———. *Report of the Second Assembly on Ageing*. Madrid: United Nations, 2002b.

———. *The World's Women 2010: Trends and Statistics*. New York: United Nations Statistics Division, 2010.

United Nations Development Fund for Women. *World Poverty Day 2007: Investing in Women; Solving the Poverty Puzzle*. New York: United Nations, 2007.

United Nations Development Program. *Human Development Report, 1993*. New York: Oxford University Press, 1993.

United Nations Educational, Scientific and Cultural Organization. *Gender and Education for All—The Leap to Equality*. Paris: UNESCO, 2003.

———. *Education for All. Literacy for Life*. Paris: UNESCO, 2005.

Vaid, Urvashi. *Irresistible Revolution: Confronting Race, Class and the Assumptions of LGBT Politics*. New York: Magnum Books, 2012.

Valentine, David. *Imagining Transgender: An Ethnography of a Category*. Durham, NC: Duke University Press, 2007.

Valian, Virginia. *Why So Slow? The Advancement of Women*. Cambridge, MA: MIT Press, 1998.

Valk, Anne M. *Radical Sisters: Second-Wave Feminism and Black Liberation in Washington, D.C.* Urbana: University of Illinois Press, 2008.

Vance, Carol S. "Negotiating Sex and Gender in the Attorney General's Commission on Pornography." In *Uncertain Terms: Negotiating Gender in American Culture*, edited by Faye Ginsburg and Anna Lowenhaupt Tsing. Boston: Beacon, 1990.

Vargas, Lucila, editor. *Women Faculty of Color in the White Classroom*. New York: Peter Lang, 2002.

Vega, Marta Moreno. *The Altar of My Soul: The Living Traditions of Santería*. New York: One World, 2000.

Vetterling-Braggin, Mary. *Sexist Language*. Totowa, NJ: Littlefield, Adams, 1981.

Waite, Linda, and Maggie Gallagher. *A Case for Marriage: Why Married People Are Happier, Healthier, and Better Off Financially*. New York: Doubleday, 2000.

Wald, Kenneth D., and Allison Calhoun-Brown. *Religion and Politics in the United States*, 5th edition. Lanham, MD: Rowman & Littlefield Publishers, 2007.

Waldman, Ayelet. *Bad Mother. A Chronicle of Maternal Crimes, Minor Calamities, and Occasional Moments of Grace*. New York: Doubleday, 2009.

Walker, Alice. *The Color Purple*. New York: Washington Square Press, 1982.

Walker, Rebecca. "Becoming the Third Wave." *Ms.* (January/February 1992): 39–41.

———, editor. *To Be Real: Telling the Truth and Changing the Face of Feminism*. New York: Anchor, 1995.

Wallace, Michele. *Black Macho and the Myth of the Superwoman*. New York: The Dial Press, 1978.

Wallerstein, Judith, Julia Lewis, and Sandra Blakeslee, editors. *An Unexpected Legacy of Divorce*. Boulder, CO: Hyperion, 2000.

Wang, Wendy. *The Rise of Intermarriage*. Washington, DC: Pew Research Center, February 16, 2012.

Warner, Marina. *Joan of Arc: The Image of Female Heroism*. New York: Knopf, 1981.

Warnock, M. "Glass Ceiling for Women in Middle East Hotels." *Hotelier Middle East*, September, 2009. Accessed November 1, 2010, from http://www.hoteliermiddleeast.com/5537-glass-ceiling-for-women-in-middle-east-hotels/.

Warrant, T., E. Fox, and G. Pascall. "Innovative Social Policies: Implications for Work-Life Balance among Low-Waged Women in England." *Gender, Work and Organization* 16, 1 (2009): 126–50.

Washington, Mary Helen. *Black-Eyed Susans: Classic Stories by and About Black Women*. Garden City, NY: Anchor Books, 1975.

———. "How Racial Differences Helped Us Discover Our Common Ground." In *Gendered Subjects: The Dynamics of Feminist Teaching*, edited by Margo Culley and Catherine Portuges. Boston: Routledge and Kegan Paul, 1985.

Watson, Tom. "The New Networked Feminism: Limbaugh's Spectacular Social Media Defeat." Forbes online. 03/05/2012. http://www.forbes.com/sites/tomwatson/2012/03/05/the-new-networked-feminism-limbaughs-spectacular-social-media-defeat/2/.

Watts, J. H. "'Allowed into a Man's World' Meanings of Work-Life Balance: Perspectives of Women Civil Engineers as 'Minority' Workers in Construction." *Gender, Work and Organization* 16, 1 (2009): 37–57.

Waylen, Georgina. "A Comparative Politics of Gender: Limits and Possibilities." *Perspectives on Politics* 8, 1 (2010): 223–31.

Weiler, Kathleen. "Reflections on Writing a History of Women Teachers." *Harvard Educational Review* 67, 4 (1997): 635–57.

Wekker, Gloria. *The Politics of Passion: Women's Sexual Culture in the Afro-Surinamese Diaspora*. New York: Columbia University Press, 2006.

Welchman, Lynn, and Sara Hossain. "Introduction: 'Honour', Rights and Wrongs." In *'Honour': Crimes, Paradigms, and Violence against Women*, edited by Lynn Welchman and Sara Hossain. London: Zed Books, 2005.

Welter, Barbara. "The Cult of True Womanhood: 1820–1860." *American Quarterly* 18, (1966): 151–74.

Wenger, Nanette K. "You've Come a Long Way, Baby: Cardiovascular Health and Disease in Women: Problems and Prospects." *Circulation* 109 (2004): 558–60.

Wertz, Richard W, and Dorothy C. Wertz. *Lying-In: A History of Childbirth in America*, expanded edition. New Haven, CT: Yale University Press, 1989.

West, Candace, and Don H. Zimmerman. "Doing Gender." *Gender and Society* 1 (1987): 125–51.

West, Jessamyn. *The Woman Said Yes: Encounters with Life and Death: Memoirs*. New York: Harcourt Brace Jovanovich, 1976.

Weston, Kath. *Families We Choose: Lesbians, Gays, Kinship*. New York: Columbia University Press, 1991.

White, Deborah Gray. *Ain't I a Woman: Female Slaves in the Plantation South*. New York: Norton, 1985.

White, Jacquelyn W., and James M. Frabutt. "Violence against Girls and Women: An Integrative Developmental Perspective." In *Handbook of Girls' and Women's Psychological Health*, edited by Judith Worell and Carol D. Goodheart. New York: Oxford University Press, 2006.

WHO (World Health Organization). *An Update on WHO's Work on Female Genital Mutilation (FGM): Progress Report*, 2011. http://whqlibdoc.who.int/hq/2011/WHO_RHR_11.18_eng.pdf.

WHO, UNICEF, UNFPA and The World Bank Trends in Maternal Mortality: 1990 to 2010, 2012.

Wichterich, Christa. *The Globalized Woman: Reports from a Future of Inequality*, translated by Patrick Camiller. London: Zed Books, 1998.

Wilcox, Joyce. "The Face of Women's Health: Helen Rodriguez-Trias." *American Journal of Public Health* 92, 4 (2002): 566–9.

Williams, D. "Racial/Ethnic Variations in Women's Health: The Social Embeddedness of Health." *American Journal of Public Health* 92 (2002): 588–97.

Williams, Patricia J. *The Alchemy of Race and Rights*. Cambridge, MA: Harvard University Press, 1991.

Wilson, E. O. *On Human Nature*. Cambridge, MA: Harvard University Press, 1975.

Wilson, Robin. "The New Gender Divide." *The Chronicle of Higher Education*, January 26, 2007.

Wilson, Sarah. "When You Have Children, You're Obligated to Live: Motherhood, Chronic Illness and Biographical Disruption." *Sociology of Health and Illness* 29, 4 (2007): 610–25.

Winterson, Jeanette. *Oranges Are Not the Only Fruit.* New York: Grove Press, 1985.

Wirth, Linda. "Women in Management: Closer to Breaking through the Glass Ceiling?" In *Women, Gender, and Work*, edited by Martha Fetherolf Loutfi. Geneva: International Labour Office, 2001.

Wiseman, Rosalind. *Queen Bees & Wannabes.* New York: Crown, 2002.

Wolf-Wendel, Lisa E. "Women-Friendly Campuses: What Five Institutions Are Doing Right." *The Review of Higher Education* 23, 3 (2000): 319–45.

———. "Gender and Higher Education: What Should We Learn from Women's Colleges?" In *Gendered Futures in Higher Education: Critical Perspectives for Change*, edited by B. Ropers-Huilman. Albany, NY: State University of New York Press, 2003.

———, and Becky Eason. "Women's Colleges and Universities." In *Gender and Higher Education*, edited by Barbara J. Bank. Baltimore: The Johns Hopkins University Press, 2011.

Wolf, Naomi. *The Beauty Myth: How Images of Beauty Are Used Against Women.* New York: William Morrow, 1991.

———. "Father Figures." *New Republic* 22 (October 5, 1992): 24–5.

Wolfinger, Nicholas H., Mary Ann Mason, and Marc Goulden. "Stay in the Game: Gender, Family Formation and Alternative Trajectories in the Academic Life Course." *Social Forces* 87, 3 (2009): 1591–621.

Wollstonecraft, Mary. *A Vindication of the Rights of Woman.* New York: Norton, [1792] 1967.

Women's Environment and Development Organization, 2001. (http://www/wedo.org/factsheet1.htm).

Woo, Terry. "Confucianism and Feminism." In *Feminism and World Religions*, edited by Courtney W. Howland. Albany, NY: SUNY Press, 1999.

World Health Organization (WHO). *World Health Organization Constitution: Introduction.* New York: World Health Organization, 1946.

———. *Women and Health: Today's Evidence and Tomorrow's Agenda.* Geneva: World Health Organization, 2009.

World Heart Federation. *Women and Cardiovascular Disease.* Accessed September 18, 2012. www.world-heart-federation-org/press/fact-sheets-women-and-cardiovascular-disease/.

Wortman, C. M., K. Wolff, and G. A. Bonanno. "Loss of an Intimate Partner through Death." In *Handbook of Closeness and Intimacy*, edited by D. J. Mashek and A. Aron. Mahwah, NJ: Erlbaum, 2004.

Wright, Elizabeth. *Lacan and Postfeminism.* Cambridge, UK: Icon Books, 2000.

Wylie, Alison. "Feminist Science Studies." *Hypatia* (Special Issue co-edited with Lynn Hankinson Nelson) 1, 2 (Winter 2004a).

———. "Why Standpoint Matters." In *The Feminist Standpoint Theory Reader: Intellectual and Political Controversies*, edited by Sandra Harding. New York: Routledge, 2004b.

Yalom, Marilyn. *A History of the Wife.* New York: Harper Collins, 2001.

Yanagisako, Sylvia Junko. *Transforming the Past: Tradition and Kinship among Japanese Americans* Stanford, CA: Stanford University Press, 1985.

Yates, Barbara A. "Church, State and Education in Belgian Africa: Implications for Contemporary Third World Women." In *Women's Education in the Third World: Comparative Perspectives*, edited by Gail P. Kelly and Carolyn M. Elliott. Albany, NY: SUNY Press, 1982.

Yezierska, Anzia. *Bread Givers: A Novel.* New York: Persea Books, [1925] 2003.

Young, Neil. "'The ERA Is a Moral Issue': The Mormon Church, LDS Women, and the Defeat of the Equal Rights Amendment." In *Religion and Politics in the Contemporary United States*, edited by R. Marie Griffith and Melani McAlister. Baltimore: Johns Hopkins University Press, 2008.

Yuval-Davis, Nira, and Flora Anthis, editors. *Woman-Nation-State.* New York: St. Martin Press, 1989.

———. *Gender and Nation.* Thousand Oaks, CA: Sage Publications, 1997.

Zakuan, Umma Atiyah Ahmad. "Women in the Malaysian Parliament: Do They Matter?" *Intellectual Discourse* 18, 2 (2010): 283–322.

Zalk, Sue Rosenberg. "The Re-emergence of Psychosexual Conflicts in Expectant Fathers." In *Pregnancy, Birthing and Bonding*, edited by Barbara Blum. New York: Human Science Press, 1980.

———. "Women's Dilemma: Both Envied and Subjugated." Paper presented at the Third International Interdisciplinary Congress on Women, Trinity College, Dublin, Ireland, June 1987.

———. "Harassment on the Job." *Dental Teamwork* (1991): 10–15.

———, and Janice Gordon-Kelter, editors. *Revolutions in Knowledge: Feminism in the Social Sciences*. Boulder, CO: Westview Press, 1992.

Zernike, Kate. "Gains, and Drawbacks, for Female Professors." *The New York Times*, March 21, 2011.

Zetkin, Clara. *Clara Zetkin: Selected Writings*. Foreword by Angela Y. Davis. New York: International Publishers, 1984.

Zikmund, Barbara Brown. "The Feminist Thrust of Sectarian Christianity." In *Women of Spirit: Female Leadership in the Jewish and Christian Traditions*, edited by Rosemary Ruether and Eleanor Mc Laughlin. New York: Simon & Schuster, 1979.

Zuger, Abigail. "The Brain: Malleable, Capable, Vulnerable." *The New York Times*, May 29, 2007. http://www.nytimes.com/2007/05/29/health/29book.html.

ART CREDITS

Page 6 Collage of Female Politicians: Tammy Duckworth, Getty Images; Nitza I. Quinones Alejandro, courtesy of Nancy Ravert-Ward and the Widener University School of Law; Elizabeth Warren and Tammy Baldwin, ASSOCIATED PRESS. **Page 11** Co-authors of *Women's Realities, Women's Choices*. Photograph by Dylan Gauthier. **Page 32** Lady GaGa. © Henry Ruggeri/Corbis / APImages. **Page 35** Judith and Maidservant with the Head of Holofernes. Photograph © 1977 The Detroit Institute of the Arts. Gift of Mr. Leslie H. Green. **Page 36** (top) Maria Martinez. © Horace Bristol/CORBIS; (bottom) pot by Maria Martinez. Courtesy of Mark Sublette, Medicine Man Gallery. **Page 37** (top) Vietnam Memorial, by Maya Lin. Bettman/CORBIS; (bottom) Maya Lin. Photo Courtesy of Cheung Ching-Ming. **Page 44** (left) "Mother India" movie poster. Mary Evans/MEHBOOB PRODUCTIONS/Ronald Grant/Everett Collection; (right) "London Dreams" movie poster. ©Viacom/Courtesy Everett Collection. **Page 52** Hypatia of Alexandria. Ancient Art and Architecture Ltd. **Page 63** Barbara Smith. Skip Dickstein / Times Union. **Page 66** Vandana Shiva. Getty Images. **Page 79** Dominique Strauss-Kahn and Nafissatou Diallo. ASSOCIATED PRESS. **Page 80** Kimblerlé Crenshaw. Peter Kramer, Getty Images. **Page 86** Anna Julia Cooper. © Hipix / Alamy. **Page 89** Gloria Anzaldúa. Photograph by Annie Valva. From the Nettie Lee Benson Latin American Collection, the University of Texas at Austin. **Page 96** Minnie Bruce Pratt. © Marilyn Humphries. **Page 97** Gender and the 99%. Photograph by L. Alcoff. **Page 99** Portrait of Louis XV. Giraudon. **Page 108** South Asian hijras. AFP/Getty Images. **Page 119 (left)** Barbie. ASSOCIATED PRESS; (right) Action figure. Associated Press. **Page 122** Alternative Gender Arrangements. Kae Deezign. **Page 130** Exotic Asian Mail-order Brides. Courtesy of Jack West/ExoticAsian-Women.com. **Page 137** Caster Semenya. Associated Press. **Page 148** Olayinka Koso-Thomas. Courtesy of Radio Netherlands Worldwide. **Page 149** (left) High Heels, Croisy; (right) Foot Deformation, courtesy of Foot.com. **Page 152** Michelle Obama. REUTERS/Jonathan Ernst. **Page 165** The Arnolfini Wedding (1434) in Flanders, Oil Painting by Jan Van Eyck. Erich Lessing/ Art Resource. **Page 168** Elizabeth Cady Stanton. Time & Life Pictures/Getty Images. **Page 169** Reunion of Hemings Family. ASSOCIATED PRESS. **Page 180** Loving Family. Bettman/Corbis/AP Images. **Page 182** Rhonda Otten and Debra Curtis. Photo by Erica McDonald. **Page 192** Sacagawea Dollar. Scott Rothstein. **Page 196** (left) Anti-war Activist Cindy Sheehan. AP Photo/ Waco Tribune-Herald, Duane A. Laverty; (right) Plaza de Mayo Mothers. AP Photo/ Waco Tribune-Herald, Duane A. Laverty. **Page 198** (top) Asian Mother Breastfeeding. © duron0123 / www.fotosearch.com; (bottom) Woman Breastfeeding Outdoors. Alexey Losevich. **Page 202** (top) Woman in Historic Billowing Maternity Dress. John, Augustus Edwin (1878-1961) / National Museum Wales / The Bridgeman Art Library; (bottom) Angelina Jolie in Maternity Dress. © Kevin Lamarque/Reuters/Corbis. **Page 207** Maternity Leave Map. Courtesy of ThinkProgress. **Page 221** Western Influence on Ads in China. AP Photo/Ng Han Guan. **Page 223** "Bacha Posh." Adam Ferguson/ VII. **Page 226** Russian Dolls. Photo by Richard Zalk. **Page 228** (top/left) Christabel Pankhurst, © National Library of Australia; (top/right) Sylvia Pankhurst, photo by Topical Press Agency/Getty Images; (bottom) Adela Pankhurst, © National Library of Australia. **Page 233** The Delaney Sisters. Photo by Marianne Barcellona/Time Life Pictures/ Getty Images. **Page 249** The Broken Column. Fundacion Dolores Olmedo, Mexico City. Photo: Schalkwijk/Art Resource, NY. © 2013 Banco de México Diego Rivera Frida Kahlo Museums Trust, Mexico, D.F. / Artists Rights Society (ARS), New York. **Page 253** Henrietta Lacks. OBSTETRICS & GYNAECOLOGY/ Science Source. **Page 255** The First "Official" Female Distance Runner. © Bettmann/ Corbis. **Page 285** Malala Yousafzai. AFP/ Getty Images. **Page 290** One of the Little Rock Nine. © Bettmann/CORBIS. **Page 301** (top/left) Rose Tseng, PR NEWSWIRE; (bottom/left) Shirley Ann Jackson, AP Photo/ Jim McKnight; (top/right) France Cordova, AP Photo/AJ Mast; (bottom/right) Drew Gilpin Faust, AP Photo/Michael Dwyer; [e] Cassandra Manuelito-Kerkvliet, Joy Massey @ Ball Studio. **Page 318** Muslim Women Praying. AP Photo/Dita Alangkara. **Page 332** Papyrus. AP Photo/Harvard University, Karen L. King. **Page 337** The Penitent Magdalene (C. 1560) by Titian. The J. Paul Getty Museum, Los Angeles. **Page 340** Bishop Andrea M. Johnson. Photograph by Michael Myer. Courtesy of Andrea Johnson. **Page 344** Reverend Ellen Barrett. Copyright Bettye Lane. **Page 346** Rabbi Sally Priesand. Bettman/Corbis/AP Images. **Page 353** Women Carrying Urns. AFP/Getty Images. **Page 357** Inuit Women. Hinrich Baesemann/ picture-alliance/dpa/AP Images. **Page 360** Women Strikers. Copyright Bettmann/ Corbis/AP Images. **Page 363** Female Soldier in Uniform. Getty Images. **Page 370** C. J. Walker. Michael Ochs Archives/Getty Images. **Page 372** Women Factory Workers. SSPL via Getty Images. **Page 373** Women of Lesotho. UN Photo/Mudden. **Page 382** (top/left) Nadine Heredia, Hillary Clinton and Michelle Bachelet. AFP/Getty Images; (top/right) Angela Merkel. ASSOCIATED PRESS; (bottom/left) Aung San Suu Kyi. ASSOCIATED PRESS; (bottom/right) Ellen Johnson Sirleaf. AFP/Getty Images. **Page 387** Hillary Clinton. AP Photo/Mary Altaffer. **Page 399** (left) Alice Paul. Library of Congress, Prints & Photographs Division, photograph by Harris & Ewing, LC-DIG-ds-00180; (right) Helena Hill Weed. Women of Protest: Photographs from the Records of the National Woman's Party, Manuscript Division, Library of Congress, Washington, D.C. **Page 403** (left) Sandra Day O'Connor. AP Photo; (right) Ruth Bader Ginsberg. AP Photo/Charles Dharapak. **Page 404** (left) Sonia Sotomayor. AP Photo/Pablo Martinez Monsivais; (right) Elena Kagan. AP Photo/Pablo Martinez Monsivais. **Page 407** Aung San Suu Kyi. AP Photo/Richard Vogel.

INDEX